Food Cultures of the World Encyclopedia

Food Cultures of the World Encyclopedia

EUROPE

Volume 4

KEN ALBALA, EDITOR

 GREENWOOD

AN IMPRINT OF ABC-CLIO, LLC
Santa Barbara, California • Denver, Colorado • Oxford, England

Copyright 2011 by Ken Albala

All rights reserved. No part of this publication may be reproduced,
stored in a retrieval system, or transmitted, in any form or by any means,
electronic, mechanical, photocopying, recording, or otherwise, except for
the inclusion of brief quotations in a review, without prior permission
in writing from the publisher.

Library of Congress Cataloging-in-Publication Data

Food cultures of the world encyclopedia / Ken Albala, editor.
   v. cm.
  Includes bibliographical references and index.
  ISBN 978-0-313-37626-9 (hard copy : alk. paper) — ISBN 978-0-313-37627-6
(ebook) 1. Food habits—Encyclopedias. 2. Food preferences—
Encyclopedias. I. Albala, Ken, 1964–
  GT2850.F666 2011
  394.1'2003—dc22   2010042700

ISBN: 978-0-313-37626-9
EISBN: 978-0-313-37627-6

15 14 13 12 11   1 2 3 4 5

This book is also available on the World Wide Web as an eBook.
Visit www.abc-clio.com for details.

Greenwood
An Imprint of ABC-CLIO, LLC

ABC-CLIO, LLC
130 Cremona Drive, P.O. Box 1911
Santa Barbara, California 93116-1911

This book is printed on acid-free paper ∞

Manufactured in the United States of America

The publisher has done its best to make sure the instructions and/or recipes in this book
are correct. However, users should apply judgment and experience when preparing
recipes, especially parents and teachers working with young people. The publisher
accepts no responsibility for the outcome of any recipe included in this volume.

Contents

List of Abbreviations

c = cup

fl oz = fluid ounce

gal = gallon

in. = inch

lb = pound

mL = milliliter

oz = ounce

pt = pint

qt = quart

tbsp = tablespoon

tsp = teaspoon

Preface

This encyclopedia is the culmination of nearly a decade's work on the *Food Culture around the World* series. As that project expanded to 20 volumes, we realized that many peoples and places, fascinating and important in their own right, had not been covered. Considering that the cultural study of food has become more sophisticated and comprehensive over the past decade, that food has become a legitimate academic topic in curricula at every level of education, and that we seem to become more obsessed with food every day, we recognized that we simply could not leave out much of the planet. The only way to satisfy this growing demand is the set you see before you, which includes material covered in the series plus new articles that span the globe. We have gathered food scholars from around the world—people whose passion and expertise have given them deep insight into the ingredients, cooking methods, and ways of eating and thinking about food in their respective countries.

A number of questions regarding breadth and depth naturally arose in planning this work, particularly about the level of analysis for each article. Could we do justice to the vast array of distinct cuisines on earth? Could we include regional coverage for well-recognized food cultures? That is, rather than the nation-state as the criterion for inclusion, why not add Alsace, Provence, and Burgundy with France, or Sichuan, Hunan, and Canton with China? It became apparent that we would need another 20 volumes or risk very brisk, superficial coverage and that as arbitrary as the construction of nation-states has been historically, in particular the way minority cultures have tended to be obscured, the best way to organize this encyclopedia was by nation. Regional variations and minority groups can, of course, be discussed within the framework of nation-based articles. On the other hand, some groups frankly demanded separate entries—those who stood out as unique and distinct from the majority culture in which they happen politically to be included, or in some cases those people who either transcend national boundaries or even those very small places, whose great diversity demanded separate coverage as truly different from the culture around them. Thus we include the Basques separate from Spain and France, and the Hmong. We have not, however, included every single people merely on the basis of national status. This should not be taken to suggest that these cultures are unimportant but merely that many places share a common culture with those around them, though divided by national borders. In such cases we have provided cross-references. This seemed a preferable solution to suffering repetitiveness or unmanageable size.

The format for each entry also raised many questions. "Eating Out," for example, is simply not relevant in some places on earth. Would forcing each article into a common structure ultimately do injustice to the uniqueness of each culture? In the end it seemed that the ability to conduct cross-cultural analysis proved one of the most valuable assets of this set, so that one could easily compare what's for lunch in Brazil or Brunei. Moreover, tracing the various global currents of influence has been made possible since a shared set of parameters places each article on a common footing. We can trace, for example, the culinary influence of various peoples as they spread around the world. In this respect this work is unique. There are several excellent food encyclopedias on the market, all of which cover individual ingredients, topical themes, cooking methods, and sometimes recipes. None, however, treats individual food cultures as discrete units of analysis, and for students hoping to find an in-depth but succinct description of places, or for those hoping to compare a single food topic across cultures, this is the only source to which they can turn. We anticipate that this work will be invaluable for students, scholars, food writers, as well as that indomitable horde popularly known as foodies.

The other major question in designing this encyclopedia was how to define what exactly constitutes a *food culture*. This term should be distinguished from *cuisine,* which refers only to the cooking, serving, and appreciation of food. Naturally we include this within each entry and in doing so have taken the broadest possible definition of the term *cuisine.* That is, if a people cooks and recognizes a common set of recipes and discusses them with a common vocabulary, then it should be deemed a cuisine. Thus there is no place on earth without a cuisine. A nation, continent, region, and even a small group may share a common cuisine. This encyclopedia, however, covers much more. It explores the social context of consumption, the shared values and symbolic meanings that inform food choices, and the rituals and daily routine—indeed everything that constitutes a food culture. Thus we include religion, health, mealtimes, and special occasions, as well as the way certain foods confer status or have meanings beyond simple sensory gratification. Nor have we neglected the gastronomic angle, as recipes are an essential expression of what people think is good to eat, and their popularity is the outcome of decisions made at every level of society, from the farmer who grows food, and the environment and material resources that make it possible, to the government policy that promotes certain ingredients, to the retailers who market them, to the technologies by which they are transformed, and to the individual preference of family members at the level of the household. To this end we have added food culture snapshots to each entry, which puts a human face on the broader topics under discussion.

As with the series that preceded this encyclopedia, our aim is to present the panoply of human experience through the lens of food in an effort to better understand and appreciate our differences. We will find remarkably common experiences among us, especially as the world increasingly falls under the sway of corporate multinational food industries, but we will also find deep, profound, and persistent distinctions, ones that should and must be preserved because they are essential to who were are and how we define ourselves. These are differences that should not be effaced nor lost as our tastes become increasingly cosmopolitan. I hope that in reading these articles you find, like me, that the world is a marvelously diverse place and what people eat tells us about them in such an immediate and palpable way that in a certain sense you feel you know the people at some level. This, of course, is the first step toward understanding, appreciating, and living with each other peacefully on this small lump of turf we call earth.

Ken Albala
University of the Pacific

Armenia

Overview

The Republic of Armenia, bordered by Azerbaijan, the Republic of Georgia, Iran, and Turkey, is the smallest and most ethnically homogeneous nation of the former Soviet republics. Ethnic Armenians compose 95 percent of its population, while Kurds and Russians make up less than 2 percent of the three million total inhabitants. Armenia is highly urbanized, with more than 70 percent of the population living in cities and towns. Most urbanites are no more than a generation or two removed from rural peasant roots.

Armenia is one of the oldest nations in the world and was the first to adopt Christianity as its official religion. Except for brief periods of unification and relative prosperity, for most of its history Armenia has been under foreign domination, subjected to Arab, Byzantine, Ottoman, Persian, and Russian influences. After becoming independent from the Soviet Union in 1991, the Republic of Armenia went through many painstaking changes from its centralized, Socialist economy to the free market system. Despite yearly government reports indicating economic growth, Armenia is still a poor country, with at least 35 percent of its population living below the official poverty line.

Armenian society is divided between a very small upper class that benefits from the market economy and a very large underclass. In turn, the poor are divided into those who can regularly afford staples such as cereals, pasta, bread, and cheese and the poorest, whose main source of nourishment is potatoes. While there are signs that a small Armenian middle class is emerging, it is not yet well defined.

Armenians have often sought security and prosperity beyond the boundaries of their homeland. Large or small Armenian diaspora communities can be found in almost any country of the world. Thus, Armenian cultural territory is much larger than the physical size of the modern Armenian republic, which is smaller than Belgium. Armenian Americans played an important role in promoting Middle Eastern culinary traditions in the United States. The challenge for the modern Republic of Armenia is not only to carve out its own culinary personality based on locally available foods and traditions but also to embrace the rich culinary heritage of Armenian communities outside its borders.

🍽 Food Culture Snapshot

Vahram Ananian, age 55, an engineer in a road-construction company, and his wife, Roza, 53, an elementary school teacher, live in a three-room apartment with their children: 26-year-old Vahan, a manager at a Yerevan bank, and their 24-year-old daughter, Marina, a project coordinator for a Western nongovernmental organization. Vahram and Roza feel very fortunate that their children were able to find decent jobs in Armenia, unlike many other young Armenians who must emigrate in search of better opportunities.

The Ananians are a typical Armenian family whose standard of living is far above the poverty line but is not quite at the level of a comfortable middle-class lifestyle. Most of the family earnings are being saved since the future is uncertain and they will need to spend a lot when the children get married.

Roza takes all the responsibility for food shopping and cooking in the family, though on weekends

Vahram goes with her to the farmers' market. Using saving strategies honed during Soviet and post-Soviet times of food scarcity and hardship, Roza prefers to buy food from the farmers' market rather than from higher-priced supermarkets in the downtown district.

Summer and fall are busy months for Roza. Like many Armenian women, Roza throws herself into a frenzy of canning called the *zakati sezon*, "the time for preserving." Most fresh produce available in summer and autumn from the farmers' market is preserved for enjoyment in the winter and spring months. Roza gets a helping hand from her daughter and other relatives, who also stock up with homemade canned foods. Some families exchange jar sets of their fruit compotes and pickled vegetables for variety's sake.

The Ananians buy meat from a small butcher's shop near their residential area. The owner of the shop, Armen, knows the preferences of his loyal customers very well. He is ready to offer Roza fresh ground beef that serves as a filling for stuffed vegetables or pieces of cut beef for soup. Rosa is known in the shop as "Kufta Rosa" because she often asks for well-kneaded ground meat to make *kufta*, Armenian meatballs. By Armenian standards, the Ananians are doing very well, since, for many of their neighbors who live in the same high-rise apartment block, meat is unafford-able and accounts for only a small proportion of the average weekly purchases.

In the spring and summer seasons, twice a week Roza buys *khar kanachi*, an attractive bouquet-style bunch of fresh herbs consisting of those most often used by Armenian cooks: cilantro, dill, basil, and parsley. She also buys tarragon and other fresh herbs in bulk and dries them in the sun on her apartment balcony for later use. At the top of Rosa's vegetable list are eggplant, bell peppers, and tomatoes. They are fried, stuffed, or baked and can be served as either a side dish or a main course at the dinner table.

Though usually not involved in the family chores, the Ananians' children often do some after-work shopping in the supermarkets and treat their family with expensive, imported foods. Sometimes they arrange a day off for Rosa by ordering pizza delivery or take-out grilled meat for the family or their guests to enjoy at dinnertime.

Major Foodstuffs

The Republic of Armenia is a highland country, with only 10 percent of its territory lying below an altitude of 3,280 feet. Sharp changes in altitude bring variations in weather and the types of soil, creating a diversity of agricultural produce. The three main zones of agriculture are the Ararat Valley and its surrounding foothills and mountains, the Shirak Plateau, and the plains around Lake Sevan. The Ararat Plain, part of the Ararat district with metropolitan Yerevan at its center, is the most fertile region. It makes up 4 percent of the total arable land but yields 40 percent of all agricultural production.

Of all the fruits grown in Armenia, the most celebrated is the apricot, *tsiran.* People buy apricots in buckets and wooden crates during apricot season, which lasts from the beginning of June until the end of July. Out of 200 types of grapes grown in Armenia, the most famous is the *areni,* a black grape grown in Vayots Dzor. The special taste of Armenia's produce is attributed to its mineral-rich soil and continental climate, which is drier than in neighboring Georgia and Azerbaijan. Armenians enjoy an average of 2,500 hours of sunshine per year. Northern Armenia is famous for its wild, delicious miniature pears, which are called *panda* because it was once erroneously believed they were a favorite fruit of panda bears.

Dried fruits are historical foods of Armenia and were used as a replacement for sugar in old times. *Chuchkhel* is made by repeatedly dipping strung walnuts or hazelnuts into grape juice. Once coated, they are removed and hung vertically to dry. Another delicacy is *alani,* dried peaches stuffed with a filling of walnuts, sugar, and cinnamon.

Chuchkhel, Armenian national candy made by dipping walnuts hazelnuts into grape juice then dried. (Shutterstock)

Since Armenia is in the northern limit of the sub-tropical zone, there are no native citrus fruits. Bananas, citrus fruits, and pineapples have not yet become items of mass consumption. Eating oranges and tangerines is an exclusively winter ritual, not a year-round activity, and many families indulge in them only during the New Year holiday.

The Shirak region in the northwest is known as the Armenian granary. Armenian women used to be true experts in grinding grains with stones and sieving them to create many varieties of wheat products. Historical reports mention 15 types of sieves used in Armenian households. In modern Armenia, the most popular grains are *dzavar,* hulled wheat; *atchar,* also known as German wheat; *korkot,* grits made by crushing hulled wheat kernels; and *blghoor,* made by boiling wheat until it swells, then drying and grinding it. Rice was once locally grown in the lowlands around Yerevan and was even a main export item, but in Soviet times all the wetlands around Yerevan were drained in an effort to end epidemics of malaria. Armenians eat rice imported from India and Iran.

Armenia is a landlocked country, but it has 100 mountainous lakes; the largest, Lake Sevan, is in the northeast. Out of the 31 fish species that reportedly exist in Armenia, the whitefish called *sig,* originally introduced to Armenia from Russian lakes, and the trout called *ishkhan* are the most popular. Gentle poaching is the main cooking method for fish. "Leave well enough alone" is the guiding principle for cooking any freshwater fish, since elaborate sauces or dressings are regarded as disguises that may hide the quality of the catch.

The Gegharkunik Province around Lake Sevan is the country's main supplier of potatoes, cabbage, and barley. For many families in this region, the winter diet consists mainly of fried or mashed potatoes accompanied by sauerkraut. Both foods appeared in the Armenian diet a century ago as a result of Russian influences. Throughout Armenia tomatoes and cucumbers are so tasty and flavorful that they are not only used in salads but also eaten whole and raw, as if they were fruits.

Cheese and traditional plain yogurt are the most frequently consumed dairy products. The two tra-ditional types of cheeses are *lori* and *chanakh.* Both require short periods of fermentation and are aged in brine. Other traditional Armenian cheeses are string cheese, *chechil;* mold-ripened cheese with a crumbly texture, *mklats;* and the fresh, naturally fermented sheep-milk cheese, *vochkhari panir.* Salty, fetalike goat cheese, *aitsi panir,* packed in small clay pots, is one of the success stories of modern Armenian cheese making.

Armenia is home to an incredible variety of herbs. A wild indigenous sorrel, *avelook,* is collected in the spring, dried in braided ropes during summer, and used in winter. Fresh tarragon sprigs are served at almost every meal during spring and summer. Other popular herbs are horse fennel, sage, *malva* (mallows—a leafy green), goose foot (like spinach),

Roasting kebabs in a roadside cafe in Armenia. (Radist | Dreamstime.com)

falcaria (or sickleweed, in the carrot family), and lemon balm. Greens are usually sautéed with onions and eaten with garlic-seasoned yogurt. Mountain greens are gathered in the wild by low-income villagers to sell in local markets. Lately, Armenian ecologists have taken issue with the widespread picking of wild herbs out of fear of the damage caused by overharvesting.

Mutton is not a popular food choice for Armenians. Only young lamb is in demand with tradition-bound Armenians who follow an age-old symbolic ritual meal of animal sacrifice, called *matakh* in Armenian. Small meat shops near churches in Armenia sell young sheep to accommodate this dining practice. The sheep-breeding businesses are mainly oriented to the export of both live sheep and meats to markets in Iran and the United Arab Emirates. Most Armenians prefer pork over any other meat, another example of the Russian influence on the Armenian diet. Consumption of pork soars closer to the New Year holiday because a roasted piglet (*gochi* in Armenian) is a traditional part of the festive table. Pork is the preferred meat for popular indoor and outdoor barbecues, too. Roasted pork chops called *chalagach* are a favorite part of the barbecue menu.

Cooking

Depending on the family's economic circumstances and on the specific occasion, the same dish can be cooked in a plain or a more sophisticated style. If a stew is made as a dinner meal for the family, the meat and vegetables will be cooked in a broth relying on the natural flavors of the ingredients. But if a stew is meant to be enjoyed by guests or is made for a special occasion, then the cook will make special efforts to enrich its flavor by frying or sautéing the meat and vegetables before adding them to the stockpot and by using more varied ingredients.

For religious observances, the style of cooking is always plain, without seasoning other than salt, itself a symbol of purification. *Khashlama* is a generic name for any dish of boiled meat. The name stems from the verb *khashel,* the Armenian word meaning

"to boil." Compared to roasting over fire with its connotations of primitivism and paganism, boiling was regarded as a more refined cookery appropriate for Christian rites. If khashlama is offered on restaurant menus or cooked at home for celebrations, it is fancied up by addition of seasoning, herbs, and vegetables.

The most common and quick method of preparing a grain dish is to boil the grain in chicken broth or water and then season it with butter and onion. The two methods of cooking rice are called *kamovi* and *kashovi.* Kashovi requires the rice to be cooked in water, butter, and salt until the liquid is fully absorbed, with the heat reduced just before it boils. Rice cooked in the kamovi style is boiled just long enough to be tender but still firm, then drained and cooked using dry heat with butter. Again, for special occasions or on restaurant menus, grain or rice dishes are more elaborately prepared.

Another traditional cooking style is the blending and combining of ingredients in one-pot cooking. The components of Armenian casserole-type dishes should be packed closely together and in a special order. The traditional flavor of Armenian stews is defined as *ttvash,* meaning "tart." A good stew should be enlivened with the right touch of tartness. Usually plums, the juice of unripened grapes, or cornelian cherries provide a hint of tartness. Stews and casseroles are delivered to the table in a two-handled crock called *kchooch.* Large clay pots are designed for efficient heat retention, allowing food to stay piping hot for many hours and preserving its juicy flavor. *Chanakh* and *putuk* are stew dishes named after earthenware pots or bowls.

The crown jewel of the Armenian menu is the barbecue (*khorovats*). Barbecuers usually don't bother to marinate meat before grilling as the exquisite taste needs no enhancement. A simple dash of salt and pepper allows the flavor to shine through. Vinegar is not used for marinating as, according to barbecue vendors, it kills the natural meat taste and raises a customer's suspicion about its freshness. A good cut of fresh meat, professional skewers, and the glowing embers of a natural hardwood fire are enough for making good barbecue. Cheese, fresh herbs, tomato-cucumber salad, and pickled green

An Armenian man enjoying khash, a dense soup of beef tripe and trotters lavishly seasoned with garlic. (Shutterstock)

vzh-tzh," so they named their popular dish of liver fried in hot oil *tzhvzhik.*

Typical Meals

Soviet modernization in the early 1920s radically changed eating habits in Armenia. The table etiquette of drinking out of a common cup and handling food with fingers was now considered déclassé. Instead of a single meal prepared to be eaten throughout the day, the tradition of serving three distinct meals—breakfast, lunch, and dinner, with appropriate foods for each meal—became the daily habit.

Armenians have a light breakfast or no breakfast at all. Wraps made by spreading a cheese and herb filling on *lavash,* a traditional flatbread of Armenia similar to the tortilla, and rolling it tightly, is the traditional breakfast or lunch. An example of an Armenian-style breakfast is a lavash wrap of boiled eggs and tarragon.

The lunch break is usually at noon for office workers. Snack-food shops and fast-food eateries serve those who have busy schedules and need to buy a quick lunch. Others manage to go home for a light meal. Dinner, the main meal of the day, is served usually after 6 P.M.

No matter what else graces the Armenian table, *panir* (cheese) should be there. Having a meal of bread and slices of cheese is an Armenian emblem of simple, happy, and unpretentious living. *Hahts u panir,* bread and cheese, is the national snack of Armenia, served and eaten at any time of the day. For many low-income Armenians, bread and cheese has always compensated for the lack of meat.

Along with bread and cheese, common to the dinner table is a plate of fresh herbs with radishes, tomato, and cucumber, served as a salad or just cut into pieces. In winter, homemade canned goods serve as a replacement for fresh vegetables and herbs from the farmers' market. *Basturma,* dried slices of lean, salt-cured, pressed beef coated with a mix of peppery powdered spices, and another traditional Armenian cold meat, *soojookh,* a spicy, dark brown sausage made from ground lamb and lots of garlic, used to be made at home. Nowadays, they are mostly bought from stores. A table platter

chili peppers are traditional side dishes that enhance the flavor of barbecue.

The traditional Armenian oven, the *tonir,* is a ceramic cylinder sunk into the ground; it is used in rural households. Country families in modern Armenia use *atar,* dried cow dung briquettes, to fuel the tonir. The tall heaps of bricks made of cow dung mixed with straw, stacked next to country homes, are a striking detail of the Armenian rural landscape. In urban households, refrigerators are used to store perishable foods, and cooking is usually done on a gas range. It is more common for food to be prepared over heat than to be baked or roasted in an oven. The flavors of most Armenian cooked dishes are delicate and subtle, not fierce.

Frying is done in a one-handled skillet, the *tava.* When meat is frying in the skillet, the English-trained ear hears the sound "siz-siz-siz," thus the word "sizzling" in English. Armenians hear "tzh-

of alternating rows of thinly sliced basturma and soojookh immediately upgrades the level of respect shown by a host toward guests.

Meat *tolma* (leaves or vegetables stuffed with meat) or a Lenten version (filled with a rice or lentil mixture) is a mainstay of the dinner table. Methods of tolma preparation have become badges of identity within Armenia. Tolma from Echmiadzin showcases a trio of stuffed vegetables: eggplants, tomatoes, and peppers in a tart sauce. In the Ashtarak region, tolma is meat-stuffed apples stacked on top of stuffed quinces, with dates and dried apricots placed in-between. Armenians share with the neighboring Iranians the predilection and skill for combining the textures and flavors of meats with fruit.

Many Armenian meatless dishes originated from the tradition of fasting. The culinary repertoire evolved around legumes, grains, fruits, vegetables, and herbs in different combinations. Unlike Russians, Armenians don't include mushrooms in their diet as a replacement for meat during fasting. Out of 300 edible mushroom species identified by Armenian specialists, only 10 are actually commonly used in modern Armenia.

After dinner, Armenians usually serve desserts. The choice of pastry often depends on the availability and price of baking supplies. Light sponge cakes are preferred whenever the price of eggs goes down since the recipes require lots of eggs. Coffee not only marks the end of hospitality for guests but also is a very popular morning fix. Armenians are heavy

coffee drinkers. Tea with *mooraba,* preserves made of any fruit or berries, is also served, especially in cold winters. Armenian homemade fruit preserves are thinner in consistency than Western-style jams and contain much less sugar.

A classic dish of Armenian cookery, a yogurt soup called *spas* is made of hulled wheat and yogurt, usually seasoned with cilantro. Egg yolk and flour are added to the soup to prevent the yogurt from curdling. In many Armenian villages, spas was made in a large pot and eaten as a one-dish meal for several days. An enduring symbol of earth and home, spas continues to have a deep emotional significance for modern Armenians. And, like so many other Armenian dishes, it is proclaimed to have curative powers.

Spas (Yogurt Soup)

1 c korkot wheat (dried or roasted cracked wheat, similar to bulgur)

7 c water

Salt to taste

1 large onion, finely chopped

3 tbsp butter or vegetable oil

1 tbsp fresh mint, finely chopped

1 tbsp cilantro, finely chopped

1 tbsp parsley, finely chopped

2 c plain yogurt

2 eggs, beaten

Combine korkot with water in a saucepan. Bring to a boil, and lower the heat. Add salt to the liquid, and let simmer for about 1 hour. Sauté the chopped onion in butter or oil until it is golden brown. Remove the skillet from the stove, add seasonings to the onions, and mix well. Pour the contents of the skillet into the saucepan when the korkot becomes tender.

Place yogurt in a bowl. Beat with a spoon until it is smooth. Beat in the eggs. Gradually add a little of the hot liquid from the saucepan to the yogurt mixture while continuously stirring to prevent the

Gata, a mildly sweet, flat coffeecake, is a traditional Armenian pastry. (Mirvard | Dreamstime.com)

egg from curdling. After about 2 cups of liquid have been added to the yogurt, pour the mixture back into the saucepan. Stir for a few minutes until the yogurt is blended. Remove from heat. Serve hot or chilled.

Eating Out

The restaurant scene in Armenia was similar to the deplorable state of dining in the Soviet Union as recently as 1990. But it has radically changed and developed at a rapid rate in recent times. There are about 200 restaurants, cafés, and bars in Armenia, the best of which are mostly concentrated in downtown Yerevan. The restaurant industry is considered one of the fastest-growing sectors of the Armenian economy. Restaurants offer eclectic menus mixing European modernity with more Armenian traditional cuisines, revived to stimulate tourism.

Hot, hearty dishes served in a pleasing oven-to-table presentation are meant to entice diaspora Armenians, who make up the majority of tourists visiting Armenia. Fine restaurants serve food in clay bowls to assure that the dish is authentic and obviously ethnic in origin. It is very chic to offer guests wine poured from a clay pitcher. Antiqued earthenware is used as an artistic decoration, prominently displayed as a means of attracting customers. Like in many post-Soviet countries, local restaurants are not affordable for locals and are mainly oriented toward tourists or expatriates.

Yerevan is famous for its summer downtown cafés, which are open around the clock. Armenia, the smallest republic of the former Soviet Union, was a pioneer of café culture in the Soviet Union. In the more permissive atmosphere of the 1960s, cafés were a sign of modernity, added to a relaxed lifestyle after so many years of Soviet austerity. Though cafés were a sign of social sophistication at first, they were still, in Soviet times, a place for male gathering. In the more liberated times of the independent republic, and with the proliferation of cafés and restaurants, Armenian women feel more comfortable going out to eat or having a cup of coffee without the company of men.

Nonetheless, there are still a lot of eateries where men get together to have parties. Small establishments attended by locals offer *khash,* a dense soup of beef tripe and trotters lavishly seasoned with garlic, for winter early-morning parties. Winter khash parties lend some excitement to those dreary months when the majority of the population is waiting for warmer days to come.

Summers in Yerevan are hot and dry, with temperatures often topping 100 degrees Fahrenheit. People stop by small shops or stores to quench their thirst with *tahn,* a lightly viscous drink made of yogurt blended with chilled water and salt. Produced commercially in plastic containers, tahn competes with soft drinks sold in store coolers.

Special Occasions

Food is placed at the center of relationships in Armenia. The word for friend, *enker,* means "eating together." A host treats guests as if they honor their host by their presence. The Armenian word for "party" is *utel-khmel,* meaning literally "eat-drink."

Like people all over the world, Armenians celebrate important events with food. Different occasions call for particular dishes or delicacies. Salty bread, *aghablit,* is the main culinary emblem of Saint Sarkis Day, celebrated 63 days before Easter, in January or February, in memory of the martyr Sergius of Caesaria in Cappadocia (now in eastern Turkey). Saint Sarkis was executed in 304 A.D.

A banquet of ethnic Armenian foods and drinks. (Corel)

during anti-Christian persecutions by the Roman emperor Diocletian. During his saint day, it is customary for young ladies to eat salty bread and go to sleep thirsty in the hope that dreams will reveal a special romantic someone in their future.

The culinary symbol of Trndez, another ancient Armenian festival of love and marriage, which is celebrated in February, 40 days after Christmas, is *aghandz,* a snack made with roasted, salted grains, nuts, and different kinds of seeds. Married and recently engaged couples not only eat aghandz but also jump over a bonfire for good fortune.

Another symbolic dish is *harissa,* a thick porridge made from korkot (dried or roasted cracked wheat) and fat-rich meat. It is slowly simmered and stirred all night long to ensure a viscous consistency. Like other ritual dishes, the time taken for its preparation is part of its cherished value. Harissa is a symbolic dish of resistance that commemorates those who died during the Turkish siege of Musa Dag Mountain in the Adana Province of the Ottoman Empire, at the beginning of the 20th century. Survivors of the tragedy who still live in Armenia celebrate the deliverance of Musa Dag by sharing harissa. Over 100 cauldrons of harissa are cooked each year in September for crowds of up to 5,000 people. Overnight, participants take turns stirring the commemorative porridge.

Food is also central in Armenian mourning customs. It is customary not only to have a wake after the burial but also to get together again 7 days after the death, and again 40 days later. In the strong belief that when food is shared or given, it is a comfort to the souls of the dead, families take food to the cemetery and leave it there as a *hogebazhin,* literally "soul-part." The rising cost of living has made it difficult for many to honor their dead lavishly, but the pressure not to lose face obliges them to lay the food table, at least for a close circle of people.

The most important time in the entire year is the New Year holiday, that special time when the dinner table should be loaded with sweet treats representing optimism for the future. The essential part of Armenian celebrations is drinking and toasting. Because Armenia is famous for its brandy and, to some extent, wine, there has been a broad misconception that

Armenians are avid consumers of wine and cognac. In fact, they mostly drink vodka. *Tti oghi,* mulberry vodka, is considered a real man's vodka. Another strong, time-honored alcoholic drink is vodka made of cornelian cherries, *honi oghi.* Vodka consumption is three times higher than wine consumption. One might blame the Russian influence, along with the availability of low-priced vodka. In recent years, local consumption of wine has increased due to aggressive marketing campaigns by the Armenian wine industry.

Armenians invest a special symbolism in their brandy, the best of which matures in oak barrels for a minimum of 10 years. The sale of the national brandy factory to the French Pernod Ricard company caused a heated debate in Armenia. To its credit, Pernod Ricard modernized the factory, promotes Armenian brandy internationally, and supports Armenian farmers by using only local varieties of grapes for its brandy production.

The line by the legendary Armenian bard Sayat Nova, "If one gives you bitter bile, you, in return, serve him with a sweet," encapsulates the symbolic importance of sweets in Armenian culture. With a flourishing pastry business in modern Armenia, many urbanites prefer buying ready-made pastries from shops instead of baking them. But still, for special occasions, women make them from scratch at home to show off their baking skills. *Gata,* a mildly sweet, flat coffee cake, is a traditional Armenian pastry. The most popular type contains *khoriz,* a layer of filling made from flour, butter, and sugar. Simpler versions of gata used to be a popular snack carried by travelers since it keeps for a long time. Ornate gatas made for weddings and ceremonies were imprinted with decorative designs.

Gata

Dough

1 tbsp dry yeast

1 c sour cream

1 c butter

1 egg

1 tbsp vegetable oil

1 tbsp vinegar

3 c sifted flour

Filling

1 c butter, melted

2 c sifted flour

1¼ c sugar

½ tsp vanilla

Glaze

2 egg yolks, beaten

To make the dough, combine the yeast with sour cream. Set aside for 10 minutes. Add the butter, egg, oil, and vinegar. Mix well. Add flour gradually. Knead the dough well. Refrigerate overnight.

To make the filling, mix butter and flour. Add sugar and vanilla. Stir well.

Preheat the oven to 350°F. Divide the dough into 8 equal balls. Roll each ball out as thinly as possible. Brush each sheet with melted butter. Cut the sheet in half, and fold each half into a square. Spread filling in the center, and fold the square in half. Press along the edges to seal in the filling. Roll out the square until it is ½ inch thick. Place pastry about 2 inches apart on a lightly floured baking pan. Brush the surface of each pastry with the beaten egg. Bake until golden brown. Remove pan from oven and allow the pastries to cool.

Diet and Health

Armenian food culture is deeply embedded with medical beliefs and prescriptions for good health. In old times, treatment with food was often the only hope for recovery, not just in rural households, but also in towns. The first hospital did not open in Yerevan, the capital of Armenia, until 1890.

Myths about the healthy qualities of herbs are passed from generation to generation. A person who did not know the medicinal and healthful values of herbs and plants was offensively called *angitats,*

"ignorant," by Amidovlat Amasiatsi, the 15th-century Armenian physician. Mhitar Heratsi, a famous Armenian physician of the 12th century, mentions in his writings the primacy of food for survival in both the healthy and the sick.

Fruits are rich in vitamins, and doctors prescribe them for people on low-calorie diets. Armenians used many foods not only to prevent illness but also to cure diseases. Jerusalem artichoke, *getnakhndzor,* is a good substitute for potatoes and starches in diabetic diets. It is sold in large bags during August and September and advertised as a natural insulin. The Chinese date (*Ziziphus jujuba*), called *unab* in Armenian, is a medicine for high blood pressure and chronic cough. Hawthorn, *alotch,* is known as a treatment for heart conditions and high blood pressure.

Meat did not figure prominently in the traditional Armenian diet, not only because it was unaffordable to peasants but also because meatless religious fasts were strictly obeyed by the faithful. In the past, fasting was strictly followed in Armenian communities. Devout Armenians abided by the dictates of the Armenian Orthodox religious calendar and not only fasted before major holidays but also kept weekdays as abstention days. Keeping off meat and dairy products for 158 fast days freed up more resources to be given and distributed to the village community on festive days. Feasting was an extreme activity because it was about overindulgence following the periods of hunger, plus the value placed on

Broiled fish from an Echmiadzin restaurant in Armenia. (Corel)

certain foods was heightened because they were denied for so long.

Rarely do modern Armenians fast as they did in olden times. Some families do make minor changes to their diets, such as replacing butter with oil or showing a preference for kidney beans or herb soup in the period before Easter or Christmas. The modern pattern of overeating at parties and consuming generous portions of meat, when it is available and affordable, harkens back to the ascetic practices of fasting and abstinence followed by heavy feasting in Armenia.

Irina Petrosian

Further Reading

Antreassian, Alice. *The Forty Days of Lent: Selected Armenian Recipes.* New York: Ashod Press, 1985.

"Armenian Cuisine." Avarayar Tour Company. http://www.avarayr.am/armcuis.html.

Baboian, Rose. *Rose Baboian's Armenian-American Cook Book.* Lexington, MA: Mary Baboian Balyosian, 1964.

Kleinteich, Sully I. *The Oriental Cookbook.* New York: Artashes Keolian, 1913. http://digital.lib. msu.edu/projects/cookbooks/books/oriental cookbook/orie.pdf.

Petrosian, Irina, and David Underwood. *Armenian Food: Fact, Fiction and Folklore.* Bloomington, IN: Yerkir, 2006.

Wise, Victoria Jenanyan. *The Armenian Table: More Than 165 Treasured Recipes That Bring Together Ancient Flavors and 21st-Century Style.* New York: St. Martin's Press, 2004.

Austria

Overview

If geography is destiny, as some historians believe, then Austria proves the case, at least in respect to its gastronomy. The republic, an area of approximately 32,377 square miles, lies in southern central Europe. It is landlocked and bordered by eight countries, many of which, or portions of which, were part of the vast Austro-Hungarian Empire at its peak of central European domination in 1914. These include Germany, the Czech Republic, Slovakia, Hungary, Slovenia, Italy, Switzerland, and Liechtenstein. Austrian culture, and, in particular, its food culture, draws from all of these neighbors and more. It seems that all who passed through this central hub over the past two millennia left their imprint on the land and its cuisine.

The Danube, the second longest of Europe's rivers, flows eastward as it meanders through Austria's western and north-central plains and valleys, then constricts through the Wachau Valley before passing through the Vienna Plains as it heads toward Hungary. The Danube has long been a major byway between central and eastern Europe, transporting ships, great barges laden with goods, and travelers. With the completion of the 106-mile Europa Canal connecting the Rhine and Main rivers of Germany with the Danube in 1992, a direct shipping passage now allows transport of goods from the North Sea to the Black Sea.

Because of Austria's central location, plains, and waterway, perhaps no other country in western Europe has been, from its earliest beginnings, so traversed by others. Countless groups passed through and often settled within the flexing borders of this great commercial hub. Etruscans, Visigoths, and Romans inhabited what is now Austria. In 500 B.C., Celts came to extract salt from its mines, later yielding them to the Romans, who, in 15 B.C., settled Vindobona, a military outpost that grew into present-day Vienna. Later, Slavs, Turks, Huns, Magyars, and Bohemians invaded. In recent years, refugees from eastern Europe and the former Soviet Union have sought harbor in this generous and neutral land. Each of these groups has left its mark on Austria's culinary heritage.

Austria became one of Europe's strongest powers under the long-reigning Babenberg and Hapsburg emperors, the latter having ruled the country from the 1200s until 1918, and uniting its nine independent provinces. Throughout a succession of wars and conflicts, the empire's boundaries were redrawn many times. By the early 1900s the Austro-Hungarian Empire had expanded to become the largest power of all of Europe. But following its defeat in World War I, Austria was reduced to its current size, which is slightly smaller than the state of Maine.

The Federal Republic of Austria consists of nine provinces: Vienna, Burgenland, Styria, Carinthia, Tyrol, Vorarlberg, Salzburg, Upper Austria, and Lower Austria. Each has a distinct geography and culinary specialties. The country's terrain is two-thirds alpine, with northern highlands that form part of the Bohemian massif and lowlands to the east. The Alps dominate the western and southern regions of the country. Though most of the area is covered with forests and mountains, the country is almost fully agriculturally self-sustaining. The flatter northern and eastern parts hold the greatest concentration of the population, with 67 percent living in urban areas, yet Austria's smaller towns and villages are considered to be among the most picturesque and livable in all of Europe.

Today, tourism is a pillar of Austria's economy, and the country's varied cuisine and high-quality wines are an important attraction. Viennese pastries, first prepared by the pastry chefs of the emperors, are among the country's most famous contributions to world cuisine, but many other specialties are also renowned.

Austria's population in 2007 totaled 8.3 million inhabitants, with an annual growth rate of 0.4 percent. Ethnic groups included Germans, Turks, Serbs, Croats, Slovenes, and Bosnians; other recognized minorities included Hungarians, Czechs, Slovaks, and Roma. The major religions are Roman Catholic (73.6%), Lutheran (4.7%), and Muslim (4.2%). All but 10 percent of Austrians speak German as their primary language. Sizable concentrations of Croatian (in Burgenland), Slovene (in Carinthia), Hungarian, Czech, and Slovak minorities live within the country, with the preservation of their language and culture guaranteed by Austria's constitutional law. Literacy is high (98%), as is life expectancy (76.6 years for men and 82.6 years for women). In 2007, 4.2 million were employed in Austria's workforce, with 67 percent performing service jobs, 28 percent engaged in industrial work, and 5 percent in agriculture and forestry. As of 2006, Austria was the fourth-richest nation among all European Union countries in terms of its gross domestic product per capita. In 2008, Austrians' per-capita income was the 16th highest in the world, according to World Bank figures.

🍽 Food Culture Snapshot

Johann and Annamarie Baumgartner have a home on the outskirts of the industrial and contemporary arts city of Linz, in Upper Austria. Johann is an accomplished violinist and plays in a major orchestra as well as teaching at a private music university. Annamarie is a physical therapist and works with children and adults with physical disabilities. The Baumgartners' twins, a son and daughter, attend a renowned public technical high school, where Felix studies information science and Catarina studies communications. Annamarie, Felix, and Catarina are avid amateur musicians and each play one or two instruments, so the family enjoys making music together, whether at home or at gatherings of family or friends.

Annamarie does all of the cooking, with some help from Catarina and Felix, and Johann and the children welcome a variety of foods, including Austrian traditional fare and foreign specialties. On vacations, the family has hiked in the neighboring Alps and Dolomites in several nearby countries. Johann has also traveled extensively throughout Europe and England for musical performances and has a cosmopolitan appetite. Although they occasionally order pizza or chicken takeout, the family reserves fine dining for special occasions. There are many excellent restaurants in Linz, and Salzburg, with its fine offerings, is only about an hour's drive from Linz.

Linz has a wide variety of stores available for food shopping, from large supermarkets to artisanal food shops where Annamarie can find excellent local produce in season or imported produce throughout the year; top-quality meats, fowl, and freshwater fish; excellent cheeses and dairy products; and many kinds of spices and condiments. She buys organic products as much as possible. There are excellent bakeries in the city, and specialty stores feature many types of foods

Close-up of coating a raw veal cutlet in breadcrumbs to make Wiener Schnitzel. (Carmen Steiner | Dreamstime. com)

and specialties, so she has a wide selection of food to inspire her cooking. She especially enjoys preparing Italian dishes, especially when fresh, vine-ripened tomatoes are available. She has collected many recipes from magazines and has several favorite cookbooks from which she prepares Austrian, Hungarian, French, and Italian dishes.

Because of Austria's diversity and wealth, and the resulting range of choice, it is difficult to typify an Austrian family and its food habits and cooking styles. However, as most Austrians live in cities or large towns, the typical urban-dwelling family has access to good farmers' markets, supermarkets, local bakeries, and specialty stores. Most are likely to keep coffee or tea, yogurt, fruit, milk, rolls, bread, butter and jam, and perhaps packaged muesli or whole-grain cereal, as well as cheese and sliced sausage, on hand for a light early breakfast or late-morning snack consisting of any combination of these foods.

A home cook might choose veal, chicken, beef, pork, fish, or sausage to prepare for the entrée of the main meal. Wiener schnitzel (breaded veal cutlets fried quickly in butter), or one of its many variations, is a typically popular dish. It is frequently available pre-prepared, along with various other entrée choices, at deli counters in larger supermarkets and specialty food stores. Vegetables, noodles, potatoes, rice, or dumplings might accompany the main course, and for these, a home cook might have purchased potatoes and other vegetables (fresh in season or frozen) at a local market or supermarket. Convenience foods and packaged mixes abound in today's Austrian supermarkets, and many busy home cooks keep them on hand and use them readily. For the salad that may accompany or follow the main course, lettuce, cucumbers, and tomatoes are available much of the year owing to imports and greenhouse production.

Many Austrians, particularly city dwellers, often take a mid- or late-afternoon break for coffee and a snack, such as a delectable pastry enjoyed at a favorite coffeehouse. Coffeehouses have been a distinctive part of Austrian social culture since soon after coffee was introduced in Vienna. A Polish hero, Franz George Kolschitzky, purportedly opened the first coffeehouse after the failed siege of the Turks in 1683. The Turks, for whom coffee was a customary beverage, fled so quickly they left behind sacks of beans; Kolschitzky, a translator, at first tried to sell the beverage as the Turks prepared it: ground and boiled several times. Only when he strained it and served it with added milk did it gain acceptance. Today, coffeehouses are popular venues for breakfast, light lunches, or snack meals in the late morning or afternoon.

For light suppers, cold meats, cheese, or smoked fish might have been purchased at the market, to be served with bread and a variety of sauces or condiments such as a range of mustards. Fruit, fresh or stewed (sometimes with rum, as for the traditional *Rum Topf*), served either alone or with heavy cream, is a popular dessert, as are strudels, fruit-filled flaky pastries with or without *Quark* (a smooth, fresh sour cheese, not unlike yogurt). Wine, beer, fruit juices, and mineral water are the common beverage choices.

Austrian home cooks buy a variety of cooking vegetables, herbs, cheeses, and condiments to keep on hand. These include onions, red and green cabbage, chives, mustards (of which there are a great variety, including sweet, horseradish-flavored, spicy, and wine- or herb-flavored types), and spices or packaged spice mixtures. For the spice rack, a home cook would have parsley (for soups); caraway, paprika, and marjoram (used in making meat stews and Hungarian goulash); and cinnamon (for rice puddings and compotes). Fresh or dry lovage might also be purchased for use in soup stocks or in dishes calling for a light celery accent. Lemons accompany some schnitzels or are purchased for the rind to be used in flavoring desserts.

Lean, dry cured or smoked ham called *Speck* is purchased for seasoning many dishes such as noodles and dumplings. Home cooks buy eggs to have on hand for omelets, soufflés, soups, and puddings. Freshwater fish (carp, pike perch, lake trout, and salmon) and chicken are prepared in many traditional ways, and turkey has gained popularity as a substitute for chicken or even veal. Beef, especially cut for *Tafelspitz* (a distinctive boiled beef dish prepared from a special cut of fine-grained meat from the leg), and pork are also popular. Good-quality veal is plentiful and is used for schnitzels, though chicken, pork, and turkey are also frequently used for this popular breaded and panfried meat preparation. Lamb is neither as plentiful nor as popular as other meats.

Sour cream and whipping cream are staples for cooking. Cheese purchases in 2001 averaged 10 percent of a household's fresh-food bill. Austrian cheeses have received many world cheese awards. Popular cheeses include Quark, Pinzgauer Bierkäse, Salzkammergut Käse, and Vorarlberger Bergkäse.

Major Foodstuffs

Farms are mostly family owned and small (45 acres, or 18.4 hectares, in 2005) in comparison with the U.S. average (445 acres, or 180 hectares). The average dairy herd is comprised of just 12 cows. Still, Austria's self-sufficiency for major agricultural products exceeds 100 percent. The top three products are beef and veal, drinking milk, and sugar. Self-sufficiency is lower for poultry, fruit, and vegetables. The total value of Austria's agricultural production in 2006 was 5.68 billion Euro (US$8.4 billion), with a little over half from animal production and the rest from plant production. About 5 percent of the nation's gainfully employed persons worked in agriculture or forestry.

Austria's agricultural production includes cereals such as maize, wheat, and barley, much of which is grown in the eastern plains. Oilseed production, including rapeseed, sunflower, soybeans, pumpkin, poppy, linseed (flaxseed), safflower, and sesame, has been increasing since the mid-1990s. Root crops such as potatoes and sugar beets are also plentiful.

Organic fruit display at a farmers market in Austria. (Shutterstock)

In 2006 about 835,000 tons of fruit were harvested from intensive and extensive fruit farming, with apples, plums, peaches, apricots, pears, and garden strawberries of major importance. Viticulture in Lower Austria, Burgenland, Styria, and Vienna has a long tradition dating back to the Roman age. Production and exportation of Austrian-produced wines are both on the rise.

Mountain farmers are federally subsidized to assure quality, agricultural continuity, and food security. Thus, especially for mountain farmers, milk and cattle production constitute a major source of income. Grazing lands are cultivated organically, and Austria is recognized as a leader in high-quality dairy and cheese production.

Livestock of predominantly combined milk/meat breeds are bred, and beef production exceeds domestic consumption by 40 percent. Pork production meets domestic consumption needs, and poultry and egg production nearly do (84% and 74% respectively in 2005). Sheep farming has been on the increase since 1975; most lamb is sold via direct marketing.

Domestic production of fish is limited to freshwater species such as trout and carp. Seafood consumption is rising due to health awareness, and marine fish, shellfish, and crustaceans are imported from other European suppliers such as Italy, Germany, the Netherlands, Denmark, and Norway.

In 2005, Austria ranked third among the top European spenders for organic foods. About 15 percent of Austria's agricultural land is certified organic, and the Ministry of Agriculture, Forestry, Environment and Water Management encourages further development of organic production through active agri-environmental research and marketing assistance. The number of organic farms is on the rise, and in recent years, Austrian consumers have increasingly favored *bio,* or organic, ingredients and products for home cooking.

Cooking

Kitchens range from basic to ultramodern. Cooktops and ovens are heated by electricity or natural gas or by propane in more remote locations. In a corner of the kitchen there is often a nook with a table and built-in bench seating at which the family eats its daily meals. In addition, a formal dining room, where fine dinnerware may be kept in a freestanding buffet, is a common feature of many homes. The extended family traditionally gathers for a large midday meal on at least one weekend afternoon, usually with the eldest woman or women doing the cooking. Outdoor grilling of meat, sausages, or fish may be done by men or women.

The female head of the family traditionally prepares the daily meals, possibly with her daughters' assistance. Children of both sexes often are expected to help with setup and cleanup. Today, many working couples, with or without children, may share in preparation and cleanup duties.

Soups and stews are simmered on modern stoves and cooktops. Meats and fish may be roasted, fried, or grilled in roasters, grills, or frying pans. For example, chicken paprika, roast chicken with paprika sauce that came from Hungary, is a popular Austrian dish. In some health-conscious homes, whole grains for use in baking are milled using a small household grain mill. Many home cooks enjoy baking, although working women have fine bakeries from which to choose a wide variety of baked goods, and they very often do. Potatoes are commonly served boiled or roasted. *Nudeln* (noodles) and various forms of dumplings, are common starch accompaniments. Rice is also served but not as often as potatoes.

Typical Meals

A light, early breakfast (*Frühstück*) in Austria might consist simply of a roll with butter and jam; bread with sliced cold meats or cheese; or cereals with milk or yogurt, all accompanied by coffee, tea, cocoa, or fruit juice. Traditionally, those who have eaten their breakfast early might take a break from their work around 10 A.M. to have a second light meal (*Gabelfrühstück*) consisting of a sausage or other snack.

Noontime has traditionally been when the main meal of the day (*Mittagessen*) is served at home, in a restaurant, or in a workplace cafeteria. Today's busy work schedules allow less time for a leisurely

multicourse noontime meal, however, so a quicker and lighter meal may be taken at noon, with a more relaxed larger meal consumed in the evening. Whenever it is served, the main meal might consist of soup and a main course followed by a small salad of mixed vegetables with lettuce and a dessert.

Stews or roasted, grilled, or panfried fish or meats such as veal, beef, or pork are most commonly served for the main meal entrée. Schnitzels (breaded and fried veal, pork, or chicken cutlets) are very popular entrée choices. Root vegetables or green vegetables in season or from hothouses, and noodles, potatoes, or dumplings (large, boiled ones, or tiny ones, such as *Spaetzle*) usually accompany the main course, and the meal may be served with bread. Some restaurants add a small cover charge for a dinner roll with butter. A small mixed-vegetable salad, either in vinaigrette or mayonnaise, may follow or accompany the main course. Wine, beer, or mineral water is also served. Wine is most popular in the eastern provinces, and beer is favored in the west. The meal concludes with dessert, which Austrians, and particularly the Viennese, enjoy immensely. Today's increasingly health-conscious Austrians might favor fruit desserts, but cakes, sweet dumplings, and puddings, as well as strudels and other pastries, are also served.

Many Austrians, particularly city dwellers, often take a midafternoon break to enjoy *Jause,* a light snack of coffee and a delectable pastry enjoyed perhaps at a favorite coffeehouse. Coffeehouses are also popular for breakfast, snacks, or light lunches. A more elaborate afternoon social gathering, like an English tea, including small sandwiches, cakes, and coffee or tea and enjoyed either in a home or in a coffeehouse or café, is also called a Jause.

For the evening meal (*Abendessen*)—traditionally consisting of lighter fare unless the main meal could not be eaten at noon—cold meats, sausage, cheese, or smoked fish might be purchased, then served with bread and condiments such as a selection of mustards. Or leftovers from a heavier meal might be served. Wine, beer, and fruit juices are the beverages of choice.

The food of Vienna is among the most cosmopolitan of all of Europe, with especially strong influences from Hungary, Bohemia, and Italy. Starters

A vast array of pastries being sold in a shop in Vienna, Austria. (iStockPhoto)

may include clear soups, perhaps with strips of cooked egg or small dumplings, noodles, vegetables, or sausage. For main courses, the popular Wiener schnitzel, a breaded cutlet of veal that is fried, is served with potatoes. Favored stews include *Gulyas,* a thicker variation of the paprika-spiced Hungarian goulash. Austrian Gulyas is mainly made from beef, veal, or pork, but one famous restaurant in Vienna specializes in Gulyas and prepares it with beans, mushrooms, turkey, fish, or chicken livers and even offers a vegetarian version. *Wiener Backhendl,* lightly breaded fried chicken that is served with lemon, is also a popular Viennese specialty.

Wiener Schnitzel

Meaning "Viennese slice," Wiener schnitzel is a breaded meat cutlet. It can be made of veal, pork, or chicken. Schnitzels are enjoyed in Germany as well as Austria, but a true Viennese Wiener schnitzel is a thinly pounded, perfectly crispy veal cutlet that's been fried in butter or a mixture of butter and oil and is then garnished with lemon and possibly anchovies, capers, and parsley.

To prepare Wiener schnitzel, allow one 6-ounce cutlet per person. Fill the bottom of one large salad plate with flour, and fill a flat soup bowl with beaten eggs to which a splash of water has been added, and then a second salad plate with crispy breadcrumbs.

Pound the cutlets evenly on both sides with a meat mallet until about 3/8 inch thick; they will spread out in size considerably. Lightly season the meat with a sprinkling of salt and pepper. Dip each first into the flour (patting off extra), then into the egg (allowing the excess to run off), then into the breadcrumbs—again shaking gently to remove excess. Make sure that all the meat is covered with crumbs. (If a thicker coating is preferred, dip the crumb-coated meat back into the egg, then into the crumbs a second time.) Place the breaded cutlets on a cake rack as you coat them, then chill on the racks, uncovered, in the refrigerator for about 20–30 minutes before cooking. This will dry the coating slightly to assure a crispy crust and moist meat.

Heat a frying pan large enough to accommodate one or two cutlets at most. When hot, add enough butter (or half butter and half canola or other oil with a high smoke point) to coat the bottom of the pan to at least 1/8 inch. When the butter begins to foam, or the oil and butter combination ripples with heat (do not allow it to smoke), put cutlet(s) in the pan and fry each side for a few minutes just until browned. Additional butter may be required before each turning. Keep cooked cutlets hot in a prewarmed oven until serving. Garnish with sliced lemon and a parsley sprig, along with a few capers and an anchovy, if desired, and serve with parsley-buttered potatoes.

Viennese pastries are world famous, and there are said to be over 100 varieties of cakes made. These include the famous *Sachertorte,* a chocolate cake with apricot filling; *Erdbeeroberstorte,* or strawberry cream torte; the layered *Dobostorte* that originated in Hungary and is frosted with chocolate buttercream; *Malakofftorte,* or ladyfinger torte with rum cream; and *Esterhazytorte,* or a Hungarian-style wafer torte filled with chocolate mousse and apricot jam. In addition, there are various strudels, or rolled flaky pastry filled with fruit or sweetened cheese. These also originated in Hungary, and the most famous of these is *Apfelstrudel* (apple strudel).

Viennese cuisine sets the national standard, and many of its dishes are served throughout Austria.

However, each of Austria's nine *Bundesländer,* or federal states, boasts its own specialties. A marketing initiative, GENUSS ("Region of Delight"), led by the Ministry of Agriculture, Forestry, Environment and Water Management, aims to bring visibility to the culinary specialties of each region.

Vorlarlberg, the westernmost federal state, is related more closely to Switzerland in respect to gastronomy than it is to the rest of Austria. The mountainous region produces over 40 cheeses, many of which win awards in international cheese-making competitions. Cheeses and plenty of carbohydrates find their way into hearty Vorlarlberg dishes. One of the most popular is *Käsknöpfle,* or cheese noodles made with potatoes and regional cheeses. Others include cheese dumplings and fried breads.

The Tyrol, which is also mountainous, is known for its fortifying foods as well. These include dumplings made with ham, spinach, and *Graukäse,* or Tyrolean mountain cheese. *Kaspressknödel,* a cheese dumpling, is served in soup or with sauerkraut. *Tiroler Gröstel,* a hashlike mixture of meat, potatoes, onions, and herbs, and *Melchermuas,* a large dessert pancake, are two dishes that are traditionally served in the heavy cast iron pans in which they're cooked. *Kiachl,* doughnut-like fried cakes, are another favorite specialty of the region.

The federal state of Salzburg encompasses the beautiful Salzkammergut Valley with its many beautiful lakes. The northern part of Salzburg leans toward Bavarian influence, whereas the southern part is alpine and Tyrolean influenced. Because of its long independence under the rule of Catholic archbishops until 1816, the cuisine of Salzburgerland has been influenced greatly by church practices, particularly during Lent.

In the southern part, meals are cheese-centric with very little meat or fish, with the exception of *Tiroler Leber mit Polenta,* or calf liver fried with onions and served over cooked cornmeal. Tyrolean mountain valleys produce wild mushrooms that are popular in dishes such as wild mushroom stews. Local fruits and berries are blended into sweet dumplings of Bohemian origin. *Nidai,* or fried potato dough, and *Schlutzkrapfen,* or spinach ravioli with butter and Parmesan cheese, are also specialties of the region.

Salzburgerland's northern lakes yield fresh fish and crayfish. The best Austrian beers are produced here. Perhaps the most famous Salzburger specialty is *Salzburger Nockerl,* a light, sweet soufflé that is dusted with vanilla-flavored powdered sugar.

Upper Austria's specialties include its dumplings, which may be made of wheat flour or potato and are filled with sweet or savory fillings. Sauerkraut and cabbage salads and potatoes are frequent Upper Austrian accompaniments. *Linzertorte,* a raspberry jam–filled almond-flour cake from Linz, is a popular pastry that is served throughout the country. Schnapps and *Most* (apple or pear cider) are also specialties of the region.

Specialties of Carinthia, Austria's southernmost province, include *Schlutzkrapfen,* cheese ravioli with mushrooms; *Kasnudeln,* potato ravioli filled with Quark and mint; *Ritschert,* a bean and barley stew flavored with smoked meat; and *Reindling,* a traditional cake filled with cinnamon, sugar, and raisins.

In Styria there are vast vineyards and pumpkin fields. Light omelets, both savory and sweet, that are torn before serving are a specialty. Collectively, they are known as *Schmarrn* and include the most popular, *Kaiserschmarrn,* a sweet pancake-like omelet with raisins that is served with fruit preserves. Savory specialties include *Steirisches Wildschweinernes,* or wild boar simmered with onion, root vegetables, and spices; and *Heidensterz,* or fried buckwheat groats with cracklings. Pumpkin seeds and pumpkin oil are produced in Styria and used for salads and to garnish pumpkin soup. Many fruits and nuts are grown in Styria.

Lower Austria possesses world-famous vineyards along the Danube Valley. The region's specialties include white asparagus, venison, pheasant, boar, rabbit, poppy seeds, and apricots.

Burgenland's broad plains came under Hungarian administration in the days of the Austro-Hungarian Empire. Carp, pike perch, chicken, duck, and goose are popular dishes. Wild mushrooms, wild asparagus, and polenta are widely used in this wine-producing region. A favorite dish is *Eszterhazy-Rostbraten,* filet of beef with a root vegetable and sour cream sauce. *Mohntorte,* or poppy seed cake, is also a specialty.

Kaiserschmarrn, a sweet omelette with raisins and served with fruit preserves. (Shutterstock)

Eating Out

Stift St. Peter Weinkeller in Salzburg, founded in the year 803, is the oldest inn and restaurant in Europe. The monastery and wine cellar are chronicled in the writings of Alcuin, Charlemagne's leading adviser. Austria has long been a mecca for dining and today offers many excellent restaurants from which to choose.

Many types of restaurants can be found, and although most meals are prepared at home, Austrians love to dine out and usually have favorite local restaurants they especially enjoy. A *Heuriger* is a rustic wine tavern, often associated with a winery. Many can be found in the suburbs of Vienna such as Stammersdorf, Grinzing, Semmering, Nussdorf, Neustift, and Ottakring, as well as in other wine-producing areas throughout the country. Foods served at these pleasant wine-garden restaurants are generally limited to cold buffet items and are accompanied by the slightly spritzy new wine of the latest vintage. Folk music known as *Schrammelmusik* is featured in many Viennese Heurige. Few evenings in Vienna can be more memorably spent than with good food and wine, and the lovely Austrian tunes one enjoys at a Heuriger.

For a light meal, there is a *Kaffeehaus* or *Konditorei*. Similar to a café, a coffeehouse is a social gathering place that specializes in coffee drinks and pastries but often offers light lunches as well. A Konditorei specializes in pastries and confections, though many such shops have expanded their menus and now resemble cafés.

Biesl are cozy restaurants where typical Viennese specialties are served. These might include Tafelspitz (boiled beef with horseradish applesauce), *Beuschel* (stewed organ meats: calf lung and heart served with a bread dumpling), *Leberknödel* (liver dumplings), or other dishes. A *Wurstlstand* is a street stand at which steaming sausages with rolls and mustard and other condiments may be bought throughout the evening. They are mostly found in the larger cities. In addition to various casual dining choices such as these, there are fine-dining restaurants as well, and many Austrian chefs have been recognized around the world for their creativity and skill. There are numerous Michelin-starred and other highly rated choices.

Special Occasions

Austria is nearly two-thirds Roman Catholic, and the church's holy days are observed, with Easter, Advent, and Christmas being special times for family gatherings. For Easter, braided breads with raisins are enjoyed at the Easter dinner, for which a whole suckling pig, ham, lamb, or rabbit may be roasted. Dessert might be a special cake such as Sachertorte, a chocolate cake with apricot filling and dark chocolate frosting.

At Christmastime, a pre-Christmas fast may be observed, and on Christmas Eve and Christmas Day, families celebrate with special meals, mulled wine, and Christmas cookies shaped like stars. For Christmas Eve supper, a light meal of clear or vegetable soup, fried carp, potatoes, cucumber salad, and mushroom rice may be served before the family attends midnight mass. On Christmas Day, some families still serve the traditional roast goose with red cabbage, potato dumplings, and dried fruit–studded Christmas breads and sweetmeats. But in some homes, turkey or Wiener schnitzel may be substituted.

For New Year's Eve, the extended family will gather for a noisy and fun celebration. Good-luck charms such as marzipan pigs may be given, followed by champagne or sparkling wine at midnight, and dancing. New Year's Day will be quieter, with many enjoying the annual Vienna Philharmonic

Orchestra's New Year's concert from Vienna on television.

Many cities also celebrate patron saints' feast days. In Burgenland, for example, roast goose is served on Martinsdag, or St. Martin's Day, on November 11. In fall, vintage festivals are held in various wine-producing areas.

Diet and Health

An old Austrian epithet advises against eating too much and too late: "Frühstücken wie ein König, zu Mittag essen wie ein Bürger und zu Abend essen wie ein Bettler" (Eat breakfast like a king, lunch like a townsman, and dinner like a beggar). During World War II and the subsequent occupation, rationing was severe and Austrians didn't have much to eat at all. Following the war, sugar, butter, and other goods became available, and some Austrians overcompensated for their wartime deprivation. The national sweet tooth grew with increasingly available and excellent pastries and confections. Although the daily consumption of sugar in Austria remains somewhat higher than in many other European countries, it has declined in recent years.

The Austrian diet today is generally well balanced, although still excessive in carbohydrates and fats in some regions, leading to the development of diabetes, high blood pressure, and heart disease in some people. Austrians in general, however, are very active and healthy. Many Austrians today, particularly younger, better-educated, and health-conscious citizens, enjoy sweets in moderation and engage in activities such as walking, hiking, cycling, skiing, and other cardiovascular exercise in order to maintain their energy intake/output balance. With their high life expectancies, most Austrians live long, productive lives. Many might gladly admit that they also live very well.

Pamela Elder

Further Reading

Austrian Federal Ministry of Agriculture, Forestry, Environment and Water Management. http://www.lebensministerium.at.

Austrian Ministry of Education, Science and Culture Austria-Forum. http://www.aeiou.at/.

Austrian National Tourist Office. http://www.experienceaustria.com.

Barer-Stein, Thelma. *You Eat What You Are: People, Culture and Food Traditions.* Buffalo, NY: Firefly Books, 1999.

Bouley, David, Mario Lohniger, and Melissa Clark. *East of Paris—the New Cuisines of Austria and the Danube.* New York: HarperCollins, 2003.

Gastronomy in Salzburg. http://www.salzburg.info/en/gastronomy/.

Gieler, Peter. *Culture Smart Austria.* London: Kuperard, Bravo, 2007.

Hughes, Helga. *Cooking the Austrian Way.* Minneapolis, MN: Lerner, 1990.

"Linzer Torte." Linz Tourism. http://www.linz.at/english/tourism/873.asp.

Mayer-Browne, Elisabeth. *Best of Austrian Cuisine.* New York: Hippocrene Books, 2001.

Millstone, Erik, and Tim Lang. *The Atlas of Food.* Berkeley: University of California Press, 2008.

Polvay, Marina. *All Along the Danube.* New York: Hippocrene Books, 2000.

Rodgers, Rick. *Kaffeehaus: Exquisite Desserts from the Classic Cafes of Vienna, Budapest, and Prague.* New York: Clarkson Potter, 2002.

Scheibenpflug, Lotte. *Specialities of Austrian Cooking.* Innsbruck, Austria: Pinguin, 1995.

"Vienna: Wining and Dining." Welcome to Vienna. http://www.wien.info/en/shopping-wining-dining.

Vorarlberg Turismus: Gastronomy. http://www.vorarlberg.travel/xxl/_area/382733/_subArea/382770/_subArea2/407289/_lang/en/index.html.

Basque Territory

Overview

The Basque territory occupies an area that spans adjacent sections of northern Spain and southwestern France, and the population is around three million. It comprises three provinces in France: Lapurdi (Labourd), Nafarroa Beherea (Basse Navarre), and Zuberoa (Soule), and four in Spain: Bizkaia (Vizcaya), Gipuzkoa (Guipúzcoa), Araba (Alava), and Nafarroa (Navarra). The first three Spanish provinces are autonomous, having a large degree of self-rule at the provincial level. Navarra has a different legal status, allowing it to join the other three by a popular vote. Thus far that has not happened. The Basque word for Basque country is *Euskadi,* meaning "land of the Basque speakers."

The Basque civilization is ancient and enigmatic. Its exact origins are unknown, and the Basque language (Euskara) is unlike any other spoken on Earth. Research suggests that Basques may descend from the earliest human settlers of the region, predating Indo-European arrivals, since the Basque language is the only surviving pre–Indo-European language in Europe. The Basque people have never had a country of their own, although the medieval Kingdom of Navarre might qualify, yet they have managed to preserve their language and rich culture over the course of millennia. Throughout history they have existed with various degrees of autonomy from and varying levels of hostility toward different rulers and the many invading armies that have passed through the region, all of which have influenced their culinary traditions.

Much of the terrain in Basqueland is rugged, so agriculture has historically mostly been limited to small plots and grazing, though the river valleys are quite fertile. The relative austerity of the land has made the sea a central focus for Basque culture and food. Basques have been famous throughout history as mariners and anglers; they made early contact with Vikings and may have had a significant presence in the Americas before Christopher Columbus arrived. Several members of Columbus's crew were Basque, as were many of the men who crewed the Spanish Armada.

Food and cooking are centrally important to Basque culture; a passion for cooking and eating is a defining characteristic of the Basque people, and they are fiercely proud of their culinary traditions and accomplishments. Basque cuisine has benefited from many influences. The cuisines of France and Spain are obviously important, and before them the Romans and Moors brought ingredients and cooking techniques. From the Vikings, the Basques learned about cod and the location of the great fisheries off of northeastern North America. Basques eagerly adopted peppers, both sweet and hot varieties, as well as tomatoes, chocolate, and spices from the Americas into their cooking. The very inclusive and open-minded attitude toward ingredients and an improvisational streak that always tinkers with and tests new possibilities accounts for the quick adoption of New World foods.

🍽 Food Culture Snapshot

María and Esteban Etxeberria live in Bilbao. María works as the office manager for an architecture firm, and Esteban is an accountant. They have two sons in grade school. As middle-class residents of a bustling city, their dietary habits are broadly reflective of their fellow urban citizens. Their day typically begins with coffee or hot chocolate with croissants, cold cereal, or a baguette with butter and jam. Most Basque families eat lunch together every day; schools let out for two hours at lunchtime, busing kids home, and many businesses close for the same period. Lunch will usually be a soup, freshly made or reheated, followed by sandwiches or, time permitting, a fish or meat stew, with cheese and fruit to finish. After the family returns from work and school at the end of the day, they have a snack: a simple sandwich, or tea and cookies or pastry. Dinner might be a whole grilled fish, a roast chicken with rice, or *marmitako* (a fish stew with potatoes). On a weekend, a slow-cooked lamb stew might make an appearance, or the family would go out to meet friends at a local bar for *pintxos* (as tapas are called here). Both parents shop for food, and it's often a challenge, since many stores are closed during the lunch break. They stock up on fresh produce, cheese, bread, fish, and meat as needed and make sure that the pantry is never without dried peppers, *bacalao* (salt cod), olive oil, and other staples.

As in the rest of Europe, supermarkets are gradually supplanting the traditional open-air markets, with shopping now done less often than the previous norm of every day. Supermarkets also tend to stay open throughout the day, allowing more opportunities for working people to shop there. As more women enter the workforce, traditional roles and institutions are changing in response. Home cooking was traditionally the exclusive territory of women, while restaurants, cider houses, and the all-male gastronomic societies gave the men a forum in which to cook for each other. Today, the traditional gender roles are much less strict than they used to be, especially in the more urban areas, but for the most part Basque women still spend an average of nearly twice as much time cooking and doing housework as men. These roles are best viewed in the larger context of Basque tradition, which is nuanced; women controlled domestic and civic finances and sat in the nave in church, while men had to sit up in the balcony.

Major Foodstuffs

Basque cuisine, like much of the territory, faces the sea. The areas farther inland feature more meat, but it is from the sea that Basque civilization gained its sustenance and fortune. Basque country can roughly be divided into three geographic regions, each of which has a different type of cuisine. The coastal areas feature seafood of all types, treating it with a light touch so that the beauty of the catch can shine: usually grilled, baked, or sautéed with a simple sauce. This simplicity—letting the freshness and quality of ingredients speak for themselves—is a trademark of Basque cooking from any region and has proved very influential for modern chefs worldwide. Farther inland, in the mountains, meat (especially mutton and lamb) and game feature more prominently, along with cheese, foraged mushrooms, and legumes. The inland regions share more foods with Castilian Spain, especially beef, pork (including cured ham and sausage, like the famous chorizo), and the red wines of Rioja. The ease of transport today has allowed each of these formerly distinct culinary regions to borrow liberally from each other, making for a somewhat more homogeneous cuisine than in the past.

Seafood is central to Basque cooking, especially in the coastal regions. Tuna, cod, squid, crab, eels, and shellfish are all prized. Onshore, where other ingredients are more easily available, more complex preparations evolved. Marmitako is a traditional stew made from tuna, potatoes, onions, and peppers and is a perfect example of a now-classic dish that originated on fishing boats. Fresh tuna is gently stewed with the precooked vegetables so that all the ingredients are perfectly tender upon serving. Squid (*txipirones*) are often grilled or stewed in their own ink. Baby eels (*angulas*) are prized and very expensive due to scarcity and demand. The eels, hatched in the Atlantic, swim thousands of miles back to the same rivers their parents lived in. Caught in the fall, at about three inches long, they are usually quickly cooked *a la Bilbaina,* or Bilbao-style, in hot garlic-infused olive oil and then served immediately.

Salt cod, or bacalao, is one of the most important foods of the Basque people. Basques were originally whalers, hunting in the Bay of Biscay. Their success depleted the whale population, so they ventured farther north, where they met and traded with Vikings who told them of the great cod fishing grounds off of Newfoundland. One of cod's defining characteristics is its lack of fat, meaning that if salted it will not go rancid over time. As a result of this, salt cod became both a crucial commodity and a means by which a ship could stay at sea for long periods without any fresh food. Salt cod offered a versatile meat substitute after the Vatican imposed a ban on Friday meat consumption, and it quickly became a staple all over Europe. Basques developed a wide range of dishes using salt cod that elevated this humble ingredient to luxurious heights. This, combined with their legendary marketing prowess and business acumen, helped to popularize cod all over Europe. As a result of cod, the ports, and manufacturing, the Basque provinces continue to be the wealthiest in Spain.

Basques were among the first Europeans to embrace the foods that colonists brought back from the Americas, among them tomatoes, peppers, and potatoes, all of which now form the basis of many dishes, including the classic *pipérade* (*piperrada*), a sauce of peppers, tomatoes, and onion, seasoned with dried hot Espelette peppers, and sometimes with eggs cracked in toward the end. Various kinds of peppers can be seen drying all over the region in the summer and fall, and they form an essential component of all kinds of Basque food. Fire-roasted *piquillo* peppers in jars are a principal export of the town of Lodosa in Navarra, and they are often stuffed with everything from seafood to sausage to cheese. *Piparras* are long, thin, slightly hot green peppers, often pickled like Italian *peperoncini;* they are natural accompaniments for ham and sausage. Probably the most famous Basque pepper is the *piment d'Espelette* (Espelette pepper), grown in the eponymous town in Labourd. Dried and ground, the complex heat and flavor of the peppers form an integral part of many Basque dishes, including the cured hams of Bayonne. Espelette peppers have received the *appellation d'origine controlee* (AOC) designation, in common with fine wines, that regulates exactly where any peppers bearing the name must be grown.

Corn and beans—two other imports from the Americas—were also thoroughly embraced by Basque cooks. Especially in Guipúzcoa, corn and beans are still often grown together in the American Indian fashion, allowing the beans to climb the cornstalks. *Talos* are thick corn tortillas used by farmers and shepherds to wrap their lunch, and

cornmeal is used in a variety of cakes. Beans are eaten both fresh and dried in a multitude of preparations. Among the most prized are beans that are mature but not yet dry; called *pochas,* during their short season they are often featured in a stew with quail. In Tolosa, the local black beans are called *alubias* and are so revered that the town holds an annual festival to celebrate them and vote for the best grower. The traditional Tolosan method of preparation is to simmer the beans in an earthenware crock with garlic and olive oil and then serve them on braised cabbage.

The varied landscape and climate of the Basque region are ideal for many species of edible mushrooms. Many Basques are avid mushroom hunters, especially in the spring and fall when the best conditions make for bountiful harvests. Among the most cherished species are truffles, cèpes (porcini), and a delicate species called *perretxiku,* which grow in the spring, but there are many more. Traditionally, and in keeping with the practice of minimal intervention, mushrooms are served simply: grilled, scrambled in eggs, or added to soup.

The Pyrenees and Cantabrians are home to deer, wild boar, and a number of species of game birds. Venison is a popular ingredient in sausage and is also often grilled and served with one of the traditional sauces. Boar is also used in sausages and to make *civets,* or stews. In the steep mountain passes, a unique method of bird hunting has evolved: White decoys—which doves mistake for hawks—are thrown into the air. The birds respond by flying down close to the ground, where they are caught in nets stretched across the narrow ravines. The doves are usually served grilled or stewed.

Basques have been shepherds since before recorded history. Goats are rarely kept, which explains the relative scarcity of Basque goat cheeses, but sheep are ubiquitous. Lamb is an integral part of any special meal, often roasted whole or quartered on iron stakes driven into the ground next to a large fire. Lamb is also commonly made into stews and sausages. A dish using both methods, and highlighting the resourceful frugality at the core of traditional Basque food, is *txuri-ta-beltza,* or "black and white." The small intestine of a lamb is cooked, chopped with garlic and onions, bound with eggs, and stuffed into the large intestine. The sausages are then gently stewed in the lamb's blood. Poultry is widely raised, though eggs tend to feature more prominently in Basque cooking than do the birds. The pink-and-black Basque pig was very nearly extinct in 1981, with only 20 left in the world. A few enterprising producers brought the breed back into widespread use, and now many of the great hams of Bayonne are made from Basque pigs.

Bayonne ham (*jambon de Bayonne*) has received a Protected Geographical Indication from the European Union and is thus carefully regulated in all aspects of its production. The pigs from which the jambon de Bayonne is made are free-range, foraging for tree nuts to supplement their grain. After slaughter, their legs must be rubbed with local sea salt and cured for at least seven months, though many are cured longer, for up to a year. They are often rubbed with ground Espelette pepper during curing to impart a slightly piquant complexity. Bayonne ham is expensive but extremely popular both as charcuterie and as an ingredient in many dishes. The ham shank bones are prized for soups.

Basque sheep cheeses are famous, and several have received either AOC or *denominación de origen* (DO) designation, depending on which side of the border they are made. *Idiazábal,* made in Guipúzcoa, is probably the best-known Basque cheese. Made mostly from Latxa sheep, after aging, it is often smoked to add complexity and deepen the flavor. Other well-known examples include Roncal (from Navarra) and Etorki, Ossau-Iraty, and P'tit Basque (from the French side). Roncal is a semihard cheese made from the milk of Latxa and Aragonesa sheep grazed around the seven villages in Navarra's Valle de Roncal. Etorki, made from the milk of black-headed Manech ewes in Mauléon, has an orange rind and a smooth texture with a subtle flavor and notes of burnt caramel. P'tit Basque is a mild, semisoft cheese developed in 1997 and marketed aggressively as an alternative to stronger-flavored sheep-milk cheeses.

Cheese, along with quince paste (*membrillo*), fruit, and nuts, traditionally concludes a meal. Sweets are more often eaten in the late afternoon around teatime, or an hour or so after dinner. Traditional

Basque desserts range from *mamia*—a junket with fruit originally made in wooden milk pitchers by shepherds, who heated the milk with hot rocks—to simple walnut, chestnut, or rice puddings and custards flavored with seasonal fruit. In addition to grapes, apples, and cherries, other berries and tree fruits are widely grown in gardens and on farms, and walnuts, almonds, and chestnuts are all traditional staples still used whole, roasted, or ground into flour for both sweet and savory preparations. Honey is also produced all over the region, though not traditionally used much in cooking. Chocolate came to the Basque territory with Jews who fled the Inquisition in Spain and Portugal and settled in Bayonne. These refugees had learned to sweeten and emulsify the cacao and soon had mastered making solid bars; prior to this, chocolate had only been drunk. As a result, Bayonne became famous for its chocolates, a reputation that endures. Probably the best-known dessert on the French side is the *gateau Basque* (*biskotx*): two layers of pastry baked with either pastry cream or cherry jam between them. The cherries, if used, should be from Itxassou, which is famous for them. There are as many versions of the recipe as there are Basque bakers and much good-natured disagreement about which filling is superior. Cherries are also often made into *gerezi beltza arno gorriakin,* a soup of the fruit poached in sweetened wine.

Cider has historically been as important as wine, if not more so; every Basque farmhouse had an orchard. Dozens of varieties of apples thrive in Basqueland, and the *sagardotegi* (cider houses) are important institutions. Over the years, they have evolved from simply being houses where cider was made into something closer to a restaurant; patrons would originally bring some food along when stopping in to buy cider, since the drink is meant to accompany food. Over time, a traditional meal took shape around the tasting, and the cider houses began to prepare food themselves. Now they are something like brew pubs, offering a three-course meal of a salt cod omelet, then a grilled steak, and then cheese with nuts and quince paste for dessert.

The cider is stored in large barrels with a tap about six feet from the floor. Periodically during the meal, patrons are called to gather at the barrel, catching the thin stream from the tap in their glasses, which aerates the cider. This is called a *txotx*. Since Basque cider is almost all still, this aeration helps to enliven the flavor and gives some temporary effervescence to the drink. The cider season lasts from mid-January through May, after which the cider houses close. Other times of the year, cider is bought in bottles. Bottles are traditionally held high while the cider is poured into glasses held low, mimicking the effects of the txotx. Most Basque cider is produced and consumed in Guipúzcoa.

Over time, as Basque tastes were influenced by outsiders, production of wine far exceeded that of cider. Txakolí, a slightly fizzy, low-alcohol white wine meant to be drunk in the year it is made, is the most famous Basque wine. Made mostly from the Hondarribi Zuri grape, it is produced in Alava, Vizcaya, and Guipúzcoa. Each region uses different grapes to supplement the Hondarribi, and differences in climate and terrain between the regions also make for variations in flavor and quality. Some red is made, from Hondarribi Beltza, but the vast majority of Txakolí production is white. It is also an ingredient in many dishes, especially seafood, which take advantage of its bright acidity to build sauces.

Irouleguy is the only Basque wine made on the French side to have received AOC status. Reds (about 70% of the total production) are made mostly from Tannat, Cabernet Franc, and Cabernet Sauvignon grapes, as are the rosés, making up another 20 percent. Some whites are made from Corbu and Manseng grapes. The best reds can age well for up to 10 years. Wine production dates back at least to the Romans and used to be far more widespread; in the Middle Ages the great pilgrimage routes led through this area, and the pilgrims required a great deal of wine. Though the quantity produced has declined dramatically since then, there is no doubt that the quality has improved a great deal both before and since the AOC designation. Some producers of note include Brana, Abotia, and Ilaria, where grapes are grown organically.

Much of Basqueland's southern border is defined by the Ebro River, along part of which lies the famous Rioja wine region. Though not specifically Basque, Rioja is commonly drunk throughout the area, as it complements the more meat-oriented food found farther from the coast. Rioja Alavesa, the northernmost of the three areas within the Rioja DOC (Denominación de Origen Calificada—a legal protection of the wine's origin), falls within the Basque province of Alava. The wines tend to be lighter and more acidic than those made farther downstream where the climate is hotter, but the poor soil and low yields make for wines with strong character. Rioja is made primarily from Tempranillo grapes, with Garnacha (Grenache), Mazuelo, and Graciano added to tailor the blend. White Rioja consists mostly of Viura grapes, blended with smaller amounts of Malvasia and Garnacha Blanca. Most *rosados* (rosés) are made from Garnacha, which has lighter flavors than Tempranillo and is better suited to rosés. Some Rioja rosés can age well for a remarkably long time.

Patxaran is an old liqueur from Navarra that originated as sloe berries (wild plums or blackthorn) macerated in anise-flavored liquor. Over time the recipe was refined and now usually includes a few coffee beans and vanilla to round out the flavor. Patxaran (*pacharán* in Spanish) is popular throughout Spain. On the French side, Izarra is a digestif made in Bayonne that is flavored with mixtures of local herbs and botanicals. It comes in green or yellow. The green is minty, with a higher alcohol content, while the sweeter almond-based yellow version includes saffron and honey. It is usually drunk neat or on ice, though more recently it has found favor as an ingredient in cocktails and desserts, including chocolates and ice creams.

Cooking and Typical Meals

A typical meal near the coast might begin with *porrusalda,* a leek and potato soup, followed by a fish stew: marmitako, *bacalao a la vizcaina* or *bacalao al pil-pil,* or txipirones (squid) stewed in their own ink. Bacalao al pil-pil is a signature Basque dish, embodying the refinement and alchemy borne of humble ingredients for which the cuisine is renowned. It features salt cod, the longtime staple around which much of the Basque economy and foodways were built. The desalinated fish fillets, cut into pieces, are gently sautéed in olive oil in which garlic and peppers have been lightly browned. The trick to the dish is creating a silky emulsion between the olive oil and the juices given off by the fish, an operation that involves gently agitating the pan over heat for some time. Gelatin from the skin of the fish helps with the emulsification, so cod with the skin on is essential. The name of the dish comes from the popping sound that results from adding wet fish to hot oil. When properly prepared, bacalao al pil-pil transcends its simple components to become something extraordinary and thus exemplifies the Basque approach to cooking.

Marmitako

2 dried *choricero* chilies (substitute ancho if needed)

1 lb tuna steak

2 lb potatoes, peeled

½ c olive oil

1 Spanish onion, chopped

1 green bell pepper, julienned

2 cloves garlic

2 teaspoons *pimentón* (smoked paprika)

Soak the chilies in warm water to soften. Remove and discard seeds and chop flesh coarsely. Cut tuna into roughly 1-inch cubes. Cut potatoes into similar cubes. Heat olive oil and add onion, pepper, chilies, and garlic, and sweat them for 5 minutes until soft. Add potatoes, paprika, and enough water to just cover, and simmer for 20 minutes until the potatoes are soft. Add tuna and cook gently for 5 more minutes, then remove from heat and let sit, covered, for 30 minutes or so to marry the flavors and thicken a bit. Reheat if needed before serving.

Basque seafood sauces are deceptively simple. They are often made with just a few ingredients, but proper execution requires attention to detail and much practice. *Merluza en salsa verde* (hake in green sauce) is a perennial favorite, where hake steaks are quickly browned and then finished in a garlicky herb sauce flavored with parsley, chives, and peas. Potatoes and clams are also frequently prepared in green sauce. *Vizcaina* is another classic Basque sauce, made from rehydrated *choricero* peppers, onions, and ham simmered with garlic, olive oil, parsley, and wine and then blended smooth. It is used for salt cod, cod-stuffed peppers, and many other dishes.

Farther inland, the ingredients shift to those from the farm: birds and mammals, vegetables, and legumes. Dinner might begin with an omelet—with ham, peppers, or asparagus—or a pipérade, then feature a steak or roast bird with foraged mushrooms, or a stew of lamb or game with chorizo or other sausage. Corn and beans are much more likely to make an appearance, whether as talos to mop up the sauce or slow-simmered beans in or apart from the stew. Cheese with nuts and membrillo is a standard dessert. Pipérade, like the seafood preparations, is deceptively simple. Onions, peppers, and tomatoes are humble ingredients, but the quality thereof and the subtleties of cooking technique can transform them into a dish of great depth and richness. The freshness of the vegetables is paramount; produce not in season is simply not used. The olive oil, the herbs, and the dried peppers are all from the region, and the result is an encapsulation of the flavor of the place. Letting the ingredients speak for themselves through artful, reverent manipulation is probably the most important and influential aspect of Basque cooking.

After fisherman, shepherds have had the biggest influence on Basque cuisine. Lamb is as centrally important to the inland food tradition as seafood is to the coast, appearing as meat (whole and sausage) and as sheep-milk cheese in a wide variety of subtly different variations. *Sauce Basquaise* is a variation on pipérade that is pureed smooth and used in many meat dishes, especially with lamb. Nuts—almonds, walnuts, and hazelnuts—are often paired with lamb as part of a pesto or as flour to thicken a stew. Easter lamb is traditionally stuffed with olives and almonds, and lamb holds a special status as the meat of special occasions. Steaks are fixtures on the standard cider house menu, and pork, especially ham and chorizo, is also ubiquitous. Many farms still hold an annual communal winter hog slaughter, called a *txarriboda,* at which the whole animal is processed into ham, chorizo, chops, and other cuts. Nothing, not even the blood, is wasted.

There are some differences in ingredients between the French and Spanish sides. The wines tend to be consumed fairly close to where they are produced, so one is unlikely to find much Txakolí used in French cooking, for example. Bayonne ham is not common in Spain, where there is plenty of *jamón iberico* instead. Most fresh vegetables do not travel far from their source, so regional differences are still significant, setting towns apart from each other in terms of what they are best known for making. The French side of Basqueland is smaller and more culturally integrated into France than the Spanish side is into Spain—the Basque language is much less used in France—but the food remains distinct from that in the rest of the country. In Spain, the dietary divide increasingly is more between urban and rural rather than between coast and mountains; the urban population has access to all of the ingredients and restaurants (Basque and foreign) common to any European city, while residents of smaller, more rural towns tend to eat more traditionally.

Eating Out

Eating out is an integral part of the social fabric of Basque culture; Basques spend twice as much of their discretionary income on food outside the home as Americans do. Pintxos (the Basque word for tapas, from the Spanish *pinchar,* "to skewer") represent the essence of Basque cooking: the freshest ingredients, combined in nearly infinite ways using refined technique and playful imagination, and served as many small courses along with drinks. A common evening ritual is *ir de pintxos*—to go from bar to bar, having a plate and a drink or two at each before moving on. It's a mix of conviviality and competition, as the patrons socialize and the bar owners try to outdo each other with creative and delicious preparations.

Pintxos are traditionally served on a slice of bread, the topping held in place with a toothpick: hence

A typical type of tapa, a pintxo, from San Sebastian, Guipuzcoa, Spain. (Shutterstock)

the name. More recently, though, especially in and around San Sebastián, presentations have become decidedly more adventurous, and ingredients can get quite exotic as chefs experiment with ingredients and techniques from around the world. This is a logical continuation of the history of Basque cuisine, which has assimilated so many ingredients and made them quintessentially Basque. Most eating outside the home will be casual, in bars, with more or less perambulation depending on the mood of the group. For more formal events, there are many restaurants offering more refined interpretations of standards as well as adventurous departures from tradition. In urban areas, options like pizza, Chinese food, and sushi are now normal, especially for young people.

Influenced by the French nouvelle cuisine of the 1970s, which featured lighter, smaller-portioned interpretations of classic dishes, Basque chefs responded by updating some traditional dishes and inventing many new ones. Their efforts, along with those of some equally talented Catalan chefs from northeastern Spain, were crucial to the development of the *Nueva Cocina* ("new cooking") in Spain. Recently, this approach further evolved to propel Spain into the vanguard of cutting-edge culinary techniques and presentation. Basque chefs preside at several Michelin-starred restaurants, and the guide rates Juan Mari Arzak's three-star restaurant Arzak in San Sebastián as the third-best restaurant in the world. Martin Berasategui, chef and owner of the eponymous three-star restaurant outside San Sebastián, has another in the Guggenheim Museum in Bilbao and recently opened a new one in Shanghai. These two chefs are hugely influential and revered in Spain and around the world for their understated virtuosity at combining traditional Basque dishes with the exotic ingredients and technological techniques of contemporary haute cuisine. Not all chefs embrace the status such awards convey; some have expressed concern after receiving a star that the attention might pressure them to change their very personal and nonaristocratic approach to cooking.

Another unique and important component of Basque culinary culture is the widespread presence of *txoko,* or gastronomic societies. Traditionally limited to men (though women are now allowed into some, especially at lunchtime), they are communally owned places where men can gather and cook for each other on a regular basis. The societies originated in 19th-century San Sebastián when friends rented a space in which to eat and drink outside the home and unfettered by cider house hours. All members had keys to the space, and all costs were shared communally. The idea spread quickly, and most sizable towns now have several. Members sign up to cook on a given night and may invite guests. Each member is responsible for purchasing any main ingredients for the meal but may use anything from the communal pantry. He must make a careful accounting of all communal ingredients used so that supplies can be replenished.

The gastronomic societies combined dishes and techniques from the two main influences on Basque cuisine: fishing boats and farmhouses. Over time they have grown into influential institutions that keep old recipes alive while also constantly innovating, with both new twists on standard fare and bolder, more experimental efforts. Though amateurs, many members are very skilled and put enormous effort into the meals they prepare; some societies have influenced professional chefs, spurring them to innovate. The gastronomic societies make annual trips to vineyards to taste the new vintages and place orders, and they are active in the community, hosting parties and organizing festivals.

Special Occasions

Basques are a celebratory people, and most foods, no matter how humble, are honored with an annual festival in some town or another that produces a key ingredient. Even the simplest dishes are treated with respect, and since festivals mostly include competitive cooking, the techniques and recipes are preserved throughout the years. No festival, saint's day, or party is complete without a feast. *Garbure* is a vegetable soup that features white beans, cabbage, and ham. At different times of the year, other seasonal vegetables are added depending on what is available. The town of Anglet, near Biarritz, holds an annual garbure festival. Olite, a town in Navarra, celebrates *menestra,* a spring vegetable stew with ham, every April. Tolosa celebrates its beans, Tudela its artichokes, Itxassou its black cherries, and Espelette its peppers, featuring them in *axoa,* a beef or veal stew. Mardi Gras, or Jueves Gordo, is enthusiastically celebrated by Basques. They are the most devoutly Catholic of Spain's citizens, and yet they also embrace the pagan roots of the festival with raucous dancing and feasting. The Tamborrada is a festival held every year on January 20 in San Sebastián. Adults dress as chefs and soldiers and parade through the town beating drums. All of the gastronomic societies participate and open their doors to all for the one night. The combination of military and culinary imagery symbolizes the degree to which the cultural pride and fierce independence of the Basque people are connected to their food.

Diet and Health

The increasing popularity of processed convenience foods has made healthy eating more difficult; obesity and the resulting illnesses are increasing among Basques as they are in the rest of Europe. Street markets, a central Basque commercial and social institution, are losing customers to supermarkets. Daily shopping at outdoor markets is exercise; weekly shopping at supermarkets is not. As the traditional roles gradually break down and yield to more European norms, the health problems that beset modern

Western societies are tending to increase. While the traditional Basque diet and lifestyle are extremely healthy, it remains to be seen how they will adapt to the pressures and changes of 21st-century life.

Peter Barrett

Further Reading

Barrenechea, Teresa. *The Basque Table.* Cambridge, MA: Harvard Common Press, 1998.

Hirigoyen, Gerald. *The Basque Kitchen.* New York: HarperCollins, 1999.

Hirigoyen, Gerald. *Pintxos.* Berkeley, CA: Ten Speed Press, 2009.

Kurlansky, Mark. *The Basque History of the World.* London: Penguin Books, 1999.

Sevilla, María José. *Life and Food in the Basque Country.* New York: New Amsterdam Books, 1989.

Uberuaga, Blas Pedro. "Basque Gastronomy." Buber's Basque Page. http://buber.net/Basque/Food/.

Belarus

Overview

The Republic of Belarus is a landlocked nation in eastern Europe. It is bordered by Russia, Poland, Ukraine, Lithuania, and Latvia. For much of its history it has been a part of either the Polish–Lithuanian Commonwealth or the Russian Empire, and later the Soviet Union. It has a population of almost 10 million people, about 80 percent of whom are native Belarusians. Its two major religions are Russian Orthodox Christianity (80%) and Roman Catholicism (almost 20%). Until World War II Belarus had a significant Jewish population (8% of the total population, and up to 40% of the urban population), which by the end of the 20th century became as small as 0.3 percent of the population. There is also a small but significant Muslim Tartar population (0.1%), which has also influenced Belarusian cuisine. The official languages are Russian and Belarusian. About 70 percent of the population lives in cities. Belarus is flat and heavily forested. It has many lakes and three major rivers: the Dnepr, the Neman, and the Pripyat'. It also has significant marshland.

The position of Belarus between Russian, Baltic, Ukrainian, and Polish lands, as well as the influence of two major branches of Christianity and Judaism, profoundly affected its cuisine. Belarusian food features ingredients and recipes familiar to all eastern Europeans—potatoes, beets, rye bread, borscht, and porridge. The climate, forests, marshes, and relatively poor soil ensured that Belarusian cuisine emphasizes mushrooms and game, potatoes and river fish. Many dishes have been borrowed from western Europe through the influence of its westernized, Catholic nobility and from the Caucasus and Central Asia during the Soviet period. What distinguishes Belarusian cuisine from those of other eastern European countries is the great emphasis on potatoes and mushrooms, as well as some unique methods of preparing these ingredients.

🍽 Food Culture Snapshot

Alesya Kupala and her husband, Vasil' Kupala, live in Minsk's Serabranka neighborhood. Alesya works for the Minsk Kristall wine and liquor factory. Vasil' used to work for the electrical repair plant nearby but now runs a computer sales and repair business from their apartment. Their son, Serhiy, studies at the Belarusian National Technical University and, like many other young Belarusians, lives at home with his parents. The Kupala family meals include both traditional Belarusian foods that Vasil' and Alesya's parents prepared, as well as foods introduced through Soviet influences and the global economy. They have three major sources of food: modern supermarkets, farmers' markets, and a garden plot just outside of Minsk.

All members of the family do some shopping, but it is mostly Alesya who shops for food and cooks the family meals. On a typical day, she is likely to stop at the local supermarket to buy bread and milk. The family shops together at a large "hypermarket" at the edge of Minsk. For this weekly shopping trip they use their car. At the hypermarket, they stock up on meat and poultry, cheese, and sausage, as well as grains such as buckwheat and oats. The men of the family also buy recently introduced convenience foods such as ramen noodles that they prepare when Alesya is not home. She buys most of the vegetables for the family at the

Belarus woman and her husband pick potatoes in the field in the village of Pererov, 2010. (AFP | Getty Images)

farmers' market, hoping that these will be tastier grown in soil that is not polluted. She is careful to ask where the farmers come from, trying to avoid areas known for their industrial pollution.

Major Foodstuffs

Belarusian soil is poor, and the climate is relatively cool. Therefore, the traditional source of grain for bread was rye, not wheat. Oats and buckwheat are also commonly used for flat cakes, soups, and porridges. Wheat bread was traditionally reserved for the nobility and became more commonly accessible only in the 20th century. Oats were used for almost all foods requiring flour that are not bread. From the 19th century on Belarus has been dominated by the potato, its most common and iconic ingredient. It is used to prepare soups, main dishes, and snacks. Among other vegetables, beets are used, but to a lesser extent than in the Ukraine. Carrots are

also often added to dishes. Cabbage is extremely common—both fresh and fermented as sauerkraut. It is used in soups, stews, and stuffed with various fillings. Sorrel and beet greens are used in soups as well. Mushrooms are, along with potatoes, one of the most distinctive elements of Belarusian cuisine. Depending on the type of mushroom used, they are marinated, salted, dried, or cooked fresh. Traditionally, they were used as a flavoring agent in soups and other dishes, but today they are also used in salads and main dishes, and often combined with meat and fish. Berries are another traditional ingredient in Belarusian cuisine, with cranberries a common ingredient in the marsh Palesye region. Fruit such as apples, pears, and cherries is used to sweeten dishes, to stuff dumplings, and to make drinks that are either fermented (kvass) or thickened with potato starch or flour. Belarusians collect birch sap in the spring and drink it as a healthy and refreshing beverage (*biarozavik*), sometimes after fermentation.

Meat has been generally a food for the well-to-do, becoming gradually more common in the 20th century. Pork is the most popular meat, often eaten roasted and stewed. Blood and meat are used in sausages. Pork fat, like elsewhere in eastern Europe, is salted or smoked and then used as a flavoring agent for starches, as a cooking fat, and, in more recent years, as an appetizer and a delicacy. Game, small and large, has also been a popular ingredient. Belarus has a large population of the *zubr,* or European bison, which are under government protection today but in the past were hunted along with boar. Boar, or domestic pork instead, along with cabbage, sausage, mushrooms, and spices, is used in the traditional hearty stew, *bigas,* that is common in Poland and Lithuania as well. Pork is not eaten by Belarusian Tartars and Jews.

Unlike Tartars who live elsewhere in eastern Europe, Belarusian Tartars do not eat horse meat, which, therefore, has not been a part of Belarusian cuisine. Beef became more popular thanks to the Soviet influence, but it was also common in Jewish cooking, often prepared in a sweet and sour sauce. Jewish influences are also seen in the preparations of poultry with fried chicken fat and stuffed necks of chicken and geese, popular dishes introduced by

Jewish innkeepers. The Catholic influences are seen in the popularity of roast geese, especially on St. Martin's Day. Until the 20th century, Belarusians ate only river fish and salted fish from the Baltic, particularly herring. While fresh fish was made into soups or baked, it was also used as a stuffing for dumplings prepared in the marshes of Palesye. Herring is especially associated with the Jewish culinary heritage in Belarus, but it has passed into the cooking of all ethnicities. Fish would be commonly eaten during the numerous Catholic and Orthodox fasts and Lent.

Milk and eggs also play an important role in Belarusian cuisine. Milk was used as a condiment to "whiten" soups, stews, pierogi, and potatoes. It is also used to prepare soft farmer's cheeses (*tvaroh*), which are either eaten plain or in dumplings and fritters. Eggs are eaten as well, added to soups and fried, often with pork fat. Painted eggs form an important part of Easter celebrations.

Generally, the flavors of Belarusian cuisine are quite mild. Salt, pepper, onions, garlic, bay leaf, dill, and occasionally coriander and caraway seed are the primary spices, and these are used sparingly. Most of the flavors in food are derived from the cooking techniques and not spices.

Cooking

Traditional Belarusian cuisine divided ingredients into five categories according to the role they played in the recipe. The main ingredients, usually vegetables or grains, constituting the bulk of the dish, were known as *privarki,* while meat, mushrooms, or fish, which imparted the dish its main flavor, were called *zakrasy. Zakolota,* or the thickening agent, consisted of flour or pieces of potato, and *vologa* were liquid fats added to moisten the dish. Finally, spices were called *prismaki.* This system of five categories of ingredients is directly related to the traditional preparation of many Belarusian dishes: the stewing of all ingredients in one pot inside a large oven, producing a kind of thick soup or stew. The simplest example is *zatsirka,* a soup of the poor, made of water and flour, with milk added as flavoring. Today, this soup is prepared with milk and egg dumplings.

Other cooking techniques are also important. Some of the oldest recipes call for the preparation of large pieces of meat or fish, while the relatively newer recipes, borrowed from Polish cooking, use finely minced ingredients, for either dumplings, fritters, sausages, or stuffing. An entire goose stuffed with porridge and mushrooms and then roasted remains an exemplary dish. *Piachisto* is the general name for a large part of an animal or an entire bird or fish that is stewed, usually in the same pot with peeled whole potatoes. A stuffed *yutz* is a stuffed stomach of a cow, pig, or sheep, prepared similar to a Scottish haggis. Instead of oats, however, buckwheat is used. A good example of a dish using ground meat is *zrazy,* baked or fried chopped meat or potato, usually wrapped around some stuffing. These can also be prepared with thin meat strips rolled up around the filling. *Kalduny,* a kind of stuffed dumpling, similar to Italian ravioli or Russian *pel'meni,* are also popular; these are stuffed with a finely chopped filling of meat, fish, mushrooms, or vegetables. The local Muslim Tartar population favored particularly large kalduny in their cooking. Contact with the Western, Catholic world brought a pasta casserole similar to the Italian lasagna, known as *lazanki.* Remnants of past contact between the Slavs and the Greeks can still be seen in the Belarusian preparation of cucumbers with honey. A traditional snack of white or black radish with honey, oil, or Jewish-style with chicken fat is also very popular.

Food is often preserved, since the growing season is fairly short. Fish and mushrooms are dried and then used during the cold seasons of the year. Belarusian Tartars also dry lamb and beef. Herbs are dried as well, to be used in medicinal teas. Salted and marinated mushrooms were introduced from Russia and Poland and are now common. Fruit and berries are dried or are made into fruit preserves.

Many otherwise-simple ingredients are subjected to lengthy preparatory processes before becoming part of a dish. Thus, many dishes call for a fermented solution of oat flour and water called *tsezha.* Milk and buttermilk are also often fermented. Fruit and grains are used to produce fermented malt beverages, kvass. Potatoes are either boiled or stewed with lard. For some recipes, raw potato is grated and used with the resulting potato juice; for others, the raw, grated potato is drained in a cheesecloth bag (*klinok*). The third method is to use boiled and mashed potatoes. These three types of preparation can also be combined for some recipes. *Dranniki,* an iconic Belarusian dish, are fritters made from drained raw, grated potato. Dumplings, or *galki,* are made of mashed potato with some egg and flour added or with mushrooms or fish and then boiled. Potato *babka,* a baked pudding made out of potato and eggs, with or without additional ingredients, is a popular dish originating with Jewish Belarusians. Tvaroh, like potatoes, may be additionally processed, strained, and hung in the klinok bag. The curds are then dried and used to flavor foods, rather like Parmesan.

Desserts are not common in Belarus. Pies and cakes were introduced fairly late. Sweet dishes are usually simple preparations of baked fruit or berries with cream or honey. *Kaldunki,* a smaller version of the kalduny dumplings, are filled with sweet cheese or cherries and served as dessert, particularly during holidays. Fruit juices are boiled and thickened with starch to make *kissel. Kulaga* is a mixture of apples and berries cooked in water with rye flour, left to ferment, and then cooked again. For weddings a large sweet bread (*karavay*) is baked. Everyday treats may also be baked crispy cookies called *korzhiki,* common to Russian and Ukrainian cuisines as well. Modern Belarusians have absorbed Russian and Western-style desserts as well. Rich cakes and pastries are popular, as are chocolate candies produced by large factories such as Spartak in Minsk.

Typical Meals

Traditional peasant meals in Belarus would be simple and as high in calories as the family could afford. Like their neighbors, Belarusians would eat plenty of bread with kvass or, in the 20th century, tea. Lard on bread, fried or boiled potatoes, porridge with milk, and eggs fried with lard or simply boiled could all serve as breakfast. *Vierashchanka* or *machanka,* a meat and flour gravy used as a dip for pancakes made of oats, potatoes, or later wheat flour, was another traditional breakfast food. The rich families' version of this dish contained more spices, as well as sausages. The main meal of the day in poor and well-to-do families would include a rich soup and a main dish, usually a stew cooked in a pot. Kvass, a very lightly fermented beverage made from rye bread, sometimes flavored with fruits, would serve as a main beverage, but vodka (*harelka*) could also be served, as could fermented birch juice. The poorest would eat bread and perhaps zatsirka. Supper would be similar to breakfast, including porridge, bread, potatoes, and milk. The noble upper class would usually identify with the monarch and so would eat either as the Polish nobility did or, later, as the Russian nobles would. However, many Belarusian nobles adapted traditional recipes for more elegant meals. Hence, kalduny à la

A plate of traditional dranniki. (Shutterstock)

Count Tyshkevich is similar to normal Belarusian dumplings but has a rich filling of eggs, ham, and mushrooms.

Modern Belarusians still tend to have a filling breakfast. They are likely to eat bread, either spread with butter or as sandwiches with pâté, sausage, and cheese. Porridge made of buckwheat, farina, or oats with milk or sugar is also eaten. Eggs, boiled or scrambled, are also popular breakfast foods. Western-style dry cereal is growing in popularity. Tea or coffee is the drink of choice. Lunch was still the main meal of the day for much of the 20th century. A salad or herring was served as an appetizer, along with a thick soup such as *borshch* (cooked in Belarusian, Russian, or Ukrainian style), then a main course with a meat and a starch, followed by a simple dessert. Today, more people are likely to have a smaller, Western-style lunch. Instant convenience foods such as ramen noodles are becoming more popular. Dinner is now more commonly the largest meal of the day. The food can be similar to either breakfast or lunch, with bread, porridge, eggs, soup, and especially potatoes served. Following a common Soviet tradition, grilled shish kebabs (*shashlyk*) are cooked when picnicking outdoors or when eating at the summerhouse, called a *dacha*.

Dranniki (Potato Fritters)

2¾ lb potatoes

½ c rye or wheat flour

1–2 eggs

1 tbsp rye bran or fine breadcrumbs

3 tbsp vegetable oil (preferably sunflower)

½ c sour cream

Wash, peel, and grate the potatoes raw. Do not drain the liquid. The rye flour in this recipe will make it the proper consistency. Mix the potatoes with flour and eggs. Form into small, thin patties. Cover on both sides with bran or breadcrumbs, and fry in oil on both sides until cooked through and nicely browned. Place into a warm dish until all dranniki are cooked. Serve topped with sour cream.

Kalduny (Dumplings)

For the Dough

2 c flour

¼ c warm water

1–2 eggs

Salt

Mix ingredients well into a strong, thick, and elastic dough. Chill slightly. Roll out very thin. Cut out small circles, place a small ball of filling (following) in the middle, fold the dough pocket into a half-circle, and pinch closed. Place prepared kalduny into salted boiling water. The kalduny are ready 5 minutes after they float to the surface. Serve with melted butter.

Tyshkevich-Style Filling

5 oz dry porcini mushrooms

2 onions, minced

Some fat (bacon fat or oil) for frying

7 oz ham, finely chopped

2 hard-boiled eggs, finely chopped

1 raw egg

Salt and pepper

Soak mushrooms in warm water for 3–4 hours. Strain the mushrooms, reserving the liquid. Rinse the mushrooms well, and boil in the soaking liquid for 1½–2 hours until soft. Chop the mushrooms finely. Sauté the onions in fat until they become translucent, add the mushrooms, and sauté together for a minute or two. Remove from heat and cool. Add the ham and the hard-boiled and raw eggs. Season and mix well.

Eating Out

In the 19th century and earlier, eating out in Belarus generally meant eating in a tavern. Many of these were kept by Jewish Belarusians, who were barred from many other professions. Along with alcoholic drinks, they served foods that have now been absorbed into Belarusian cuisine: *sheykas,* stuffed goose neck, various preparations of herring, and sweet-savory *tzimmes,* or carrot stew. Jewish emigrants have spread Belarusian cuisine as well. Dranniki, for instance, are more commonly known as latkes in the United States.

In modern Belarusian cuisine, traditional recipes are prepared for special occasions in cities and more often in the countryside. Since the 19th century, Belarusian cuisine has been greatly influenced by Russian food. In the 20th century, foods from the rest of the Soviet republics reached Belarus. Today, Belarusian cuisine is more influenced by Russian and modern Western traditions than by the past. This is especially noticeable in foods served outside the home in Belarus. At the same time, patriotic and nostalgic restaurants serving traditional foods have become common.

There are plenty of Soviet-style cafeterias left, serving dishes borrowed and simplified from Slavic, Caucasian, and Central Asian cuisines. The same menu could contain Ukrainian borshch as well as *azu,* Tartar-style sliced steak served with pickles. Restaurants serving food from the Caucasus are very popular. They specialize in grilled meats and make much more prominent use of spices than Belarusian cuisine. Central Asian foods, especially from Uzbekistan, are served in many restaurants. Recently sushi restaurants have also appeared. This variety of restaurants can be found primarily in the capital city of Minsk, as Belarus remains fairly poor and its regions isolated from the globalized economy. Most Belarusians still do not eat out in restaurants very often.

Various forms of fast food are affordable and common. Belarusian fast food developed in the Soviet period and featured baked or fried pies with meat, egg, cabbage, or potato fillings. *Bul'bianki,* Belarusian-style pies made of potato dough with fillings similar to Russian pies, were and remain very popular. Today, Belarus has a few very popular branches of McDonald's restaurants. Pizza can also be found, along with European-Turkish *doner kebabs* (ground meat on a vertical rotisserie, similar to gyros). *Bliny* stands serve crepes with various fillings, sweet and savory. Finally, inexpensive but high-quality, high-fat ice cream made from recipes developed during the Soviet period remains a popular treat to eat on the go.

Special Occasions

Special occasions in Belarus can be classified as traditional, usually religious, holidays; Soviet-introduced holidays; and life events. All holidays are likely to have both traditional holiday foods and also Soviet-period holiday foods served. Christmas is a holiday celebrated with feasting, caroling, and fortune-telling. Homes are decorated with straw, in remembrance of Jesus of Nazareth's birth in a manger. Christmas dinner features stuffed carp, fancy borshch with mushroom-filled dumplings (*vushki*), and desserts. These are fragile cookies called *lamantsi* and traditional barley or wheat-berry pudding with poppy seeds and honey, called *kuttsia,* often served with an almond soup-sauce *poliuka.* Shrovetide, or Mas'lenitsa, is celebrated by Orthodox Christians but has recently become popular among otherwise-secular Belarusians. An equivalent to Western Mardi Gras, this holiday is a week of feasting and carnivals, with revelers eating pancakes, butter, and eggs but no meat, which is forbidden during this week for believers. During Lent, rich foods, especially meat, are forbidden for Orthodox and Catholic Christians alike. Potato and mushroom dishes dominate the menu during this time. Fish, especially herring, is eaten by itself or with potatoes. In the past, beaver tails, due to their fishlike appearance, were allowed to be eaten during Lent and were seen as a delicacy. On Easter, *babka,* a rich egg bread with raisins, is served. Eggs are served as well, some decorated to become *pisanki.* Egg and cheese dishes, such as cheesecake-like *syrniki* fritters, are also served, along with springtime favorites like sorrel soup and birch sap. Catholic-influenced holidays bring other special foods to the Belarusian table.

Kupalle, or St. John's Eve, is an ancient festival related to the sun and fertility. Today, it is marked with a mixture of pagan and Christian elements. Catholic Belarusians celebrate the holiday on the night between June 23 and 24, while the Orthodox celebrate between July 6 and 7. The day following

Babka, a spongy yeast cake that is traditionally baked for Easter Sunday in Belarus. (Mariusz Jurgielewicz | Dreams time.com)

the celebration is meant to commemorate the birth of John the Baptist, but the celebrations of the night before hark back to pre-Christian fertility rituals. The holiday is directly related to food, as its rituals are meant to help the harvest. Women go into the ripening fields and gather wildflowers for wreaths. At night, fires are lit and many games are played, all involving jumping over the flames. These rituals are meant to please the sun, which will warm the crops as they grow. Dishes of fried eggs—cooked on a fire and resembling a burning sun—are cooked, along with fruit-filled dumplings. On All Saints' Day (November 1) sheep are slaughtered and prepared, while on St. Martin's Day (November 11) geese are eaten, with their giblets cooked in plum sauce.

Weddings feature a rich, large bread called karavay, similar to an Easter babka. Kuttsia since ancient times was served not only at Christmas but also during funeral meals. A rich egg and flour dish, drachena, has often been served in villages on special occasions. It is part omelet and part pancake and can be either sweet or savory. Its rich ingredients made it a special-occasion food. Belarusian Tartars prepare bialushi, round meat pies stuffed with fatty lamb and spices. These became popular quick snacks during the Soviet period. Otherwise, the Tartar population has been largely integrated into the ethnic Belarusian population and eats similar foods during their own holidays such as the Bairam festival.

Soviet holidays have become very important to modern Belarusian identity. The New Year now has essentially replaced Christmas as the most important holiday of the year. It is celebrated with gift giving, a decorated pine tree, and a large celebratory meal. The meal is likely to include traditional winter holiday foods, as well as Soviet celebratory classics, such as olivie or stolichnyi salad made with potatoes, meat, carrots, peas, and pickles and generously dressed with mayonnaise. A similar salad, sometimes called Minskyi, is made with potatoes, chicken, grated cheese, and mushrooms and is also dressed with plenty of mayonnaise. All celebrations now tend to feature imported wines and domestically produced harelka. Soft drinks, both the traditional kvass, syta (honey and water combination), and uzvar, a drink made of dried fruit and oat flour, are supplemented by mineral water and sodas. A similar menu is served to celebrate Victory Day (May 9), marking the defeat of Nazi Germany—an extremely important event to Belarusians, who suffered greatly under German occupation.

Diet and Health

Food has been seen as medicinal in Belarus. For instance, combinations of vegetable or herb juices with honey and alcohol are common folk remedies for many illnesses. Many medicinal plants were gathered on Kupalle night, as it was believed that their power is then at its peak. These beliefs remain today as well. Major newspapers, books, and calendars contain articles, often submitted by the readers themselves, about various folk remedies. Mint or lime-tree tea is considered helpful for dizziness. A plaster made of hot mashed potato mixed with vodka and honey applied to the chest and back is said to prevent colds and coughs.

Belarusians eat many starchy foods and a lot of fatty pork. In the past, heavy work in the fields made this traditional diet a necessity. In the past, access to fresh herbs and berries from the woods aided Belarusians in obtaining enough vitamins in their diet. Today, most of the population lives in cities and is relatively poor. Belarusians rely on inexpensive foods to provide most of their daily energy intake.

Due to the fairly cold climate they have little access to or inclination to eat more fresh fruit and vegetables out of season, and poor exchange rates prevent their importation. Heavy drinking and smoking, imported from the former Soviet Union, remain serious problems. These factors lead to about half of Belarusians dying in their mid-sixties from cardiovascular diseases.

Industrial pollution and remaining radiation from neighboring Ukraine's Chernobyl nuclear disaster in 1986 have tainted some Belarusian farming land, water, and the food supply. The concern about pollution remains strong for many people, who ask farmers about the origins of food in farmers' markets. These concerns are also addressed by the marketing of many food brands as coming from "ecologically pure" sources.

Anton Masterovoy

Further Reading

Belaruskaia kukhnia [in Russian]. http://culinary. org.ua/index.php?act=cat&id=4.

Bely, A. *The Belarusian Cookbook.* New York: Hippocrene Books, 2009.

"Cuisine of Belarus." Belarus. http://www.belarus. by/en/about-belarus/cuisine.

Belgium

Overview

Bordered by the Netherlands in the north, Germany and Luxembourg in the east, France in the south, and the North Sea in the west (with England nearby), the Kingdom of Belgium (12,500 square miles) has three distinct geographic regions: lower, central, and upper Belgium. Lower Belgium is flat (under 350 feet above sea level), with 40 miles of coast and very fertile lowlands. Central Belgium (up to 700 feet above sea level) has very fruitful clay plateaus and many gentle hills. Upper Belgium (700 feet or more above sea level) is full of woods, with large, fertile valleys and plateaus.

Belgium gained its independence from the Netherlands in 1830. This brought together two regions into the Belgian nation: Flemish-speaking Flanders in the north and French-speaking Wallonia in the south. The new state had a long-standing urban and trade tradition, with Roman, medieval, and early-modern cities like Tongeren, Tournai, Bruges, Ghent, and Antwerp. Later, industrial areas around Mons and Liège and the service city of Brussels generated huge wealth as well as social inequality. Today, Belgium is one of the most urbanized and densely populated countries of Europe, ranking as the 15th-richest nation in the world. Antwerp is the third most important harbor of Europe, and Brussels hosts the headquarters of many international organizations and corporations. Once an essentially Catholic country, religious control has greatly diminished since the 1950s, except for moderately growing Muslim influence that came with migrants. State reforms reorganized the nation into three communities based on language (Flemish, French, and German) and three regions (the Flemish region, the Brussels Capital region, and the Walloon region), with each having a parliament and government. Reforms did not abolish the federal parliament and government, so this little country of about 10 million people now has seven parliaments and six governments.

🍽 Food Culture Snapshot

Sylvie Delfosse, from Liège, and Hans Martens, from Bruges, have lived in Brussels since university. They fell in love, easily ignoring linguistic and cultural differences. She is a teacher, and he works in the advertisement business. They earn enough, but the children (Jaak, seven years old, and Evy, four years old) cost more than Sylvie and Hans expected. They rent an apartment in a trendy neighborhood, regularly set aside time for themselves, and are trying to save money to buy a house. The family represents the average European urban lifestyle of a couple with young children.

Weekdays begin in chaos. Everybody needs to be somewhere by 8 A.M., and breakfast is often limited to a cup of coffee for the parents, orange juice for the children, and a piece of toast with jam for all. Consequently, Sylvie, Hans, Jaak, and Evy need a snack around 11 A.M. (a chocolate bar or a waffle). Lunch is eaten in cafeterias or sandwich bars, although Hans occasionally has a business meal in a fancy restaurant. The children pay a small amount for a hot school meal (soup, a meat dish or pasta, and dessert), Sylvie uses the salad bar at her school, and Hans is happy with the sandwiches he purchases near his firm. Returning from her school at 4 P.M., Sylvie fetches the children and buys food in the supermarket, which offers a very rich variety. Around 6 P.M. the family is home. Sylvie and Hans cook together, serving fresh and healthy food every day. They try to limit meat, although Evy and Jaak like hamburgers, sausages, and chicken nuggets. The evening meal is limited to a hot dish, but occasionally there's dessert, mostly fruit. The children drink water or soda; Hans is keen on a glass of beer, but Sylvie prefers wine.

On weekends the family takes more time for cooking and eating, although outdoor activities sometimes take precedence. Sunday breakfast consists of fresh croissants. Sylvie loves to experiment for lunch and often reads through cookbooks from around the world. A treat on weekends is visiting the local open market where exotic food is sold. Occasionally, the family goes to a restaurant; before they had children, Sylvie and Hans very often ate in restaurants, which they adored.

Major Foodstuffs

As in most European countries bread forms a staple food in Belgium. Not that long ago, most of the tilled land was utilized to grow grain, mostly wheat, but today it occupies only 20 percent of all agricultural land. Importation of grain has always been significant. Bakers sell diverse sorts of bread and are continuously expanding their offerings. For a long time, the most common bread (*pain de ménage*, a 1¾-pound oval bread) was made of highly refined wheat flour. Until 2004 the government controlled its price by setting a maximum. Gradually, customers began to prefer so-called improved or special bread made of a mix of grains or containing raisins, nuts, or honey. Within a couple of decades, the hierarchy of bread types has totally reversed: Today, dark bread is much more appreciated and expensive than the wheat bread that had been the bread of the rich people until the 1950s.

For a long time, turning milk into cream and then into butter was time-consuming and very costly, so until the 1950s many people spread lard on bread. When more milk was produced and dairy machines

appeared, the price of butter fell, and specialized dairy factories produced more and more cheese, cream, and, later, desserts like ice cream. Butter comes in diverse forms. Some people could not do without salted butter, but others profoundly dislike the salty taste. Margarine is available in numerous brands and types, and it is marketed as a health-conscious choice (for example, advertised as lowering cholesterol). Belgium produces three types of cheese: cottage cheese, soft cheese, and hard cheese. Quite popular is cottage cheese mixed with salt and pepper and garnished with thin slices of radish. Pungent, soft cheese made with unpasteurized cow milk, *fromage d'Herve,* has had the European Union's certificate of Protected Designation of Origin since 1996. Belgian hard cheese is similar to Gouda. Processed meats, such as ham, salami, sausages, pâté, or *kipkap* (minced, seasoned meat), are much appreciated. These have a very long tradition that catered to both affluent consumers, in the case of ham and salami, and more modest ones, with preparations made of offal. The latter, enriched in various ways, are gaining new appreciation recently.

Konijn met Pruimen or Lapin Aux Prunes (Rabbit with Plums)

I rabbit (about 2½ lb)

I tbsp butter

Salt and pepper

5 shallots

I bottle dark beer (1½ c)

Thyme and bay leaf

Prepared mustard

I slice bread

½ lb dried plums (about 2 c)

Cut the rabbit into large pieces, and fry in butter until the meat is brown; sprinkle with some salt and pepper. Then, chop the shallots and add them. After 10 minutes, put in the beer, thyme, and bay leaf; spread the mustard on the bread and add to the meat. Simmer for at least 40 minutes on a very moderate flame, then add the plums. Cook for another 15 minutes. Serve with floury potatoes or croquettes.

Before 1800 potatoes were eaten with reluctance as they were seen as pig fodder, but by 1850 they had become a staple food, eaten by rich as well as poor people. Nowadays, *pommes frites* (French fries) are very popular. In particular, the "fries shack," mostly small, separate constructions with a window on one side where the fries are sold in paper cones and eaten while standing outside, is typical of Belgium. Rice and especially pasta have become popular but do not challenge the potato's position.

Belgians see meat as the centerpiece of a hot meal. Pork, beef, and poultry are very popular. Lamb, horse meat, and goat are rarely eaten, while game, rabbit, and other sorts are limited to particular seasons or social groups. Ground meat, mostly a mixture of pork and beef, gained great importance because of its use in sausages and hamburgers. All meat together adds up to an annual consumption of 220 pounds per person. Meat has always been a strong marker of social status, which is also true of fish: Rich people consume expensive species (like turbot or crustaceans), but poorer people buy cheap ones (like herring or mussels). Mussels have become very popular among all classes since the 1920s.

Carrots, turnips, and cabbage were the ingredients of a simple, hot meal, forming the base of today's well-liked *hutsepot* (stew). Gradually, other vegetables like cauliflower, asparagus, brussels sprouts, and witloof (Belgian endive) have been increasingly consumed, marking largely present-day Belgian identity. Most vegetables are bought fresh, leaving the canned and deep-frozen supply far behind.

Chocolate in Belgium is a matter of both daily and special consumption. It is everywhere: in shops, advertisements, people's minds, and household cupboards. The 1.4-ounce chocolate bar is a classic. In addition to plain milk chocolate and dark (*fondant*) chocolate bars, there is an enormous selection: white, extra dark, with nuts, and with fillings (cream, banana, strawberry, cherry, and more). Pralines, or small filled chocolate bonbons, are particularly popular and have long been considered the perfect gift.

Table display of chocolate-covered nuts, almonds, and raisins at a chocolate shop in Brussels, Belgium. (Jborzicchi | Dreamstime.com)

There are dozens of brewers and hundreds of beers in Belgium, together with many beer museums and beer restaurants. Belgian beers are famous worldwide, with several brands appearing in recent top 100 lists of best beers. Their international success contrasts with the continually declining consumption in Belgium over the last century. Of all the beer consumed in Belgium, about 70 percent is plain pilsner beer. Then come the renowned Trappist beers made by monks and abbey beers, the specialty beers (regional varieties), and the *lambics* (fruit beers). Declining beer consumption is due to the success of wine and soft drinks.

Cooking

The way Belgians obtain and prepare food is constantly changing, depending on such factors as agriculture, imports, manufacturing, retailing, and kitchen technology. Because of its open, international character, Belgium quickly picks up new trends and serves as a region for market testing. Hence, Belgian foodways are particularly sensitive to international changes. Today, most Belgians buy food in supermarkets of various types, where they make 94 percent of total food purchases, with the remaining 6 percent of sales coming from traditional ("corner") shops, open markets, and farmers. Almost all towns and villages have a weekly market offering vegetables, dairy products, and fruit. Individual bakers and butchers are able to compete with the huge sale of bread and meat in supermarkets by offering highly specialized products. Within Belgian supermarkets the supply differs, but all sell food: the bigger the supermarket, the more choice, variety, and price diversity. Apart from their size and supply, the hierarchy between brands of supermarkets is equally important. Crucially, because of their scale and international network, supermarkets are the places of food innovation. Through purchases in supermarkets, many people for the first time experience frozen products, convenience foods, foreign spices, unfamiliar fish or meats, organic and health foods, beverages, and other items.

Today, almost 80 percent of Belgians regularly buy ready-made food. Frozen pizza is extremely popular. Buyers of convenience food are primarily young families with little children, who appreciate the taste, the speed and ease, the variety, and the recent price decrease. However, most consumers think convenience food is too sweet, salty, and fatty; still quite expensive; not very healthy; and of average quality. The rapid growth of ready-to-heat dishes goes along with new technological devices that have become very familiar in many Belgian kitchens. Microwaves embody this. Yet traditional home cooking remains the rule. Today, almost two-thirds of Belgians cook with electric stoves and ovens, while the remainder use gas.

Home cooking in Belgium is primarily done by women, and most learned their cooking skills from their mothers by watching and imitating. However, they do not follow recipes or procedures exactly: Most interpret, modify, and innovate. In the 1990s, women reacted to the industrialization and globalization of the food business by revalorizing their mothers' techniques. Since mothers and daughters take less time for cooking, daughters have to learn the skills elsewhere. Most women rely on cookbooks to experiment and learn. Belgian cookbooks have been published since the 1850s, and some were particularly successful, such as *Ons Kookboek* (Our cookbook), which has the reputation of being present in every Flemish household. In many Belgian bookstores the gastronomy section is one of the largest. In addition to cookbooks, housewives may find recipes, ideas, and ingredients in magazines and newspapers and on daily television programs and numerous Web sites. Relatively new are the very popular cooking classes for adults.

Professional cooking is taught in so-called hotel schools, and today Belgium has about 35 of these. Boys and girls between 12 and 18 years of age are trained as cooks, pastry chefs, waiters, or butchers and may receive one year of further training (in *cuisine gastronomique,* for example). Pupils of these schools often win international prizes. Also, they are invited to provide the catering for special occasions. Belgian restaurants are highly appreciated by both Belgians and foreigners, to which the many stars, forks, or *toques* in international eating guides testify. Some of these guides claim that Belgium is, in gastronomic terms, the "best-kept secret of Europe."

Typical Meals

Since the late 19th century, cookbooks and school manuals have presented a three-meal pattern as traditional and optimal: breakfast (*petit-déjeuner* or *ontbijt*), lunch (*dîner* or *middagmaal*), and dinner (*souper* or *avondmaal*). Four to five hours between each meal are recommended, which implies breakfast around 7:30 A.M., lunch around noon, and dinner at 6 P.M. Eating between these meals is discouraged. Rigid eating times were highly encouraged as enhancing digestion and thus promoting good health. In general, eating hours are shifting, and more and more people skip breakfast and eat lunch and dinner later in the day than they used to.

The proportion of total family expenditures spent on food eaten at home fell from 17.6 percent in the late 1970s to 12.3 percent in 2006 (whereas housing, communication, and leisure expenses rose significantly). The lowest-income groups spent 3.2 times less on food than the highest-income groups. Compared with a decade earlier, this gap has widened.

Breakfast time is between 7:30 and 10 A.M., which is later than in the mid-1980s. On average, Belgians take 11 minutes for breakfast (a couple of minutes more on the weekends). Only one-fifth of Belgians have a regular breakfast, which worries nutritionists, since they assume that breakfast is the most important meal of the day. This should consist ideally of light and varied food that should be consumed in a relaxed setting. A glass of milk, some yogurt, two to three slices of whole wheat bread with a little jam, cheese, or ham, and some fresh fruit make the perfect breakfast. In fact, most Belgians limit themselves to coffee, some bread, or a bowl of cornflakes with canned orange juice. A sweet snack later in the morning often replaces the breakfast. On Sundays, Belgians love to have a full breakfast with fresh coffee and croissants, *pistolets* (a little, round, crusty bread), and other *viennoiseries* (little sweet breads) bought at the bakery.

Lunch may be eaten hot or cold. Many Belgians prefer a hot lunch, although outdoor activities force people to have a cold lunch in a cafeteria or a sandwich bar. A typical hot lunch is still considered ideal. One-third of Belgian people eat a meal at home between 12 and 1 P.M., and in general, lunch takes about 25 minutes. Since the 1960s, lunch has been later and shorter. Belgians tend to linger at the table on Sundays. As with breakfast, nutritionists advise people to pay ample attention to lunch and to reinstate it as the freshly prepared family meal that it once was supposed to be. Soup is a classic opener. Then comes the main dish, which includes the "golden trio" of potatoes, meat, and vegetables, all put onto one plate and covered with gravy. Plenty of potatoes are crucial, and these come in many forms, including steamed, fried, boiled, simmered, mashed, and baked. Pommes frites (fries) are increasingly viewed as an identity marker for the nation. Vegetables form another part of the hot meal, although many Belgians, particularly those with lower incomes, eat only small portions out of a feeling of obligation (caused by dieticians' great emphasis on the nutritive and digestive value of vegetables). Perhaps Belgians' low enthusiasm for vegetables should be explained by the fact that plain, overcooked vegetables formed the core of hot meals for most people in past centuries. The Belgian top three vegetables are tomatoes, carrots, and various types of lettuce. Quite popular is the combination of mashed potatoes with carrots, beans, or leeks.

Meat is the central part of the typical Belgian hot midday meal. It has always been highly valued by all social classes. Even today, after the weakening of meat's status since about 1980, there are still noticeable differences in family expenditures, with high-income families spending more on meat than low-income households. After World War II, beef and veal became popular, reaching a peak in the 1970s, but now poultry has taken over. Nutritionists see fish as a healthy alternative to meat, but although average fish consumption rose recently, meat's position remains largely unaffected. Commonly, light beer is drunk with the hot meal, but recently wine and sodas have challenged beer's position. A small dessert ends the lunch. This may consist of fruit, but increasingly dessert is bought in the supermarket, which offers an astonishing supply, including a gigantic variety of containers of yogurt, ice cream, puddings, sweet rice, and cheese.

Blinde Vinken or Oiseaux Sans Tête (Blind Finches)

½ lb minced pork

Salt, pepper, and nutmeg

1 lb veal

3½ tbsp butter

1 onion

Bay leaf and thyme

Flour

3 tbsp Madeira wine

1 tbsp tomato puree

Mix the minced pork thoroughly with some salt, pepper, and nutmeg. Cut four to five thin slices of the veal, put the minced pork on it, and roll to make cylinder-like shapes. Bind each piece with a thin thread, and brown the meat in a hot pan with butter (2 teaspoons). Dice the onion, and put it in the pan, together with the thyme, bay leaf, and some salt and pepper. Add half a cup of water, and simmer for half an hour. Meanwhile, prepare the sauce: Melt the remaining butter, add flour, and stir well, adding some water if the sauce is too thick. Gently pour in the Madeira, add the tomato puree, and leave on low heat for about 5 minutes. Serve with potato croquettes.

___

Belgians tend to eat their dinner much later nowadays than they used to, while they also take less time for it, about 25 minutes. Nutritionists worry about Belgians eating late, having television dinners, and snacking individually, and they recommend eating varied, light foods, with little or no sweet toppings or fillings. Many Belgians limit their dinner to slices of bread with ham, bacon, pâtés, salami, or meat salads with mayonnaise, with hardly any salad or fruit. Several times a year, freshly made pancakes or waffles with sugar, whipped cream, or jam may replace the bread meal. Light beer, but especially coffee, is drunk.

Eating Out

As in most European countries, since about 1970, Belgians increasingly eat out. A reliable indicator of this increase is the share of total household expenditures spent on eating out. This reached 1.9 percent in 1961, rising to 3.3 percent in 1978, to attain 5 percent in 1990. Since 1990, this proportion has remained fairly stable. Urban dwellers, couples without children, and big earners eat out the most. The 1.9 percent of 1961 reflects a very different way of eating out than the recent 5 percent does, with the big change being that since about 1970 many more people eat out for pleasure. Before then, this had been the privilege of richer people, whereas eating out related to work has long been common for many people.

There are crucial differences with regard to the location and style of eating out. In the late 1980s, 27 percent of meals eaten out were eaten in restaurants, 8 percent in snack bars, 57 percent in the cafeterias of schools and companies, and 8 percent in other places such as milk bars or fries shacks. Most eating out is thus work related. White- and blue-collar workers away from home buy snacks in a sandwich bar. This is a small shop with a large display

window, divided into two parts by a counter, selling slices of bread or baguette with cheese, meat, or fish salads and drinks such as coffee or soda. Other snack bars sell simple dishes such as *roll mops* (salted herring fillet)*, oeuf à la Russe* (hard-boiled egg with cold chopped vegetables and mayonnaise), *tomate aux crevettes* (fresh tomato with North Sea grey shrimp), or *filet américain* (raw minced beef with capers, Worcestershire sauce, pickles, small onions, salt, and pepper). Snacks may also be eaten at fries shacks, which sell fries in paper cones, with salt and mayonnaise and some meat. The coming of American-style fast-food outlets in the early 1970s only added to the wide choice for snacking. School and company cafeterias appeared in the 1950s in response to the desire to have a hot lunch at noon. Initially, they served a cheap, often overcooked lunch, but nowadays they offer a growing choice of tasty, healthy, and relatively cheap food.

Eating out for pleasure is relatively new. Many of the aforementioned eateries offer food also during nonwork occasions. Shoppers, students, theatergoers, or soccer supporters may enjoy a cone of fries, a cheeseburger, or a sandwich with tuna salad before, during, or after their activities. In the entertainment districts of the big towns one may indeed find a wide assortment of food almost 24 hours a day. About two centuries ago, however, a new form of eating out appeared in Europe, one that was exclusively oriented toward enjoying gourmet eating: the restaurant. This became such an extraordinary event that it made a special trip to another city or country worthwhile. The legendary Michelin guide labels this as *vaut le détour* (worth taking the detour). For decades now, Belgian restaurants are worth the detour.

Belgium followed closely the Parisian restaurant model because of its close bonds with France. By 1820, French chefs and waiters owned restaurants in Brussels, cooks from Paris worked in Belgium, and Belgians moved to France to learn the French way of cooking. Today, many restaurants in Belgium depict themselves as serving Belgian-French cuisine. This French character has always been highly appreciated by travel guides, which have assigned French

French-inspired restaurants, bars, and coffee shops along the old streets of Brussels, Belgium. (Rostislav Glinsky | Dreamstime.com)

cuisine the highest status. Belgian restaurants generally have done well in these guides.

Not all restaurants in Belgium have been influenced by French cuisine, however. Throughout the 19th century many restaurants, brasseries, cafés, and cabarets had a German, English, or Swiss ambiance. In the 1890s fancy Italian and Jewish restaurants appeared in Antwerp and Brussels, and in the course of the 20th century many more ethnic restaurants were opened. Today, there are about 80 different ethnic cuisines in Belgium.

Until the 1890s, gastronomic restaurants disregarded any reference to local dishes, ingredients, or methods of preparation, the French influence being absolutely dominant. This changed by 1900. More popular restaurants opened and were appreciated by tourists, while fancy cuisine became aware of

local ingredients and foodways. Culinary reviewers then described these restaurants as places where Belgians and foreigners adored eating informally and copiously, enjoying mussels with fries, *carbonnades à la flamande* (a beef stew with beer), or *waterzooi de poulet* (a souplike chicken dish with vegetables). Beer was typically drunk, and prices were moderate. Many other old and new *plats belges typiques* (typical Belgian dishes) are served nowadays, some of which had been prepared in the estaminets (small cafés) of the poorer town quarters in the early 19th century and some in petit bourgeois kitchens, although others are quite recent creations that are promoted as authentic and traditional. Belgian chefs eagerly responded to the increasing interest in Belgian cuisine, and they readily incorporated local ingredients and ways of preparation in the fancy cuisine.

Stoemp met Spruitjes or Stoemp Aux Choux de Bruxelles (**Mashed Potatoes with Brussels Sprouts**)

This is a typical Belgian dish that is prepared in many homes but increasingly also in Belgian top restaurants.

4 medium-sized onions

1 green cabbage (about 1 lb)

10 big carrots

5 big turnips

4 stalks celery

About ½ lb leeks

1 lb brussels sprouts

7 tbsp butter, melted

6 c chicken stock

Bouquet garni of thyme, bay leaves, and parsley

Salt and pepper

2¼ lb potatoes

Clean and wash the vegetables. Mince the onions and the green cabbage very fine, and chop the carrots, turnips, celery, and leeks into coarse chunks. Cut the brussels sprouts in two. Put a large pot on low heat, and melt the butter, then add all the vegetables to sweat (*suer*) for 10 minutes. Meanwhile, stir regularly. Then add the chicken broth, the bouquet garni, and some salt and pepper. Heat until boiling, cover the pot, reduce the heat, and leave for about 30 minutes. Peel and cut the potatoes into little pieces, and put these into the pot; cook for another 20 minutes, stirring regularly. Finally, heat the pot and stir well, and add salt and pepper. Serve really hot. Salted bacon is a typical accompaniment.

There are common features of eating out in Belgium. Bread is always abundant and close by, second helpings of pommes frites are free, and the choice is wide. But there is more. Fancy restaurants affect the way food is prepared, presented, and named in snack bars and cafeterias. Haute cuisine seems to be everywhere: not just in the street but also in the media and the everyday talk of the common people.

This presence leads to a diffusion of the restaurant culture, to which even the food in sandwich bars and cafeterias testifies.

Special Occasions

In the past, stringent traditions regulated eating and drinking during celebrations in Belgium. Restrictions on drinking alcohol were mostly connected to the numerous Catholic festivities throughout the year. There were about 40 "high days" in Belgium in the past, but regulations in the 1780s limited this number. Today, only six Catholic celebration days remain as public holidays. Belgians now have 10 official holidays when shops, schools, and firms are closed. Of course, Belgians do not celebrate only the official holidays. In addition to these, which aim to foster religious and regional communities, local and private feasts are celebrated, which contribute to regional and intimate group identity. A renewed wave of local celebrations emerged in the early 1950s and particularly in the 1970s, which has led to a "feasting culture" nowadays, meaning that virtually every village and city district has its feast.

All of these public and private occasions include food in diverse forms and quantities. An average year means 10 festive dinners for the Belgians, with at least 5 grand meals for Christmas Eve, New Year's Eve, one's birthday, Easter, and a life-cycle ritual like a first communion or wedding. The highest-income group spends 6.3 times more on feast eating than the lowest-income group does, and a lot of this money is spent on champagne, of which Belgians are the fifth-highest per-capita consumers in the world.

Since the mid-1990s, the traditions and rules of the older celebrations have tended to disappear totally. Fasting and its corollary, excessive eating, are virtually gone, whereas only traces remain in the link between feasts and the eating of particular foods, such as fresh eggs on Easter. Old traditions remain or are rediscovered during carnival feasts (Mardi Gras), which are organized in about one-third of the Belgian communes in February, including famous parades such as those of Aalst (East Flanders, going back to the 16th century but with an annual parade since 1851) and Binche (Hainault, maybe appearing in the 14th century; in 2003 it was put on UNESCO's World Heritage list). While making fun of the rich and famous via decorated floats, funny masks, and clothing, thousands of people eat pancakes, waffles, and pies but also eels, mussels, *smoutebollen* (doughnut balls; called beignets or *croustillons* in French), and sausages in little breads, while they consume quarts of beer.

Smoutebollen or *Beignets* (Doughnut Balls)

I tbsp yeast

⅓ c milk

1⅔ c flour

I egg

I tsp sugar

½ tsp salt

I small bottle **witbier** (white beer, Hoegaerden type)

2 tbsp butter

Oil for deep-frying

Dissolve the yeast in the lukewarm milk, and add the flour, sifting it well. Separate the egg, and add the egg yolk, sugar, salt, and beer to the milk-and-flour mixture; stir well, and add the melted butter. Then, beat the egg white and fold it gently into the dough. Cover the dough, and let rise until its volume has doubled. Keep it out of the cold. Heat the oil to 350°F. Very gently stir the dough, then drop teaspoonfuls of the dough gently into the frying oil and fry until golden brown, which takes about I minute. Use a slotted spoon to remove the doughnuts from the fryer, lay on a plate covered with a paper towel to absorb excess oil, and serve with powdered sugar.

In general, rites of passage give rise to plentiful eating and drinking, providing the opportunity for families to gather and to renew or intensify ties. Christian families celebrate First and Holy Communion, whereas nonbelievers have the Spring Feast and the Feast of the Secular Youth. Today, there are no longer fixed rules with regard to the food at communion feasts, which may mirror perfectly well the persisting trend toward innovation.

Belgian's declining religiosity implies the loss of traditional eating and drinking associated with Easter, Christmas, and other Catholic holidays. Since the 1950s the increasing purchasing power of Belgians has allowed them to abandon the traditional fasting and the correlated short-lived excesses after breaking the fast, while growing individualization has freed people from long-established community constraints. Yet Catholic high days are still moments of special eating.

The biggest festive meals in Belgium are those around Christmas and New Year's. Generally, Christmas Eve, Christmas, and New Year's Day are spent with family and close friends at home, while New Year's Eve is often spent eating out with friends. In December 2007 a survey found that 89 percent of the interviewees celebrated Christmas, and 77 percent celebrated New Year's Eve. Most people prepare familiar food, although they search for inspiration in cookbooks, Web sites, and magazines, which pay a lot of attention to grand feasts. Christmas dinners are rather traditional, with turkey, shellfish, salmon, game, and foie gras, along with wine and champagne. Since the 1970s, however, magazines and newspapers emphasize innovation with regard to the December feasts: the latest aperitif, an out-of-the-ordinary soup, or a fashionable dessert. In general, New Year's Eve dinner is less elaborate than the Christmas meal.

The food eaten on special occasions not only mirrors the general development of the Belgian diet but also shapes it in that many home cooks wish to excel in preparing special food. This leads to a continuous quest for new tastes, combinations, dishes, and ingredients when the festive days come into sight. Web sites, magazines, television programs, books, and specialized sections of newspapers are oriented toward guiding the home cook in this search. Often, new festive dishes have been tried out on the close family. If the meal was a success, particular dishes or ingredients may make their way into the daily cooking of the family. Festive eating thus introduces and diffuses new things. This contrasts with old traditions, when most feasts were linked to particular

Belgians eat and shop during the annual International Christmas Market in Belgium. (Richard Elliott | Getty Images)

foods. Still, many people prefer to stick to familiar festive food with such classics as asparagus, game, lobster, croquettes, salmon or turbot, cranberries, foie gras, and, most certainly, champagne.

Diet and Health

Today, in Belgium, food is on sale 24 hours a day, and most Belgians may eat whatever, whenever, and wherever they want. Compared with the past, this is a drastic change. If the pre–World War II food-related problems are viewed in terms of shortage and imbalance, with lack of calories, vitamins, and protein, leading to loss of weight and strength, edema, anemia, lethargy, and, for children, slow growth, the post-1950 abundance has caused problems of a new kind related to body shape and health: Being

overweight and obese increases the risk of diabetes, cardiovascular diseases, hypertension and stroke, and some cancers.

Today, 52 percent of the Belgians are considered to have a "normal" weight according to the body mass index (BMI, or the relation between a person's weight and height). The number of obese people, however, is growing slowly but constantly, and about 13 percent of Belgians are considered obese (with a BMI over 30). This worries nutritionists, doctors, and health workers, and public organizations regularly launch information programs aimed at convincing Belgians to move more such as by using the stairs instead of the elevator, while eating less sweet and fat food. Belgians have many ways of trying to lose weight. Slimming products such as laxatives are popular, but starting exercise, or simply more physical effort, is rarely considered. A minority of Belgians calls on a physician for help with losing weight, and stomach reduction has gained popularity. However, the most popular way of losing weight is dieting. This takes many forms: eating less in general, eating less sweet and/or fat food, eating more fruit and vegetables, skipping meals, starting to use diet products, and/or following, strictly or loosely, the latest fad in dieting.

Slimming is not necessarily prompted by health concerns but may be purely cosmetic, to attain the ideal body. Slim ideals appeared among the higher social classes in Belgium in the 1920s but spread to all classes in the 1950s. By the end of the 1930s, many cookbooks suggested a reduction in consumption of meat, cheese, and eggs, for both health reasons and slimming. Calories started to rule the lives of thousands of people.

The public authority's influence on what Belgians eat has largely increased in terms of safety monitoring, information, and recommendations. Belgians nowadays eat more safely than ever before, and, above all, they are much more informed about the tiniest food risk, food-safety procedures in supermarkets, organic foods in cafeterias, and dieting schemes. Yet despite the greater sensitivity regarding health and safety of food, recent crises have shown the very feeble trust most people have in the food chain. For some, eating copiously provides the badly needed security in today's uncertain times.

Peter Scholliers

Further Reading

Belgian Beer Paradise. http://www.beerpara dise.be.

Devriese, S., I. Huybrechts, M. Moreau, and H. Van Oyen. *Enquête de consommation alimentaire Belge* [Food Consumption Survey, Belgium]. Report # D/2006/2505/16. Brussels: Scientific Institute of Public Health, 2005. Available at: http://www.iph.fgov.be/epidemio/epifr/foodfr/ table04.htm.

Gastronomica.be. http://www.gastronomica.be.

Jacobs, Marc, and Jean Fraikin. "Belgium: Endives, Brussels Sprouts and Other Innovations." In *Culinary Cultures of Europe: Identity, Diversity and Dialogue,* edited by Darra Goldstein and Kathrin Merkle, 75–85. Strasbourg, France: Council of Europe Publishing, 2005.

Resto.be. http://www.resto.be/ware/index.jsp.

Scholliers, Peter. *Food Culture in Belgium.* Westport, CT: Greenwood Press, 2008.

Van Waerebeek, Ruth, and Maria Robbins. *Everybody Eats Well in Belgium Cookbook.* New York: Workman, 1996.

Bosnia and Herzegovina

Overview

Bosnia and Herzegovina, one of the six federal units constituting the former Socialist Federal Republic of Yugoslavia, has been an independent nation since 1994. It is located at the center of the Balkan Peninsula with an area of some 19,741 square miles and a population of about four million. Bordered by Croatia, Serbia, and Montenegro, Bosnia and Herzegovina is landlocked, except for about 15 miles of Adriatic Sea coastline around the town of Neum. Bosnia makes up about four-fifths of the country, Herzegovina the remainder. The capital and largest city is Sarajevo.

Bosnia and Herzegovina became independent during the civil war of the 1990s and the breakup of Yugoslavia. The country is currently divided into the Federation of Bosnia and Herzegovina and Republika Srpska. The 1991 census, before the civil war, reported 43.47 percent Muslims (1,902,958), 31.21 percent Serbs (1,366,104), 17.38 percent Croats (760,852), 5.54 percent Yugoslavs (242,682), and 2.38 percent other (104,439). According to 2000 data, Bosnia and Herzegovina comprises 48 percent Bošnjaci (Bosnian Muslims), 37 percent Serbs, 14.3 percent Croats, and 0.6 percent other. There has not been a census since the war, but estimated figures show a significant loss of population. All speak the same language, though each group calls it by its own name; because of historical circumstances, groups have different religious affiliations. Serbs are associated with Serbian Orthodoxy, Croats with Roman Catholicism, and Bošnjaci with Islam. Each group also includes nonbelievers. The declared Yugoslavs in the census are those who ranked their citizenship in the nation over their ethnicity, and "others" refers to Roma, Jews, Albanians, and other minorities. The term *Bosnian* refers to all residents of the country, but with the rise of nationalism spurred by the civil war, Muslims are now referred to as Bošnjaci, the term used in the Ottoman period and in modern Turkey.

If one discounts the pre-Islamic medieval state that preceded the Ottoman conquest, the area now comprising Bosnia and Herzegovina was never an independent state until the recent civil war. This means that the area has always been open to the free exchange of cultures, including food and foodways. The region has served as a crossroads between East and West for armies, invaders, migrations, and travelers. Slavs arrived in the region in the late sixth and early seventh centuries, and before and after settlement, control over the region was frequently contested by outside forces. There is an overlay of Ottoman culture throughout the Balkans, but it is particularly thick in Bosnia and Herzegovina, where Ottoman rule lasted from the mid-15th century until the area was occupied by the Austro-Hungarian forces in 1878 and annexed in 1908. Ottoman cultural influence was not just Turkish as is so often assumed. The Turks were a nomadic people until their conquest of Anatolia and the Byzantine Empire and sedentarization. It can be assumed that much of the foodways they carried throughout the Balkans were Byzantine in origin. But the Ottoman Empire also incorporated cultural elements of the various components of the empire. Examples in foods are many, such as pilaf (originally a Persian rice specialty), *burek* (a Persian word for *pita*, while the word for pita dough, *jufke*, is Arabic), and *musaka* (known in the United States

51

Burek, a Bosnian specialty made with pita and meat. (Blacksnake | Dreamstime.com)

as a Greek dish, spelled moussaka, but Arabic in origin). Regardless of origins, however, the foods are Bosnian today. Austro-Hungarian rule lasted until World War I. Austrian culinary influences were much less evident in Bosnia and Herzegovina than in nearby Croatia, where their rule lasted much longer. The best examples can be found in pastry.

The Yugoslav period, both the Kingdom of Yugoslavia, established in 1929, and the Socialist state (1945–1990), was a time of South Slavic integration, particularly during Tito's life, when great attention was paid to "brotherhood and unity" (*bratsvo i jedinstvo*) and free cultural exchange between the various constituents of the nation. In the post–World War II period, with increased travel abroad and work in western Europe, there was greater openness to the cultures, including the foodways, of the wider world. In the 1970s, for example, a cultural exchange between China and Yugoslavia resulted in the first Chinese restaurant in the country, located in Sarajevo. A Chinese chef was brought to teach local chefs about Chinese food, after which the Chinese chef returned to China and the restaurant was left in the hands of local chefs, with a rapid Balkanization of Chinese dishes.

Food Culture Snapshot

In Sarajevo, the weekly food purchases for the Dudo family—two working adults and three school-age children—include bread (15.5 pounds) and other starches such as flour, rice, potatoes, pasta, rice pasta, cornflakes, and manufactured jufke. They buy dairy products, including not only milk, cream, brined cheese, fresh cheese, premade ghee, and soured milk (*kiselo mleko*) but also imported Gouda cheese and flavored yogurts. Meat might include ground beef, hot dogs, baked chicken, several varieties of beef sausage, mutton, veal, beef steak, canned chicken pâté, and sardines. They also purchase eggs. Even in January, the Dudos' access to fruits and vegetables exceeds what is available to villagers. Fruits include a variety of citrus, bananas, and dried figs. Besides the basics of cabbage, carrots, and onions, the vegetables also include tomatoes, spinach, red peppers, and mushrooms. Other essentials are garlic, lentils, kidney beans, pickles, granulated and cubed sugar to serve with coffee, sunflower oil, Hellman's mayonnaise, peach marmalade, mustard, sea salt and other salt, chicken soup mix, chicken bouillon, coffee beans, Nescafé, and cocoa. Snack foods consist of raisins, peanuts, and candy, and beverages include sodas, mineral water, and concentrated and powdered fruit juices.

In contrast to villagers, the Dudos' diet includes many imported foods, a fair amount of processed food, and some industrial food. In cities and towns, many residents like the Dudos maintain close ties with family in villages, from whom they often receive meat, vegetables and fruits, *šljivovica* (plum brandy), and other home-produced supplements to their diet.

Major Foodstuffs

Except for the Islamic prohibition against alcohol and pork, there is little difference between ethnic groups in the major foodstuffs. In Bosnia and Herzegovina, the prohibition of pork is much more rigorously observed than that of alcohol. People eat seasonally. Fruits and vegetables are very important in the diet, and vegetable gardens are very popular; on the smallest plots of ground, people find space for a garden. There is also a widespread system of periodic markets that provide both local products and those from other regions of Bosnia and Herzegovina and the former Yugoslavia. In the summer, melons, especially watermelon, are very popular. In late summer women buy large quantities of peppers that they stuff, freeze, pickle, make into *ajvar* (a red pepper spread, also eaten as a condiment and salad), and roast and freeze for future salads. Cabbage is put up as sauerkraut, to be cooked or used as salad, and the fermented liquid (*raso*) is drunk between and at meals and in the summer as a thirst quencher. Whole-head sauerkraut is used for cabbage rolls (*sarma*). Fruits are preserved for winter use as compote; fruit butter (*pekmez*), which is especially made from prunes; and fruit syrups. Northeastern Bosnia is known for its smoked prunes from which a distinctive pekmez is made. Fruit brandy (*rakija*) is a very popular use of fruit; in particular, plums are used for šljivovica. Milk and milk products are important in the diet, especially in those zones given to sheep husbandry. This includes sweet milk, soured cultured milk (*kiselo mleko*), yogurt, sour cream, fresh white cheese, and brined white cheese (often made of sheep milk or a mixture of cow and sheep milk), butter, and *kajmak* (cream skimmed off heated milk, used sweet or soured). The whey left after churning butter (*mlaćenica*) is very important to the diet of families who keep sheep and cows.

Bread is the most essential component of everyday meals; it is said that without bread, one has not eaten. At every meal, except with pita and burek (see the following), slices of bread are placed at each table setting and eaten without butter. In cities and small towns, bread is often purchased, and locals know when bread comes out of bakery ovens. In villages bread is often baked at home. In isolated villages of western Bosnia, at elevations where wheat was not adapted, the everyday bread was of barley; wheat bread was also made, especially for holidays. Cornbread, too, was a favorite food. When these villagers went to market, they would often treat themselves by buying a loaf of white wheat bread for lunch.

Certain foods are emblematic of Bosnia and symbolic of Bosnian identity. These foods include *Bosanski lonac,* pita, stuffed vegetables, and certain sweets such as *halva* and *urmašice* (biscuits soaked in syrup). They are eaten in most homes and found on both everyday and ceremonial tables. The national dish of Bosnia, Bosanski lonac, is a stew of combined meats (typically lamb, veal, and beef) and

vegetables slowly cooked for many hours or overnight in a special covered earthenware pot. The pot (*lonac*) is so much a part of the dish that the dish is named after it. Pita is the generic name for ingredients rolled into a very thin, stretched dough (*jufke*). The dough is made at home or can be purchased in two thicknesses, depending on the dish to be prepared. Common fillings are spinach, fresh cheese, squash, potato, and cabbage. Pita made with meat (chunks or ground) is called burek. Without filling, it is *maslenica* or *maslenjak.* There are many variations. Spinach and white cheese, for example, are often combined; Christians make a potato and pork pita; and one can improvise with fillings such as chopped lamb intestines. Stuffed vegetables are very popular, of which cabbage rolls (sarma) are the most common. A meat and rice mixture is wrapped in cabbage leaves to form a sausage-like shape no

Sarma, a traditional Bosnian dish made with cabbage and meat. (Shutterstock)

bigger than a fat thumb. This beloved dish is favored throughout the Balkans as well as in Bosnia. Other stuffed vegetables include peppers (*punjene paprike*), onions (*sogan dolma*), eggplant, and tomatoes. Balkan peppers are light green, thick walled, and very flavorful, the opposite of bell peppers. Bosnians like sweets, and most households have sweet pastries on hand for guests. Mass-produced cookies and cakes are available at supermarkets, but homemade sweets are favored.

Buying in the marketplace from the growers and producers of products is the preferred way and a natural part of daily life. There are also small grocery stores and, today, supermarkets where staples are obtained. Traditionally, women shopped every day for food, but as refrigerators and freezers became more available and larger and more women entered the workforce, weekly shopping has become more prevalent for urban dwellers.

Cooking

Bosnian traditional cuisine has certain distinguishing characteristics: Dishes are not made with a roux; strong and hot spices are seldom used; spices are used in small amounts to enhance, not hide the taste of the meats and vegetables; foods are lighter because most are cooked in their own juices rather than in fat; and a wide variety of sweets are consumed. Cookery styles do change, and contemporary cooking styles may modify these generalizations.

The primary home cook is the female head of the household, whose tasks are to plan and prepare the meals. This is especially the case in traditional regions of Bosnia and Herzegovina; however, in contemporary urban settings, more and more men can be found in the kitchen.

Hearth cooking was still viable into the 1970s in isolated mountain villages of western Bosnia. In one example, the stone hearth was approximately 10 feet long and 4 feet wide and stood about a foot high off the ground. It was backed by a stone wall; the smoke from the hearth escaped through the roof of the passageway that divided the lived-in rooms and the storerooms. Wood was stacked at the end of the hearth; a fire burned in the center of it. When

they had burned down, the glowing embers were swept aside, the hearth was carefully cleaned, and the ready bread dough was placed on the hot hearth and covered with a *sac* (a convex metal cover similar in function to a Dutch oven), which was then covered with the glowing embers from the fire. Pita and other foods were also baked under the sac. Foods such as eggs (*cimbur*) and soup (*corba*) were cooked in pans over low fires. For long slow-cooking foods, a pot was hung from a heavy chain over the hearth. Eventually, villagers acquired wood-burning sheet metal stoves with ovens. The sac is still available in Bosnia, and sometimes in Bosnian markets in the United States, though it is now seldom if ever used in daily cooking.

In contemporary Bosnia and Herzegovina, both rural and urban stoves are electric, burn wood or coal, or use bottled gas. Grills and barbecues are popular, and Bosnians can follow their passion for grilled meats. Spit-roasted sheep is everyone's favorite, and meat, sausage, and cheese are smoked in backyard smokehouses to provide popular accompaniments to rakija. Suckling pig, spit-roasted or roasted in the oven of the local bakery, is popular among Christians.

Sarma, possibly the food that most symbolizes Bosnia and Herzegovina, is one of those dishes that frequently appears on everyday tables and is requisite at celebratory meals. The rolls are made with ground pork, or a mixture of pork and beef, and rice by Christians, and with beef or lamb (or a mixture) and rice by Muslims. The cabbage- or sauerkraut-wrapped rolls are stacked in a pan, which ideally is lined with bones or ribs, to which tomatoes or tomato sauce is added; they are then simmered until done. When whole-leaf sauerkraut is not available, chopped sauerkraut can be added to the pan.

Also symbolic of Bosnia and Herzegovina, pita is the most common dish. It is eaten throughout the former Yugoslavia, but Bosnians are especially known for theirs. Like sarma, pita is eaten every day as well as at celebratory meals. When making pita, it is traditional to place the filled dough into a large round pan with sides about one to two inches high (*tevsija*), starting in the center and coiling it around itself until the pan is full. It is cut into wedges for serving to individuals, but if it is eaten from the tevsija, people break off pieces with the right hand. It can also be made in individual servings.

Trahana or *tarhana* is a special food prepared in Muslim homes, and it is considered a specifically Muslim food, a belief reinforced by a traditional saying, *tarana, Turska hrana* (tarana, Turkish food). Regardless, some Christians buy it from Muslim families. Trahana is a small granular dumpling used in soup and as gruel for babies. Production takes about a week for the dough to sour before it is forced through a traditional sieve (*sito za trahanu*) to form the grains. It is then dried and stored in a dry place.

Typical Meals

A similar meal pattern can be defined for most of Bosnia and Herzegovina, regardless of ethnicity. The diversity is greatest when comparing rural with urban dwellers. Sunday meals often differ from those on weekdays, and what one eats depends on the season.

The same raw materials are available to every group, with the exception of pork and alcohol, which are prohibited by religious law to Muslims, and the cuisine shows only slight differentiation. A few dishes are, or at least are regarded as, specific to one group or another. Sometimes these foods are linked to distinctive practices; for example, a mixture of a shortening and sugar was traditionally eaten and used for divination by Serbs at Christmas. More commonly, the differentiation occurs in daily diet. Pudding-like dishes such as cooked fruit thickened with flour (*eksija*) and rice pudding (*sutlijaš*) are regarded as typical Muslim sweets, as is halva, a cooked paste of flour, sugar, and oil or butter. As already discussed, trahana is another food closely associated with Muslims. Christians, more so than Muslims, prepare a variety of cakes and cookies.

Of the meals, breakfast varies the most. Coffee is commonly the first thing consumed in the morning, but many Christian men, especially in villages, will start the day with a shot of šljivovica. Children rushing off to school might have a bowl of cold cereal, such as cornflakes, now available throughout the country. A favorite breakfast, if time permits, is pita without filling (maslenjak or maslenica), which is eaten alone or might be accompanied with fresh cheese or eggs (cimbur). This is a typical Sunday breakfast. In cities, few women know how to make maslenjak anymore, or, because they work, they do not have time to make it. A common urban breakfast is coffee with milk and bread with jam. There are, however, frequent coffee breaks throughout the workday. Urban coffeehouses send boys with coffee to businesses. Coffee is usually Turkish, although espresso is increasingly common in urban centers.

The midday meal depends on where one lives and whether one goes to school or works in town or on a farm. Many families eat their largest meal at midday. Some might go home from 12 to 3 P.M. for the largest meal of the day. They might have stewed chicken or Bosanski lonac, one-dish meals that can be prepared the evening before and quickly reheated. If a family works the fields, the woman left at home may bring hot food to the field. Working individuals who do not go home to eat might take leftovers from home or buy something to eat. When they get home after a day at work, they attempt to make a quick meal, the main one of the day for them— soup, fish or meat, a starch, and bread—or they reheat one-dish meals made the evening before.

Sunday dinner is eaten in early afternoon, and it is usually larger than those during the week. It might begin with soup followed by an entrée or two: chicken baked with rice or potatoes, vegetables cooked with meat (*djuvec*), sarma or another stuffed vegetable, and bread. It is fairly common to have more than one meat dish. A salad of greens or raw vegetables would be dressed with sour cream or oil and vinegar. There is always something to drink, such as mineral water, pop, beer, or wine. Dessert is seldom eaten, but coffee usually follows the meal.

When the main meal is eaten at midday, the evening meal is usually light, often consisting of leftovers from midday or possibly the day before, or soup with bread, sometimes with a red pepper spread (ajvar). Desserts are not commonly part of a meal, but rather sweets and pastries are enjoyed as snacks and with coffee or other beverages. Ceremonial meals are an exception to this pattern.

A complex of distinctions exists in drinking habits. Coffee, the variety called Turkish coffee in the United States, is prepared by all groups throughout the former Yugoslavia, but it is especially typical in Bosnia and Herzegovina and has the greatest importance among Muslims. Bosnian Muslims would say that when Yugoslavia again acquired access to coffee after World War II, the first shipments were sent to Bosnia and Herzegovina "because Tito [the former leader of Yugoslavia] knew how much we liked it."

The importance of coffee seems related to the Islamic prohibition on alcohol rather than to differential diffusion. Plum brandy (šljivovica), the national drink of the former Yugoslavia and widely consumed in Bosnia, has strong ritual use in Christian homes. It is served to all guests and at all ceremonies, and elaborate codes of serving and drinking behavior have evolved. Although many urban and lowland Muslims drink alcohol, the šljivovica syndrome is much less elaborate among them and carries little of the ritual importance. Muslims in Bosnian and Herzegovina generally are less observant then those in the Middle East, although a revival followed the civil war.

Upon arriving in a Serbian household, guests traditionally are served a spoonful of a whole-fruit preserve (*slatko*) with water, followed by šljivovica and coffee. In an observant Muslim home the place of alcohol was traditionally filled by sherbet (*serbe*), cold water sweetened with sugar and flavored with lemon or fruit syrup, served in small glasses and drunk immediately, followed by coffee. The ritual significance of serbe in Muslim homes was just as important and as elaborate as that of šljivovica in Christian homes. Serbe is never served in Christian homes, except perhaps for a Muslim guest. Today, in Muslim and Serbian homes, especially in urban centers, serbe and slatko seem to have been replaced by pastries served with coffee. Ideally, women always have pastries and sweets on hand for guests. Bošnjaci might serve Turkish delight (*rahat lokum* or *ratluk*) instead of pastries.

Most of the differences between ethnic groups are unrelated to differential diffusion of Turkish patterns. Turkish influence in all cultural spheres was greatest in the urban centers where Ottoman power

An assortment of Turkish delight or lokum. (Alaettin Yildirim | Dreamstime.com)

was centralized. Like many other aspects of culture, Turkish influence on eating habits follows a rural-urban dichotomy rather than a Muslim-Christian one. Turkish-style dishes, traditionally cooked and served in tinned copper utensils, are perhaps most commonly prepared in the homes of urban Muslim families, but they are more prevalent on the tables of small-town Christians than those of rural Muslims. The exception to this pattern is the use of pork and pork products. The cooking fats among Muslims are butter, clarified butter, and vegetable oil, whereas Christians usually use lard and vegetable oil. Therefore, Christians commonly claim that Bošnjaci have a distinctive body odor because they cook with butter.

One distinction most prevalent among Muslims in small towns and villages rather than in large urban centers is the use of a *sofra*. A sofra is a low, round table large enough to seat 8 to 10 people around it on the floor. Traditionally, people would eat from a common dish, using only a spoon, and Muslim etiquette required that individuals take food only from directly in front of them. In village homes in western Bosnia in the late 1960s, village Muslims used only sofras for eating and some food preparation. When not in use, they were hung on the wall. These villagers did not use table and chairs. Christian villagers in the same area used tables and chairs except for large celebratory meals when they, too, brought out the sofras.

Traditionally, coffee was served in small handleless cups (*findzani*). Coffee is made in a special long-handled copper or brass pot (*džezva*) with a lip but no lid that is used only for coffee. Christians tend to make coffee with sugar, while the Bošnjaci style is without sugar, but the coffee is otherwise the same. Bošnjaci serve sugar cubes with coffee; these are either dipped into the coffee cup, or they are placed in the mouth and coffee is drunk through them. Granulated sugar is also available for those who stir sugar into the cup. These distinctions are highly variable.

Eating Out

Bosnians go to restaurants, but the most popular establishments are eateries that specialize in specific dishes. One food that most if not all Bosnians eat outside the home is the much-loved *ćevapčići* or *ćevapi*, for which one goes to a *ćevabdžinica*. This is finger-sized ground meat grilled and served in a split *lepinje/somun* (Bosnian yeast bread about 10 inches in diameter) and eaten with chopped onions. Typically an order comes with either 6 or 10 ćevapi. This food is so tightly integrated into Bosnian culture that some of the first restaurants established by post–civil war immigrants to the United States usually sold nothing but ćevapi. There are many opinions on what makes the best ćevapi; some say it should be a mix of veal and lamb, others that it should also include beef. In the United States packaged ćevapi are available wherever Bosnians settled, and although it is now grilled at home and is a favorite picnic food, Bosnians also eat it at local Bosnian American restaurants. There has been a general replacement of lamb with beef among Bosnian Americans, and this has included ćevapi, which are generally all beef.

Some restaurants are known for having an exceptional mixed grill: ćevap, a meat patty with onion (*pljeskovica*), shish kebab (*šiš-ćevap*), small pieces of veal on a skewer (*ražnjići*), pork cutlets (*culbastija*), and lamb kidney. Bosnians are not big meat eaters, but they like meat and mixed grill is a treat. Proportionally, meat makes up about 40 percent of the Bosnian diet.

Another eatery popular in urban Bosnia is the *aščinica*, which some believe appeared in Sarajevo with the Ottomans in the mid-15th century. Like the historical aščinica, which consisted of a butchery, bakery, and restaurant, today's aščinica offers a buffet with precooked foods, many of which are meat and vegetable one-dish offerings, kept warm in hot water baths. The food is inexpensive, familiar Bosnian fare.

Bosnians like sweets, and to fulfill their wants, they go to special sweet shops (*slastičarnice*), where they choose from a variety of Turkish-style sweets, Austrian-style pastries and cakes, and ice cream. In the fall, one of the specialties is pureed chestnut topped with whipped cream, and on cold winter days one can indulge in *salep*, a hot, sweet drink made from orchid roots. Most of the slastičarnice in the former Yugoslavia were owned and run by Albanians, regarded as specialists in making sweets.

Special Occasions

The most important celebratory, ritualized occasions in Bosnia and Herzegovina are Ramadan (Ramazan), Eid al-Fitr (Ramazanski Bajram), and Eid al-Adha (Kurbanski Bajram) for Bošnjaci, Christmas and saint's days for Christians, and, in the case of the Serbs, Krsna Slava. These occasions are commemorated with tables overflowing with carefully prepared, often special foods.

Ramadan, the monthlong Muslim fast, is the major event in the Bošnjaci ritual calendar. Believers do not eat, drink, smoke, or have sex between sunrise and sunset. Families wake while it is still dark and eat a larger-than-usual breakfast, often including types of dishes served at midday and evening meals. Their evening meals also consist of more dishes than usual and often include dessert, which is not part of everyday meals. Ramadan is a period of intense devotional activity centered in the mosque and with much socializing in homes in the evenings. The evening meals, which break the day's fast, for example, are often shared with friends and neighbors. Eid al-Fitr is the celebration of the end of Ramadan, and Eid al-Adha is the commemoration, 40 days after Ramadan, of the saving of Abraham's son through the sacrifice of a lamb instead. Both commemorations consist of three days of lavishly prepared meals shared with friends. For Eid al-Adha, an animal, usually a lamb that is perfect in every way, is sacrificed and the meat distributed to the poor and needy. According to Greater Islamic tradition, one-third is given to the poor, one-third is given to friends or relations, and one-third (the right front shoulder) is retained by the family.

Meals for the Eids are elaborate, with as many as 20 or more dishes. A traditional meal began with a soup (corba) with trahana and lamb. This was followed by dishes served one at a time to the men seated on the floor around the sofra, who ate from the common dish using soup spoons. When everyone stopped eating, the dish was removed and another was put in the center of the sofra. After the soup came eggs (cimbur), bread soaked with lamb juice and covered with pieces of cooked lamb (*potkriža*), unfilled pita (maslenica), cookies soaked with sugar syrup (urmašice), cabbage rolls (sarma), rice pudding (sutlijaš), sauerkraut cooked with dried lamb (*kalja*), cheese pita (*sirnjaca*), a pudding-like dish (eksija) with prunes, buttermilk (mlaćenica), coffee, and serbe. The alternation of sweet and savory dishes is traditional in Muslim feasts.

Urmašice (Bosnian Dates)

Among Bosnians this sweet is also known as *hurmašice, nabrdnjace, brdarice,* and *hurmadzik.* The word derives from *hurma,* meaning "date," and the shape of the sweet is somewhat like that of a large date. Urmašice should be made at least 24 hours before needed.

Dough

1 c yogurt

1 lb unsalted butter

2 egg yolks

1 lb flour

Use cheesecloth to drain all the water off the yogurt, which can be done in a sieve over a bowl. This will require about 1 hour. Cream the butter. Mix in the yogurt and egg yolks. Add as much flour as the mixture will take (about 1 pound). The dough should hold together and be firm. Break off pieces of dough the size of an egg, and with your hands form into a ball. On a floured grater, press the dough into the shape of a date. Lift the date off the grater and place grater-side up in a pan with sides at least 2 inches high. Bake in a hot oven until a light golden brown, about 20 minutes.

Syrup

1½ lb sugar

2½–3 c water

1 tsp vanilla

Juice of ½ lemon

While urmašice are baking, prepare the syrup. Simmer sugar, water, and vanilla until it forms a light syrup. Add the lemon juice. When the urmašice come out of the oven, let them cool for a couple of minutes. Then, with the syrup simmering, slowly ladle it over the pan of urmašice. Keep urmašice in the pan until all the syrup is absorbed, about 24 hours. They should not be dripping with syrup.

After the meal, the host and other men of the family brought well wishes to their closest neighbors and kin. By custom they were supposed to visit each household in the village during the three days. The visits were seldom longer than 30 minutes, and at each home they would be served coffee, serbe, cigarettes, and Turkish delight (rahat lokum). The next two days the women visited from house to house.

For Eid today, the meal begins with corba (a lamb or chicken soup with vegetables, noodles, or trahana). Subsequent dishes in the order served are cimbur (an egg dish), *djulnari* (a sweet soaked with sugar syrup), okra (*bamija*) with veal, lamb with quince (*ćevap sa djunjama*), pita with spinach, baklava, rose-flavored serbe, stuffed onions (sogan dolma), *gurabije* (a cookie-like sweet), rice and lamb (*janjeci pilav*), rice pudding (sutlijaš), and sour cherry compote (*hošaf od višanja*). All the dishes remain on the table throughout the meal. Bread is taken for granted. After the meal, coffee is served.

A lavish, plentifully laden table is also integral to the most important Serbian celebration, the Krsna Slava, an annual commemoration of the day a family's ancestors were baptized and became Christian and a celebration honoring the saint on whose day this conversion took place. Serbian Orthodox churches, families, and communities have their own Krsna Slava. This celebration requires the presence of an icon of the patron saint and four ritual symbols: a lighted candle, a dish of cooked sweetened wheat kernels (*Slavsko žito* or *koljivo*), a special round loaf of bread (*Slavski kolač*), and red wine. The bread is decorated on top with a large cross. On its Slava, the family attends church for communion, after which the priest is invited to the family's home, where he blesses the bread, cutting a cross into the bottom and pouring wine onto the cut edge. The bread is then torn in half and everyone present tears off a small piece. The koljivo is shared by all guests, who each take a spoonful. A table is laden with food, which is replenished throughout the day and into the night for well-wishers who stop in. Traditional appetizers to be consumed with šljivovica and wine included bite-sized pieces of roasted suckling pig, raw bacon, cooked ham, pickled peppers, homemade fresh cheese, baklava, urmašice, mixed cookies, and white bread. The meal that follows often includes spit-roasted lamb or suckling pig and a large variety of pastries.

The most important day of the year for Croats is Christmas. A traditional serious celebration began on Christmas Eve and continued through the three subsequent days. A meal began with toasts and considerable šljivovica served with appetizers of white cheese and roasted sheep. Food was brought to the sofra in the following order: noodle soup, burek, sarma, unfilled pita sweetened with sugar, cheese pita (sirnjaca), cabbage and ham, boiled wheat with chicken, sutlijaš, and a variety of homemade cookies. Coffee was served at the end.

A very old traditional food, once a common dish of Dinaric herders regardless of ethnic affiliation, has become a ritual dish among Bosnian Christians with the introduction of a cash economy and migrations; it is called *cicvara* or *masla* in Bosnia and Herzegovina and *gotovac* in Montenegro. Corn, rye, or, less often, wheat flour is poured into a mixture of water and milk into which butter and cheese are melted. Even today, some Croats in western Herzegovina and Serbs in eastern Herzegovina prepare cicvara for Christmas.

Secular occasions, such as hosting visiting in-laws or family members from overseas, a work bee (mowing hay or building a house), and a village son's return from military service, are important events that call for roasting a sheep. Throughout the former Yugoslavia, a spit-roasted whole sheep is an integral part of most festive occasions. The act itself, usually accompanied by jovial visiting, drinking, and singing, is as important as the food prepared. It is no wonder that Bosnian immigrants to the United States, with jobs that afford some luxuries, are roasting sheep more frequently than they did in Bosnia. Aside from these festive occasions, spit-roasted sheep is a favorite food anytime. It is not unusual for restaurants in market towns to roast lamb on market day, and shoppers eagerly wait for it to be done. It is usually eaten with bread and fresh green onions or a salad of chopped onions and tomatoes. Marketgoers buy roasted sheep by the kilogram to eat while in town or to take home. Roasting sheep on water-driven spits are prominently placed in front of special restaurants located along well-traveled roads.

Diet and Health

The traditional Bosnian diet is basically healthful. Instead of being fried, for instance, meats are often simmered, and vegetables are cooked in the meat juices. These vegetable and meat one-dish meals are very common. The diet is grain based; bread, whether made of wheat, barley, or corn, is an essential part of nearly every meal, and polenta (*pura*) and buckwheat mush are surviving traditional foods. Meat makes up about 40 percent of the national diet, though in mountain villages the amount may be far less. In villages fresh meat generally is eaten on auspicious occasions but otherwise used sparingly. Milk products are essential to the diet. Soured cultured milk is heavily consumed in urban centers, and whey from churned butter in villages. Bosnians shop regularly at open markets where they buy seasonal fruits and vegetables, which they eat fresh and preserve for winter. Buying local without being particularly conscious about it is a Bosnian tradition.

Yvonne R. Lockwood and William G. Lockwood

Further Reading

Bradatan, Cristina. "Cuisine and Cultural Identity in Balkans." In "Food and Foodways in Post-Socialist Eurasia." Special issue, *The Anthropology of East Europe Review: Central Europe, Eastern Europe and Eurasia* 21, No. 1 (2003): 43–47.

Bringa, Tone. *Being Muslim the Bosnian Way: Identity and Community in a Central Bosnian Village.* Princeton, NJ: Princeton University Press, 1995.

D'Aluisio, Faith, and Peter Menzel. "Bosnia and Herzegovina: The Dudos of Sarajevo." In *Hungry Planet: What the World Eats,* 46–51. Berkeley, CA: Ten Speed Press and Material World Books, 2005.

Fabijanic, Radmila. "Identity on the Table." *The Digest: A Review for the Interdisciplinary Study of Food* 10, No. 2 (1990): 4–6.

Lockwood, William G. *European Moslems: Economy and Ethnicity in Western Bosnia.* New York: Academic Press, 1975.

Marin, Alma. "The Unbearable Lightness of Wartime Cuisine." *Gastronomica: The Journal of Food and Culture* 5, No. 2 (2005): 27–36.

Tanovic, Nenad. "Bosnia and Hercegovina." In *Culinary Cultures of Europe: Identity, Diversity and Dialogue,* edited by Darra Goldstein and Kathrin Merkle, 87–93. Strasbourg: Council of Europe Publishing, 2005.

Bulgaria

Overview

Lying between Romania and Turkey but also sharing borders with Macedonia and Serbia, Bulgaria lies on the western edge of the Black Sea with 220 miles (354 kilometers) of coastline. Bulgaria is a southeastern European country on the Balkan Peninsula. Bulgaria's terrain is mountainous, although lowland plains occupy 30 percent of the landmass in the north and southeast. Bulgaria's temperate, warm climate, fertile lands, and diverse environments (a third of the country is forested, and there are deep, fertile valleys and lowland plains) mean that Bulgarian food culture is diverse. Greek and Turkish culinary influences predominate. South Slavic and rooted in southeastern Europe, Bulgarian food is similar to Balkan food in general. The long period of association with other Balkan countries aligned under the dominance of the Ottoman Empire in the 16th and 17th centuries is evident in the presence of baklava, moussaka, and *gyuvetch* (an eggplant dish). Bulgarian food culture is a confluence of influences, coalescing into Balkan-style food in which one can taste the influence of the Greeks, Slavs, Bulgars, Romans, and, even further back, the Thracians.

Within a total population of 7,204,687, ethnic Bulgarians constitute 83.9 percent of the population, Turks are 9.4 percent, and Roma, Tartars, Macedonians, Circassians, and Armenians make up the remaining 6.7 percent. The religious demographic of Bulgaria is as follows: Bulgarian Orthodox, 82.6 percent; Muslim (Pomaks), a sizable 12.2 percent; and remaining Christian denominations (Protestants, Roman Catholics) and other theistic (such as Armenian Orthodox Christianity), agnostic, and atheistic groups, the remaining 5.2 percent. In 2003 it was estimated that 14.4 percent of the population lived below the poverty line.

Bulgaria's main agricultural output (agriculture accounts for 7.3% of the gross domestic product, using 7.5% of the labor force, while the majority of the population—57%—works in the service industries and 35.5% in industry) consists of the following crops: fruits and vegetables, barley, wheat, sunflowers, and sugar beets. The challenges faced by the Bulgarian agricultural industry include deforestation, industrial waste products and heavy metal contamination from metallurgical plants, the pollution of rivers with raw sewage, damage to forested land from acid rain and air pollution, and industrial emissions and the air pollution associated with these. However, the prohibitive costs of chemical fertilizers and pesticides mean that food products are generally free-range or organic. In contrast, for urban centers of agricultural production, the many decades of collectivization and state planning under the erstwhile Socialist regime in Bulgaria mean that these sites of agriculture are more conformist and less diverse in their produce.

The fall of Communism in 1989 caused a seismic disruption in Bulgaria's economy. In consequence, agricultural production declined following the dispersal of cooperative farms, unemployment increased, and the real monetary value of wages decreased; this was coupled with exponential growth in private-sector activity. Although Bulgaria is capable in principle of self-sufficiency in food production, the demise of collective farming has led to a decline in the agricultural production of key crops such as

Traditional Bulgarian moussaka before baking. (Shutterstock)

wheat, as have unpredictable weather patterns. Following further economic change in the 1990s, substantial increases can be seen in the production of food needed for individual household subsistence.

Although there is very little vegetarianism as a lifestyle choice, Bulgarian food culture (*bulgarska kuhnya*) tends to involve lower meat consumption than in other European countries. New European Union member states consume twice as much meat; the monthly per-capita average meat consumption in Bulgaria is 6.7 pounds (3.06 kilograms).

🍽 Food Culture Snapshot

George and Anna live in Sofia, the capital city of Bulgaria. As a middle-class couple, George works in information technology, and Anna is an administrator. George's day starts at 7 A.M. The impact of modern, fast-paced living means that they travel to work separately, working slightly different shifts. The amount of time George spends commuting and working outside the home means that he buys coffee for his breakfast, to drink as he travels. This he buys from a café not far from his work, along with a cheese *banitsa* (pastry). Anna, because she has a later start, at 9 A.M., and because her work is not in the distant business district of Sofia, has yogurt, *kifli* (a flaky pastry made from sweet dough with a jam filling), and coffee at home, all bought in advance from one of the small supermarkets that now proliferate in large cities in Bulgaria.

Lunch, for which they both go to Anna's mother's house, is at midday. As this is the largest meal of the

day, Anna's mother has made a starter of *sa'lati shopska* (shopska salad, made from tomatoes, cucumber, onion, and white cheese called *sirene*, similar to feta), meatballs stewed in a *kavarma* (stew with tomatoes and paprika), boiled *kartofi* (potatoes), peppers stuffed with cheese, bread, and yogurt. Anna's mother bought the ingredients for these dishes from the supermarket: The supermarkets have taken a bigger market share, so more processed food is now available and eaten, although most people still cook their evening meal from scratch. The local markets typically sell fruit and vegetables, and as more and more of the Bulgarian ones are exported, more and more is imported from Turkey, with a lower quality. However, Anna's mother bought the meat for the kavarma from a local specialized shop for meat and the sirene cheese for the shopska from a minimarket run by an individual owner.

For dinner, George and Anna return home and eat a light meal of meze (small plates)—this means Anna has to prepare rather than cook the meal, although she did make the baked eggplant the weekend before. The cod roe appetizer and the *pasterma* (air-dried, pressed, and cured beef, flavored with paprika) they eat, along with cornmeal *kačamak* balls, were bought in the small local market, although the pasterma was bought in a large supermarket. As the intricate nature of some meze dishes involves more intensive kitchen-based labor than Anna has time for during the workweek—and it is still the expectation that Anna will take responsibility for domestic arrangements—Anna opts instead to buy in some meals. In Bulgaria, both lunch or dinner can begin with meze, the series of small dishes that link Bulgaria to Turkey: Some meze are baked eggplant, pickles, and the carp or cod roe appetizer *tarama* that resembles Greek *taramosalata*. Bulgarian pasterma is a centerpiece of meze along with other cured meats such as dark Dalmatian ham. Hot cheese, meat, or spinach banitsa may also follow meze. Savories such as kačamak balls, cornmeal-based snacks, stuffed with a local ewe-milk cheese, such as *bryndza*, also feature in meze.

Major Foodstuffs

Although key staples and ingredients inform the corpus of Bulgarian food, regional culinary differences are apparent and mirror localized environmental conditions. Along the coastline of the Black Sea, a food culture that depended on fish consumption is evident, despite the diminishing fish stock of the Black Sea. The mountainous landscapes of Bulgaria are a source of dairy products, while fertile plains supply Bulgaria's substantial fresh-vegetable consumption. The everyday diet of Bulgarians is founded on seasonal, local products.

The northern reaches of Bulgaria provide root crops, while the south yields the summer crops of peppers, tomatoes, okra, zucchini, and eggplant. This range of vegetables figures largely in Bulgarian food culture. An extensive array of vegetables is grown locally in Bulgaria and appears on a seasonal basis. The seasonality of vegetables and food means, for instance, that spring sees a rise in the use of wild and domesticated green plants for food, such as dock leaves, sorrel, nettles, and spinach. There has been an increase in the domestic production of vegetables, and some of this produce reaches the open market. These include varieties of potatoes, onions, tomatoes (*domati*), garlic, okra, peppers (*piperki* and *chushki*), carrots, cauliflower, lettuce, cucumbers (*krastavitsi*), cabbage (*zele*), peas, mushrooms, celery, eggplant, zucchini, radishes, spinach, lima beans, pumpkins, turnips, green beans, and olives.

Major fruits include blueberries, melons, apricots, blackberries, raspberries, quinces, medlars, watermelons, muskmelons, strawberries, plums, peaches, cherries, grapes, and pears. Early summer sees the harvest of strawberries and cherries, followed by the harvest of apricots, figs, and numerous other fruits.

In preparation for winter, and the increase in price and decrease in availability of vegetables, vegetables can be canned, bottled, preserved, and stored through the production, for example, of sauerkraut. Indeed, the processing of vegetables into meals can reveal the many influences on Bulgarian food. Turkish nuances are evident in dishes such as stuffed vine leaves; Greek and Turkish tones are clear in zucchini stuffed with rice. The tradition of *turshiya* or *torshi* unites Bulgaria in the pickling of vegetables with wider Balkan and Middle Eastern food culture. Persian influence can be found in the etymology: The Persian word *torsh* means "sour." Turshiya is an appetizer of dried aromatic herbs, peppers, ginger, vinegar, and salt—acting as antibacterial agents—and

various proportions of chili, celery, beets, cauliflower, cabbage, garlic, and small onions. Its two most popular incarnations are *selska turshiya* (country pickle) and *tsarska turshiya* (king's pickles). Turkish-style turshiya, called *tursu,* uses a higher concentration of salt. In contrast, Persian-style turshiya, known as *torshi,* has a higher vinegar content. It can be made within the home—much domestic industry goes into its production in the autumn, even in urban centers—but a processed version of turshiya can be bought in large supermarkets. Served both at home and in restaurants, turshiya will be placed in a bowl alongside the main dishes on the Bulgarian table. Vegetables can also figure in popular vegetable mixtures or relishes such as *lyutenitsa,* which is particularly popular in the summer in northern Bulgaria. Tomatoes, roasted peppers, onions, garlic, and sunflower oil are combined in a mortar and pestle until they are of a rough texture. Parsley is added. The distinctively pungent taste is what stands out most clearly about lyutenitsa—etymologically, *lyut* means "piquant." The mass production of lyutenitsa has flourished in recent years.

High in antioxidants and nutrients, walnuts and almonds are harvested in abundance in Bulgaria. They find their way into the pastry-making industry in such pastries as baklava with its interlayering of phyllo pastry and chopped nuts, sweetened with honey or syrup. Baklava consumption spans food cultures from Turkey to the Middle East, the Balkans, and parts of Central Asia.

Dairy products, in many different forms, are widely consumed but with a particular emphasis on white cheeses preserved in brine, as well as types of yogurt. Feta cheese, popular throughout southeastern Europe, is associated in popular consciousness with Greece, but in fact it originated in the Trakia region, currently designated as southern Bulgaria. Existing in Bulgaria under the appellation *sirene* and made from sheep milk, goat milk, or, more frequently, from cheaper cow milk, with a fat content of 40–45 percent, this brined, grainy-textured white cheese is featured in banitsa and shopska salad. *Kashkaval,* a hard, yellow ewe-milk cheese, also predominates. Popular when dipped in egg and rolled in breadcrumbs, then fried, kashkaval is, in this incarnation, known as "fried cheese."

Yogurt (*kiselo mlyako,* meaning "sour milk") is an integral part of much Bulgarian food and is sold in various grades and qualities. A particularly buttery version, found most often in mountainous regions, such as Shipka and Gabrovo, is the water buffalo–milk yogurt called *bivolsko mylako. Arjan,* a mixture of water and yogurt, is also popular, particularly at breakfast. Purportedly, yogurt originated in Bulgaria, when the ancient inhabitants, the Thracians, carried sheep milk in lambskin bags; *yog* and *urt* translate in Thracian as "thick" and "milk." The high number of centenarians in the Bulgarian population was attributed to the high yogurt consumption in Bulgaria, related to the *Lactobacillus bulgaricus* bacteria used in the process. Although yogurt consumption has decreased in Bulgaria, it still exports some 200,000 tons of yogurt annually to Japan.

Rice cultivation in Bulgaria dates from the 14th century, although rice consumption predates this by some thousand years. Rice is mainly grown in the Pazardjik and Plovdiv regions, due to their proximity to the Maritsa (or Evros) River—at 298 miles (480 kilometers), the longest river in the Balkans' interior—and the Chaia and Goiolnitsa rivers. In relation to grain prices, meat prices have risen markedly, making it financially advantageous to buy grain for family consumption. Rice dishes often incorporate spinach or zucchini in contemporary Bulgaria.

Staples include rice, corn, beans, and lentils. Cornmeal-based kačamak (known as *mămăligă* in Romania) is a traditional Bulgarian dish, made from dried, ground corn grown near the Black Sea. Cornmeal and salt are boiled in water and mashed to a variety of consistencies, but in every incarnation it is a bread substitute and is similar to Italian polenta. In its drier version it can be sliced like bread, and in its more watery version it is resembles a thick ochre-colored porridge and is served dotted with sirene cheese, or with fried pork crackling, *prăzhki.* It can also be accompanied by yogurt and sour cream. It is also baked with meat or with yellow kashkaval cheese (similar though often superior to Italian *cacciocavallo*). Kačamak balls containing cheese, salami, or ham are a popular snack. Traditionally, kačamak was a staple food for impoverished sections of the population, but it has now

reemerged as a hip and stylish appetizer dish available in upmarket restaurants.

A key staple is bread, eaten with every meal—Bulgarians consume more than 22 pounds (10 kilograms) per person monthly—but rather than being home baked, bread is often purchased. Such bread would be both leavened and unleavened and uses millet, rye, and, predominantly, wheat. A type of plain donut is also consumed, called *mekitsi,* and a croissant-type roll filled with sweet preserves is popular, called kifli.

Core herbs and spices inform Bulgarian food culture. Summer savory, *čubrica,* is commonly used in Bulgaria and is preferred to winter savory. Similar in taste to oregano, čubrica is dried or ground and sprinkled on soup just before eating. It can be used as a spread on bread in a manner similar to the use made of *za'atar* in Palestine. The Bulgarian table does not have the simple duality of salt and pepper but will, instead, have a triad of condiments: salt, paprika, and dried summer savory. Mixed together, this is called "colorful salt" (*sharena sol*). Parsley, *magdanoz,* is used throughout Bulgarian cuisine, as is thyme, euphemistically also called "shepherd's basil" and "granny's soul;" thyme is used both fresh and dried as a seasoning in such dishes as broad bean stew. Also used sparingly for flavoring soups, and in a number of other dishes, is dried mint, called *djodjen* (*Mentha spicata*). The type of oil most frequently used for cooking is sunflower oil, but olive oil and cow-milk butter are available.

Meat consumption in Bulgaria is relatively low and, per capita, is among the lowest in Europe. Commonly used meats are pork (*svinsko*), chicken (*pile*), and veal (*teleshko*). Beef, however, is less commonly consumed, as cattle breeding focuses on milk as opposed to meat production. This means that veal is readily available and recurs throughout Bulgarian food culture. The availability of meat products shows some seasonal differentiation: lamb during the production period in the spring (Bulgaria is a net exporter of lamb); chicken in the summer; and pork during the winter months. Despite the minority Muslim population's objection to eating pork, it remains the most prevalent meat consumed in Bulgaria. Some explanation is offered in that, during the period in which the Ottoman Empire dominated Bulgaria, the only livestock animal to be exempt from the "natural tax" was the pig. Meat is stewed with vegetables in kavarma, a stew served in earthenware pots; stewed lamb and vegetables are *gyuvech* dishes; or meat is minced and shaped into spicy meat patties (*kyufteta*) or sausage-shaped grilled meat like *kebapcheta*.

Fish predominates in the coastal region of the Black Sea but is eaten widely throughout Bulgarian cuisine. Fried, grilled, or stewed, varieties such a bream, grey mullet, and scad predominate, as do freshwater varieties such as carp and trout. Shellfish attracts only limited consumption—mussels are a case in point. In 2009, construction of Europe's most extensive black mussel farm began in the Bay of Kavarna: Ironically, mussel output will be channeled to export, as Bulgarian consumption is very limited.

The rivers of Bulgaria produce freshwater fish such as carp, which may then be baked with walnut paste or poached with caraway seeds. Trout caught in a river may be wrapped in dampened leaves or paper, packed beneath hot ashes, and cooked.

Coffee consumption follows the Turkish model of imbibing intensely flavored and thick coffee, often with an accompanying sweet. Hot tea is, additionally, a popular beverage. Lying between the alcoholic and nonalcoholic is roseate sweet-sour *boza,* or millet ale, a fermented drink with a very low alcohol content (1%), made with a millet-flour base. Boza, unusually, occupies a special place as a winter breakfast dish, ideally accompanied by a pastry (banitsa).

Bulgarians consume a variety of wines and often region-specific alcoholic drinks such as *mastika, menta,* and *rakiya.* Mastika, which is 90 proof, derives its name from "to chew or gnash the teeth" and

A traditional wine cellar in the village of Melnik in Bulgaria. The village has been famous for its wines for centuries, especially during the Soviet regime. (Asafta | Dreamstime.com)

is usually made from grapes, figs, plums, or raisins. Mastika derives its flavor from resin produced by the small, evergreen Mediterranean Chios mastic tree. The method used for extracting mastic sap is very similar to that of extracting maple sap: collection of sap dripping from incisions made in the tree's bark. Menta is a liquor flavored with spearmint oil. Contrary to the expectations set up by its name, rakiya is not an aniseed-flavored liquor like Turkish raki but instead a fruit brandy, usually based on fermented grapes (*pomorska rakiya*), but also on plums (*slivova rakiya*) and apricots (*kaisieva rakiya*), which are then twice distilled. The Stara Planina region produces the notable Elena plum brandy. Vodka is also produced and a cognac called *pliska*. The most popular types of beer are *zagora, pleven,* and *astika.*

There are several main wine-producing regions, each distinctive, and there are approximately 12 producing wineries in Bulgaria, exporting to over 70 countries. The southwestern region is famed for *melnik,* a red wine—and red wine remains the most popular Bulgarian wine type. The southern reaches of the Middle Balkan mountain range are grape-rich. Intersecting Bulgaria from east to west is the Valley of the Roses, established in the 17th century by the Turks and now the core producer of rose attar, a rose water that is the basis for a small-scale industry in rose liquor and soap.

Cooking

Women do the majority of household cooking, in both urban and rural contexts. Traditional cooking pots of clay for oven baking, called gyuvech, are used to make the eponymous slow-cooked dish. Western-style cooking utensils and pans are used, in fact, for most cooking. Purportedly, a feature of Bulgarian food culture is that the cooking of one course can be accomplished in one saucepan. To a large extent, sautéing and deep-frying are rare activities: Many Bulgarian dishes are oven-baked, stew-based, or, when called for, steamed. Grilling is also a common practice both in the preparation of fish for the table and in the treatment of varieties of meat, for instance, the preparation of *kébabchés* (kebabs).

Typical Meals

Bulgarian food culture dictates that the majority of Bulgarians will eat at home but much more so for Bulgarians in a rural context. As the service industry sees restaurants and fast-food outlets grow and expand in cities, so, too, do opportunities for eating beyond the home. Domestic food in Bulgaria tends to emphasize the production of soups, salads, stuffed vegetables, and stews, while bread, sausage, and cheese might be more frequently produced and purchased outside the home.

While there are regional and socioeconomic factors to take into account, most Bulgarians eat three meals a day—breakfast, lunch, and dinner—although these meals may well be supplemented by a midmorning snack and coffee in the afternoon. Breakfast is a light meal, combining yogurt, cheese-based pastries, and fruit. A strudel-like banitsa (pastry) is eaten, which is an interlayering of sirene cheese with phyllo pastry—though it may also contain leeks or spinach (*spanachena banitsa*). There is also a sweeter version of banitsa stuffed with pumpkin (*tikvenik banitsa*) and a milk-based banitsa called *mlenchna banitsa.* Another breadlike product, *krenvirshka,* a frankfurter-style sausage in a light pastry, may also be eaten, as well as the breadlike *kozu'nak,* sprinkled with sugar, accompanied by coffee and yogurt or thick, slightly acidic boza or *airan,* a yogurt drink. A breakfast for children might have, as part of it, *popara,* made from bread soaked in hot milk and mixed with butter, sugar, and sirene cheese or clotted cream called *kajmak.*

Midday is the time for lunch. This is the preferred point for a family meal; if it is such, then it will follow the three-fold linear structure of a salad or soup, followed by a main course, and then dessert. Bulgarian soup has both hot and cold incarnations, the most famous of which is *tarator* soup. Most popular in the summer, this appetite-stimulating cold soup is based on a combination of soured milk (yogurt), walnuts, cucumber, dill, water (which can occasionally replace the sour milk entirely), and sunflower or olive oil. Bread can be used instead of walnuts to thicken this soup, and the soup may even be served with ice in order to keep the tarator's temperature down. Tarator may be served alongside shopska salad, although a tarator-based salad does exist in the form of *salata snezhanka* (snow-white salad), made using the same constituents and with thicker yogurt and less finely chopped ingredients. Vegetable-based soups (*zelenchukova supa*) dominate, and forest mushrooms appear in *gubena supa.* Bean soups feature in Bulgarian food culture, the most famous being *smilyanski fasul* using Smilyan beans. *Bob chorba,* Bulgarian hot bean soup, is a combination of dried white beans, such as haricot or fava beans, with tomatoes, peppers, chili, onion, and djodjen (mint) or even čubrica (summer savory). Indeed, bob chorba was a favored staple in Bulgarian monasteries. Sourness can be added to produce some of Bulgaria's distinctive hot and sour soups, such as *pacha* soup, a sour lamb's-trotter soup, through adding pickles, bitter fruits, or even vinegar to the broth. Other offal-based soups are also popular, such as *shkembe chorba,* made with tripe and milk.

Sa'lati shopska, typically the salad first course for lunch or eaten with meze or to accompany an aperitif such as rakiya, is made of a core combination of chunks of tomatoes (domati), onion, and cucumber (krastavitsi), with, sometimes, a yogurt dressing. Additionally, cabbage (*zele*) and peppers (*piperki* or *chushki*) can be added. This can then be garnished with a topping of grated white ewe-milk cheese. If dressed with yogurt and nuts and made with ingredients resembling those in tarator soup, this is called *mlechna salata,* and if consisting only of yogurt-dressed pickled cucumbers, this is called *snezhanka.* Furthermore, if a sa'lati comes with the trio of cucumbers, tomatoes, and peppers, this is a *meshana sa'lati.* The salad is often a communal dish, eaten by all participants from a common platter, with diners using their own forks to eat from it. When individual plates are used, the emptiness of the diner's plate will be taken as the signal for more food; a small amount left discreetly on the plate indicates the eater's appetite is sated.

The central course may be kavarma, which may come as casseroled veal or pork with onions and mushrooms, or pork with paprika (*slav gyuvech*). Or it might be spicy pork or veal sausages grilled on skewers with onions and peppers or beef patties

in their own sauce, called *kyufte.* All of these grilled meats come under the generic title kebapcheta but vary regionally from Sofia to Dobrudja. Kebapche may consist of minced chicken or veal, combined with onion and cumin and served with fried potato. Also on the table may be rice-stuffed cabbage, chard, or vine leaves, called *sarmi* (derived from the Turkish word *sarmak,* meaning "to wrap or roll"). Potatoes (kartofi) or some stewed, hot vegetable dish such as *gyuvech zarzavat* will be served, accompanied by bread.

Dessert may be a Turkish-style pastry such as baklava (a confection of phyllo pastry with crushed pistachios and sugar syrup) or *kadayif* (a pastry of shredded wheat with syrup and nuts). Peaches may come dotted with butter, baked, spiced with cloves,

Traditional Bulgarian kavarma in a gyuvetche. (Shutterstock)

and drizzled with a brandy, such as kaisieva rakiya (apricot brandy). Rice pudding–style desserts also feature and may be scented with rose water, laced with cinnamon, or flaked with lemon: all distinctively Bulgarian flavors. This lunch structure can always be abbreviated with the impact of modern living, making lunch a lighter meal, eaten at a fast-food outlet, such as a café or kiosk, although such fast-food venues remain relatively uncommon in Bulgaria, concentrated mostly in urban areas.

Dinner is eaten between 7 and 8 P.M. As it is not the central meal, dinner is light; it may include the same foods as at lunch, sometimes excluding the first and third courses: the soup and the dessert. If dinner is a meat stew, fruit may be cooked with the meat, for instance, pork with quince.

Both lunch and dinner may be accompanied by a dish of the spicy vegetable relish lyutenitsa, made from a mixture of peppers, eggplant, and tomatoes, or the similar relish *ajvar,* which is slightly less spicy in Bulgaria than in other Balkan countries.

Western eating styles are most common: Eaters will sit around a table, and each will hold a fork in the left hand, a knife in the right. Meals can last for variable lengths of time—although it is always a given that lunch lasts the longest—except on celebratory occasions, when meals can span several hours and are accompanied by *nazdrave* (toasting), which will occur sporadically throughout the meal.

Although Bulgaria is a small country, there are regional differences in food culture. The Black Sea coast influences the food culture of this coastline in the wealth of fish dishes and the wide range of fish available. Dishes such as the tomato-based mackerel stew *skumriya n keremidi* or a batter-encased whitefish served with fried potatoes (*tsatsa*) appear, as well as turbot, mussels, crab, and shellfish soups, and swordfish steaks grilled with lemon and oil. Dishes utilize the many varieties of fish sourced in the Black Sea such as scad (resembling whitebait) and grey mullet, used in onion and mullet casserole. Nessabar, lying on the Black Sea coast, produces a famous fish soup, made from four or five different kinds of fish, while Sozopol, on the southern section of the Black Sea coast, produces renowned mussel soup.

The southwestern mountainous Pirin region produces its own regional dishes: for instance, Bansko's unusually named sausages *starets* (old man) and *babek* (old woman). Bankso has a reputation for its meat stews such as *kapama,* a stew that combines pork, veal, and chicken, or the veal, onion, and potato dish *chomlek.*

The central Plovdiv region produces sausages, primarily in Karlovo, namely, the red-brown, square shaped semidried sausages *karlovski sudjuk* and *karlovska lukanka.* Made of chopped or minced cumin-spiced beef, pork, and grainy fat, when it is finely sliced, lukanka functions as an appetizer. Cooked sudjuk is used as a breakfast dish, fried like bacon and accompanied by eggs. The central Bulgarian Stara Planina mountain area, particularly centering

Traditional Bulgarian meal made of spinach, feta, and kori (phyllo). (Shutterstock)

on the town of Elena, is famed for its production of the national delicacy *elenski but,* a dry-cured ham, its taste accounted for in part by the climatic conditions of Stara Planina.

The Rhodope mountain region, close to the border with Greece, has many distinctive local dishes. The Rhodope town of Smilya is famed for the beans produced in the upper Arda Valley: a large white or purple streaked bean, used in salads or fried in a light batter; and a smaller brown bean with blue streaks that is a key ingredient in corn and bean *trahna* stew. Also from Rhodope are vegetarian dishes such as *patatnik,* a pulverized potato cake, in which some sheets of potato act as banitsa-style layers, all of which is flavored with mint and summer savory and may be interspersed with crumbled sirene cheese, peppers, and grated onions. *Rodopski klin* is a phyllo pastry dish, enclosing rice and white cheese. Regional varieties of pancakes are popular in this area, too; Rhodope inhabitants make thick pancakes called *marudnitsi* and *katmi.*

Eating Out

In urban areas and large cities, such as Sofia, Varna, Burgas, or Plovdiv, there are many multicultural restaurants. In Sofia alone it is possible to eat Italian, Russian, Korean, German, Japanese, and Vietnamese food. There is even an Indian restaurant in Sofia: Ramayna, in the Lozenets quarter of Sofia. The roadsides are dotted with stands selling Bulgarian street food in the form of kebapcheta and kyufteta. Patisseries sell tea, coffee, pastries, and cakes such as the chocolate cake *garash.* Along with coffee bars and pubs, these outlets remain popular meeting places. McDonald's and other fast-food outlets are taking hold in Bulgaria, and a recent study published in *USA Today* revealed that as many as 68 percent of Bulgarians interviewed admitted to fast-food dependence.

Traditionally, be it in an urban or rural context, *mehana,* traditional Bulgarian hostelries, would be popular sources of food, along with offering folk dancing and folk music. The mehana also exists in cultures connected to that of Bulgaria, such as Turkey, where such restaurants and drinking establishments are called *meyhane,* with both names deriving from the Persian *may,* meaning "wine," and *χāna,* meaning "house."

Special Occasions

Fasting is central to the observance of two of the religions of Bulgaria: the dominant theism of Orthodox Christianity and the minority religion of Islam. Orthodox Christians may adhere to the observance of the Lenten fast before Easter, while Muslims may observe the daylight fast of Ramadan (Ramazan). Specific dishes are exchanged at the end of each fasting day: Sugared delicacies are exchanged in the nondaylight eating hours of Ramadan. Both religions also mark celebration, devotion, and rebirth through food. The willing sacrifice of Ishmael by Abraham is relived through food metaphor in the Eid al-Adha (Kurban Bairam) practice of preparing a spit-roasted sheep or goat. This religious observance is the Turkic equivalent to the Muslim "feast of sacrifice," Eid al-Adha (Arabic). Indeed, the word *kurban,* meaning "sacrifice," also denotes a ceremonial meat dish. Spanning the whole year is the Muslim refusal of pork.

The rebirth of Easter is celebrated in the visual extravaganza of braided and dyed *kozunak* bread, dotted with dyed eggs and tasting of warmed rum, raisins, and lemon zest. The joy of Christmas and the Nativity is expressed through a greater number of vegetarian dishes, such as stuffed vine leaves (sarmi) and stuffed peppers, and through visual food "tricks," surprises, and games, such as hiding slips of paper within banitsa. There is the familiar danger of swallowing one's fortune or luck as one of the coins or charms hidden in cakes and pastries made for Christian holidays. Cabbage will be consumed on New Year's Eve. On St. Barbara's Day, December 4 (to honor the saint who protects against smallpox), it is customary to bake unleavened bread, spread it with honey, and offer pieces of this on the roadside to passersby, with the salutation to strangers of "May God bless you, your family, your people, your cattle and all!" The morning of St. Barbara's Day should be marked by an odd number of children boiling kidney beans in a broth with salt and onion; when ready, the youngest child would put three of the beans on the knees of each of the other children. They then had to eat the beans without using their hands.

On the day of the great winter festival, December 6, Nikulden (St. Nicholay's Day), fish—blessed carp baked in pastry (*ribnik*)—is consumed, having been baked with two loaves of bread per household, and the table is open to all guests. Carp is considered the saint's servant. As St. Nicholay is the saint of the seas, fishermen offer the day's catch to the saint, and the first fish caught will be cooked and eaten, ritually, on the shoreline by the fishermen. After the fish has been blessed, and after incense has been given, the local priest is, traditionally, offered the tail end of the carp. The cross-shaped *krakhche* bone of the carp used to be sewn into children's caps to guard them against malevolent spirits. The bones of the carp must be either burned, buried, or returned to the river. In a similar way, on May 6, Gergyovden Day (St. George's Day, the most popular name day in Bulgaria: Over half of Bulgarian men are named after St. George, farmers bake round bread in honor of the patron saint of farming, and roast lamb is on the table. There is even a special liquor for the day: *rakia Gergyovden.* All of the dishes mentioned should be cooked by the participants: Store-bought, ready-to-cook foods are not examples of genuine veneration.

Diet and Health

While herbalism has long held an honored place in Bulgarian home treatment, the economic hardships of the 1990s placed Western prescription medicines beyond the financial reach of many Bulgarians, leading many to look inwardly to traditional methods of medical care once again. For instance, čubrica, summer savory, is said, when rubbed on an insect sting, to soothe the skin's painful reaction, but it is also used more generally as a pick-me-up, as an expectorant to help clear phlegm in the lungs and sinuses, and as a preventative of diarrhea and reliever of colic and flatulence. Although there has been debate in Bulgarian food culture about whether the onion should be considered a spice, its efficacy is not questioned. Onion is considered to have some medicinal properties and to stimulate the secretion of gastric juices. It appears raw in salads and travels through Bulgarian cookery, appearing in stews, sauces, and preserves. Bulgaria has great resources of mineral waters, most notably the spring-fed water in a number of towns that cluster around Plovdiv: Brasigovo and Hisarja. Used to treat gastrointestinal disorders, such water is also bottled and distributed commercially. Soup also holds a place in the panoply of anecdotal food "cures" in Bulgaria: The tripe soup shkembe chorba reputedly alleviates the gastrointestinal problems associated with hangovers.

Fiona Ross

Further Reading

Davies, Trish. *The Balkan Cookbook: Traditional Cooking from Romania, Bulgaria and the Balkan Countries.* London: Anness, 1999.

Croatia

Overview

As with every aspect of life in the Balkans, cuisine in Croatia has political and cultural connotations. During the period of government-enforced harmony when the Serbs, Croats, Slovenes, Bosnians, ethnic Albanians, and Macedonians were all enveloped in Yugoslavia, cultural differences were officially minimized and almost invisible to outsiders. Since the breakup of Yugoslavia into separate republics, partisans have made exaggerated claims for the uniqueness of each ethnic and religious group's foodways. Although the foodways are superficially similar, Croatia's history and geography have given it a cuisine with subtle differences from its neighbors'.

All cuisines of the former Yugoslavia were influenced by three occupiers: the Ottomans, the Austro-Hungarians, and the Venetians. Though known by different names in the various languages and dialects of the Balkans, Turkish-influenced kebabs such as *čevapčići* and *ražnjići* are enjoyed everywhere. They are made with beef and pork in Croatia, lamb in Bosnia and Macedonia, and all three in Serbia, but the spicing and preparation are essentially the same. All are served either plain or in a domed bread loaf, a *somun,* with or without onions on the side. Similarly, each country has its own version of schnitzel, with only the most minor differences in preparation to distinguish one from the other.

The situation with Croatia is more complex than with most other states of the former Yugoslavia because from medieval times until less than 100 years ago, the coastal and inland regions were often ruled by different empires that fostered cultural ties with faraway capitals. Inland Croatia was occupied by the Austro-Hungarians longer than any other part of the Balkans, and there is a correspondingly strong Germanic influence in the cuisine of that region. Meanwhile, the coastal counties of Istria and Dalmatia were part of the Venetian Republic and later the Kingdom of Italy, and as late as 1910, more than a third of the population of the coastal regions spoke Italian as their native language. Only a tiny section of the coast around the city of Dubrovnik and a few offshore islands, collectively known as the Republic of Ragusa, remained independent and under native Croatian control for any substantial period.

The ease of travel by sea, the wealth of nearby Venice, and the relative difficulty of crossing the Balkans meant that trade links from the sea to the interior were few, and luxury goods and imported spices were more plentiful on the coast. Inevitably, the coastal cuisine contains more complex and sophisticated dishes using seafood, while the cuisines of the mountains and the Pannonian Plain near the Hungarian border are simpler and use more meat.

🍽 Food Culture Snapshot

Dusan and his wife, Dijana, start their day with an early and modest breakfast, rolls with some cheese or smoked meat, yogurt, and a small cup of very strong coffee. She grew up on the Adriatic coast and considers a bowl of soft polenta the best way to start the day, but he is from Zagreb and prefers bread. After he leaves for work, Dijana checks the pot of pork and

Goulash, often made with pork and pumpkin, is a popular Croatian dish. (Shutterstock)

potato stew that was left on low heat overnight. Their apartment is modern and has gas, but through the open window she can hear the neighbor raking out the embers from the stone hearth in their medieval house. She envies that neighbor sometimes for the beauty of her old home, but the sound of the hearth being shoveled out every morning reminds her of the virtues of new construction.

Dijana works part-time, and she spends a few hours around the house in the morning. When she is just about to go shopping for groceries, her neighbor invites her in for *marenda,* the traditional late-morning snack. A meal with a friend is a more attractive proposition than stopping at a street stall at the market, so she gratefully accepts. After fruit and a cup of *jota,* the minestrone-like soup, her neighbor pours a glass of *bevanda,* wine diluted with water. Her husband

can't have this traditional accompaniment to marenda because he works for a multinational company that frowns on any consumption of alcohol during working hours. She has no such problem, and she sits over a glass and chats with the neighbor for a few minutes before going to the market.

Although modern supermarkets (often called hypermarkets, in the European fashion) are nearby, she prefers the traditional street market because the selection of fresh fish is usually better. She gets fresh sardines at an excellent price, but the find of the day is at a nearby vegetable stall. There is *blitva,* fresh young Swiss chard, a specialty of the Croatian islands, which will be a good accompaniment to dinner. At another stall an old farmer sells *misanca,* a mix of wild onions, forest herbs, and edible flowers. With a few salted anchovies, a sliced hard-boiled egg, some capers, and olive oil, it will make an excellent salad for dinner.

Dijana makes it home in plenty of time to increase the heat under the stew, mix the misanca into a salad, and make a few quick side dishes before Dusan comes in for lunch. He arrives just after 2 P.M., and they sit down for the largest meal of the day. Dusan mentions that his company's new manager, who is not Croatian, will be hosting important American clients for dinner tomorrow and wants him to join them. The Americans often are confused by the tradition of the marenda and taking the main meal in the middle of the day, and Dusan and the other Croatian managers have to make allowances for their odd habit of having the main meal late. The Croatians think it is unhealthy to eat heavily at night, but business is business.

Dusan goes back to work, and Dijana heads to her job at a local computer store. Like most urban retail businesses, it closes at 7:30 P.M., and she and Dusan are both home by 8 P.M. She fries the sardines in olive oil and herbs, puts them on a bed of sautéed chard, and serves it with some of the leftover stew and glasses of wine. They finish with slices of cherry strudel that she picked up in the market—a simple, light, and satisfying meal to finish the day. Dusan has some friends coming over to play *belot* and other card games, so she sets out glasses and a bottle of *rakija* (a strong clear liquor). Some of the men who are coming don't drink, but offering alcohol is part of hospitality. Dijana knows that the brass coffee grinder and the ensuing Turkish-style coffee will be popular with everyone.

Major Foodstuffs

Coastal Croatia is a continuous Mediterranean-type ecosystem with Slovenia and Italy to the north and Macedonia, Albania, and Greece to the south, and all the Adriatic cuisines share the same elements. Ocean fish of many kinds is abundant, particularly tuna, mullet, sardines, squid, octopus, and mackerel, as well as shellfish such as shrimp, mussels, clams, crabs, and lobster. Frogs, eels, and river crabs are all eaten in Dalmatia. Fish is also popular inland, with freshwater species such as carp, catfish, and pickerel predominating.

Pigs and sheep are raised everywhere in the country, while cattle are raised mainly on the inland and northern plains. Venison is a specialty of the alpine and coastal regions, and rabbit is widely eaten in the north. *Prst,* the local version of prosciutto, based on beef, mutton, goat, venison, or goose and turkey, is a popular appetizer.

Cow-, goat-, and sheep-milk cheeses are made throughout the country, mostly by small producers, but the salty, hard sheep-milk cheese from the island of Pag, called *Paški sir,* is the most prized. The taste and texture are similar to Parmesan, and it is eaten as an appetizer with olives and used in cooking. Several soft cheeses and cottage cheeses are used for vegetable casseroles that are a popular side dish. *Kajmak,* a fatty, crumbly cheese based on cream, is universally encountered, even, occasionally, on so-called cheeseburgers.

The principal vegetables include bell peppers, onions, eggplant, green beans, cabbage, and tomatoes. Potatoes are boiled, roasted, fried, used in soups, and pounded into flour for gnocchi (*njoki* in Serbo-Croatian). Other common vegetables and pulses/legumes include beans, peas, lentils, carrots, artichokes, mushrooms, and asparagus. The Istria region produces small amounts of white truffles, which are highly prized. A type of seaweed known as *motar* (rock samphire or sea fennel in English) is a delicacy along the coast; it fell out of favor for many years but has recently enjoyed a rediscovery.

City families often have a *vikendica* (weekend place), where they may grow vegetables and fruits, as well as harvest wild plants, or they may have a city allotment. Spring and summer weekends are usually spent at the vikendica, and fresh foods are brought home either from the family plot or from visits to country cousins.

High-quality wheat is grown in inland areas of the country, and Croatia is a net exporter of winter wheat, spelt, and related products such as pasta. Corn (maize) is widely cultivated and eaten locally, and production has been increasing. Street vendors may be found selling corn on the cob. Buckwheat has been cultivated in Croatia since the Neolithic period and is a staple in the mountainous regions. Modest soybean and barley crops are grown for domestic consumption.

Croatian cuisine as a whole is not highly spiced, but almost any meal might include paprika and other red pepper–based condiments. Other spices that will be found in any kitchen are rosemary, parsley, salt, and pepper. Apples, almonds, chestnuts, plums, cherries, walnuts, grapes, raisins, and elderberries are all used in desserts and in some savory dishes.

Cooking

The center of a traditional Croatian kitchen is a woodstove known as a *commine,* which is under a domelike hood called a *peka.* Here, pots and skillets sit right on the embers of the fire or hang from hooks, and meat can be roasted on spits or smoked by hanging it in the chimney. Meats prepared in this fashion are known as *na pekara.*

Most families also have a *kotao* (boiler), a wide, shallow cauldron built on top of an iron pot-bellied charcoal stove, usually used outside. Modern homes might have a gas kotao. Items cooked on this stove are called *kotlovina,* meaning "food from the cauldron." Many kotlovina recipes are slow-cooked all day, and a few require more than one day to prepare. Another outdoor cooking method that is popular in the coastal regions is cooking lamb or fish on spikes at the edge of a fire.

Inland parts of the country are famous for pickling in vinegar, and there are many regional varieties of sauerkraut. Cabbage leaves are also pickled whole and used for the stuffed cabbage called *sarma.* Other vegetables that are pickled are cucumbers, onions, eggplant, beets, and bell peppers. Large plastic tubs of pickled winter vegetables, *zimnica,* are found stored on patios throughout the country. Meats are pickled, too, or made into sausages, dried, or smoked. In the colder parts of the country people still keep a *lodrica ili tiblica*—literally, "big wooden bowl"—with cooked meats preserved under a layer of lard.

The northwest is noted for jams and jellies, particularly from plums, cherries, and rose hips. These are used to spread on bread or are sandwiched in cookies, some of which are then coated in chocolate. Brewing, winemaking, distilling brandy, and making the mead known as *gvirc* are all popular hobbies. In winemaking season, the smell of crushed grapes fills the air in many neighborhoods. It sometimes seems that everyone who owns a plum tree—or knows somebody who has one—is making *slivovitz* (brandy) in their cellar. *Dedo*'s (Grandpa's) is always the best.

Typical Meals

In common with other cultures throughout the eastern Mediterranean and Adriatic, on the coast all but the simplest main meals begin with appetizers similar to the Greek meze. Favorite items are olives, pickled octopus, slices of sausage or cured meats, and bread. A popular starter anywhere in Croatia is *Štrukli,* cheese raviolis that are fried with butter and breadcrumbs in Zagreb, boiled in the Alps, and usually baked along the coast. A variant on the Štrukli is the *borek,* a baked turnover made with phyllo dough and stuffed with cheese or ground meat.

The Italian influence on Istria and Dalmatia has left a legacy of mildly spiced but rich seafood dishes, including risottos, squid ink pasta, seafood ravioli, and various permutations of grilled fish with olive oil, garlic, and herbs. The most interesting and characteristic Dalmatian dish is *bakalar,* a stew of dried salted codfish and potatoes that is similar to some Iberian preparations. Codfish are caught in the North Atlantic rather than the Adriatic, and

this traditional Christmas specialty is a legacy of the maritime tradition during the era when Ragusan sailors traded between the Ottoman Empire and Spain. Other rustic seafood specialties include mussels poached in olive oil with parsley and garlic, finished with white wine, sea salt, and pepper (*dagne na buzaru*).

Besides seafood, coastal Croatian cuisine uses vegetables that thrive in the mild Mediterranean climate, and local olive oil is used liberally in marinades and sautés. Arborio rice is imported from Italy and used in risottos and the locally popular *rizi-bizi,* rice cooked with peas, butter, onions, and herbs.

The stuffed cabbage known as sarma is made throughout Croatia, but while it contains chopped meat and rice in the inland versions, in Dalmatia it has no rice, just ground meat spiced with cloves, cinnamon, and pine nuts. Here it is called *arambašići,* named after Turkish soldiers—*harambaše.*

Sarma (Stuffed Cabbage)

Ingredients

For the Cabbage

1 whole head cabbage

1 qt water

8 tbsp salt

¼ c vinegar

For the Filling

1 lb finely chopped pork (not ground)

1 lb finely chopped beef

1 large onion, chopped

1 garlic clove, chopped

1 egg

½ tsp cloves

½ tsp cinnamon

½ c pine nuts

Juice of 1 lemon

Salt and pepper

1 8-oz can tomato sauce

To Pickle Cabbage

Remove the core from the whole head of cabbage, and place cabbage in a bowl. Add water, salt, and vinegar. Make sure the cabbage is submerged under the liquid, held down with a plate. Keep covered in a cool place for 2–3 weeks. The longer it pickles, the sourer it will be. When ready to assemble, drain and rinse the cabbage and carefully separate the individual leaves from the head.

To Stuff

Mix all the ingredients except the tomato sauce, and add salt and pepper to taste. Fill each cabbage leaf with a few tablespoons of the mixture. Roll them up into tidy cigar shapes and line a greased casserole. Cover them with the tomato sauce, adding salt and pepper to taste. Cover the casserole and bake at 350°F for 1½ hours.

Other meat specialties include Dalmatian dried ham, game dishes made with pheasant and wild duck, and *janjetina*—spit-roasted lamb prepared with Mediterranean herbs.

One of the signature dishes of Istria is jota, a soup of beans, onions, sauerkraut, and garlic boiled in an earthenware pot with whatever shreds and ends of bacon and pork are handy. The oldest written jota recipe dates from 1890, from an octogenarian named Bagatina, who described it as a dish of her childhood. Though this soup probably evolved as a way to use up leftovers, in the 1980s gentrified versions of jota became popular in upscale restaurants. Another peasant dish that has flourished in upscale variants is *Dalmatinska pašticada,* a hearty braised dish similar to a French daube. It consists of beef marinated overnight in vinegar, lemon, and rosemary, then stewed with spices and red wine.

One legacy of the long Italian influence on the coast is the popularity of wine there, while all the country's major breweries are inland. Wine production is an ancient tradition, and both the Zinfandel and the Primitivo grape are cultivars of the Crljenak grape that originated in coastal Croatia. During the Soviet era winemakers were instructed to focus on volume rather than quality, and the reputation of Croatian wine has not entirely recovered. White wines make up the majority of the production inland, while red and white wines are both produced near the coast. Grape and plum brandies known as rakija or slivovitz are common and of highly variable quality, and liqueurs are also made from figs and other fruits. The most famous alcohol from the region is maraschino liqueur from cherries and almonds, which has been made in the Dalmatian town of Zadar since the 1500s.

Coastal Croatia is rich in desserts, of which the most famous is probably the Rab cake (*Rapska torta*) of marzipan and spices rolled in short pastry and folded into a spiral. It is claimed that this confection has been made since 1177, and the exact recipe is a secret known only to a few women on the island of Rab. For everyday meals, people enjoy *palascintas,* crepes filled with jam, cheese, or fruit. Other desserts abound—sour cherry strudels, wal-

Traditional Rab cake from the Rab region in Croatia. (Jasna01 | Dreamstime.com)

nut spiral rolls, spicy pepper cookies, and locally made chocolates.

Palascintas

Ingredients

For Pancakes

3 eggs

9 c flour

1 c milk

1 c mineral water

For Filling

3 eggs, separated

½ c sugar

Peel of one lemon, grated

12 oz cream cheese

Directions for Pancakes

Beat eggs with a pinch of salt. Gradually add flour, milk, and mineral water until the mixture forms a thin batter.

Heat a small amount of oil in a small frying pan. Pour about ¼ cup of batter into the pan, and cook the pancake until small holes appear in the surface.

Loosen the edges of the pancake and flip it over carefully. Cook on the other side for about 30 seconds.

Directions for Filling

Separate eggs, pouring the yolks and whites into two different bowls.

Beat egg yolks and sugar together until thick. Add grated peel from a lemon. Beat in softened cream cheese.

Beat egg whites until they form stiff peaks. Carefully fold (mix using a gentle stirring motion) egg whites into cheese mixture.

Directions for Assembling Pancakes and Filling

Spread about 2 tablespoons of filling near one side of the pancake. Roll the pancake up to enclose the filling. Place the filled pancakes, side by side, in a buttered baking dish or casserole. Keep warm in a 250°F oven until ready to serve.

Serve warm. May be topped with jam (a Croatian favorite is plum jam), powdered sugar, or sour cream.

There is only one pass from the Adriatic across the beautiful but sparsely populated Dinaric Alps to inland Croatia, and it leads to Zagreb, seat of the viceroys during the long Austro-Hungarian domination. While this is now the capital of Croatia and the largest city in the country, the linkage to the coast is relatively recent. Roads and rail lines between the two areas had been rudimentary until the 20th century, and the first modern paved highway from Zagreb to the Adriatic was not built until the 1970s.

It is therefore no surprise that seafood plays little part in the inland dishes. Game from the mountains and beef from the Pannonian Plain that extends toward the Hungarian border are major elements of this cuisine. Hungarian-influenced dishes are popular, including *game cobanac* (shepherd's stew), *gulyas* (goulash) and other paprika-laced stews, garlicky pickled vegetables, and poppy seed or cottage cheese strudels.

Zagreb specialties hark back to the days of empire, with heavy, bland main dishes like *Zagrebacki odrezak* (stuffed veal schnitzel with gravy) and venison cooked with prunes. These are paired with the local sauerkraut and other pickled vegetables; Zagreb is famous for mild, sweetish sauerkraut, which is served with almost everything. Another accompaniment is buckwheat groats, which are grown throughout the alpine regions and are eaten with mushrooms in soup and casseroles. They also feature in goose Medimurje-style, which is stuffed with buckwheat and nuts.

Mlinci, torn pasta fried in turkey, duck, or goose fat, is native to the area near the Slovenian border but popular throughout Croatia. It is usually a side dish with roasted meats but is occasionally served as a main dish with chunks of poultry.

Desserts are usually pastries in the style of an Austrian *Konditorei*—sweet cheese, sour cherry, or poppy seed strudels and buns, and other flaky, sweet confections. *Kremsnite,* custard topped with flaky pastry sprinkled with powdered sugar, is among the richest sweets, typically washed down with many cups of strong coffee.

The most famous edible product of the Zagreb region is the *licitar,* beautifully decorated gingerbread cookies that are often bought as souvenirs and used as wall hangings. Licitar making originated in Hungary but was brought to a high art in Zagreb, and the gift of a heart-shaped licitar to someone one admires is part of traditional courtship. This practice has been celebrated in popular culture, including a ballet called "Licitar Heart" by Krešimir Baranović. To drink, Zagreb natives enjoy beer, mead, and fruit brandies such as slivovitz, all widely available in home-brewed versions.

As one goes to the north and east from Zagreb into Slavonia, the land becomes flatter, the people poorer, and the cuisine simpler. Beans, potatoes, bell peppers, and cabbage are rounded out with fresh or smoked meats and brittle, garlicky, air-dried sausage. The Hungarian influence is strong here, and popular dishes include stuffed peppers and gulyas stew made with lake fish, beef, chicken, or rabbit. This area has the spiciest food in Croatia, such as the *kulen,* a hot paprika-laced salami. Sausages, blood puddings, and pickled meats use every part of the pig; an example is *hladetina,* a Pannonian headcheese made of jellied meat with hard-boiled eggs, salt, pepper, garlic, and paprika. Offal such as liver and kidneys features in soups and in *svargl,* a kind of Croatian haggis. This consists of a pig's stomach filled with minced meat, pig's blood, and herbs, then air-cured—it is an acquired taste even in the region where it is made. The turkey is an import that has become very popular and is roasted in the same way as is traditional in the United States, including the giblet gravy. Only the accompanying sauerkraut and mlinci would remind one that this is Croatia rather than New England.

In the 20th and 21st centuries, a new Croatian nationalism led to an emphasis on cultural and national unity. The quest for a distinct pan-Croatian cuisine has been explicitly reflected in a recently invented dessert called *croaterra,* made by a commercial bakery of the same name. This cake uses ingredients from everywhere in the country; the principal ingredients are spelt grain, olive oil, walnuts, honey, fruit, and fennel. The first three items are associated with Slavonia, Istria, and Pannonia, respectively, and the remaining items come from the Croatian coast and islands. The company's promotional literature is explicitly nationalist and advises giving croaterra cakes to foreigners as a symbol of Croatian unity.

As political arguments simmered in the former Yugoslavia, local commentators discerned or invented differences between inland Croatian and Serbian cuisines. This trend has occasionally resulted in international friction with Serbia, particularly involving a company called Podravka, headquartered in Koprivnica in northern Croatia. Podravka's most famous product is a mix of dried vegetable, herbs, monosodium glutamate, and salt called Vegeta. Vegeta went on the market in 1959 and is the most popular seasoning among both local and overseas Croats. In 2002 Serbia briefly banned the sale of Vegeta in that country, claiming it was unfit for human consumption. The real differences between modern Croatian and Serbian food is that Serbian food is generally blander, uses less seafood, and has more Germanic and pan-Balkan and less Italian influence.

Eating Out

The expanding tourist industry has made a growth industry of traditional-style restaurants in Croatia, and all over the country old residences and shops have been remodeled into replicas of antique inns. Coastal Croatian-style restaurants have become popular in inland cities like Zagreb, especially the Dalmatian-style taverns called *konobas.* These are similar to Spanish tapas bars and serve fried sardines and anchovies, vinegary octopus salad, smoked ham, fried olives, and similar salty dishes that encourage the consumption of alcoholic beverages. The popularity of konobas and other coastal cuisines in the inland regions has been a one-way cultural transfer, and few restaurants in the coastal areas offer only inland cuisine.

More sophisticated versions of coastal, Italian, and Hungarian cuisine are also popular throughout the country and are served at establishments called *restaurans.* A lively dining scene in Zagreb and other cities means that young Croatians are also exposed to cuisines that are not available elsewhere in the Balkans, including Chinese, Indian, and Mexican food. Croatians are also innovating on traditional cuisine. The naming of chef Lida Bastianich, who was born in Istria, as America's Top Chef in 1994 was a cause for national pride, and the international success of other Croatian-born chefs has inspired many restaurants that go outside traditional paths. Fast food is hugely popular, and pizza and kebab places selling *cevapčići* (*cevapi*) are full at all hours. A few sell horse burgers, a specialty of Slovenia, along with international standard sandwiches and snacks.

One beverage that has spread across Croatia is *bambus,* an unlikely mixture of half red wine, half Coca-Cola. Exactly where and when this concoction was created is a matter of debate, but bars in the Istrian region probably deserve the credit or blame. While bambus began as a way for bars and restaurants to use up otherwise-undrinkable harsh red wine, it has become popular nationwide and has a reputation as a ladies' drink.

Special Occasions

The population of Croatia is overwhelmingly Catholic, and the calendar of the saints offers plenty of excuses for feasts and festivals that are popular even with nonreligious Croats. Easter is celebrated with braided breads called *primorski uskrsne bebe,* which are often in the shape of a baby with a colored egg for the head. Otherwise, there are few ritual traditions that are associated with a specific food; the feast day of St. Blaise, patron of Croatia, is celebrated everywhere but with lavish portions of everyday foods. There are a few exceptions, such as Christmas Eve, when codfish stew is the traditional meal, and the *makovnjaca,* a poppy seed roll, and the fruitcake known as "bishop's bread" are made nearly everywhere. In inland Croatia, goose and duck are specialties for St. Martin's Day. This

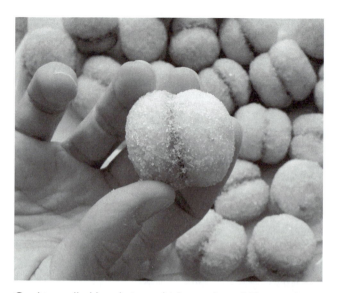

Cookies called breskvice, which are shaped like peaches and filled with jam, are often served at Croatian weddings. (Landd09 | Dreamstime.com)

celebration comes at the end of the harvest season and is celebrated by winemakers, who stage elaborate ritual feasts at which mock bishops "christen" their new wines.

There are also special dishes for weddings, mostly sweets. A cookie called *breskvice,* which is shaped like a peach and filled with jam, is a must; while these were traditionally filled with jam, Nutella is now far more popular. Other secular celebrations that involve food include the completion of a house, which is celebrated with wine and cakes.

During the Yugoslav period, the government fostered nonreligious food and music festivals, many of which have remained popular even after the breakup of the country. These often combine culinary interests with the Soviet mania for all things oversized. At the asparagus festival in April, a highlight is an omelet made with 1,000 eggs and 66 pounds (30 kilograms) of asparagus. The cherry festival in Lovran in May is celebrated with a 33-foot- (10-meter-) long cherry strudel, and other events feature similar outsized entrées.

Diet and Health

Croatia has a long tradition of folk medicine and home remedies, many of which are still adhered to among the highly educated elite. In June 2009, health minister Darko Milinovic surprised his colleagues by saying at a press conference that honey, tea, and lemon along with frequent showers was a cure for swine flu. He retracted that claim almost immediately, but it did reveal a typical belief that a simple good diet promotes health.

Croatia has a long tradition of using herbs such as caraway, juniper, and walnut kernels for intestinal problems; mallow, chamomile, mint, and lemon balm for sore throats and cough; and elderflower to improve circulation. Other remedies have more of a magical aspect, as in the burning of alecost with wormwood and rose petals; supposedly, inhaling the smoke has special healing powers. *Raki,* the grape brandy, is used to make herb infusions and also externally to heal wounds or bruises. Wrapping a sore throat in a towel soaked in *lozovac,* a locally produced brandy, is said to aid in healing.

Still, the best folk remedies in the world are powerless against unhealthy modern dietary practices. Changes in the Croatian diet have had a strong negative effect on coastal Croatians; a study conducted in 2003 showed that the percentage of overweight people among residents of Dalmatia had increased to 54 percent of men and 48 percent of women, and 27 percent of both genders were obese. The authors of the study theorized that this was because the islanders now eat much more meat than their ancestors and have not changed their lifestyle accordingly.

Islanders are still healthier than inland Croats. Cardiovascular disease is the leading cause of death in Croatia, and a study from the Croatian Public Health Institute in 2005 showed that inland Croats were far more likely to suffer a heart attack. A poor diet was cited as a major factor. A 2009 study of multiple sclerosis and cancers in Croatia showed that both diseases were twice as common in the inland areas where the diet is rich in meat and fat and suggested that the high intake of olive oil among coastal residents was protecting them from the same fate. The government has been trying to encourage a return to traditional healthy practices such as increased consumption of fish instead of meat. This includes financing a campaign called *Srdela snack,* encouraging people to eat sardines instead of other fast food. It has been relatively successful, but sardine sandwiches still have not replaced hamburgers and cevapi as the most popular quick meals.

Regardless of their region, Croatians have a very high rate of smoking and consumption of alcohol, and the government is taking steps toward discouraging these unhealthy practices. A tobacco ban in restaurants went into effect in 2009 but has been widely ignored; nevertheless, a study by Euromonitor predicted that this ban, combined with an increase in tobacco taxes, will start to reduce tobacco use. An increase in the tax on hard alcohol went into effect in 2007 but has had little social effect for several reasons. It doesn't apply to wine and beer, can't be imposed on the brandy and other liquors that are widely homemade, and, even when it is applicable, is widely avoided. These statistics aside, the general level of health in Croatia is superior to that in most of the other former Yugoslav republics, and the life expectancy of 73 years is not far from the European Union average.

Richard Foss

Further Reading

Evenden, Kate. *A Taste of Croatia.* Ojai, CA: New Oak Press, 2007.

Novak-Markovic, Olga. *Yugoslav Cookbook.* Ljbljana, Slovenia: Cankarjeva Zalozba, 1984.

Pavicic, Liliana. *The Best of Croatian Cooking.* New York: Hippocrene International Cookbooks, 2000.

Radin, George. "Traditional Ways of Living in Yugoslavia." *Journal of the American Dietetic Association* 20, No. 6 (1944): 373–75.

Cyprus

Overview

A small nation with a big history, Cyprus lies at the eastern end of the Mediterranean between Europe, Asia, and Africa, an island gatekeeper to three continents. Its position has proven an irresistible draw to larger and more powerful empires throughout history. Egyptians, Assyrians, Persians, Phoenicians, Greeks, Romans, Franks, Venetians, Turks, and Britons invaded or annexed the island seeking outposts for military use and trade.

Cyprus today is a divided country. In 1960, the Republic of Cyprus attained independence from Britain, but intervention by both Greece and Turkey provoked over a decade of violence and division. Today, the Republic of Cyprus, occupying the southern two-thirds of the island, is recognized internationally and is a member of the European Union. The Turkish Republic of Northern Cyprus occupies the north and is recognized internationally only by Turkey.

Years of settlement, occupation, and interaction with other civilizations have left Cyprus with a rich culinary tradition. Though close association with Greece has left an obvious imprint, it is geographically closer to Turkey, Syria, Lebanon, and Egypt, and much of its food culture betrays strong Middle Eastern influences. But Cyprus brings a great deal of its own to the table. Slashed east to west by two mountain massifs, this small country harbors numerous ecosystems and a rich biodiversity including edible plants unknown elsewhere. Foraging remains a way of life in the countryside and a popular activity for townsfolk.

Today, a new kind of international influence flourishes in the larger towns and cities. With modernization, supermarkets have blossomed beside or instead of traditional markets. Meanwhile, tourism has spawned American-style fast-food restaurants like McDonald's, Pizza Hut, T.G.I. Friday's, and Kentucky Fried Chicken. But the interior villages preserve Cypriot cuisine in its purest forms, and, even in town, family meals and traditions reflect a culinary culture shaped over millennia by indigenous ingredients and the influences of civilizations near and far.

🍽 Food Culture Snapshot

It is a Saturday in springtime, and the market is bursting with fresh vegetables and fruit. The Demetriou family heads out to select the very best for the next several days: chard, spinach, cauliflower, and artichokes. Some of the artichokes will be shredded fine and eaten raw, while others will be cooked. This is citrus season, which means oranges, grapefruit, and mandarins are plentiful. They select some of each, along with lemons, a necessity in Cypriot cooking year-round.

For Sunday's dinner, the Demetrious hunt down a Cyprus anomaly, *kolokassi,* known elsewhere as taro, a root product that has migrated all the way from the Pacific Islands. Stewed with pork, it is one of the country's favorite dishes. Then the yogurt supply must be replenished. In Cyprus it is made from the milk of goats and sheep, which thrive much more easily here than cows. The family stops to pick up some freshly made *halloumi,* the country's signature cheese. Traditionally served either grilled or fried, this cheese maintains its shape even when heated.

Then they are off for a foraging expedition, a favorite Cypriot activity. Out in the countryside, both herbs and greens are there for the taking. *Rigani* (wild oregano or marjoram) grows in multiple varieties. Arugula, fennel, purslane, nettles, dandelion, and amaranth fill up the foraging baskets. Like the vegetables from the market, they will be eaten raw in salads, sautéed simply, perhaps with eggs, or mixed with staples from the family's pantry.

Major Foodstuffs

A typical Cypriot family keeps its larder well stocked with legumes such as lentils, garbanzos, black-eyed peas, and dried fava beans. Grains of choice are cracked wheat (or bulgur) and rice. Other staples include pastas and *trachanas,* wafers made of ground wheat and soured milk used for porridges and soups in the winter. A plentiful supply of local olive oil is a must.

Many of the spices kept on hand reflect the country's proximity to the Middle East. They include coriander, cinnamon, cumin, and black pepper, along with the less-known mastic—a resin from a small evergreen tree—and *mahlepi,* kernels from the pit of the tiny black cherry. Sesame seeds are used in various ways by themselves, crushed into tahini paste, or pressed for their oil. Favorite herbs, grown at home, foraged, or purchased from the market, are oregano, marjoram, cilantro, parsley, thyme, bay leaf, and mint, which is used both fresh and dried. Important flavoring agents for sweets are rose water, orange flower water, and carob syrup.

Vegetables are key to the country's diet, and Cypriots eat what the seasons offer. In addition to spring's bounty, favorites include tomatoes, eggplant, summer and winter squash, peppers, potatoes, okra, beets (both roots and tops), many members of the cabbage family, and greens, both cultivated and wild. Dairy products are essential to the diet, not only yogurt and halloumi, but other cheeses such as feta and *anari,* which is made from whey.

Residents of this island nation are great lovers of seafood, which is no longer as abundant as it once

Traditional halloumi cheese being grilled in Cyprus. (Ron Zmiri | Dreamstime.com)

was. Still, calamari, shrimp, octopus, cuttlefish, and finfish of all sorts find their way onto the table in homes for special occasions and in restaurants. Meats, too, are eaten only once or twice a week at home, though they star on special occasions. Pork is the favorite of the Christian southerners, while the Muslims of the north prefer lamb for religious reasons. Cypriots also produce a delicious variety of sausages and preserved meats.

Cooking

Frying, braising, baking, roasting, and grilling are all important techniques in preparing Cypriot food, but many of the most popular dishes require little to no cooking at all because Cypriots are great lovers of salads. Their own version of what is known in the United States as "Greek salad" is called "village salad," and it often contains wild greens, shredded cabbage, arugula, or purslane in addition to the predictable cucumber, tomatoes, olives, and feta cheese. Ingredients are sometimes chopped, a Middle Eastern tendency. Other simple raw salads include artichoke hearts, carrots, and kohlrabi that are shredded and tossed with olive oil. Vegetables like beets are boiled first, then receive similar treatment.

Cypriots are also great lovers of dips and spreads. *Skordalia* mixes garlic, breadcrumbs, olive oil, and lemon juice. *Tzadziki* combines yogurt, cucumbers, garlic, and olive oil. Hummus, a Lebanese or Syrian import, blends mashed, cooked chickpeas (garbanzos) with tahini paste, lemon juice, and garlic.

Grains, legumes, and vegetables dominate the daily menu, but there is much variety in their preparation. Legumes are used in stews, soups, and purees. Bulgur pilaf is a delicious accompaniment to any meal. The cooked grain is also made into *koupes,* or cigars, and stuffed with ground meat. Vegetables are baked, stuffed, fried, sautéed, or braised. Greens are scrambled with eggs. Potatoes, mushrooms, cauliflower, and artichoke hearts may be seared, then simmered in red wine and coriander to make a stew called *afelia.*

Cypriots use a similar range of techniques for cooking seafood and meats, but roasting and grilling are usually reserved for holidays, celebrations, and family outings. Essential to every kitchen is a *tava,* a terra-cotta oven fitted with a tight lid, often shaped like an old-fashioned beehive. Once used outdoors over coals for long, slow cooking of meats, it has successfully made the transition indoors to the oven. Most households also keep a portable grill outfitted with electrically powered spits that turn slowly to produce pork or lamb kebabs or souvlakia, whether at home or off in the countryside.

Souvlakia Me Pitta (Kebabs in Pita Bread)

Serves 6

This preparation is equally good with pork or lamb. Be sure to purchase high-quality, tender meat.

2 lb pork or lamb in 2-in. cubes

4 cloves garlic, crushed

2 medium-sized onions, quartered

2 bay leaves

2 tsp plus 1 tbsp dried oregano

1 tsp cinnamon

3 tsp salt, divided

Red wine to cover

2 tbsp olive oil

Juice of 1 lemon

1 large tomato, chopped

½ cucumber, chopped

Leaf lettuce, shredded

Pita bread

Lemon wedges and yogurt

Place the meat in a large nonreactive bowl. Add garlic, onions, bay leaves, 2 teaspoons oregano, cinnamon, and 2 teaspoons salt. Cover with wine, and toss. Marinate for 2 hours to overnight.

Blend olive oil and lemon juice. Mix 1 tablespoon oregano and 1 teaspoon salt. Mix vegetables together and set aside.

Thread meat and large onion pieces onto either metal skewers or wooden skewers that have been soaked in water for 20 minutes. Grill over moderate heat or broil 5 inches from the heating element, turning from time to time. When meat has lost its color, baste with olive oil/lemon juice mix and sprinkle with the salt/oregano mix. Continue basting and sprinkling every 15 minutes or until meat is done.

Cut the pita bread in half, grill briefly, and remove.

To serve, fill pita halves with meat. Top with vegetable mix, and serve with lemon wedges and yogurt on the side.

Typical Meals

Everyday meals in Cyprus consist of grains, legumes, vegetables, fruit, and dairy products, with fish or meat appearing on the menu once or twice a week. Vegetable entrées include an assorted variety layered with cheese and baked in addition to stuffed peppers, eggplants, tomatoes, and squash. As with stuffed grape leaves, or *koupepia,* the essential fillings are rice, onion, and herbs, while meat is optional. Mixing sweet and savory flavors in a single dish does not appeal to the Cypriot palate, so addition of raisins and other dried fruits is rare.

Legumes, simply prepared, are the primary source of protein in everyday meals. A puree of split peas and potatoes, a soup of sharply flavored lentils, a rich fava bean stew, or a mound of black-eyed peas studded with chard makes for a hearty meal, particularly when accompanied by a plate of seasonal vegetables, bulgur or rice, and a slice of crusty bread.

For a springtime dinner the Demetriou family begins with a lentil soup flavored with cilantro, scallions, and vinegar. But this is the last of the individual courses; family-style service prevails in Cyprus. All remaining dishes are spread on the table at once. Anchoring the meal is a bulgur pilaf.

Tonight's pièce de résistance is mushrooms afelia, a dish in which browned mushrooms are simmered in red wine and crushed coriander seeds. Also on the table are uncooked artichoke hearts shaved finely and tossed in olive oil and lemon juice, as well as sliced beets with skordalia, a sauce made with garlic, bread, ground almonds, and olive oil. A dish of goat-milk yogurt drizzled with olive oil completes the spread. A bowl of mandarins is passed around the table for dessert.

Black-Eyed Peas with Chard

1 c black-eyed peas, picked over to check for stones or debris and rinsed

5 c water

1 lb chard, washed

2 cloves garlic, pressed, or chopped and mashed with salt in a mortar

¼ c olive oil

Juice of 1 lemon

Salt and pepper to taste

Additional olive oil and lemon wedges for serving

1. Add enough water to cover the black-eyed peas by an inch, bring to a boil, drain, and throw away the water. Add the 5 cups of water, and bring back to a boil. Begin checking for tenderness at 30 minutes. Peas should be tender within 40 minutes.

2. Meanwhile, trim chard stems, and remove them from the leaves. Slice the stems into ½-inch pieces and shred the leaves.

3. When the peas are just tender, add chard stems along with salt and pepper to taste. Simmer for another 10 minutes. Add shredded leaves, and simmer for 10 minutes more until chard is tender.

4. Drain peas; whisk garlic with olive oil, and drizzle over peas and chard, gently tossing. Pour lemon juice over the dish, and toss again. Adjust salt and pepper. Serve with additional olive oil, lemon wedges, a bowl of whole-milk yogurt, and slices of rustic bread.

Eating Out

Dining out in Cyprus means a visit to a nearby taverna for a riot of *mezedhes*. These small plates of food are known throughout the eastern Mediterranean, but in other countries they serve as appetizers to the main event. Not so in Cyprus, where a meze means an entire meal consisting of 20 to 25 different dishes. The parade begins modestly with olives, dips, and spreads, moves to salads, and finally ends with hot preparations. In many places, the diner has the option of ordering a seafood or a meat meze. In either case, the preparation will become more elaborate as the evening proceeds, with a skewer or two of souvlakia toward the end.

As recently as 1960, mezedhes were the property of men, the regular taverna customers. These small bites provided nibbles to accompany *zivania*, the native spirit distilled from the pomace of grapes pressed in the winemaking process. With the loosening of social restrictions and the growth of tourism, tavernas have become the principal dining establishments, welcoming everyone, young and old, men and women, and the beverage accompanying the meal is likely to be one of the local Cyprus wines.

Special Occasions

The Cypriot diet may be largely vegetarian, but weddings, birthdays, name days, and holidays in Cyprus call for meats and sweets. The smell of pork and lamb wafts through the air, either roasting in the oven or turning on the spit. Celebratory dishes include kebabs, *souvla* (skewered bone-in lamb chunks), and *sheftalia* (ground meat sausages bound together with pork caul).

The biggest holiday of the year is Easter with its attendant buildup of Carnival and Lent. The first day of Carnival is known as "Smelly Thursday" because of the amount of meat grilling throughout the towns and cities. Other Carnival specialties include small cheese-stuffed pastries, known as *bourekia*, and *ravioles*, a gift of the Venetians during their 15th- to 16th-century occupation.

With the beginning of Lent, meat, fish, and dairy disappear from the menu. Tahini cakes and little pies filled with pumpkin and spinach are popular at this time. The first post-Lent meal in the early hours of Easter Sunday is *avgolimono* soup, broth swirled with egg and flavored with lemon juice. Later in the day, the feasting begins. Souvla is the main dish, while the classic pastry is *flaounes,* cheese-stuffed buns sprinkled with sesame seeds.

Christmas in Cyprus once called for the slaughter of a carefully fattened pig, which was turned into hams and sausages to create a supply for the year. Today, the tradition continues in the countryside, but even city dwellers are likely to buy meat for *loukanika,* traditional sausages soaked in red wine. On Christmas Eve, families share a specially baked bread flavored with raisins, nuts, brandy, and orange rind called *Christopsomo.* On Christmas Day,

a favorite treat is a spicy cake studded with dried fruits and nuts, inherited from the British.

Diet and Health

Traditional Cypriot cuisine is an ideal example of the widely praised Mediterranean diet. Its foundation is a healthful mix of grains, legumes, vegetables, and fruits, with meat and fish eaten sparingly once or twice a week. Holidays and celebrations call for richer, more indulgent foods throughout the island, but they are balanced in both the north and the south by religious days of fasting and abstention, such as Ramadan in the north and Lent in the south.

That pattern is likely to be challenged, however, now that tourism has become an important driver in the country's economy. Today, restaurants supply holiday foods every day of the week to visitors and Cypriots alike. As the Cypriot standard of living rises, this temptation will become increasingly difficult to resist.

Nancy G. Freeman

Baking bourekia in preparation for Easter celebrations in Cyprus. (Shutterstock)

Further Reading

A. M. Filagrotiki Consultants. Cyprus Food & Drinks. http://www.cyprusfoodndrinks.com/cgi bin/hweb?-A=1321,intro.html&-V=authentics.

Davies, Gilli. *The Taste of Cyprus: A Seasonal Look at Cypriot Cooking.* Hertfordshire, UK: Interworld, 1994.

Mallos, Tess. *The Complete Middle East Cookbook.* North Clarendon, VT: Tuttle, 2006.

Sakkadas, Savvas. "Cyprus: Culinary Traditions throughout the Year." In *Culinary Cultures of Europe: Identity, Diversity and Dialogue,* edited by Darra Goldstein and Kathrin Merkle, 119–28. Strasbourg: Council of Europe Publishing, 2005.

Weaver, William Woys. "Bold Flavors, Ancient Roots." *Saveur* 111 (May 2008): 54–65.

Czech Republic

Overview

The Czech Republic's food and foodways are a fine balance between its folk traditions and cosmopolitan culture. The country's history, geography, and ethnicity have influenced the "meat and potatoes fare" and a rapidly evolving Continental cuisine brought on by its recent entrance into the European Union.

The Czech Republic for much of the 20th century was the first part of the famous portmanteau, Czechoslovakia. In 1993, it peacefully split with Slovakia in what is called the Velvet Divorce. Now, the country is a parliamentary democracy with a population of 10.3 million, split into two regions, Bohemia and Moravia, with 14 administrative districts. The country has 30,449 square miles (78,864 square kilometers) of landlocked, hilly, and low mountainous terrain and is bordered by Poland, Austria, Slovakia, and Germany. Traditional Czech foods are heavy, simple dishes that reflect the cultivation and preservation of a strong national folk culture but with influence from the changing empires of its neighbors. Schnitzel from Austria, sausages from Poland, goulash from Hungary, and roast goose from Germany are commonly found in Czech cuisine.

Unlike its former counterpart, Slovakia, the Czech nation was an established state until the 16th century, when it came under Hapsburg rule, lasting until 1918. The Czech national movement started with the pre-Reformation leader Jan Hus and came to head in the Czech national revival of the early 19th century when Czechs upheld cultural markers such as language, poetry, and literature as tools to unify all Slavs in the country. These markers tie Czechs to folk traditions, which in turn value home

food preservation, household animal husbandry, and gardening.

The 45 years under Soviet influence, from after World War II until 1989, limited the amount of commercial food goods into the country as the food chains were incorporated into an organized economy. As such, food lines, uniform prices, and limited amounts of meat and fresh produce became common. This period drastically changed the cuisine, and only since 1990 has a diverse food retailing and restaurant culture revived as the country draws tourists and business leaders from within the European Union and around the world. Today, Prague is the sixth most visited city in Europe, and foods from around the world are available for foreigners and residents. The country joined the Schengen area (border-free zone) in 2007, and the free flow of people and goods across borders pulls the cuisine of western Europe into the Czech Republic.

The Czech Republic was one of the first nations to industrialize in the early 19th century, losing a large part of its agricultural labor force to mining and manufacturing facilities. Today, agriculture makes up less than 5 percent of the gross domestic product. Since few people are involved in modern commercial farming, rural food nostalgia is tied to an identity cultivated centuries ago in the hills and fields of Bohemia and Moravia. However, harvest festivals, cottage gardens, and simple countryside fare are still valued as strong Czech identifiers.

Only 39 percent of the population considers themselves Roman Catholic, while 40 percent are confirmed atheists and 16 percent more are religiously uncertain. Despite this, many Catholic traditions are still popular during Lent and Christmas. Meatless fasting meals consist of various vegetable soups and freshwater fish. The Easter meal eaten throughout the country has strong Catholic symbols.

The Czech Republic has had many ethnic groups move and settle throughout the region, but today the country is ethnically uniform, with 94 percent of the country claiming Czech nationality. The repatriating of its large prewar German population was forced by the harsh Beneš Decrees, which economically punished foreign, specifically German, settlers and encouraged Czechs to move back within its borders. As such, strong German food traditions have disappeared. Currently, the significant minority ethnic groups are Roma, Slovak, Polish, German, and Vietnamese.

Many Czechs recognize Vepřo-Knedlo-Zelo as the national dish of the country and will serve it at family meals or special celebrations. (Ingrid Heczko | Dreamstime.com)

🍽 Food Culture Snapshot

Martin is a 46-year-old father of two sons, who lives in an apartment in Prague with his girlfriend, Katarina. Since he finished his mandatory military service as a young man, he has worked in the growing hospitality industry. He recently left his work as a manager at an international hotel chain to open a small café in the middle of a newly renovated shopping center in the center of the city, serving espresso coffee drinks and panini sandwiches in the style of an Italian eatery.

Martin's breakfast includes black tea with muesli and milk, bread, ham, and cheese, followed by an espresso in midmorning. As Martin works in the busy city center, he chooses to eat at a cafeteria for lunch. This cafeteria has selections of food from around the world, including Indian, Chinese, Italian, and Thai. Lunch is the heaviest meal of the day. For dinner he eats a lighter meal at home with his family.

Martin saves his long lunches for the weekend when he cooks with his family. He prefers to cook international foods such as Chinese noodles or Thai chicken, while Katarina makes traditional Czech fare, specializing in the complex baked goods such as *vánočka,* a spiced yeast bread commonly served at Christmas. Martin always drinks Czech beer, his favorite being Pilsner Urquell, with these meals.

Vepřo-Knedlo-Zelo (Pork Dumplings and Vegetables)

Part of the influence of the Czech national revival is the naming of certain national foods. Many Czechs recognize *vepřo-knedlo-zelo* as the national dish of the country and will serve it at family meals or special celebrations.

For the Meat

2 lb pork roast

2–3 cloves of garlic

Salt

1 tsp caraway seeds

⅓ c water

1. Preheat oven to 325°F.

2. Rub the meat with crushed garlic and salt. Sprinkle with caraway seeds. Put in a roasting pan with the water.

3. Roast in the oven for approximately 2 hours until the internal temperature reaches 160°F.

4. Let it rest and slice open.

For the Dumplings

1½ c milk, divided

1 package yeast

1 tsp sugar

1 egg

½ tsp salt

3½ c flour

3 slices white bread, cubed

1. Take ½ cup milk, and scald it on the stove, then let it cool. Add the yeast and sugar, and let stand for 10 minutes.

2. Heat the remaining milk until warm. Add this to the yeast mixture with the egg and the salt.

3. Mix the flour and bread cubes in a dry bowl. Add the liquid to the flour, and knead it like you would regular bread dough.

4. Leave it in a warm place to rise for 2 hours. It should double in size. Knead again, dividing the dough into three long loaves, each about 2 inches thick. Let these rise for 45 minutes.

5. Boil salted water in a large pot. When the dough has risen, drop one of the loaves into the water and cook for 15 minutes. Remove with a slotted spoon onto a greased platter. Repeat with the two remaining loaves.

6. To slice, take a thread, loop it around the loaf, and pull it together. Each slice should be about 2 inches thick.

For the Vegetables

1 head cabbage

2 tbsp lard

1 small onion

1 tsp caraway seeds

1 tsp salt

2 tbsp vinegar

1 tbsp sugar

1. Boil water in a pot. Cut the cabbage into thin strips, and blanch in boiling water and strain.

2. Melt lard in a frying pan. Add chopped onion, and sauté until translucent. Add cabbage and caraway seeds, and cook until strips are tender. Season with salt, vinegar, and sugar.

3. Put warm dumplings on the plate, topped with pork and cabbage.

Major Foodstuffs

Food-retailing structures in the Czech Republic look very different from 1990 and before. The former Communist government demanded a minimum profit margin in the retailing sector; therefore, food marketing was virtually nonexistent: Grocery stores on average had one-third of the space of their Western counterparts, and food goods were priced uniformly across all of Czechoslovakia. So when in 1992, Globus opened its first store in the center of the Czech Republic's second-largest city, Brno, the hypermarket format became an instant success. Leading European retailers, such as Tesco, Ahold, Globus, and Kaufland, quickly moved into the country, and these retailers are still in heavy competition for a market share in the region. In addition, traditional farmers' markets populate the centers of most cities, offering wholesale produce and locally processed and harvested foods. Smaller grocery stores, convenience stores, and fruit stands can be found in most residential neighborhoods.

In general, Czech food is simple and rich with limited spices and heavy sauces. But it is also extremely seasonal and tied to local food production. Meat dishes dominate Czech entrées, with beef, pork, and venison as the proteins of choice. A popular beef dish is *svíčková,* marinated beef served with spiced cream sauce and preserved fruit. Pork is processed into smoked sausages and a wide range of deli meats and bacons. Poultry is more and more popular as a healthy alternative protein. As the Czech Republic is a landlocked country, saltwater fish is rare, but river fish such as trout and carp are commonly eaten.

Potatoes and wheat flour provide most of the starch on the plate. Rice is commonly served with chicken and fish. Soups and dumplings are made from potatoes. The wheat is processed into pasta and rye and brown breads. Children especially enjoy spaghetti topped with ground poppy seeds and powdered sugar.

Traditionally, vegetables were pickled or processed or eaten only during the harvest season, but this is changing with the availability of more fresh produce from the new retailing structures. More Czechs are eating fresh vegetables and salads with their meals. In the summer and fall, Czechs use the forests to forage for mushrooms for soups and casseroles. Fruits are eaten fresh when they are in season, while most are saved for preserving and pickling. Long gone are the lines for bananas and mandarins, which were available only during the Christmas season, but tropical fruits are still valued as a holiday treat because of their past scarcity.

Lard is the most traditional cooking fat. A slice of brown bread spread with lard and topped with onions, salt, and paprika is a common dish found in pubs and markets. Recently, with the increased knowledge of the health benefits of monounsaturated fats, olive and vegetable oils are becoming more popular. Butter is used in baked goods.

Czech cuisine is not particularly known for its spices except for caraway, paprika, and poppy seeds. These usually make up the only spice for the dishes, other than salt and pepper. Garlic is liberally used in most meat dishes and makes a very popular soup, *cesnekova polevka.*

Cesnekova Polevka **(Garlic Soup)**

6 cloves garlic

3 tbsp butter

14 oz chicken stock

I egg per person

Spring onions, sliced

3 oz semisoft, mild cheese, like Gouda

3 oz ham, diced

I c hard white bread, diced and fried for croutons

Fry the garlic in butter until aromatic, add stock, and bring to a boil for 10 minutes. Turn the burner to low. Add the egg(s) softly to the pot, and let sit for 5 minutes. Spoon eggs with broth into serving bowls. Add spring onions, cheese, and ham. Add croutons to the soup.

Cooking

Most Czechs have modern kitchens with stoves, refrigerators, and sinks with potable water. As such, the cooking methods reflect the Continental style found in western Europe. But many city dwellers like to keep country homes with the traditional kitchens for weekend vacations. They can have wooden stoves and open fires to make stews, roasted fatty meats and root vegetables, and preserves.

Frequently, these small homes have gardens and kitchens with tools to preserve food by canning, pickling, and distilling alcohol. Popular preserves include cherry, peach, and plum jams; pickled beets; horseradish; and pickles. Alcohols are distilled into brandies, more specifically eau de vies, made from plums (*slivovice*), apples (*jablakovice*), pears (*hruskovice*), and peaches (*broskovice*).

Typical Meals

Czechs usually eat three meals a day: breakfast, lunch, and dinner. Tradition calls for all meals to be eaten at home, but many people take weekday lunches at school or work. It is not customary to eat a meal alone. Even at the workplace or at school, there is one lunch hour in which everyone eats together.

Breakfast can be savory or sweet. Ham and cheese sandwiches on *roky,* fresh-baked white-flour rolls, are served with mustard. The breakfast sausage, *parky,* is also served with mustard. Children eat sweeter breakfasts of rolls with butter and honey or cereals that are found in the aisles of the large hypermarkets.

Lunch and dinner fare are similar. Both meals have two courses, a soup and an entrée, and both are served hot. Potato, garlic, and cabbage soups are popular starters. This can be followed by a stewed meat such as svíčková, spiced beef, with *knedlicky,* potato-flour dumplings, or by roasted chicken with rice or pasta. Usually, lunch is a larger meal than dinner.

Midday Sunday, the family gathers for a large meal and eats more traditional Czech fare such as vepřo-knedlo-zelo and Wiener schnitzel. Beers and spirits are included in this meal along with dessert pastries and cakes made from poppy seeds, nuts, dried fruits, or chocolate. Coffee and tea are served after all leisurely meals.

Eating Out

Restaurants essentially died under Communist control, and today the heart of Czech cuisine is not to be found in the restaurant but in the home. Due to the opening of trade with the West, Czech restaurants have experienced a renaissance in both the variety and the quality of the foods. Visitors to the city centers have dined in Japanese, French, and Italian restaurants since soon after the Velvet Revolution, but more recently classically trained chefs are transforming humble Czech fare into fine dining. These chefs have taken the traditional ingredients like mushrooms, organ meats, and venison and applied French cooking techniques for the modern diner.

The pub is the true gathering place outside the home. The country has a long tradition of beer brewing that is well respected around the world. Western European and American corporations bought many of the most famous Czech beer brands, such as Pilsner Urquell, Staropramen, and Zlatopramen. Furthermore, many pubs in the city centers have exclusive tapping contracts with these large labels. A growing independent beer movement, *ctvrta pipa,* "the fourth pipe," embraces the local microbrewery. Still, Czechs are loyal to these large brands. Beer will always be an intimate symbol of the Czech eating experience whether it is mass-produced or microbrewed.

A sign outside a Czech pub for the popular beer, Pilsner Urquell. Nine out of 10 beers produced and consumed worldwide are made according to a method directly derived from the Pilsner style of brewing. (Sepavo | Dreamstime.com)

Special Occasions

Wedding celebrations are long events with an abundance of food. A three- or four-course sit-down meal is served, starting with soup. The bride and groom are bound together and must eat the soup with one spoon. It is common for the wedding party to go well into the next morning, and another meal will be served around 1 or 2 A.M. It is usually a simple stew to sustain the guests for the party. In the countryside, some homes may slaughter their own pigs and prepare homemade dishes and desserts for months preceding the wedding. In the city, it is more common for these affairs to be catered.

Easter is tied to strong Catholic traditions. A wicker basket is brought to the church to be blessed by the priest. Different foods represent elements of the Easter story such as joy, mercy, moderation, resurrection, and generosity. This basket includes *paska,* a sweet, rich yeast bread, marked with a cross; *hrudka* or *sirets,* a type of bland spread of cheese and eggs; *šunka,* ham; *maslo,* butter shaped to look like a lamb; *kolbasi,* sausage; and bacon, eggs, salt, and horseradish.

Diet and Health

Traditional Czech cuisine is heavy in salt and saturated fats. As such, the Czech Republic has one of the highest rates of death due to cardiovascular disease in the developed world. As more awareness is given to health and diet, more and more Czechs are dieting or watching their weight.

To eat dietetically, Czechs increase their consumption of fresh fruits and vegetables. Grapefruit and pineapple are considered "fat eaters" and are popular diet foods eaten at breakfast. This is in contrast to eating foods that have the fat or sugar removed. Cheeses, potato chips, milks, and yogurts are all full fat. It is believed that the fat is more natural in these foods.

Czechs have a long tradition of using spas as a health and wellness resource, both for treatment of chronic medical conditions as well as for relaxing vacations. These spas, mostly located around natural mineral springs, take advantage of mountainous forested areas. These resorts have special spa food with more fresh vegetables and lower-fat meats and fishes. It is not uncommon to go to one for several weeks to a month to recover from an illness.

Brelyn Johnson

Further Reading

Brizova, Joza. *The Czechoslovak Cookbook.* New York: Crown, 1965.

Cornej, Petr, and Jiri Pokorny. *A Brief History of the Czech Lands to 2000.* Prague, Czech Republic: Prah Press, 2000.

Czech Tourism.com. http://www.czechtourism.com.

My Czech Republic. http://www.myczechRepublic.com.

Polvany, Marina. *All along the Danube: Recipes from Germany, Austria, Czechoslovakia, Yugoslavia, Hungary, Romania and Bulgaria.* New York: Hippocrene Books, 1994.

Pynsent, R. B. *Questions of Identity: Czech and Slovak Ideas of Nationality and Personality.* New York: Central European University Press, 1994.

Trnka, Peter. *The Best of Czech Cooking.* New York: Hippocrene Books, 1996.

Denmark

Overview

The northern European kingdom of Denmark is one of the oldest surviving monarchies in the world. It was first recognized as a unified territory in the 10th century under the rule of Gorm the Old, said to be a direct ancestor to Denmark's present monarch, Queen Margrethe II. Gorm was succeeded by his son, Harald Bluetooth, who erected runestones in the town of Jelling to commemorate his parents' death and to celebrate Denmark's conversion from paganism to Christianity. Dating from around 965, the Jelling Stones represent Denmark's "birth certificate" and are today recognized as a UNESCO World Heritage site. Denmark's first constitution was introduced in 1849.

The smallest country in Scandinavia, Denmark is made up of three main landmasses (the Jutland Peninsula, connected to Germany, and the islands of Funen and Zealand), as well as a number of smaller islands, including Bornholm, off the south coast of Sweden. The former colonies of Greenland and the Faeroe Islands continue to be Danish protectorates but are now both governed by politically autonomous parliaments.

Denmark's location between the North and Baltic seas secures a rich source of seafood, which features prominently in its food culture. Its temperate climate and largely flat landscape also account for Denmark's long agrarian history, particularly dairy, livestock, and cereal farming. Evidence of animal husbandry and grain cultivation in the area dates to the Neolithic period (3900–1700 B.C.), while the famous "Tollund" man (the fourth-century body found preserved in Jutland's peat reserves in 1950) was found to have soup containing seeds in his digestive tract.

Now predominantly an industrial economy, with agriculture accounting for less than 20 percent of Danish exports and remaining exports mainly dedicated to machinery, pharmaceuticals, electronics, and environmental technology, Denmark is at once a thoroughly modern and a proudly traditional country. Denmark was twice rated the Best Country for Business by *Forbes* magazine (2008–2009) and twice voted the "happiest" country in the world (2006, 2008). Visitors to Denmark will find global brands and products well represented in cosmopolitan centers, including the predictable array of food franchises like McDonald's, KFC, Subway, and Pizza Hut, not to mention a thriving sector of "ethnic" eateries. Immigrants constitute almost 10 percent of Denmark's population of 5.5 million.

Visitors will also find a strong sense of history in the cobbled streets where pretzel signs heralding Danish bakeries outnumber the golden arches and where one hardly ever needs to walk more than a block to find another *pølsevogn* (hot dog stand), a century after they were first introduced in 1910. Inside modern homes, tradition continues in the form of *hygge,* that famously untranslatable sense of comfort and well-being that Danes thrive on creating. Both a verb and a noun, *hygge* can describe a feeling, a situation, or an activity, but more often than not it takes place around a table, where candles may be lit day or night, in summer or in winter, for special occasions and for simple family meals.

Just a few decades ago there existed a clear polarity between "fancy" food—typically the kind

Windmill in a field of barley in Denmark. Sixty percent of land in Denmark is used for agricultural development, but the industry contributes only to just over 4 percent of the gross domestic product. (Corel)

served in restaurants, inspired by French haute cuisine (Queen Margrethe's husband, His Royal Highness the Prince Consort, is French)—and the more hearty "traditional" fare, often in the form of meat, potatoes, and gravy, if not the time-honored *smørrebrød* (open-faced sandwiches), which continue to feature fish and meat toppings preserved by salting, smoking, and brining, techniques probably used by the Vikings. Today, the so-called New Nordic Cuisine is fast gaining the world's attention, particularly after Copenhagen's Noma was voted *Restaurant* magazine's Best Restaurant in the World in 2009. The manifesto of the New Nordic Cuisine stresses local and seasonal cooking and eating. With initiatives such as these—and others, like *smushi,* the playful combination of sushi and smørrebrød pioneered by the Royal Cafe in Copenhagen—Denmark's food culture is fast coming to entail more

than pork and potatoes, and rye bread and herring. But in the tradition of the fairytales that Denmark is equally proud of, these culinary innovations are not so much novelties as they are retellings, with a modern twist, of age-old stories. Whether plated old- or new-style, the flavors of sea, smoke, and earth continue to dominate Danish food.

🍽 Food Culture Snapshot

A young couple with small children in Copenhagen, Thomas and Bente both work full-time, so they do most of their shopping on Saturday afternoons. A standard part of their shopping is for *pålæg* ("put on top," or bread toppings), both sweet and savory. Their two children insist on bread with Nutella or *pålægschokolade* (wafer-thin sheets of chocolate) for breakfast whenever they can, but Bente tries to make them eat cereal more frequently. For her own breakfast she prefers one of the many cultured dairy products available, like yogurt or buttermilk, with a little muesli or the combination of toasted rye crumbs and sugar known as *drys* ("sprinkle"). Apart from Sunday mornings, when he cooks American-style pancakes with maple syrup for the family, Thomas eats a toasted bread roll with cheese and jam for breakfast. He likes the wide variety of ready-to-heat bread now available in supermarkets, so he alternates between ciabatta-style rolls one week and something "healthier," like carrot and bran, the next.

Thomas and Bente both eat lunch at their workplace canteens, but the children take packed lunches to school, as well as a midmorning snack of fruit or a dried fruit stick and a flavored drinking yogurt (chocolate milk when they are lucky). For lunch they generally have open sandwiches, so a packet of presliced rye bread is always on the shopping list, along with their favorite toppings. Hans, age six, gets either salami topped with rémoulade (a tartar-like relish) and crispy onions, liver pâté, or a sliced *frikadelle* (meatball) on his bread. His eight-year-old sister, Pernille, prefers fish and white meat—her favorite is tinned mackerel with a liberal squeeze of mayonnaise, or any kind of herring. But fishy toppings do not travel well, so these mostly stay at home for weekend lunches, and she gets turkey, chicken, or ham sandwiches for school. Sometimes they get leftovers like pasta or lasagna.

Dinner usually consists of meat and some form of vegetable, so the family buys a selection of products that can be stored in the freezer if not used right away, especially minced meat, which can easily become frikadeller, *hakkebøf* (hamburger patties served with fried onions), or a pasta sauce. Bente does occasionally buy fresh vegetables on her way home from work, but they rely mostly on frozen vegetables. They also buy frozen pizza bases that at least once a week they have fun building into "gourmet" pizzas with whatever *pålæg* needs using.

They do not generally eat sweets, but Thomas and Bente do sometimes enjoy a few pieces of dark chocolate with their evening coffee after the children have gone to bed. On Saturdays Hans and Pernille each choose a DVD to watch in the afternoon, when they are also allowed a small bowl of sweets and maybe some potato chips or microwave popcorn, so there are always some goodies in the shopping cart along with the week's supply of food, coffee, and fruit juice. Thomas and Bente rarely feel like cooking when they come home with their purchases, so on Saturdays the family typically gets a take-out meal in the evening for a bit of hygge in front of the television. They take turns choosing what everyone eats, and the cycles are predictable enough: Thomas likes his *döner kebab* (meat on a vertical spit, similar to gyros), Bente her pizza, Pernille chooses Chinese food, and Hans invariably requests McDonald's.

Major Foodstuffs

Denmark is famously home to more pigs than people and, in addition to dairy, is probably best known for its pork. These are arguably two of its most important foodstuffs, both on Danish tables and in terms of agricultural exports. Denmark prides itself on a highly efficient and technologically advanced agricultural sector that produces enough food annually to feed 15 million people, approximately two-thirds of which is exported, mainly to the European Union. The industry is dominated by large, mechanized farms run by cooperatives, meaning complete ownership by Danish farmers, whose annual turnover contributes 10 percent to the country's gross domestic product. The Danish Agricultural Council puts a high priority on food safety and animal welfare.

Danish Crown, a cooperative comprising 15,000 farmers and 25,000 employees, is one of the largest companies in Denmark and the world's leading meat exporter. It represents 8 percent of the European Union's total pork production, with two million tons of pork processed annually, as well as 150,000 tons of beef. The joint Danish-Swedish Arla Foods is Denmark's biggest dairy cooperative and one of the few remaining after nationwide mergers decreased the number of cooperatives from almost 1,500 in 1935 to just 12 in 2007. Arla is also the world's largest producer of organic dairy products and counts Lurpak butter and Buko cream cheese as some of its most popular products, both at home and abroad.

Whereas the country's soil used to be poorly suited to grain cultivation, years of applying livestock manure have helped to fertilize the land to the extent that Denmark no longer relies exclusively on grain imports. Now, more than half the arable land is devoted to cultivating grains: some rye and rape but mainly wheat and barley, which are important for the bread industry and for that other Danish favorite, beer. Sugar beet farming occupies less than 2 percent of agriculture, though imported sugar has remained an important foodstuff since it was brought over in the 1600s, when Denmark began to occupy the Virgin Islands, which most certainly helped to fuel a nationwide sweet tooth that can today be satisfied by a number of proudly Danish specialties ranging from pastries to cookies, sweets, marzipan, and chocolate.

Potatoes have featured heavily in the Danish diet since they were introduced from France in the 18th century. For years they have been the main starch of a "proper" meal, and many of the older generation would today still prefer potatoes over rice, pasta, or noodles. Danes are particularly fond of new potatoes, or the first crop of the season, which produces delicately flavored small tubers. The island of Samsø is well known for its new potatoes, although with modern farming and transport, potatoes from the island are available in Danish supermarkets throughout the year. Potatoes have also historically been used in the production of *snaps,* or aquavit, but the spirit is now mostly grain based.

Beyond bread, meat, potatoes, and dairy (and beer and snaps to wash it all down), fish continues to be an important component of the Danish table, with evidence of herring and oyster consumption dating to the Stone Age. The Baltic Sea provides herring—the island of Bornholm is famous for its herring smokehouses—and the North Sea a variety of cold-water fish, like cod, mackerel, plaice, eel, and crustaceans, while the Limfjord Sound is renowned for its oysters. Despite these local resources, Denmark still imports fish, including herring from Norway and shrimp from Greenland, though European Union fishing quotas have made seafood generally more expensive and less abundant in recent years.

A smokehouse and restaurant on Bornholm Island, Denmark. (Collpicto | Dreamstime.com)

A final significant foodstuff in Denmark is fruit. While not a major component of domestic industry, fruit picking on private smallholdings is both a popular tourist activity and a form of seasonal employment for young travelers who help to make the season's best fruit available for Danish consumers. Strawberries are plentiful in summer, as are a number of other berries such as black currants, red currants, blueberries, and cherries, which are enjoyed fresh or made into jams and compotes, if not frozen for later in the year. Hibiscus fruits are popular for making jam, and rhubarb for compotes that are eaten as a dessert with cream or milk or served as an accompaniment to grilled meat or fish. Rhubarb is also a possible ingredient of *rødgrød med fløde,* "red pudding with cream," probably more famous as a Danish phrase that is notoriously difficult for foreigners to pronounce. Essentially a mixture of lightly stewed fruit—mostly red berries—slightly thickened with corn or potato starch and served with a drizzle of cream, rødgrød med fløde is the perfect expression of Danish summer hygge.

Cooking

Despite the increased availability of fast, convenience, pre-prepared, and frozen foods, cooking continues to be an important and widespread activity in Denmark. Danish women who work or go to school full-time reflect a variety of attitudes toward cooking: Some cook for pleasure, some as a chore, some to ensure optimal healthiness. Consistent is the regularity of some form of cooking, even if the category of homemade is becoming more ambiguous with the convenience of prepared components of a meal that simply need to be assembled or finished at home. The popular birthday *lagkage* (layer cake), for instance, is often assembled at home using store-bought sponge cake and powdered custard, while potatoes are available by the jar, peeled and preboiled. So while it is entirely possible to produce a lot of food at home with minimal cooking from scratch, or even with minimal cooking skills, the act of regularly preparing food at home remains an essential part of Danish food culture—particularly when it comes to smørrebrød, basically an act of assembly.

Even when made entirely from scratch, cooked Danish food is not traditionally time- and labor-intensive in the style of haute cuisine or other food cultures that rely on heavy spicing and/or marinating. Joints of meat or whole chickens are roasted with minimal preparation, while fish, steaks, and patties are panfried and typically served with boiled potatoes and a simple gravy of cooking juices, cream, and coloring. Salt and pepper are the most important seasonings in a Danish kitchen, and dishes are often finished with a garnish of herbs like chives, dill, or parsley. Baking of bread, cakes, and cookies is perhaps the most time-consuming kitchen activity and also the most popular, although the very labor-intensive pastry making is generally left to professional bakers. When a general strike shut down bread

factories for two weeks in 1998, fresh yeast was the first commodity to be sold out in supermarkets, and the event was dubbed the "yeast strike." Most Danes may prefer to buy bread for the sake of convenience, but this episode suggests that a majority of them can bake if they need to.

Following widespread industrialization at the turn of the 20th century, when it became normal to buy bread rather than to bake it (rye bread, in particular, takes a very long time to bake), home-baked bread became fashionable again only in the 1960s and 1970s when Denmark, like many other Western countries, began paying more attention to both flavor and healthiness. In 1972 the Dairy Board published the first of a very popular series of cookbooks called *Karoline's Køkken* (Caroline's kitchen). Compiled from recipes developed to promote the use of dairy products, eight new cookbooks (complete with nutritional information and meal plans) were published between 1980 and 2001, all distributed free of charge to Danish households. Free distribution was discontinued after the firm was taken over by Arla in 2003, but these cookbooks remain the most comprehensive account of Denmark's changing food culture in the final decades of the 20th century. Most obvious is the increasing number of "exotic" recipes as Danes began to embrace and exhibit a more comfortable relationship to food from around the world as a combined result of increased travel, immigration, and access to foreign ingredients and restaurants in Denmark. Changing attitudes about health are also evident in the recipes themselves, as they begin to include less cream and butter and more low-fat dairy products, as well as in the loss of the friendly cartoon cow that was Karoline's icon from the first edition until the 1990s, when she was dropped because a cow was considered inappropriate for connoting good health.

Long before *Karoline's Køkken,* the first Danish cookbook was published in 1616. As with many early cookbooks, the first century or so of Danish culinary guides were written mostly by men for other male chefs, after which women became more common as authors of largely didactic volumes aimed at young housewives. By the end of the 19th century, cookbooks were most frequently authored by women, written with a less moralizing tone, and included general household tips for an audience presumably more at ease in their kitchens. The most popular book from the early 20th century was *Frøken Jensen's Kogebog* (Miss Jensen's cookbook, written by Kristine Marie Jensen), which went through 75 editions by 1975, in addition to a special centenary edition in 2001. *Frøken Jensen's Kogebog* may be old-fashioned, but it is not outdated. A number of the classic dishes she included continue to be cooked and eaten by many Danes, and perhaps increasingly by non-Danes around the world, thanks to globally best-selling cookbooks like Trine Hahnemann's 2009 *The Scandinavian Cookbook,* which includes a recipe for *æbleskiver* (small, round doughnuts traditionally eaten around Christmas) that is only marginally different from Miss Jensen's century-old recipe for the same.

Typical Meals

Open-faced sandwiches are extremely versatile in Denmark, extending beyond smørrebrød proper to be a potential component of every meal: a slice of bread or a bread roll eaten as two separate halves with cheese and jam at breakfast, for instance, followed by rye bread with toppings for lunch. Alternatively, if lunch has been a main warm meal, then it is not unusual to have a light dinner of bread or *knækbrød* (crispbread) with cheese and a cup of tea.

Unless it is oatmeal porridge, a Danish breakfast is seldom a hot, cooked meal. Following a general preference for reserving the heavier rye bread for lunch, *morgenbrød* ("morning bread") is a blanket term that refers to bread eaten for breakfast—typically some form of white roll from a bakery. Given the cost of bakery bread, morgenbrød is often a weekend treat, or it is reserved for special occasions like birthdays and anniversaries when it is also standard to bring bakery bread or pastries to work to share with colleagues. Although recent surveys suggest that one in four Danes skip the first meal of the day, a typical everyday breakfast is as likely to feature store-bought bread, cereal, and some form of cultured dairy product.

Denmark's equivalent to the Swedish *smörgåsbord* is the *kolde bord,* or "cold table," which also signals the main difference between them: Most of the items on the Danish table are cold—or if not, just *lune,* or gently heated—rather than properly hot like some dishes on a Swedish table. The cold table, traditionally served at lunch, is a spread of bread and toppings required to make and eat smørrebrød and includes a range of seafood (pickled herring; smoked salmon, eel, or herring; boiled shrimp; crumbed fillets of plaice), cold meats (salami, roast beef, corned beef, ham, roast pork, liver pâté), and a number of condiments including prepared salads (including Italian salad, a mixture of mayonnaise, carrots, peas, and asparagus; Russian salad, with beets; mackerel salad, canned mackerel in tomato sauce topped with mayonnaise; curry salad, mayonnaise mixed with chopped, hard-boiled eggs, apple, and mild curry powder); and rémoulade, sliced beets, capers, onions (raw and fried), bacon, mushrooms, pickled cucumber, red cabbage, and grated horseradish. Warm foods may include panfried slices of pork loin, meatballs, and beef patties. Cheese, including the Funen specialty of smoked curd cheese, is often served with grapes as an end to the meal.

To the uninitiated, this cornucopia can be as confusing as it is tantalizing, but there are strict sequences and combinations to be observed. As a general rule, fish is eaten before meat, and rye bread is used for herring, whereas white bread is reserved for shrimp and cheese. Beyond these, a number of classic combinations exist that Danes seem to know instinctively: Crumbed plaice needs rémoulade, as do salami and roast beef, both of which are topped with crispy onions; liver pâté is topped with bacon and mushrooms and maybe beets; Italian salad goes with ham, roast pork with red cabbage, and so on. Beer and snaps are the traditional accompaniments to a cold table, together with regular toasts. The oft-repeated *Skål!* requires everyone to lift their glasses and drink.

This typical meal is not an everyday meal, but it does contain elements of the kinds of foods that many people eat on a daily basis, either as a packed lunch or from work cafeterias, where employees can choose a few pieces of prepared smørrebrød if not the salad buffet or a hot meal of the day. Eating smørrebrød for lunch on the job began as a worker's habit in the early 19th century, and it was not until it appeared on the first restaurant menu in 1883 at Nimb, in Tivoli Gardens, that it became fashionable as a high-class restaurant food as well. Now it exists as both, with many high-end restaurants in Denmark serving classic combinations, and the profession of being a *smørrebrødsjomfru* (literally "virgin," *jomfru* refers to young maidens who were historically trained in the art of constructing smørrebrød) continues as a respected trade in Denmark.

Dinner is usually a hot meal and often features some of the same foods that, as leftovers, can be reused as bread toppings, such as meatballs, roast pork, beef, or chicken, with potatoes or other vegetables. In more rural areas, it used to be common to begin the evening meal with some form of porridge or gruel to curb the appetite—at Christmas it was fairly common to eat pudding before the main meal—but this has given way to the more universal practice of an early dinner followed by coffee

Brændende kærlighed ("burning love," mashed potatoes topped with crispy bacon and fried onions). (Jörg Beuge | Dreamstime.com)

and a slice of cake or a few cookies later in the evening. Other traditional evening meals include *æbleflæsk* (pork fried with apples and onions), *forloren hare* ("mock hare," or meatloaf), *boller i karry* (pork dumplings in a mild curry sauce), and the evocatively named *brændende kærlighed* ("burning love," mashed potatoes topped with crispy bacon and fried onions). A favorite light summer meal is *koldskål* (buttermilk flavored with eggs, sugar, vanilla, and lemon) sprinkled with *kammerjunkere* (small vanilla cookies). Whatever the food or occasion, two phrases are important to any meal: *tak for mad* ("thank you for the food") and *velbekomme* ("you are welcome").

Eating Out

Given a price structure that includes taxes, service fees, and staff wages, dining in restaurants has generally been considered expensive in Denmark and therefore a regular habit only for the very wealthy, and otherwise reserved for special occasions—the older generation commonly celebrates so-called round birthdays (50, 60, 70) at great expense by reserving an entire restaurant to cater for a family party. The restaurant business nevertheless continues to thrive, thanks to both locals and tourists, who have the choice of newer establishments like Noma and also historic sites like Det Lille Apotek (The small apothecary), the oldest restaurant in Copenhagen, founded in 1720 and said to have been regularly patronized by author Hans Christian Andersen.

Added to these are the now-countless options for eating out offered by international franchises, smaller foreign restaurants, and an abundance of local pavement cafés, which are particularly trendy during summer. The historical *kro,* or inn, typically located outside major towns and often the main attraction of smaller towns, is also a popular place to eat out and typically specializes in traditional Danish fare. The ubiquitous hot dog stands and "grill bars," offering a variety of foods from hot dogs to hamburgers and fries, toasted sandwiches, and ice cream, represent the more casual and affordable side of eating out, as do the many fast-food outlets selling döner kebabs, pizza slices, and Chinese food.

Special Occasions

No special occasion in Denmark is observed without special attention to food and drink, and some foods also denote special occasions. Christmas Eve is the biggest food event of the year, although items from the Christmas table are often eaten repeatedly in the preceding months. The November 11 celebration of Morten's Aften (Martin's Evening, named after the French St. Martin of Tours, who tried to hide in a goose pen to avoid being anointed bishop), for instance, looks very much like a Christmas table, with roast duck, caramelized potatoes, red cabbage, and pickled cucumber. Duck is also eaten at Christmas, if not turkey, goose, or pork. *Julefrokost* (Christmas lunch) refers not to lunch on December 25 but to end-of-year parties arranged by employers, students, or any other social group. Generally hosted at lunch, and generally entailing the big "cold table" (which can be used for any festivity), it is not unheard of for a julefrokost to be held in the evening, nor for it to feature the hot meal traditionally eaten on Christmas Eve.

Birthdays are celebrated with lagkage, a cake layered with custard, cream, and fruit, or the more traditional *kringle,* a large pretzel-shaped cake filled with fruit or custard and made with a similar yeast dough to Danish pastries called *wienerbrød,* or Vienna bread, after the 19th-century baker's strike that brought a number of Germans and Austrians to work in Danish bakeries, who introduced the flaky, buttery dough that Danish bakers would later appropriate. Special events like anniversaries are often marked with an open house where friends and family can visit throughout the day to enjoy a piece of pastry or cake with a cup of coffee and a small glass of *Gammel Dansk* ("Old Danish"), an herbal bitters. Another sweet item for special occasions is the *kransekage,* or wreath cake, an elaborate pyramid of cake rings made from ground almonds, egg whites, and sugar. Today, smaller kransekager

are widely available from bakeries and supermarkets and generally offered with champagne at midnight on New Year's Eve, but for many years it was splendid enough to mainly be a wedding showpiece. Like many special and everyday events in Denmark that are no longer restricted to Danish food alone, guests at modern weddings, christenings, and confirmation parties are as likely to feast on "foreign" food as they are on anything specifically Danish.

Diet and Health

With an average life expectancy of 78 years, low infant-mortality rates, and an HIV prevalence of less than 1 percent, Denmark has a generally healthy population. Cancer is the leading cause of death, followed by heart disease. This good health is thanks in large measure to a highly efficient public health system, partly funded by Denmark's global leadership in diabetes treatment, antibiotics, and psychotropic medication. It is also thanks to a general lifestyle that includes a fair amount of physical activity—cycling is the most common mode of transport, for children and adults alike, and large parts of most cities are reserved for pedestrians. However, in recent decades, Denmark has also experienced increasing numbers of people who are overweight or obese, particularly children. This is most often explained as a result of increased consumption of fast food, sweets, and convenience products.

The country does have a long history of monitoring food and diets in the interests of public health. The first major study of the nutrient values of foods was undertaken by physiologist and pathologist P. L. Panum in the 19th century. Panum's work was developed by a number of scientists over the next century or so, notably Christian Jürgensen (author of the first table of "Common Recommendations for the Healthy and the Ill" in 1888) and Richard Ege, whose 1932 nutrition tables incorporated the then–newly discovered vitamins and who continued to publish significant work until the 1970s, when Peder Helms's computerized tables paved the way for the first national Danish Food Composition Database, which published its first official tables in the

1980s. These nutritional databases have been instrumental in compiling dietary recommendations for the Danish population.

The first official food pyramid was launched in 1976 by FDB, a retail cooperative that has been involved in consumer welfare for more than a century. In 1996 they introduced the "S" symbol on supermarket products that were certified as healthy choices (*sundhed* is the Danish word for health). In 2009, following a merger with other Nordic countries, this was replaced by the keyhole symbol that had been introduced in Sweden some years earlier. Criteria for the keyhole include acceptable amounts of fat, sugar, fiber, and salt. Its effectiveness is yet to be measured. As the rest of the world tunes in to not just the gastronomic delights but also the supposed healthfulness of the so-called new Nordic diet with its emphasis on local grains, berries, and fish, it remains to be seen whether Danes themselves will find the fairytale compelling enough to prefer rye bread and herring to a frozen ready-made portion of Moroccan-spiced chicken from the supermarket.

Signe Rousseau

Further Reading

Davidson, Alan. "Recipes from Denmark." In *North Atlantic Seafood: A Comprehensive Guide with Recipes,* 385–93. Berkeley, CA: Ten Speed Press, 2003.

Gold, Carol. *Danish Cookbooks: Domesticity and National Identity, 1916–1901.* Seattle: University of Washington Press, 2007.

Hahnemann, Trine. *The Scandinavian Cookbook.* Kansas City, MO: Andrews McMeel, 2009.

Halkier, Bente. "Performances and Positionings in Cooking Practices among Danish Women." *Food, Culture and Society* 12, No. 3 (2009): 357–77.

Meyer, Claus. "Manifesto for the New Nordic Cuisine." Claus Meyer's Web site. http://www.clausmeyer.dk/en/the_new_nordic_cuisine_/manifesto_.html.

Notaker, Henry. *Food Culture in Scandinavia.* Westport, CT: Greenwood Press, 2008.

Finland

Overview

Finland is said to be a country between East and West, a small nation sharing a border with Russia in the east and the Scandinavian countries in the west. Cultural influences have come from both sides, sometimes dividing the country east to west when it comes to architecture, customs, religion, and food. Also politically Finland has a western and an eastern history, belonging to Sweden until 1809 and then being a part of Russia until 1917. Even so, national borders don't necessarily create new customs or habits; it is more a question of contacts between people, trade routes, migration, and geographic features that form the culture. The Baltic Sea has, for example, been an important area for trade, and some influences have come from Germany, especially feast traditions.

The climate in the north and the traditional dispersion of the population in rural areas are, however, the most essential factors influencing Finnish food culture. Large forest areas have offered hunting opportunities (birds, hare, moose), berries to gather (blueberries, cowberries, cloudberries), mushrooms, and even bark to mix with flour for baking bread in times of famine. Finland is also known as the land of the thousand lakes, and therefore fish has been an important part of the meal not only for the coastal population but also for the inlanders. Potatoes came to Finland with Swedish officers in the 18th century and soon became an important base for every meal. Before that, the turnip was the main root. Meat, milk, and butter are also traditionally important products from cattle breeding among the agricultural population. Since self-sufficiency was a

fact for the majority nearly until World War II, islanders also kept cows for milk and butter even if fish dominated as the main food in the archipelago. In the north of Finland both Finns and the Saami population (once referred to as Lapps, though this is considered derogatory) have kept reindeers as their main industry, which is naturally reflected in the diet.

Food Culture Snapshot

Pekka (38) and Mari (36) live in Helsinki with their two children, Seppo (7) and Satu (5). After a quick breakfast of coffee and two sandwiches, on his way to work, Pekka takes Satu to kindergarten, where she also gets her breakfast, a sandwich and hot chocolate. Mari sends Seppo, who has eaten cereal for breakfast, off to school and then gets ready for work. During the day Pekka eats fried whitefish with potatoes for lunch at a nearby restaurant, whereas Mari chooses to eat a take-out shrimp salad at her desk since she was a little late for work in the morning. Seppo eats sausage soup at school and Satu a spinach crepe at her kindergarten.

On her way home Mari hurries to the nearest market to buy milk, bread, fruit, and some minced meat. She picks up Satu (Seppo is already home from school) and starts to prepare dinner, which is spaghetti and meat sauce. When Pekka arrives, dinner is ready; they eat together, but since Mari takes Satu to her gymnastic lesson this evening, Pekka is left with the quite messy kitchen to take care of.

Pekka and Seppo go by car to a supermarket in a mall outside town and do some shopping for the weekend. In the supermarket Pekka calls up Mari to check if she thinks it would be a good idea to buy chicken fillets as they are on sale and also whether he also should buy wine for Friday and Saturday. Before they drive back home, Pekka and Seppo eat ice cream in the mall. Back home from the gymnastics lesson, Mari makes Satu porridge for her evening meal before bedtime. The rest of the family eats sandwiches and drinks tea before it is time for sleep.

Cooking

In old times both fish and meat were mainly salted, as a conservation method, to last through the winter. In western Finland bread was baked only a couple of times a year, and therefore it was dry most of the time. In eastern parts of Finland bread was baked more often, perhaps every week, and therefore eaten fresh. Cooking over an open fire in a pot was the norm until the iron stove became more common in the 1920s in the countryside. At the same time, during the period of independence after 1917, national awareness grew strong and many organizations that took an interest in the welfare of the population started to propagate a healthier and more diversified diet. New schools focusing on giving youngsters education in practical tasks were founded, and the girls participated in cooking courses and in this way spread new recipes and food habits to their families. Since the 1950s both girls and boys have been educated in housekeeping and cooking as a school subject. Since the majority of Finnish women work outside the home, the responsibility for the family cooking, at least among young and middle-aged men and women, is shared quite equally.

Boiling, frying, and baking are still the main cooking methods. The oven has an important role when preparing food. Many common dishes are baked, today mostly in electric ovens. The Finns have quite easily accepted new technology. The microwave oven became a big hit in the 1980s. Since Finland is an industrialized Western country, time is always too short; everything has to be done in a hurry, even cooking. At first, cookbooks for how to cook with microwaves were published, but soon the traditional electric stove and oven proved better for cooking. Gas is also used in Finland but mostly in some areas

in bigger cities and in the many holiday cottages used during the summer and on weekends. The microwave oven is still, however, an important article in nearly every Finnish kitchen and has come to stay. The market offers a lot of ready-made food that can be heated quickly, even by the children in the family. Another important use for the microwave oven is to defrost food, since nearly every family has a freezer, not only for ice cream and ice for drinks but also for berries and mushrooms gathered in the forests, garden products, or fish and meat. Finns still love to make their own food supply for the winter, to have raw material of their own, and to take advantage of what nature can offer for free.

Typical Meals

Since Finland has been mainly a receiver of cultural influences, not much can be seen as typically Finnish when it comes to food. However, typical Finnish bread is made of rye. Every Finn who lives abroad, or even just stays abroad for a vacation, at some point misses dark rye bread. It is eaten in both the morning and the evening as a sandwich with butter and cheese or ham, or as a complement to the main dish, usually then also spread with butter. Not all bread is made of rye, but some kind of whole grain is often preferred. Bread completely made of wheat is not very popular except for sweet coffee bread called *pulla*.

Finns are known as heavy drinkers, but when it comes to everyday meals a typical drink to go with the food is milk, even for adults. Water and nonalcoholic malt liquor or beer are also common, while wine has been accepted among the general public quite recently during the last decades, and even then merely at festive occasions and weekend dinners. A more traditional way to mark a festive dish is to drink a shot of vodka, in Finnish called *ryyppy* and among the Swedish-speaking population known as *snaps*; it is drunk after singing a special snaps song.

Domestic fish is no longer a cheap ingredient for everyday meals. The traditional wild fishes, such as Baltic herring, northern pike, pike perch, whitefish, and pollan, called *mujkku*, are more and more being replaced by imported, mostly Norwegian salmon or trout grown in net cages by local fishermen in the archipelago; this imported fish is actually cheaper. The latest statistics show that Finns eat 26.5 pounds (12 kilograms) of foreign fish and 11 pounds (5 kilograms) of domestic fish a year. Salmon and trout are used in the same way: baked in the oven, grilled, smoked, or fried, and very often just raw, salted, and served in thin slices with potatoes or rye bread. Salmon and trout are also used for soups and as fillings in pastries, often mixed with rice. It is, however, very popular to catch one's own fish, as the lakes are many and the seashore long. At people's vacation cottages fishing is an important way to relax and to spend time, especially among men, in a way that usually results in food on the table. Depending on what kind of fish one catches, it can be grilled or fried and eaten with potatoes and perhaps with a sauce made of sour cream and herbs (for grilled fish) or a warm sauce made of butter, cream, and white wine (for fried fish). Fish soup is also popular. In the supermarkets highly refined products such as fish nuggets and other ready-made frozen fish dishes are available. These are popular especially among children because the possibility of swallowing fish bones is eliminated. There is also an environmental and ethical question today when choosing frozen fish. Finnish salmon are sent by airplane to Asia for processing and then returned to the Finnish market, requiring a considerable expenditure of fossil fuels and causing unnecessary pollution. This is, of course, a global problem and not significant only for Finland.

Many tourist guides recommend that visitors eat bear when visiting Finland. There may be a few restaurants, mainly in Helsinki, that occasionally do have bear on their menus, but it is definitely rare. Big wild or semiwild animals are indeed served, especially moose and reindeer. The moose population is reduced every year, or at least officials try to keep it in control, by a special moose hunt that many men in the countryside participate in. Moose meat can be bought in the autumn in market halls or well-supplied supermarkets, but mostly it is a product that the participants in the hunt share among themselves and fill their freezers with. It is used like any other meat, in a casserole, in soups, or as minced

meat. Reindeer is often marketed as typical for Finland. In the north of Finland reindeer is a natural product, but farther south mainly one dish, called *poronkäristys,* or sautéed reindeer, is really common. It consists of a thin sauce with a lot of very thin slices of reindeer meat, eaten with mashed potatoes and cowberries. A reindeer steak can also be an alternative to beefsteak and is then often served warm or cold-smoked.

Like in many other countries, meatballs are popular among both children and adults; on the whole minced pork, beef, or most often a mix of both is used a lot. Ground meat is quite cheap, easy, and fast to make a sauce of, eaten with spaghetti or potatoes. Pork is common as well, especially grilled in summertime. Both pork and beef are often used in casseroles. Ground meat mixed with rice forms the

Poronkäristys, a thin sauce with a lot of very thin slices of reindeer meat, eaten with mashed potatoes and cowberries, common in the south of Finland. (Shutterstock)

filling for cabbage rolls, a popular dish in autumn. About the same taste, but with less skill needed, can be achieved by mixing cabbage, minced meat, milk, and egg together in a mold and baking it in the oven. Both are served with cowberry jam. Sausages are a popular everyday food as well. A typical Finnish sausage seldom contains much meat, however, and is therefore jokingly even said to be the most popular vegetable in Finnish cuisine.

In almost every supermarket there are ready-to-eat grilled hens and broilers. Mostly, chicken is a cheap product sold in slices, as parts, or breasts, either plain or in different marinades. Poultry is often seen a lighter form of meat and therefore healthier. As for so many products mass-produced as food, ethical considerations now influence people's decisions, however. Broilers are produced and forced to grow quickly, an ethical question, but also a question of taste. Especially when it comes to egg production, eggs from "happy hens" are sold, meaning hens are free-range and not kept in small cages.

Fish, meat, and sausage are all ingredients for making soups. They are traditional everyday dishes, but the younger generation is not so enthusiastic about these, especially if it involves cooking their own dinner. Pea soup is, however, very common and even has its own day, when it is served at lunchtime and in workplace restaurants. Thursday is the day for pea soup, which in Finland is green, compared with a yellow pea soup in Sweden. It is the most common canned soup as well and often eaten in conditions where the cooking facilities are limited.

Pancakes with jam are traditionally served as a dessert after the pea soup. The jam can be made of strawberries, raspberries, blueberries, or cloudberries and is often homemade. Berries are an important part of Finnish food culture. There are 37 edible species of wild berries in Finland, of which about 20 species are picked for consumption. The tradition of picking berries in the woods or home gardens or buying them at the market is well preserved, even among younger generations. Berries are eaten alone or with cream, milk, and a little sugar. A Finnish specialty is *leipäjuusto,* a kind of cheese baked in the oven or warmed in a frying pan and eaten with cloudberries. A cake with strawberries and whipped

cream is the ultimate symbol for summer and a must at birthday parties in June and July. Blueberry pie is also a must for most people, eaten with vanilla cream. A specialty originating in Russia is frozen cranberries eaten with hot caramel sauce called *kinuski.* Berries of any kind are also eaten with *Quark* (a smooth sour-milk cheese like yogurt) or ice cream. Ice cream is extremely popular. Among Europeans, Finns eat the most ice cream, despite their northern and mostly cold climate.

Eating Out

Eating out usually means going out with friends or family. Eating is, of course, an important task, but equally important is the social dimension: One goes out to spend some time together. Finland is one of very few countries where schoolchildren, from first grade to high school, are served a free lunch every day. It is considered the most important part of the national health plan. This means that every child can eat at least one warm, nutritious meal a day. Most Finns are used to eating lunch at noon. Some workplaces have their own cafeterias, and if not, there are dishes with special prices at restaurants during lunchtime. A typical menu for one week at a lunch restaurant in Helsinki can be as follows: Monday—fried salmon with spinach and egg sauce, Tuesday—black salsify soup, Wednesday—sausage soup, Thursday—meatloaf with mushroom sauce, Friday—fried Baltic herring with chive sauce.

Otherwise, the tradition of eating out is quite young in Finland. There are, of course, restaurants with old and fine traditions that the bourgeoisie, civil servants, businessmen, and other groups higher up in society have frequented as long as restaurants have existed. Families have also celebrated special occasions by eating out. Still, a bigger change in eating-out habits has occurred only since the late 1980s. An economic boom and a new generation with money to spend in a new way found their way to the restaurants, not only for feasts and family celebrations but also as a way to spend time, enjoy good food and wine, and relax, even in the middle of the week. Despite the recession in the 1990s, eating together as a form of social act had come to stay. A pizza or a meal at the gas station is an inexpensive option. There are alternatives for everyone. Ethnic restaurants have a quite young tradition, due to the fact that immigration was very limited until the late 20th century. The first pizzeria opened in the 1960s, but they became common in the 1980s. Indian, Chinese, Turkish, and other restaurants became more common about the same time. The first hamburger restaurant, Carrols, was established in Helsinki in the late 1970s, and McDonald's came about 10 years later.

Today, Helsinki and the larger towns elsewhere in Finland are like any other town in the Western world, and it can be hard to find something special and local when it comes to eating out. Chefs are influenced by international cuisine and follow the same trends worldwide. One new trend is to promote the use of local products for both ethical and ecological reasons. Despite that, in Finland, exotic dishes are commonly served at restaurants such as tuna fish, pilgrim scallop, or even ostrich meat. One specialty of Finland before the "new" ethnic restaurants was a proliferation of Russian restaurants. They were, and perhaps still are to a certain degree, for tourists, when the Iron Curtain made Russia quite exotic but difficult to visit. Finland, as a neighbor, could offer good Russian cuisine and thereby something of the exotic atmosphere as well, at least inside restaurants. Cabbage, mushrooms, pickled cucumber, and of course vodka are ingredients in both countries. There are still a few popular Russian restaurants with a good reputation in Helsinki.

Special Occasions

Christmas and Easter are the most food-centered festivities in Finland, like in so many other Western countries. There are, however, occasions during the year with culinary traditions and delicacies such as special dishes, pastries, early vegetables, crayfish, and so forth. January and February are a time for blini, a small pancake with Russian origins made of buckwheat and eaten with caviar, *smetana* (sour cream), and chopped onion. These months are also a time for fishing burbot from underneath the ice

on the lakes. Burbot is eaten in soup or with white sauce.

A special tart, called Runeberg tart after Johan Ludvig Runeberg, who is the national poet of Finland, is sold some weeks before February 5, his birthday. It is a small cake made of breadcrumbs with a dab of raspberry jam inside a ring of frosting on the top and moistened with arrack liquor.

On Shrove Sunday and Shrove Tuesday, it is time for another pastry, a cream bun with almond paste, lately also sold with jam, and eaten plain or with warm milk from a plate. Pea soup is the natural main dish these days. On Annunciation Day there is an old tradition of eating waffles, not perhaps common in every family but still known in some regions.

The Easter traditions reflect influences from both West and East. Perhaps the only thing really unique to Finland is *mämmi,* a malt-flavored oven-baked pudding, black in color and eaten with cream and sugar. Mämmi originates from the western parts of Finland, while *pasha* (molded sweetened curds with raisins and almonds) originates from Russia and the eastern parts of Finland. Today, these two delicacies are eaten in both western and eastern parts and are sold in markets all over the country. Pasha and a bun called *kulitj* belong to the Orthodox tradition, the Orthodox Church being the second state church in Finland beside the majority Lutheran church. Traditionally, hens started to lay eggs again at Easter time after a long, dark winter, and eggs still play a central role in Easter meals. Other typical things to eat on Easter are lamb, smoked ham, and fish, especially on Good Friday. For children, but also very popular among adults, are Mignon eggs, real eggshells filled with chocolate.

The first of May is celebrated with mead and a kind of fried pastry called *tippaleipä*, similar to funnel cakes. It is also time to welcome springtime and come together, eat a buffet meal, and drink a lot. Summer is the high season for all kinds of fresh vegetables, new potatoes, pickled herring, foods grilled outdoors, smoked fish, strawberries, rhubarb, and later on mushrooms, apples, and things to pick from the forests or home gardens. Midsummer in late June is the biggest summer festival, celebrated with a lot of food and drinks, and nearly everybody escapes the cities for a weekend in the countryside. In summertime Finns enjoy eating outdoors if possible; they improvise and eat lighter fare and just enjoy the time of nearly endless daylight. The long daylight hours give vegetables, berries, and fruits grown in the north an especially good flavor. A popular vegetarian dish is "summer soup," consisting of potatoes, carrots, cauliflower, peas, and spinach. These are cooked in milk, thickened with flour and egg yolk, and topped with a pat of butter and parsley and sprinkled with salt.

Crayfish season starts on July 21. Once many lakes and creeks hosted a lot of crayfish, but a disease, easily spread by fishing tackle from lake to lake, has made the original crayfish rarer. Another more resistant species has been brought into lakes, but still crayfish parties are a quite expensive feast to arrange considering that the size of the local crayfishes is small and the guests can be hungry. An alternative to domestic crayfish are much cheaper frozen ones, imported mostly from Spain or China. One can also eat crayfish as a starter and then move on to a mushroom tart and berries for dessert. The magical feeling at a crayfish party comes, however, not only from the eating but also from a lot of lights and decorations in the darkening evening; a lot of vodka, beer, or white wine; songs; and happy friends being together. Dill and toasted bread are also essential ingredients for a crayfish party.

Autumn is hunting season. Wild duck and moose are most common to hunt, and lately the deer population has increased. Mushrooms and berries are free to collect for everyone everywhere under a special law. In the cities along the coast special fish markets are held, where fishermen sell pickled and salted herring, a special dark and sweet bread, and even some handicrafts. The fish market is a popular event with over 100 years of history, a time when fishermen and town dwellers meet.

The greatest focus on food is, however, concentrated in December and Christmastime. Gingerbread and mulled wine, served with raisins and almonds, are served both in homes and at restaurants. Friends, business associates, colleagues, and society and club members meet for pre-Christmas lunch or dinner, either at restaurants or for covered-dish suppers at club rooms. The time from Christmas Eve until Boxing Day is reserved for the family and close relatives. Because one is supposed to be surrounded by dear ones, Christmas socially can be quite a hard holiday for single people, of whom there are many in Finland. Typical ingredients on a Christmas table, often served as a buffet similar to the Swedish smorgasbord, are pickled herring, freshly salted or cold smoked salmon, roe with smetana (sour cream), pâtés, and *rosolli,* which is a salad of boiled beets, potatoes, carrots, onions, apples, and pickled cucumber. Then follows Christmas ham, potato casserole, carrot casserole, rutabaga casserole, meatballs, and for some also boiled ling *lipeäkala* (lutefisk), with white sauce, and so forth. The lutefisk can, however, be left for another day if it seems like too many dishes at the same time. Some people can't stand the odor of the lye used to preserve the fish; others love it. In the archipelago the old tradition is to eat pike instead of Christmas ham. Every family has its own specialties with small but ever so important differences, and it is said to be quite difficult to agree on what should be on the Christmas table when a young couple moves in together and both want to take their old family traditions from childhood into the new household.

Rice porridge can be served for lunch at Christmastime but also as a dessert together with cinnamon, sugar, and cold milk or with a sweet fruit soup made of dried apples, prunes, and pears. Puff pastries formed as a star with prune jam in the middle are called *joulutorttu* and are served at every occasion where mulled wine, coffee, or tea is drunk in December. Chocolate, marmalade, raisins, nuts, dates, figs, and cranberries rolled in egg white and icing sugar are all sweets that are associated with Christmas as well.

When New Year finally comes, everyone is tired of Christmas food, and it is time for something fancy and delicious, perhaps a starter of shrimp and lobster salad, a spinach-filled hen with rosemary potatoes as a main course, and a lime cheesecake for dessert. The New Year starts fresh, with promises of a healthier life in the coming year.

Joulutorttu, puff pastries formed as a star with prune jam in the middle and often served at Christmastime. (Shutterstock)

Diet and Health

Diet and health are important issues in Finnish society and are often mentioned when talking about food. In the 1960s mortality due to heart disease was very high among men, and a major health-promoting project to prevent cardiovascular disease in North Karelia started in the 1970s. It was a big success. Butter, whole milk, and fatty dishes were abandoned in favor of lighter oil-based products, vegetables, and fibers. Still, as in so many Western countries, being overweight is a big problem that causes many health problems such as diabetes. The Development Program for the Prevention and Treatment of Diabetes (DEHKO, 2000–2010) is a national program, the first worldwide to include and implement the prevention of type 2 diabetes. Life has become easier in a way; food is everywhere, and most people don't burn all the calories they take in. Physical work is replaced by sitting still all day long

in an office, and people need a lot of information to be able to take care of their health.

Finland is a pioneer developer of health-enhancing foodstuffs. Nutrition research is internationally recognized at a high level, and also many remarkable inventions in functional food development have been made. Probiotics, prebiotics, plant flavonoids, plant sterols, dietary fiber, and more are important ingredients in functional food, seen as a new possibility to promote well-being by using "tailored" foods. Benecol, Xylitol, and Lactobacillius GG are officially approved examples of Finnish food innovations.

Finnish researchers have also pointed out several products that are naturally health enhancing such as rye bread, berries, rapeseed oil, oat products, and buckwheat products. Finnish meat, grain, vegetables, and berries are considered to be very clean. Pollution is limited, and not many insecticides are used compared with many other southern countries because of cold winters and strict regulations. There are also about 4,500 organic farms in Finland, representing 6 percent of all farms. The organic food production has a reliable reputation since the authorities enforce strict regulations throughout the whole organic food chain.

There is an increasing demand for special diet food as well. Many clients in restaurants, patients in hospitals, and students in school need a special diet because of their diseases. High cholesterol, diabetes, celiac disease, and many food allergies have united developers in the food industry and medical scientists to find solutions for dietary needs in society. In fact, Finland has one of the oldest dietary industries in the world.

The reason public authorities focus on nutrition and eating habits is for the prevention and treatment of diseases. The National Nutrition Council in Finland makes statements and recommendations, but Finns wonder about the relationship between food and pleasure and health. In the south of Europe, food and eating are considered to be pleasurable. The Nordic tradition is more spartan; food has for a long time been merely a nutrient, something one needed to survive but not for pleasure. If one is really enjoying a meal, there must be some reason to feel guilty. Something being both healthy and good tasting seems impossible.

Yrsa Lindqvist

Further Reading

Bourret, Joan Liffring-Zug, Jerry Kangas, and Dorothy Crum, eds. *Finnish Touches: Recipes and Traditions.* Iowa City, IA: Pennfield Press, 2002.

"Finland." Global Gourmet. http://www.global gourmet.com/destinations/finland/.

Food from Finland. http://www.foodfromfinland. com/.

Hill, Anja. *The Food and Cooking of Finland.* London: Anness, 2007.

Previdi, Tammi. *The Best of Finnish Cooking.* New York: Hippocrene Books, 1996.

Zug, John, Sue Roemig, and Beatrice A. Ojakangas. *Fantastically Finnish: Recipes and Traditions.* Iowa City, IA: Pennfield Press, 1998.

France

Overview

Located in western Europe, metropolitan France occupies an area smaller than the size of Texas and has a population of only 62 million. Yet the country has long enjoyed an outsized reputation for its cuisine. Historical, geographic, political, and social factors account for the rich gastronomic and culinary culture, a key element in the French way of life.

The fertility but also the diversity of the geography and climate permit a broad scope in agricultural production. Coasts along the cool North Sea, English Channel, and Atlantic Ocean, and also along the warmer, saltier Mediterranean Sea, yield fish, shellfish, and aquatic plants. Landscapes range from alpine mountains to continental plains, with a full third of the land area considered arable. Climates include the temperate oceanic west but also the drier Mediterranean south.

The agricultural tradition in France is ancient and has been continuous up to the present day. The cultivation of wheat, grapes, and olives for bread, wine, and olive oil—the basis of the ideal diet of classical antiquity, the forerunner of today's Mediterranean diet—is traceable to Greek settlements of around 600 B.C. at Massilia (Marseille) and Agde. Over the centuries, successive migrations to the territory broadened the agricultural traditions and diet. Contemporary to the Greeks, Celts migrated from the area of Hallstatt, Austria, bringing their agriculture and animal husbandry as well as hunting. Celts raised animals for milk, cheese, butter, and lard as well as meat. They preserved fish and meat, especially pork, by drying, smoking, and salting. Today, the taste for charcuterie (cured meat products, es-

pecially from pork) remains pronounced. By the Roman era, the lands inhabited by Celtic peoples were famous for their agricultural potential.

The victory of the Roman army over Gallic forces in 52 B.C. resulted in the division of the fertile Celtic territories into Gallo-Roman provinces. The Roman administration opened up the provinces to trade routes extending as far as India and China. Thus, elite diners in what would later become France had early access to exotic spices, such as black pepper, and to foreign foods, which were soon adapted to local cultivation, such as Persian peaches and Numidian guinea fowl. Wealthy Gallo-Romans followed the Roman custom (drawn from Greek precedent) of eating meals in two to seven distinct courses, a practice that would prove lasting. Sophisticated and wealthy eaters tracked local specialties such as coastal shellfish and yearly variations in wine production, their discernment prefiguring that of today's knowledgeable *fines gueules* (gastronomes or food connoisseurs). Barbarian (from the Greco-Roman perspective) Frankish or Germanic tribes that migrated into the Gallic provinces further cultivated the taste for meat, ale (beer without hops), apples, hard cider, spelt, rye, butter, and poultry.

As the Roman Empire declined in the early centuries of the Common Era, Christianity penetrated into Gaul from the south, where the pagan Germanic traditions held less sway. With Christianity came a revitalized emphasis on bread and wine, now symbols of sacrifice and redemption in the communion ritual, and a new asceticism. The ninth-century Carolingian emperor Charlemagne embodied the full, if sometimes uneasy, merging of the primary cultures—Gallo-Roman, Frankish, and Christian—in early-medieval France. Charlemagne encouraged agriculture with the aim of renewing the achievements of imperial Rome within the Christian empire. His biography shows the effort to negotiate customs from Frankish warrior feasts, which featured meat and alcohol in quantity, along with classical moderation but also Christian asceticism.

In the 15th and 16th centuries, European voyages resulted in the import of New World foods that would become staples in French cooking, such as potatoes, tomatoes, and turkey. The French drive toward overseas territorial and economic conquest began in the 17th century. At this time, Mexican chocolate, African coffee, Chinese tea, and sugar cultivated in Atlantic colonial outposts became fashionable, initially among elites. France's greatest colonial expansion occurred during the 19th through the mid-20th centuries. Rapid contraction followed, and France ceded territories in North Africa and Asia; however, the old politics of imperialism informs the postcolonial era. Beyond metropolitan or European France, the tentacular reach of today's French Republic includes the overseas departments Guadeloupe, Martinique, Réunion, and French Guiana. The population of metropolitan France includes about 9 percent immigrants, of whom about 40 percent trace their origins to the former colonies of the Maghreb.

Contemporary French culture and cuisine have continued to assimilate exotic elements, while attitudes remain ambivalent. Contact with extra-European territories has made such dishes as *accras,* or Caribbean fried codfish balls, into familiar appetizers. Couscous, or semolina-flour pasta that is steamed and served with a choice of meats, fish, seafood, pulses, greens, and vegetables, is eaten in the former colonies of Tunisia, Morocco, and Algeria. So familiar and so popular is couscous across France that it has become a *plat national,* a national dish. Yet exotic foods can also stigmatize. Consider the characters of North African origin in the film *La graine et le mulet* (*The Secret of the Grain,* 2007, directed by Abdellatif Kechiche). They identify themselves as French, yet their food marks them as foreign—and as outsiders and interlopers—to

the characters of European origin. Ironically, such staples as tender young haricots verts (French green or string beans) depend on economic ties inherited from the colonial past; today, most French beans are in fact grown in northern and western Africa and imported into the Hexagon (a nickname for France). Tension between the politics of assimilation and the experience of difference is a constant in France today. Nowhere is this clearer than at the table.

A distinguishing feature of food culture in France is the grand cuisine that has been elaborated over centuries. In the 17th century, cooks working for distinguished patrons emphasized tastes and techniques that differed noticeably from court cooking elsewhere in Europe and from older practices. Their recipes show the emerging preference for plants, such as onions, garlic, and herbs, rather than spices, for flavoring, a feature that remains typical. Court cooks developed sauces and broths that combined in a modular fashion to produce a range of dishes. In the 18th century, the court ceded its role as the center for cultural production, and cooks employed in the great bourgeois houses took up the tradition of grand cuisine. In the 20th century, Auguste Escoffier installed fine cooking as a feature of commercial luxury hotels. Professional chefs still consult Escoffier's cookbook as the reference for standard techniques and recipes. His repertoire, with its lineage to that of the court cooks, underpins the *cuisine gastronomique,* or elaborate fine restaurant cooking, that is now the most prestigious, highly worked expression of French food culture. Following the Revolution of 1789, shifts in the social structure and the acceleration of consumerism birthed a newly powerful figure: the food critic. The mutual dependence between producer and consumer, chef and informed diner, fostered by Grimod de la Reynière, avatar of contemporary food critics, continues to characterize gastronomic culture. The American animated film *Ratatouille* (2007, directed by Brad Bird with Jan Pinkava), set in Paris, amusingly parodies but also quite accurately depicts the prestige and pratfalls of grand cooking and its critics in France.

Essential, yet often overlooked, factors in shaping the contemporary French diet and food culture are the transition to industrial agriculture, combined with the completion of urbanization and modernization, in the mid-20th century. In the 18th century, four-fifths of the population of France lived in villages and rural areas. As recently as the late 19th century, two-thirds of the population still lived in or near the countryside. In rural areas, bread and vegetables from the kitchen garden—especially turnips, carrots, and cabbages—were the building blocks of daily meals. Animal protein was likely in the form of eggs, milk, or cheese, although meat consumption varied by region. Throughout the 19th century, meat consumption increased in cities, but prices fluctuated. During World War II, rationing and the export of meat and dairy products to the German Reich reduced the average caloric intake and drastically diminished life expectancies. In the mid-20th century, hunger and diseases that result from dietary deficiencies persisted, public health was at a low point, and the food supply was unstable.

Beginning in the late 1940s, postwar rebuilding heralded a shift in agricultural practices and the dietary paradigm. Under the Common Agricultural Policy of 1962, the European Union began subsidizing French grain, dairy, and beef farmers. The subventions, along with new industrial agricultural practices, resulted in overproduction and a reliable, inexpensive supply of beef, dairy products, and grains. Now, about 77 percent of the population lives in urban and ex-urban settings, while the country's gross domestic product ranks in the top 10 among nations worldwide; France is now an affluent, urban, modern consumer society. It is also the foremost agricultural producer in Europe and a net exporter, although less than 4 percent of the population works in the agricultural sector. Meat competes with bread for the central place in the diet and as the dominant alimentary symbol. Although France is a pillar of the European Union, it has maintained a strongly protectionist stance regarding agricultural production. Against the liberal European approach to free trade and privatization, France has notoriously refused to relinquish European farm subsidies in place since the 1960s. In 2009 it continued to defend its farmers and fishermen, who received French subventions during the 1990s and the early years of the 21st century.

Regional specialization in cuisine is both a fact and a nostalgic idea in contemporary France. Travelers have long remarked on regional variations in French cuisine, while in the 19th and 20th centuries, regionalist movements and then the tourism industry set out self-consciously to cultivate these differences. Lyonnais *quenelles* (poached fish dumplings), heavy Jura wines, *boeuf à la Bourguignon* (beef stew from Burgundy), or an Auvergnat or Aveyronnais *aligot* of potatoes whipped with cheese to a smooth elastic texture can certainly be found in their places of origin. But a Parisian restaurant and the table of a creative home cook anywhere in France are nearly as likely venues. France is the premier tourist destination in the world, receiving approximately 75 million visitors annually. The gastroculinary arts—in their local variations but also their national and international forms—play a major role in the tourism industries, while the appreciation for good food is a distinguishing feature of the culture.

Food Culture Snapshot

Solange and Denis live outside of Paris in a community of professional and working-class residents. Originally from Bordeaux, Denis attended university in Paris, then stayed to pursue his career. He is a computer programmer who works at a multinational firm outside the city. Solange, a native of Paris, is a lawyer who advises a branch of the police force in the capital. Their lifestyle and foodways exemplify those of the middle and upper-middle classes. When it comes to food, quality but also convenience are primary considerations.

On weekdays, Denis and Solange eat lunch with colleagues at their workplaces or nearby restaurants. After work and on weekends, they shop for the meals they eat at home: breakfast, dinner, and weekend lunches. On weekends, they drive to a supermarket to buy staples and items that will keep for several days in the refrigerator: ground coffee to brew and cartons of milk to heat up for the morning café au lait, butter and fruit jams to spread on bread at breakfast, sunflower oil for cooking, olive oil and vinegar for dressing salads, dried pasta, yogurt, eggs, and bottles of table wine. Thinking ahead to the busy weeknights that leave little time for cooking, Denis and Solange stop at Picard, the chain store specializing in frozen meal components. Here, they pick up raspberry ice to eat with fruit for dessert and puff pastry shells to fill with cheese or vegetables, such as mushrooms, for a tasty appetizer.

The couple most enjoys the shopping they do on foot on an as-needed basis. Upon returning from work at about 6:30 P.M., they have just enough time to walk to the shops in the town center. Denis and Solange buy fresh bread daily at the *boulangerie* located a few blocks from their townhouse. A baguette, a long, crusty, white bread, accompanies dinner. For breakfast they may try a country loaf made with whole wheat flour, a *pain aux noix* enriched with walnuts, or, for a weekend treat, a buttery yeasted *pain brioché* or a *pain de mie* (white bread).

A stop at the cheese shop follows. They rely on their *affineur* (specialist in aging and storing cheeses) to tell them which cheeses are at their seasonal peak. The couple usually prepares a cheese plate to conclude dinner and the weekend lunches. At the cheesemonger's, they choose a flavorful goat cheese, a semisoft cheese with a white-mold rind made from cow milk, a hard cheese made of sheep milk, and a blue cheese.

At the grocer's shop, Denis and Solange find the quality better than at the supermarket. The fruits are unblemished and ripened to a fine bouquet. The vegetables are flavorful and selected with regard for the season. They purchase a head of lettuce for salad; onions and garlic to use in cooking; green peas, fava beans, and new potatoes to serve as vegetables; and cherries and apricots for dessert.

The last stop is a visit to either the butcher's or the *traiteur*, the caterer specializing in prepared foods. At the butcher's, the couple selects steaks to be panfried for a main course. On the butcher's recommendation, they have tried his rotisserie chicken, which they found to be excellent. When time is short, the caterer can provide further components for the evening meal. They relish his prepared seafood salads and pasta dishes. Both work as main courses, which the couple will supplement with vegetables, a salad, cheese, and bread.

Major Foodstuffs

France is the premier wine producer in the world, responsible for a fifth of global production. As recently as the late 1930s, wine consumption averaged 45 gallons per person yearly, or the better part of a pint each day. Today, the average stands at about just under 16 gallons yearly, or less than one glass per person per day. Wine has long been practically synonymous with France, as a staple beverage and a symbol, along with bread, associated with the Catholic communion. For the French, wine sets off food, and vice versa; each brings out the taste and textures of the other to best advantage.

For centuries, bread was a staple of the diet, as well as a powerful religious symbol and symbol for life itself. White wheat bread has always been considered the most desirable. Recently, health concerns and the revival of artisanal bread making have created interest in whole wheat and in spelt, rye, and buckwheat. In the last 100 years, average bread consumption has declined from one to two pounds per person per day (historical estimates vary) to about three or four slices. Despite the radical decline in consumption, fresh bread appears on the table for almost every meal. Bread satisfies the French appetite—physical but also psychological—as nothing else can.

Despite the historical, symbolic, and psychological importance of bread, meat is now the centerpiece for most main meals and the cornerstone of the contemporary diet. France is the foremost producer of meat in the European Union, yet the country must import additional meat to meet demand for choice cuts such as chops, steaks, and roasts. On average, each person eats about 220 pounds yearly, slightly behind America and Australia as the biggest consumers of meat in the world. The French eat beef, lamb, goat, horse, pork, and game such as venison. Offal such as veal liver and veal, pork, and lamb kidneys is appreciated. France exports more chicken than any other country in the world. Other popular fowl are turkey and goose for holidays but also guinea fowl, capon, duck, and quail. Rabbit and hare are sold alongside fowl.

Fish and shellfish are popular, particularly in the coastal regions, where specialties vary by location. Markets across the country sell standbys such as cod, monkfish, salmon, sole, skate or ray, trout, mullet, and hake. The tradition of eating snails is

A sprawling vineyard in Alsace, France. France is the premier wine producer in the world, responsible for a fifth of global production. (Shutterstock)

ancient, while eponymous frogs enjoyed a surge in popularity during the 18th and 19th centuries. Neither snails nor frogs can be considered a staple of the modern diet, however.

In the past, *légumes à gousses,* or pulses, were staple foods. Peas and beans provided protein when eaten in combination with grains, contributing to a healthful diet with little or no meat. Today, pulses along with legumes are considered vegetables. Vegetables appear in the entrée course, as side dishes to a meat-based main course, and in salads. Orchard fruits and berries, both European and exotic ones such as bananas, mangoes, and kiwis, are eaten out of hand and as desserts. Fruits figure prominently in pastry making.

Cheese, like wine, immediately evokes France. Dairy products have long been cheaper than meat, while providing protein and, in the case of cheese,

preserving milk over time. Today, the taste for cheese, milk, and cream is general. Cheese and cream are used in cooking and baking. Cheese appears as a distinct course in the typical meal.

Cooking

Cooking at home was long the province of women. The education of women, their entry into the professions, and contemporary notions of gender equality have brought men, as well, into the home kitchen as cooks and nurturers for families and households. Nonetheless, nostalgia centered around home cooking retains an association with mothers and grandmothers. *La cuisine grand-mère* (grandmother's cooking) describes dishes thought to be old-fashioned and soul-satisfying, familiar and comforting, such as the simple dessert *compote de pommes* (stewed apples) and homey meat stews. Traditional roles still continue in cooking outside the home. Despite the entry of women into the workforce and the prominence of a few female chefs, men dominate professional cooking.

In home kitchens, quick dishes have largely replaced the economical, slow-simmered soups or stews of past centuries. Modern cooking technology, affluence, and time pressures factor into this trend. Searing or sautéing, baking for items that do not require long exposure to heat, steaming for vegetables, and pressure cooking are preferred methods.

Supermarkets sell items suited to the fast cooking methods, such as fish in fillets, meat in fillets and chops, and produce that can be eaten raw in salads. Ready-made, prepared, and semiprepared elements further facilitate the task of cooking and serving meals at home. Bread is almost never made at home, although it is a part of nearly every meal. Other staples purchased ready-made include jams, yogurt, cheese, charcuterie, and mustard, used in vinaigrettes and as a condiment for meat. Home cooks take advantage of fresh preparations from specialty shops, such as a butcher's mixture of fresh, loose, raw sausage meat or ground pork seasoned with spices and herbs. At home, one simply spoons the flavored meat into hollowed-out tomatoes or zucchini, then gives the stuffed vegetables a turn on the stove in an inch of liquid or pops them into the oven. Minimal fuss yields a fresh, home-cooked main dish.

As in the United States, the media extension of food and cooking in France is vast and influential. Food shows appear on television. Web sites catalog and celebrate food and cooking. Food and cooking periodicals have multiplied. Formerly, families owned one or two cookbooks used as references. In contrast, recent years have seen a marked increase in the sale of books on French cooking but also on the cuisines of Thailand or Japan and on foreign foods, such as British muffins, Moroccan tagines, and the Chinese stir-fry. The phenomenon indexes the social prestige of food connoisseurship in the affluent society.

Typical Meals

Three meals each day is typical in France. This pattern has been common across the population since the mid-20th century. Through the late 19th century, eating schedules varied widely to reflect the profession, region, and income of individuals; season and religion also played a role. Elites might eat twice daily and manual laborers up to four times each day; however, the pattern was inconsistent. Now, school and work schedules are arranged in broad synchrony. Most people eat meals at about the same time, resulting in a strong shared feeling of the day's rhythm.

The *petit déjeuner* (breakfast), eaten in the morning before school or work, is insubstantial. Adults drink café au lait, heated milk mixed with strong, hot, brewed coffee. A section of baguette spread with butter, jam, honey, or Nutella to make a *tartine* is eaten along with the coffee. For a treat, pastry such as a croissant replaces bread. Children drink hot chocolate. Adults wishing to avoid caffeine stir powdered roasted chicory root into their morning hot milk.

A main meal, eaten at noon or in the evening at about 8 P.M., or both, has a typical structure: Dishes appear in a succession of separate courses. An entrée, or first course, might consist of a potage (soup), a plate of crudités (raw vegetables) served with an oil and vinegar dressing, or a cooked salad of warm lentils or carrots. This is followed by a *plat principal,* or main dish. The main dish usually contains animal protein: meat, poultry, fish, shellfish, or eggs. Home cooks prepare sautéed chops with a light sauce made from the pan juices, a chicken stewed in wine, or a grilled or baked fish. Eggs appear as an omelet flavored with chives or bits of *lard* (fat bacon). The main course may be accompanied by a cooked vegetable, potatoes, or beans. Afterward comes a green tossed salad, a cheese course (some substitute yogurt as a lighter alternative), and perhaps a fruit or sweet to finish. Bread is placed on the table throughout the meal, and people take a slice or break off a piece of the loaf as desired. For a main meal, portions are relatively small. The

Cooking the traditional French summer stew. (Shutterstock)

appetite is not overwhelmed by the succession of different edibles.

Because both men and women work outside the home, dinner is often the only weekday meal for which the whole family can gather together. In this case, to accommodate busy working schedules, the luncheon may well consist of a sandwich eaten on the run. For children, an effort is made to serve a full meal at noon, either at the school canteen or at home if it is feasible for the child to return over the lunch recess.

Ratatouille (Summer Vegetable Stew)

This is a typical entrée for cooking and eating at home.

7 tbsp olive oil

1 lb zucchini and/or yellow crookneck squash, sliced into rounds

2 green or red peppers, seeded, membranes removed, and sliced

1 eggplant (about 1 lb), cut into 1-in. cubes

1½ c chopped onion

2 tbsp chopped garlic

2 lb tomatoes, halved and seeded

6 sprigs thyme, leaves stripped from the stems

6 tbsp chopped parsley

8 tbsp chopped basil

Salt

Ground black pepper

Heat 2 tablespoons of the olive oil in a large skillet over moderate heat. Sauté the zucchini about 6 minutes until lightly browned. Using a slotted spoon, transfer to a large bowl.

Add 1 tablespoon of oil to the skillet, then sauté the sliced peppers for 5 minutes, and transfer to the bowl.

Add 3 tablespoons of oil to the skillet, then put in the eggplant. Stir to prevent the eggplant from sticking to the pan. Cook until the eggplant is soft, light-colored, and smooth in texture (about 8 or 9 minutes). Add to the bowl with the other vegetables.

Pour the last tablespoon of olive oil to the pan, and sauté the onion and garlic for about 3 minutes, watching carefully to prevent them from browning much. Add the tomatoes, thyme, and half the parsley. Simmer for 10 minutes. Return all the vegetables in the bowl back into the pan with the tomatoes, stir gently to mix, and cook for 10 more minutes. The vegetables should be cooked through and tender but not mushy.

Take the pan off the heat. Stir in the rest of the parsley and the basil. Season with salt and pepper. Serve hot, cold, or at room temperature.

Poulet Aux Poireaux (Chicken with Leeks and Tarragon)

This is a typical entrée for cooking and eating at home.

2 large leeks

Salt

Ground black pepper

6 individual chicken breasts on the bone

2 tbsp unsalted butter

2 tbsp olive oil

4 c chicken stock or white wine

1 tbsp chopped fresh tarragon

Cut away the bearded root and tough, dark green end of the leeks. Slit the leeks in half lengthwise and wash them under cold running water, removing any dirt trapped between the leaves. Slice the leeks thinly.

Salt and pepper the chicken breasts. Heat the butter and olive oil in a large skillet over moderate heat. Cook the chicken skin side down until brown (about 10 minutes), then turn and cook 5 minutes more. Transfer chicken to a plate.

In the same pan, sauté the leeks until soft. Add 3 cups of stock and the tarragon. Bring the liquid to a simmer and cook until stock reduces by about half.

Return the chicken to the pan, and add the remaining cup of stock. Bring to a simmer, then reduce the heat to medium low and cover the pan. Cook until the chicken is done, basting occasionally with the pan juices (about 15–20 minutes).

To serve, ladle the sauce and leeks over the chicken. Serve with rice or noodles.

Balance and harmony are sought when planning a meal. The French palate prefers rich, deep flavors over sharp or spicy ones. Edibles seek complements. A course or finished dish is more than the sum of its parts. For a summer entrée, crisp peppery radishes are balanced with creamy dairy butter spread on bread and finished with a sprinkle of salt. For a main dish, the clean acidity of tomato and the aroma of aniseed complement the marine flavors in a fish soup. Durable combinations of flavors and textures are sought. A hot main dish may be followed by a crisp, cool salad. The mixing of sweet and salty flavors within a single dish is unusual. Sweets appear at the end of a meal.

A sense of leisure and conviviality is prized as integral to meals. This is true across the population. The French value sociability and community. Eating is considered a convivial activity par excellence. The community aspect of meals strengthens social ties and expresses shared values. The family meal or meal with friends or colleagues is a central feature of daily life, despite circumstances that mitigate against it, such as fast-paced work schedules and larger numbers of people living alone.

In addition to the main meals, two smaller meals are served primarily to children. For the *collation du matin* (morning snack) at about 10:30 A.M. and the after-school or late-afternoon *goûter,* at about 4:00 P.M., children eat a tartine, a piece of fruit, or a yogurt, and in the afternoon perhaps a pastry. Adults may take a coffee or tea break and in the afternoon eat a light snack such as fruit or yogurt, although snacking between meals is otherwise frowned upon.

Eating Out

Eating at home is the norm, yet traditions of eating out go back centuries, and the practice is typical. In the Middle Ages, especially in urban areas, people purchased foods from street stands and boutiques. They ate out in taverns and inns and at *tables d'hôte,* which featured meals served at common tables, at fixed times, and with a single menu, giving diners hot food but no choice in the matter of what they ate. Establishments calling their products and then themselves *restaurants* emerged in France in the 1760s. Here, the diner ate at a private table but in a public venue, choosing foods and beverages from a menu, or list of what the kitchen offered, for a price.

With the spread of industrialization in the 19th century came inexpensive restaurants where workers could eat a full meal in two to four courses but without breaking the bank. The end of the century saw the development of the extensive *cantine* or cafeteria system in businesses and schools. Today, many French employees eat their daily noon meal in the *restaurant d'entreprise* (in-house work cafeteria). As a separate or a substitute benefit, they receive *tickets* (restaurant coupons) from their employer. Schoolchildren who cannot return home for the noon meal eat in the school canteen.

Today, the average person eats 120 meals outside the home each year, or one meal out approximately every three days, and spends just over a fifth of his or her total food budget on eating out. The French eat outside the home less frequently than residents of some nations with a comparable standard of living, such as the United Kingdom. Yet the trend from about 1970 has been to spend less on food to be prepared and consumed in the home. The modern trend to eat outside the home results from affluence but also from the fast pace of life and the incursion of work into mealtimes.

The prominent restaurant culture offers extensive choices for eating out. Bistros and brasseries, formerly associated with beer brewing, tend to offer an informal dining experience. Restaurants serving foreign cuisines reflect the presence of the dominant immigrant groups in France, such as Algerians, Moroccans, Vietnamese, and Chinese. In the cities, restaurants serve cuisines hailing from Tibet to Peru, attesting to the influence of the global economy, migration and immigration, and the interest in foreign cultures associated with travel. A renowned feature of the French restaurant scene is the high-end *restaurant gastronomique,* with its refined, complex cooking. An equally remarkable element of the French restaurant scene is the general availability of a reasonably high-quality meal. The system of apprenticeships for cooks under the early-modern trade guilds, and the development in the 19th century of organized cooking schools, contributed to the robust tradition of professional cooking and *restauration.* In turn, the French population maintains high expectations, looking for an advantageous ratio of *qualité* (quality) to *prix* (price) when eating out.

Eighteenth-century Paris saw the rapid rise not only of restaurants but also of urban cafés. Cafés provided a meeting place for people from all walks of society, as well as a space to read newspapers and debate the latest in politics and the theater. The café remains an institution in French life, as a welcoming spot to drink coffee or an aperitif, eat a light meal, socialize, and watch people and the world go by. Cafés are widespread, although statistics from 2009 indicate that they are seeing a slow decline in popularity and in viability as businesses.

The media have extensively covered protests against fast-food restaurants, symbols for the French of the American way of life that is publicly deplored and highly controversial. Yet both French and foreign fast-food chains have been successful within France and continue to grow.

Special Occasions

The care, interest, and enjoyment that the French bring to cooking and eating can add a certain reverence and revelry to nearly any meal. This is typical *savoir-vivre* (knowing how to live well) applied at the table on a daily basis. A holiday atmosphere prevails for the Sunday family lunch and at the dinner party given on a Friday or Saturday evening for close friends. These meals begin with a leisurely aperitif and feature the full sequence of courses. They center around a large dish such as a roast leg of lamb studded with garlic and perfumed with sprigs of rosemary, or a *pot-au-feu.* Pot-au-feu, or mixed boiled meats, yields a soup that appears as a first course. The succulent sliced meats are served as the main course, along with pickles, horseradish, and mustard as garnishes. Holidays and special occasions have their rituals marked with particular foods. The holiday calendar attests to France's history as a strongly Catholic country but also its contemporary identity, which is officially secular.

Varzy, Burgundy: Preparing the festive lunch sponsored by the village to celebrate the national holiday on July 14, 2008. Méchoui, spit-roasted lamb typical of the Algerian Berbers, is the centerpiece. The meal includes ham and melon for an entrée, the lamb along with fried potatoes and beans, apple cake, wine, and coffee. The mix of local and naturalized exotic elements is typical. (Photo courtesy of Julia Abramson.)

The federal government mandates 11 holidays. July 14, popularly called Bastille Day, is the national holiday. The day brings tremendous collective celebration, including municipal meals, parades, fireworks, and outdoor concerts and dancing. Since *le quatorze* falls during the heat of summer when people turn out of doors, menus often feature grilled *merguez* (North African lamb or beef sausages), steaks, lamb chops, pork cutlets, spit-roasted fowl, and even whole spit-roasted pigs and lamb.

Like the other Christian holidays, Christmas, celebrated on December 24, was formerly a day of abstinence or fasting in Catholic France. Like nearly all holy days, it is now marked with a feast rather than a fast. The old lean dishes are replaced by festive foods that suggest prosperity and sensual indulgence but are now within reach of many wallets. Oysters and foie gras often appear as appetizers, despite the controversial status of the latter; the ancient practice of gavage, or force-feeding geese to produce the unctuous, silky, fatted liver, is held by some to be inhumane, by others to be a defensible part of the *patrimoine,* or cultural heritage. For the main course there is roasted turkey stuffed with chestnuts. Wines accompany the meal, with champagne saved for the dessert. Many families eat a *bûche de Noël,* or rolled cake decorated to resemble a Yule log. Traditional dishes vary by region, such as the group of 13 Provençal desserts based on local winter fruits, dried or preserved summer fruits, and nuts.

Epiphany, or the *fête des Rois,* demands a *galette des Rois,* or 12th-night pastry, a puff pastry shaped into a crown that may be filled with a semisweet almond paste. The Chandeleur (Candlemas) on February 2 and Mardi Gras (Shrove Tuesday) preceding Lent are marked with egg-, butter-, and oil-rich treats such as stuffed crepes, butter cookies, and, for Fat Tuesday, beignets (doughnuts). Easter brings a new round of celebrations with spring foods such as roast lamb, *blanquette de veau* or *blanquette d'agneau* (white stew with veal or lamb), and, in the south and on Corsica, roasted kid goat. Eggs, symbolizing renewal, appear in rich breads and pastries and in omelets, hard-boiled in salads, and baked whole into savory dishes. November 11, the Saint-Martin, marking the traditional end of the harvest season, is celebrated with a thanksgiving meal of roast goose and new wine.

New Year's Eve, *la fête de Saint-Sylvestre,* is as often spent with friends as with family. An elegant festive meal concludes at midnight with popping corks from champagne bottles to bring in the New Year. The meal repeats many of the Christmas foods. It may feature a roast beef or ham instead of a large fowl.

People used to observe their saint's day or name day as a religious holiday. Given the trend toward secularism and the emphasis on the personal in modern life, families and circles of friends now celebrate personal days such as birthdays and wedding anniversaries. Milestone birthdays are often celebrated with a large party for family, friends, and colleagues. The birthday person plays host and offers a formal celebration dinner served in several courses.

Progress through the old religious cycle of sacraments, including baptism, communion, and marriage, brings festive luncheons or dinners crowned by a pièce montée, or showy dessert. A typical example is the *croquembouche,* an assemblage of puffpastry balls filled with cream or custard that are built up into a pyramid. At wedding feasts, like at feasts for Christmas and the New Year, foods are high-status items presented as elegantly as possible. Menus often include foie gras, lobster, roasted monkfish, and boned and stuffed fowl such as a guinea hen or capon. A dessert of layer cake or the pyramidal croquembouche includes champagne.

Since the 1990s a trend to revive traditional agricultural and regional celebrations has served to affirm local identity and maintain the sense of history. Most villages and small towns have a *fête votive, fête patronale, fête du pays,* or *kermesse* celebrating the town's patron saint. The festivals usually take place on a Sunday during the warm season (May through October). In the past, such celebrations marked the communal agricultural events of planting and harvest. Today, they are valued as community and civic events, and as a way of preserving and teaching about local customs from dress and dancing to gastronomy.

Diet and Health

Variety has characterized the French way of eating since the end of World War II. The diet is relatively high in fruits, vegetables, grains, and legumes, in addition to meats, cheeses, and other dairy products. The use of butter fats, animal fats such as lard and goose fat, and vegetable oils used to vary largely by region. At present, the broad preference for cooking with vegetable oils such as sunflower oil stems from their lower prices, on the one hand, and information about health benefits associated with unsaturated vegetable oils and the Mediterranean diet, on the other. Wine was long viewed as a healthful, strengthening beverage and in this sense was perceived as different from distilled alcohols. Despite this perception, rates of alcoholism and diseases such as cirrhosis of the liver were high through the mid-20th century. In this nation of wine drinkers, the *crise de foie* (liver crisis) was a classic complaint, extensible to nearly any malaise. The view that wine is healthful has not disappeared, but consumption has declined. Water is the most widely consumed beverage.

The French associate eating the full three-course meal with a sense of well-being and with good health. The structured family meal provides nutritional balance. It conditions daily eating while contributing to the highly valued quality of life. The benefits of eating the full three-course family meal are thought of in a holistic fashion. The American practice of counting calories and weighing portions would seem strange to most French. Rather, eating a broad selection of fresh foods is understood as key to *une bonne nutrition* or *une alimentation saine* (good nutrition, a healthful diet). And variety is precisely what characterizes the full meal with its complement of three or four different dishes.

Beyond nutrition, culinary quality and the appreciation of food are essential to the perception of eating well. Conviviality and social connection to family and friends are equally necessary ingredients. The respite imposed by the slow rhythm of the full meal cannot be discounted. People use the terms *équilibre* (balance), *modération* (moderation), and *plaisir* (enjoyment, pleasure) to name the salient

A long-time French delicacy, foie gras is the liver of a duck or goose that has been fattened through the process of force-feeding. Although popular, the process remains controversial. (Shutterstock)

features of eating well, and *harmonieuses* (harmonious) to describe the ensemble of practices that go into eating well. These ideas guide practical aspects of cooking and serving, such as determining the relatively small portion sizes for meal components.

In the past, most health care was given at home, including for severe illnesses. Home cooks and cookbooks had a repertoire of foods for the sick, such as "pectoral" broths to strengthen the lungs. Today, there remains little concept of specific foods appropriate for the ill. Adjustments are made to the diet, such as excluding greens and salads, in favor of plain boiled rice and cooked carrots, until a stomach ailment has passed, or reducing protein on a daily basis in the case of a chronic kidney problem. To improve digestion, people take mineral waters high in magnesium, salads, fresh fruits and vegetables, yogurt, or a drink of pastis (anise liquor).

The general health of the population is relatively good. To be sure, as in other affluent nations, abundance, the modern lifestyle, and agricultural and manufacturing practices create dietary dilemmas. For some, *grignotage* (snacking) replaces or augments the cycle of three daily meals. The sedentary lifestyle combined with an unbalanced diet contributes to rising levels of obesity and diabetes. Pathological behaviors related to eating and having psychological causes, such as anorexia and bulimia, are on the rise. Genetically modified foods and agribusiness practices are perceived as threats to health. Yet other indicators remain quite positive. The life span for women is more than 83 years, the longest in Europe. The national health system, which provides nearly universal access to high-quality medical care, emphasizes prevention. The state, which regulates health care, has stressed intervention, such as removing vending machines from public schools in 2005 to reduce young people's consumption of sugar, salt, and fat as empty calories in junk food. In France, the precautionary, preventive, and interventionist attitude plays a role in maintaining public health, while the shared strong emphasis on food culture enhances *la vie à la française*—the French way of life.

Julia Abramson

Further Reading

Abramson, Julia. *Food Culture in France.* Westport, CT: Greenwood Press, 2007.

Chef Simon. http://www.chefsimon.com/.

de la Pradelle, Michèle. *Market Day in Provence.* 1996. Translated by Amy Jacobs. Chicago: University of Chicago Press, 2006.

Fischler, Claude, and Estelle Masson. *Manger: Français, Européens et Américains face à l'alimentation.* Paris: Odile Jacob, 2008.

Garrier, Gilbert. *Histoire sociale et culturelle du vin.* 1995. Paris: Larousse-Bordas, 1998.

Institut National de la Statistique et des Études Économiques [National Institute of Statistics and Economic Studies]. http://www.insee.fr/.

Kaplan, Steven L. *Good Bread Is Back: A Contemporary History of French Bread, the Way It Is Made, and the People Who Make It.* 2002 Translated by Catherine Porter. Durham, NC: Duke University Press, 2006.

Marmiton. http://www.marmiton.org/.

Mathiot, Ginette. *Je sais cuisiner.* 1932. Paris: Albin Michel, 2003.

Mériot, Sylvie-Anne. *Nostalgic Cooks: Another French Paradox.* 2002. Translated by Trevor Cox and Chanelle Paul. Boston: Brill, 2006.

Régnier, Faustine. *L'Exotisme culinaire: Essai sur les saveurs de l'Autre.* Paris: Presses Universitaires de France, 2004.

Georgia

Overview

Geographically part of Asia yet professing Christianity, the tiny nation of Georgia has for centuries stood at the confluence of East and West. The capital city of Tbilisi (Tiflis) was situated on the major trade routes between the Caspian and Black seas and in the 19th century was celebrated as the Paris of the Caucasus for its elegance and sophisticated tastes. Thanks to the country's agricultural riches and long tradition of hospitality, Georgia has long been an object of desire for outsiders.

The Georgians date the beginnings of their culture to the sixth century B.C. The ancient Greeks established colonies along the Black Sea coast in a region they called Colchis. In 66 B.C., when the Roman general Pompey invaded and brought the area under Roman rule, Greek control came to an end, but the outposts in Colchis remained important links in the trade route to Persia. Tbilisi was founded in the fifth century A.D. According to legend, King Vakhtang Gorgaslani, on a hunt near the Kura River, killed a pheasant, which he retrieved fully cooked from the hot springs where it had fallen. Toasting his good fortune, Gorgaslani vowed to create a city on this auspicious site. He called it Tbilis-kalaki, or "Warm City" (hence the name Tbilisi; outside of Georgia, the city was known as Tiflis into the 20th century).

Following a mid-7th-century invasion, Tbilisi fell under Arab control, and between the 8th and 11th centuries the city was controlled successively by Arabs, Khazars, and Seljuks, even though the populace remained Christian. By the early Middle Ages Tbilisi had become a major stopover on the medieval trade routes, a midpoint between the Muslim East and the Christian West.

As an important stopover on the trade routes, Tbilisi both benefited and suffered from repeated waves of migration and invasion, each of which left its traces on Georgia's cuisine. By the late 16th century, the country was effectively split in two, with western Georgia falling under the Turkish sphere of influence and eastern Georgia politically part of northwestern Iran. Repeated attacks by the Persians, the Turks, and Muslim tribesmen in Dagestan finally caused the Georgians to turn for help to Russia, their mighty Christian neighbor to the north; in 1801 Russia incorporated Georgia into its empire. The Russian presence in Georgia lasted until 1918 when, following the October Revolution, Georgia declared its independence. But in 1921 Bolshevik troops invaded, and once again Georgia was incorporated into the empire of its more powerful northern neighbor, this time the Soviet Union.

Until the dissolution of the Soviet Union in 1991, Georgia existed as a constituent republic of that country, with its economy dependent on the Soviet system. Georgia's citrus fruits, fresh vegetables, herbs, tea, and wines found a ready market in Russia and the other Soviet republics, and the Georgian economy flourished. When the Soviet system collapsed, the country suddenly experienced severe economic distress, which was exacerbated by political conflicts in the breakaway regions of Abkhazia and South Ossetia. These conflicts have led to continued unrest. In 2005 Russia embargoed Georgian agricultural products, including citrus fruits and the Borzhomi mineral water

Weighing section at a tea factory in Chakva, Georgia. Under Soviet leadership, Georgian farmland was collectivized. The region specialized in growing such export crops as tea, citrus fruits, and grapes, making farmers dependent on importing such necessities as meat and grains. (Library of Congress)

that provided an important source of export revenue; in 2006 Russia extended the embargo to Georgian wines, claiming that they had been adulterated. This move was, in fact, political retaliation for Georgia's desire to ally itself with the West by seeking membership in the North Atlantic Treaty Organization and the European Union; the Russians were further displeased by the Baku-Tbilisi-Ceyhan oil project and the Baku-Tbilisi-Erzerum natural gas pipeline, both of which bypass Russian territory. Nevertheless, Russia's attempts to control Georgia must be seen in historical perspective, as the Russians are only the latest in a series of outsiders to covet this rich land.

 Food Culture Snapshot

Georgian society is rapidly changing, but until the 21st century most families followed traditional patterns of eating. Even urban dwellers had country cousins or a small plot of land outside the city to supply them with fresh produce and meat, by necessity organically grown, as there was no money for chemical fertilizers. Because there were no mega-supermarkets, people

frequented local specialty purveyors or the central farmers' market in their town for items they could not produce themselves. Typical of this largely self-sufficient way of life is the Lataria family, Guram and Gulisa, who, until being forced to relocate due to the war with Abkhazia, lived in the town of Khobi, near the Abkhazian border. Today, the Latarias live in Tbilisi, where they run a beautiful guesthouse. In Khobi their table was always amply spread with vegetables harvested from their backyard garden; in Tbilisi they shop at the city's produce markets, where they have developed close relationships with purveyors who set aside their best produce, meats, and cheeses for them.

Their daily breakfast is leisurely, featuring shimmering yogurt made from water buffalo milk, aromatic orchard fruits (plums and apricots in summer, apples in the fall), and crusty bread baked in a *toné*, a tandoor-like clay oven. Lunch typically consists of a soup or stew—perhaps a tart summer lamb soup with eggplant, green beans, and handfuls of fresh herbs, or spicy *kharcho* (meaty soup) seasoned with the classic Georgian spice mixture, *khmeli-suneli*. Dinner is the grand meal of the day, especially when guests are present. The table is laid with an array of local specialties like cabbage, carrot, and eggplant slices stuffed with walnuts, spices, and pomegranate seeds; *adzhapsandali,* a ratatouille-like mélange of eggplant, peppers, potatoes, and tomatoes; *khachapuri,* the famous Georgian cheese bread; chicken *satsivi,* which is roasted, then topped with a sauce of ground walnuts; boiled kid; and *gomi,* a cornmeal pudding. Bread again accompanies this meal. Although supermarkets now offer packaged bread, most Georgians still prefer the traditional *shoti* and *lavash* baked in a toné. In Khobi, Guram and Gulisa had a toné in their backyard; in Tbilisi they buy bread from a traditional bakery or at the farmers' market.

Adzhapsandali

Adzhapsandali is a spicy Georgian vegetable medley, like ratatouille with a bite.

Serves 6

1 small eggplant (1 lb)
1 large boiling potato
1 medium onion, chopped

2 tbsp vegetable oil

1½ lb ripe tomatoes

1 medium green pepper, seeded and chopped

3–4 garlic cloves, minced

3 tbsp minced dill

3 tbsp minced cilantro

3 tbsp minced parsley

3 tbsp minced basil

¾ tsp salt

¼ tsp paprika

¼ tsp cayenne (or less, to taste)

Freshly ground black pepper to taste

Pierce the eggplant, and bake in a preheated 375°F oven for 35 to 40 minutes, until soft. Allow to cool.

Meanwhile, boil the potato in salted water until just tender. Cool, then peel and cube.

Sauté the onion in the oil until soft.

Drop the tomatoes into boiling water and cook them until soft, about 10 minutes. Drain, then force through a sieve to make a puree. Add the tomato puree to the onion, along with the chopped green pepper and the minced garlic. Simmer uncovered for 10 minutes, until slightly thickened.

Peel the eggplant and cut it into cubes. Add the cubes to the tomato mixture along with the cubed potato. Stir in the remaining ingredients and heat gently for 5 minutes more. Cool to room temperature before serving.

Major Foodstuffs

Remarkably, through all the invasions, sieges, and subjugations, Georgia has maintained a strong national identity and a distinctive national cuisine, even though the presence of so many outside rulers and visitors inevitably introduced foreign ways. Georgian food is reminiscent of both Mediterranean and Middle Eastern tastes, the result of a rich interplay of culinary ideas carried along the trade routes by merchants and travelers alike. Some borrowed practices are easily recognizable. The pilafs of southeastern Georgia echo those of neighboring Iran, and the meats simmered with fruit are similar to variations of Persian *khoresh* (stew), though to yield the tart taste they prefer, the Georgians more often stew meat with sour plums or pomegranates than with sweeter fruits like quinces or prunes. Many savory dishes are flavored with khmeli-suneli, Georgia's aromatic mixture of ground coriander, basil, dill, summer savory, parsley, mint, fenugreek, bay leaf, and marigold. Like the turmeric used in curry blends, the dried marigold petals—known as Imeretian saffron for the region where the flowers are grown—add a rich yellow cast to many foods; their use may reflect a culinary legacy from the Moguls. The prized Georgian *khinkali*—the overstuffed boiled dumplings of the mountainous zones—reveal the culinary influence of Central Asian Turks. Along the Black Sea coast in western Georgia, the stuffed vegetable *tolmas* resemble Turkey's various dolmas. But the Georgians never developed a taste for the elaborate oriental sweets from Turkish, Persian, or Armenian kitchens; instead, they limit dessert mainly to fresh fruits and nut preparations.

Not yet fully documented is the kinship of Georgian food with that of northern India. The ruling Moguls of northern India invaded Georgia in the 13th century. The correspondences in culinary terminology between contemporary Georgian and Hindi are especially notable in a language like Georgian, which is not even Indo-European but South Caucasian, an entirely separate linguistic group. The Georgian word for bread, like the Hindi word, is *puri;* and the Georgians use the toné for baking bread and roasting, much as Indians of the Punjab use the tandoor. The Georgian *tapha,* a special pan for making the succulent, flattened chicken *tabaka* that is so emblematic of Georgian cuisine, is related to the cast iron skillet, or *tava,* of northern India.

But differences often reveal more than similarities. What most distinguishes Georgian cuisine from that of its neighbors is the use of walnuts, not merely as garnish, but as an integral component in a wide variety of dishes. To offset what might otherwise be a cloying richness from the nuts, many recipes call for a souring agent. Yogurt (*matsoni*), pungent cheese, and immature wine (*machari*) often serve as counterpoints to ground walnuts; vinegar or fruit juices and fruit leathers similarly lend balance. Marigold lends an earthy depth to Georgian dishes and sets them apart from those of other culinary cultures. For instance, cinnamon and vinegar regularly flavor meat in the Georgian diet, just as they do in Middle Eastern cuisines, but marigold rather than true saffron adds the distinctive touch.

Other differences are visible in the staple foods. Where Persian cooks turn to rice and Armenians use bulgur, Georgians rely on wheat and corn. And instead of the legumes typically found in the Middle East and the Mediterranean—lentils, chickpeas, and favas—Georgians favor kidney beans, like corn a New World crop. Walnuts predominate over pine nuts and almonds. So well loved are walnuts that many standard dishes prepared without nuts, such as the spicy beef soup kharcho or the chicken stew *chakhokhbili,* often include walnuts in their western Georgian renditions. Freshly pressed walnut oil provides a necessary supplement of fat, as do the rich *suluguni* and *imeruli* cows' milk, served in place of butter with cornbread in western Georgia.

Stretching as it does from the Black Sea nearly all the way to the Caspian, the Republic of Georgia has numerous climatic zones, from the mountainous to the subtropical. Western Georgia, bordering on the Black Sea, endures high precipitation and steamy temperatures. Here, tea and citrus fruits thrive. Eastward the climate grows progressively drier, until sere Central Asian winds buffet the plateaus to the east of the Likhi chain. This hot, dry atmosphere produces the lush stone fruits and grapes of the Kartli and Kakheti provinces. The boundary between east and west is also visible in the relative degree of spiciness in the food. Eastern Georgians prefer a cool, fresh taste, thanks in part to their hot, arid summers, while western Georgians add generous amounts of fresh and dried hot pepper to their food, consuming nearly twice as much as eastern Georgians. A second difference lies in the western Georgian preference for corn over wheat. Here, *mchadi,* or corncakes, are prepared instead of puri. In the mountainous regions, when wheat flour is scarce, the roots of wild plants are first dried and then ground for use as bread additives, creating a rather coarse, though tasty loaf.

As is evident from their reliance on such ingredients as corn, peppers, and beans, western Georgian cooks put crops originating in the Americas to good use. Another transplant from the Americas, the tomato, is highly appreciated by eastern and western Georgians alike. Kartli, the eastern province in which Tbilisi is located, is known for its orchard fruits, especially apples and peaches, the best of which come from the environs of Gori, where dictator Joseph Stalin was born. The local markets abound with seasonal golden lady apples, pink gooseberries, red and black currants, many varieties of plums (sweet and sour; purple, yellow, green, and red), apricots, pears, berries, sweet cherries, and sour *shindi* or cornelian cherries, the juice of which Georgian warriors once drank before battle to fortify their blood. Mounds of dried fruits and locally grown walnuts, almonds, and hazelnuts are available year-round.

Cooking

Georgian dishes evolved naturally from the produce available, and traditional methods of preparation have hardly changed over the years; high tech does not yet have a solid place in the Georgian kitchen. To an extraordinary degree, Georgians still integrate the outdoors into their lives when they cook and eat. Grilling remains a preferred way to cook meats in Georgia—recalling the Promethean legend: Prometheus is said to have given fire to mankind when he was chained to a rock on Mount Elbrus in the Caucasus. Georgians frequently cook not only meats and vegetables but also breads and stews over an open flame.

A second standard method of preparing food is by slow cooking, and Georgian cuisine has an extensive repertoire of soups and stews. The heat remaining in the toné after bread baking is used for dishes like *purnis mtsvadi,* lamb braised slowly in a clay pot. In western Georgia, *chkmeruli* (fried chicken) and corncakes are baked in special red clay dishes called *ketsi,* which range in diameter from 6 to 12 inches. The use of ketsi is another way in which the Georgians continue to practice time-honored cooking methods. This technique can be traced back to the ancient Egyptians, who stacked earthenware pots filled with food atop one another to seal in moisture—creating an oven, in effect—before baking the food over an open fire. Today, in urban apartments, the foods traditionally prepared in ketsis can successfully be made indoors on the cooktop.

Perhaps the single most important implement in the Georgian kitchen is a mortar and pestle for grinding nuts and spices. Although many affluent families now have food processors, the best Georgian cooks swear by labor-intensive hand-grinding, which yields the finest texture.

Bread is still baked in the traditional round toné, for which a very hot fire is made from dried grapevines on the oven floor. By the time the flames die down, the sides of the oven have been coated with black ashes, which soon turn white, indicating that the oven has reached the proper temperature. Salted water is then splashed against the sides of the oven to test the temperature. When it instantly sizzles, a metal lid is placed over the burning vines. Water is sprinkled onto old ashes to make a rather dry mix that is spread over the lid to cool down the fire. The baker then runs a piece of wet burlap along the sides of the toné to clean it of ashes. Ovals of dough are sprinkled lightly with salted water and slapped directly onto the inside walls of the oven. The bread bakes on one side only. When it is done, taking less than 10 minutes in the first round of baking, each loaf is secured with a hook before being removed from the oven wall with a spatula.

Typical Meals

The most typical and distinctive Georgian meal is the formal feast, or *supra,* which is organized at the slightest excuse—a birthday celebration, a good report card, or the arrival of a guest. The supra is a ritual affair that calls for the skillful exercise of moderation in the face of excess—no small feat, considering the meal's extravagances. The shared table is meant, above all, to promote a feeling of kinship and national unity. Centuries of gathering around the table to affirm long-standing traditions have helped the Georgians preserve their culture even under foreign subjugation. The supra represents the collective public face the Georgians proudly present to the world even as it reflects the honor of an individual household.

The rules for commensal celebration are strict. Most important, a *tamada,* or toastmaster, is chosen to orchestrate all but the most informal meals. This practice may have evolved from the ancient Greek custom of choosing a symposiarch to guide the progression of the feast. The role of the tamada is taken very seriously, and he is accorded great respect, for it requires skill to keep all the guests entertained, ensure that the meal is proceeding apace, and see to it that no one drinks or eats to excess, as drunken guests bring shame on the host. The best tamadas are renowned for their wit and eloquence, including an ability to improvise. The tamada guides the company through a series of toasts, which can be brief or complex. Each calls for downing a glass of wine. Georgians do not sip, and drinking out of order or at random is not allowed. A *merikipe* is appointed to make sure that diners' glasses are filled at all times.

The rules of the Georgian table call for uplifting toasts, so that each occasion, even a sad one, becomes an affirmation of life. Traditionally, toasting begins with glasses raised heavenward in acknowledgment of God's presence. Then the host family is toasted, particularly the lady of the house responsible for the meal. The tamada's ability to pace the evening is crucial. Each time a toast is pronounced, whether by the tamada or someone else, wine is drunk as a mark of honor. But if inebriation seems likely, the tamada must slow down the succession of toasts. The traditional meal is punctuated by breaks for entertainment, often a cappella singing, a holdover from medieval patterns of feasting when entremets were actual diversions.

Given such ritualized drinking, the apparent chaos of the food service can seem surprising to outsiders. Courses are not always presented in the fixed order of the *service à la russe* that western Europeans, and later Americans, adopted in the 19th century, and which still prevails in Europe and America today. By contrast, the Georgian style of service is intended to dazzle the eye and pique the

An old man serves as the tamada at a funeral in Osetia, Georgia. (AFP | Getty Images)

palate through contrasting colors, textures, and flavors. When diners sit down to eat, the table is already laid with a wide variety of dishes. As the meal progresses, the hostess does not remove serving plates that still contain food but rather continues to pile new dishes on the table, balancing some on the edges of others, so that by the end of the evening the table is laden with a pyramid of plates, ensuring plenty at every stage.

Georgian Wine

If food is the heart of the Georgian feast, then its spirit resides in wine. For a Georgian, wine evokes both culture and community. Based on evidence of grape pips unearthed from archaeological sites, viticulture is an ancient art in Georgia, practiced as early as the fourth millennium B.C. Scientists believe that the species *Vitis vinifera,* the original wine

grape, is native to the Caucasus region, and many linguists consider the Georgian word for wine, *ghvino,* the prototype for such Indo-European variations as *vino, vin, wine,* and *Wein.* The grapevine symbolizes life and faith, a belief that Saint Nino of Cappadocia adapted to Christian doctrine when she introduced it to Georgia in the fourth century. Bearing a cross plaited of dried vines and tied with her own hair, Saint Nino seemed to represent divine approval for the winemaking that had been practiced for centuries. The vine and the cross became inextricably entwined, each an object of devotion.

The center of wine growing in Georgia is Kakheti, in the eastern half of the country. The region is known for its traditional method of winemaking, which differs considerably from standard European practices because it is so labor-intensive; it is dying out as a commercial process. After the grapes are pressed, the juice is fermented together with the skins, stems, and seeds to yield distinctive wines of a lovely, deep amber hue and a raisiny taste with a hint of Madeira.

Traditionally, wine was made in large, red clay amphorae known as *kvevri.* Nearly every Georgian country household has a *marani,* a place where the temperature remains cool and steady. Here, the kvevris are buried up to their necks in the earth. If the house lacks an earthen cellar, the kvevri are buried directly in the ground outdoors. To make wine by the Kakhetian method, the freshly pressed juice, along with the skins, stems, and seeds, is poured into the buried amphorae and stirred four or six times a day for three to five months. The resulting new wine is called machari. When the wine has achieved the desired degree of fermentation, it is drawn off from the lees. If produced commercially, the wine is transferred to oak barrels to age for at least a year, but homemade wine is usually ladled by means of a special long-handled gourd from the first kvevri into smaller ones for aging. These kvevris are topped with a wooden lid, then sealed with mud. Dirt is mounded all around the lid to keep air out, lest it spoil the wine. Whenever wine is taken off from a kvevri in any quantity, the remainder is transferred to progressively smaller vessels.

Some Georgian families still use special vessels to bring wine to the table, such as the *chapi,* a two-handled jug with a squat neck and bulbous body tapering to a narrow base. From this transitional vessel the wine is poured into a variety of other containers intended either for pouring or drinking. Quite common are a single-handled pitcher and the more elaborate "mother jug" (*deda-khelada*) composed of a central pitcher with several smaller pitchers affixed to the sides, like a mother with numerous breasts.

The most widespread red wine grape of Georgia is Saperavi, which, depending on its treatment, can yield wines ranging from dry to semisweet. For white wines, the indigenous Rkatsiteli grape makes nicely acidic wines with a fresh, green taste. Both varietals predominate in Kakheti's Alazani River valley, which lies between the high peaks of the Greater Caucasus to the northeast and the foothills of the Tsiv-Gombori Range to the southeast. They are made into wines bearing such controlled

appellations as Mukuzani, Kindzmarauli, and Tsinandali. Today, artisanal producers like Mildiani make some extraordinary wines that blend ancient traditions with modern technology.

Eating Out

The great 19th-century Russian poet Alexander Pushkin once said that "every Georgian dish is a poem." Similarly, nearly every occasion offers cause for celebration. Most gatherings still take place in private homes, although since the collapse of the Soviet system a lively restaurant culture has developed in Tbilisi. Most villages and towns feature at least one hole-in-the-wall café offering tasty local food such as khinkali, the famous oversized dumplings that are a specialty of taverns along the old Georgian Military Highway. As soon as the weather turns nice, Georgians like to gather for impromptu picnics, even just by the roadside. They consider al fresco dining the best way to eat, a chance to appreciate nature while consuming its gifts. Georgians also enjoy street food. Appealing stands along the Black Sea coast offer corn on the cob, which is either grilled or boiled to order. The national fast food is khachapuri, a cheese-filled bread that comes

Khachapuri, a cheese-filled bread that comes in a variety of shapes and sizes and national fast food of Georgia. (Sergey Zavalnyuk | Dreamstime.com)

in a variety of shapes and sizes. One specialty is the Adzharian version, *adzharuli khachapuri*—an open, boat-shaped loaf brimming with fresh sheep-milk cheese, with a still-runny egg baked on top. It is a meal in itself. To eat it, a piece of crust is broken off and dipped into the near-liquid cheese in the center of the loaf.

Khachapuri

Most cafés sell the appetizer khachapuri made with yeast dough—Georgia's answer to pizza. At home, baking soda, a European import, or yogurt is often used to tenderize the dough, resulting in a rich, flaky pastry.

Serves 16

2 c unbleached white flour

½ tsp salt

12 tbsp cold butter, cut in pieces

2 eggs

¼ c plain full-fat yogurt

1¼ lb mixed Muenster and Havarti cheeses

1 egg yolk, beaten

Put the flour and salt in a medium bowl, and cut in the butter until the mixture resembles coarse cornmeal. Beat 1 egg, and stir in the yogurt, then add to the flour mixture. Form into a ball, and chill for 1 hour.

Grate the cheeses coarsely, beat the other egg, and stir it into the cheese. Set aside.

Preheat the oven to 350°F. Grease a large baking sheet. On a floured board roll the dough to a rectangle about 12 x 17 inches. Trim the edges. Spread the cheese mixture over half the short side of the dough. Then fold the other half over to enclose it. Roll the extra dough on the edges up over the top and pinch the edges decoratively to seal.

Transfer the bread to the baking sheet and brush with beaten egg yolk. Bake for 50 minutes, until nicely browned. The bread is best served slightly warm, cut into small squares.

Diet and Health

Throughout most of Georgia's history, meat was a luxury, so the Georgians took great advantage of copious fruits, vegetables, and herbs. The bulk of the Georgian culinary repertoire is made up of preparations for vegetables, both cultivated and wild. Over 100 varieties of such wild greens as sarsaparilla, nettles, mallow, ramp, and purslane are still gathered in season and prepared in a surprising number of ways—cooked, marinated, dried for seasoning, or steeped in water for a nutritious drink. But above all, the Georgians enjoy their greens fresh, and no Georgian table is complete without a large platter of leafy cilantro, dill, tarragon, parsley, basil, summer savory, and peppery *tsitsmati,* or falseflax (*Camelina sativa,* similar to arugula). Often there is also *dzhondzholi* (Colchis bladdernut, *Staphylea colchica*), an edible ornamental plant with long stems of tightly furled, beadlike tendrils redolent of garlic. The greens, which are rich in nutrients, provide a refreshing counterpoint to the heavier foods in the meal.

These foods are washed down with wine and local mineral waters like Borzhomi and Nabeghlavi, which have long been touted for their health benefits. To diners used to the mild taste of Perrier or Pellegrino, these waters seem heavy and salty (so much so that Borzhomi is now bottling a Borzhomi Light), but Georgians have traditionally put them to therapeutic use in addition to serving them at the table. Certain foods are also considered especially nutritious. The benefits of yogurt have been touted by Madison Avenue in ads featuring the long-living inhabitants of the Caucasus. Georgians more frequently prescribe *khashi,* a much-loved tripe soup, for digestive problems; it is also a favored hangover remedy when consumed early in the morning following a drinking bout. The marigold petals used in place of saffron are also said to aid in digestion, while *nadugi,* the delicious whey derived from cow milk and often served mixed with fresh herbs, is virtually fat-free and is considered a sclerosis preventative. The traditional Georgian diet is notable for its high amount of omega-3 fats, found in walnuts, walnut oil, and purslane. Purslane contains more omega-3s than any other leafy green vegetable.

The 1991 collapse of the Soviet Union ushered in an era of civil unrest and economic pressure. A new generation of Georgians is working to overcome the problems that still plague the country after so many years of dependence on the larger Soviet economy, which provided a ready market for Georgian produce and prepared foods. Although small-scale farms never died out in Georgia, there was plenty of industrial farming to supply the needs of the Russian market, and activists are now working to reestablish sustainable agricultural practices and revive the legendary wines that had either disappeared from the market or been restyled for the Russian palate. In the 21st century Georgia is a small country with a shattered infrastructure, but it is placing a good measure of economic hope on fairly traditional, organic agriculture.

Darra Goldstein

Further Reading

Allen, W.E.D. *A History of the Georgian People.* 2nd ed. New York: Barnes and Noble, 1971.

Burney, Charles, and David Marshall Lang. *The Peoples of the Hills: Ancient Ararat and Caucasus.* New York: Praeger, 1972.

Goldstein, Darra. *The Georgian Feast: The Vibrant Culture and Savory Food of the Republic of Georgia.* Berkeley: University of California Press, 1999.

Holisky, Dee Ann. "The Rules of the *Supra* or How to Drink in Georgian." *Annual of the Society for the Study of Caucasia* 1 (1989): 22–40.

Mars, Gerald, and Yochanan Altman. "Alternative Mechanism of Distribution in a Soviet Economy." In *Constructive Drinking: Perspectives on Drink from Anthropology,* edited by Mary Douglas, 270–79. Cambridge: Cambridge University Press, 1987.

Suny, Ronald Grigor. *The Making of Modern Georgia.* Bloomington: Indiana University Press, 1988.

Germany

Overview

Germany is situated in the middle of the European continent: east of France, west of Poland, north of Switzerland, and south of Denmark, between Slavs and Romans, cold and heat, sea and mountains. Over the course of history it has been enormously influenced from all sides—one could even say it is composed of those influences. Although Germany is not particularly large (in terms of land area, it is slightly smaller than Montana), its culture is very complex. In addition to geographic, climatic, and religious reasons, this is mainly due to migrations throughout history, with new peoples bringing their foods and foodways with them, as well as the fact that until the declaration of the German Empire in 1871, Germany was composed of countless small individual kingdoms, fiefdoms, and free cities. This made for a variety of regional cuisines. Unlike, for instance, its neighbor France, Germany has no single national, overarching haute cuisine, not even a national dish.

When industrialization reached Germany around 1850, compared with almost a century earlier in England, the effects were far-reaching. In the process, agrarian Germany was quickly and thoroughly urbanized and came to rely more and more on "modern" food industries. As 19th-century industrialization gave way to 20th- and 21st-century globalization, German food culture shifted once more to contend with worldwide food trends. Despite heated debates about the rights and wrongs of fast food versus "real" food, world cuisine versus home-style regional cooking, food scares, and one of the highest standards of living worldwide, culinary

Germany today at last seems to have reached a more balanced normality.

Germany is no agricultural idyll—with more than 81 million inhabitants it is densely populated, thoroughly urbanized (72% of Germans live in towns of more than 10,000 inhabitants, 32% in large cities of more than 100,000), and heavily industrialized. Although the general standard of living is high, differences in income are rising steadily. Competition is steep because of the European single market as well as imports from non–European Union countries. With strong trade unions, labor is expensive and, in spite of high unemployment, difficult to find (today, viticulture and asparagus cultivation, for instance, would be unthinkable without foreign workers from Poland and Russia), which leads to further attempts to increase efficiency through concentration, mechanization, and rationalization.

🍽 Food Culture Snapshot

Petra and Jan are in their mid-thirties and live with their children Paul, seven, and Maria, three, in a leafy Berlin suburb. Jan comes from Hamburg; Petra is a Berliner. They are both architects, running an office in the center of town together with a colleague. Since they are freelance, their income varies quite a lot, but they have learned to adapt to that and prefer to forgo long, expensive vacations rather than stint on food. Like many other Germans, they make a big shopping trip with the car to a large supermarket once a week, mostly on Friday afternoon, to stock up on basics like flour, sugar, cereals, yogurt, ice cream, frozen pizza, dried pasta, canned tomatoes, and the like, as well as mineral water, beer, and fruit juice. Petra used to have a subscription to have a box of fresh vegetables delivered every week from an organic farm not far from Berlin, but recently going to the farmers' market in their neighborhood has become a family ritual on Saturday mornings. Here, they buy vegetables, fruit, eggs, bread, meat, and cheese from the vendors they have come to know and trust, after which they meet friends for a coffee and a pastry. During the week, they tend to combine shopping with driving to work and dropping the children off at school and kindergarten. For fresh food like bread, milk, and vegetables, they frequent an organic store that is situated near their office, and on their way home, they often stop at a small independent wine shop. Both Petra and Jan remember many more independent butchers and bakers from their childhood, and for special occasions like dinner parties with friends they sometimes drive to one of the few remaining ones. On the whole they feel that shopping has become much more relaxed since shop hours are no longer strictly regulated. Until the end of the 20th century, shops had to close at 6:30 P.M. on weekdays and 1 P.M. on Saturdays, and were completely closed on Sundays and public holidays. As they often worked late before having the children, a small store run by a Turkish family was frequently their last resort, as those shop owners tended to take their time closing up. Now most stores stay open until 8 or 9 P.M. (6 P.M. on Saturdays), and some are even open on Sundays.

Major Foodstuffs

Bread is arguably the most significant German food. The traditional multitudinous variety of bread and rolls is based on different grains (wheat or rye, pure or in all possible mixtures with oats, spelt, buckwheat, linseed, and millet), coarse or finely ground flours, and varying fermentation methods (sourdough or yeast) and baking methods, as well as shapes and seasonings in the form of nuts, seeds, or spices, all developed through specific regional conditions. All over Germany, darker, whole-grain breads have seen a renaissance during the last decades through the organic and health movements. For breakfast, fresh rolls are for many people almost a necessity.

Next to bread, potatoes are the most important staple food. Although the potato repertoire includes ever more finished products like chips, fries, dumplings, ready-to-serve fried potatoes, or dried mashed potatoes, Germans still see themselves as potato eaters and distinguish between *fest, halbfest,* and *mehlig kochend* (waxy, semiwaxy, and floury) varieties. Broadly speaking, in the north, potatoes are regarded as a staple food, a starch in the same league as rice or pasta, traditionally served with every warm meal on principle. In the south, however, they are treated as a vegetable. Potato soup is perhaps the most German of all soups, sometimes refined with cream and often served with small rounds of *Frankfurter* or *Fleischwurst* (a larger type of scalded sausage).

Kartoffelsuppe (Potato Soup)

1 onion, diced

2 tbsp bacon, diced

2 tbsp butter

1 carrot, diced

1 small leek, sliced

2 tbsp celeriac or celery, diced

1 tsp dried marjoram

Sea salt

White pepper

Nutmeg

1 lb floury potatoes, peeled and diced

1 qt water

½ c heavy cream (optional)

Fresh parsley, chopped

Sauté onion and bacon in butter until translucent, adding carrot, leek, and celeriac or celery after a little while, together with seasonings. After some minutes, add potatoes, cover, and let cook for 10 minutes. Add water, and bring to a slow boil. When vegetables are soft, add cream, if desired, and puree the soup in a blender to the desired consistency—it should not be too smooth. Serve with parsley and possibly sliced frankfurters.

Dumplings are found mostly in southern and central Germany. In their countless versions and variations, they are comparable to the multitude of pasta shapes and uses in Italy. They are made from flour and/or potatoes. Confusingly, they are occasionally called *Nudeln* (noodles), which also designates Italian-style pasta, also widely consumed in Germany (15.65 pounds per person in 2006). Rice is not grown in Germany but has long been imported. German stores carry all the usual varieties of mostly Italian and Asian rice, with risotto being very popular.

Pork is the favored meat of Germans, although since World War II, beef and poultry consumption has risen with affluence and health awareness, and mutton and goat meat are slowly gaining ground. *Schlachteplatte* is the German version of Alsatian *choucroûte,* combining all kinds of salted and boiled pork cuts, served with sauerkraut and boiled potatoes. In spite of the low pork prices of today, *Schweinebraten* (pork roast, frequently a leg) with crackling crust is still considered something special in the southeast, whereas beef is more common in the north, center, and west. Panfried meat patties that are called *Buletten* (in Berlin), *Frikadellen* (all over Germany), or *Fleischpflanzerl* (in Bavaria) are very popular eaten warm or cold, often as a snack with beer. Ground meat is also made into all kinds of dumplings served in sauce.

Sausages served with sauerkraut, a popular German dish. (Shutterstock)

Following the same model as sugar, poultry was once considered a high-prestige item, but its consumption has soared with cheaper, industrial production. Erstwhile festive dishes like *Hühnerfrikassee* (chicken fricassee) are still popular but have become much less special. Offal can be everything from a lowly substitute for "real" meat to an expensive delicacy. Although the gusto for eating steak in modern Germany rivals Texas or Chicago, there is no particular tradition for raising and maturing beef that corresponds to that in the United States. Veal is often panfried as *Schnitzel* and roasted as *Kalbshaxe* (shank). Although venison is widely available and affordable today—also with imports of farmed venison from New Zealand—the meat of roe, red, and fallow deer, as well as wild boar, is still seen as special, and a venison roast is a marker for festive occasions. Besides that, *Gans* (goose) and *Ente* (duck) account for a large part of festive winter roasts and often take pride of place on Christmas dinner tables.

The variety of sausages and ham in Germany is overwhelming and dominated by pork. Ham and sausage are mostly eaten as cold cuts with bread, but some varieties are also served warm. Very broadly speaking, *Wurst* (sausage) in the north tends to be made from raw meat. In the south, many sausage varieties are made from finely cut meat, possibly with larger pieces of ham or pickled tongue added afterward, and scalded in a fashion similar to mortadella or bologna. *Würstchen* (smaller, individual sausages like frankfurters) are served heated and whole, often in pairs. All over Germany, sausage is also made from cooked meat, often seasoned with marjoram and/or onion. *Leberwurst* (liver sausage) is always spreadable, resembling chopped liver. Ham is mostly made from pork leg or shoulder and smoked or cooked; some types are boiled or baked, as the climate permits air-drying only for smaller sausages rather than larger cuts like in Italy or Spain. There are versions matured on the bone and deboned varieties like *Schwarzwälder Schinken* from the Black Forest.

Germans are not great fish eaters, consuming only about 30 pounds per capita annually, about a sixth the amount of meat consumed. Although with modern transportation, fresh and frozen fish of all international varieties is readily available throughout Germany, northerners still consume more than southerners. Most offerings today come from aquacultures around the world. Of the fish consumed in Germany, 85 percent is imported, and *Lachs* (salmon) is as common as chicken. *Karpfen* (carp) is perhaps the most traditional fish dish and still plays a role on special occasions, especially those historically related to fasting. *Salzhering* (salted herring) today mostly survives as *Matjes* (caught young and fat).

Dairy farming is generally highly industrialized. Except for a very small number of estates that, under strict controls, offer untreated *Rohmilch* (raw milk) and *Vorzugsmilch* (special milk) for sale, milk in Germany (by definition cow milk; other kinds have to be designated as such and do not play an important role) has to be pasteurized and most often is homogenized as well. Milk is still seen as a healthy product, important for infants and children, whereas adults consume less than 0.53 pints per day. *Schlagsahne* (whipping cream) is used for cooking and eaten with cake. Yogurt in all its modern forms is a favorite for breakfast and snacks and seen as very healthy. In contrast to American-style cottage cheese (in Germany less common and called *Hüttenkäse*), *Quark* is smooth and homogeneous in texture with a more or less pronounced acidic tang. A multitude of regional names for Quark attest to its traditional importance in the daily diet. It is also used for *Käsekuchen* (cheesecake), which is either baked or made with gelatin, and combined with all kinds of fruit for desserts.

Germans eat 48.28 pounds of cheese per capita annually; the cheese ranges from industrial, rubbery slices to the most sophisticated imports from France and Italy. Traditionally, cheese is consumed on bread as cold cuts, but more and more it is also taking the place of dessert. German cheese culture was so quickly overwhelmed by industrial production at the end of the 19th century that it has only very recently begun to search for a distinctive character. A growing number of German dairy farms, predominantly small and organic, are developing new regional cheeses. Prior to industrial farming methods, butter was considered a luxury product.

With the onset of modern technology, it became more affordable but kept its high reputation. Most German butter, which is always made of cow milk and rarely salted, tastes rather bland and is quite soft to assure good spreadability. Germans consume 14.77 pounds of butter per person per year, spreading it on bread and rolls with jam and cold cuts, as well as using it in baking and cooking. Until butter became widely affordable, most of the fat consumed was in the form of *Talg* (suet) and *Schmalz* (lard). Schmalz in Germany is made from the rendered flare, back, and belly fat of pigs as well as the much softer goose fat. It is still popular, often homemade, but also commercially available. Margarine, introduced as a cheaper butter alternative in the 1870s, now covers all sorts of lower-fat spreads and butter substitutes and is mostly promoted as a healthier alternative to butter. However, in that respect, it cannot beat *Olivenöl* (olive oil) in German kitchens. Olive oil is seen as very healthy and is offered at all price levels. Consumption of olive oil stands at 1.8 pints per person per year, which puts Germany significantly behind Mediterranean countries. Besides other seeds and nuts, *Mohn* (poppy seed) is especially popular in eastern Germany and is used for cooking and baking.

Eggs are used in pastries and desserts but are also eaten boiled or as scrambled eggs for breakfast, or as an alternative to meat. Today, consumption averages 290 eggs per person per year. However, eggs are constantly surrounded by concerns about production methods and scares about food safety, raw eggs now being considered very risky.

Vegetables in general accompany meat or fish as a side dish, are eaten raw as *Rohkost,* or are made into salads or soups. The proverbial Germanic preference for cabbage reaches back at least to the Middle Ages. Round white and red cabbages are traditional standard fare all over Germany during autumn and winter. Sauerkraut is found throughout Germany.

Kohlrouladen (Cabbage Rolls)

½ lb ground meat (half pork, half beef)

1 egg

I onion, finely diced

Half a stale white roll, soaked in water or milk, squeezed dry, and torn into small pieces

Sea salt

Black pepper

I tbsp parsley, chopped

2 small or I large head white cabbage or savoy cabbage

2 tbsp butter or lard

4 thin slices bacon

I c water

I tbsp dried porcini mushrooms

Mix the meat with the egg, onion, and bread, and season well with salt and pepper. Add the parsley, and divide into four parts. Cut cabbage(s) in halves, and cut out the core liberally, taking out enough of the heart of the cabbage as well to create a hollow for filling. Season cabbage with salt and pepper. If working with two small heads, fill each of the four halves with one part of the stuffing, fold gently to form rolls and tie with string. If using one large head, the halves first need to be gently separated into two layers. Brown rolls on all sides in butter, cover each with a bacon slice, add water and mushrooms, and cover and braise for about I hour. Serve with boiled potatoes. Optional: Cooking liquid can be slightly thickened with some potato starch.

Besides cabbage, root vegetables such as beets and turnips as well as French beans play an important role. Legumes are seen as time-consuming to prepare and hard to digest and have never been as popular in Germany as they are, for instance, in India. For Germans they rather represented an answer to the problem of storage and winter food supply. *Spargel* (asparagus), however, is a national passion in Germany. It is cultivated in all the states, but Schwetzingen near Heidelberg and Beelitz southwest of Berlin arguably enjoy the highest reputation. Although the green version is now produced and eaten as well, and fresh spears are imported from Israel, California, and Peru in the off-season, asparagus in Germany is still clearly defined as white, something

special, and strictly seasonal. Omnipresent today, albeit mostly in an industrialized, robust, long-life version, tomatoes count among the most popular vegetables. Bell peppers, eggplant, zucchini, and fennel are all common (mostly imported) and available year-round. *Kürbis* (designating both pumpkin and squash) has recently been experiencing a culinary renaissance, furthered by the offerings of organic gardeners growing smaller, more flavorful varieties. *Salat* (lettuce, although in German *Salat* also means salad) is omnipresent, with all the modern varieties available, increasingly also in ready-to-eat bags. Fresh herbs, most commonly parsley, chives, and dill, are used as a garnish, as well as in all kinds of dishes, and are widely available commercially in small bunches or pots. Cèpes/porcini, chanterelles, and bay bolete are seen as very special, either gathered privately or bought in the market, where they are often imported from eastern European countries.

As for seasoning, the salt shaker is an essential part of the table setting in Germany. More often than not it is joined by a pepper shaker or mill. Otherwise, spices are used sparingly compared with practices in other countries. Apart from salad dressings, vinegar is used in traditional cooking for purposes of seasoning, preserving vegetables and meat, or tenderizing. Mustard above all is an important accompaniment for all kinds of sausages. In the south, freshly grated, pungent horseradish often replaces mustard with boiled beef or sausages.

As with fresh vegetables, fresh fruit was deemed not very nourishing in the 19th century, and it was even more perishable than vegetables and thus difficult to store and transport. Consumption really picked up only toward the end of the 19th century. Today, Germans annually consume about 165 pounds of fresh fruit, about a quarter of which is produced in Germany, mostly around Hamburg and on Lake Constance, plus about 88 pounds of citrus fruit, much of it in the form of juice. Apples are probably seen as the most "German" fruit, with local varieties enjoying a revival, but strawberries are the great favorite (at least strawberry is Germany's favored yogurt flavor) and a symbol of spring or early summer. For jam—on buttered rolls or bread a necessity for breakfast and often homemade rather than purchased—strawberry seems to top an enormous variety of other flavors in popularity.

Sugar in Germany is commonly white refined beet sugar. Brown, unrefined cane sugar is perceived by some as healthier although it is more expensive, and thickened fruit syrup is used in health food. However, as in other Western cultures, sugar generally has a negative image and is seen as a major culprit in obesity and related health problems. Artificial sweeteners are widely available, as are sugar-free diet versions of soft drinks and all kinds of food. Honey is spread on buttered bread as an alternative to jam and is used to sweeten herbal tea as well as in baking gingerbread for Christmas.

Although tea has a long tradition in the north, coffee is the hot caffeinated drink of choice in Germany. It is drunk at breakfast, during numerous breaks throughout the day, and especially for *Kaffee und Kuchen* (coffee and cake) in the afternoon. Italian espresso machines have become fashionable, but the standard is less concentrated *Filterkaffee* (filtered coffee), drunk with milk or condensed milk and sometimes sugar. International coffee chains as well as most bakeries offer take-out coffee in all the modern latte versions. With few exceptions, tea is prepared using bags of undifferentiated black tea, with various herbal types as a healthier alternative, lately joined by green tea and caffeine-free rooibos tea from South Africa, also available in a multitude of flavored versions.

Beer has been *the* German drink since ancient times. Today, an average of 274.84 pints per person are drunk annually, whether with meals or on its own, at home or in pubs and bars. Most beer today is bottom-fermented and sold in bottles, although draft beers are more highly valued by connoisseurs. *Pilsner* (frequently shortened to *Pils*) is almost a synonym for beer in the north and tastes in general much bitterer than the light *Kölsch* of Cologne. Brown *Altbier* is the specialty of Düsseldorf, and there are various local specialties like *Gose* in Leipzig or *Berliner Weisse,* both slightly sour wheat beers, the latter served flavored with a dash of red or green fruit syrup. In Bavaria, where beer consumption is the second highest (following Saxony),

beer is considered a food more than an alcoholic beverage, and Bavarian varieties tend to be lighter than in the north.

Generally, wine complements beer in regional consumption, with the exception of the north, where spirits play a more important role in total alcohol consumption. Riesling is the most important variety of German wine in terms of quality. Traditionally, and in complete contrast to Roman culture, wine, produced in Germany at least since the first century A.D., was and to some extent still is drunk by itself, for instance, in the afternoon or after dinner, and in general does not require food as an accompaniment. Since the 1990s, Germans have developed a keen interest in all kinds of wines from around the world, as well as wine and food combinations. Wine service and wine lists in restaurants have become much better, and wine shops with a very good international selection are common now.

German amber beer being poured into a glass. (Shutterstock)

Around Frankfurt and in the southwest, traditional apple and sometimes also pear cider is made and mostly consumed locally like beer. Most spirits, commonly called *Schnaps,* are drunk in the north in the form of a clear grain spirit often flavored with juniper. They are often accompanied by beer. In the southwest, all kinds of fruits are distilled to make fruit brandy, of which *Kirsch(wasser),* a type of cherry brandy, is perhaps the best known.

In 2006 Germans drank 627.27 pints of alcohol-free beverages on average (up 3% from the previous year, and second behind Spain for all of Europe) and spent slightly more on them than on alcoholic beverages. Although tap water is perfectly safe everywhere and unchlorinated, today many prefer to buy bottled mineral water. Apple juice is a big favorite, followed by orange juice, often available freshly squeezed.

Cooking

In Germany, as in most societies and cultures worldwide, the private kitchen where cooking and related tasks take place has traditionally been women's domain. According to a time budget study from 2001–2002, German women on average still invest one hour and six minutes daily in household tasks, of which 45 minutes are spent on food preparation. German men spend just 23 minutes daily on food preparation and directly related tasks like setting the table and washing the dishes. In families with children and working mothers, fathers contribute even less time, and almost half of the male population is being looked after by women. Young people show the same gender pattern, with 72 percent of young men between 20 and 25 years of age not getting involved at all in food preparation. At least there seems to be a tendency for retired (pensioner) couples to share food-related tasks more evenly. Obviously, these numbers would have been much higher in the past. The decrease in food-preparation time is related on the one hand to the availability and use of prepared food and meals—ever less is prepared from scratch or made into preserves—and on the other hand to the logistics and technicalities of the kitchen and its equipment.

In spite of the dominant pattern in which women are responsible for the food, cooking and eating are changing from a pure necessity to a freely chosen option of how to spend one's time. In the 1970s, men discovered cooking as a hobby with high prestige. Most of these *Hobbyköche* (hobby cooks) are not interested in the everyday routine of the kitchen but instead plan and produce complicated meals on the weekend. However, younger Germans have a more relaxed approach; they see cooking not as a task but as a trendy, relaxed, and delicious pastime of choice, to indulge in during free time or on the weekend. Meeting with friends to cook or inviting them for meals is a popular social activity. In recent years, cooking schools and courses have become very popular.

In German apartments and houses, the kitchen is seen as the second most important room after the living room: It is often described as the most used room, with the best atmosphere or feeling, and it is the room most used to receive visitors. Younger Germans especially use the kitchen in a very multifunctional way; many a party ends there. The *Einbauküche* (fitted kitchen) still is the ideal for the majority. However, most of them like to combine its functionality and technical potential with more *Gemütlichkeit* (homey contentment). Most people have at least breakfast in the kitchen, and often a separate dining room is used only for more formal or festive occasions or when guests are invited.

Germans love electric kitchen gadgets, and kitchens are generally fitted out well. Although many everyday dishes are made without consulting a recipe, cookbooks are deemed essential, with a multitude of cookbooks published every year, directed at all social groups, ages, and budgets. Most households own a liter measure as well as (electric) scales for baking, as recipes are given in (kilo)grams and (milli)liters.

The techniques used to prepare food in Germany are by and large the same as in other Western cultures. *Dünsten,* which is stewing in its own juice with a little fat and some liquid like wine, stock, or simply water added, is perhaps the method most commonly used for vegetables and meat. It combines dry heat for roast flavors with wet heat to tenderize and yield some sauce. This is also the case with *schmoren* (braising), most often used for ragouts, goulash, and large cuts of meat: The meat is browned, and then some vegetables like carrots, celeriac, and onions are added and lightly sautéed as well before the *ablöschen,* when a little liquid is added. Then a lid goes on the pan, and the meat is slowly finished, often in the oven, where it yields the gravy deemed essential for a traditional "real" meal with dumplings or potatoes.

Typical Meals

Frühstück (breakfast) is mostly eaten at home, consisting at its most basic of a hot beverage, more often coffee than tea, with milk and hot chocolate as alternatives, in particular for children, and some kind of starch. This can be—depending on the preference for sweet or savory—bread or rolls spread with butter, then topped with jam or honey, cheese, Quark (sometimes with herbs), sausage, ham, or, more luxuriously, smoked salmon. Sweet pastries are also popular as are various cereals with milk.

At school or at work, a break is taken during the morning around 10 A.M. It could be just a *Kaffeepause* (coffee break) for a cup of coffee and perhaps a cigarette. Schoolchildren might have a sandwich they brought from home, but in rural areas, where there is a greater number of manual laborers, more solid fare is consumed. *Brotzeit* might consist in Bavaria of *Weißwurst und Brezel* (scalded white veal sausages and a pretzel) or in Swabia of a slice of freshly baked *Leberkäse* (baked meatloaf) in a roll. Both might be washed down with a beer.

In rural areas and traditional households, *Mittagessen,* the meal around noon, is on principle a warm meal, and more importance is given to it than to dinner. At its most classic, Mittagessen consists of meat or fish accompanied by a vegetable and a starch, often preceded by soup or a salad and followed by a dessert like stewed fruit, yogurt, custard, or ice cream. A recent survey of favorite dishes among Germans aged 14 to 60 years produced a hit parade that is headed by global dishes like spaghetti Bolognese but dominated by regional fare like asparagus and sauerbraten.

Traditionally, meatless dishes, like soft-boiled or fried eggs on spinach with boiled potatoes, are served on Fridays, although today they are probably chosen by vegetarians rather than for religious reasons. In urban surroundings and among office workers, long breaks for an extended meal at lunchtime are rather unusual. Most people have time only for a snack—the business lunch offered by many restaurants is by definition quick. Sunday lunch tends to be a more sumptuous and family-oriented affair than meals during the week, often accompanied by a glass of wine.

In the afternoon, two very different in-between meals are possible. On the one hand, between 3 and 4 P.M., it is time for Kaffee und Kuchen, that is, coffee (or exceptionally tea, mostly in the north) and cake. On the other hand, a bit later, between 4 and 5 P.M., especially in the southern, more rural areas, *Vesper* or Brotzeit is taken after the day's work, traditionally between the day's work in the fields and the evening milking of the cows. This cold snack can consist of all kinds of sausages, ham, or brawn (headcheese-like sausage); bread, rolls, or Brezeln; sliced and salted long white radish (in Bavaria); and/or cheese, and it is often accompanied by beer or wine.

Abendessen or *Abendbrot,* the evening meal, can either be cold, resembling the afternoon snack, or warm, above all on days and occasions when lunch has been cold. It tends to be structured similarly to a warm meal at lunchtime but will probably evolve in a more leisurely fashion and be eaten in a larger group, with family or friends. This is the occasion for enjoying food and drink in a relaxed way.

Table manners became much more relaxed in Germany during the last decades of the 20th century. However, some basics still apply. It is considered bad taste to start eating before the head of the family or the person of highest rank at the table says *Guten Appetit* (bon appétit), wishing all an enjoyable meal.

Roughly one out of every nine people in Germany is not of German heritage and thus probably eats differently, to varying degrees. The Turkish are by far the most numerous of this group, making up more than 25 percent of immigrants, followed by immigrants from Asia (12.2%), Italy (8.0%), and Greece (4.6%). Most Germans are of Christian background, and Christian traditions still dominate foodways, although religious rituals, especially in urban surroundings, are superseded by a secular lifestyle. Only 0.013 percent of all Germans are Jewish, and their influence on the food available and consumed in Germany is hardly noticeable. Their number is currently increasing, however, because of Jewish immigrants, mainly from Russia.

Eating Out

For most Germans, eating out in a restaurant is not just another everyday meal option but is widely regarded as something special. Generally it is a luxury to be indulged in only when the most important status symbols like a nice home, car, and vacations are already guaranteed. Although Germany is generally perceived as an almost-classless society, the strong opinions and delicate decisions about who eats out where and with whom, as well as anxiety about being at the "wrong" place or not dressed "right" for the occasion, betray the subliminal existence of a distinctive social hierarchy. In fact, the term *ausgehen* (to go out) still designates both eating out and entertainment such as concerts or the theater.

Whereas in West Germany until today schools tend to end around midday with no meals provided, day schools—and with that school cafeterias—used to be the norm in East Germany but are currently on the rise throughout the country. However, eating in cafeterias or schools is regarded as an unavoidable necessity when studying or working. The same applies for food in hospitals and nursing homes: Its quality obviously varies, but its overall reputation is bad.

But in general the profession of chef has become very attractive, with stereotypes changing from unreliable drunkard to star artist. New technical equipment has made kitchen work less physically demanding, and during the 1980s the almost exclusively male profession slowly opened up to include women, although they are still in the minority. Some German chefs are as much influenced by the Spanish chef Ferran Adrià and his futuristic cuisine, commonly called molecular cuisine, as their colleagues in other Western countries, but most of them are very aware of their origins and surroundings. They use all kinds of ingredients, elements, and styles but tend to integrate them into a regional culinary pattern, striving for a clear, straightforward taste. Beginning as a necessity for travelers, eating out in Germany has developed into a plethora of possibilities.

Hot food is served in most places during fixed lunch and dinner hours. It is the exception for German restaurants to do two seatings in the evening as is common in American cities, and guests decide for themselves how long to linger after the meal. Be it in the beer gardens in Bavaria, in the traditional *Ausflugsgaststätten* (gastronomic day-trip destinations) around the larger cities, or in their own gardens and on their balconies, Germans love to eat and drink outside. When the weather permits in the summer months, many German meals on the weekend revolve around the barbecue. Younger Germans and Turkish citizens flock to public parks for this occasion, loaded down with a grill, table, and chairs as well as victuals. However, the majority of Germans prefer to retreat to their private yards. Weekend barbecues are a good occasion to invite neighbors and friends, as they are much less formal than normal dinner invitations.

Café culture is not quite as developed as in the Austrian *Kaffeehaus,* but most cafés in Germany open in the morning and offer breakfast and some menu of simple hot and cold food all day long. Some double as a bar and stay open until late. Affordable, informal restaurants in Germany are often run by immigrants, and in spite of all regional influences, the chances of finding a pizzeria or a Greek or Asian restaurant are probably higher in most of Germany than those of coming across a traditional inn. Even in the southwest with its more indulgent food culture and higher density of restaurants of all categories, people love to go *zum Italiener* or *zum Griechen* (to the Italian or the Greek). Besides Italian and Greek restaurants, French, Austrian, Chinese, Thai, Vietnamese, Lebanese, Japanese (sushi), and many other ethnic eateries abound.

Until about a decade ago, with the exception of ice cream and food at fairs, eating while walking in the street was considered unacceptable behavior and was rarely seen. Drinking from a beer bottle in public was just one step further down the social ladder and a sure sign of a homeless person. Today, it is quite normal and socially acceptable to walk around German streets eating or with a drink in one's hand, although admittedly most take-out and street food is offered in busy city centers, in open-air markets, around large department stores, near tourist attractions, and in or around train stations, largely replacing the *Bahnhofsrestaurant* (train station restaurant) of old.

Today, fast food carries with it notions of fun and social freedom. It is an affordable alternative, especially for allowing young people to escape family restraints and meet with friends over a meal. Turkish *Döner Kebab* (meat on a vertical spit, similar to gyros), Lebanese falafel, Berlin *Currywurst* with French fries, and pizza dominate the offerings.

Special Occasions

The differentiation between *Alltag* (everyday) and *Festtage* (holidays or special occasions) used to be much more marked in Germany. It was mostly based on Christian religious rules and prohibitions. One used to dress better, go to church, and eat differently and more sumptuously on holidays or special occasions. However, with the onset of industrialization and the dominance of mechanical production, new time patterns and eating groups emerged. New developments were furthered by general affluence: Modern wealthy people moved away from religious holidays spent with the family or a larger social group toward a more globalized and nation-transcending celebratory culture (witness the rise of Halloween in Germany, unknown until a few years ago), accompanied by a loosening of social taboos and peer pressures.

There are relatively few nationwide public holidays in Germany besides those celebrated on weekends. As religion plays less of a role in most Germans' lives, many originally religious holiday rituals survive as almost-secular events, including

Christmas. Furthermore, the wide availability of most foodstuffs nearly throughout the year makes it difficult for distinctive food traditions related to holidays to survive. But even if the reasons might not be as clear as they once used to be regarding holiday fare, special occasions—which, of course, also include personal festivities such as birthdays or weddings, more official occasions like fairs, and private gatherings, mostly on the weekend—still include special food.

As a general rule that remains valid until today, however, holiday meals tend to involve larger gatherings than weekday meals and tend to be richer and longer, for instance, including a more sumptuous dessert. Sweet baked goods, such as pastries, cakes, and cookies, are the most obvious and continuing markers for special occasions in Germany. They range from a *süßes Stückchen* (sweet pastry), eaten as a private treat on the go, to Sunday afternoon cake, traditional Christmas cookies, and extravagant wedding cakes. Before private households were generally equipped with an oven, all the baking was done at a communal oven or at the bakery. Deep-frying pastries in lard was the housewife's alternative then and represents a category of its own, above all associated with Carnival time.

For most Germans the weekend is experienced as a short holiday, as the contrast between work and free time tends to be strongly felt. Friday night, Saturday, and Sunday, when most people do not work, are a highlight to look forward to. Besides household chores, gardening, do-it-yourself car and house projects, and larger shopping trips, these days are spent going out (Friday and Saturday are the busiest nights in German restaurants), meeting friends, or going on day trips to the countryside or other destinations.

Kaffee und Kuchen is the least formal way to mark a special event with a meal. Unlike most American cakes, German *Torten* tend to be somewhat lighter, favoring whipped cream and some buttercream over the popular American cream icing. The best-known German Torte, without doubt, is *Schwarzwälder Kirschtorte* (Black Forest cherry gâteau), at its best a glorious combination of chocolate sponge cake, tart cherries, Kirschwasser (cherry brandy), and freshly whipped cream. However, frequently it is only a poor imitation of the real item, relying on cheap and longer-lasting buttercream and maraschino cherries.

Christmas undoubtedly is the most important holiday of the year, connected to special foods of all kinds. At its core, its present form goes back to the bourgeois families of the 19th century. It is still very much a rather quiet family affair, *eine besinnliche Zeit* (a time of contemplation), but also the occasion for a *Weihnachtsfeier* (Christmas party) at businesses and offices during the Advent weeks. During the whole Advent period, *Weihnachtsbäckerei* (Christmas baking) plays an important role. It is often an occasion for friends to gather, with children joining in the mixing and stirring and especially the cutting and decorating of cookies. The most traditional German Christmas cake is the *Stollen.* Looking at today's recipe, heavy with butter, almonds, and dried fruit, it is hard to believe that Stollen originally started as a cake for the Advent fasting period before Christmas. *Lebkuchen* (gingerbread) is rarely made at home. Its tradition goes back to when the crusaders brought exotic spices home with them. Marzipan (almond paste) is generally regarded as special. For Christmas it mostly takes the shape of *Marzipankartoffeln* (literally, marzipan potatoes), small balls coated in cocoa powder, or other imitations of fruits and vegetables. Christmas lunch on December 25 is for most Germans quite a grand affair, depending on personal means. Restaurant dining is more of an option than on Christmas Eve, but, for the most part, geese, ducks, or venison legs or saddles are roasted in private ovens, to be served with brussels sprouts or red cabbage.

A multitude of *Volksfeste* (fairs) all over Germany offer a mix of fun rides, amusements, and food and drink, the most important being Oktoberfest in Munich, which centers around huge amounts of beer and accompanying *Schmankerl,* hearty fare like grilled chicken and pork shanks.

Inside one of the many beer tents at Oktoberfest in Munich, Germany. (Shutterstock)

Diet and Health

For most Germans, diet and health are closely linked. This could be traced back to the holistic approaches to medicine that were practiced in medieval times, and thus to its roots in India, where it is still alive in the Ayurvedic school. But with collective morality loosening, moral obligations have become more individualized and today include the obligation to eat right, that is, healthily.

Life expectancy in Germany is increasing; currently, it is at more than 75 years for men (of which more than 68 years are spent in good health) and more than 81 for women (of which 72 in good health). But it is still thought that nutritional knowledge is insufficient. Overall alcohol consumption is decreasing, and there is a trend toward eating poultry and fish instead of red meat, but fat consumption remains too high and not enough vegetables and fruit are eaten. Varying levels of education, financial means, and gender make for different patterns. The higher social classes and women have significantly better nutritional knowledge than the lower classes and men, respectively.

According to a survey conducted in 2003, 66.9 percent of all German men are overweight, with a body mass index (BMI) of 25 or above, including 17.1 percent who are obese, with a BMI of 30 or above. As in most Western countries, slimness is seen as an ideal and is projected as such in the media. In its most excessive forms, for instance, in fashion advertising, it is also publicly criticized. The link to eating disorders, which are seen as psychological in origin, is widely accepted. Seventy percent of girls between 14 and 15 years are thought to have a diet history. Indeed, diets are an ever-present subject in newspapers, magazines, and books.

Food production, preparation, and trade are strongly regulated in contemporary Germany. The *Lebensmittelrecht* (food law) is a federal law falling under the jurisdiction of both the Ministry for Consumer Protection and the Ministry for Health. Its main purpose is to guarantee food safety as well as a certain level of quality. Looked at rationally and put into a larger perspective, most food scares and scandals seem somewhat overblown when set against the actual casualties. Undoubtedly, objective food safety in Germany has never been as high as today, and the crisis surrounding bovine spongiform encephalopathy (mad cow disease), for instance, became a turning point in German food politics, as from that point transparency and organic agriculture were heavily promoted.

Genetically engineered food is a very controversial topic in Germany, where the first experimental plantings have only recently been allowed. Another discussion concerns ingredients seen as potential allergens or for those who are subject to lactose, gluten, and other food intolerances.

Insecurity and angst resulting from the inability to understand the often-complex interrelations between diet and health combine with a romanticization of supposedly pure natural food versus artificial human-made food. This has led to a rise in vegetarianism—these days about 8 percent of all Germans are vegetarians—as well as growing environmental awareness, apparent in a multitude of ecological groups, notable among them the Green Party.

But many today apply *gesunder Menschenverstand* (literally, healthy common sense) to seek a balance between human-scale artisanal and industrial perfection in food. Healthy alternatives take different forms for different people. Abstention from smoking, alcohol, and/or sweets during Lent (the weeks leading up to Easter) is not necessarily linked to religious practice. Homeopathic treatment is gradually being recognized by health insurers. Pharmacies expand to become health centers. Ayurvedic treatment is in, and yoga schools are booming. But most important is the growing market for organic and biodynamic food, led by small chains of organic supermarkets. Customers are mainly families with young children from the middle to upper classes, but generally, in spite of discussions about what is acceptable as such, the organic alternative, though not affordable for all, is seen as the better option for reasons beyond personal health.

Ursula Heinzelmann

Further Reading

Anderson, Jean, and Hedy Würz. *The New German Cookbook.* New York: HarperCollins, 1993.

Dr. Oetker. *German Cooking Today.* Bielefeld, Germany: Dr. Oetker, 2006.

German Foods. http://www.germanfoods.org.

Heinzelmann, Ursula. *Food Culture in Germany.* Westport, CT: Greenwood Press, 2008.

Metzger, Christine, ed. *Culinaria Germany.* Cologne, Germany: Konemann, 1999.

Scharfenberg, Horst. *The Cuisines of Germany.* New York: Poseidon, 1989.

Schulze, Hagen. *Germany: A New History.* Translated by Deborah L. Schneider. Cambridge, MA: Harvard University Press, 1998.

Wildt, Michael. "Promise of More: The Rhetoric of (Food) Consumption in a Society Searching for Itself: West Germany in the 1950s." In *Food, Drink and Identity,* edited by Peter Scholliers, 63–80. Oxford: Berg, 2001.

Great Britain

Overview

Great Britain is an island with a heavily indented coast situated on the northwestern continental shelf of Europe, with Ireland to the west. It contains three countries, England, Wales, and Scotland, which, together with the Province of Northern Ireland, make up the United Kingdom. Colloquially, Great Britain refers to the political unit of the United Kingdom as well as to the island. Global interaction through trade and empire has affected food and taken British ideas about it to former colonies. In the 1970s the United Kingdom joined the European Union, whose policies on agriculture have had a significant impact on food production.

The population of the United Kingdom is about 61,383,000; between 4.5 and 5 million are of Asian, Caribbean, African, Chinese, or other non-British origin. The country is heavily urbanized and industrialized and dominated by London as a source of new ideas.

Southeast Britain is a mixture of flat or rolling land and low hills; the west and north contain areas of low mountains, the highest just over 4,000 feet. Soil types are varied, reflecting a complex geology. The climate is temperate, although the west and north are significantly wetter. About 25 percent of agricultural land in Great Britain is arable, principally in southern and eastern England, and northward up the east coast into Scotland. In the west and north, the emphasis is on cattle and sheep.

Agriculture is intensive but fulfills only about 60 percent of the county's food needs and employs under 1 percent of the labor force. Processing, distributing, and retailing food are important sources of employment, as is catering. Food production generally is industrialized. Dependent on imports, both of raw ingredients and ideas, current food trends tend to be inspired by other cultures and subject to fashion, and they spread across the country in a few years. British food culture has changed markedly since the 1960s, as interest in dishes and ingredients from all over the world and a vibrant restaurant scene displaced an earlier reputation for plain, bland, poor-quality food.

The traditional diet is based on bread, potatoes, dairy produce, and meat. Regional ideas related to food survive but are nuanced and sometimes difficult to detect. More obvious is a reliance on imported food, including many tropical crops and fruit and vegetables. Migrant communities, cheap foreign vacations, media interest in food, and supermarkets' marketing strategies have influenced and altered eating habits significantly. Personal taste is important in food choice; ideas relating to health or to ethics about production systems and animal welfare are influential among some groups. Religion has a weak influence, except among minorities, for instance, those from religious backgrounds such as Hinduism or Islam.

Economics are important. Money spent on food as a proportion of income, and in real terms, has fallen over the past 50 years. It has also declined as a proportion of household expenditure. Food and drink accounted for about 25 percent of consumers' total spending in 1976 but in 2001–2002 was down to about 16 percent.

Fish and chips, a classic dish in Great Britain. (Shutterstock)

🍽 Food Culture Snapshot

John and Kate Smith live in an outer suburb of London. John works in information technology for the local council and walks to work; Kate commutes into central London. Her journey takes an hour each way, and she sometimes works late, until 7:30 P.M. Neither was born in London. Like many of their friends, they have little time for shopping and food preparation and rely on the supermarket, take-out food, and eating out. Their weekly one-stop shopping trip includes bread, milk, tea, coffee, pasta, rice, breakfast cereal, fruit juice, yogurt, biscuits (cookies), cheese, margarine, and meat or fish, usually in portions—steaks, chops, chicken pieces, salmon steaks. Vegetables include peppers, tomatoes, onions, carrots, frozen peas, and prewashed salad in bags; they stock the fruit bowl with bananas, apples, and oranges or buy whatever soft fruit (strawberries, raspberries, blueberries) is on special offer. Pre-prepared meals, chilled or deep-frozen, also go into the basket.

On working days Kate rises at about 6:30 A.M. and leaves the house an hour later. John eats cereal or toast and drinks tea at home; Kate buys a pastry and a cappuccino at the station and sees this as a reward for early starts and long days. She packs a lunch; it might be sandwiches filled with cheese and chutney or cold roast chicken, or a salad based on pasta or rice from the previous evening. John eats a subsidized lunch in the work cafeteria. He tries to make a healthy choice from the salad bar but often ends up with chips (French fries) on his plate.

On weekday evenings, they eat dinner when Kate returns. They tried not to rely on expensive pre-prepared meals, but new or exotic-sounding dishes in the supermarket freezer are tempting. Otherwise, they favor pasta or rice dishes, quick-to-prepare heat-and-serve pizzas, or meat such as chicken portions baked in a ready-made curry sauce. When Kate works late, she often collects a take-out meal from a nearby Indian or Chinese restaurant on her way home, and they consume it with a bottle of wine while watching a cookery program on television. They rarely eat dessert or pudding during the week, except ice cream, fruit, or yogurt, although both are fond of biscuits and chocolate. On weekends they look through their collection of cookbooks and shop for fresh ingredients for more ambitious fish or meat dishes, or they make a Sunday roast of beef, lamb, or chicken, followed by apple crumble or a chocolate cake, or eat out at a favorite pub.

They would like to cook more and are conscious that their diet is reliant on processed food and tends to be high in fat and salt, but long working hours seem to leave little time and energy for this or for local shopping. There are few of these local shops left, although a street market still thrives about a mile away. This reflects a recent influx of migrants from sub-Saharan Africa, and sometimes they look at the stalls and wonder how to cook cassava.

Major Foodstuffs

Diversity is the only word to describe contemporary British food. The most obvious influence is multiculturalism, and cuisines from all over the world are raided for ingredients and techniques. The growth of vegetarianism, foreign travel, and the work of chefs and writers inspired by other cultures have influenced choices, as have changes in retailing and an intense media interest in food. The long-standing reliance on wheat, potatoes, meat (especially beef), and dairy produce was evident well into the 1970s, and these are still important, but their proportions in the diet have fallen, while intakes of poultry, rice, and pasta have risen.

Flour always means white wheat flour, unless otherwise stipulated, and products made from it are important sources of carbohydrates. It is used in bread, cakes, pastry, biscuits, sauces (for thickening), and many other items. Bread means white wheat bread, the popular choice, in the form of soft, oblong, thin-crusted loaves, sold presliced and wrapped. As toast or sandwiches, together with related products—rolls, buns, teacakes—it is the basis for snacks and light meals. Other important items are scones, crumpets or pikelets, and muffins (all types of griddle breads, i.e., what are called English muffins in the United States).

Breads made using continental European and eastern recipes are popular: croissants, focaccia, ciabatta, pita, nan (a flat, tear-shaped leavened bread), and chapati (thin, circular, unleavened bread); pizza is also common. Rich fruitcake made with flour, butter, eggs, sugar, and dried fruit, covered with marzipan and icing, is a celebration food. Cakes and pastry are treats and the basis for some puddings (desserts). Many types of sweet biscuits are made commercially and at home and are eaten with tea or coffee.

Oats are used in traditional baking and for breakfast porridge. Barley is important in brewing beer and making whiskey. Maize is little used, although its derivatives have numerous applications in the food industry. Other important cereal products are breakfast cereals, pasta, and rice; quickly prepared, they fit in with a perceived time shortage in British life and with growing tastes for Italian and Southeast Asian food.

Pulses are most popular as canned baked beans, usually eaten on toast. Dried peas and beans are used in soups, and interest in vegetarian and ethnic foods has stimulated interest in dishes such as dal, a staple of Indian cuisines, and hummus. Soybeans are less popular, although tofu is used to a limited extent.

For centuries meat has been eaten by all who could afford it, and nutritional theories about the importance of it as a protein source enhanced its status. Attitudes are also influenced by price, farming methods, and perceptions of health risks. Beef, lamb, and pork provided the basis for most main meals in the mid-20th century; poultry and game were luxuries. Chicken is now inexpensive and the basis of many routine meals, and beef and lamb have become more costly.

Roast beef is a dish for Sunday dinners; steaks are also, as a treat. Beef goes into stews, pies, burgers, and sauces for pasta, but veal is little used. Lamb or mutton (from older sheep) is also used as roasts, chops, or steaks, or in stews and in dishes inspired by French, Middle Eastern, or Indian cookery. Fresh pork is used for roasts or is grilled or fried as chops or steaks. Pork products include pies that are prepared with pastry made using lard melted into hot water and mixed with flour, filled with chopped pork and jellied stock. Fresh sausages are made from lean and fat pork, seasonings, and rusk. Salted, the meat becomes bacon and ham, the former essential for a traditional British breakfast and in sandwiches eaten as snacks or quick meals.

Chicken is cheap and ubiquitous. It is roasted, baked with a bought or homemade sauce, or made into stews, curries, or stir-fries. It is especially popular in curries developed by Indian restaurants, and one of these, chicken tikka masala, is quoted as the nation's favorite dish. Thai dishes, especially green chicken curry, are popular, too. Convenience foods, from supermarket versions of curries to heat-and-serve nuggets, use chicken as a base, and cold cooked chicken is used in salads and sandwiches. Turkey is mostly served roasted at Christmas but is also made into convenience products for a year-round market. Guinea fowl, quail, and duck are available, but consumption is relatively small, and goose is restricted to Christmas.

Game, once a high-status food, is widely available and compares well in price with farmed meat. Venison, hares, rabbits, pheasants, partridges, grouse, and several other bird species are all available in season. Offal (internal organs) from all meat animals is eaten but has declined in popularity over recent years. Beef, lamb, and chicken are used in curries, *kofta* (meatballs), and kebabs by ethnic minorities, especially Muslims from the Indian Subcontinent. Versions of these, and of Chinese-influenced stir-fries, have been adopted by the wider population.

Fish, another source of protein, has become less important. Cod, haddock, and herring, once important, are all overfished, and salmon, much farmed off northern Britain, is now relatively inexpensive and used in many routine meals with different sauces and flavors. The taste for smoked fish like kippers has declined, but smoked salmon, formerly a luxury, is easily available. Shellfish are popular but vary widely in price, with crabs, prawns, and mussels being relatively cheap, and lobsters and oysters expensive. Tastes generally have moved toward convenience. Fish products such as frozen fish fingers or fish cakes are popular. Commonly used canned fish types include salmon, tuna, sardines, pilchards, and anchovies.

Eggs cooked in various ways are a component of a full breakfast and the basis for light meals. They are essential ingredients in baked goods, puddings, and other dishes, as bindings, batters, food coatings, and pastry glazes.

Milk (mostly cow milk) and milk products are important, though changes in agriculture induced by European Union policies have increased interest in sheep and goat milks and their products. Liquid milk is available as whole milk (about 3.5% fat), semiskimmed, and virtually fat free, although consumption of it is declining. It is used as a drink, poured over breakfast cereal, and much used in cooking for sauces and custards.

Cream of various thicknesses is used in or to accompany many desserts and in cooking. Clotted cream is very thick and rich, a traditional product of southwestern England. Yogurt was virtually unknown until the 1960s but is now widely consumed, as are various dairy desserts such as ice cream, mousses, and *fromage frais* (a cultured semiliquid dairy product not unlike yogurt).

Cheese is eaten alone or as an ingredient. Cheddar is most important. Much cheese, especially the "territorials" (nine traditional recipes for hard cheese), is made in creameries (factories). Changes in the dairy industry led to the growth of artisan cheese making, and hundreds of recently developed cheeses, including sheep- or goat-milk ones, are now produced. Cheese is also imported, both from former colonies and from continental Europe.

Fats and oils include butter and margarine, spread on bread and used for frying and as ingredients, especially in baking. Choice is dictated by price, flavor, and perceptions of healthiness. Other solid fats include lard for frying and pastry, drippings (rendered beef fat, for frying), and suet in pastry and puddings, but these are losing importance and vegetable oils have gained ground. Olive, corn, sunflower, soy, and rapeseed (canola) oils are all used for frying and in dressings.

Vegetables are recognized as providers of vitamins and minerals but received little attention in traditional British cookery. Potatoes are most important, cooked in many different ways and popular as products such as crisps (potato chips). They are most important as a source of carbohydrates but are often eaten in large enough quantities to contribute useful amounts of vitamin C to the diet.

Green vegetables, mostly belonging to the cabbage family, are important. Beans and peas, whether homegrown, flown in from warmer countries, or frozen, are also popular, as is asparagus. Onions, celery, and garlic are important for flavoring. Carrots, turnips, and parsnips are winter staples, often added to soups or stews or used as accompaniments.

Mushrooms are usually cultivated, although an interest in wild ones has developed recently. Fresh salad leaves and herbs of many kinds are used, including the traditional English specialty of watercress. A taste for green cilantro is recent, stimulated by the taste for Indian and Thai food. Tomatoes and vegetables that were once highly seasonal or exotic, such as peppers, eggplant, zucchini, and squash, are readily available. Supermarkets have helped to develop the market for exotic vegetables. Some vegetables, especially onions and beets, are pickled in vinegar, and others are made into chutneys (spiced sweet-sour relishes). Tomato products are important in sauces and flavorings.

Fruit is consumed raw, cooked, and as juices or is made into sweet puddings, preserves, and jams. Apples are a quintessential British fruit. There are many varieties, but in practice only a few commercially successful ones grown in southern England or abroad reach the market. The best known is Cox's Orange Pippin. Some are grown specially for cooking; these varieties, such as Bramleys, are acidic and used in sweet dishes such as pies and crumbles. Apples are also pressed for juice, and special varieties are grown for cider, which is always a fermented drink.

Pears are also grown for both eating and cooking. Many are imported, as are most species of stone fruit, though some plums and cherries are grown in southern England. Damsons (a small, acidic, juicy plum) grow well over much of the country but reach the market in relatively small quantities. Peaches, nectarines, and apricots are imported from continental Europe and further away.

Strawberries and raspberries are popular, both homegrown and imported. They are eaten with cream for dessert and are used for filling cakes and to make jams. Red and black currants are also used in desserts and jams. Gooseberries (*Ribes grossularia*) grow easily throughout Britain and are cooked for puddings. Pink forced rhubarb is a delicacy available only in the late winter and early spring.

Citrus species (oranges, lemons, limes, and grapefruit) are vital and have been imported fresh or preserved for centuries. Most are consumed raw, as fresh fruit or juice, or are used in desserts and some savory dishes. Lemons are especially important in flavoring sweet dishes such as lemon meringue pie, lemon curd, syllabub, mousses, and ice creams. Seville (bitter) oranges are grown in southern Europe for the British market and make orange marmalade essential for breakfast.

Other imported fruits include grapes, figs, melons, dates, bananas, pineapples, mangoes, papayas, kiwi fruit, avocados, and other tropical species such as lychees, some of which have a limited market among ethnic minorities. Fruit-based preserves are widely used, both alone and as flavorings.

Baking includes dried fruit: Sultanas, raisins, currants, prunes, dates, and candied orange, lemon, and citron peel are all essential for fruitcakes, traditional enriched breads, plum puddings, and mince pies. Nuts—hazelnuts, almonds, walnuts, Brazil nuts, pistachios, and pine nuts—are also essential. Almonds are the most important and are the basis for marzipan, which is used for decorating fruitcakes. Coconut is another popular flavoring.

Sugar is the principal sweetener. Cane sugar is imported from tropical countries; beet sugar is produced within the European Union. Its use in hot drinks, as a preservative for jams, and a bakery ingredient has declined, but soft drinks, processed food, and confectionery keep the intake relatively high. Corn syrup and other sweeteners are used in industry. Black treacle and golden syrup give characteristic flavors and textures to some baked goods. Honey is mostly used as a spread on bread and toast.

Vinegar is an essential souring agent and pickling liquid. Malt vinegar (made from malted barley), with a characteristic flavor and brown color, is used to pickle vegetables and eggs as well as in chutneys, and it is sprinkled over chips, fried fish, and other foods. Wine or cider vinegar is used for salad dressings and dishes in which a gentler flavor is required.

Spices of many types are widely used. In traditional cookery they are most important in sweet foods. Cinnamon, nutmeg, allspice, and cloves are used in baking. Vanilla is used for flavoring sugar, custards, and ice creams, and ginger is used in biscuits and gingerbreads. Pepper is ubiquitous in sauces and stews, and a mixture of black and white peppercorns, mustard seeds, and whole dried chilies flavors pickling vinegar. Allspice and pepper occur in mixtures for salting meat. A little chili powder and mustard are often added to cheese dishes. "English" mustard is a fine, pungent yellow flour, mixed to a smooth paste with water to accompany cold ham and beef; milder coarse-grain mustards and French mustards are popular as well.

Curry powders, originally arriving with the East India Company, have been a part of British food culture for over 200 years. Recent immigration from India and Southeast Asia has brought new ideas about spice mixtures. Sauces and pastes, bottled or chilled, are sold as convenience products for use with meat, vegetables, and rice or noodles. Varieties include tikka or tandoori pastes and *rogan josh,* derived from Indian traditions, and Thai green curry paste. Chinese mixtures such as sweet and sour sauces and Italian-type cook-in sauces based on tomatoes, cheese, or pesto are also common.

Another British tradition is the use of bottled sauces such as Worcestershire sauce and mushroom ketchup, used for savory dishes, and brown sauces such as HP, which is thick, sweet-sour, and spicy and is used as a table condiment, as is tomato ketchup. Commercially produced chutneys and pickles, soy sauce, and mixes for making gravy, stuffing, custards and other desserts, cakes, and breads are all to be found.

Hot drinks include tea, closely identified with British food culture. It is drunk with food, after meals, and any time in-between. Most is black tea of Indian origin, purchased as teabags. Coffee, mostly instant, is equally important. Chocolate-based drinks are also common, although consumed with less frequency, and chocolate confectionery (often very sweet and low in cocoa solids) is ubiquitous. Sugar confectionery is also widely consumed.

Alcoholic drinks are widely purchased, ranging from canned lager-type beers to artisan-produced real ales, including bitter, porters, and dark beers. Wine is mostly imported, though a small amount is produced in the United Kingdom. Of spirits, whiskey (closely associated with Scottish and Irish cultures) and gin (frequently consumed as an aperitif with tonic water) are perhaps the most typically British. Alcoholic drinks are also used in cookery, as liquids or flavoring agents. Bottled mineral waters and soft drinks, both as cordials for dilution and as carbonated products, are also widely consumed. Neither drinks nor confectionery are seen as food in the sense that meat, bread, and potatoes are, but, with the exception of mineral water, they contribute energy, and sometimes other nutrients, to the diet.

Cooking

Domestic cookery was always considered to be women's work, and it is still largely a female

A traditional British pub in Cornwall. (Shutterstock)

responsibility to maintain basic stocks of food and put meals on the table at the expected time. However, men are more willing to cook than formerly, particularly for special occasions, and restaurant chefs are often men.

In practice, much cooking is now actually heating of purchased prepackaged meals. These have been developed by an innovative and powerful food-retailing sector exploiting a desire for convenience, long working days, a rise in car ownership, and a tendency to dislike or feel inadequate about cooking as a task. Ethnic minorities tend to have more obviously gendered and traditional food cultures and to adhere more to their communities' food traditions.

Despite this, kitchens are important rooms, often expensively fitted and equipped. Gas or electric cookers are usual, but ranges such as Agas have a following. Microwave ovens are common, usually supplementing conventional ones. Perishables are generally stored in a fridge. Small appliances always include a kettle, usually electric, for heating water for tea and other drinks, and a toaster or grill for bread. Ownership of cake mixers, bread makers, slow cookers, pressure cookers, espresso machines, spice grinders, rice cookers, food processors, juicers, and liquidizers depends on individual means and interests. Their presence does not always mean that they are used. Meals are often eaten in the kitchen, or in front of the television.

Basic kitchen utensils are similar to those from much of the Western world: pots, pans, casseroles, and roasting pans of various sizes and shapes. A traditional emphasis on baking means that most kitchens have bowls and pans for mixing and shaping cakes, pies, and tarts, as well as a wooden rolling pin for pastry. Scales are routinely used for measuring. Metric measurements are officially used, but imperial ones of pounds, ounces, and pints (20 fluid ounces) are still quoted. Nonindigenous communities such as the Chinese and groups from the Indian Subcontinent have brought their own utensils, and some of these are found in the wider British domestic sphere; the wok is probably the most widespread.

Recipes are as likely to come from television chefs, magazines, newspapers, or promotional leaflets as from previous generations. Quick and easy preparation is favored. Many basic raw ingredients can be bought in a semiprepared state, for instance, peeled potatoes vacuum-packed in plastic, ready-washed salad leaves, or trimmed and ready-cut beans or carrots, all reducing the time taken to cook a meal but not the expense.

Roasting is always the first choice for prime cuts of meat, such as beef sirloin, a leg of lamb or pork, and birds such as chicken or turkey. This usually takes place in an enclosed oven and is, more correctly, baking, but it is usually called roasting. Gravy, based on the sediment left by the meat in the roasting pan, often augmented by a packaged mix containing thickeners and flavorings, is an important part of a roast meal. The remains of a roast are often expected to provide one or two subsequent meals, eaten cold or reheated in various ways with or without sauces.

A perceived shortage of time means that steaks and chops, or convenience foods such as sausages, bacon, or burgers, are popular, grilled or fried. These methods are also used with fish. Frying is used for cooking eggs, as well as vegetables such as tomatoes, mushrooms, and potatoes, and also for reheating leftovers. Beef, pork, and chicken are now used extensively in stir-frying, and barbecues have become increasingly popular for cooking in summer.

Boiling is a common method for cooking vegetables. Braising or pot roasting is sometimes used for large pieces of meat. Poaching—cooking gently in water, milk, or wine—is often used for fish, with the cooking liquid being used in a sauce (fish pie is usually this type of recipe, topped with mashed potatoes). Meat is often cooked in casseroles and stews, usually flavored with onions, herbs, and sometimes other vegetables. More complex methods and seasonings derived from southern European or Indian cookery, or marinades or sauces, either home-prepared or purchased, are used by more ambitious cooks. Fish and vegetables are also cooked this way, as are beans for vegetarian dishes.

Baking is a traditional culinary strength. Until the 1970s, the making of bread and yeast products varied across the country as to whether this was carried out at home or by a professional baker. The further one was from the southeast and metropolitan influence, the more likely this was to be practiced at home, and the more varied the products, with numerous regional types of bread rolls and buns. Soda bread, leavened with baking powder, is regarded as an Irish specialty, and *girdle* (griddle) baking as characteristic of Wales, Scotland, and the northernmost part of England.

Cakes and other products raised with baking powder were frequently made at home and still are, though in smaller quantities. There are numerous recipes for fruitcakes, sponge cakes, tea breads (plain cakes of the banana-loaf or date-and-walnut type), scones, gingerbreads, and biscuits, all enormously popular. They were eaten as snacks, offered to guests, and served for evening teas; now, they are more likely to be occasional treats or are made when guests are expected.

Another branch of sweet cookery in which the British have a long interest is making puddings or desserts. Pudding can refer to any sweet item eaten at the close of a meal, including fruit or ice cream, but it also denotes a cooked dish, often some combination of fruit with a sweetened cereal mixture. Typical examples are crumbles (apples, rhubarb, gooseberries, or any other fruit with a topping of flour, butter or margarine, and sugar); fruit baked under a cake or gingerbread mixture; concoctions of fruit, custard, and cream; or suet puddings, now best known as Christmas plum pudding, but also including sweetened mixtures of suet, flour, and fresh fruit, spices, or jam. Pastry is used for both sweet and savory dishes, mostly pies of fruit or meat. A basic short type is often made at home, but puff pastry is usually purchased ready-made.

Home preserving has been rendered less important by the year-round availability of frozen or imported fresh fruit but was another traditional skill, and many people still make small amounts of sweet fruit preserves. Orange marmalade is perhaps the most characteristically British of these items.

Typical Meals

Food is organized into several named meals. Breakfast begins the day; lunch is always a midday meal,

although older people and those from provincial and rural backgrounds sometimes refer to this as dinner. This word implies the main meal of the day, once routinely taken at midday but now much more likely to be an evening meal. Those who eat dinner at midday call their evening meal tea—not to be confused with afternoon tea, which is essentially a snack between lunch and a midevening dinner.

Breakfast eaten at home on a working day is usually a snack of fruit juice, coffee or tea, and breakfast cereal with milk or yogurt, or toast with butter or margarine and jam or marmalade. On weekends or vacations, especially if staying in a hotel, breakfast is often a cooked meal. Fried bacon and eggs are most important in this; sausages, black pudding (blood sausage), fried bread or potatoes, mushrooms, tomatoes, and baked beans are added in any combination, and toast and marmalade are expected as well. Alternative cooked breakfasts include eggs in various forms and fish such as kippers or kedgeree (a mixture of smoked fish, rice, and fried onions, derived from Indian *kichri,* a mixture of rice and lentils).

Lunch depends entirely on individual means, tastes, and schedules. Sandwiches are probably most common; light meals of salad, soup, or a pastry-based snack are also common choices, but in practice the meal can range from a chocolate bar and a drink to an elaborate meal of several courses. Dinner is the largest meal. British food culture contains

A typical breakfast in England including blood pudding, baked beans, bacon, eggs, and sausage. (Shutterstock)

the notion of a "proper meal" or a "cooked dinner." At its most basic, this is meat, potatoes, and vegetables. A sweet pudding often, but not invariably, follows. The savory course could stand as a meal on its own but not the pudding.

The idea of a proper dinner is most developed in the "roast"—roast meat, gravy, roast potatoes, and boiled green vegetables, closely associated with Sundays, although less of a ritual than it once was. The format is relatively stable. Accompaniments are Yorkshire pudding, horseradish sauce, and mustard for beef; mint sauce for lamb; and applesauce and sage and onion stuffing for pork, which is cooked to ensure the skin makes crackling. Pudding for Sunday dinner is often trifle, a layered dish of wine-soaked sponge cake, fruit preserves, custard, and cream.

Roast Beef and Yorkshire Pudding

About 5 lb beef sirloin or rib, preferably from a traditional breed fed on grass

Salt, pepper, and a little dry mustard powder mixed with about 1 tbsp flour

For the Pudding

4 oz (1 scant cup) all-purpose flour

Pinch of salt

2 eggs

5 fl oz milk and 5 fl oz water, mixed

Dust the fat of the meat with the flour mixture. Put the joint in a roasting pan and start in a very hot oven (475°F), for about 20 minutes. Turn the temperature down to 375°F, and cook for 15 minutes per pound (rare), plus 15 extra minutes (for medium-rare), plus 30 minutes extra (for well-done). Remove the meat from the oven, and put it on a heated plate in a warm place. Leave to rest for 30 minutes before carving.

While the meat cooks, put the flour for the pudding in a bowl, and add a pinch of salt. Break in the eggs, and stir well. Add the milk and water slowly, stirring well. The batter should be the consistency of light cream. When the meat comes out of the oven, take a roasting pan and add about a tablespoonful of drippings from the meat. Heat it in the oven for a few minutes at 450°F. Remove the pan from the oven, and pour in the batter (wear oven gloves, as the fat may spit). Return to the oven, and bake for 30–40 minutes, until golden and rumpled. Cut into squares for serving.

Make the gravy in the pan the meat was cooked in. Pour all the fat and juices into a small bowl. Spoon off the fat, and reserve the juices. Add about a tablespoon of fat back to the pan, and stir in a tablespoon of flour. Stir over gentle heat until the mixture is lightly browned. Then blend in the juices from cooking the meat and some stock (or water from cooking vegetables or a gravy mix) to make a thin sauce. Cook gently for a few minutes, adjust the seasoning, and serve with the beef and Yorkshire pudding.

Choices for weekday meals include meat pies, sausages, chops or steaks, meat stews, and fish, egg, or cheese dishes. Salads are unusual as main meals. Choices for dinner now also include many nontraditional foods: pasta or rice dishes, stir-fries, or curry for cooking meat. These have sometimes been adapted to the idea that the meat and carbohydrates are most important, with vegetables in third place. Purchased fish and chips, or hot food from a take-out place (usually relating to an ethnic minority community), is often chosen as a minor treat or when time is short.

Afternoon tea, like cooked breakfast, now survives mostly in hotels, but snacks consisting of drinks, especially coffee or tea, or soft drinks, plus biscuits, crisps, confectionery, or fruit are taken at almost any time of day.

Eating Out

In the 1980s, the nation's favorite meal out was prawn cocktail, steak, and chips followed by Black Forest gâteau; it is now claimed to be curry, especially chicken tikka masala, a dish developed from Indian tandoori cooking under the influence of British tastes, but these clichés disguise the extraordinary complexity, dynamism, and eclectic nature of eating out in contemporary Britain.

A table set with tea and sweets for a classic British afternoon tea. (Dreamstime)

London has an especially vibrant and interesting eating-out culture, with numerous excellent restaurants, cafés, and pubs. The capital sets the fashions for Britain generally, but recently provincial restaurants have shown more interest in reflecting their locality. The other side of this picture is one of a nation that can be sold the latest fad and that consumes fast food in enormous quantities.

Places to eat out take many forms: pubs, hotels, sandwich bars, coffee bars, tea shops, carveries (where they carve large roasts buffet style), pizzerias, kebab houses, snack bars, fast-food outlets, motorway service stations, and restaurants from basic to Michelin starred, plus a substantial noncommercial sector providing food in institutions. Eating out is seen on one level as a pleasurable, social activity. Drinking, on the other hand, is often seen as a pastime that does not necessarily involve food.

Inevitably, income plays a part in choice. Lower-income groups tend to spend more on takeout than other groups, but eating out has accounted for a steadily increasing percentage of household expenditures over the last 50 years. Most money is spent on eating out in southeastern England, where both wealth and premium-priced restaurants are concentrated.

Restaurants identify themselves in terms of cuisine (French, Italian, Indian, Mediterranean, modern British), type of food (pizzeria, kebab house, steakhouse), or mode of operation (fast-food restaurant, carvery). They can be independent or part of a large chain. Being a chef is now seen as a route to celebrity and a lucrative media career. The food in the best restaurants is excellent in quality and expensive; wine is also expensive. Most restaurants offer vegetarian options on their menus.

Ethnic restaurants began to spread during the 1950s, as Chinese and Italians, followed by Indians (mostly Punjabis) and Greek or Turkish immigrants, opened eating places. Most communities bigger than villages have restaurants serving Chinese, Indian, or Thai food. The success of these restaurants lies partly in the ability to adapt their cuisines to dishes that suit the British palate and notion of a proper meal, with large portions of meat in sauce and less emphasis on the smaller dishes that make up a meal in their native traditions.

Indian restaurant menus include kormas (mild and creamy), vindaloos (hot with chili), and tandooris (spiced meat cooked in a tandoor, a clay oven) as well as rice, Indian breads, *pakoras* (vegetable fritters), and samosas (deep-fried pastries). "Going for a curry" is an inexpensive night out with friends or a good way to round off an evening's drinking. Balti houses, developed in Birmingham, offer *baltis,* curry sauces containing onions, tomatoes, and sweet peppers and meat such as chicken, served in *karhais,* traditional cooking dishes shaped like small woks.

Bar meals in pubs have become an increasingly important element in eating out. Food provides additional profit and has made pubs, traditionally a masculine environment concerned with beer, more attractive to women. The flippant term *gastropub* indicates a place with the character of a pub that also offers good and imaginative food at reasonable prices. Menus include classics such as sausages and mash, steak pies, calf's liver and bacon, or fish and chips, as well as more exotic items. Some pubs specialize in Thai food.

Fish and chips (French fries) have been street food since the late 19th century. Usual options are cod or haddock fried in batter. Sprinkled with salt and vinegar and wrapped in paper, they are usually carried out, either consumed with the fingers while walking down the street or taken home. Mushy peas (dried peas cooked to a puree), curry sauce, chicken portions, sausages, squid (popularized by cheap vacations to the Mediterranean), pies, and, in Scotland, sausage-like puddings are usually available as well.

Special Occasions

The most important calendar festival is Christmas, on December 25. A typical Christmas Day menu is imposed by tradition. Usually a midday meal, it involves roast turkey with stuffing, gravy, bread sauce, sausages, rolled-up bacon rashers, roast and boiled potatoes, brussels sprouts, and other vegetables. A minority favor alternatives such as goose, game, or a large piece of beef. A steamed Christmas pudding made with suet, breadcrumbs or flour, dried fruit, eggs, and sugar follows. This is flambéed with brandy and contains a coin, which is lucky for the finder. The Scots have their own version, *clootie dumpling,* cooked by wrapping it in a *cloot* (cloth) and boiling.

Other Christmas foods include mince pies, small double-crusted pies filled with currants, raisins, sultanas, candied peel, sugar, spices, apples, and suet minced together, offered with coffee, sherry, or mulled wine at almost any gathering between late November and early January. New Year is important in Scotland; food plays a secondary role to drink, although shortbread (a rich shortcake) and black buns (raisins, currants, almonds, candied peel, and spices, wrapped in pastry) are midwinter specialties.

Other foods associated with the season are nuts, dried fruit, candied fruit, oranges, and sweets and chocolates generally. Certain cheeses are also important, especially Blue Stilton, which is sold in vast quantities at this time, as is Christmas cake, a rich fruitcake. Decorated with appropriate motifs, this is also important for other celebrations, such as Easter, weddings, christenings, and birthdays.

Rich Fruitcake

12 oz (2¾ c) flour

Pinch salt

1 tsp ground cinnamon

1 tsp mixed spice (similar to pumpkin pie spice)

10 oz butter

10 oz caster sugar (superfine sugar)

6 large eggs

2 tbsp brandy or rum

4 oz mixed candied peel, chopped

4 oz blanched almonds, chopped

1 lb currants

1 lb seedless raisins

8 oz sultanas

4 oz glacé cherries, halved

Line a cake pan about 8 inches in diameter with a double thickness of greased paper. Sieve flour, salt, and spices together. Put the butter and sugar in a large bowl, and beat until light and fluffy. Beat the eggs in separately, blending each well before adding the next. Stir in the dry ingredients and the spirit. Add a little milk if the mixture seems stiff. Turn into the prepared pan. Bake in a slow oven at 300°F for about 1½ hours, then reduce the heat to 275°F and bake for a further 4–5 hours. When fully cooked, the cake should be coming away from the sides of the pan a little, and a fine skewer inserted in the center will come out clean. Wrap and store in an airtight tin; the cake can be unwrapped and a little brandy sprinkled over it at intervals. Before eating, cover with a layer of marzipan or almond paste, and ice and decorate as desired.

Other calendar festivals include Burns Night dinners of haggis, neeps, and tatties (turnips and potatoes, boiled and mashed), washed down with whiskey, held around January 25 to celebrate the life of Scottish poet Robert Burns. Shrove Tuesday, immediately before Lent, is a time for pancakes. Easter is celebrated with hot cross buns (light, spiced, and yeast-leavened, marked with a cross) on Good Friday, and chocolate eggs and simnel cake, fruitcake with a layer of marzipan in the center, on Easter Sunday. Gingerbread and toffee are traditional autumn foods for the time around Halloween and November 5 in some parts of the country. Ethnic communities celebrate their own festivals, including Diwali, the Chinese New Year, and several other community-specific events.

Births, marriages, and deaths also have special foods. Weddings are the most visible. The cake (generally rich fruitcake, piled up in tiers) is important. Wedding breakfasts have no specific menu but are composed with the disparate tastes of different generations in mind; they are generally either of the roast dinner type or a cold collation of meats and salads, followed by creamy desserts.

Christenings are generally low key and vary widely, from drinking sessions for the father and his friends to a decorous tea party for family and older relatives. A funeral, too, is generally followed by a gathering involving eating and drinking. It is generally impossible to predict the number of guests, so an afternoon tea or finger buffet-type meal is usually provided.

Most families celebrate birthdays, especially for small children, with a birthday cake and candles appropriate to the birthday on top. Families celebrate other events as individual tastes and inherited customs dictate. Engagements, graduations, and anniversaries all provide an excuse for parties, but there are no traditional forms for these to follow.

Diet and Health

There are variations in diet according to region and income group—the Scots eat especially high levels of salt, sugar, and fat, while people in the southeast of England spend the most on fruit and vegetables. Low-income families tend to resist change

and avoid experiments with new foods. Substantial minorities observe special diets, based on religious (kosher, halal, Hindu) or ethical (vegetarian, vegan) requirements.

A lack of food is rare, as are diseases due to dietary deficiencies, although nutritionists express concern over intakes of certain micronutrients, particularly vitamin D and iron in some groups of the population. More problems are related to overnutrition including high intakes of fat, refined carbohydrates, and salt and the associated obesity, cardiovascular disease, diabetes, and hypertension. Levels of obesity (a body mass index of over 30) have increased significantly in the past three to four decades, especially among children and adolescents. Cardiovascular disease is a major cause of premature death in the United Kingdom, and there is evidence for a link to diet, as with the high incidence of type 2 diabetes. High alcohol intake among some groups is also a concern.

The official advice is to reduce the proportion of energy derived from fat and increase that from complex carbohydrates in the diet, and to increase intakes of vegetables and fruit. Encouraging higher consumption of these is an official priority, promoted in various ways, including provision of fruit in primary schools and a campaign called "Eat Five a Day" (five portions of fruit or vegetables).

Consciousness of food hygiene has become increasingly important, as more food is pre-prepared and held in a partially or fully cooked state; intensive farming and industrial processing have also given rise to concerns about pathogens ranging from salmonella in eggs to bovine spongiform encephalopathy (BSE, or mad cow disease) in beef. Responses have ranged from public health measures, such as tightening legislation relating to food safety, to individual choice in pursuit of organically grown food. Most food-borne illnesses are probably related to *E. coli* 0157, salmonella, *Listeria monocytogenes*, campylobacter, and *Clostridium perfringens*. Less quantifiable threats are BSE, pesticide residues, irradiation, and genetic modification, all recurrently the subject of intense debate and suspicion.

Relative perceptions of the risk to health from diet vary between health professionals, the media, and the public. Health professionals consider poor diet and food-borne bacteria or viruses as the highest risks. The media concentrate on "scares" and stories with sensational and sinister implications. The public, nervous of an industrialized food supply and cynical of advertising, tends to choose on the basis of personal likes and dislikes, fashion, and convenience.

Laura Mason

Further Reading

Food Standards Agency. http://www.foodstandards.gov.uk.

The Great British Kitchen. http://www.greatbritishkitchen.co.uk.

Historic Food. http://www.historicfood.com.

Lawrence, Felicity. *Not on the Label: What Really Goes into the Food on Your Plate.* London: Penguin Books, 2004.

Mason, Laura. *Food Culture in Great Britain.* Westport, CT: Greenwood Press, 2004.

Mason, Laura, and Catherine Brown. *Taste of Britain.* London: HarperCollins, 2007.

Oddy, Derek. *From Plain Fare to Fusion Food: British Diet from the 1890s to the 1990s.* Woodbridge, UK: Boydell Press, 2004.

Slater, Nigel. *Toast: The Story of a Boy's Hunger.* London: Harper Perennial, 2003.

Greece

Overview

Greece is located in the south of Europe and makes up the majority of the Balkan Peninsula. Its size is 50,949 square miles (131,957 square kilometers), and it falls within the Mediterranean climatic zone. Greece as a geographic region is characterized by 1,400 islands as well as the mainland. In addition, it is located at the meeting point of the continents of Europe, Asia, and Africa. Its neighboring countries are Italy to the west, Albania, Bulgaria, and the former Yugoslav Republic of Macedonia to the north, Turkey to the east, and Libya and Egypt to the south. Greece has an estimated population of 11,262,539, of whom approximately five million live in the capital city, Athens. The population is rather homogeneous, with 93 percent being Greek and only 7 percent of different ethnic and cultural backgrounds, mostly Albanian, Bulgarian, some African, and some Pakistani and Indian. As a nation, Greece is relatively new. Its present geographic form was established right after World War II in 1947. The current constitution was formed on June 11, 1975, under the presidency of Konstantinos Karamanlis, who was also head of state in 1981 when Greece entered the European Union.

Keeping in mind the geographic location of Greece, its long history, and its current state, one can argue that it is the place where Western cuisines and Eastern cuisines meet. In historical terms, the ancient Greeks were avid traders, which acquainted its people with new foodways and exotic ingredients. Historical accounts refer to the regions where one was able to find the best products. One example is by Archistratos, who gives a detailed description of the best place to find the top-quality *amia* (small tuna fish) and how to prepare it. He claimed that the best specimens were found around Byzantium and that it should be cooked as simply as possible. Greek cuisine was also influenced by Asia, especially after the conquests of Alexander the Great, who introduced to the Greeks new fruits and vegetables as well as spices from as far as India.

After the fall of the Roman Empire and its division into eastern and western parts, Greece was part of the Byzantine Empire, which encompassed much of the Middle East. This relationship brought together various cuisines and exotic ingredients in different parts of Greece. At the same time some islands of Greece were under the influence of the Venetians, who brought their own cultural and culinary traits. Finally, with the fall of the Byzantine Empire in 1452, the Ottoman Turks took over Greece for approximately 400 years, and they in turn introduced many culinary traditions. After the Greek revolution in 1821, Greece started to regain its autonomy, and in 1922 the creation of the state of Turkey brought to Greece thousands of ethnically Greek immigrants from Asia Minor who in turn brought with them their cultural and culinary traditions.

🍽 Food Culture Snapshot

Greek dietary habits are similar throughout the country. People usually start their day at around 7 to 7:30 A.M. with a cup of coffee, which is a crucial beverage in Greek culture. It can be cold or hot. Cold coffee is referred to as *frappe,* which is shaken instant Nescafé

Shaving gyro meat into a pita. (Shutterstock)

For Greeks, the first proper meal is at about 11 A.M. and includes a fresh *tiropita* (cheese pie), spanakopita (spinach pie), or *koulouri* (bagel), which they purchase from bakeries or various snack places on the street. These products, together with fresh orange juice, compose the first meal of the day. Lunch is served between 2 and 4 P.M. This is the time of day when everything closes in Greece. It is the first more important meal of the day, and it is highly valued. Lunch will usually include bread, salad, cheese, a main course, and some fruit at the end. Lunch being the first complete meal of the day, there is an effort to include all nutrients in it, from protein to carbohydrates and fat. In between lunch and dinner, people might enjoy another cup of coffee and some fruit to keep them going. Between 8 and 9:30 P.M. dinner is served. Dinner is the final meal in a Greek person's day. It is usually made up of small meze, which are small plates of various kinds of foodstuffs. These include bread, cheese (just like with lunch), light varieties of some spreads like *tirokafteri* (spicy cheese salad) or *tzatziki* (yogurt sauce with cucumber and garlic), maybe some small meat meze like *keftedakia* (meatballs) and *bekri meze* (pork chunks; literally translated as the "drunken snack"), and always some fruits and vegetables.

It is normal for routine shopping to take a long time. Shopping is done predominantly by women. While supermarkets are modern and designed to satisfy all consumer needs, Greeks prefer to divide their shopping among various stores. Supermarkets are used for dry staples such as pasta or flour, or for products that are very specific, such as cheese for sandwiches or ham. Shopping for fresh produce is done in specialized shops. For fresh fruits and vegetables people go to the *manaviko*, a shop that specializes in fruits and vegetables. For meat, they go to the *kreopolio* (meat shop), for fish to the *psaras* (fisherman) or the *psaradiko* (fish shop), and for bread to the *fourno* (bakery). The reason for this is not that the products found there are necessarily of better quality than those found in a good supermarket. Instead, sale of fresh products in Greece is very much based on personal relations. These shops are found locally in one's own neighborhood, and each neighborhood has its own manaviko, fourno, and so forth, or they are found in a concentrated block of similar shops,

and is never made from any other kind of coffee. Among younger generations cold variations of coffee may also include *fredo,* which is iced espresso, and *cappuccino fredo,* which is iced cappuccino. Hot coffee is mainly consumed in winter months and includes all the Western forms of coffee (cappuccino, instant coffee, filtered coffee, and so on) and also Turkish coffee. Greek people refer to Turkish coffee as Greek coffee, and they are very sensitive about that. Waiters will refuse to serve it if not ordered as Greek coffee. Whatever the name, Greek coffee is consumed frequently, and Greek people prefer to buy it fresh. Coffee for Greeks is not considered just a drink. It is thought to be part of a meal. It is perceived as highly nutritious (especially Greek coffee) although somewhat difficult on the stomach by itself. For this reason Greeks take their coffee with a cookie or a piece of cake.

in which case the entire neighborhood is named after the shops: *perasa apo ta psaradika gia na ertho* (To come I passed the neighborhood of fish shops).

Major Foodstuffs

Greeks have three basic ingredients that have throughout history been used in their cuisine: bread, wine, and olive oil. Since ancient times they were considered to be the essential elements of Greek cooking. The ancient Greek god Apollo had three daughters: Spermo (Grain), Elais (Olive), and Oeno (Wine). Even today among Orthodox Christians, who make up 98 percent of the population, it is believed that Jesus especially blessed *arton* (bread), *oinon* (wine), and *eleon* (olive oil). These three ingredients are the foundation for modern Greek cooking as well. Everyone buys them and uses them as is, or they add them to recipes. Olive oil especially is the essential ingredient for cooking. Greeks use oil to fry, add it to boiled dishes, and even baste meat or fish before roasting. It is used in practically every recipe, whether cooked or raw.

Bread is also an integral part of Greek cuisine. It is the companion to every food. Greeks often eat bread for breakfast with some cheese. Different varieties of bread are used, such as *xoriatiko* (bread from the village), *lefko* (white), *polisporo* (with different seeds), *mavro* (black), and so on. Greeks are very fond of dry bread as well. In this case fresh bread has been sliced up and put back in the oven to dry at low temperatures. This is a technique people used so they did not waste any bread that was leftover and going stale. Bakeries are always busy, and a good bakery can make a fortune just by selling good bread. Bread symbolizes life, and even prayers of the Orthodox Church use bread as a metaphor for life, especially in Holy Communion.

Proteins come from various sources in Greek cooking. People usually consume sheep or goat meat, but beef and pork are also widely used. Fish on the islands and anywhere near the sea is a principal protein source and may be prepared in various ways. The occupations of shepherd and fisherman are still very common in the country. People tend to look for and appreciate homegrown meat products, believing that since the animals run free in the lands, they must be cleaner and healthier. The same goes for fish. Local fishermen are very much trusted, and fish consumption is based on how fresh the fish is. In the majority of cases fishermen will not have every kind of fish but only what they can catch, and thus buyers adjust their purchase accordingly.

Meat has not always been the main protein source for Greeks. In the recent past, poverty was widespread across the country, and not everyone had the financial means to buy meat. Thus an essential element of Greek cuisine that contains the necessary nutrients is *ospria* (legumes—beans and peas). *Fasolia* (beans), *fakes* (lentils), fava beans, and other, similar legumes were known to Greeks from ancient times. Today, they exist in almost every household together with later arrivals such as snap peas, sweet peas, chickpeas, and so on. Even more recently a wide array of beans, such as the kidney bean, arrived from the Americas. They are prepared in various ways and are very popular during the fast of Lent and other times when consumption of meat is forbidden by the church.

Cheese is also found in every grocery store and supermarket. Greeks are enthusiastic consumers of cheese, and several varieties are native to Greek cuisine. Every location has its own unique type, but there are some varieties that are used across the country—from the well-known fresh sheep cheeses like feta, which are soaked in brine, to others such as *kefalotiri, graviera, anthotiros,* and *mizithra.* Cheese can also be used as part of a recipe like *saganaki* (fried breaded cheese). Every Greek refrigerator has a chunk of cheese in it, and it is a main part of all meals of the day.

Greeks pay special attention to the fruits and vegetables they consume. Shopping for fresh ingredients is seasonal and highly localized. It is very rare to see a Greek person buy nectarines, watermelons, or grapes in winter or oranges, apples, and mandarins in summer. This means that Greeks do not trust fruits and vegetables that come from abroad unless they do not exist in Greece. Vegetables are also bought only when in season. Tomatoes, for example, are not eaten in winter as often as in summer, nor cabbage in summer. Each region has its own special products that are highly valued in the rest of the country. Peaches from northern Greece and parts of Greek Macedonia are greatly appreciated, and the same applies to tomatoes from Crete and cherries from Aigio.

Herbs and spices are considered very important in Greek cuisine. Major flavorings include oregano, thyme, coriander, cumin, and rosemary. Some of these ingredients can be found growing in almost every uninhabited rocky space in the country since the climatic conditions and the soil are perfect for them. Other spices are used only in particular areas of Greece but are not common everywhere. Saffron, for example, is widely used in Kozani (northern Greece) and is most widely known in Greece as *krokos Kozanis,* which means the flower that comes from Kozani. Bay leaves, parsley, fennel, basil, and sage are also used widely for their special taste and aroma.

Last but not least are olives and olive oil. Olive trees are grown throughout Greece along with vineyards. Olives have been considered sacred and the essence of life since ancient times. The myth suggests that when it was time to name Athens, there was a battle between the goddess Athena and Poseidon. The one that would offer the most important present to the city would be the one to give it its name. First, Poseidon knocked the rock of Acropolis, and fresh water started to spring forth. Then it was Athena's turn, and she threw a seed that turned into an olive tree. Athenians thought of the olive tree as the most important gift since it symbolized wisdom and prosperity, and thus they named their city Athens. Olives and olive oil are still central to Greek cuisine, and Greeks use olive oil everywhere. It is highly appreciated for its nutritious and healthy properties. Different varieties of olives are grown around the country, but not all of them are used for olive oil. Some of them are just for eating, while others are cultivated only for making olive oil. There are many expressions in Greek that emphasize the importance of olive oil. Such expressions are used when people go to eat and suggest *pame na*

Men enjoy fine bread, wine, and a spread of olives, classic ingredients in Greek food. (Shutterstock)

fame gia na ladosi to anteraki mas (Let's go eat, so some oil will go to our intestines).

Cooking

Most cooking in Greece is done by women, and it involves a great deal of time and skill. It is very common for someone to hear conversations between people praising their mother's or grandmother's cooking. Cooking skills are considered as something to be very proud of. Kitchens in Greece are perceived as the areas where meals take place and women do their magic. Greek women are very proud of their kitchens and, most important, their cooking, even among those who work outside the home and consider themselves equal to men.

Kitchen appliances are modern and electric. Kitchen stoves are also electric since Greece has only recently started to import natural gas from Russia. In the recent past stoves used propane from very big, heavy, external cylinders. In addition, cooking was also done outside in the garden or the front yard, where a fire was made and pots or grills were put on it in order to prepare food.

Many different cooking techniques are used, and there is no distinctive way of cooking in Greece. Boiled, fried, oven-baked, and grilled food is prepared everywhere. Greeks are not fond of raw food, though. A raw or medium beef steak is not considered a food cooked at home in Greece. Possibly the only raw protein Greeks consume is sea urchin eggs or the red fish egg pastes called *taramas*.

Garlic and onion are essential in cooking as well. Tomatoes, although from the Americas, arrived via Italy in 1815, and they are now essential in Greek cooking. The combination of tomatoes and onions is referred to in Greek cooking as *stifado;* if tomatoes are the dominant taste in the sauce, then it is called *kokinisto* ("made red"). Other cooking techniques involve frying (*tiganito*) or baking in the oven (*psito*). All techniques use olive oil as a basis, and the seasoning changes according to the recipe. Preparation of food through salting and air-drying is also common in Greece. Usually dry salamis and sausages such as *salami aeros* or *pasturma* are air-dried. Salted preparations involve foodstuffs such as haddock (*bakaliaros*) and are referred to as *pastos* because of the technique used.

Kitchen utensils vary depending on the technique, but they are the same as in any other modern European kitchen. Frying pans (*tigani*), pots (*katsaroles*), and pans (*tapsi*) are the predominant kitchen tools. In addition, pressure cookers (*hitra taxititos*) are used to shorten the cooking time of products such as fresh beans or goat meat. However, Greeks use another pot that is not widely used in Europe, used only to cook Greek (Turkish) coffee. This is called *briki* and is a small pot that can hold 8.5 ounces (250 milliliters) of water. After water is put in the briki, it is placed on a hot fire to boil. Immediately after the water is put on the fire, coffee and sugar are added, and it is stirred well. Once the mixture starts to rise, the coffee is ready to be served. Because of this cooking technique Greeks ask people whether they should cook them a coffee rather than make them one.

Typical Meals

Greeks have two main meals, lunch and dinner, and two supplementary snacks in the late morning and early afternoon. The two main meals take place either in the kitchen, which is the most common eating place, or in the dining room. In addition, every house in Greece has small shot glasses for *raki* (alcohol made of distilled grape pomace left over from winemaking) or *tsipouro* (similar to grappa) and slightly taller and wider ouzo glasses. Ouzo is similar to raki but is flavored with aniseed and may be single or double distilled. Also, coffee glasses are found in every household for serving Greek coffee. These glasses are somewhere between a mug and an espresso cup.

There are a few typical meals in Greece. This is due to different climatic conditions, which affect the natural resources and thus culinary practices. Furthermore, migration, especially from Asia Minor and Pontus, together with the dominance of many different empires in the country (Roman, Venetian, Byzantine, and Turkish), has affected what Greek people eat in various locales. In northern Greece and Greek Macedonia, for example, there is an extensive use of pies. The pastry used is phyllo pastry, and the pies can be filled with anything from meat, to cheese, to vegetables and several different kinds of wild green leaves. In addition, food in this part of the country is much spicier than in the rest of Greece. In Epirus, in contrast, people eat more meat of all kinds. The climatic conditions there favor rearing of cattle, as well as pigs, lambs, and sheep. Thus, meat is the main ingredient in almost every dish. In the Peloponnese and Crete consumption of vegetables and wild herbs is most common. People use products that come from the earth since the ground is very fertile. There is widespread production of olives and grapes; thus, meals based on olive oil and vegetables are available. With the exception of Crete all the people who live on the islands of Greece eat fish most often. Due to their surroundings and the strong winds in the Aegean and Ionian Sea the soil is not very fertile. Thus, the sea itself provides much of the necessary foodstuff for people on the islands to survive.

Recipes typical of this cuisine are common everywhere, though it varies from place to place. Fish is consumed everywhere, and so are vegetables. One such example of a typical Greek meal that is consumed all around the country is *gemista* (stuffed vegetables). One can find it in households as well as restaurants and tavernas. The word *gemista* in Greek means "stuffed," and it refers to tomatoes, zucchini, eggplant, and even occasionally potatoes that are stuffed with a mixture of rice, herbs, and vegetables.

Gemista (Stuffed Vegetables)

4 medium-sized ripe tomatoes

2 large zucchini

2 medium eggplants

1 medium green pepper

1 onion

1 carrot

3 tbsp olive oil

1½ tsp oregano

Salt and pepper

½ c parsley

1 tsp celery

1 c basmati rice

1 tsp vinegar

Take the tomatoes, zucchini, eggplants, and green pepper, and cut the tops off so you have access to the inside, but do not throw the tops away. Take a soup spoon and scoop out the inside of each vegetable carefully, making the walls as thin as possible without cutting through to the outside. Discard only the ribs and seeds of the pepper, but keep everything else. For the zucchini, slice off a thin top lengthways and scoop out the insides like a canoe. Scoop out the inside of the vegetables into a bowl. Arrange the hollowed vegetable shells in an ovenproof pan or a baking dish.

Chop or thinly slice the onion and the carrot, and add the vegetables' insides with olive oil, oregano, salt, and pepper. Chop the parsley and celery, and add. Finally, add the rice and vinegar, and stir well. Be careful not to use more rice than the amount listed; otherwise, when the rice starts to cook, the vegetables will split and the stuffing will go everywhere. Once the mixture is well stirred, use the spoon to stuff the vegetables. Fill the vegetables only ¾ full so the rice has enough space to expand. Cover the vegetables with their tops, and add some olive oil on the top. Once they are ready, put them in a preheated oven at 350°F for an hour and a half.

Optional: For a better visual effect you can add some breadcrumbs on top of the vegetables to make a tasty crust.

Another typical and highly characteristic meal consumed in Greece is an omelet called *sfougato*. This literally translates as something that becomes spongelike: Its texture and appearance when ready make it look like a big yellow sponge.

Sfougato (Omelet)

1 large potato

1 onion

4 eggs

Oregano, salt, and pepper

½ c milk

1 c salty cheese (white or yellow) with rind trimmed, diced

1 tomato

Cut the potato in pieces as for French fries or in round slices, and fry them in oil. Just before they are crispy take them out and drain them on a plate covered with a paper towel or kitchen towel. Sauté the onion, and add the potatoes. Then take the eggs, oregano, salt, pepper, and milk, and mix them in a bowl all together. Add this to the onions and potatoes, and cook over very low heat. Make sure the mixture has solidified in the frying pan and then turn it so it gets crispy on the other side. Add the cheese and some slices of tomato. Cook on low heat for another 10–15 minutes, and serve on a large platter.

In general, there are many dishes that could be argued to have great importance in Greek cuisine. Dishes such as moussaka and *pastitsio* (macaroni casserole) are very popular. However, products such as okra (*bamies*) are very widely used. There are also several types of foods that combine vegetables or legumes with meat, such as beef cooked with green beans in tomato sauce in a casserole or lamb cooked with artichokes in egg and lemon sauce.

Sweets are also important in Greek culinary culture. One such sweet is baklava. Although there is an argument whether it comes from Greece or Turkey, Greek people love it. Baklava is a sweet made of several different layers of phyllo pastry and nuts

Stuffed vegetables in the Greek style filled with meat and rice and served with French-fried potato chips. (Paul Cowan | Dreamstime.com)

of different kinds (commonly walnuts, almonds, and pine nuts) and the addition of syrup. A very similar sweet but with different pastry is *kadaifi*. The main difference between baklavas and kadaifi is that in the latter the dough is shredded phyllo.

Other syrup-based sweets are also predominant in Greece, such as *ravani* (semolina cake), but as a general rule all these sweets fall under the category of *syropiasta* due to the syrup that adds the sweetness. Another popular sweet in Greece is *glika tou koutaliou* ("sweets of the spoon"). The name derives from the serving size, since they are so sweet that they are served in small amounts. These sweets are usually ripe fruits and vegetables boiled in water and then cooked again with sugar syrup. Most famous are sweet figs, grapes, oranges, carrots, and young eggplants.

There are non–syrup-based sweets in Greece also. Greeks enjoy *koulourakia* with their coffee. These are sweet small cookies of different shapes made from a mixture of flour and water, sugar, and nuts. They are fast and easy to make. Other types of sweets come in different seasons. For example, *kourampiedes* and *melomakarona* are types of sweets mainly cooked for the Christmas holidays. Kourampiedes are sweet cookies with almonds covered with powdered sugar. Melomakarona are honey and spice cookies with the addition of semolina, cinnamon, and orange juice, which gives them a special soft texture.

Another very popular Greek sweet is *mpogatsa*. This sweet is very similar to the tiropita, but instead of cheese cream is added. In some regions in northern Greece they eat mpogatsa with a salty stuffing as well, but the most common way is with cream and sugar or cinnamon. A very similar variation of mpogatsa is *galaktompoureko,* with the difference that the cream is much sweeter and it is served with honey.

Eating Out

Eating out has always been very popular in Greece. Even in difficult times under Turkish rule there were many small places where men could gather and enjoy a glass of wine with some food. In addition to those places there were *hania,* or inns, where travelers could stop and enjoy a warm meal and some rest. Although eating out used to be the privilege of men, after World War II women became entitled to spend time eating out.

In modern Greece eating out is part of the local culinary culture. For this reason there are several different types of places where people can enjoy good food outside their homes. The most popular are the *giradika* or *souvlatzidika,* which sell a very popular Greek dish, gyros, or the widely known souvlaki. Gyros is made out of pork and more specifically out of the meat that surrounds the shoulder blade, which is ground with the addition of several different spices such as cumin, oregano, thyme, and rosemary. (In the United States, it is usually made with ground lamb.) It is formed around a vertical rotary spit, which is heated slowly by burners from behind as it turns. Meat is sliced off as it cooks. It can be served on its own with fried potatoes or, the most popular way, in Greek pita bread with potatoes, yogurt or tzatziki (a yogurt, garlic, and cucumber sauce), fresh tomatoes, onions, and parsley. Souvlaki, on the other hand, is made out of the leg of the pig cut into cubes and placed on small skewers. It is prepared on the grill, and it can also be served on its own with some fried potatoes or in the same way as gyros. Places that sell this food are very busy. They are a meeting point for young people who want to eat cheap and heavy food full of taste or for people who need something to eat after a night of heavy drinking.

Other popular places for Greek people to eat out are tavernas. These are medium-sized restaurants that offer cheap, homemade food. They used to be very popular between the 1970s and 1990s because they offered good food at very reasonable prices. Now, although still popular, they have to compete with modern restaurants and gourmet choices that are advertised by the mass media. Similarly, there are the meze restaurants. These are something like a tavern, but instead of serving food in big portions or personal dishes, they offer small menus with several different tastes that accompany drinks. When someone visits a *mezedopolio* (meze restaurant), the first thing to notice is that drinks arrive first, which

can be wine or raki, tsipouro, or ouzo, and then the food. Some meze restaurants do not have a menu and serve whatever is prepared for the day, in this way making sure that they always serve fresh food.

A custom that has become popular since the 1990s is fine restaurants. Greeks, especially the younger generations, enjoy eating out in restaurants. The haute cuisine of famous chefs, despite being expensive, is nonetheless popular. In addition, there are restaurants offering international cuisines such as Italian, Chinese, or Mexican. However, restaurants that offer alternative or refined Greek food are more popular.

Eating out also receives great attention by the Greek mass media. There are many publications about what defines good food, and almost every magazine offers an article on the best places to visit based on what one can afford. Television shows are dedicated specifically to places to eat, and these are very popular.

Special Occasions

In Greece food is connected to special occasions in every way, shape, or form. From social events to religious celebrations food is integrated with expressions of every emotion. Special types of food are prepared according to the type of celebration, both in the home and outside the home. On some occasions, markets adjust to the occasion and sell food products that are appropriate to the time of the year and what is being celebrated.

One such occasion is what Greeks call Kathara Deftera, which is literally translated as "Cleansing Monday," that is, the beginning of the 40-day fast of Lent leading up to Easter. On this day the Greek Orthodox Church prohibits olive oil and all kinds of animal products from the table. Although modern Greeks do not strictly follow this rule, almost everyone abstains from meat and uses vegetables and grains, as well as seafood, instead. Because of the restriction on olive oil, a different type of bread is sold on this day: *lagana.* This bread is made from just flour, water, and sesame seeds. It is flat and drier than regular bread. Mostly bakeries produce this bread and sell it in large quantities.

Another special religious occasion connected with food is Easter. The entire Great Week (Megalobdomada) and Easter Day (Pasha) are characterized by activities in the kitchen. The most significant days with regard to food are Great Thursday, Friday, Saturday, and Easter Sunday. On Great Thursday eggs are painted red to symbolize the coming Resurrection. In addition, this is the day when *dolamdes* (vine leaves stuffed with rice and vegetables) are prepared. This is a very typical food eaten in Greece, but on this day it initiates the beginning of summer since it the first point in the year when fresh vine leaves can be collected. On Great Saturday there is a very lengthy preparation of food. Greeks celebrate Easter not only on Sunday but also on Saturday after midnight. In the Greek Orthodox Church, Easter mass is performed on Great Saturday at midnight, and there is a second celebration on Easter Sunday afternoon. However, the most popular one takes place on Saturday. Thus the entire day is spent in preparation for that evening and the day that follows. In the early morning *tsourekia* are prepared. These are Easter breads that take a rather long time to prepare and are made of sweet dough. In some parts of Greece tsourekia take the form of *kalitsounia* or *diples*. These are sweets made out of sweet dough stuffed with white sweetened cheese and mint. Once the tsourekia are made, the typical midnight food called *magiritsa* is prepared. This is a soup made out of the boiled kidneys, liver, and stomach of a sheep or goat with the addition of fennel, parsley, and young onions. Once they are boiled, lemon juice is added as well as eggs, which thicken the soup.

The peak of celebrations takes place on Great Easter Sunday. Men start the day early with roasting a whole lamb. The entire animal is skewered on a big iron spit and fastened on with wires. Once it is stable it is placed on the fire for five to six hours where it roasts as it turns. Men suggest that to properly cook the lamb, the fire has to be situated most prominently beneath the head and the legs of the animal so the heat is evenly distributed all over. During cooking men smear the skin with a mixture of olive oil, oregano, and lemon, using branches of rosemary so all the aromas of the herbs are transferred to the meat.

A special type of food is prepared for all religious and personal occasions. Marriages and funerals or memorials have special food. For example, at all memorials for people, even years after their death, *koliva* are distributed. Koliva is boiled wheat that is left to dry for a couple of days. Once it is dried, pomegranates, raisins, cinnamon, almonds, walnuts, and granulated sugar are added, and this makes a very sweet mixture. It is served outside the church after the memorial.

Diet and Health

For Greeks, food is basic for the healthy balance of the body and mind. This is obvious in the relationship that Greek cuisine has with natural products. Fresh produce and ingredients are fundamental to Greek cuisine not only for their better taste but also for their nutritional value.

Greek food is highly seasonal and localized. Greeks believe that local products are always best. In addition, the long history of farming and well-established traditions assure its people that the products they get are appropriate for their health. The diet has even been recognized throughout the world as the so-called Mediterranean diet, which is based on fresh local products, eaten in moderation. Modern industrialized farming makes Greek people unsure about the quality and safety of products since, according to their beliefs, when money is involved in such mass production, there is little personal care by the farmers for their products.

Greeks believe that healthy food means cooked food and that the longer it cooks, the better it is. It is only recently that Greek people might enjoy a medium-cooked steak, and even now it is highly unlikely to find this as a home-cooked meal. For Greeks, the application of fire kills any type of bacteria or germs that might exist on vegetables.

In addition, religion is highly connected with diet and health in Greece. In the Greek Orthodox Church there are several long periods of fasting (*Sarakosti*). There is a period before Christmas for about 30 days; the *megali sarakosti* (Lent) before Easter, which lasts for a bit longer than 40 days; and finally the 15-day sarakosti before August 15, when the Virgin Mary is celebrated. Although many people do not actually believe in these long periods of abstinence from animal products, they do follow it since they believe that it is very good for the body and cleans out all the toxins. At the same time, the church has carefully devised the diet so people get all the necessary nutrients.

A healthy diet and the use of natural products are also important for medical purposes. Greeks are generally aware of the nutritious properties of foods. For example, they know that tomatoes, lentils, and beets contain a lot of iron. Thus they try to combine or use ingredients so as to include all the important nutrients in their diet. However, certain combinations are used for various more serious health issues. Greek coffee dissolved in lemon is highly recommended for diarrhea. *Glistrida* (purslane) is considered to be medicine for high cholesterol, onions for people with high blood pressure, garlic for those with low blood pressure, and so on.

Evidently, although Greece is a modern, westernized, progressive country, people have a special bond with food and as a consequence with nature. They follow the seasonal life cycles with the celebration of different occasions, and they understand food as the transformation of nature into something tasty that fulfills, follows, and emphasizes important phases of life.

Giorgos Maltezakis

Further Reading

Bober, Phyllis Pray. *Art, Culture, and Cuisine: Ancient and Medieval Gastronomy.* Chicago: University of Chicago Press, 2001.

Dalby, Andrew. *Food in the Ancient World from A to Z.* Oxford: Routledge, 2003.

Garnsey, Peter. *Food and Society in Classical Antiquity.* Cambridge: Cambridge University Press, 1999.

Mackley, Lesley. *The Book of Greek Cooking.* Los Angeles, CA: HP Books, 1993.

Psilakis, Nikos, and Maria Psilakis. *Cretan Cooking.* Herakleion, Greece: Karmanor, 2003.

Sterling, Richard, Kate Reeves, and Georgia Dacakis. *World Food Greece: For People Who Live to Eat, Drink, and Travel.* Oakland, CA: Lonely Planet, 2002.

Gypsies

Overview

After their departure from India sometime around 1000 A.D., Gypsies dispersed throughout Europe and beyond. In the process they were fragmented into a great number of national and tribal groups lacking sustained contact, and consequent cultural exchange, with one another. Therefore, one finds little if anything in common between what is eaten, for example, by Gitanos in Spain, Romnichals in England, and American Kalderash. Much of the descriptions that follow of Gypsy food are true only of the particular group being described and cannot be generalized.

The very name by which Gypsies call themselves is a good example of this cultural heterogeneity. The majority of Romani speakers are properly called by the name they call themselves, Roma (singular Rom, masculine, or Romni, feminine). With the development of greater Romani political consciousness, this has gained wider usage, both among other Romani groups and among the general public. But a number of other groups, including those that speak one of the several creolized Romani languages, use other terms. Most Anglo-Romani speakers prefer to be called Romnichals, Romanies, or simply Travellers. Almost all Spanish Gypsies identify themselves as Gitanos. Most Sinti and Manouche, the majority of whom are located in Germany and France, respectively, strongly object to being called Roma. There is no term in Romani that denotes all these people despite their common history, hence the use of the term Gypsies here, which many consider pejorative.

Despite the general misconception that Gypsies are nomadic, only a minority are. Ever since their arrival in Europe, the majority have been settled, sometimes in cities, sometimes on the periphery of peasant villages or in separate hamlets. Of those who were nomadic, some traveled more or less fixed annual routes, while others wandered internationally to the extent they were allowed. Then and now any nomads travel only seasonally.

Gypsies remained in the Balkans for 200 years before some dispersed throughout western Europe during the 14th and 15th centuries. Those in Romania and some adjacent regions were enslaved until the mid-19th century. This period in the Balkans left an indelible imprint on the culture, including the foodways, of many contemporary groups of Gypsies. Others, like the Gitanos of Spain or the Romnichals of England, eat a variant of the national cuisine of the country they live in. There is often an evident culture lag, in which the elements of the cuisine are more reflexive of the foodways of a nation in which they used to live than of that in which they live now. Kalderash Americans still prefer a Russian-style tea, drunk from glasses with pieces of preserved fruit. Some still use an heirloom Russian samovar to prepare it.

Each Gypsy community developed its own distinct foods and foodways, often completely unrelated to one another. Nevertheless, there are some common patterns that can be broadly, if not universally, applied. Those groups that are still nomadic place a natural emphasis on stewing and frying, rather than baking, steaming, or roasting, other than whole animals on a spit. They also incorporate into their diet wild foodstuffs, both vegetable and animal, to which they have ready access. Romnichals have a reputation, in part deserved, of poaching rabbits and game birds from private property. All over Europe, nomadic or recently nomadic Gypsies will collect young nettles in the spring, which they cook as a green.

By far the most important and far-reaching factor shaping what Gypsies eat and how they prepare their food is a complex of beliefs concerning pollution and ritual purity that originated in India. These are more stringently held in some groups than others, and specific practices vary from one group to another, but all Gypsy life has been shaped to some degree by these beliefs, and this is particularly true of food and food preparation. American Roma (including Kalderash, Machwaya, and Kunéshti) are particularly strong adherents and serve as a good example.

Roma believe in a bifurcated world divided into Gypsy and non-Gypsy, men and women, ritually clean (*wuzho*) and unclean (*marime*). The body above the beltline, especially the head, is considered sacred; that below, especially the genital area, is marime. A woman is marime during and six months after childbirth and during menstruation. A marime woman

A Gypsy woman cooking stew over an open fire. (Shutterstock)

cannot cook or serve food to men. She cannot step over anything belonging to a man or allow her skirt to touch his things. For a woman to throw her skirt at a man or to lift her skirt to him is a defiling act. Women's and men's clothing must be washed separately. Upper garments must be washed separately from lower garments. A tablecloth would never be washed with underwear. Dishes could never be washed in the same sink or washpan as clothing. All food is prepared, served, and eaten with the greatest concern for ritual quality. Anything brought into the home from outside is considered possibly polluted and is, therefore, scrutinized with care. Only freshly grown foods are considered safe, but everything, including meat, is cleansed thoroughly before use. People who, for some infraction, have been declared marime cannot eat with others. Roma do not eat with strangers or with those they don't trust. To refuse to eat with a Rom is a sign of distrust, implying that he is not ritually clean. Non-Gypsies follow none of these proscriptions and are, therefore, considered marime. Many Romani households will keep a separate coffee cup and other tableware that they reserve for the use of non-Gypsy guests. Some will destroy or discard a cup that a non-Gypsy guest has used.

There are also certain qualities of lifestyle that are emphasized in most Gypsy communities, though these are not necessarily true for all groups or for all members of any group. These include spontaneity, adaptation, improvisation, and extravagance even in the face of poverty. These can be seen as adaptive strategies that have allowed Gypsies to cope more easily with problems such as discrimination, poverty, and pariah status. These qualities are present throughout Romani culture, including food and foodways.

Spontaneity in Gypsy cultures is such that dishes are never exactly the same. One uses what is available or what comes to mind. No one uses a cookbook or written recipe, so recipes are never standardized. Moreover, the common practice of not storing foodstuffs ahead of time, either because of not having money to build up stores or through lack of facilities to store them, means fewer options when cooking. One must think creatively.

While there is a strong tendency to hold onto tradition, Gypsies are very quick to adopt and adapt those features of mainstream culture that fit into their own way of life. Thus, in some areas, Gypsies more quickly adopted the cell phone than did their non-Gypsy neighbors. In England, Romnichals took the notion of the travel trailer and adapted it to their own needs along the lines of their traditional horse-drawn, highly ornate *vardos* (living wagons). So, too, in food. Bosnian Xoraxane in Italy, used to produce purchased in farmers' markets, quickly learned to make use of tubes of tomato paste and bouillon cubes produced in Italy.

There are Romani lawyers, doctors, university professors, and well-to-do businessmen, but a disproportionate number of Gypsies are poor, some extremely poor. Nomadic Xoraxane in Bosnia expect some sort of meat at every meal, while the villagers among whom they wander, who raise the meat they eat, tend to reserve meat for special occasions. Nomadic Kalderash in Sweden eat only butter, never margarine, no matter how poor they might be. On special occasions Kalderash Americans produce lavish displays of food, including numerous whole roasted animals, that put the Thanksgiving and wedding feasts of non-Gypsies to shame.

🍽 Food Culture Snapshot

Halil and Hanifa Salkanović are Xoraxane (Muslim) Čergaši (nomads) from Bosnia. They speak the Gurbeti dialect of Romani but are equally fluent in Bosnian and Italian and speak a number of other European languages to some degree. Like other members of their group, Halil was a peripatetic coppersmith who traveled from village to village, market town to market town, repairing and retinning the copper utensils that were traditionally used in Bosnia for cooking and serving. Hanifa told fortunes by reading palms. When these copper utensils were replaced by plastic and enamelware in the late 1960s and early 1970s, they and many of their relatives moved into western Europe seeking other forms of livelihood. Almost none have been able to obtain regular employment because of discrimination, lack of education and marketable skills, and

government obstructions. Halil and his family manage by buying and selling various objects and by collecting scrap metal, and they benefit from some social services. Several members of the larger group make fanciful copper vessels sold as mantle pieces rather than cookware. Children beg or wash car windows at traffic lights.

After much traveling, including in North Africa, and extended stays in Germany and the Netherlands, they settled down in a rough campground designated for Gypsies on the outskirts of Rome. Their dwelling is similar to others in the camp: a travel trailer, now immovable, with extensions built of scrap lumber and sheets of plastic. Their four surviving sons and their daughter, all now adults with their own families, are settled in adjacent campsites. There is no kitchen or special area set aside for food preparation. There is a propane cookstove in one corner, but much of the cooking in good weather is done at the campfire in front. Similarly, there is no special area for eating. Usually, diners will just take their plate to a chair or upturned bucket to eat by the campfire. There is no refrigerator, and there is a strong tendency to shop for each meal. Leftovers are often discarded. Meals are very irregular, with no set schedule and not everyone eating at the same time. Each of the six adult women of the extended family shops and cooks individually, but food, both raw and cooked, is very commonly shared.

The day starts with coffee, if there is any. In camp, the women prepare Turkish-style coffee. The men will very often go to a nearby café for espresso, both upon rising and repeatedly throughout the day. This was especially true before the acquisition of cell phones, when the café telephone was essential for keeping in touch with family members scattered throughout Europe. Those who want breakfast will eat leftovers from the previous day's supper and perhaps a piece of fruit.

Halil will often drop by Rome's central market, sometimes making a purchase that strikes his fancy, such as some turkey wings, a chicken, or some fatty cuts of beef. The younger women of the extended family will go to the market just prior to closing time to ask for items of produce, most often seconds or items that may spoil before the next day. They usually return with enough for a mixed bowl of fruit and a combination of vegetables to comprise the stews that are the most common dish prepared. In mid- to late afternoon, when all have returned to camp, supper will be prepared. If a man or a family group is hungry before they can return, they might stop for pizza, but restaurants are seldom patronized otherwise.

Supper may consist of a stew of turkey, potatoes, string beans, and tomatoes heavily seasoned with black pepper, or "pasta *suta,*" consisting of a package of *zita* mixed with a couple of cans of Campbell's *ragu di carne* and a cube of margarine. Eggs are much used for their convenience and low cost. One preparation is to crack half a dozen eggs into a melted cube of margarine flavored with garlic and cook them sunny side up. Supper almost always includes a typical Bosnian salad of tomatoes, cucumbers, peppers, and onions dressed with vinegar, oil, and salt, but they will make do with whatever combinations of these vegetables is available. If they are out of vinegar, the salad is dressed with oil and salt; if there is no oil, then just salt. In a pinch, just a raw onion will suffice. There is always bread. Beer, or more often wine, is drunk before, during, and after the meal by the men and sometimes the women. Most evenings conclude with the men seated around the campfire drinking wine while the women do household chores.

Trgance

Trgance is considered a Bosnian Xoraxane Čergaši specialty. Mix 3–4 eggs into 2 double-handfuls of flour. Meanwhile, prepare a chicken or meat broth. On the day observed, the cook used a chicken carcass left from the previous day's dinner. It is said to be even better to add a couple of packages of the commercial soup base "Brodo Ricetta Sapore" instead of salt. For a change of taste, some tomato paste can be added. The broth is thickened with flour fried in lard or oil. When the broth is boiling, add irregular lumps of the trgance dough, varying in size. Cook approximately half an hour.

Major Foodstuffs

The culinary raw materials used by Gypsies are as unlimited as those of the nations they live in. Even international nomads are quick to adapt to local availabilities. There are few restrictions governing what they can or cannot eat. Some groups refuse to eat horse meat, presumably because of their close association in the past, but other groups do. American Roma consider birds that fly, such as doves or pigeons, marime and therefore inedible, while chickens, turkeys, and other fowl that do not usually fly are edible.

Meat is of special importance in the diet of most Gypsies. Many Gypsies of many groups expect some sort of meat at every meal. Meat is especially important at any Gypsy feast. The feast (*slava*) honoring the patron saint of a New Jersey family that was attending the annual pilgrimage at the Basilica of Sainte-Anne-de-Beaupré, near Quebec, included roast beef, turkey, salmon, hot dogs and hamburgers, and spit-roasted sheep and pigs. Another family's feast at the same event included nine sheep roasted on spits in the parking lot. Spit-roasted meat, either sheep or pigs, is obligatory at any feast in many Romani communities.

Fatty meat is generally preferred to lean. Except among Muslim Gypsies, who generally observe the Islamic prohibition, there is a widespread preference for pork. The many poor Gypsies often make use of cheaper cuts: turkey wings instead of breast, calf lungs, pig tails and feet, sheep's heads, soup bones, and offal such as tripe and kidneys. Historically, some groups in eastern Europe ate "dead meat" (*mulo mas*), a pig or some other livestock that they secretly poisoned and then offered to dispose of for the hapless owner.

A meat that is iconic in the cuisine of many European Gypsies is the hedgehog, though it is seldom if ever eaten today. It is now a protected species in many European states, though its decreasing importance in the Romani diet may have less to do with its rarity than with Gypsies' increasing sedentarization in urban places and other modernization processes. Various ways of preparation have been reported, but the most common is packing the gutted but unskinned animal in clay and burying it in the coals. When the fire dies down, the clay is cracked off, taking the skin and quills with it. Others report laying the carcass on its back in the coals, after which the quills can easily be removed. The animal can then be cut into pieces and fried or roasted on a stick over the fire.

Vegetables are not particularly important in most Gypsy diets, though some groups or individuals greatly appreciate them. American Roma believe black pepper, red pepper, salt, vinegar, garlic, and onions to be lucky (*baxt*) foods, and they make much use of all of these. Many Gypsies like spicy food, and this is especially true of American Roma. Celery is believed by American Roma to promote virility. At feasts, a stalk of celery is laid at every place setting. Bread is essential at every meal, and there is a general appreciation of quality bread. There are a number of home-baked traditional breads, including some made by nomads without the benefit of an oven. Kalderash in Mexico have adopted tortillas (along with many other items from the Mexican menu), though they have not given up bread.

Cooking

In an extended-family household, the most recently arrived daughter-in-law is usually expected to do the cooking. Otherwise, the mother or eldest daughter may be the designated cook. Although cooking is generally considered woman's work, men are not restricted from the kitchen or from cooking when called upon, as when the usual female cook is prohibited to do so because of marime conventions. Some men take great pride in their cooking abilities. Among American Roma, men cook all festival food, thereby ensuring that the food is ritually safe.

Gypsies of many groups, both travelers and semisettled, prefer to cook outside. Many travelers, from Xoraxane Čergaši to English Romnichals, will cook outside even when they have a perfectly good stove inside their caravan.

Gypsy cooks seldom if ever employ cookbooks. Although illiteracy rates vary from country to country, until recently Romani women could not have used Romani cookbooks even if they had existed. Gypsy cooking tends to be spontaneous, and recipes are very loose. Australian Romnichal Rosemary Lee-Wright, in what is apparently the first cookbook by a Gypsy, explains that Gypsy measurements are "a handful," "a palm" (level or heaped), and "a pinch." For a number of years, Lee-Wright's

was the only authentic Gypsy cookbook, though it was quite limited in the contextual information provided with the recipes. Several other books by non-Gypsies were extremely fanciful and offered no sources for their recipes, which appear not to have had ethnographic validity. Since 2000, however, a number of Gypsy cooks have provided authentic pictures of Romani food in a variety of countries, such as England, Spain, Palestine, and the United States. Elsewhere, sympathetic and knowledgeable non-Gypsies have worked together with Gypsy cooks to collate and publish their recipes, such as in France, Italy, and Slovakia.

Stews are a particularly common dish. They are convenient, especially for travelers—a one-pot meal incorporating a wide variety of available foodstuffs. Stews can be lavish, utilizing a variety of meats, or very inexpensive. They can be cooked on a single burner or a campfire. Frying is also common. Roasting tends to be reserved for festive occasions. Steaming or oven roasting is rare, though the latter is becoming more popular as Gypsy populations become more settled with modern kitchen stoves.

Cooking pots were sometimes suspended from a tripod of iron stakes driven into the ground around the campfire. Romnichals also used the *chitty,* an iron rod in the shape of a shepherd's crook that was driven into the ground with a chain suspended from the crook at the top. Cast iron pots with a bale were preferred. Romnichals also used a cast iron skillet with a fixed bale with a ring at the top so it could be

A typical Gypsy stew made with vegetables and beans. (Shutterstock)

suspended from a tripod or chitty. These also came in the form of a griddle. An alternative mode of cooking that was sometimes utilized by Romnichals was the hay pit. A hole was dug a foot deeper and wider than the cookpot and lined with hay or straw. The hot pot was placed in the hole, and more hay or straw was packed tightly around. A sack stuffed with more hay or straw was placed on top. In this way the family could be gone for the day, reheating the pot prior to eating.

Typical Meals

There is little or no resemblance between the meals typical of one group and those of another. Some examples from specific groups follow:

An American Romnichal. His ancestors came to the United States from England in the mid-19th century. He grew up on the road but now is long settled in Ohio, where he works as a painter of barns, a traditional American Romnichal occupation, and commercial buildings.

Breakfast: coffee, frozen waffles or Special K cereal

Lunch: on the job, goes to a fast-food restaurant

Supper: fried pork chops, fried potatoes with onions, bread and butter, iced tea

Sedentary basketmakers in Izmir, Turkey.

Breakfast: *Simit* (sesame rolls that a street vendor delivers every morning), rolls filled with sweetened sesame paste, tomatoes, cucumbers, olives, honey, and tea

Gitanos in Barcelona.

Dinner, around 2 or 3 P.M.: bean soup with noodles (*fideos*), garlicky *bacalao* (dried salt cod) and potatoes, tomato salad, bread, stewed fruit, red wine

Eating Out

The amount of eating out varies considerably from group to group, though in general eating in restaurants is not particularly common among most Gypsies. Those still forced to live in poverty, as in eastern European ghettos and western European designated camps, seldom have the funds for more than an occasional snack at a marketplace stand or a local shop. At the same time, many wealthier Gypsies, like the Kalderash and Machwaya of North America, try to avoid food prepared by non-Gypsies because of presumed impurity. They will usually not eat in non-Gypsy homes or eat food prepared by non-Gypsies and brought to their homes. If forced to buy cooked food while traveling, they prefer food wrapped in plastic or clean paper rather than food on plates. If forced to eat in a restaurant, many will avoid eating utensils, preferring to eat with their fingers. Often they will ask for paper or plastic cups, which they can be sure have not been used previously by a non-Gypsy. If food is suspect for any reason, it will be rejected. The preference is for well-lit restaurants where the food preparation can be observed.

Special Occasions

Special occasions among Gypsies, as among other groups, call for special foods. Even the poorest will do their best to provide as lavishly as they can. Bosnian Xoraxane, both when they were still peripatetic coppersmiths in Yugoslavia and now, when they are currently encamped semipermanently in western Europe, consider a spit-roasted sheep essential for any wedding.

The Balshaldra (sometimes called Slovak-Hungarian in the literature) came to the United States from villages in Slovakia, which was then a part of Hungary. Most settled in Midwestern industrial cities, at first in Hungarian neighborhoods. Most of the men are professional musicians, and music, both as professionals playing for others and for their own community, is an important unifying factor. They are unusual among American Gypsies in the emphasis they place on education, including but not limited to advanced musical training. Music has been instrumental in their maintaining a strong Romani identity, even though an increasing number are now entering other professions. Their cuisine, including that for special occasions, does not vary greatly from that of other fourth- and fifth-generation Americans of eastern European background. A wedding feast provides a good example: roast chicken, pasta with tomato sauce, cabbage rolls, mashed potatoes, string beans, green salad, Jell-O salad, relishes (including celery, carrot sticks, dill pickles, and pickled beets), walnut torte (purchased from a local Hungarian baker), wedding cake, coffee, and an open bar.

It is among American Roma that Gypsy feasting reaches its highest expression. Of special importance is the slava, a saint's-day feast most often fixed according to the Orthodox calendar. A slava feast brings good luck, good health, and prestige to the family that gives it. Over time, some slavas have become traditional for some families or groups of related families. In other cases, a slava is given because of a promise to a saint for curing a person in ill health. Food for a slava, which must be of the utmost ritual purity, is prepared the night before by the family giving the slava (an occasion called *tšinašara* by Kalderash and *večera* by Machwaya). Each slava features a specific meat: roast pig for Saint John's Day, fish for Saint Nicholas, roast lamb for Saint George, Saint Mary, Saint Anne, and Easter. A slava feast should also include certain auspicious foods: *gushvada* (cheese strudel), *pirogo* (noodle cake), and especially *sarmi* (stuffed cabbage). An excess of food is very important, and great attention is paid to its display. Lavish feasts are also obligatory at weddings, funerals (*pomana*), baptisms, *pakiv* (a feast honoring some important individual), and *kris romani* (the trials at which laws governing social behavior are resolved). Newly arrived Romani immigrants were also quick to adopt Thanksgiving and New Year's celebrations. Some Romani families like feasts so much they will celebrate both Catholic and Orthodox Christmas and Easter. Photographs from special-occasion feasts, especially weddings, are commonly displayed on YouTube. Feasts have great social significance. Guests number in the hundreds and may come from across North America. The sharing of food at a feast table expresses mutual respect, friendship, and acceptance of one another's ritual cleanliness.

Pork stuffed cabbage rolls, or sarmi. (Shutterstock)

Over the last several decades there has been a steady conversion to evangelical Protestantism. The majority of American Roma are now members of evangelical churches with Romani pastors. Since saints are not recognized in these churches, those who have converted no longer celebrate slava, though the other feasts are still held.

Sarmi

The most important dish of the American Romani menu, served at all feasts, is stuffed cabbage (sarmi). There is much variation, but the following is typical. Core and boil a large head of cabbage together with ½ pound lard, 2 cups vinegar, and sufficient water to cover. When soft, remove the cabbage, saving the water. Cut pork into small pieces, and fry with rice in lard until slightly brown. Add chopped bell peppers, jalapeño peppers, onion, celery, parsley, and black and red pepper, and sauté briefly. Add a can of tomato paste and some of the reserved water, and cook until rice is about half done. Roll mixture in cabbage leaves, one handful to a leaf. Place sarmi in a pot, cover with reserved water, 3 more cans of tomato paste, and a can of tomatoes. Cook till done, an hour or longer.

Diet and Health

The many impoverished Gypsies of eastern Europe and the camps of western Europe have poor health due to inadequate and unbalanced diets as well as generally poor living conditions and poor health care. But even middle-class and wealthier Gypsies often have health problems resulting from unhealthy diets and lifestyles. Studies of American Roma have demonstrated that the diet, which is high in salt, sugar, and animal fat, together with a lack of aerobic exercise and a nearly universal prevalence of smoking, leads to very high levels of blood cholesterol, triglycerides, and blood sugar. Abnormally high blood pressure usually begins before 30 years of age. By age 50, nearly 100 percent are afflicted with diabetes and vascular disease. Roma generally are considered old if over 55. Heart attacks occur in the early thirties, even the late twenties. Some Romani families eat only fish and vegetables for Lent, but there is a general opinion in the community that this Lenten diet is unhealthy, even for patients with cardiovascular disease. In recent years there has been some improvement as many members of the community have become more health conscious and as smoking has somewhat decreased, but as yet there are no recent studies to confirm this.

Dietary problems have been compounded historically by a cultural bias for obesity. To be fat was to be powerful; thinness was a sign of weakness. The term in Romani for a traditional leader is *Rom Baro,* or "big man." While meant in the sense of political power, it is also almost always literally true.

William G. Lockwood

Further Reading

Cooper, Keziah. *Favorite Romany Recipes: Traditional Food and Country Lore.* Sevenoaks, UK: J. Salmon, n.d.

Edwards, D. M., and R. G. Watt. "Diet and Hygiene in the Life of Gypsy Travelers in Hertfordshire." *Community and Dental Health* 14 (1997): 41–46.

Gropper, Rena. *Gypsies in the City: Culture Patterns and Survival.* Princeton, NJ: Darwin Press, 1975.

Hancock, Ian. "Romani Foodways: Gypsy Culinary Culture." *The World and I* (June 1991): 666–77.

Hancock, Ian. "Romani Foodways: The Indian Roots of Gypsy Culinary Culture." *Roma* 35 (1991): 5–19.

Kudlickova, Lydia. *Romañi Tavl'ard'I / Rómska Kuchárka.* Bratislava, Slovakia: Minority Rights Group—Slovakia, 1997.

Lee-Wright, Rosemary. *The Gypsy Cookbook.* Sydney, Australia: Wentworth Books, 1978.

Leo, Jacey. *Gypsy Open-Fire Cookbook.* Baltimore, MD: PublishAmerica, 2005.

Miller, Carol. "American Rom and the Ideology of Defilement." In *Gypsies, Tinkers and Other Travellers,* edited by Farnham Rehfisch, 41–54. London: Academic Press, 1975.

Miller, Carol. "Macwaya Gypsy *Marimé.*" Master's thesis, University of Washington, 1968.

Palmerini, Maurizo. *Kuhinja romani / Cucinazingara.* Rimini, Italy: Pietroneno Capitani Editore, in collaboration with the Comune di Rimini, Assessorato al Servizi Sociali, 2001.

Pickett, David. "The Gypsies of Mexico, Part 2." *Journal of Gypsy Lore Society,* 3rd ser., 45 (1966): 6–16.

Poueyto, J. L., and S. Didier. *Latcho rhaben; Cuisine tsigane.* Serres-Castets, France: Editions De Faucompret, 1994.

Salo, Matt, and Sheila Salo. *The Kalderas in Eastern Canada.* Canadian Centre for Folk Culture Studies Paper No. 21. Ottawa: National Museums of Canada, 1977.

Santiago, Amalia, Julia Fernández, Luisa y Paqui Perona, Paqui y Manoli Cortés, and Pepi Castro. *Cocina Gitana.* Barcelona, Spain: Icaria Editorial, 1996.

Sleem, Amoun. *The Domari Cookbook: Recipes from the Dom Gypsy Community in Jerusalem.* Cyprus: Dom Research Center, 2003.

Sutherland, Anne. *Gypsies: The Hidden Americans.* New York: Free Press, 1975.

Sutherland, Anne. "Health and Illness among the Rom of California." *Journal of the Gypsy Lore Society,* ser. 5, 2 (1992): 19–60.

Thomas, James. "Disease, Lifestyle, and Consanguinity in 58 American Gypsies." *Lancet* 2 (1985): 377–79.

Thomas, James. "Health Care of American Gypsies: Social and Medical Aspects." In *Papers from the Eighth and Ninth Annual Meetings,* edited by Cara DeSilva, Joanne Grumet, and David J. Nemeth, 128–38. New York: Gypsy Lore Society, North American Chapter, 1988.

Tillhagen, C. H. "Food and Drink among the Swedish Kalderaša Gypsies." *Journal of the Gypsy Lore Society,* 3rd ser., 36 (1957): 159–60.

Hungary

Overview

The Republic of Hungary is in central Europe, landlocked between seven neighbors: Romania, Ukraine, Austria, Croatia, Serbia, Slovenia, and Slovakia. Hungary is a parliamentary democracy, consisting of 19 counties. The country's population is nearly 10 million, and about one-fifth of the population resides in Budapest, the capital city.

Hungary is roughly the size of the U.S. state of Indiana, and much of the country consists of flat to rolling plains and some low mountains. Though Hungary is blessed with fertile soil—nearly half of the country consists of arable land—and agriculture plays an important role in the economy, cooking with fruits and vegetables takes a back seat to meat. Hungarians are avid meat eaters, with pork being the preferred meat. Very few Hungarians are vegetarians, and at traditional Hungarian restaurants, vegetarian dishes are rare.

Slightly more than half of Hungarians are Roman Catholic, about 16 percent are Calvinist, and small percentages are Lutheran, Greek Orthodox, and Jewish. Religion does not have a major effect on eating habits in Hungary, although Catholics do not eat meat on Good Friday and Christmas Eve. Very few Hungarian Jews follow a kosher diet.

Hungary has the distinction of being one of Europe's unhealthiest countries, largely due to the traditional diet, which is high in animal fat, cholesterol, sugar, and salt and is generally low in fiber, fruits, and vegetables. Obesity is an increasing problem. There is a sharp difference, however, between the lifestyles and eating habits of the younger generations of Hungarians and those of the older generation who came of age during Communism. There is also a clear difference between the eating habits of those in Budapest and those in the countryside.

Food Culture Snapshot

Katalin and László Kovacs live in an affluent Budapest suburb with their three young children. Katalin—originally from a village called Bőny in northwestern Hungary—is currently in graduate school. László—originally from the town of Kecskemét in central Hungary—owns a midsized software-development company. Although they can afford to spend a significantly higher amount than the average on food, their diet still reflects the traditional elements that they grew up with in the countryside. But they eat significantly less sugar, salt, and fat than their parents' generation did. They do occasionally splurge on expensive imported food, but for the most part, their daily meals consist of typical Hungarian dishes and ingredients. Unlike their parents' generation, Katalin and László enjoy dining out at restaurants on a fairly regular basis, while the children stay at home, with either their grandparents or a babysitter.

Breakfast in the Kovacs' household is at around 7:30 A.M., when Katalin and the children eat toast, cold cuts, biscuits, or cereal. László rarely eats breakfast at home during the week since he leaves early for work. During the week the children eat lunch at school, which consists of two courses: a soup followed by a main course, which is often a vegetable stew (*főzelék*). During the week, Katalin doesn't cook lunch for herself. She will eat whatever is around, such as leftovers from the night before. Like many who work in offices, László eats at restaurants for lunch. Dinner is served around 7 P.M., and it usually consists of something warm but uncomplicated: warm sandwiches, ham and eggs, or a homemade stew or soup pulled from the freezer.

On weekends, when the whole family is at home together, the Kovacs eat big lunches together as a family, which include a soup and a meaty main course accompanied by rice and either pickled vegetables or a salad. When the family hosts guests, Katalin will prepare something special and more time-intensive such as a roasted duck with red cabbage, foie gras, and a cake.

As is common in Hungary, both Katalin's mother and László's mother, who both live in the countryside, often come to visit to help with the children. While they are in town, the two mothers do all of the family's cooking, even preparing extra dishes to store in the freezer. Katalin and László also frequently travel to the countryside to visit their families, and their mothers always send them home with several containers full of leftovers, baked goods, and fruit, vegetables, and eggs from the garden.

Katalin does the grocery shopping every two or three days. She shops at a midsized supermarket where she can do one-stop shopping for things like dairy products (yogurt, kefir, butter, milk, cheese, and sour cream), kitchen staples (flour, rice, sugar, and salt), and meat (sausage, cold cuts, various cuts of pork). When she has time, she goes to the neighborhood farmers' market, where she prefers to buy her fruit and vegetables. Although Budapest has a variety of international food shops, Katalin doesn't shop at them. She prepares mostly the same traditional foods as her mother did, although with a lighter touch.

Major Foodstuffs

Agriculture is an important element of the Hungarian economy, and a significant amount of the produce for sale at the markets is grown in Hungary. The most important agricultural products are wheat, corn, sunflower oil, potatoes, sugar beets, pork, beef, poultry, and dairy products. Hungary has no sea, but water is important to the Hungarian psyche, and the main rivers—the Danube and the

Tisza—essentially split the country into three vertical sections. Hungary's Lake Balaton is the largest lake in central Europe, and Hungarians are fond of their local freshwater fish such as carp, catfish, trout, and pike perch.

The diet in Hungary is meat-centric, and meat is often accompanied by potatoes, which are abundant in Hungary. By far the most popular meat is pork, and a wide variety of types of bacon and sausage are available. Other commonly eaten meats are chicken, duck, goose, foie gras, beef, and mutton. Lamb, veal, and game are less common but are easily available at the markets. Butchers and markets in Hungary carry all parts of the animal, and offal, tripe, and other cuts infrequently seen in the West are easy to find and commonly used in Hungary. The preferred cooking fat is pork lard, but sunflower oil is gaining popularity.

Important vegetables include root vegetables, particularly for soups (celeriac, carrots, parsley root, kohlrabi, etc.); squash and zucchini; peppers; and tomatoes. Plums and apricots are plentiful and are eaten plain, as well as turned into jam and *pálinka* (fruit brandy). For many home cooks, particularly older ones, canning fruits and vegetables is still an important part of their cooking routine. They turn fruit into jams, sugary syrups, and compote; peppers into paprika paste; and tomatoes into juice. They can *lecsó* (stewed peppers and tomatoes) to last the whole year.

A man makes sausage by hand in a Hungarian deli. (Shutterstock)

Milk products are an important part of the Hungarian diet. Sour cream is a common addition to soups and salads, and some stews and even meat dishes are topped with it. Yogurt and kefir are also commonly eaten. *Túró,* curd cheese, is made from both sheep and cow milk and is a major ingredient in many Hungarian dishes, both savory and sweet. It is served with pasta and lecsó in a dish called *túrós csusza;* used as a filling for a ravioli-like pasta called *derelye;* or turned into a spread spiked with paprika and garlic, called *kőrözött.* Desserts featuring it include *rétes* (strudel), *túró gomboc* (dumplings), and *palacsinta* (crepes).

Paprika is, by far, the most important spice in Hungarian cuisine. It is used in abundance in many of the best-known Hungarian dishes. As the saying goes, "All good Hungarian recipes begin by sautéing onions in bacon and then adding paprika." Most commercially produced Hungarian paprika comes from the southern towns of Szeged and Kalocsa. It is never smoked in Hungary, and it comes in a range of varieties from sweet through hot, and finely ground through coarse. At home, people make paprika by simply grinding peppers. Hungarian cuisine has a reputation for being hot, but in reality it is not. Sweet paprika is always used in cooking, and hot paprika or paprika paste is provided at the table for diners to individually add heat. Caraway seeds, nutmeg, and cinnamon are also frequently used. The most common herbs are flat-leaf parsley, dill, and marjoram.

Hungarians like to say that anywhere one drills in Hungary, thermal water will be found. Mineral water is abundant in Hungary, and there are dozens of commercially bottled varieties. Additionally, in some areas there are public springs where locals can bring bottles to fill. Hungarian mineral water is known for its high mineral content. In restaurants it is common to drink mineral water, while at home Hungarians drink both mineral water and tap water.

Hungary is a wine-drinking country, with 23 different wine regions producing a wide range of wines. The wine industry has grown up considerably in the past two decades, and Hungarian wine is being increasingly recognized for its quality.

Cooking

Hungarian food is generally uncomplicated to prepare. There are no laborious sauces or preparation methods. Throughout Hungary's history cooks were forced to be economical with ingredients, and they developed ingenious ways of doing things when little was available. This is still evident in the way that most people cook at home, which is why there are animal parts like tails, necks, and feet at the markets in Budapest. Many of the most typical—and traditional—Hungarian dishes require long, slow cooking, such as stews (*pörkölt*) made from beef, pork, or other meats and roasts made with the less-than-tender cuts.

Many Hungarian recipes begin with onions slowly cooking in fat, with a healthy portion of paprika stirred in. It's a combination that gives off a distinctively Hungarian aroma. Then the meat is added and browned, and a variety of dishes can result. Hungarian food has a bad reputation for being heavy and greasy. But it doesn't have to be. Pörkölt and goulash (*gulyás*), for example, use very little fat. Deep-frying is a common technique, as are panfrying and roasting.

Soups are thickened with either sour cream or a *rántás* (roux) of flour slowly browned in hot lard. Sour cream is a favorite Hungarian ingredient—in addition to soups, it's also added to stews like *paprikás* (made with paprika), *székelykáposzta* (a stew with sauerkraut), *főzelék* (vegetable stew), and even some sweets. Vinegar is often added to soups at the table.

Hungarians generally do not use as many kitchen utensils and appliances as Americans do. Most Hungarians have a battery of aluminum pots, but Hungarian cuisine doesn't require any special utensils (other than a *spaetzle* plane—a device that batter is passed through, into a pot, to make rough noodle-dumplings. Since kitchens tend to be small, avid home cooks often have large cutting boards that they pull out to use as temporary additional counter space when preparing large meals. Grilling is not common in Hungary, but during the warm months Hungarians like to cook soups and stews outdoors in a cauldron. Another outdoor cooking event is the *szalonnasütés,* in which a fire is built and participants stick slabs of bacon along with onions on the ends of sticks, hold them in the fire, and catch the drippings on pieces of bread. Traditionally, bread was baked in an outdoor wood-burning oven (*kemence*), but these days most people buy bread from the grocery store. Pickling is important and is done in abundance with both fruits and vegetables. During the summer, cucumbers are also fermented in large jars set out in the sun to make *kovászos uborka.*

Typical Meals

Hungary is a small, relatively homogeneous country, with few regional specialties or differences. But typical meals for Hungarian families will vary greatly depending on their economic and social standing, age, and location such as rural or urban. Traditionally, breakfast in Hungary has been a substantial meal, typically consisting of a "cold plate" of a variety of sliced cheeses; cold cuts, dried sausage, and salami; Hungarian banana peppers and tomatoes; bread and butter; and strong espresso-style coffee. For those living in the countryside as well as for many blue-collar workers in cities, breakfast still looks like this. But urban Hungarians will often have a more westernized breakfast such as cereal, eggs, or yogurt. Or they will buy scones (*pogácsa*) or sweets from a nearby pastry shop to eat on the way to work. Increasingly, as lifestyles become more hurried, Budapesters will do what was unthinkable not long ago: get their coffee in a to-go cup rather than sitting and relaxing with it. A midmorning snack called the *tíz órai* is customary in Hungary and generally consists of coffee or tea and either something sweet to eat or something simple like toast.

Lunch at around noon is typically the main meal of the day in rural Hungary, where, if they are able to, people go home for a home-cooked family lunch. Increasingly, however, this habit is eroding. In Budapest, most workers either bring something from home or have a restaurant lunch. Many restaurants specialize in delivering hot prepared lunches to offices. Eating a large Sunday lunch, however, remains an important family custom, in both cities and rural areas. Children generally eat hot lunches at school, which are fairly nutritious and varied.

Traditionally dinner was a lighter meal than lunch, eaten around 7 P.M., and often it was a cold plate, similar to breakfast. In rural areas, this is still typical. In Budapest, dinner habits have become more westernized, with a large dinner becoming the main meal of the day, around 7 or 8 P.M. Hungary produces a significant amount of wine, and wine or beer is usually drunk with dinner.

Soup is an important element in a Hungarian meal, and no Hungarian meal is complete without it. Bread is never served on its own, but it is always served with soup. Despite the stereotypes, very few Hungarian dishes feature hot paprika. However, a bit of hot paprika powder or paste is always placed on the table for diners to add heat to their food individually. Vinegar and sour cream are also added to soups at the table.

Traditional Hungarian goulash, or beef stew, served from a crock pot. (Shutterstock)

Gulyás (Goulash)

Goulash is an everyday dish served at nearly every Hungarian restaurant. It is so simple to make that any Hungarian who cooks can do it. Many also cook it over an open fire in a *bogrács* (cauldron), which adds a smoky flavor. Some cooks add pinched pasta (*csipetke*) before serving. If you were to continue cooking the meat without adding water or potatoes, the resulting dish would be pörkölt, which is the stew that foreigners tend to think of as goulash. Gulyás is an everyday meal, eaten with thick-crusted white bread.

4 tbsp sunflower or canola oil

2 yellow onions, chopped

1½ lb beef chuck, trimmed and cut into ½-in. cubes

Kosher salt and freshly ground black pepper, to taste

¼ c sweet paprika

2 tsp dried marjoram

2 tsp caraway seeds

2 cloves garlic, finely chopped

2 medium carrots, cut into ½-in. cubes

2 medium parsnips, cut into ½-in. cubes

1½ lb medium-sized new potatoes, peeled and cut into ½-in. cubes

1 tomato, cored and chopped

1 Italian frying pepper, chopped

Heat the oil in a pot over medium heat. Add the onions, cover, and cook, stirring occasionally, until soft and translucent, about 10 minutes. Increase the heat to high. Add the beef, and season with salt and pepper. Cook, uncovered, until the meat is lightly browned, about 6 minutes. Stir in the paprika, marjoram, caraway, and garlic, and cook until fragrant, about 2 minutes. Add the carrots, parsnips, and 5 cups water. Bring to a boil; reduce heat to medium. Simmer, covered, until the beef is nearly tender, about 40 minutes. Add the potatoes, and cook, uncovered, until tender, about 25 minutes. Stir in the tomatoes and pepper; cook for 2 minutes. Season with salt and pepper to taste.

The main course of a Hungarian meal is always a big portion of meat—whether it is a roast, a stew, or vegetables such as cabbage or peppers stuffed with meat. Potatoes are the most common accompaniment, and sometimes these are even served with rice. Stew (pörkölt) has historically played an important role in the Hungarian meal. Stews can be accompanied by buttered parsley potatoes, flour and egg dumplings (*galuska*), or tiny pieces of pasta the size of barley (*tarhonya*). Almost always, they are served with a few pieces of *savanyúság* (pickled vegetables) to aid the digestion of so much fat and starch. Leafy salads are rarely eaten, although Hungarians do eat salads made of sliced cucumbers or sliced tomatoes in a briny dressing made with vinegar, salt, and sugar. Salads are always served with the meal, never as an appetizer.

Lunch will nearly always end with coffee. Hungarians have a legendary sweet tooth, and leisurely meals will nearly always end with cake, strudel, cookies, or some other home-baked sweet. Pálinka (fruit brandy) is a traditional spirit in Hungary, made both commercially and at home. In traditional Hungarian households drinking shots of pálinka is common and done in a variety of situations: to welcome guests, to begin a meal, or to end a meal.

Depending on location and affluence, the types of meals eaten will vary. Hungarians who are well traveled are more likely to add non-Hungarian recipes to their repertoire, while rural Hungarians and those with little exposure to international cuisine will rely more on the diet laden with pork and potatoes. Likewise, the less educated and less affluent will rely on a diet of processed and prepared foods, which are also abundant in Hungary.

The following are examples of typical meals in middle-class families in Budapest and in rural Hungary. Budapest is a bustling, cosmopolitan city of nearly two million people. Life for many residents is fast-paced, which is reflected in the differences between the eating habits and diet here and in the countryside. In Budapest, breakfast varies from the traditional cold plate of sliced meats, vegetables, and cheeses to simple toast and jam or a quick bite on the way to work. There are bakeries and pastry shops on nearly every corner, where people often stop in for pogácsa (savory scones), cheese rolls, or some other type of baked goods. Hungarians tend to drink lots of strong coffee, made at home with a stovetop coffeepot or purchased at a café. A midmorning snack at around 10 A.M. can simply be coffee or tea, a crescent roll (*kifli*), or a sandwich.

For workers, lunch in Budapest is usually eaten at a restaurant, an *étkezde,* a type of restaurant open only for lunch and serving inexpensive, simple Hungarian dishes, or at a *büfe,* where prepared food sits under heat lamps in chafing dishes. Many who work in offices will order food daily from a delivery service. Restaurants in Budapest cater to workers, with inexpensive and quick two- or three-course lunch menus.

A family dinner now serves the function that lunch once did in Budapest, with most families eating a dinner that is larger than lunch. Some examples of common everyday dinners include pasta with curd cheese and lecsó (stewed peppers and tomatoes with paprika), roasted or fried pork, or beef pörkölt (stew) with potatoes. Dinner may also include foods that are typically considered breakfast foods in Western countries: ham and eggs, savory French toast, rice pudding, and semolina pudding. With the arrival of ethnic ingredients, international cooking shows, and scores of international restaurants, Budapesters are apt to experiment with cooking more exotic types of food.

In the countryside, no matter the region, eating habits are similar. Hungarians tend to rise early, eat breakfast as a family, and, whenever possible, have lunch together. Breakfast is a hearty but cold meal, with smoked bacon, paprika-spiked dried sausage, and salami served alongside sliced banana peppers and tomatoes, cheese, bread, and coffee. Bread with butter, jam, and honey might also be served.

Lunch in rural Hungary is traditionally the main meal of the day and consists of a first course of soup and then a meat-centric main course, usually accompanied by potatoes and pickled vegetables. Dessert could be *almas lepény* (apple tart), a yeasty cake, or walnut cake.

Dinner in rural Hungary is typically served around 7 P.M. and is lighter than lunch. It sometimes features sweet dishes such as pasta with poppy seeds or palacsinta (crepes) with apricot jam, sweetened

curd cheese, or ground walnuts. Alternatively, it could be a cold plate, similar to breakfast. Local wine is typically drunk with dinner. Often, pálinka (fruit brandy) is drunk before or after dinner.

Paprikás Csirke (Paprika Chicken)

Paprika chicken is one of the most classic of Hungarian dishes. Named for the large amount of paprika that goes into the sauce, the *paprikás* method can also be applied to veal. In Hungary, this dish is usually eaten with galuska (or spaetzle—a kind of ragged noodle made by dropping batter into boiling water) and a cucumber salad. The best type of pot to use is a cast iron casserole, but any pot with a tight-fitting lid will do. Cooking the chicken with the skin intact greatly benefits the flavor. For best results use a high-quality Hungarian sweet paprika.

2 tbsp lard (or oil)

2 large onions, peeled and minced

1½ tsp salt

2–3 tbsp sweet paprika

1 or 2 tomatoes, chopped

2 lb chicken pieces

1 banana pepper, sliced into rings

2 tbsp sour cream, plus more for garnish if desired

1 tbsp flour

2 tbsp heavy cream

Heat the lard (or oil) in the pot, add the onions, sprinkle with half of the salt, and cook, covered, over very low heat until the onions are glossy but not browned. Turn off the heat (so the paprika doesn't burn and become bitter), and stir in the paprika. Add the tomatoes and ½ cup of water, and mix. Turn the heat back on low, and place the chicken pieces in the pot. Sprinkle the remaining salt on the chicken, cover, and cook for about 30 minutes, checking every few minutes to see whether it needs more water. Remove the lid, add the sliced pepper, and cook for 10 more minutes. In a small bowl, mix the sour cream, flour, and heavy cream. Remove the pieces of chicken, and place the pieces on a serving platter. Add the sour cream mixture to the paprika sauce, and stir until blended. Cook for a minute or two, but don't let the sauce come to a boil. Pour the paprika sauce over the chicken pieces. Garnish with a spoonful of sour cream, if desired, and sprinkle with paprika.

Eating Out

Restaurant culture in Hungary suffered horribly during Communism. Businesses were privatized, the quality was poor, and most people wouldn't have had the money to eat out even if there were restaurants. Now, Budapest has a sophisticated restaurant scene with an increasing number of ethnic eateries to cater to both foreigners and Hungarians. There are Western fast-food chains, as well as a few local Hungarian fast-food chains specializing in főzelék. In the countryside, however, restaurants haven't advanced as much. Traditional Hungarian restaurants reign, and the quality is usually not as high.

There are several types of restaurants in Hungary, but these days the lines between them have been blurred. An *étterem* (the most common word for restaurant) can mean anything from a fancy white-tablecloth place to a fast-food eatery. Originally it referred to a more upscale restaurant, but it has now taken on a more all-encompassing meaning. Historically, a *vendéglő* was a step down from an étterem, in terms of both price and decor. It was the kind of place that served hearty portions of classic Hungarian food, and now it might still be decorated with folksy knickknacks and have red-and-white-checked tablecloths.

Étkezdes and *kifőzdes* are simple no-frills places that serve lunch on weekdays, and sometimes Saturdays. They're usually one-room restaurants with little decoration and a home-style menu. These types of restaurants have loyal regulars who share tables when needed. Coffee and alcohol are rarely served since the idea is to eat quickly and leave. The short menu usually changes daily, offering a few soups, ready-made dishes like stew or roasted meat, freshly prepared dishes like big slabs of fried meat, pickled salads, főzelék, a pasta, and one or two desserts. There are many simple fast-food stands (büfé), which are basically snack counters serving basic things like cold sandwiches, drinks, and sweets. Chinese buffets (*kínai büfé*) are ubiquitous and usually serve Hungarianized Chinese food. Butchers (*hús-hentesáru*) serve sausage and bread, and possibly roasted chicken or pork belly, at stand-up counters.

Hungary is also famous for its coffeehouse culture. A *kávéház* can be a trendy place serving breakfast, lunch, and dinner along with an extensive wine list. Or it can be a classic kávéház where coffee is served on silver trays with tiny glasses of mineral water and the decor is lavish with gold gilt, fancy plasterwork, and crystal chandeliers. These are the places that were plentiful at the end of the 19th and the beginning of the 20th century, popular with writers, artists, and revolutionaries. During the 1930s the elegant kávéház was replaced by the simpler *eszpresszó* (also called *presszó*), which was (and still is) a smoky, unattractive place, serving cheap alcohol and strong coffee. *Cukrászdas,* pastry shops, are usually small places with a few tiny tables just big enough for a cup of coffee and a piece of cake. A *pékség* is a bakery, but there are few dedicated bakeries left, since most people buy their bread in the supermarkets.

Special Occasions

In Hungary it seems as if festivals with food or wine as their focus are constantly taking place throughout the country. Villages and regions hold festivals honoring important crops, ingredients, or dishes, and there are competitions for cooking gulyás and fisherman's soup (*halászlé*) in many regions. Holidays are closely associated with traditional foods, and the food can be more important than the holiday itself. In Budapest, holiday traditions and customs are generally less elaborate than in the countryside, but customs differ with every family.

The Christmas (*karácsony*) season kicks off in Hungary with Mikulás nap (St. Nicholas's Day) on December 6, when children polish their shoes and set them out for Mikulás (St. Nick) to fill with chocolate and toys. If they've been bad, Mikulás's helper, Krampusz, will leave twigs instead. In December bakeries and home cooks bake enormous amounts of roulade cakes filled with walnuts or poppy seeds (*bejgli*), which are a crucial part of the holiday season. December 24 is the big celebration, when the children are banished from the living room, and the angels and Jézuska (baby Jesus) bring the presents and decorate the tree with shiny pieces of *szaloncukor* (candies wrapped in colorful foil wrappers). It's customary to abstain from meat on Christmas Eve, so dinner revolves around fish. The meal most often starts with halászlé, followed by whole roasted fish or breaded carp and potato salad with tartar sauce. Christmas Day dinner was traditionally turkey, but these days it is anything from stuffed cabbage to roasted duck. Dessert is bejgli or *mákos guba* (bread pudding with poppy seeds).

Hungarians greet the New Year (called Szilveszter, because it falls on St. Szilveszter's feast day) with sparkling wine. Traditionally, roast suckling pig with horseradish and braised red cabbage was eaten on New Year's Day. Now, the most significant

Bejgli, a traditional Hungarian folk cake. (Shutterstock)

food to consume is some form of lentils, which are said to bring money in the coming year. *Korhelyleves*—a tangy sauerkraut and sausage soup with sour cream—and sausages (more commonly frankfurters) are also eaten in the early morning hours. At midnight everyone gathers around to sing the Hungarian national anthem.

The Easter (*húsvét*) meal is one of the biggest of the year, with boiled smoked ham, freshly grated horseradish, boiled eggs, deviled eggs in homemade tartar sauce, light and fluffy Easter bread (*tejes kalács,* similar to challah bread), potato salad in tartar sauce, pickled vegetables, and bejgli. Most Catholics abstain from eating meat on Fridays during Lent, and they often give up something else throughout the Lenten period.

Harvest festivals and processions are held throughout the country during September and October, but the harvest in Tokaj for the famous sweet wine only begins at the end of October, when many festivities are held. November 11 is the feast day of Saint Martin (Szent Márton nap), who was born in what is now Hungary but was then the Roman province of Pannonia. Legend has it that Martin was a devout hermit when he was asked to become the Bishop of Tours. He refused, hid in a goose pen, and then killed and ate one of the geese after their squawking gave away his hiding place. Ever since, it has been a Hungarian tradition to mark the day by eating goose (*liba*) and drinking the season's first wine (*újbor*).

Diet and Health

Like much of central and eastern Europe, Hungary is struggling with the long-term effects of its traditional diet, as well as of the Communist-era agricultural policies and lifestyles that resulted in meat-centric and fat-heavy diets. Obesity is the number-one public health problem in Hungary, according to studies, with some estimates putting the number of obese adults at more than 15 percent of the population.

Both age and location greatly affect the way that Hungarians cook and eat. Hungarians living in rural areas tend to eat in the most traditional manner and, ironically, often have less access to a variety of fresh fruit and vegetables, as well as the many organic food shops that stock whole grains, than Budapest residents do. Although sunflower oil is increasingly being used, pork fat remains heavily used by many older people who don't take advantage of healthier options now available.

Age is also an important factor in determining lifestyle and health. While the older generation is fairly set in its ways in terms of cooking and eating, younger Hungarians, particularly those living in urban areas, are more likely to cook non-Hungarian and lower-fat recipes. They tend to avoid the abundance of deep-fried dishes and sugary sweets, and they like to shop at organic shops and markets when they can afford to.

In addition to the diet, since the fall of Communism, experts have noted that lifestyles have become less active—in part due to the easier access to cars and the arrival of multiple television channels—with people walking less and not exercising enough.

Alcoholism, too, is a serious health problem in Hungary, with mortality due to alcoholism three times higher than the European Union average for males and 2.5 times higher for females.

Carolyn Bánfalvi

Further Reading

Bánfalvi, Carolyn. *Food Wine Budapest.* New York: Little Bookroom, 2008.

Gergely, Anikó. *Culinaria Hungary.* Cologne, Germany: Könemann, 1999.

Koerner, Andras. *A Taste of the Past: The Daily Life and Cooking of a Nineteenth-Century Hungarian Jewish Homemaker.* Durham, NH: University Press of New England, 2003.

Kovi, Paul. *Transylvanian Cuisine.* New York: Crown, 1985.

Lang, George. *The Cuisine of Hungary.* New York: Penguin Books, 1971.

Iceland

Overview

Iceland is a 40,000-square-mile island country of 320,000 people, which in 2007 the United Nations named the world's best country to live in. It was one of the first to establish a parliamentary democracy; its capital, Reykjavik, is one of the most fashionable urban enclaves on earth; and Icelanders write, publish, purchase, and read the most books per capita globally. The country boasts a landscape of spectacularly unspoiled scenery that includes mountains and oceans, wildlife and glaciers, not to mention volcanoes.

The Norse settlers who founded Iceland between 874 and 930 A.D. came upon mostly the same geography present today, which is 63 percent tundra, 14 percent lakes and glaciers, and only 23 percent vegetation. Located as far north up the Mid-Atlantic Ridge as it is, Iceland saw few ships and explorers at that time, which meant very few imported goods made it to the island. The lack of fertile, arable land also made sustainable agriculture a huge challenge and forced locals to subsist on whatever they were able to forage. And so the way Icelanders eat is mostly a result of the way they were, and are—the cold climate and long winters result in a typical Icelandic diet that is low in vegetables and high in cereals, seafood, and lamb meat, as well as a bounty of preserved foods.

🍽 Food Culture Snapshot

Pétur Galdur and Freyja Andersson are a couple in their early thirties living together in Reykjavik's Old Town neighborhood, an upscale, happening district where shopping, culture, and late-night cafés thrive. Pétur is an architect; he grew up in the suburbs of the city and easily absorbed its progression from an old-world reputation to a hip center of music, nightlife, and cosmopolitan cuisine. Freyja is from Ísafjörður, known for its charming dining culture, and embraces traditional Icelandic cuisine as much as the fusion options available in the capital. While many typical local dishes may seem old-fashioned and very much off the beaten path to visitors, they are a mainstay of urban dining, despite the variety of Asian and other European options available. It's typical for big city dwellers such as Pétur and Freyja to embrace what they ate in their childhood as comfort food while continuing to explore new palates.

Breakfast in Pétur and Freyja's modest one-bedroom loft takes place a little before 8 A.M. It is a hearty affair that includes cold cuts of meat, cheese, *sild* (pickled herring), cottage cheese, and wheat toast or oatmeal, with nibbles of dried fruit and, on the colder days, a banana for an extra boost of energy to battle the icy temperatures. Because Iceland runs on coffee, Pétur and Freyja without a doubt would have already had a cup or two of the country's world-class, gourmet *kaffi* from delicately roasted beans, which come in handy when days are short and dusk falls early. For lunch, eaten around noon, they have an easy meal of soup, bread, and salad from a deli or café near their respective offices, or a hot dish of meat or fish with potatoes, followed by a sweet fruit soup and accompanied with a glass of milk. Between 2:30 and 4 P.M., they will grab an afternoon break of an open-faced sandwich or bread and butter with some sweets, typically selecting from layer cakes, tortes, or cookies. Because dining out is expensive in Iceland, Pétur and Freyja often cook and eat in, saving trying a new restaurant or visiting a favorite for a fun night out every two weeks or so. Dinner is similar to lunch and finishes with *skýr,* a yogurt topped with sugar and cream. With some of the freshest meats, seafood, and produce in the world, it's easy to shop nutritiously at supermarkets or special produce markets for a fulfilling home-cooked meal. Before they head to bed, coffee and pastries are enjoyed at about 9:30 P.M., sometimes with friends over, other times during a sojourn to one of Reykjavik's beloved coffee shops, which run the gamut from bohemian to trendy, sometimes with live music, but always a comfortable home away from home.

When they do eat out, Pétur and Freyja are never at a loss for where to go. A culinary destination, Iceland has the most wine stewards per capita, and innovative young chefs know no bounds in fusing and creating ingredients to produce wildly new interpretations of global cuisine. Freyja is always amazed at dishes such as pizza topped with alfalfa and snails at Elðsmijan, herring sushi at Apótek, and tuna tandoori at Thorvaldsen—Iceland's famously fresh seafood taking a worldly stage.

Major Foodstuffs

The two key items on any Icelandic menu are lamb and fish. In a country where sheep outnumber people by four to one, lamb is never lacking, and few parts of the sheep are left out of the kitchen. And with the Atlantic Ocean and the Arctic Ocean as the perimeter, fish of all varieties is a common sight all year round.

The low industrial output and high environmental consciousness in Iceland mean that Icelandic meat and seafood are some of the healthiest in Europe and entirely organic. In fact, this slogan exists

A commercial salmon fishing facility in Iceland. Fishing is the country's economic staple. (Corel)

in a bid to attract interest in exports and tourism: "Sustainable Iceland since 874." Because the waters around the island are unpolluted, the fish is delicious and fresh—most common are cod, haddock, catfish, monkfish, halibut, trout, arctic char, and salmon in the local catch. The lamb has a distinctly wild flavor due to being raised free-range in the country, free of hormones, and purists insist you can taste the wild berries, moss, and herbs the flock feeds on. Apart from lamb, beef and reindeer are robust alternatives, and seabirds such as puffins and guillemots often feature in local dishes.

Dairy makes up a large part of the Icelandic diet as well, with more than 80 types of cheeses produced in the country, Camembert and blue cheese being the most famous. With milk just as wholesome as the cows they come from, it is a popular beverage that accompanies most meals and skýr, a yogurt-like product, is de rigueur daily.

Although agriculture is more challenging than in other parts of the world, hothouse technology has given rise to a decent range of vegetables and some fruit, particularly tomatoes, cucumbers, and bell peppers. That being said, salads in Iceland tend to be a by-the-way sideshow rather than a main attraction.

Cooking

Because of the country's history and lingering cold climates, preserving food is a long-standing tradition in Iceland—any meat, fish, and produce not eaten fresh are pickled, preserved, and spiced using all possible means. It's no surprise that Icelanders typically like their food saucy, salty, and well seasoned and that traditional cooking methods transform meat and seafood into hearty, heavy dishes. Fish is typically dried, smoked, salted, or baked, with garlic as a common ingredient. The pinnacle of Icelandic preservation practices must be the *hakarl,* shark meat that is buried from anywhere between three and six months until putrefied, breaking down the high levels of toxins in the flesh. While connoisseurs liken the taste to strong cheese, the flavor often makes the eyes water, and chasing a bite with *brennivin* (brandy) is often recommended, although

it is too overwhelming even for many locals. A favorite way of serving lamb is in a mustard sauce or cut into filets, as well as in stews, roasts, grilled dishes, and cutlets. Of course, it wouldn't be Iceland if there were not an outstanding way of presenting lamb—*svid* is sheep's head that is first singed to remove the wool, then cut in two to remove the brain, and then boiled to be eaten fresh or pressed into jelly (*svidasulta*).

With bread and pastries an important complement to meals and coffee breaks, baking is a significant part of Icelandic cooking. Milk is also a common ingredient, to add a robust and wholesome taste, and cheese is very popular as a side dish or addition, as well as the ubiquitous skýr. In addition to milk as a drink with meals, strong alcoholic drinks are favored, such as brennivin and other types of vodka.

The utensils in an Icelandic kitchen are similar to those used in other Western cultures, since few traditional dishes require innovative methods of preparation. Consistency is characteristic of Icelandic cooking, as a local cuisine that has thrived on homogeneity with few exterior influences.

Typical Meals

The structure of meals in an Icelander's day is not unlike that in many European countries, consisting of three main meals with an afternoon snack and a nightcap to top things off. Eating takes place at tables with individual settings of the usual silverware. The long winters and unusually cold temperatures necessitate hearty meals to stay strong and robust, and to keep the chill out, which explains the long tradition of heavy meals. Conveniently enough, the lack of a wide variety of agriculture does not make much of a difference since grains, breads, meats, and seafood are key nutritional items for Iceland's climate. As Iceland's cuisine grows more cosmopolitan, pastas and pizza have become a popular option for carbohydrates.

Interestingly enough, despite how quickly Iceland's culinary scene has been elevated on an eclectic scale, strong traditions remain, such as the constant imbibing of kaffi and skýr for dessert. The latter is now available in all sorts of berry varieties, shakes, and even a more liquid form to complement cereals. And what may appear to be delicacies, such as *fillsegg* (seabird eggs), *lundi* (puffin), *hreindýr* (reindeer), *hrútspungar* (pickled ram's testicles), *slátur* (leftover lamb parts cooked like haggis), and *hestur* (horse), are common ingredients in the daily repast. In fact, *harðfiskur* (wind-dried haddock or cod) is a popular snack and the local equivalent of gum, eaten by tearing off a piece and chewing away, sometimes with a spread of butter.

Eating Out

The exorbitant price tag attached to dining out in Iceland, mainly because of high labor costs, makes it challenging for the typical local to regularly sample the burgeoning gourmet scene in major cities such as Reykjavik, which leads the charge (a midscale meal begins at 3,125 kr, or $50). However, when Icelanders do venture into restaurants, the eclectic and innovative range of options, running from contemporary spins on traditional dishes to a fusion of international tastes, is endless. The hallmark of real Icelandic restaurants can still be found in cities outside of Reykjavik, especially in coastal areas, where these are identified by their nautical decor and wide selection of seafood and seabirds, always served with potatoes, familiar vegetables, and rich sauces in large portions and dramatic presentations. These traditional restaurants serve the dishes that are harder to create at home as well as fancier, more expertly prepared versions of comfort favorites.

The focus on modern Icelandic dining is strong and conspicuous—in Reykjavik restaurants, the waitstaff passionately introduce and engage in discourse about their specialties. Service is impeccable and welcoming, the warmth an immediate antidote for the climate, and a fantastic entrée into this wild new (for Iceland) art. Dining hours tend to run on the late side, with most breakfast places opening only after 10 A.M. on weekends and dinner service starting no earlier than 8 P.M.

There is perhaps no better indication of how far the Icelandic culinary scene has come than the Reykjavik Food & Fun Festival, held yearly in February (note that winter does not prevent Icelanders from going out and indulging in great food). Now one of the city's major events, prominent chefs from all around the world descend on the city to collaborate with their local counterparts to produce one-time-only prix fixe menus, at regular prices, in Reykjavik's best restaurants, infusing local Icelandic ingredients with global spices, flavors, and methodology.

In a country where delicacies come all the way out from left field, and with an abundance of fresh meats and fish, it is surprising that hot dogs are revered as an epicurean icon. After dancing a Saturday evening away, with more than a few nips of brennivin, many Reykjavik dwellers can be found in line at Bæjarius Beztu Pylsun, which literally translates as "the best hot dog in town," in the country that considers its hot dogs the best in the world. For only $2, you get lamb, pork, and beef in a super-snappy casing—the addition of lamb mellows and deepens the flavor—and crunchy fried onions, rémoulade, chopped raw onions, ketchup, and mustard nestled in a sweet, soft, and light white bun, the basic construction for *ein með öllu* ("one with everything").

Special Occasions

There's perhaps no better time than *Þorramatur* to see a parade of Iceland's finest foods. *Þorramatur* is a selection of local dishes comprising meats and fish cooked in the ways already described and served with *rúgbrauð* (dense and dark rye bread), butter, and brennivin, usually buffet-style. *Þorramatur* is usually eaten from January through March, particularly during the midwinter feast of *Þorrablót*, but it is interesting to note that Icelanders enjoy their delicacies so much—the sheep's head, putrefied shark, pickled ram's testicles, and so on, all highlights of *Þorramatur*—that it is not uncommon to see this served any time the mood arises, particularly since locals truly embrace tradition.

Christmas Eve is a big occasion in Iceland, when a maelstrom of baking is done leading up to the holiday, featuring special spicy cookies. Each family will have at least 10 different types of cookies to offer visiting guests, and the centerpiece on the Christmas

Eve dinner table is usually ham, *hangikjöt* (smoked lamb), or *rjupa,* a grouselike ptarmigan that takes the place of turkey. It is also a long-standing tradition for the family to make *laufabrauo* together, a pancake eaten at Christmas. Pudding with hidden almonds is served for dessert, and the person who gets the portion with the nuts wins a prize.

Although the smell of hangikjöt cooking is a sure sign of yuletide, the feasting begins on the eve of Christmas Eve, St. Thorlakur's Day, celebrated with a skate lunch. Originally eaten to mark the end of the Catholic Christmas fast, the tradition of the skate lunch continued even after Iceland converted to Lutheranism because this was a busy day and a dish that was easily and quickly cooked was needed. Beginning in the fall, skate is pickled and fermented to be ready by December 23 and is then served in chunks with boiled potatoes on the side. While the odor of ammonia is strong and the taste must be acquired, the skate lunch remains one of the most celebrated events of the holiday season.

Diet and Health

There is no better indication that the Icelandic diet has been lauded and commended for its organic, hormone-free nature than the fact that many countries are importing its meats and fish—in fact, with Whole Foods Market in the United States heavily marketing its selection of Icelandic lamb and skýr, these mainstays of the country's diet have indeed entered mainstream popular culture.

The strong reliance on fish, pasture-raised lamb, and wild game for food means the Icelandic diet is rich in omega-3 fats; some experts attribute the low depression rates, despite the bleak climate, to this.

Some traditional Icelandic food (plate to the left: Hangikjöt, Hrútspungar, Lifrarpylsa, Blómör, Hákarl, Svid; plate to the right: Rúgbrau, Flatbrau). (Shutterstock)

By consuming geothermally grown vegetables, wild berries, and whole grains such as barley and rye, Icelanders absorb a lot of antioxidants, which keep them healthy during the icy months.

Desiree Koh

Further Reading

Anthony Bourdain: No Reservations [DVD]. Zero Point Zero Production for Travel Channel. Chatsworth, CA: Image Entertainment, 2007.

Rognvaldardottir, Nanna. *Cool Cuisine: Traditional Icelandic Cuisine.* Reykjavík, Iceland: Vaka-Helgafell, 2004.

Wilcox, Jonathan, and Zawiah Abdul Latif. *Iceland.* New York: Marshall Cavendish Benchmark, 2007.

Ireland

Overview

Ireland is the most westerly country in Europe and part of the British Isles. For many centuries, the British Crown has exercised dominion over parts of the island and at times the whole. The island of Ireland has 32 counties, 6 of which form Northern Ireland, which is part of the United Kingdom. The other 26 counties gained independence from Great Britain in 1921, and the division of the island into two countries has been contentious ever since. Ireland has a mild temperate climate in which grass grows nearly all year long. Ireland also has over 3,500 miles of coastline, which is teeming with fish. It has been suggested that the Irish are more connected to the land than any other western European nation. Although there are only 5 million people living on the island of Ireland, more than 80 million people around the world claim Irish lineage.

Ireland has one of the most interesting culinary traditions in western Europe, which has been influenced by the interaction of climate, geographic location, geology, tradition, conquest and colonization, and commerce. Ireland was the first European country to adopt the potato as a staple crop, which transformed Ireland from an underpopulated island of 1 million in the 1590s to the most densely populated country in Europe in 1840, with 8.2 million inhabitants. The overdependence on the potato, particularly on one variety, the lumper, which was not resistant to the fungal disease *Phytophthora infestans,* led to the disaster known today as the Great Famine (1845–1849), with the result that, by 1851, at least one million of the Irish poor had died and another million had emigrated. Long before the introduction of the potato to Europe, however, the Irish were renowned for their tradition of hospitality, which was enshrined in the ancient Gaelic laws. Parallel food traditions existed in Ireland before, during, and after the famine, in which the middle classes and the Anglo-Irish gentry enjoyed a varied diet that would be hard to surpass in contemporary rural France or Britain. Traditional Irish food is essentially solid country cooking using the freshest of ingredients and treating them simply, letting the food speak for itself. The traditional fresh home-baked breads and scones served with butter, jams, and marmalades form a staple of Irish cuisine. The Irish attitude toward food has transformed dramatically, particularly since the early 1990s. In 2005, Irish people for the first time in history spent more on food to eat outside the home than they did on eating in the home.

🍽 Food Culture Snapshot

Fergus and Niamh Dunne are a typical middle-class family with two children; they live in Dublin. Their breakfast consists of either porridge (oatmeal) or breakfast cereals such as shredded wheat, which is served with milk and sugar. Beverages at breakfast time include orange juice and either tea or coffee. Lunch for both the children and Fergus normally consists of a sandwich (with a ham or cheese filling) served with a fruit smoothie (fruit pureed with natural yogurt and fruit juice) and perhaps some popcorn. Niamh would normally eat some pita bread with hummus or some cream cheese, apple, and crackers for her lunch. As a family they go through phases of using their fruit juicer

Shepherd's pie served with sautéed potatoes and broccoli. (Shutterstock)

or the bread maker but then don't use them again for a while. Like in many families, the evening dinner follows a weekly pattern in which meat, potatoes, and vegetables (for example, chicken breasts, mashed potatoes, and broccoli) would be served around three times a week, with either spaghetti Bolognese or lasagna on another day, fish (salmon normally) served with potatoes and vegetables on Wednesdays, and pizza on Thursdays. One day a week, they would eat dinner from either a fish and chip shop or an Indian or Chinese take-out place. Dinner is usually completed by a cup of tea and some biscuits (cookies) or a slice of cake. Once a week, the children might also eat pasta, chicken nuggets, or slices of pizza when they return from school.

The Dunnes do their main supermarket shopping online and have it delivered. This includes their breakfast cereals, milk, sugar, oil, rice, pasta, fruit (apples, oranges, and bananas), fresh vegetables, frozen foods (peas, sweet corn), jams, and cleaning products. This main weekly shopping is supplemented by about four visits to smaller local shops, including a local butcher, a convenience store, and a weekly farmers' market. During the summer months, salads feature within their diet, and they grow lettuce in the back garden. The children dictate much of the diet; Niamh and Fergus don't eat as much of the ratatouilles or stir-fries they used to eat before the children came along. Fergus makes homemade soup once a week, and they

entertain friends for dinner about twice a month. Daily guests, however, are always offered a cup of tea or coffee, which would normally be accompanied with some biscuits or a slice of cake.

Major Foodstuffs

Potatoes, dairy produce, cereals, meat, and vegetables remain the staples of Irish cuisine, despite the wave of immigration the country experienced in the last two decades. Ireland is now a truly multicultural country where dishes such as lasagna, chicken tikka masala, fajitas, or Thai green curry are as much part of the Irish culinary canon as bacon and cabbage, Irish stew, or shepherd's pie. Ireland's residents are among the highest per-capita consumers of tea, butter, potatoes, pig meat, and milk in the world. Some foodstuffs, which historically had been luxury items, such as chicken, beef, and salmon, have become increasingly popular and affordable in the last few decades. Oatmeal porridge, which has been eaten in Ireland since ancient times, remains a popular breakfast dish, often served with cream and honey. Despite Ireland's island location and the richness of its coastal waters, the Irish have never fully exploited its marine resources. The majority of the Irish catch is exported, and Ireland is on par with landlocked Austria in per-capita consumption of seafood.

Irish cuisine has been influenced by history over the centuries. The Vikings helped to popularize seafood, whereas the Normans introduced new varieties of animals, birds, and fish, including the white-fleeced sheep, domesticated duck, mute swan (as opposed to the native Hooper swan), pike, rabbits, pheasants, pigeons, and fallow deer.

By the late-medieval period, a number of dietary systems were in place in Ireland, according to social rank, region, and access to the market. Areas of direct Norman influence aligned their palate to the medieval European norm. Trade records testify to the use of imported luxury goods like spices, sugar, almonds, pepper, figs, verjuice, and rice. Almonds were used on fast days to make almond milk as a substitute for dairy milk. The older Gaelic diet of dairy produce, oats, and salted meats coexisted with the newer, more elaborate Norman diet.

Detailed accounts of food eaten before the arrival of the potato in the 17th century exist. Among the vegetables listed, both wild and cultivated, are watercress (*biolar*), sorrel (*samhadh*), nettles, celery, parsley, charlock (*praiseach*), kale and cabbage, shamrock, wild garlic, leek, onion, chives (*foltchep*), peas and beans, carrot and parsnip (*meacan*), beets (*biatas*), dulse (*duileasc*), and sloke (*sleabhcán*). Fruits listed include the blackberry, sloe, wild cherry, raspberry, strawberry, rowan, crab apple, elderberry, whortleberry, and cranberry. Native hazelnuts and imported walnuts are mentioned, but the most frequently mentioned fruit in the early Irish documents is the apple. Orchards were widely distributed, particularly in Leinster but also in the counties of Donegal, Mayo, Armagh, and Fermanagh. Apple tarts and crumbles remain extremely popular as sweet dishes with the Irish, with rhubarb, strawberries, and blackberries also popular when in season.

Potatoes

There were four main phases in the potato's acceptance into the general Irish diet. Stage one (1590–1675) saw the potato used as a supplementary food and standby against famine; in stage two (1675–1750), the potato was viewed as a valuable winter food for the poorer classes; in stage three (1750–1810), the poorer classes became dangerously reliant on the potato as a staple for most of the year; and stage four (1810–1845) saw mounting distress as localized famines and potato failures became commonplace. Two centuries of genetic evolution resulted in yields that grew from 2 tons per acre in 1670 to 10 tons per acre in 1800. The potato was useful for cleaning, restoring, and reclaiming the soil and also for fattening pigs. It has been suggested that increased potato consumption may simply and paradoxically reflect the fact that cereal cultivation intensified in the 1750s and 1760s, resulting in a growing reliance on the potato as a cleaning and restoring root crop. The potato provided food for the growing labor force needed for the move from

pasture to tillage that occurred at this time, but this shift resulted in high levels of unemployment following the Battle of Waterloo (1815) when the demand for grain exports fell. During the 18th century there was a steady export demand for Irish salt beef and butter. As dairy herds grew, cattle were drawn out of the poorer household, denying them an important food source, but this gap was filled by the potato, which was a noncommercial subsistence crop.

By the 19th century the potato had established itself as a staple of one-third of the population, an overdependence that led to the devastation of the famine in the 1840s when successive harvests failed. The period 1810–1845 saw the adoption of new, inferior varieties of potatoes, notably the lumper, which promised excellent yields. With this new variety, a family of six could exist for a whole year from one acre of even the poorest land that had been well manured. However, the lumper was not resistant to the potato blight, and this resulted in the dramatic potato failures of 1845, 1846, and 1847.

The potato was enjoyed by rich and poor alike. The custom of preparing potato puddings, both sweet and savory, was particularly noticeable among the wealthy, where extra ingredients like saffron, sugar, and spices differentiated this potato dish from the plain boiled potatoes of the cottiers. Among the poorer classes, who consumed an average of 11 pounds (5 kilograms) of potatoes each a day, it was not uncommon, it was said, to see individuals "eating one potato, peeling a second, have a third in his fist and an eye on the fourth." Boiled potatoes were eaten with a restricted variety of foods—butter, buttermilk, occasional bacon, herring, and seaweed (dulse and sloke) and shellfish in coastal areas. The Irish have traditionally favored floury potatoes over waxy potatoes. Mashed potato dishes such as *champ* (with spring onions), colcannon (with shredded cabbage), and *kala* (with onions and soft-boiled eggs) were popular with those of moderate means and have become very popular in recent times on the menus of Irish restaurants. Another traditional Irish potato dish that remains most popular in the northwestern counties of Ireland is *boxty,* which is made from a mix of cooked and grated raw potatoes. In 1845 there were over 2 million acres (829,875 hectares) under potato cultivation, but this had fallen to about 50,000 acres (20,000 hectares) in 1991. Popular potato varieties in Ireland include Kerr Pinks, Wexford Queens, Records, Pentland Dells, and Golden Wonders, but the most widespread variety is an all-purpose potato called the Rooster, which was developed in Oak Park, County Carlow. However, pasta, rice, and noodles are beginning to challenge the dominance of potatoes on the carbohydrate front.

Pork

In Ireland today, pork is the most commonly eaten meat. It is eaten in a number of forms, including fresh pork steaks and chops, pork sausages, bacon, hams, rashers (bacon), and both black and white puddings. Historically, potatoes were cooked as feed for pigs. Pigs were also fed whey, the by-product of both butter and cheese making. Some of the pigs were kept for home consumption, but the rest were a valuable source of income and were shown great respect as the "gentleman who paid the rent." Until the early 20th century most Irish rural households kept some pigs. From around the mid-18th century commercial salting of pork and bacon grew rapidly in Ireland. Irish bacon was the brand leader, and the Irish companies exported their expertise to countries like Denmark and Russia. Nowadays, pigs are reared mostly in large factory farms. Pork features strongly in the Irish breakfast, on sandwiches at lunchtime, and in the famous Dublin dish *coddle*. The popularity of pork products became particularly apparent through the amount of empty shelf space in Irish supermarkets in December 2008 when there was a food scare concerning dioxins in pork and all products were recalled.

Dublin Coddle

Serves 4

½ lb sausages (cocktail sausages are nice)

½ lb bacon (cut in chunks)

½ lb onion (cut in chunks)

I lb potatoes (cut in chunks)

I large carrot (peeled and cut in chunks)

34 oz chicken stock or water

½ leek, finely sliced (using green and white of leek)

3.5 oz cream (about ½ c)

Seasoning (mostly ground pepper as little salt is required due to the salt in the meat and stock)

Put all ingredients (except leeks, cream, and seasoning) into a pot, and bring to a boil. Reduce heat and simmer for 25 minutes. Skim any impurities that rise to the top. Add the cream and the chopped leeks, and cook for a further 3 minutes, then season and serve.

Milk and Dairy

Ireland traditionally has excelled in the production of dairy produce—milk, sour milk, butter, buttermilk, curds, and both soft and hard cheeses. Evidence of the Irish fondness for *bánbidh*, "white foods," is found in the 12th-century poem *Aislinge Meic Con Glinne,* where reference is made to a delectable drink "of very thick milk, of milk not too thick, of milk of long thickness, of milk of medium thickness, of yellow bubbling milk, the swallowing of which needs chewing." In both the medieval and the early-modern periods, the Irish were the highest per-capita consumers of butter in the world. Irish butter is sold under the Kerrygold label all around the world. Cheese making has an ancient tradition in Ireland, but it had all but disappeared until the resurgence of an artisan farmhouse cheese industry, led by a number of farmers' wives who had more milk than the European Union quotas allowed them to sell. Prior to this, the cheese industry in Ireland was almost exclusively confined to large-scale production of mainly cheddar cheese in factories, which were mostly owned by dairy cooperatives. Ireland today has over 300 types of farmhouse cheese, which on a per-capita basis is higher even than the production in France. The most popular of these are Cashel Blue, Gubbeen, Milleens, Ardsallagh, Gabriel, Durrus, and Coolea.

Tea, Breads, and Cakes

From ancient times in Ireland, oatcakes, flatbreads, and griddle breads were popular staples. There was no evidence of the built-up oven until the Norman arrival, and leavened yeast bread was common only in areas of Norman influence. During the latter half of the 19th century, there was a general growth in food-related stores and in the number of commercial bakeries and dairies in particular. During this time two items that had been the prerogative of the wealthy, white yeast-leavened baker's bread and tea, became increasingly popular among the working classes. White bread was held in esteem over homemade bread and was offered at special occasions such as wakes, Christmas, and Easter, or when special guests such as a priest visited the home.

A parallel development was the appearance of raised wheaten soda bread that was produced on the open hearth in a *bastible* pot (a type of Dutch oven), due to the increased availability of chemical leaveners (particularly bicarbonate of soda), which along with the soft flour and buttermilk produced a product that is considered to be uniquely Irish. The addition of other ingredients—eggs, butter, dried fruit, and spices—led to the growing repertoire of Irish breads, scones, and cakes. Some regional variation was also evident, with potato breads such as boxty most popular in the northwestern counties. A yeast-leavened bread bap (bun) called *blaa* is considered to be unique to Waterford and may be Norman in origin. Soda farls (a type of scone cooked on a hot plate rather than in the oven) are particularly popular in Northern Ireland and form part of the famous Ulster fry, along with fried bread. Two Irish brands of tea, Barry's and Lyons, have dominated the market from the early 20th century to the present day, and the Irish are still the highest per-capita consumers of tea in the world today.

Cooking

Roasting, boiling, baking, stewing, and frying are the main methods of cookery used in Irish cuisine. The prime cuts of meat (beef, lamb, pork) are roasted and often served with roasted potatoes and

Traditional Irish soda bread. (Shutterstock)

roasted root vegetables (carrots, parsnips, and turnips). Most vegetables are boiled, although some people prefer to steam floury potatoes. Bacon and corned beef are boiled, and the cooking liquor is often used to cook the accompanying cabbage or as an addition to the parsley sauce. Stewed meats are particularly popular in wintertime, with the most famous Irish stew classically containing only mutton, onions, potatoes, and water. Stewed apples are very popular as a sweet, scented with some cloves and served with custard. The frying pan holds pride of place in the Irish household, for it is used to fry sausages, rashers, eggs, black pudding (blood sausages), and tomatoes for the famous Irish cooked breakfast, commonly called a "fry." The more health-conscious broil their breakfast, and some lamb cutlets with butter, pepper, and mustard are also commonly cooked under the broiler. Many children learn to bake by making fairy cakes (little buns) and gradually progress to sponge cakes, apple tarts, and crumbles. It is hard to beat the taste of oven-fresh scones with fresh butter and strawberry jam, washed down with a nice cup of tea.

Typical Meals

The typical meals in Ireland are breakfast (7:30–9 A.M.), lunch (1–2 P.M.), and dinner (6–7 P.M.). Some people also take a supper (9:30–10 P.M.). There have been changes in the mealtimes and structure in recent years due to the rising female participation in the workforce. Many families ate their main meal in the middle of the day and then took a meal they called tea in the evening. The main family meal is now most commonly eaten in the evening, albeit sometimes in front of the television.

Breakfast can include one or many of the following: fruit juice, breakfast cereal (cornflakes, Weetabix, Special K, Rice Krispies, and so on), oatmeal porridge, toast, scones, brown or white soda bread with butter, jam or marmalade, yogurt, fruit, croissants, and Danish pastries. A full hot Irish breakfast includes sausages, rashers, fried eggs, grilled tomato, black and white pudding, and mushrooms. The Ulster fry also includes soda farls and fried bread. Boiled or poached eggs are also popular breakfast items, served with toast and butter. Omelets are occasionally served for breakfast as are fried kippers or dishes such as kedgeree. This would be more common on weekends, particularly as a form of brunch on Sunday. Breakfast beverages include tea, coffee, and fruit juices.

The traditional main meal based around meat and two vegetables has not disappeared despite the growing popularity of ethnic dishes such as Thai curry, lasagna, or chili con carne. The most popular meats are bacon (with parsley sauce), chicken (normally roasted with stuffing and gravy), beef (with horseradish sauce), lamb (with mint sauce), and pork (with applesauce). Smaller cuts of meat are also popular, such as beef steaks, pork chops, lamb chops and cutlets, and individual chicken breasts, thighs, or drumsticks. Minced beef is very popular and is used by most families at least once a week to make burgers, shepherd's pie, spaghetti Bolognese, lasagna, meatballs, or chili. Mutton is not as widely available or as popular as in previous times. There has been a decrease in the consumption of offal (liver, kidneys, heart, oxtail, tongue, pig's trotters) among the native Irish since 1990, but they have become more visible in butcher's shops due to the growing multiethnic population (or the new Irish, as they are known), who still value offal for both culinary and economic reasons.

Potatoes are served boiled, steamed, baked, and mashed. Deep-fried chipped potatoes, known as chips, are particularly common but are usually purchased alongside fried fish in batter from fish and chip shops. Common vegetables include cabbage, carrots and parsnips, turnips, broccoli, cauliflower, French beans, and peas. Onions, celery, and carrots are particularly popular as a base for stews (both brown and white). Casseroles are also popular one-pot dishes, particularly in wintertime. It is customary to finish dinner with a cup of tea, which is normally accompanied by a biscuit or a slice of cake. Apple tarts or crumbles might be served with whipped cream or with custard. Sponge cakes and fruit cakes are also popular.

Children are increasingly being fed separate food from what their parents eat, with pizza, pasta, noodles, chicken nuggets, chips, and potato waffles well established as foods most Irish children regularly eat. Another regular snack for children are crisps (potato chips), which come in cheese and onion, salt and vinegar, prawn cocktail, and barbecue beef flavors mostly. Most elementary schools now take part in a government program in which the children grow some food in their schoolyard or classroom. Milk is also delivered free of charge to primary schools to encourage dairy consumption for calcium intake and healthy bones. Childhood obesity and related diseases are, however, becoming an increasing issue in Ireland.

Eating Out

There has always been a market for eating outside the home in bars, taverns, eating houses, restaurants, cafés, canteens, and clubs. This market grew dramatically from the 1970s, and in the last 15 years, eating out moved from an occasional event to a regular pastime for most Irish people. In 2005, for the first time in history, Irish people spent more money on food consumed outside rather than inside the home. Many Irish public houses (pubs) sell food as well as alcoholic beverages. The most common form is the *carvery,* where roast meats are carved to order and served with potatoes, vegetables, stuffing, and gravy. Wet dishes such as stews and curries are also served at a carvery. The carvery provides the most authentic public form of Irish cuisine. Most Irish people prefer to go to a Chinese, Thai, Italian, Indian, or

French restaurant when dining out. There is also a gradual growth in sushi bars and bagel bars in the large cities. Ireland now has some excellent restaurants and is steadily building a reputation as a culinary destination for travelers. A growing number of restaurants serve what is called modern Irish cuisine, where the best Irish produce is cooked and served using contemporary techniques. There has been a long tradition of a café culture in Irish cities, but in recent years the famous cafés such as Bewley's, where a pot of tea and an almond bun might be consumed, have been replaced by smaller cafés where cappuccinos and Danish pastries or muffins are more popular.

Fast-food restaurants such as McDonald's, Burger King, and Kentucky Fried Chicken are popular in Ireland, but some indigenous chains such as Supermac's and Abrekebabra have proved to be equally popular, serving particularly Irish versions of fast-food items, such as curry chips, taco fries, or garlic and cheese fries. Most Chinese and Indian restaurants also offer take-out menus. The most common take-out place in Ireland is the fish and chip shops, which are mostly run by Italian families. These establishments serve deep-fried fish in batter, battered sausages and onion rings, burgers, southern fried chicken, and sometimes also kebabs. Chips are usually served with salt and malt vinegar. Another source of food outside the home that has become extremely popular in recent years is the deli counters in convenient shops, where fresh sandwiches, rolls, and wraps are made to order. At lunchtime, there are regular queues at such counters throughout the country. A particularly Irish morning offering popular in such establishments is the jumbo breakfast roll, which is two sausages, two slices of bacon, and black pudding placed in a buttered bread roll with tomato ketchup.

Special Occasions

There are a number of special occasions within the year or social calendar that call for specific foods. Christmastime revolves around the family; the traditional Christmas dinner of roast goose has been replaced by turkey and ham with stuffing, cranberry sauce, roast potatoes, vegetables, and gravy. This meal is often preceded by some smoked salmon on brown bread or a prawn cocktail (cooked prawns on shredded lettuce topped with a cocktail sauce). The Christmas meal is followed by Christmas pudding, also known as plum pudding, which is a rich fruit-based boiled or steamed pudding served with either brandy butter or custard. Later on, with a cup of tea or coffee, you might be offered a slice of Christmas cake, which is a rich baked fruitcake topped with both almond and royal icing. Another popular Christmas food is spiced beef, which was traditionally eaten on Christmas Eve. Both the spiced beef and the turkey and ham are excellent for either cold salads or sandwiches when guests come to visit at Christmastime. Another popular sweet served at Christmas is sherry trifle.

The turkey and ham meal is also often served at family occasions such as weddings or at funerals. Families often invite mourners back to a hotel for either soup and sandwiches or a sit-down meal after a funeral. At other occasions such as christenings, first communions, confirmations, or 21st-birthday parties, it is more common to serve either a cold salad buffet or a hot dish such as chicken curry with rice.

The next food-related date in the calendar is Shrove Tuesday, which marks the beginning of Lent (40 days of fasting from Ash Wednesday to Easter Sunday). On this day it is customary to eat pancakes, a custom that originated to use up eggs, which would not be eaten again until Easter Sunday. Pancakes were eaten with sugar and lemon or with honey, but nowadays children increasingly prefer Nutella (a hazelnut chocolate spread) on their pancakes. Ash Wednesday, Good Friday, and Holy Thursday were all traditionally black fast days when no meat was consumed. Fridays were also traditionally fast days when fish was normally consumed, but these traditions are quickly being lost in an increasingly secular Ireland. Many Irish people continue the tradition of abstaining from some foodstuff during Lent, normally sweets, sugar, cakes, or alcohol. Saint Patrick's Day falls in the middle of Lent, and Irish people are given a special dispensation from whatever they avoided for Lent on this day. On Good Friday, it is customary to eat hot cross buns (yeast-leavened spiced fruit buns topped with a cross of pastry), and the tradition of eating many eggs on Easter Sunday has been almost replaced by the gifts of chocolate eggs for children. On Easter Sunday it is customary to eat roast leg of spring lamb, which is seasonal.

The arrival of summer is marked with the availability of fresh strawberries and of new potatoes, which are as welcomed in Ireland as the Beaujolais nouveau celebrated by the French. New potatoes are often eaten simply with their skins still on, with butter and salt. Summer is also about eating wild salmon, which is becoming less available due to overfishing. Rhubarb and blackberries are at their best in the summer months also. The tradition of eating goose at Michaelmas (September 29) has all but disappeared, but the game season (venison, pheasant, grouse, etc.) in the winter months is still influential in the diet of the countryside and in gourmet restaurants.

The next special occasion for food is the festival of Halloween (October 31/November 1). Many foods and food rituals are associated with this festival. Many of the traditions are linked to divining the future. From the mid-18th century, colcannon, a dish made from mashed potatoes with curly kale or cabbage, was a traditional supper dish on Halloween night, often containing items such as a coin, stick, or rag to predict the future prospects of the consumers. Another traditional foodstuff at Halloween is *barmbrack,* which comes from the Gaelic *bairín breac,* or speckled loaf. The fruit loaf traditionally contains charms that foretell future events. Finding a ring in the cake meant marriage within the year, a rag symbolized poverty, a bean meant riches whereas a pea meant poverty, a stick forecasted a future beating by one's spouse, and a thimble discovered by an unmarried girl indicated life as a spinster. Most barmbracks nowadays contain only a ring. The American Halloween tradition of the jack-o'-lantern made from a pumpkin is Irish in origin. The Irish used to carry a sod of turf from a sacred fire to their houses inside a hollowed-out turnip (rutabaga), and this tradition was carried on by Irish immigrants in America, using the pumpkin where no turnip was available.

A dish of colcannon. (Shutterstock)

Diet and Health

Cardiovascular disease is the main cause of death in Ireland, accounting for 36 percent of all deaths and including heart attacks, strokes, and other circulatory diseases. The government has been working with the food industry to reduce salt levels in processed food and is involved in promoting a more active lifestyle among the population. Research shows that certain segments of the community are more likely to suffer from diet-related illnesses. In a study, the contribution of fat to total energy intake increased as socioeconomic status decreased, a finding reflective of the higher consumption of foods high in fat by respondents from socially disadvantaged groups. Energy from carbohydrates was greatest among those from socially advantaged groups and was close to the recommended 50 percent of the total energy intake. Conversely, energy from protein decreased with increasing social status in groups. The mean intake of vitamins and minerals was generally close to or above the recommended values. Another diet-related health issue in Ireland is the amount of alcohol consumed, which is significantly higher than the European average.

Máirtín Mac Con Iomaire

Further Reading

Andrews, Colman. *The Country Cooking of Ireland.* San Francisco: Chronicle Books, 2009.

Clarkson, Louis A., and E. Margaret Crawford. *Feast and Famine, Food and Nutrition in Ireland 1500–1900.* Oxford: Oxford University Press, 2001.

Cowan, Cathal, and Regina Sexton. *Ireland's Traditional Foods: An Exploration into Irish Local and Typical Foods and Drinks.* Dublin, Ireland: Teagasc, The National Food Centre, 1997.

Mac Con Iomaire, M. "The History of Seafood in Irish Cuisine and Culture." In *Wild Foods: Proceedings of the Oxford Symposium on Food and Cookery 2005,* edited by Richard Hoskings, 219–33. Totnes, Devon, UK: Prospect Books, 2006.

Mac Con Iomaire, M. "The Pig in Irish Cuisine Past and Present." In *The Fat of the Land: Proceedings of the Oxford Symposium on Food and Cookery 2002,* edited by Harlan Walker, 207–15. Bristol, UK: Footwork, 2003.

Mac Con Iomaire, M., and A. Cully. "The History of Eggs in Irish Cuisine and Culture." In *Eggs in Cookery: Proceedings of the Oxford Symposium on Food and Cookery 2006,* edited by Richard Hoskings, 137–49. Totnes, Devon, UK: Prospect Books, 2007.

Mac Con Iomaire, M., and P. Gallagher. "The History of the Potato in Irish Cuisine and Culture." In *Vegetables: Proceedings of the Oxford Symposium on Food and Cookery 2008,* edited by Susan Friedland, 111–20. Totnes, Devon, UK: Prospect Books, 2009.

O'Sullivan, Catherine Marie. *Hospitality in Medieval Ireland 900–1500.* Dublin, Ireland: Four Courts Press, 2004.

Sexton, Regina. "Ireland: Simplicity and Integration, Continuity and Change." In *Culinary Cultures of Europe: Identity, Diversity and Dialogue,* edited by Darra Goldstein and Kathrin Merkle, 227–40. Strasbourg, France: Council of Europe Publishing, 2005.

Sexton, Regina. *A Little History of Irish Food.* Dublin, Ireland: Gill and Macmillan, 1998.

Italy

Overview

Italy is located at the heart of the Mediterranean Sea. After years of relative underdevelopment, the country has become one of the most industrialized countries in the world, despite its dysfunctional political structure. Various areas differ in terms of economic activities, social structures, and culture, although some habits, especially those connected with Catholicism, are widespread and widely followed. Because of its long history, the diverse and prolonged influences of neighboring populations, and local differences, Italian cuisine presents a stunning variety of products, foods, and dishes. Italians are usually quite knowledgeable about foods and dishes that have nationwide diffusion and distribution, but they are also very proud of their local products and traditions. In recent years, local foodways, and above all artisanal products, have been rediscovered. However, large sections of the population are abandoning the traditional Mediterranean diet, mainly based on carbohydrates and vegetables, and adopting a diet rich in protein, fat, and sugar; as a consequence Italy is experiencing a growth in obesity and heart disease.

🍽 Food Culture Snapshot

Massimo and Francesca live in downtown Rome with their four-year-old daughter, Caterina. It is Saturday, and on weekends they take the time to go grocery shopping. Like most Romans, they buy different things in different places, depending on what they are looking for. They start early at the outdoor market, the best place for fresh fruit and vegetables. Some produce comes from the central wholesale market, but some stalls belong to farmers from the nearby villages on the hills, who have been bringing their products into the city for years. Now, immigrants manage many stalls, but they are familiar with their Italian clients' foodways and habits. Massimo and Francesca decide to get some fresh fish, too; the best day to buy it is Friday, but today it is still good, and they trust their fishmonger. For meat, although it can be bought at the outdoor market, they prefer to go to the neighborhood butcher's, where they can get the cuts they need in a quieter environment. They also like to patronize the local bakery, where they buy fresh bread and also pizza by weight: Caterina loves it. After taking care of the fresh food, Francesca and Massimo drive to the supermarket, where they buy products that can be stored: canned and frozen food, flour, cookies, and pasta, which are cheaper at the supermarket. Tomorrow they are having friends over, so on their way back they decide to stop at their favorite gourmet shop and get some cheese and cold cuts for the guests. It is expensive, but for special occasions they do not mind spending a little more. A final stop at the wine store to get some good bottles, and they are good to go.

Major Foodstuffs

Grains, such as wheat, rice, and corn, constitute the main staple in Italian cuisine. Wheat, both the hard and soft varieties, provides the bulk of dietary calories in the form of flour, bread, pasta, pizza, and such. Breads, both salted and unsalted, vary in size from single-portion breads to big loaves. They are used during meals, and single-portion breads (*panini*), filled with all kinds of food, are eaten as a snack or a light meal. Leavened dough is also used to make pizza, which can be baked in the oven and simply seasoned with a dash of olive oil, salt, and some herbs or enriched by all kinds of toppings. Pizza can be either eaten at a restaurant, in which case it is round and served on a dish, or bought from shops, where it is cut according to the client's request and sold by the weight.

Pappa al Pomodoro (Tuscan Tomato and Bread Soup)

$^1/_3$ c extra-virgin olive oil

1 medium onion, finely minced

1 stalk celery, finely minced

1 medium carrot, finely minced

1 clove garlic, finely minced

1 tbsp parsley, finely minced

3 c stale Italian bread, crust removed, cut into 1-in. cubes

1½ lb red tomatoes, peeled, seeded, and chopped

3 c chicken broth

Salt and pepper

4 basil leaves, minced

Heat the olive oil in a soup pot over medium heat. Add the onion, celery, carrot, garlic, and parsley, and sauté until the vegetables are soft. Add the bread, and stir for a couple of minutes. Add the tomatoes, let cook for 5 minutes, and then add the warm broth. Season with salt and pepper. Reduce the heat and let simmer, uncovered, till the bread dissolves into a thick, creamy soup. Remove from the heat and allow the soup to rest for 20 minutes. Serve at room temperature, garnishing each portion with a drizzle of extra-virgin olive oil and a sprinkling of basil.

The main Italian staple made with wheat flour is certainly pasta. Fresh pasta used to be made at home, but it is now available in shops. The most common types are fettuccine or tagliatelle, shaped with a knife into long ribbons. Local specialties include *tajarin* (long, flat egg noodles) in Piedmont, *garganelli* (ridged quill shapes) in Romagna, *orecchiette* (ear shapes) in Puglia, *spaghetti alla chitarra* in Abruzzo, and *bigoli* (thick hollow strands) in Veneto. There are also many types of fresh *pasta ripiena*, or filled pasta, such as ravioli, *agnolotti, tortelli,* and tortellini; *lasagne* and cannelloni, rolled squares filled with meat, mozzarella, or vegetables, are also common. Although most *pasta secca*, or dried pasta, is industrially produced, artisanal varieties are also very popular, despite being more expensive. Different shapes of pastas tend to be used with different sauces and condiments according to local tradition or nationwide habits.

Italian rice grains tend to be more rounded and release more starch than varieties from other countries and thus are particularly apt for local recipes. In the north, a traditional way of cooking rice is risotto: The grains are first sautéed in butter and onion until translucent, then hot meat broth is added slowly. The most famous is probably *risotto alla milanese,* cooked with saffron and broth. In recent years, fish-based risotto has also become very popular. In the south, there are fried balls of rice stuffed with various ingredients, like *supplì* in Rome and *arancini* in Sicily. Rice is also widely used in thick soups.

Maize was introduced into Italy in the 16th century. Although corn on the cob is appreciated and corn kernels have found their way into salads, maize is mainly consumed in the form of polenta,

A traditional Italian saffron risotto. (Shutterstock)

similar to American grits, seasoned with various sauces. Other grains used to make pastas or cooked in soups are buckwheat, barley, and *faro,* a whole grain similar to spelt.

Pulses, both fresh and dried, are important in the dietary pattern of Italian populations, the most common being beans, lentils, chickpeas, fava beans, and peas. Pulses are also used in vegetable soups, or *minestre;* other ingredients may include pasta, vegetables, and herbs. When pasta is absent, soups are called *zuppa.* Chestnuts, although a fruit, were used like a legume in the past; that is to say, they were boiled in soups or ground into flour.

Introduced in the 16th century, potatoes can be mashed into a puree, fried, sautéed, boiled, roasted, and baked. The most renowned potato-based dish is gnocchi, little dumplings made by adding flour and sometimes eggs, which are boiled and then seasoned with melted butter and cheese, light tomato sauces, or pesto. Other root vegetables, like beets or radishes, are not common, with the exception of carrots.

Together with legumes and potatoes, vegetables play an important role in Italian dietary patterns. Besides fresh salads, there are onions, garlic, celery, scallions, leeks, eggplant, sweet peppers, chili peppers, tomatoes, cucumbers, zucchini, asparagus, artichokes, fennel, chard, spinach, broccoli, broccoli rabe, and all kind of cabbages. Vegetables are consumed fresh, or pickled and conserved in olive oil, vinegar, or salt. Mushrooms and their more expensive relatives, truffles, are appreciated all over Italy. Herbs like oregano, basil, rosemary, mint, bay leaves, and parsley are commonly used to season dishes. Thyme, myrtle, dill, tarragon, and juniper berries are less frequent. Spices such as pepper, cinnamon, nutmeg, cloves, and saffron are also widely used.

Fruits play a very important role in the Italian diet, eaten all day long as a snack and consumed regularly at the end of every meal. The most common fruits are oranges, tangerines, pears, and apples in winter; strawberries and cherries in spring; peaches, plums, apricots, figs, melons, and watermelons in summer; and persimmons, grapes, and chestnuts in the fall. Tropical fruit is now widely available, especially bananas, pineapples, grapefruit, and coconuts. Almonds, hazelnuts, pine nuts, walnuts, and pistachios are widely consumed; peanuts are massively imported.

Olive trees grow well in the coastal areas of the south, in Tuscany, along the coast of Liguria, and near Lake Garda. Olives are commonly pickled and cured. Varieties of olives differ in size, taste, and growing periods, making the oils deriving from them different. The mixture of olive varieties and the *terroir* (depending on the character of the soil, the weather, exposure to the sun and wind, cultivation methods) determine the character of the final product. Olive oil is a traditionally important cooking fat, together with butter in the north and pork fat all over the country.

Wine, produced in great quantities, often employing local varieties, is a basic component in everyday meals. Wine is still bought in bulk for everyday consumption, but the general appreciation for high-quality wines is growing. Some wine is traditionally fermented into vinegar, a very common condiment; balsamic vinegar, originally produced in Emilia Romagna, is now increasingly popular. Italian spirits are made either by distilling the by-products deriving from the winemaking process or by macerating herbs and fruit in different types of alcohol. The most famous distilled spirit is the grape-based grappa, mostly produced in the north. Beer, some of it produced locally, is also widely consumed.

Consumption of meat has dramatically increased in the past decades. Ways to cook meat include frying, roasting, grilling, boiling, braising, stewing, and sautéing. The most common meats are beef, veal, pork, lamb, chicken, turkey, and less frequently rabbit, duck, goose, squab, mutton, goat, venison, game, and horse. Pork meat is cured and preserved as sausages, salami, and prosciutto (both raw and roasted). Offal is still popular, although the youngest generations are increasingly less willing to consume it.

Fish is widely available, both fresh and frozen. Among freshwater fish, Italians prefer trout, perch, carp, and eels, while the most appreciated saltwater fish are sea bass, gilthead bream, sole, turbot, skate, John Dory, and red mullet. Also very popular are salted codfish and stockfish, which are dried and reconstituted. A special category is the so-called blue fish, which includes anchovies, sardines, mackerel, tuna fish, and swordfish.

Aliciotti con l'indivia (Fresh Anchovies with Escarole)

2 lb escarole

2 lb cleaned fresh anchovies

Salt and pepper

6 cloves garlic, slivered

2 tbsp dried breadcrumbs

1 tbsp extra-virgin olive oil

Slice and salt the escarole, then drain in a colander for 2 hours. Wash and pat dry the fresh anchovies with a paper towel. Rub a 9-inch round baking dish with extra-virgin olive oil. Arrange the anchovies in one layer. Salt and pepper to taste. Distribute a few slivers of garlic over the anchovies and some of the escarole. Repeat layers of anchovies, escarole, and garlic until all of the ingredients are used up. Cover with the breadcrumbs, and drizzle with olive oil. Bake in a preheated 400°F oven for 40 minutes. Serve lukewarm or at room temperature.

Fish—usually sold and served whole, and not filleted—can be grilled, roasted, boiled, stewed, sautéed, fried, steamed, or cooked in aluminum foil. Crustaceans, shellfish, and all kinds of mollusks are appreciated, especially mussels, clams, shrimp, crab, squid, and octopus. Eggs constitute a very important element of the everyday diet, cooked in various ways.

Milk is not as popular as in the United States and is mostly drunk for breakfast. Sour cream and buttermilk are quite rare, while yogurt is increasingly popular. Plain cream is sometimes used in pastry or specific recipes. Hundreds of cheeses are available in Italy, with different flavors, textures, and aromas depending on the area of production, the grass, the habits of the shepherds, traditions, and technical know-how. Industrial cheese is also widely sold. Italians consume cheese by itself or in sandwiches, use it in many recipes, or grate it on top of pasta and soups. The most popular cow-milk cheeses include *parmigiano reggiano, grana padano,* Asiago, taleggio, Gorgonzola, fontina, provolone, mozzarella, and *scamorza;* popular sheep-milk cheeses are scamorza, pecorino Romano, pecorino Toscano, and caciotta.

Italians enjoy both mass-produced brands of ice cream, available in groceries, supermarkets, and bars, and artisanal gelato, sold in shops (*gelaterie*) that are often open year-round. A simple frozen dessert is granita, grated ice flavored with fruit, coffee, or syrups poured on top, while sorbet (*sorbetto*) is made with syrups or pureed fruit.

Pastry shops and bakeries offer a wide choice of pies, cakes, and small pastries, which vary according to the different areas. Many pastries are made of fried dough with different fillings, like *zeppole* in Naples, filled with custard cream. Doughnut-shaped fried pastries are called *frittelle.* Also, the dough for the renowned Sicilian cannoli, filled with a ricotta cheese–based cream, is fried. Baked desserts and pies are also very common, both homemade and commercial. There are many kinds of biscotto (the word means "twice-cooked") and *crostata,* a thin layer of *pasta frolla*—quite similar to shortbread—spread over the bottom of a pan, topped with homemade jam or fruit preserves, and baked. Many desserts use a sort of sponge cake, or *pandispagna,* as a base, like the famous Sicilian *cassata,* filled with a cream made of ricotta cheese, sugar, candied fruits, and pieces of chocolate, covered with a thick frosting of white sugar and decorated with candied fruits.

Several drinks made by infusion or decoction of leaves, grains, or roots in boiling water are commonly used in Italy, the most common being coffee. Other infusions include tea, chamomile tea, linden, mint, and verbena. Chocolate in all forms is also very popular.

Cooking

Women are usually in charge of food at home, helped by appliances like electric or gas stoves, refrigerators, microwave ovens, and smaller appliances like pressure cookers, frying machines, pasta makers, toasters, mixers, and food processors. Only after World War II, with the massive immigration toward the industrial north, the growing urbanization, the abandonment of the countryside, and the economic boom, did it become normal for women to work full-time outside the house. Although jobs that left time for cooking and housekeeping were still preferred, over the past decades it has become socially acceptable for women to dedicate themselves to their careers. However, men from older generations still expect the women to do the shopping, the cooking, and the cleaning. Among younger couples chores tend to be shared, especially when it comes to grocery shopping and the kitchen. It has become acceptable for young men to learn how to make at least some simple dishes.

Various dishes and culinary traditions that require intensive and lengthy preparations are slowly disappearing. To respond to these changes, food industries are investing in creating and mass-producing ready-made alternatives that still maintain some connection with the dishes of the past, banking on nostalgia. Curing and pickling vegetables in one's kitchen, or making jams and preserves at home, has become rare, more a hobby than a necessity.

In the past, women were in charge of transmitting their knowledge and experience in all culinary matters to the new generations. There was no desire for new recipes; the main task was to make the best of the limited resources available. Recipes and techniques were transmitted orally and by practical example. A woman with scarce culinary abilities was pitied and frowned on. From the 1960s, most working women had no time to teach their children how to cook, while young women did not want to perpetuate the social order that had forced their mothers into the kitchen. As a result, many young people, especially in urban environments, did not learn how to cook. Then came the 1990s, with the renewed interest in food and wine, finally considered as a major component of the Italian culture and society. People are interested again in learning about food and cooking but this time from cookbooks, magazines, televisions shows, and associations such as Slow Food, which was founded in Italy in reaction to the proliferation of fast food.

Typical Meals

The triad of meals, breakfast—midday meal—evening meal (*colazione, pranzo, cena*), is the norm all over Italy. Breakfast is often insubstantial, and often adults have only a small cup of coffee or coffee with frothed milk (cappuccino) on their way to work. Children usually have a slightly more structured meal, centered around a bowl of milk, often enriched with coffee, or less commonly tea, accompanied by plain or flavored cookies (biscotti), croissants, cake, slightly sweetened double-baked slices of bread (*fette biscottate*), or simple bread. Due to the scanty quantity of food consumed at breakfast, it is not uncommon to have a midmorning break. Brunch is a new concept in Italy. During the weekend, if people wake up late, they prefer to limit themselves to a coffee and wait till lunchtime for a more abundant meal.

The midday meal usually takes place between 12 and 3 P.M., depending on the area and the season. The traditional midday meal is structured around two main courses, called *primo* (first dish, often a pasta dish or a soup) and *secondo* (second dish, meat or fish, often served together with one or more side dishes, usually vegetables). Everyday meals usually end with some seasonal fruits, more rarely with a dessert, with the exception of ice creams or frozen desserts in summer. In the hot season, people often fix very light meals, with a preference for salads or cold dishes. Today, most people have either a primo or a secondo at midday and have both courses in the evening. A complete meal with primo and secondo, often followed by substantial desserts, also marks weekends and special occasions. Many Italians still consume their lunch at home, making it the biggest meal of the day, but children and people working 9 to 5 eat in canteens or in various kinds of eateries. It is fairly common for workers to bring their own lunches from home, consisting of a cooked dish or of a simple sandwich.

The evening meal, which in the past tended to be lighter, is now acquiring more importance, since it is often the only time of the day when the whole family can sit together. Many opt for either a primo or a secondo or prepare a single dish that includes more than one element. Some cheese and cold cuts in the fridge can be used to fix a fast, light meal, together with a fresh tossed salad, tomatoes, or other vegetables. With a seated meal, most adults may drink beer or wine.

Eating Out

Although Italians enjoy cooking and eating their meals at home, and inviting friends and family for meals is a very common custom, eating out at *ristoranti, trattorie,* and *osterie* constitutes an important element in Italian social life. The meaning of these words has changed over time. Now, a ristorante is usually an establishment that offers nice decor, good service, and an upscale menu, while trattorie and osterie tend to provide simpler food and service, at more affordable prices. Restaurants are rarely patronized by persons eating by themselves, with the notable exceptions of tourists, businessmen from out of town, or single men and women who prefer not to cook. Eating a complete meal by oneself is nevertheless considered quite unsatisfying and psychologically depressing. Restaurants thus become places to celebrate birthdays, to have dates, to mark holidays and special occasions, or just to socialize and meet friends.

With the renewed interest in traditional dishes and local ingredients, osterie and trattorie are undergoing a definite renaissance. Also, many ristoranti now offer traditional, regional, and local dishes in a more upscale environment. In this case there is greater attention to ingredients, produce, and wine, with a tangible increase in prices. Other establishments bet on new cooking styles, either by importing foreign models (as was the case for nouvelle cuisine in the 1980s and, more recently, for American steakhouses or Japanese-style sushi bars)

Cafè scene, Portofino, Italy. (Corel)

or by adopting a creative approach toward Italian cuisine.

Beginning in the 1950s, the younger generations found a relaxed and laidback place to gather in the new "American-style" bars, an evolution of coffeehouses, with a more modern decor and a less refined service, but still serving coffee rather than alcoholic drinks and offering a choice of food, pastry, and ice creams. However, many cities still boast elegant coffeehouses, usually more expensive than bars, offering great ambiance and a wider choice of sweet and savory small bites. These are places where clients sit down and take their time chatting with friends, reading, or having dates. They ensure calm and privacy, while bars tend to cater to people on the go, who often consume their drinks and their snacks standing. Nevertheless, bars often have tables and outdoor seating for the summer. The life of Italian bars revolves around coffee and other breakfast drinks, and not so much around liquor and alcohol, although the latter are regularly—and legally—sold in these places. Adults who prefer to have breakfast on the go make a quick stop in their favorite bar and have an espresso, often by itself, but sometimes also accompanied by some croissant or pastry. Most bars sell candies over the counter and offer ice cream and a choice of savory bites. In this case the bar is known as a snack bar and, more recently, as a bar *gastronomia*. The latter often offers cooked dishes at lunch, especially if it is located in an urban center near offices or other workplaces. The average bar displays panini (single-portion breads in different shapes, cut in two and filled with various ingredients), *tramezzini* (triangular, made of *pancarré*, a sort of upscale Wonder bread), toasts, slices of pizza, pieces of focaccia with *salumi* (cured meats), and sometimes salads and fruit salads.

Beside bars, there are plenty of other ways to get food on the go. The tradition of street and market food, although dying, is still present. Nevertheless, people are increasingly skeptical about hygienic conditions and have lost the taste for some of the most traditional street foods. Every area has its own traditions. Street foods are the legacy of a past when hunger and poverty were common for many city dwellers who did not even have a kitchen at home.

That is why many traditional street specialties are made with innards or employ the simplest ingredients, like bread, legumes, or fruit.

While home deliveries are still rare, some shops sell ready-made food to take out. They are called *tavola calda* when they offer cooked dishes, and they often have small tables for clients who want to eat on the premises. No service is provided: Customers buy their dishes, often served in aluminum containers, at the counter and bring them to their tables. They are often required to clean up when they are finished. A *rosticceria* specializes in fried or roasted foods that would take too long or be annoying to prepare at home.

Many rosticcerie also use their oven to make pizza, either in large metal pans or directly on the bottom of the oven. This kind of pizza, called *pizza al taglio,* is cut according to the customer's request and sold by the weight. Some shops specialize in pizza al taglio, adding very few fried items to their offer. There are also places that sell pizza à la carte, where customers can sit at their table, order their meal and their drinks from a menu, and be helped by waiters. These places are called pizzeria, a name also used for shops selling pizza al taglio. Until a few years ago pizza was served at the table only in the evening. Many establishments now offer it also for lunch. Besides, many trattorie have diversified their menus by adding pizza.

In the new millennium, wine has become the object of a renewed interest from both connoisseurs

Pizza fresh out of a wooden oven in a pizzeria in Italy. (Shutterstock)

and amateurs. Some specialized shops, called *enoteca,* cater to the needs of a growing public, curious to taste new wines and to know more about a world that until a few years ago was a realm reserved to a few aficionados. These are the direct development of the wine shops that in the past used to sell bulk wine, pouring it into bottles provided by the clients. Many enoteche have an annexed wine bar, which operates under a different business license and is also allowed to serve food to be consumed on the premises. Wine bars constitute an increasingly popular alternative to other types of restaurants, especially for high-end customers who are willing and able to spend nicely on a good bottle of wine and are knowledgeable enough to do so. Partly to meet the burgeoning demand from their clients, partly to make them even more passionate about their products, some enoteche, but above all wine bars, organize tasting meetings and classes.

Beer is also enjoying a growing success, especially among young people. New establishments have developed around this trend, called pubs, using the English word, or *birrerie* in Italian. The decor is usually quite different from that in other restaurants. Wooden tables and benches are prevalent. No tablecloth is provided but only paper towels. The service is basic. Dishes of foreign origin are served, such as sauerkraut with boiled wurst (sausages), hot dogs, hamburgers with French fries, potato salads, and chili con carne. Some pubs also serve salads, pasta, and sandwiches, to satisfy all tastes.

Fast foods appeared in Italy in the late 1980s, among heated public debates. However, foreign chains have often adapted themselves to the local tastes, adding pasta salads and vegetable salads to their menus and even offering beer and wine. Some Italian entrepreneurs found the concept appealing and created chains that operate like foreign fast-food places but serve only Italian dishes and pizza. These kinds of shops are now quite common in and around train and bus stations, airports, and service areas along the highways.

Since 1990, new forms of high-end tourism focusing on food and wine as expressions of local culture and traditions have developed. An *agriturismo* is an enterprise run by a farmer who offers food and lodging to tourists on his property, using the products from the farm and at times organizing recreational or cultural activities.

A relatively new phenomenon is the growth of ethnic restaurants. Chinese restaurants are definitely the most visible and numerous. Besides the Chinese, not many other ethnic restaurants are available: a few "African" establishments (mostly from Ethiopia and Somalia), some Moroccan or more vaguely "Arab" places, as well as some Japanese and Mexican, and very rarely Brazilian. Curiously, French restaurants are a rarity, confirming Italians' attachment to their food traditions, especially against the eternal rivals in culinary matters, the French.

Special Occasions

Italians tend to find plenty of excuses to make a special occasion of a meal, both cooking at home and going out. Close friends and family feel free to drop by unannounced or on very short notice. As a matter of fact, this is an element that characterizes close social relationships, whereas invitations ahead of time denote that the guests are in an outer circle of friends and family. Also, coffee time after lunch is a favorite time to pay a visit and have a good chat over a steaming cup of espresso.

Sunday dinners often maintain their character as a special meal. The main courses, primi and secondi, usually become more elaborate, and cooks make an effort to prepare more side dishes. Some hosts offer more than one primo and more than one secondo to prove their cooking abilities and to show appreciation for their guests.

Many ceremonies are connected with the Catholic religion, which is still prevalent by far. Even many nonreligious people do not renounce these celebrations. Christening (*battesimo*) is the first occasion to mark most children's lives. In the days preceding the rite, families send out *bomboniere,* little souvenirs parceled up with smooth confectionery sugar-coated almonds called *confetti.* After the christening ceremony, families invite relatives and friends to join them to celebrate the occasion with a meal, often in a restaurant. Also, the first communion and confirmation are marked by family celebrations, generally big lunches after the ceremony, held at home or at the restaurant. A festive lunch is also organized when a young person takes religious vows as a priest, a monk, or a nun.

Weddings are also celebrated with long, abundant, and sometimes extravagant meals. The menu starts with one or two appetizers, continuing with a couple of primi, if not three, and two or three secondi accompanied by several *contorni* (side dishes). All the dishes are served one after the other, so that guests do not need choose between the two or three primi, or between the two or three secondi, but can have a portion of each. After the main courses, desserts are served. At the end, the wedding cake is brought; the couple is supposed to cut the first slice, while the guests toast to their future happiness with sparkling wine. The cake is brought back to the kitchen, sliced, and served to the guests. The meal, which ends with liquors and coffee, can last a few hours.

Other occasions that are celebrated with food at home or meals at restaurants are birthdays, saint's days (according to the Catholic tradition, every day is dedicated to a specific saint, and the people who carry his or her name are supposed to solemnize that day), and academic and professional achievements.

Catholicism being the traditional religion in Italy, liturgical and religious festivities also marked social times, with holidays that were often connected to specific foods and meals. One of most important holidays is Christmas. At the vigil, in some areas families gather for a "lean supper," that is, with no meat courses. However, the dishes can be numerous, abundant, and delicious, usually pretty much the same year in and year out, changing according to the area. Christmas Day dinner, customarily served in the early afternoon, is dominated by meat. Meat stocks and broth are very common primi, usually with pasta ripiena with meat-based fillings. All kinds of Christmas desserts are served. While in some families it is still customary to make some desserts at home, the food industries produce most of the holiday delicacies, some of which can also be bought from bakeries and pastry shops. Many Christmas desserts are actually derived from bread:

pandoro from Verona (*pan d'oro* means "bread of gold"), panettone from Milan (*pan di tono,* "important bread"), *pan speziale* from Bologna ("spiced bread"), *panforte* from Siena ("strong bread"), *pan pepato* from Ferrara ("peppered bread"), *pan nociato* from Umbria ("bread with nuts"), *pan giallo* from Rome ("yellow bread"), and *parrozzo* from Abruzzo (*pan rozzo,* "rough bread"). As the names reveal, in time different ingredients were added to the bread to make it more festive, such as spices, nuts, raisins, candied and dried fruits, chocolate, and honey. The Christmas dessert in Naples is tiny balls of fried dough, dipped in honey syrup, arranged in a wreath, and decorated with colored spangles, called *struffoli.* Nougat candy, or *torrone,* is widespread all over Italy; it can be soft or hard, with hazelnuts or almonds, covered in chocolate or with some liquor.

New Year's Eve is celebrated all over Italy with parties and late suppers. The menu varies, but it is quite common to eat *zampone* (minced pork meat with spices, stuffed into the skin of a pig's foot) or *cotechino* (minced pork meat, lard, and skin made into a big sausage) with lentils, which represents money and abundance. Tradition requires that bottles of sparkling wine be opened at midnight on the dot. Many families also have a New Year's Day dinner, whose menus also vary but always feature rich and abundant dishes.

On January 6, the Catholic Church celebrates the Three Kings in a holiday called Epifania. This name

A selection of Italian chocolate Easter eggs in a shop in Rome. (StockPhotoPro)

was corrupted to *Befana,* which is also the name of an old ugly lady riding a broom. Coming down the chimney, she brings sweets, candies, and little presents to the good children and just coal to the bad ones. Children would hang socks and stockings from the hearth (over the stove in modern kitchens), while leaving some food in the kitchen to thank her and to let her get some rest.

For Carnival, the Italian equivalent of Mardi Gras, long strips of crunchy fried dough powdered with sugar (called *frappe, cenci,* or *chiacchiere*) and little fried balls covered in melted honey (*castagnole*) are particularly popular.

For Easter, the egg is the most evident symbol of fertility and renewal, connected to the resurrection of Christ. Boiled eggs to be eaten on Easter Day, often painted in bright colors, were brought to church to be blessed at the midnight mass. Boiled eggs are also used to decorate sweet and savory cakes. Eggs are the main ingredients in many pies. Chocolate eggs are mass-produced, containing little presents for children. All over Italy, the Easter lamb—considered a symbol of Christ sacrificing himself—is served roasted or grilled. In many areas, there is still a tradition of an Easter breakfast, featuring boiled eggs, salami, savory and sweet pies, and chocolate, together with wine. Among the desserts, *colomba* (a leavened cake shaped like a dove and covered with a sugar and almond glaze) is common all over Italy. Many desserts are still homemade, like *pastiera* in Naples (a cake filled with boiled wheat grains, ricotta, and candied fruits and flavored with orange flower water) and cassata in Sicily (the sweet ricotta cheese cake), where making little lambs out of almond paste (*marzapane*) is still a living tradition.

Diet and Health

Since the late 1950s, there have been radical changes in the amount and the composition of the foods that Italians consume. For centuries, populations around the Mediterranean Sea, including Italians, had to strive against food scarcity, tilling soils that were often less than generous and making do with what they could grow around them. As a consequence, the diet was based mostly on carbohydrates, pulses, and vegetables, with little fat and animal protein.

Then, starting from the end of World War II, even the less-well-off became able to afford a more diverse and abundant diet. Nutrition patterns changed under the influence of new packaging and conservation techniques, industrial mass production, and more sophisticated systems of distribution. A widespread economic development that led to the actual boom in the 1960s allowed many to lead better lives and enjoy a more regular intake of food, even though it often severed the ties to their traditional ways of life, including culinary habits. The daily energy intake passed from slightly below 2,000 calories in the 1950s to almost 3,500 nowadays. Italians are consuming more meat and sugar, and coronary diseases are reaping more victims than ever before, because of fattier and higher-calorie diets. Obesity, especially in children, has become a main concern for the Ministry of Health, which has launched public campaigns aiming to educate the parents and the children themselves to eat better.

At the same time, the whole world seems to have discovered that the way the Mediterranean people had eaten for centuries in their effort to fight hunger actually constitutes a very healthy diet. The international public became aware of the advantages of the so-called Mediterranean diet in the late 1980s, when scientist Ancel Keys and a group of researchers published the results of the survey they had conducted in seven countries. Then, in 1990, the U.S. Department of Agriculture issued dietary guidelines for Americans that become the basis for the 1992 Food Guide Pyramid, clearly shaped by Keys's findings in southern Italy back in the 1950s. However, because of the way the media describe it, it is unclear whether the Mediterranean diet is considered as a cultural and historical construction, as a selection of specific foods, or, more scientifically, as a nutrient profile.

Despite the changes in their dietary patterns, and the regional differences, Italians still tend to eat more carbohydrates, legumes, and vegetables than Americans do. The distribution within these categories has changed, too: From the 1950s, the growing availability of bread and pasta marked a decrease in the consumption of other cereals considered less desirable, such as barley or rye. Rice and maize maintained a certain acceptance in northern regions. The southern regions traditionally consume larger quantities of carbohydrates and vegetables than the northern ones. With regard to the consumption of different kinds of meat, beef increased until the 1970s, reaching a constant level that suddenly decreased at the end of the 1990s, due to the mad cow scare and other health-related anxieties. In contrast, consumption of chicken, pork, and rabbit is growing, on account of the lower prices of these meats and the fact that Italians now consider them as nutritious as beef.

Dietary rules change during each individual's lifetime. A very special moment for many women is pregnancy. Gaining weight in the months preceding the birth of a baby is not only considered acceptable but even recommended. Most women opt for breast-feeding, considered better for the child, since it creates a closer connection with the mother and provides the child with all necessary nutrients and a better protection against infections and diseases. For this reason, breast-feeding in public is socially accepted.

Up to five months of age, babies are fed exclusively milk or formula. From 5 to 12 months, babies are weaned, and new flavors and foods are introduced into their diet. Between 1 and 3 years of age, the babies are supposed adapt their diet to the adults' habits. The goal is to let babies get used to the taste of real food, since there is no concept of baby food per se. At this point, babies are usually more than happy to start eating what their parents and other adults eat, especially at social occasions when many people are gathered around the table. There are no children's menus in restaurants: Children are supposed to eat small portions of the same dishes the adults are having. Children are often curious to taste adult food, and in many families it is accepted to serve them even tiny drops of coffee in their milk and also wine, often diluted in lots of water.

There is no concept of food for the old. Senior citizens are supposed to eat the way they always did, unless they have specific ailments or suffer from loss of teeth. They continue to drink wine with their meals, to have their coffee in the morning, to season their dishes with salt, and to consume fried food and sweets. Since the calorie intake does not decrease, while retirement implies a less active style of life, it is quite common for older people to gain weight and to suffer from problems connected with high levels of cholesterol in the blood, high blood pressure, and diabetes.

Most physicians in Italy are not particularly interested in matters of nutrition, unless they affect some specific ailments. With the exception of pediatricians, who are definitely more involved in the subject, also because of pressure from mothers, many of them do not even take that subject during their professional training. For this reason, the advice some medical doctors give is quite vague, often based more on common sense than on study and research. Most of the knowledge people get about their food and their nutritional needs comes from less reliable sources: the media. Most television channels, newspapers, and magazine have a section on health, which often deals with food-related issues.

Fabio Parasecoli

Further Reading

Anderson, Burton. *Treasures of the Italian Table: Italy's Celebrated Foods and the Artisans Who Make Them.* New York: Morrow, 1994.

Andrews, Colman. *Flavors of the Riviera.* New York: Bantam Books, 1996.

Artusi, Pellegrino. *Science in the Kitchen and the Art of Eating Well.* 1897. New York: Marsilio, 1998.

Bastianich, Joseph, and David Lynch. *Vino Italiano: The Regional Wines of Italy.* New York: Clarkson Potter, 2002.

Bastianich, Lidia. *Lidia's Italian Table: More Than 200 Recipes from the First Lady of Italian Cooking.* New York: William Morrow, 1998.

Bugialli, Giuliano. *Bugialli's Italy: Traditional Recipes from the Regions of Italy.* New York: William Morrow Cookbooks, 1998.

Camporesi, Piero. *The Land of Hunger.* Cambridge, UK: Polity Press, 1996.

Cernilli, Daniele, and Marco Sabellico. *The New Italy.* London: Mitchell Beazley, 2000.

Counihan, Carole. *Around the Tuscan Table: Food, Family, and Gender in Twentieth Century Florence.* New York: Routledge, 2004.

Dickie, John. *Delizia! The Epic History of the Italians and Their Food.* New York: Free Press, 2008.

Flandrin, Jean-Louis, and Massimo Montanari. *A Culinary History of Food.* New York: Penguin Books, 2000.

Goldstein, Joyce. *Cucina ebraica: Flavors of the Italian Jewish Kitchen.* San Francisco: Chronicle Books, 1998.

Hazan, Marcella. *Essentials of Classic Italian Cooking.* New York: Knopf, 1992.

Heltosky, Carol. *Garlic and Oil: Food and Politics in Italy.* Oxford: Berg, 2006.

Italian Food. http://www.lifeinitaly.com/food/default.asp.

Italian Food Forever. http://www.italianfoodforever.com/.

Italian Made. http://www.italianmade.com/home.cfm.

Jenkins, Nancy Harmon. *Cucina del Sole: A Celebration of Southern Italian Cooking.* New York: William Morrow, 2007.

Mariani, John. *The Dictionary of Italian Food and Drink.* New York: Broadway Books, 1998.

Marinetti, F. T. *The Futurist Cookbook.* London: Trefoil, 1989.

Montanari, Massimo, and Alberto Capatti. *Italian Cuisine: A Cultural History.* New York: Columbia University Press, 2003.

Parasecoli, Fabio. *Food Culture in Italy.* Westport, CT: Greenwood Press, 2004.

Petrini, Carlo. *Slow Food (The Case for Taste).* New York: Columbia University Press, 2003.

Root, Waverly. *The Food of Italy.* New York: Vintage Books, 1971.

Scicolone, Michele. *Italian Holiday Cooking.* New York: William Morrow, 2001.

Serventi, Sivlano, and Françoise Sabban. *Pasta.* New York: Columbia University Press, 2002.

Slow Food. http://www.slowfood.com/.

Tasca Lanza, Anna. *The Heart of Sicily.* New York: Clarkson Potter, 1993.

Wright, Clifford. *A Mediterranean Feast.* New York: William Morrow, 1999.

Latvia

Overview

The Republic of Latvia occupies the central position among what are collectively known as the Baltic States, with Estonia to the north and Lithuania to the south. It shares borders with both Russia and Belarus to the east, and Scandinavia lies to the west, across the Baltic Sea. Latvia is a parliamentary republic divided into 26 districts. Rīga is the capital and the country's largest city. The population is just over two million people, who are mostly Latvian or Russian, with smaller percentages of Belarusians, Ukrainians, and other ethnic groups.

Geography, politics, and religion all factor into Latvia's culture and cuisine. In ancient times, native Latvians held pagan beliefs and fostered close spiritual ties to nature and seasonal life cycles. By the 13th century, German-led crusaders had forcibly Christianized the country. This paved the way for eventual Russian conquest and colonization, rendering Latvia a historical and cultural crossroads between Germanic and Slavic Europe. Latvia has been a member of the United Nations since 1991, following its independence from the Soviet Union. Though Latvia's culture and customs are inextricably linked to its history of occupation, Latvians have retained many of their ancient, pagan practices, as evidenced through their celebrations, folk songs (*danias*), and food traditions.

🍽 Food Culture Snapshot

Imants and Nina Vilcina are newlyweds living in Rīga, and they both frequent the Central Market, one of Europe's largest, located in dramatic hangars once used to house zeppelins. Shopping is done several times each week, as the freshness of food is imperative to Latvians. This is particularly so with fish, one of the country's best-loved resources, which may even be carried home from the market still living, stored in a newspaper cone with a small amount of water.

Meat is also important, and in Latvian homes such as the Vilcinas' people may stock up on various sausages or purchase cuts of pork or beef for making *kotletes*—flattened meat to be breaded and fried. However, dairy is the crucial component in Latvian cuisine, enjoyed in a variety of ways at every meal. The Vilcinas are never without milk, which they consume heartily each morning, along with cottage cheese, and perhaps fresh eggs and tomato or cucumber.

Ingredients for lunches and dinners are also purchased at the market, including more dairy for making rich cream sauces and the Latvian table's ubiquitous sour cream. Today, a wide variety of produce is available at the market; however, staples such as potatoes, carrots, radishes, onions, and dill remain the foundation of Latvian cuisine. Honey and fruit preserves are ever present, as is black tea, which is sometimes flavored with orange rose hips and is always taken with milk.

Major Foodstuffs

Latvia's climate is temperate, with long, cold winters and short, warm summers. The short growing season has resulted in an emphasis on grains, legumes, and dairy, with fresh vegetables being slightly less

This market in Rīga, Latvia, is held in five enormous hangers that were originally used for building the zeppelin airships. (StockPhotoPro)

common. This has also helped to produce a pragmatic cuisine that is high in fat with few spices and that features the products of resourceful farmers and fishers.

Before farming and agriculture, ancient peoples subsisted on foods that did not need to be cultivated, only gathered, so wild mushrooms and a wide variety of berries may still be found in today's cuisine. In winter months, sausages and salted pork may be stored in cellars, alongside salted cabbage and pickled cucumbers, mushrooms, and herring.

The importance of milk and milk products cannot be overstated, and these have been essential sources of protein and nourishment throughout Latvia's history. Milk is drunk by itself and throughout the day, as are various preparations of cultured and curdled milks. Milk soups are eaten, and sauces are made from cream, served alongside hard cheeses and dishes topped with sour cream. Butter is the most common cooking fat and is spread on bread, though safflower oil and lard are also used.

Spices are few, and flavors uncomplicated, though dishes may feature dill, caraway, black pepper, or white mustard. There were no sources of salt in ancient Latvia. It was obtained through trade and used sparingly, a practice still observed in today's cooking. Condiments include mustard and horseradish, though ketchup has become popular in more recent times. Honey is the preferred sweetener, and fresh honeycomb is a particular delicacy. Natural sweetness is found in a variety of berries, including strawberries, blueberries, loganberries, cranberries, and raspberries.

Potatoes were introduced in the 19th century and may be grown almost anywhere in Latvia; they are extremely popular. Mushroom gathering is a favorite activity, and mushrooms are pickled, boiled, fried, or incorporated into sauces. Turnips, black radishes, linseed, carrots, onions, and garlic are also grown.

Bread is a staple of the Latvian diet, and respect for it is encouraged from early childhood. It is made from either rye or wheat, typically in two varieties: white (oatmeal-colored whole-grain bread) and black (dark, tangy, and sour bread). Other grains include barley, oats, millet, and hemp. Peas and beans are consumed regularly.

Coastal Latvians rely heavily on fish, while freshwater fish caught inland is considered more of a delicacy. The most common species are herring, trout, pike, eel, sprats, and salmon. Red and black caviars are also enjoyed and may be eaten with pancakes. Pork is the most important meat, followed by beef and chicken. Available game may include deer, duck, and goose.

Mineral water and fruit juices are commonplace at mealtimes, as is milk, *rūgušpiens* (a refreshing curdled milk drink), and beer. Tea and coffee are both consumed, the latter often topped generously with whipped cream. Vodka is a staple brought by the Russians, and in summertime Latvians enjoy *kvass,* a mildly sweet fermented drink made from rye, water, yeast, and honey. A springtime specialty is *bērzu sula*—juice made from birch sap gathered each March.

Cooking

Latvian cooking is straightforward and uncomplicated, and women have traditionally prepared the meals for their families. Clay pot and hearth cookery were early techniques, followed later by bread ovens. A large pot for boiling and a large pan for frying are the primary implements.

Cold salads of potato, egg, herring, cucumber, and various meats are enjoyed alongside various pickled preparations. Soups and porridges are made from grains, peas, meat, and fish and are often laden with milk. Russian beet soup, or borscht, is eaten cold in the summer and hot in the winter. In addition to its place in soups, fish may be fried, smoked, or salted.

Meat is consumed regularly by most Latvians and may be breaded and fried, boiled into soups, or made into various dumplings. *Belashi* are a popular deep-fried snack of dough filled with beef and onions, as are *pīrāgi* (bacon rolls). Baking is commonplace and produces a variety of breads, pastries, cookies, and cakes, though these tend to be less sweet than their American or western European counterparts. Canning and preserving are methods

Rīga sprats baked in oil and served with salad. (Shutterstock)

for enjoying berries year-round. *Kisels* are produced using a technique of thickening a sweet and sour blend of juices with potato flour.

Just before the leaves appear on birch trees in the spring, some Latvians go into the country to make sparkling wine. Sap from the birch tree is filtered and then mixed with raisins, lemon peel, currants, and sugar. The blend is bottled, corked, and sealed with wax to allow fermentation to take place and is then enjoyed three months later.

A unique Latvian specialty that is still popular today is *Rīgas Melnais balzams* (black balsam), a bitter, black drink invented by a pharmacist in the 18th century. The recipe remains a secret, though among the listed ingredients are Peruvian balsam oil, arnica blossoms, raspberry juice, orange peel, oak bark, and wormwood. It is often mixed with coffee or vodka and may be served over ice cream.

Typical Meals

Latvians usually eat three meals per day, beginning with a moderate breakfast of milk, juice, coffee, or tea and either boiled eggs, sausages, or small sandwiches of cheese, cucumber, and tomato. Lunch is eaten between noon and three and tends to be served hot. It can include fried meat (pork, steak, or chicken) or fish (salmon, trout, cod), potatoes (boiled, fried, or mashed), boiled buckwheat, and salad. Sour cream is the main accompaniment. Alternatively, meat soups may be eaten. Midday drinks may be fruit juice, kefir, milk, tea, coffee, or beer.

After the workday, supper is taken at six or seven. This main meal can vary widely but could consist of soup, cold salads, a hot meal similar to lunch, or occasionally more traditional preparations such as *zivju zupa*, fish soup with potatoes and fried carrots and onions. Another traditional fish dish is *cepts lasis ar plumju kompotu*—fried salmon with plum compote. Gray peas with bacon is a cornerstone of Latvian cuisine, as is the emblematic porridge, *skaba putra*, a sour milk and barley soup that is fermented, then chilled. This may be prepared with pork fat and can contain pieces of meat or herring. Cooking large meals at home is becoming less common, however, as frozen foods, pizza, and quick sandwiches have become increasingly popular.

Skaba Putra (Sour Barley Porridge)

¼ c finely ground cracked barley

½ tsp salt

2 c buttermilk

2 c milk (whole or skim)

⅓ c sour cream

Pork fat (or bacon), sautéed (optional)

Onions, sautéed (optional)

In a large pot, mix barley and salt with 1 cup water, and slowly bring to a boil. Reduce heat to low, cover, and simmer for 45 minutes, or until barley is tender and water has been absorbed. Set aside to cool slightly.

Add buttermilk and milk, and stir to the consistency of a thick soup. Cover and store overnight (or up to 12 hours) in a warm place so that the porridge sours slightly. Refrigerate for at least one full day to continue the fermentation, which will intensify over time.

Add sour cream before serving, as well as the optional pork fat (or bacon) and onions.

At the table, certain traditional customs and beliefs are still observed, such as to always offer food to others when eating. The end piece of a loaf of bread is called the "farmer's son," which young women compete for in hopes that they may marry the son of a farmer or one who owns their own home and land. Too much salt in the food means that the cook is in love, and if salt is spilled, there will be a quarrel in the house. If a spoon or fork falls to the ground, a female visitor will appear, and if a knife falls, the visitor will be male.

Eating Out

Following World War II, many rural Latvians migrated to cities, and mealtimes began to revolve around busy work schedules, causing a decline in home cooking. Cities in Latvia today feature a vast array of European, Asian, and American cuisines, as well as traditional Latvian eateries. Eating out has become more popular in recent times, and with the emergence of pizzerias, Chinese food, and American fast food, there are more choices today than ever before in Latvia. Rural people still primarily cook at home, however.

Special Occasions

Latvian celebrations follow the rhythms of the seasons according to the solar year in the northern hemisphere and simultaneously reflect the culture's pagan past and its Christian practices. Many traditional foods and beverages carry folk or mythological significance, though these roots have become obscured over time.

St. Anthony's Day, on January 17, is not largely celebrated today, but it was one of the first festival dates on the ancient Latvian calendar. St. Anthony was the patron saint of domestic animals, particularly hogs. The ancient belief was that in order for one's animals to thrive, a hog's head must be cooked and eaten and its bones taken to the forest. The snout was boiled and typically served with apples and cabbage.

Shrove Tuesday is a movable feast day falling between February 3 and March 9 and is the equivalent to the Mardi Gras of certain nations. As the last day before the Lenten fast, it marks the end of the long Baltic winter and is the culmination of a four-day meat-eating period, called Shrovetide. For fisherman, this represents the date by which all nets and other preparations for the season should be made. In the past, if the "net-making fork" was not out of a fisherman's home by this time, a fork would be tied to his back in symbolic shame. Fisherman would also meet with their partners on this day to celebrate the upcoming season over a plate of buckwheat pancakes.

Easter in Latvia is a telling blend of the country's pagan and Christian heritage. It is a celebration of the sun, replete with songs and dances. One traditional preparation for Easter eggs is to blow their contents out through holes poked in the shell into a communal bowl. After each person has contributed an egg, they are cooked over a large open fire and eaten straight from the frying pan.

Jāņi (St. John's Day) is a summer solstice celebration with pre-Christian roots. It was believed to be a time when people and gods would come together so that Latvians might ask for a bountiful harvest and for their crops and livestock to be protected from witches and devils. Men, women, children, and animals spend this day bedecked in garlands of grasses and flowers, which are saved throughout the year to ward off evil spirits. Jumping over bonfires is done to ensure luck in the coming year. Ķimeņu siers is a caraway cheese served especially during Jāņi; it is eaten to the health of cows, while barley beer is drunk to ensure strong horses.

The masked procession of Kakatas begins on November 10 with Martin's Day and culminates around Christmas. Martin's Day is a day to respect the dead, on which, in times past, farmers would kill a rooster, give its blood to their horses, and then cook the bird for dinner. Today, kekatnieki are dancing revelers armed with homemade noisemakers. They travel through neighborhoods, wearing costumes representing traditional folkloric figures, such as the bear and the stork. Popular dishes at Martin's are sauerkraut, poultry, and Martini balls—baked balls of cooked peas, bacon, and onions, flavored with hemp. Hemp was once popular in Latvian cooking, but it is now illegal, though hemp-seed butter is readily available.

The Christmas table can include pig snout, pīrāgi, barley sausage, boiled gray peas with bacon, sauerkraut, mulled wine, soured milk, and desserts such as gingerbread and kringel, a sweet coffee cake. One should eat nine meals on Christmas Day to assure wealth in the coming year, though this is rarely observed today. If carp is served, the fish's scales are placed into pockets and purses, to ensure money in the new year.

Latvian weddings are associated with an abundance of foods, such as pīrāgi, salads, sweet pastries, fruit, and beer; the meal can also include schnitzel, rolled veal, boiled potatoes, sautéed sauerkraut, and berries with milk for dessert.

Diet and Health

In combination with a high-fat diet, modernization has led to a decrease in exercise in Latvia and therefore an increased threat of cholesterol-related health issues. Alcohol consumption is high and is one of the main causes of traffic deaths, fires, and crime. Smoking is also common, and illnesses such as emphysema, lung cancer, and asthma continue to present problems.

Neil L. Coletta

Further Reading

Doub, Siri Lise. *Taste of Latvia.* New York: Hippocrene Books, 2000.

O'Connor, Kevin. *Culture and Customs of the Baltic States.* Westport, CT: Greenwood Press, 2006.

Pigozne-Brinkmane, Ieva. *The Cuisine of Latvia.* Rīga: Latvian Institute, 2004.

Lithuania

Overview

The Republic of Lithuania is a northern European country located on the southeastern coast of the Baltic Sea. Lithuania borders Latvia, Poland, Belarus, and Russia's Kaliningrad region, and, across the Baltic Sea, it faces Sweden. Its population is 3.37 million, of which 84.6 percent are ethnic Lithuanians; the remainder includes Poles (6.3%), Russians (5.1%), Belarusians (1.1%), and other nationalities/ethnicities (2.1%). Lithuania is predominantly Roman Catholic with 79 percent of the entire population belonging to the Catholic Church, while other significant religious affiliations include Eastern Orthodox (4.9%), Protestants (1.9%), nonbelievers (9.5%), and other groups.

Despite the seeming cultural homogeneity, Lithuania has four well-defined regions—Aukštaitija, Žemaitija, Dzūkija, and Suvalkija. Each of these regions has distinctive dialects, histories, traditions, and food cultures that persist mostly thanks to the relatively large number of rural and small-town inhabitants (constituting about a third of Lithuania's population), whose local identities continue to be strong and who tend to procure a sizable amount of their own food directly from their land. In Aukštaitija, various pancakes and cottage cheese dishes are most popular, while the inhabitants of Suvalkija tend to eat more smoked meat and potato dishes. Žemaitija is famous for porridges, sour butter, and gruels, and Dzūkija is the place where one finds a lot of mushrooms and wild berries, brined and dried sausages, and buckwheat dishes. Vilnius, Lithuania's capital and the largest city, and Klaipėda, the port city, are the main melting pots featuring cosmopolitan lifestyles and international restaurants.

Lithuanian food tends to be hearty and filling. Meat (especially pork), potatoes, dairy, and dark bread are eaten almost every day in the majority of households. Of vegetarian dishes, pancakes, crepes, and dumplings filled with cottage cheese or berries are common. The most popular fish is herring, but smoked mackerel, salmon, pike, and perch are also well liked. With increasing concerns over health and diet, more fresh fruit and vegetables such as apples, cucumbers, cabbages, and tomatoes are consumed year-round.

Contemporary foodways in Lithuania have been shaped by its geography and history. The country is relatively flat with numerous lakes and rivers and rolling hills in the south. Soils range from rich loam in the north and central plains that are amenable for growing wheat, rye, and root vegetables and for pastures to poorer, sandy soil in the south, where the largest pine forests lie. After the last glacial period around 10,000 B.C., several waves of proto-Indo-European ancestors swept through the region, mixing with the older settlers and introducing their cooking methods, agricultural knowledge, tools, seeds, and, most important, animals domesticated in the Middle East and Asia. During this period Baltic tribes started to milk goats and cows, and since then milk and its products, such as curd, cheese, sour cream, butter, sour milk, and kefir (cultured milk), have been used as the key ingredients in the local cuisine. During the Viking times, Baltic tribes living in contemporary Lithuania's territory were integrated into the Baltic trade networks and traded honey along with furs for salt and herring. In the 14th century, the Great Duchy of Lithuania was the largest country in Europe, encompassing most of what is now Ukraine, Belarus, West Russia, and part of Poland. As expected, southern and eastern European food cultures such as those of the Tartars and Karaim were brought back and melded into local diets. The most popular street food in Lithuania today, *čeburekai,* large deep-fried donuts typically filled with meat, was adopted from the Tartars, while a special cake made with poppy seeds and consumed on special occasions and another popular street food, *kybynai* (a half-moon–shaped pastry with a filling made of mutton, onion, and cabbage), were borrowed from the Karaim settlers.

Starting from the 15th century, with the spread of Christianity and with Lithuania forming a common state with Poland, local nobles were drawn into the western European cultural sphere and enjoyed fashionable meals prepared by chefs trained in western Europe's capitals, while the peasantry continued to eat poor diets consisting of coarse breads, porridges, soups, various types of dumplings, pancakes, and, on rare occasions, dried or cured meats.

In terms of other cultural influences, the sizable Jewish minority played a key role in Lithuanians' diets throughout the Middle Ages and into the modern era, especially in Vilnius, one of the cultural capitals of eastern European Jews. Jewish foods such as bagels and a potato pie known as *kugelis* have been seamlessly assimilated into the Lithuanian cuisine.

The Columbian Exchange products such as tomatoes, potatoes, and chocolate as well as coffee from Africa reached Lithuania at the end of the 17th century as the country was folded into the Russian Empire. Of these products, tomatoes and especially potatoes were adopted and became local staples by the second half of the 19th century. The adoption of the potato brought a profound change in local diets, as cereal-based meals were replaced with potato dishes. Even today potatoes occupy a central place in Lithuanian food culture with the highest rate of per-capita potato consumption among the European Union countries (2008).

The adoption and popularization of the potato in the late 19th century coincided with the national revival that led to the formation of strong national identities and the establishment of Lithuania as an independent state. Not surprisingly, the most famous national dish in today's Lithuania is a potato dumpling, called the zeppelin. The peculiar name of the dish refers to the oblong shape of the dumpling and its grayish color, and also to the experiences of industrialization in the early 20th century that brought new transportation technologies (e.g., zeppelins, cars, and motorcycles) and communication devices (radios). The short-lived independent state of Lithuania (1918–1940) saw the emergence of a national cuisine and supported its institutionalization with the publication of a number of cookbooks and recipes in popular magazines.

Cepelinai (Zeppelins/Potato Dumplings)

2 large raw potatoes, peeled

2 large peeled and boiled potatoes

1½ tsp lemon juice

1 tbsp salt

Cepelinai, a Lithuanian national dish made from grated potatoes. (Shutterstock)

For Meat Filling

2 onions, finely chopped

1 tbsp butter

8 oz ground meat (beef, pork, or ham); or meat can be replaced with cottage cheese, mushrooms, herring, or smoked ham

Salt

Black pepper

Marjoram

Boil a large pot of water. Grate the raw potatoes through a fine grater. Separate the juice by squeezing the grated potatoes dry through a double layer of cheesecloth and collecting the potato juice in a separate dish. Mix the lemon juice into the dry potato mass. Set it aside. When starch settles at the bottom of the dish with the potato juice, in about 5–10 minutes, collect the starch by pouring off the liquid. Then add ½ tablespoon salt, and mix in the potato mass. Mash boiled potatoes and add to the mix.

For meat filling, sauté onions in butter and add to the ground meat. Season with salt, pepper, and marjoram. Mix well.

Take about ½ cup of the potato mix, roll into a ball about the size of an egg, and flatten into a round patty that is about ¼ inch thick. Place a tablespoon of filling mixture in the center of the round, fold over, and seal seam. Roll in your hands until the surface is even by slightly pressing in the middle to make the dumpling into an oblong shape. Gently drop zeppelins into boiling salted water. Make sure all the zeppelins are submerged. Boil for 30 minutes, stirring gently. Remove from water and serve with melted butter and sour cream or fried bacon bits sprinkled on top.

Due to perennial food shortages under Socialism, only staple foods such as bread, milk, butter, farmer's cheese, root vegetables, organ meats, and occasionally ribs and ground meats were available in stores, while better cuts of meat and sausages quickly disappeared and were saved for special occasions. Most of the population maintained close ties with the countryside or grew vegetables and fruit in private gardens to be preserved and eaten throughout the year. Even today, preserved foods—such as smoked and cured meats, jams, and pickled vegetables—continue to occupy an important role in Lithuanian diets. With the opening of the state borders and globalization of food markets, new cuisines were introduced. Restaurants serving pizza, sushi, tapas, steaks, and Chinese dishes have grown rapidly in Lithuanian cities over the last 20 years.

Major Foodstuffs

The most important ingredients in Lithuanians' diets are grains/cereals (rye, wheat, buckwheat, some oats), dairy, root vegetables, eggs, meats (especially pork and beef), mushrooms, and berries. In summer cold, sweet, and milk-based soups are popular. Breads are traditionally divided into two types, white bread made with wheat flour and dark bread made with rye or whole wheat or a mix of flours. There are also two types of salads. Starchy salads are a key dish for celebrations and social events; they are made with beets, potatoes, carrots, beans, mushrooms, herring, ham, and fermented cheeses and are dressed with mayonnaise or oil. Green salads are usually prepared in the summer using seasonal ingredients such as cucumber, tomato, shallots, chives, greens, and dill and are dressed with sour milk, kefir, or sour cream. Brand-name salad dressings and vinegar-and-oil dressings can be bought in supermarkets.

Milk is a popular ingredient in and of itself, as are sour cream, butter, yogurt and yogurt drinks, and fermented cheeses. Local cottage cheese, *varškė,* and farmer's cheese with or without caraway are popular and also available smoked. Sugar was a rare and expensive commodity until the third decade of the 20th century when the first sugar beet–processing factory was built. Today, sweet baked goods play an important role in Lithuanian diets. Multilayered cakes with yogurt and fruit fillings and elaborate decorations, rolls filled with jams, fruit pies, and cookies made with cinnamon, ginger, or chocolate can be found in even the smallest of food stores.

Herring is still a popular fish, eaten either as an ingredient in starchy salads, with potatoes, or in a dish prepared with caramelized onions, mushrooms, and tomato sauce. Among other fish, mackerel, pike, eel, perch, and shrimp can be found frozen in the supermarkets, while salmon harvested in Norway or caught wild in the Atlantic is most often sold defrosted. Eggs are used for cooking as well as hard-boiled or scrambled for breakfast.

Of meats, pork is the most popular, while veal is highly valued but is often too expensive for daily consumption. Many buy ground meat such as pork, beef, or turkey or a mix thereof to prepare cutlets or meatballs for soup. Smoked pig's ears, peas with pork cracklings, and fried dark bread flavored with garlic are favorite snacks with beer. Chicken is well liked and so is turkey. Goat and lamb meats are difficult to come by outside of a few gourmet stores in major cities. Game meat is even rarer.

Mushrooms are popular and used in a wide range of dishes such as soups, salads, and dumplings as well as for sauces or various fillings. Similarly, berries (strawberries, both wild and homegrown; blueberries; raspberries; gooseberries; cranberries; and currants) and nuts have played an important role in Lithuanian diets. Wild berry picking and mushrooming are popular activities among both those living in the countryside and the urbanites. Herbs such as dill, parsley, oregano, and bay leaves are used widely to add flavor to dishes and for marinades. Chamomile, mint, and oregano are also often used for herbal teas. The most popular vegetables are potatoes, beets, carrots, and squash, as well as onions and garlic. Among the locally grown fruits, apples, pears, cherries, and plums are the most popular. Since the early 1990s, with the increase in food imports, tropical fruits and vegetables have been introduced and incorporated into daily diets, including oranges, bananas, and pineapple.

Šaltibarščciai (Cold Beet Soup)

Serves 2

2 medium-size red beets, boiled and peeled

2 hard-boiled eggs

4 c buttermilk

1 c plain, whole-milk yogurt

4 tbsp sour cream

2 cucumbers, finely chopped

Salt to taste

For Garnish

Fresh dill, finely chopped

Fresh scallions, finely chopped

Grate boiled beets coarsely, and chop hard-boiled eggs into cubes. In a bowl mix wet ingredients including buttermilk, yogurt, and sour cream. Add grated beets, finely chopped cucumber, and salt. Mix well. Add chopped eggs. Sprinkle with chopped dill and scallions for garnish. Serve with hot boiled potatoes.

Cooking

Most of the everyday dishes in Lithuania are produced on the stovetop. Potatoes along with other vegetables are boiled in a pot or cooked in a pan with oil. Searing is used sparingly, mostly for meats. Homemade smokers were popular during the Soviet times, and today, smoked meats including hams, different types of sausages, and fish such as eel and perch are still very popular. Pickled vegetables such as homemade or store-bought sauerkraut, cucumbers, and tomatoes are consumed on a regular basis. Deep-frying is not widespread, except for some sweet products such as *žagarėliai,* "twigs." Grilling is quite trendy and is usually performed by men. The common grilled dishes include grilled chicken and a local version of shish kebabs, or *šašlykai.* Pancakes and crepes filled with cheeses, bananas, or berries are cooked in pans in vegetable oil or butter. Handmade dumplings boiled in water are also widespread.

Typical Meals

The most important meal is in the middle of the day and consists of meat or vegetable soup and a protein-based main dish such as breaded chicken, beef rolls filled with mushrooms, pork cutlets, beef stroganoff, goulash, boiled sausages, or stuffed cabbage, which would be accompanied by potatoes, pancakes, or potato dumplings, followed by a dessert. Due to demanding schedules during the day, many are shifting from a midday sit-down meal to having a heavier dinner at the end of the day. Other meals include a breakfast that often consists of an open-faced sandwich made out of dark or white bread with butter and smoked meat such as ham, sausage, turkey, or salmon or farmer's cheese. Oatmeal and breakfast cereal are becoming increasingly popular. During weekends it is common to make more time- and labor-intensive breakfasts such as crepes, pancakes, or dumplings. For breakfast, Lithuanians drink a cup of tea or coffee. In late morning and midafternoon, many share a cup of coffee with sweet or savory snacks with their coworkers or snack at home. The traditional supper is usually light and vegetarian. It may include soup, a bowl of cereal, a potato dish, or dumplings.

Eating Out

During the Soviet times an important change took place in Lithuanians' eating habits, as many started eating their main meals outside of the household, with coworkers, with friends, or alone, on a regular basis. Factory and office cafeterias became important places for socialization. Today, eating out is usually practiced as a rather expensive leisure activity, not a necessity. The opening of the global markets in the early 1990s, and especially the massive wave of out-migration of Lithuanians to Spain, the United Kingdom, and the United States, spurred local interest in international cuisine. New restaurants were opened, including tapas bars, steak houses, Mexican grills, and sushi and sashimi restaurants as well as fast-food chains such as McDonald's. Of these, pizzerias and local coffee shop–type restaurants serving snacks and a limited range of meals are the most popular.

Special Occasions

The most important celebration in Lithuania is Christmas Eve dinner, Kūčia or Kūčios. The name of the celebration is derived from the dish called *kūčia,* made from grain and pulses. The serving of the dinner starts when the North Star rises on the horizon. Hay is often placed under the white linen tablecloth. In Christian tradition it symbolizes the manger where Jesus was born. It is common to set a plate of food for those family members who passed away in the previous year. Dinner starts with all participants sharing Christmas wafers. Twelve dishes are prepared, both as a symbol of the 12 apostles and as a reassurance that the 12 months of the upcoming year will be plentiful. These dishes include beet soup with mushrooms; fish, including herring and pike; dumplings filled with mushrooms; cold soups made with whole wheat kernels, poppy seed extract, sugar, and water; dried fruit compotes; cranberry pudding; honey; and special Christmas biscuits.

Another celebration, Shrove Tuesday, is accompanied by Carnival and the universal sharing of pancakes. Food also plays an important role in weddings. *Šakotis,* known as *baumkuchen* in Germany, is a tall cake with spikes on the outside and hollow inside, and it is the centerpiece of the wedding table. Bread, salt, and vodka are still widely used as part of the wedding ritual of accepting the bride and groom into the kin. In weddings as at other significant social gatherings in Lithuania, alcoholic drinks are served. Beer is a traditional local drink, especially in the northern region. During the interwar period, the first Lithuanian wine factory was founded and

Vendors bake a giant pancake at a Mardi Gras celebration in Vilnius, Lithuania. (EPA Photo | Petras Malukas)

started producing wines made with berries, apples, and honey. During the Soviet times the old tradition of mead, a fermented honey drink, was brought back. Today's mead is much stronger than the medieval version as it is made using distilled spirits and honey flavoring rather than by fermenting a honey drink. Other distilled drinks include liqueurs with herbal essences such as *Trejos Devynerios* or berry-flavored vodkas.

Diet and Health

In response to the changing perceptions about healthy diets, since the early 1990s there has been a major change in local cooking methods, moving away from animal fat to vegetable oils. Even in the early 1990s, most of the food was still cooked either in pig fat or, on rare occasions, in butter. Rapeseed oil (canola) was used for frying fish. Today, extra-virgin and virgin olive oil and other vegetable oils have made inroads into everyday diets, and pig fat has disappeared from the supermarket shelves. While there is a widespread perception that fat is not good for one's health, health-conscious eating is mostly practiced by the younger generations, who did not experience the food scarcity in the early Socialist era. As in other places around the world, dieting is usually practiced among young women, who tend to ration their daily caloric intakes following dietary fashions. There is also an increased interest in traditional medicine, especially the use of local herbs' medicinal powers for healing. While such knowledge survived in Lithuania during the early decades of the 20th century, which brought the industrialization and professionalization of medicine, and continued to be practiced in most homes under Socialism, today it is receiving a renewed interest.

Diana Mincyte

Further Reading

Bindokienė, Danutė Brazytė. *Papročiai ir Tradicijos Išeivijoje/Lithuanian Customs and Traditions.* 1989. Chicago: Lithuanian World Community, 1998.

Imbrasienė, Birutė, ed. *Lithuanian Traditional Foods.* Vilnius, Lithuania: Baltos Lankos, 1998.

Malta

Overview

The Maltese archipelago is situated in the middle of the Mediterranean, about 58 miles (93 kilometers) south of Sicily (Italy) and 180 miles (290 kilometers) north of North Africa, and covers an area of 122 square miles (316 square kilometers). The two main inhabited islands are Malta and Gozo, while a third island, Comino, mainly comprises a hotel, an ancient watchtower, and a handful of private residences.

The resident population of the Maltese Islands stands at approximately 416,000, which translates to a population density of 3,414 people per square mile (1,318 per square kilometer). This is by far one of the highest densities in the world and is further augmented by the one million plus tourists who visit the islands annually.

Through the ages, Malta has been colonized by many different nations, including the Phoenicians and Romans, the Arabs and Normans, the pan-European Order of the Knights of St. John (also known as the Knights of Malta), the French, and the British, gaining independence in 1964 and becoming a republic in 1974. Its location at the crossroads of mercantile sea routes has made the island a staging post for trade since antiquity. A long history of greeting visitors and adapting to the demands of colonizers has made the Maltese particularly open to novelty and change, also when it comes to food. Malta's proximity to Italy and the strong cultural and commercial ties between the two neighboring countries have also left their mark, which is evident in the Maltese people's affinity for Italian culture, including food. All of this, together with the most

recent influence of nearly 200 years of British domain, has molded 21st-century Maltese cuisine and eating habits. Thus, the Maltese diet can no longer be considered typical of the traditional Mediterranean diet but is a mélange of dishes and flavors reflecting a multicultural history.

Slightly over one-third of the total land area in the Maltese Islands is agricultural, made up of arable land or permanent crops, although there is greater agricultural activity in Gozo, which is, in fact, much more rural. About half of the cultivated land is used for fodder crops, slightly less for vegetables, and most of the remainder for vines and fruit trees. The major crops are melons, tomatoes, potatoes, pumpkins, zucchini, and cauliflower. Malta is self-sufficient in fresh vegetables, processed tomatoes, eggs, poultry, pork, and fresh milk and milk products. It produces about a fifth of its food and imports the rest.

The Maltese are predominantly Roman Catholic, although the various associated rituals are practiced to varying degrees. This is also evident in the kind of food eaten. Avoiding meat and meat products on Wednesday and Fridays is perhaps followed only by a minority of elderly people; however, choosing to abstain from certain foods, such as sweets and desserts, for the whole 40-day period of Lent is a common practice among all age groups.

🍽 Food Culture Snapshot

Claire and Karl are a young married couple with two school-age children. Claire is a teacher, and Karl works in a shipping office. The family wakes up around

A selection of local Maltese produce on display in a farming village. (Shutterstock)

6:30 A.M., and breakfast will typically consist of a cup of tea or coffee and toast for the adults and a bowl of cereal with milk and a freshly squeezed orange juice for the children. Sarah, who has just turned 13, will sometimes grab a yogurt or banana on the way out and skip breakfast if she is late for school transport. Jeremy, who is 9, also sometimes skips breakfast and then buys a croissant from one of the little shops just outside his school.

The entire family takes a packed lunch. This usually consists of sandwiches with a cheese or meat-type filling, fruit, and water. Claire will sometimes take a fresh salad, and Karl sometimes opts to buy a ħobża biż-żejt from a shop just around the corner from his office. This consists of a hearty, crusty bun, spread with tomato or tomato puree, drizzled with olive oil, and then filled with chopped onions, olives and capers, tuna flakes, butter beans, and a few slivers of chopped lettuce. If Sarah is still hungry, she sometimes buys a cereal bar at the school "tuck shop." School meals are not offered in Malta, though secondary schools have little shops called tuck shops selling a variety of snack foods and drinks.

Claire arrives home first, around 2:45 P.M., followed soon by Sarah and Jeremy. The children are ready for a snack, which may consist of a slice of pizza, a sandwich, a packet soup, or leftovers from yesterday's supper. Claire might join them or just have some tea with a biscuit (cookie) or a yogurt.

Around 4:30 P.M., the three of them may have another tea or coffee. Though biscuits are always available in the food cupboard, sometimes Claire buys traditional teatime sweets, such as qagħaq tal-ħmira (soft dough rings with sesame seeds), qagħaq ħelwien (hard dough rings with sesame seeds), biskuttelli (golden brown Italian biscotti-like fingers), and biskuttini tar-raħal (baked rounds with an aniseed flavor topped with a piped pink or blue icing design). The children enjoy these treats, especially as they are great for dunking.

Supper is normally around 7 P.M. Staples on the menu are pastas with different sauces—tomato, white sauce, or pesto—with a meat or fish slant; or meat, chicken, or fresh or frozen fish with some mashed, fried, roasted, or boiled potatoes and raw or boiled vegetables in season.

In the colder winter months the family might have minestra (thick vegetable soup), kusksu (broad bean–based soup, with miniature pasta balls and ricotta), or soppa tal-armla (also known as widow's soup—consisting of potatoes, onions, tomato, cauliflower florets, and an egg or ġbejniet—little goat or sheep cheeses—cooked whole in the soup). Claire's mother sometimes makes an extra batch of these traditional soups and shares it with her daughter's family.

In the hotter summer months, the family will often opt for cold salads with a variety of vegetables, tuna or chicken, and pasta or rice. Ever since they bought their own gas-operated barbecue, summer evening barbecues have become more common, with grilled chicken, fish, and meat accompanied by fresh salads being the typical fare.

Whatever the season, fruit will always be offered as dessert with the evening meal. Puddings and other cooked desserts are typically saved for Sunday lunch or other special occasions. Wine is generally also served on the table. The children are allowed to have some mixed with a soft drink, although more often they drink water.

Major Foodstuffs

Most of the food consumed in Malta is imported. This is not a recent phenomenon. Although through the ages the Maltese are recorded as growing many of their own fruits and vegetables, hunting for wild rabbits or breeding them domestically, rearing goats and sheep for milk and for making cheese, and starting revolts to safeguard their supply of daily bread, even during the time of the Knights and the British, a lot of the food that ended up in Maltese people's stomachs had been shipped in from abroad and was influenced in one way or another by the kitchens of the colonizers. Nowadays, supermarket shelves are laden with thousands of imported processed food items, yet, luckily, local seasonal fruits and vegetables are still widely available, as is freshly baked bread, fresh fish, and fresh milk and dairy products.

However, if one ventures to the capital city, Valletta, and asks teenagers at random to identify ingredients typical of Maltese cuisine, some would probably find themselves at a loss as to how to answer straightaway. The problem is that they are being less frequently exposed to traditional Maltese ingredients and dishes due to changes in their families' lifestyles, in the availability of foods, and in the restaurants offering certain cuisines. Despite their initial hesitation, the teenagers would eventually likely name one or more of the following: *ħobż tal-Malti* (the local soft, open-textured, "holey" bread, either with a hard crust or, if unleavened, with a softer crust), ġbejniet (little sheep or goat cheeses, served fresh, dried plain, or dried and pickled in vinegar and covered in black pepper), *bigilla* (a brown paste made from boiled, mashed beans, seasoned with olive oil, salt, and red pepper, typically served as a dip), *tadam ċatt* (tasty flat-shaped tomatoes with grooves, often used to spread on fresh bread), *għaġin il-forn* or *timpana* (baked macaroni with a tomato and meat sauce, sometimes encased in pastry), and *stuffat tal-fenek* or *fenek moqli* (rabbit stew or fried rabbit in wine and garlic). They might also mention garlic and onions (especially since these are often chopped and used as a base for sauces, soups, and dips) and olives and capers (which weave their way into many dishes, both traditional and more modern).

Bigilla

Ingredients

1 lb dried fava beans

6–8 cloves garlic, roughly chopped

2 tbsp olive oil

Juice of 1 lemon

2 tbsp parsley, finely chopped

1 tbsp mint, marjoram, or basil

1 red chili pepper, finely chopped

Salt

Wash the beans and soak for 24 hours in cold water, changing water at least three times.

Cook the beans in a little water for about 1½ hours or until soft. Drain off the excess liquid.

Mash or blend the beans, adding the garlic, olive oil, lemon juice, herbs, chili pepper, and salt.

Serve hot or cold, as a spread on crusty bread or as a dip.

The youth will likely mention the local alternative to westernized fast food—*pastizzi*. These are flaky pastries shaped like diamonds or turnovers and filled with a fluffy ricotta cheese or soft mashed peas. A heavier version—called *qassatat*—is made with short-crust pastry and shaped like a rose. This is sometimes also stuffed with a mixture of spinach and anchovies or tuna.

Interestingly, historians have stated that, for reasons of shared history and proximity leading to trading and other contact, Maltese dishes have similar if

Bigilla, a traditional dish found in Malta. (Shutterstock)

not identical counterparts in neighboring countries. For example, the *kannoli*—pastries filled with sweetened ricotta and candied fruit—are nearly identical to those of nearby Sicily, and the *kapunata*—made with tomatoes, green peppers, eggplant, onions, garlic, capers, and olives—is similar to the *peperonata* and other such dishes found in many southern Mediterranean nations.

Also, for historical reasons, there is a clear British influence on foods still typically eaten in Malta. Potatoes were introduced to the islands as a cash crop by the British (though they were probably first seen locally in the kitchens of the Spanish knights), and they are now a staple food, being used in soups, stews, and pies, and also as an accompaniment to meat and fish dishes. For the latter, roasted potatoes or chips (fries) are the most common formats. Curry powder is often used to spice up sauces and stews. Bread is often buttered; olive oil is not so commonly used for cooking but more so for flavoring.

Cooking

In keeping with traditional Mediterranean principles, many traditional Maltese recipes involve slow cooking methods. The older generations will swear that soups, sauces, and stews benefit enormously from being simmered for a couple of hours over a low flame, whereas cooking using more modern equipment and utensils results in inferior dishes from the perspective of both flavor and texture.

Well into the early 20th century, Maltese households cooked food in earthenware pots on a *kenur*—a portable stone stove with four raised corners on which a pot could be placed and with a hole in the middle where twigs and thorns (and coal for those who could afford it) were burned as fuel. This was later replaced by a *kučiniera*—a paraffin-fueled stove—which allowed for easy regulation of the flame. In both cases, the food would be left to cook slowly and gently for hours, filling the house with tantalizing aromas while household chores were carried out.

A habit that was common in the 20th century and still persists in a few villages is that of preparing the food, covering the dish with a clean white cloth, and taking it to be cooked in one of the local bakeries.

In the past, this was typically done to cook enough loaves of bread to last the family for a few days or to cook the Sunday lunch. Two dishes still commonly cooked in this communal fashion are *patata l-forn* (layered meat, onion, and potato slices baked in wine), or *mqarrun* or *ross il-forn* (baked macaroni or rice). The dishes cook side by side in one large oven so that the aromas mingle, giving each dish a flavor unachievable in the home oven. For bakers to recognize which dish belongs to whom, each family is given a lead identification tag matching one attached to the dish.

Typical Meals

Meals in modern households differ quite a lot, often depending on the work status of the main food provider (very often the mother), as well as a multitude of other factors (including food availability and accessibility, culinary skills, and support from elderly relatives). Whatever the circumstances, in most cases a variety of meals are offered, some of which may take a more traditional slant and others a more modern one.

The Maltese are well known for their trait of adaptability—taking what is foreign and giving it their own mark. This likely was also the case with food over the centuries. Many Maltese were employed in the different kitchens of the Knights of Malta's eight Langues (i.e., languages, from Provence, Auvergne, France, Castile, Aragon, Italy, England, and Germany) and later in the households of the British military families stationed in Malta. Their participation in the production of different dishes for these colonizers surely influenced their own repertoire of recipes and dishes cooked at home.

Currently, in households that still present more traditional fare, a meal will typically start with *brodu* (broth), followed by a plate with meat, potatoes, and vegetables cooked in the broth itself, or else steamed on top of the broth as it simmered slowly on the flame. In winter hearty soups, such as minestra, kusksu, or soppa tal-armla, are often served as a one-dish meal. In some cases, these soups may be followed by a slice of bread with *ġobon tal-bżar* (cheese with whole black peppers). Other typical main dishes might be a variety of pies, such as *torta tal-irkotta* (with a filling of ricotta and broad beans), *torta tal-qargħa ħamra* (with a filling of pumpkin and rice), and *torta tal-lampuki* (with a filling of dorado fish chunks, tomato, onion, cauliflower, and potato). A traditional way of using leftover vegetables (such as cauliflower and potatoes) is to use them to make *pulpetti* (fritters) with tuna. Nowadays, these are often served with a fried egg and chips (fries).

A typical meal in a more modern kitchen will consist of roasted chicken drumsticks, roasted potatoes, and some vegetables or a salad. Tabletop grills are common in many households and are used with low-fat cooking in mind. Other typical meals are based on a wholesome pasta dish, such as penne, farfalle, or tortellini with either a tomato and meat (Bolognese-style) sauce or a cream, mushroom, and bacon (carbonara-style) sauce or a simpler sauce with pesto (of which many jarred varieties are available). However, pizzas, burgers, chicken nuggets, and noodles would possibly be the more common fare on the younger generation's daily menu.

In the past, red meat dishes were reserved for Sundays, feast days, and special occasions. Fish and pasta were consumed on Roman Catholic days of abstinence from meat (Wednesday and Friday). These traditions may still be upheld in some households, especially among the older generations; but in most households they are nonexistent (with the exception perhaps of abstaining on Good Friday and Our Lady of Sorrows Day—the Friday after the third Sunday following Easter).

Sunday lunch still holds a special place in many families. As a result, more traditional and perhaps labor-intensive and time-consuming meals are prepared. One such menu may be brodu, followed by timpana, and then patata l-forn. Alternatively, *braġjoli* (stuffed rolled-up beef slices stewed in a sauce of tomatoes, peas, and potatoes) or a similar plain meat stew—*stuffat tal-laħam*—will be prepared. Spaghetti is offered as a starter, over which some of the sauce from the stew is ladled; this is then followed by a plate of the stew accompanied by plenty of crusty bread for sopping up the sauce.

Though fruit is considered the standard dessert in most households, there are a number of traditional desserts that are occasionally prepared, perhaps more so on Sundays or feast days. These include *torta tal-marmurat* (a baked pie with a filling of almonds, candied orange peel, and chocolate) and *pudina tal-ħobż* (a baked pudding using stale bread with apples, raisins, and cocoa among the most common ingredients—though every family has its own secret recipe). A common dessert that shows traces of Malta's past British colonization is fruit trifle comprising layers of sponge cake, blancmange (and almond pudding), and fruit. Some families may also douse the sponge with a shot of vermouth. A typical traditional meal would essentially end with a variety of nuts, such as roasted peanuts, or hazelnuts and walnuts accompanied by dried figs and dates. During the Christmas season, roasted chestnuts are also popular.

Eating Out

Tourism is one of the major industries in Malta, and, possibly as a result of this, there is no lack of restaurants in Malta. In fact, eating out as a family is a common weekend and special-occasion activity. Recent years have seen a rapid expansion in the range of international and ethnic cuisine restaurants. Apart from the omnipresent Italian restaurants, the islands have also seen an increase in Chinese and Indian restaurants, as well as the emergence of African, eastern European and Baltic, Greek, Mexican, Japanese, and fusion restaurants, to name a few. Fast-food outlets are heavily patronized by Maltese families. Kiosks and take-out places selling kebabs are also becoming popular, especially among the younger generations.

There are still very few restaurants on the islands that offer truly traditional Maltese dishes. Very casual restaurants that offer what is called a typical *fenkata* meal have been around for a few decades. This meal revolves around the traditional stuffat tal-fenek (rabbit joints prefried in garlic and then stewed with onions, tomatoes, peas, potatoes, bay leaf, and wine). The meal may start off with an appetizer, such as crusty bread slices rubbed with tomato and olive oil (similar to the Italian bruschetta), or local *galletti* (water biscuits) served with chunks of ġbejniet or some bigilla for dipping. This is then followed by a plate of spaghetti mixed with some of the sauce ladled out from the pot of rabbit stew.

Restaurants along the waterfront in Marsaxlokk, Malta. (StockPhotoPro)

The main dish is the rabbit stew itself, served with baskets of fresh crusty local bread. Dessert consists of a variety of seasonal fresh fruit. Then the meal ends with roasted peanuts, which all the diners shell at the table.

A recent phenomenon has been the opening of wine bars, particularly in the narrow winding roads of village cores and old fortressed cities. These wine bars offer both local and foreign wines, yet a staple item on their menu is a platter consisting of local traditional appetizers such as the *ħobż biż-żejt,* galletti, ġbejniet, bigilla, and parsley-laced butter beans.

Special Occasions

The yearly calendar in Malta is punctuated with a number of public holidays, including many special *festa* days linked to the Roman Catholic religion.

Although a turkey dinner and Christmas pudding have taken over as the meal for Christmas in many households, several other festa days have retained their associated traditional dish or sweet. For example, it is not uncommon for a family to order a young lamb or kid to be roasted for Easter lunch. Easter also brings with it *figolli* (a sweet pastry filled with an almond paste and generally coated with glacé icing or chocolate). These pastries were traditionally shaped as a lamb or fish, though over the years other less religiously symbolic shapes have emerged, such as butterflies, hearts, and cars.

Carnival is celebrated just before the beginning of Lent—the period of fasting before Easter. *Prinjolata* is a sweet made from cake crumbs, sugar, egg whites, and nuts, coated with icing and decorated with glacé cherries and piped chocolate, which is typically sold as a little mound or by weight and cut from a larger mound during Carnival days.

Karamelli tal-ħarrub (carob sweets) are readily available on both Our Lady of Sorrows Day and Good Friday, two days of strict fasting. A very common meal on these days is ricotta-filled ravioli or torta tal-irkotta in observance of the no-meat rule. Either as a sign of respect or perhaps as a show of morbid humor, November 2, which commemorates All Souls' Day, is characterized by shop windows displaying trays of *għadam*—pastries in the shape of bones.

Throughout the year the various churches in the towns and villages celebrate their patron saints. These festivals involve street parades with bands and a statue of the saint carried high on men's shoulders. The main streets and especially the square in front of the church are typically lined with little wooden ornately decorated kiosks selling different types of *qubbajt* (nougat). One can choose from either a soft white nougat containing roasted nuts or a rock-hard, dark brown caramel nougat also containing nuts or sesame seeds. Now and again, one might also find a mobile vendor selling *mqaret.* These are deep-fried diamond-shaped, date-filled pastries served piping hot. Over the years, the festas have become heavily commercialized and westernized, with mobile kiosks selling hot dogs, burgers, kebabs, chips, ice cream, cotton candy, and all sorts of fast food.

Diet and Health

Since the latter half of the 20th century, Malta has witnessed a shift toward westernized dietary patterns, with an increased consumption of meat, dairy products, and processed high-fat, high-sugar, high-salt foods and a decreased consumption of pulses. Common foods in children's diets are chicken nuggets, burgers, pizzas, and packet noodles, together with a variety of packaged salted snacks, chocolate or jam-filled croissants, and cookies.

In 1988, the "National Nutrient Goals and Dietary Guidelines" document specifically recommended that Maltese eat less meat and consume fish and poultry in preference to beef; replace high-fat dairy products with low-fat alternatives; and eat fewer eggs and more fresh fruit and vegetables and whole-grain cereal products.

Following a traditional Maltese diet would go some way toward meeting these recommendations. For example, rabbit is one of the meats lowest in fat, whereas fish is used in several recipes ranging from *aljotta* (a broth-type fish soup containing rice and some vegetables), to pulpetti, to torta tal-lampuki. Moreover, fresh seasonal vegetables are used, raw or boiled and then cooled, to make vegetable salads, as well as a variety of soups. *Tadam mimli* (stuffed tomatoes), *brunġiel mimli* (stuffed eggplants), and *bżar mimli* (stuffed bell peppers) are three common traditional dishes in which the vegetables are filled either with rice and meat or with rice, tuna, olives, and capers and then baked.

Fruit, which is lauded for its health benefits, is luckily a staple in the diet. Different local fruits are available year-round, including plums, peaches, nectarines, apricots, pears, oranges, tangerines, strawberries, melons, watermelons, and grapes. Some claim that one of the best local fruits is prickly pears, which grow on the side of country lanes. Cut first thing in the morning and peeled after they have been soaked in water to tame the spines, prickly pears are delicious eaten cold from the refrigerator. They come in shades of red, green, and orange and are a feast for the eye when presented on the table in a bowl.

Local grapes are also pressed to make a variety of wines, and the elders insist that a glass of wine daily proffers many health benefits. Interestingly, some local entrepreneurs are using prickly pears, pomegranates, and various herbs to make liquors that all have a distinctive Mediterranean aroma and are marketed with an emphasis on their natural ingredients.

Suzanne Piscopo

Further Reading

Atkins, P., and M. Gastoni. "The Maltese Food System and the Mediterranean." *GeoJournal* 41 (1997): 127–36.

Billiard, E. "When Tradition Becomes Trendy: Social Distinction in Maltese Food." *Anthropological Notebooks* 12 (2006): 113–26.

Caruana, Claudia. *Taste of Malta.* New York: Hippocrene, 1998.

Caruana Galizia, Anne, and Helen Caruana Galizia. *The Food and Cookery of Malta.* London: Pax Books, 1999.

Cassar, Carmel. *Fenkata: An Emblem of Maltese Peasant Resistance?* Valetta, Malta: Ministry of Youth and the Arts, 1994.

Cremona, Matty. *Cooking with Maltese Olive Oil.* Mosta, Malta: Proximus, 2002.

Malta Tourism Authority. "Food and Drink." http://www.visitmalta.com/food-and-drink.

Parkinson-Large, Pamela. *A Taste of History: The Food of the Knights of Malta.* Lija, Malta: MAG Publications, 1995.

Moldova

Overview

The Republic of Moldova is a landlocked country that lies between the Ukraine and Romania in eastern Europe. The official language is Moldovan, which many linguists say is the same language as Romanian. The population of Moldova in 2009 was 4,320,748. With 29 percent of the population living below the poverty line, Moldova rates as one of Europe's poorest countries. Moldova gained independence in 1991 after 44 years of Soviet rule. Previous to this, the territory had been annexed into two areas, one Russian and the other Romanian. Consequently, Moldovan food culture shows clear Russian and Romanian elements. Originally, Moldova was part of the principality of Moldova. In the 14th and 15th centuries the Ottoman Empire ruled Moldova. Moldova was also part of an ongoing cultural exchange that has typified eastern Europe from the Middle Ages to the present day. The result is a cuisine that brings together Russian, Romanian, Turkish, Bulgarian, Greek, German, Jewish, and Ukrainian elements. History, agriculture, poverty, and religion all play defining roles in Moldovan food culture.

Fertile land covers most of Moldova's 13,070 square miles (33,851 square kilometers), three-quarters of which are dedicated to agriculture. Agriculture is considered the main pillar of Moldova's economy and accounts for half of Moldova's exports and a third of its labor force. Moldova has supplied food and wine to Russia, Romania, and Turkey at different times in history. Today, Moldova exports produce mainly to nearby countries. Wine is one of Moldova's most significant industries. Grapevines, maize, wheat, and a range of fruit trees and vegetables grow in Moldova's rich soils, and animals are kept for dairy and meat products.

Food Culture Snapshot

With half the population living rurally and half in urban settings, the variety of foods available is different for these two demographics. What is common is the use of produce markets to buy food. Produce markets are located in most places, from small towns to large cities like Chisinau. Cornmeal will be bought in large quantities to make into a variety of dishes served throughout the day. In a rural setting families grow much of their fruit and vegetables, and animals are reared for meat, eggs, and milk. Flour will be purchased to make pastry and bread. Food items, such as coffee, sugar, salt, and pepper, will be purchased from a supermarket or store. Since the transition to a free market economy, supermarkets selling a wide range of well-known food brands have become common in urban locations.

Major Foodstuffs

Most of what Moldovans eat is supplied domestically. Historically Moldova supplied the Soviet Union with much of its agricultural products. Today, considering the size of the country, exports are generally high. However, political and environmental reasons have caused fluctuations. For example, wine exports to Russia decreased dramatically in 2006 after Russia placed an embargo on wine imports from Moldova and Georgia. The average size of Moldovan farms is larger than western

A fountain of red wine in Moldova. (Shutterstock)

European farms, which allows for high productivity. The high percentage of foods produced in Moldova has meant that over the period of transition from being a Soviet state, food supplies were more stable than in some other eastern European countries. However, another consequence of this is that the population's food supply relies heavily on the stability of agriculture. This was a major problem in 2007 when Moldovan agricultural productivity dramatically decreased due to drought.

Even though meat features in many Moldovan dishes, it provides only half the dietary protein that cereals do. Cereals are not only the main source of protein but also the main source of dietary energy. The two main cereals grown are wheat and maize. Maize is eaten more frequently and at a higher consumption rate than wheat. Like in the neighboring country Romania, maize has historically played, and continues to play, a central role in the

Moldovan diet. The dish *mamaliga* (cornmeal polenta/porridge) is the most common way it is eaten. Wheat is made into bread, which holds a meaningful place in many special occasions. Wheat is also used to make pastry for foods, such as *placinta* (cheese-filled pastry). Wheat bran is used to make a fermented, pickled soup called *bors*. Homemade wheat noodles are commonly used in the popular Moldovan soup *zama* (sometimes called *zeama*) made with chicken and vegetables. Other grains that are eaten less frequently are rice and barley.

Poultry, mainly chicken, and pork are the most widely consumed meats. Chicken is made into a customary Moldovan dish of "jellied chicken." Mutton is used to make *ciorba* (sour soup), *ghiveci* (vegetable stew), or *musaca* (from Greek moussaka). Its use in Moldova is likely a legacy of the Ottoman Empire. Lamb is eaten for Easter and more regularly in southern areas. Beef is eaten to a lesser extent but is still seen in common dishes like *mititei* (sausage-shaped grilled patties) or bors, and it is more common in regions where the cuisine has been more heavily influenced by Russia. Eggs are also a main source of dietary protein and are served on top of mamaliga, served for breakfast, or used in cooking.

Apples, pears, quinces, apricots, and some berries are grown, and all feature in Moldovan dishes. Fruits often accompany meat dishes and are made into preserves, pickles, pies, and juices. Vegetables are often used to balance meat dishes. Tomatoes, cabbage, sweet and green peppers, garlic, eggplant (aubergine), beans, onions, and potatoes are the most popular. Walnuts and sugar beets are also major crops in Moldova.

Moldovans consume a lot of milk and milk products. According to the Food and Agriculture Organization (FAO) of the United Nations, in 2003 milk accounted for 19 percent of daily protein intake. Milk is produced in Moldova and used to make cheeses, cream, butter, and sour cream. However, many of Moldova's favorite cheeses are made using goat or sheep milk. *Brinza* is a sheep cheese, also common in Romania, which accompanies many Moldovan dishes.

Above all, Moldova is known for its wine production. Even though most of the wine is produced for export, wine is served daily at the table. Moldova has been cultivating grapevines and making wine for 5,000 years. Today, the wine-producing regions located in the south, north, and east grow mainly European grape varieties, along with a smaller quantity of local varieties, such as Rara Neagra, Plavai, and Feteasca Regala. White, red, and sweet wines are made, and due to its similar latitude to France, sparkling wines and cognacs are produced as well. Sparkling wines are commonly drunk at celebrations. Grapes are also used to make juices, and they are eaten fresh or used in cooking.

Cooking

Moldovan cooking typically balances sour tastes with some spice and aromatic herbs. Women do most of the cooking. Moldovan cooking makes use of many utensils familiar to a European or American kitchen. Kitchens are generally more basic and don't always contain the time-saving tools that are found in the West. Meat is often grilled over charcoal, which is similar to Balkan cooking. The *ceaun* (cast iron pot that is sometimes rounded at the base) is an important element to the kitchen and is used to make soups, stews, and mamaliga. Mamaliga is commonly placed on a wooden board after it is cooked, and then once it has cooled, it is cut into pieces and served.

Zama (Chicken and Noodle Soup)

Zama is a hearty but well-balanced soup made in a ceaun or large pot, and it forms the foundation for many Moldovan meals.

Ingredients

1 small whole chicken

Approximately 12 c water

Salt and black pepper

½ medium onion

1 carrot

1 medium tomato

1 medium celery stalk and some of the young leaves, finely chopped

2 c egg noodles (preferably homemade)

3 tbsp lemon juice

3–4 small branches of thyme

¼ c finely chopped parsley

¼ c chopped fresh dill

Wash the chicken, place it in a large pot or deep saucepan, and add water. Season with salt and pepper. Boil on medium-low heat until froth rises to the top. Meanwhile, clean and chop the onion, carrot, tomato, and celery stalk. Using a skimmer, remove all the froth. Then reduce to a simmer, cover, and cook for 40 minutes, or until meat is tender. Remove the meat from the pot, then chop and return to the pan along with the vegetables. Season to taste, then return to a simmer and cook for 10 minutes. Then bring to a boil and add the noodles. Continue cooking for 8 minutes, or until the noodles are just tender. Add the lemon juice, herbs and finely chopped celery leaves. Cover pot and remove from the heat. Let the soup stand for 5 minutes. Serve with cornbread.

Breads, pastries such as placinta (pastries filled with egg and brinza or curd), and pies are all baked in the oven. Baked mamaliga is a popular way to eat cornmeal; it is served topped with brinza, and sometimes with egg, bacon, sour cream, or cottage cheese.

Most rural and some urban houses have access to produce right at their door. The amount of produce available can vary depending on whether it comes from a small vegetable garden, a small plot, or a small semisubsistence farm. Preserving produce for consumption throughout the cooler months is a very common method of food preparation. Fruits are preserved in syrup, frozen, pickled, or made into beverages, either juice or brandy. Vegetables are pickled. Canning is also a popular form of preserving.

Typical Meals

Meals vary in quantity and variety depending on occupation, income, and location. Breakfast is often light and may include bread, cornmeal porridge, a pastry, eggs or cheese, and usually coffee or tea. For many people lunch is the main meal of the day. Generally lunch will start with soup. There are many different types of soups: ciorba (sour soup), *zama cutia* (wheat soup with honey), bors, and goulash. Soups contain meat, vegetables, herbs, spices, and often noodles, too. A meat dish will usually follow the soup. Meat can be roasted, baked in a pot, or grilled, for example, grilled mititei (sausage-shaped meat patties) or baked chicken. Meat is often accompanied by fruit, such as *torca* (pork stew) with apricots. *Sarmale* (stuffed cabbage leaves) are also common for lunch or dinner, as are jellied chicken, ghiveci (meat and vegetable stew), and fish. Wine is served with most meals.

At the center of most meals is maize. Having been a vital staple in times of food shortage over the last few centuries, it is now an established part of Moldovan cuisine and considered a national dish. Maize in the form of mamaliga is made into bread; it can also be served as porridge for breakfast, as an accompaniment to main dishes, or topped with cheese.

Mamaliga (Polenta)

This dish is well known in both Moldovan and Romanian cuisines, and it is very similar to Italian polenta. There are numerous ways it can be cooked, and it is served as an accompaniment in a variety of ways. This recipe makes it into a bread; therefore, it will be thicker than Italian polenta.

Ingredients

3½ c water

Salt to taste

1 c cornmeal

4 tbsp butter

In a ceaun or a pot bring water and salt to a boil. In a steady stream, sprinkle about 2 tablespoons cornmeal into the boiling water, stirring constantly. In the same manner gradually add the rest of the cornmeal while stirring continually. With the heat still on low, add small pieces of butter, one at a time, and continue to stir for about 5–10 minutes more. The mixture will start to separate from the sides of the pot. Flatten the surface with the wooden stirring spoon, remove from the heat, and let rest for 5 minutes. Turn the pot over onto a wooden cutting board to remove the mamaliga. Cut into wedges using a taut string. Serve instead of bread with meat, vegetables, or stew. It can also be served with cheese sprinkled on top. Use either brinza, feta, or a sharp, crumbly cheese.

Eating Out

There is little tradition of eating out in Moldova The reality is that many people do not have the financial means, even though restaurants and cafés are extremely cheap compared with Western standards. A variety of restaurants and cafés are found, mainly in the large cities. In Chisinau, Moldova's capital, a number of international cuisines as well as Moldovan food can be found. Food venues range from simple street vendors to fine restaurants. Pizza is ubiquitous in Chisinau, and there are also increasingly more fast-food establishments. In urban settings it is more common to eat out for lunch, when on a work break.

Special Occasions

Food is central when people gather for all major life events, such as birth, marriage, and death, as well as religious holidays. Also, in times of much poverty and turmoil, food and coming together have been very important for Moldovans. When Moldova was a Soviet state, many of these celebrations were forbidden; however, they are still practiced widely today.

Eastern Orthodox Christianity is practiced by 98 percent of the population. Celebrations and commemorations are common occurrences and involve fasting and feasting. The year is structured by many religious holidays. Christmas and Easter are the most relevant to Moldovan food culture. At Christmastime, as in Romania, pork is commonly eaten. In rural settings, a pig is usually slaughtered especially for Christmas. On Christmas Eve an exchange of food takes place. Children go to the houses of relatives and friends with food parcels, as gifts, containing *lichie/liipi* (cakes, biscuits, unleavened bread), apples, and other sweets. The host, having prepared food parcels, then gives a parcel of food to the children. On the eve of Easter, special food baskets are brought to the church to be blessed. The baskets usually contain chicken eggs painted red, lamb, *pasca* (a round cake made especially for Easter), cheese, and salt. As in many other Orthodox religions, lamb, usually grilled, is eaten on Easter Sunday.

There are over 200 different shapes of ritual bread in Moldova. This bread is similar to *colaci,* which is a braided or cross-shaped sweet bread from Romania, something like challah. Different shapes are used for specific occasions; for example, the figure eight is commonly made for Christmas Eve. Ritual bread is central to ceremonies. At births, deaths, marriages, and christening ceremonies, ritual bread is used at certain points in the ceremony. It is also given to guests. Bread accompanied by a candle is given to guests at "meals for the dead," which take place at intervals for seven years after someone's funeral.

Diet and Health

Like many other ex-Soviet states, the population of Moldova does not score as well as most western Europeans in many key health indicators. Also, like many other countries dealing with post-Soviet stresses, many of the health issues are related to lifestyle, including smoking, alcohol consumption, and diet. Food shortages are, and have been, a reality for many people and often result in inadequate nutritional intake. An example of this occurred during the recent 2007 drought, which drastically reduced food reserves. This in turn led to a national health problem because the Moldovan population relies heavily on the food it produces.

Even though Moldova produces a large amount of fruit and vegetables and these also feature heavily in the cuisine, at times consumption has been low and nutrient intake poor due to poverty and poor yields. In the time of large collective farms, Moldova had a high use of pesticides and herbicides. There may be environmental remnants from this time, but today produce is often cleaner and more organic, since Moldova now has a low use of pesticides and fertilizers. For many households, the fruit and vegetables that they grow or buy are likely to be of high quality.

Kate Johnston

Further Reading

Agriculture and Agro-Food Industry of the Republic of Moldova. Chisinau, Moldova: Ministry of Agriculture and Food Industry, 2009

Buzila, Varvara, and Teodorina Bazgu. "Ritual Breads through the Season." In *Culinary Cultures of Europe: Identity, Diversity and Dialogue,* edited by Darra Goldstein and Kathrin Merkle.

Strasbourg, France: Council of Europe Publishing, 2005.

Great Moldovan Recipes. http://moldaviancuisine.blogspot.com/.

"Moldovan Cuisine." World of Moldova. http://www.worldofmoldova.com/en/article/moldovan-cuisine/.

"National Cuisine." All Moldova. http://www.allmoldova.com/en/moldova/chisinau/cuisine.html.

Stratu, Anastasia. "Taste across Frontiers." Moldovarious.com. 2009. http://www.moldovarious.com/culture/113-taste-across-the-frontiers-main-courses.html.

The Netherlands

Overview

The Kingdom of the Netherlands is located in the northwest of the European mainland, bordering the North Sea. In the south the country borders Belgium, and in the east Germany. The Netherlands is a modern, industrialized country and a large exporter of agricultural produce. It has around 16.5 million inhabitants and has been a member of the European Union since 1951. With Amsterdam as its official capital, the government of the monarchy, which was founded in 1830 when Belgium separated, is seated in The Hague. *Dutch* refers to both the inhabitants and the language officially spoken within the country's 12 provinces. Often, and incorrectly, the Netherlands is called Holland, which refers to the (northwestern) provinces of North and South Holland. All 12 provinces have specific characteristics in regard to culture, cuisine, inhabitants, and dialects. The province of Friesland is unique in that, apart from Dutch, Frisian is also an official language. Not only the provinces but also Dutch cuisine originated in the Middle Ages. Due to the moderate climate with cool summers and mild winters, cookery traditionally follows the seasons, and until today dinner centers around potatoes, vegetables, and meat. After World War II the down-to-earth Dutch approach toward cooking changed drastically, and apart from potatoes, staple foods such as rice and pasta started to appear regularly on the dinner table. Vegetables and legumes are commonly boiled in water and remain a more important food choice than meat, fish, or meat alternatives. This is reflected in popular language, as dinner is many times referred to as *agv—aardappel, groente, vlees* (potato, vegetables, meat).

Apart from geography, until late into the 20th century poverty and religion strongly influenced Dutch eating and drinking habits. After the prosperous *Gouden Eeuw* (Golden Age, a period roughly spanning the 17th century), the country was struck by poverty, and as a result the already-existing gap and vast differences in the diets of the rich and poor grew wider. Dating back to the 16th and 17th centuries, segregation, religious freedom, and tolerance became "typical" Dutch characteristics. Toward foreigners and foreign religious dissenters, certain forms of religious freedom and tolerance were practiced, but Dutch citizens who themselves deserted religion or openly practiced otherwise were persecuted and discriminated against. Religious tolerance resulted in many people seeking a haven in the Netherlands, including Jews and French Protestant Huguenots, who could practice their beliefs openly, as well as several new religious sects, such as the Mennonites and Anabaptists. Until the late 1960s Christianity predominated in various forms of Calvinism (the Dutch Reformed Church above all), plus other denominations of Protestantism and Catholicism. Although most of the population was religious, a substantial increase in prosperity, mobility, education, and television sets resulted in secularization but never in a homogeneous nation. Still today around 60 percent of the Dutch population is faithful to religion, including more recently arrived Muslims, Hindus, and Buddhists. In the past, the Dutch diet was well intertwined with religion.

Subsequently, a large number of foods and dishes were prepared and eaten according to religious calendars, laws, and requirements. The well-known Dutch expression "fish on Friday," for instance, reflects the Catholic prohibition of eating meat during fasting days.

Central aspects of the economy are agriculture and international trade, which together with industrialization and the ongoing national and global changes strongly influenced postwar cooking. Also, migration and migrants influenced the diet and eating habits. At present approximately 3.5 million inhabitants are of non-Dutch origin. The independence of the former colonies Indonesia (in 1948) and Suriname (in 1975) resulted in a massive influx of expatriates, and as of the 1960s migrants from southern Europe started to join the workforce.

Food Culture Snapshot

Together with their two-and-a-half-year-old daughter Sophie, Sandy de Roos (38) and Bart van Dijk (45) live in an apartment in a new neighborhood in Amsterdam. Their lifestyle and foodways are typical for many young middle-class cosmopolitan urbanites in the Netherlands. Both are food, wine, and gastronomy enthusiasts and devoted hobby cooks. On holidays and weekends they enjoy eating out in modern and upscale restaurants, as well as visiting food-oriented markets and festivals.

During the week their day starts at around 7:00. Sophie eats her hot porridge followed by a *beschuitje hagelslag* (a Holland rusk with chocolate sprinkles), and she drinks a cup of hot steamed milk. Sandy eats a bowl of cereal with milk. Apart from drinking fruit juice and coffee with milk, Bart breakfasts on slices of bread with either different types of cheeses or cold cuts. After breakfast Bart leaves to work at an advertising agency where lunch is catered between 12:30 and 1:30. Together with his colleagues, Bart lunches on breads and salads. Sandy's lunch many times consists of sandwiches or a roll with melted cheese or cold cuts with a cup of tea. Sophie loves sandwiches of sliced bread with *pindakaas* (peanut butter) and a mug of semiskim milk.

The most important meal of the day is dinner, when the family gathers around the dinner table. On weekdays the cooking is shared by both; the food is prepared in 45 minutes and served around 7:30. For the preparation fresh ingredients are used, as, according to Sandy, these are more appetizing. Boiled, fried, panfried, steamed, or cooked as French fries, potatoes are prepared approximately three times a week. In wintertime, together with vegetables, potatoes are mashed into *stamppot* (hotchpotch). During the week meals vary from mussels with French fries, to Indonesian vegetarian or meat dishes, to Italian pasta, Middle Eastern bulgur, and Moroccan *tajines*. Depending on what's on the menu, supermarkets and specialized or exotic stores are frequented. As during the weekend many times friends are entertained by cooking a three- or four-course dinner with complementary wines, food shopping for leisure consumes more time.

Major Foodstuffs

The most important dietary staples in the Netherlands are dairy (milk, yogurt, cheese), bread and grains, meats, vegetables, and potatoes. A substantial part of the country's crops, dairy products, and livestock is traded and exported internationally. The country has a moderate rainy climate, and due to its position by the sea, where it can be very windy, the differences in winter and summer temperatures are not great. The draining of land has resulted in an extensive network of waterways, dams, and dikes. The overall flat country has fertile soils on which major food crops such as barley, corn, potatoes, sugar beets, and wheat are cultivated openly. Dutch agriculture is highly specialized and technologically sophisticated, which also applies to the country's intensive livestock and dairy production.

Dairy

The average consumption of dairy is very high. Milk and buttermilk are drunk by all ages, and yogurt and milk-based desserts are consumed on a daily basis. Besides for their butter, the Dutch are renowned for their yellow cheeses from cow milk that are produced in factories and by farmers. Gouda,

Edam, and Leerdammer are among the most popular varieties. Most semihard and hard cheeses have the shape of a small soccer ball or cartwheel and are sold cut in pieces. Whether young, mature, or very old, Dutch cheese is eaten thinly sliced with a cheese slicer for breakfast and lunch and on sliced bread spread with butter or margarine. Cut into dice, Dutch cheese traditionally also serves as an appetizer with drinks. Furthermore, the dairy self-sufficient country exports tons of cheese, butter, and condensed milk.

Potatoes and Vegetables

As dinner centers around potatoes, vegetables, and meat, and the Dutch cuisine and diet very much follows the seasons, the average diet is relatively high in potatoes but also in animal, processed, sweetened, and refined foods. Apart from potatoes a substantial amount of energy and carbohydrates comes from staple foods such as bread, cereals, pasta, rice, and dried legumes.

All sorts of vegetables are available year-round: fresh, frozen, and canned. Potatoes and vegetables such as carrots, leeks, cabbages, and onions are grown in the open fields, but tomatoes, cucumbers, lettuce, green beans, spinach, zucchini, eggplant, and peppers are often cultivated in greenhouses. Generally, tomatoes, cucumbers, cauliflower, and lettuce are the most consumed vegetables, but in season locally cultivated produce such as carrots, spinach, beans, peas, endive, leeks, onions, brussels sprouts, or one of the various kinds of cabbages is very popular.

Fruit

Particularly in the summer and the autumn many kinds of domestically grown apples, pears, plums,

Alkmaar Cheese Auction, Amsterdam, Holland. (Corel)

strawberries, cherries, and berries are eaten fresh. Imported bananas, citrus fruit, melons, pineapple, grapes, peaches, and kiwis are sold year-round and primarily eaten fresh. Canned fruits such as mandarin oranges, peaches, and apricots are common, and pineapple especially is very popular.

Meat, Poultry, and Game

Although most Dutch do not eat meat everyday, for most of the population meat remains the most important source of protein. Pork and beef, but also chicken, are the most popular meats; in particular, minced meats and easy-to-prepare meats such as sausages, fillets, chicken breasts, and schnitzel (cutlets) are preferred over larger cuts of meat. Veal, lamb, mutton, goat, horse meat, and turkey are also consumed. In autumn and winter, and especially for festive occasions, all sorts of game (rabbit, hare, pheasant, duck, ostrich, and deer) are served. Eggs, cheese, and meat replacements from soy are popular among the small group of vegetarians (2%) and people who avoid meat regularly.

Fish

All over the Netherlands fresh saltwater fish from the North Sea is available, in particular herring; eel, mackerel, and shrimp are also popular. Besides mussels, cod and plaice are also cultivated, and wild "exotic" fish such as salmon, tuna, tilapia, and *pangasius* (a kind of catfish that looks like a shark) are widely consumed. Smoked eel, wild salmon, and oysters are considered a delicacy. Apart from being prepared at home and in restaurants, fried fish and especially raw salted herring are popular street (snack) foods.

Spices

Roasted, ground, fresh, or dried herbs, spices, and flavorings are traditionally common but used sparingly in Dutch cooking. A wide range of so-called typical Dutch as well as exotic herbs and spices are available. These are commonly purchased in supermarkets, grocer's, and specialty stores that also sell all kinds of spice mixtures. Like most herbs and

spices, they are sold in small bags, cans, or plastic and glass bottles or containers. Curly parsley, flat celery leaves, and chives are among the most used fresh herbs. Parsley and chives are finely chopped, and parsley is particularly popular for all kinds of soups, salads, and sandwiches. Together with the celery root, celery leaves are primarily boiled and used for *erwtensoep,* a thick soup of dried peas. Due to globalization in the 1960s, foreign fresh herbs such as rosemary, thyme, oregano, basil, and cilantro became popular and nowadays are reasonably common. Most households own a salt and pepper set, and many people use a pepper mill. A number of savory and sweet dishes are traditionally prepared with both whole and ground spices such as cloves, nutmeg, and cinnamon. A dash of nutmeg on vegetables and a bit of cinnamon in desserts, cookies, and apple tarts is quite common. The Dutch spice cabinet also contains varieties of mild or spicy paprika and *kerriepoeder* (curry powder). Also widely available are ready-made dried spice mixtures for a large number of Dutch and foreign dishes such as the traditional *gehaktbal* (meatball), *hachée* (meat stew), fish, chicken, chili con carne, and a large number of potato dishes, rice, and pasta. The use of vanilla pods and cinnamon sticks is common. Typically Dutch are *koek- en speculaaskruiden,* which is a mixture of spices made from cinnamon, coriander, nutmeg, cloves, ginger, cardamom, and dried orange peel, used especially in winter for all kinds of cookies, cakes, and desserts.

Condiments

Apart from a salt and pepper set, favorite condiments are mustard, mayonnaise, vinegar, and Maggi seasoning sauce (a substitute meat extract), as well as sweet and sour pickled gherkins and onions. Popular, too, are tomato ketchup, piccalilli and garlic sauce, and *saté-saus* (peanut butter sauce).

Preserving

Until the beginning of the 20th century, since most of the population was self-supporting, food preservation was a necessity. Common methods used to preserve fish, meats, vegetables, and fruits (for example, herring, ham, bacon, and apples) were salting, curing, drying, smoking, and sugaring. At the end of the 19th century freezers were introduced and eagerly adopted by households and the growing food industry. Subsequently, mass-produced preserves started to replace homemade produce and a number of traditional preservation techniques.

Cooking

In the middle of the 19th and the first decades of the 20th century, the interior of the Dutch house started to modernize drastically. Until then most people prepared one-pot dishes on top of a coal stove. After the introduction of gas, electricity, and a separate room for the kitchen, cooking became less time-consuming. Nowadays, middle-class households have modern kitchens that contain at least a four-burner gas range, a microwave, and conventional oven. Also common are a broad variety of electronic household appliances such as a mixer, blender, coffeemaker, espresso machine, toaster, egg boiler, juicer, and water heater.

The standard kitchen equipment is the *pannenset* (set of pans). This collection of saucepans in different sizes is mostly purchased together and traditionally used for cooking potatoes, vegetables, soups, and desserts. Sautéing larger cuts of meat is done in an enameled *braadpan* (casserole). All kinds of flat cast iron and Teflon frying pans with handles are used for the preparation of panfried meats, eggs, and pancakes. Since stir-frying has gained in popularity, most households own a Teflon wok. Typical Dutch kitchen equipment is a potato knife or peeler, a potato masher, and a cheese slicer.

Potatoes, vegetables, and also fruits such as apples and pears are commonly boiled in water with salt or sugar. Meats and eggs are traditionally sautéed in margarine or butter but also in sunflower, olive, peanut, or soy oil, or a combination. Furthermore, lard and bacon are often used for sautéing. The oven is commonly used for baking a traditional *appeltaart* (apple pie), cakes, and cookies but also for savory dishes such as lasagna, pizza, and quiche. Fun cooking and eating together for the *gezelligheid* (sociability) is gaining popularity. In wintertime electric household appliances such as a table wok, grill, or fondue set are put on the dinner table, and in summer more and more people gather around a barbecue or are eating outdoors.

Breakfast, lunch, and dinner are consumed at the dinner table, which is dressed with a cloth, paper, or plastic tablecloth or place mats. Either pans or serving dishes are placed on the table. Soup is eaten from bowls or plates, the main dish is served on flat plates, and dessert is served in separate bowls. The standard tableware is a spoon, fork, and knife. The style of eating is "Continental," with the fork to the left and the knife to the right of the plate. If dinner is followed by dessert, dessert spoons are placed on the table, above the plate. Table manners are influenced by the French; thus, it is considered impolite to chew food with an open mouth, to eat food from someone else's plate, or to leave the table before all have finished eating.

Vast amounts of local and foreign beers and wine are consumed. Although drinking wine has gained in popularity, apart from on the weekend and in restaurants, drinking alcohol or any other beverages at the dinner table is not very common and usually restricted to special occasions.

At present the average middle-class Dutch woman spends around 30 minutes in the kitchen. Inspiration many times comes from a wide range of women's and specialized magazines, daily recipes in newspapers, the Internet, the television, and cookbooks. Shopping for groceries is mostly done once a week, in particular, on Friday and Saturday. During the week women usually do most of the cooking. As cooking and gastronomy have become more popular, many men and middle-class cosmopolitan urbanites engage in food and wine shopping for leisure, especially on the weekend.

Typical Meals

Since the poverty-stricken 1800s and beginning of the 1900s, the Dutch diet has improved substantially. The year-round availability and variety of food have never been greater. Also, television shows, celebrity chefs, cookbooks, and magazines have added to the development and globalization of domestic cooking and gastronomy. In the 20th century, together with industrialized foods, new and exotic products, foods, and ingredients increasingly modernized the diet. From the 1960s on, alongside the potato, rice, pasta, pizza, and quiche, a large variety of ingredients and dishes from around the world started to appear on the menu. Although Dutch cuisine and meals always have been internationally oriented, especially the younger (urban) generation prepares meals that can vary from Chinese to Italian, Moroccan to Indian.

For most people the main meal is dinner, but especially the older generation and rural families keep the traditional mealtimes. Around lunchtime they eat a hot meal starting with soup, followed by potatoes, vegetables, and meat, and a dessert. Around 6 P.M. often just a cold light meal of sliced bread with cold cuts and cheese or soup is consumed. This supper is many times followed by a cup of coffee with a cookie around 8 P.M. On Sunday afternoon many families gather around the dinner table or eat in restaurants, where they have either an extensive lunch or brunch or a three-course dinner. Especially during weekends, it is popular to order take-out food from eateries or Chinese-Indonesian restaurants.

During the week, a cold or hot breakfast and lunch are followed by a hot dinner around 6 P.M. Commonly a snack or a cookie is consumed during the 10 A.M. coffee break and 3 P.M. tea break. Both at home, at work, and in the streets, sweet and savory snack foods are very popular. A vast variety of traditional and exotic snacks such as French fries and the *kroket* (croquette) but also Vietnamese spring rolls and Middle Eastern *shoarma* (shawarma—similar to Greek gyros and served in a flatbread) are available in most cities.

Breakfast is generally consumed between 8 and 9 A.M. before people start school or the workday. Apart from convenience products such as cereal, it sometimes consists of oatmeal porridge, but more common are slices of (white or brown) wheat bread that are spread with margarine or butter and jam, sliced cheese, or cold cuts. Most kitchen cabinets and refrigerators contain an ample supply of strawberry, apricot, and other kinds of fruit jams. Popular, too, are pindakaas (peanut butter), *chocolade-pasta* (chocolate spread), *appelstroop* (apple treacle),

hagelslag (chocolate sprinkles), old and young semi-hard cheeses such as Gouda and Edam, and many types of cold meats and sausages. Also, *beschuit* (rusk) and *ontbijtkoek* (breakfast cake) are typical for breakfast. To drink, orange juice, tea, milk, or coffee is considered suitable.

Eating lunch in a restaurant or eatery is not very common; most people take their own sandwiches to work in a lunch box. The Dutch very often refer to lunch as *boterhammen uit de broodtrommel cultuur* (sandwiches from the lunch-box culture). Between 12:00 and 1:00 schoolchildren and a large part of the workforce consume a few sandwiches, soup, or a snack in a canteen, home, or workplace, or in the street.

The main meal of the day is eaten between 5:30 and 6:30 P.M. Traditionally, dinner is a sequence of three courses: soup, a main dish, and a dessert. Serving soup as a starter has lost its popularity, but dessert is rarely skipped. What is served at dinnertime many times is decided in the supermarket and day by day. Most families use dinnertime as the opportunity to sit, eat, and talk together. Apart from potatoes, vegetables, and meat, a few times each week pasta or rice is prepared. Most supermarkets carry a wealth of convenience desserts ranging from the more traditional (fruit) yogurt, vanilla or chocolate *vla* (custard), and *griesmeelpudding* (semolina pudding) to foreign desserts such as chocolate mousse and *bavarois* (Bavarian cream).

Even though vast numbers of slices of bread and rolls are consumed for breakfast and lunch, the preferred source of carbohydrates is the potato. For every taste and dish there's a Dutch potato. Of the around 90 potato varieties available, the so-called mealy types with a yellowish or red-brown skin are the favorites. Potato types are often given girl's names, such as Bintje, Irene, and Marijke. Potatoes are usually served peeled and boiled. If potatoes are eaten together with vegetables, panfried meat, and gravy, the vegetables are boiled in water and served with a *roomsaus* (literally, "cream sauce," but actually prepared with butter, flour, and milk).

Although eaten all year round, the ultimate Dutch winter foods are stamppot (hotchpotch) and soups of dried beans. In winter, soups with boiled potatoes, vegetables, meats, dried brown beans, and (broken) dried green peas are popular as *maaltijdsoep* (dinner soup). Well known are *bruine bonensoep* (brown bean soup) and erwtensoep (pea soup).

From fall to the beginning of spring, stamppot is commonly prepared by boiling and mixing potatoes together with vegetables. A few well-known local varieties, such as *hete bliksem* (hot lightning, with apples) and *blauwe bliksem* (blue lightning, with pears), are made with potatoes and fruit. In spring and summer, mixing cooked potatoes with raw vegetables such as endive is also popular. Today, there are numerous recipes for and variations of stamppot, but overall the most traditional versions include endive with bacon and meatballs, *hutspot* (carrots with onions) with *klapstuk* (boiled beef), *zuurkool met spek* (sauerkraut with bacon), and *boerenkool met rookworst* (kale with smoked sausage). Hotchpotch is commonly served with *rookworst* (smoked sausage) and/or fried bacon on the side.

The best-loved stamppot is made with *boerenkool* (kale, or "farmer's cabbage"). This is also a strictly cold-weather dish, as kale is best once the frost has softened the leaves, thus improving their taste. Most kale is purchased finely chopped in plastic bags. As a primitive version of cabbage, kale is certainly not the world's most elegant vegetable. Given its popularity stamppot boerenkool can be considered a national Dutch dish.

Vegetable hotchpotch served directly from the pan. (iStockPhoto)

Stamppot Boerenkool (Kale with Sausage and Potato)

In most parts of the Netherlands boerenkool is prepared in the same manner—by putting the potatoes on top of the kale and boiling these together—but it is eaten with a variety of condiments and in many different manners. The most common way is to serve it with a smoked sausage and fried bacon. Gherkins and/or pickled onions and yellow *Amsterdamse uien* (yellow pickled onions) are popular on the side, and because sour combines well with it, a dash of vinegar is a well-known addition. Mustard commonly accompanies the sausage. Still, some people prefer to serve kale with meatballs or fried sausages or modernize the traditional recipes by putting nuts, little pieces of cheese, duck, and even olive oil into the stamppot boerenkool.

Ingredients

2 lb mealy potatoes

1 bunch finely chopped kale

1 tsp salt

1 smoked sausage

5 slices smoked bacon in pieces (optional)

2 tbsp butter

½ c milk

Peel the potatoes, and cut them in half. Place the potatoes on top of the kale in a pot with about 3 cups of water and salt. Put the sausage on top, and cover. Bring to a boil, and boil for about 25 to 30 minutes. Meanwhile, fry the bacon on very low heat. Remove the sausage from the pot, and drain the cooking liquid. Set this aside. Heat milk, add the milk and butter to the potatoes, and mash the kale and potatoes until mixed well. Make sure the stamppot boerenkool remains moist. One by one, add a few tablespoons of the reserved cooking liquid, and if desired some extra tablespoons of butter. Stir in the fried bacon. Serve with the sausage.

Apart from being boiled in water or mixed into hotchpotch, vegetables and fruits are stewed or served pickled. Traditional stewed vegetable side dishes are red cabbage, endive, Brussels endive, spinach, and leeks. Boiled red beets are sliced and pickled in a sweet and sour dressing with oil, vinegar, and spices. Red cabbage is commonly stewed with vinegar, sugar, cinnamon, cloves, raisins or currants, and pieces of apple. Apples and pears also serve as side dishes. Popular with all ages is *appelmoes* (applesauce), for which apples are stewed with sugar and cinnamon. Pears are boiled in water or red wine, with the peel of a lemon, cinnamon, and sugar.

In spring and summer, fresh vegetables, and especially lettuce, are commonly used for salads that many times also contain thinly sliced tomatoes, cucumber, and small pieces of spring (orange) carrots, red peppers, and onion. Salads are either dressed with *slasaus* (literally, "salad sauce") or a mayonnaise- or yogurt-based dressing with mild (sunflower, soy, or peanut) oil, vinegar, salt, pepper, and a bit of mustard. Olive oil–based vinaigrettes and other foreign dressings are popular. Furthermore, together with easy-to-prepare packages of mixed vegetables for Mediterranean and Eastern dishes, finely chopped mixed vegetables are commonly used for vegetable soups.

Since the 1950s all kinds of minced meat (beef, pork, or a mixture of the two) have become popular and are used for pasta sauces, oven-baked casseroles, and hamburgers but especially for the traditional gehaktbal (meatball). Apart from being served for supper with potatoes, vegetables, and gravy, meatballs are a very popular snack. Ranging from tennis to golf ball size, and served with mustard and white bread, they are always present on the menus of eateries and bars and are sold via snack-food vendors.

Overall, pork and the easy-to-prepare parts of beef and chicken are favorites. Traditionally Dutch butchers divide meat into many more parts than elsewhere. Popular pork parts are *karbonades* (pork chops), *speklappen* (slices of fresh bacon), and *slavink* (minced beef wrapped in bacon), in addition to minced meat. Larger cuts of meats, and especially beef, are prepared on Sundays and festive occasions. Furthermore, *rollade* (rolled meat), hachée (a slow-cooked stew with onions, vinegar, and bay leaf), and (Hungarian) goulash from beef are commonplace. Soup is made from the whole (old) chicken, but for

supper panfried chicken parts (legs and wings) and especially the easy-to-prepare breast are far more popular. Eggs are hardly consumed for dinner but are commonly eaten boiled for breakfast or lunch and are also a regular in the *uitsmijter* (literally, "bouncer"—panfried eggs with bacon and cheese on slices of white bread). Especially in autumn and for Christmas, game such as rabbit, pheasant, and venison is prepared. For the more elaborate Christmas dinner, turkey and goose are popular.

Bordering the North Sea, the Dutch eat a lot of fresh and smoked fish. Most notable is the *zoute haring* (raw, salted herring). Although herring is consumed all year round, the herring season begins in June; the first herring of the season is called Hollandse Nieuwe. Herring is served with finely chopped raw onions and gherkins. Although also sold in supermarkets, traditionally herring is bought at outdoor markets and the *haringstal* (herring stall). These vendors also sell the national delicacy smoked eel, sliced smoked salmon, and shrimp, which are often eaten on the spot on a white bread roll. Many kinds of fish are fried on the spot. Furthermore, typically Dutch are *panharing* (marinated fried herring) and *rolmops* (pickled herring), cold and hot smoked herring, and mackerel. Also popular, and considered festive foods, are fish salads with herring, shrimp, or tuna and a mayonnaise-based dressing. Fresh fish such as plaice and cod are commonly filleted and panfried. The most popular crustaceans and shellfish are oysters and cooked mussels, served together with sauces and a French baguette or fries.

Typically Dutch are pancakes and *poffertjes* (silver dollar–sized pancakes). Plate-sized pancakes are eaten as a meal but considered a treat. The classic way to eat them is topped with butter and powdered sugar. There are numerous sweet and savory toppings but most common is bacon and molasses (a dark syrup from sugar beets).

Apart from apple pie, which is typically baked at home, specialty stores and supermarkets carry a wealth of cookies, cakes, and pies. Almost every city has its own pastry; well known are *stroopwafels* (treacle wafers) from Gouda, Deventer *koek* (honey cake), and the *Bossche bol* (chocolate-coated choux pastry filled with whipped cream). Another national delicacy is licorice, often quite salty compared with that found elsewhere. The annual licorice consumption averages three pounds per person.

Apart from a national cuisine, most provinces have a typical cuisine and local products. The northeastern provinces are known for rye bread, potato dishes, dried farmer's sausages, and the use of mustard. Saltwater fish such as herring, mackerel, and English whiting is eaten all along the coastal area, and the province of Zeeland is famous for mussels, oysters, and sea vegetables such as *salicornia, lamsoor* (*Limonium vulgare,* or sea lavender), and *zeeaster* (*Aster tripolium*—a spinach-like plant that grows in marshes). The southern province of Limburg is known for its *vlaai* (fruit pie), asparagus, and mushrooms.

Eating Out

With a down-to-earth approach to food, cooking and entertaining guests at home as a leisure activity was neither very common nor well established in the Netherlands until the middle of the 20th century. Eating out foremost was considered a necessity, and it was mostly restricted to eating in hotel restaurants, eateries, bars, and caterers' shops, in addition to snack foods available via street vendors and stalls. In the 1900s and especially in Amsterdam the entertainment industry and eating out as a luxury started to become popular. Besides establishments serving Dutch food, French-style restaurants appeared. Until the late 1960s the quality of the service was of greater importance than the cooking skills of the chef. The upper-middle class often dined in hotel restaurants, and eating out was restricted to weekends and special occasions such as birthdays and other celebrations.

In the 1920s in larger cities such as Rotterdam and Amsterdam a handful of poor Chinese immigrants started selling peanuts on the street, and eventually a few of these vendors started Chinese eateries and restaurants. With the postwar influx of Indonesian expatriates, in the 1960s and 1970s the Chinese restaurants were transformed into Chinese-Indonesian restaurants. By offering cheap foods, and with take-out and dining-room facilities, these restaurants lured Dutch middle-class families into their establishments, especially during the weekend. Today, most Dutch cities and shopping malls have a Chinese-Indonesian restaurant. The growing postwar middle class that was raised on take-out Chinese food still considers dining at *de Chinees* (the Chinese) a festive occasion.

For centuries the French culture and language have been well established and held in high esteem. When France became a popular holiday destination in the 1960s, the country's food and wine started to become available. French cuisine became popular among the more educated middle class via the bistro and cookbooks. In the same period self-employed immigrant entrepreneurs from Greece, Italy, Spain, and Turkey opened eateries and snack bars and started street-vending ice cream. As the Mediterranean became a popular holiday destination, eating Greek moussaka, Spanish paella, and Italian pizza and pasta became popular.

When in the 1970s the first McDonald's opened its doors, American fast food and hamburgers started to conquer the Netherlands. Subsequently, a growing number of American-inspired fast-food chains have opened, and nowadays numerous places successfully sell American pizza, muffins, chocolate chip cookies, and bagels. Ironically, McDonald's offers the Dutch-inspired Mac Kroket.

Numerous restaurant sites and guides reflect the ongoing and growing popularity of eating out and gastronomy. Especially since the 1950s, the number of restaurants and the quality of gastronomy increased significantly, and today both Gault-Millau and Michelin publish special Dutch editions. In these guides the approximately 100 best restaurants are listed. Apart from 2 restaurants with three Michelin stars, there are over 10 restaurants with two stars. Also, a number of Chinese, Japanese, and Indonesian chefs, and even a Surinamese chef, have been rewarded with Michelin stars. Chefs are educated according to the French gastronomic model as introduced by Auguste Escoffier in the early 20th century; especially in the most expensive restaurants, kitchens are organized according to the French model. Cooking is inspired by global gastronomic trends and influenced by the leading foreign chefs such as Alain Ducasse, Michel Bras, Jean-Georges Vongerichten, Ferran Adria, and Heston Blumenthal. Due to a growing number of ambitious chefs, the quality of Dutch gastronomy is steadily improving.

Special Occasions

As the prevailing religion and cultural heritage is Christian, traditionally a wide range of typical foods and dishes mark Christian holidays such as Carnival, Easter, and Christmas. Birthdays and a number of other festivities and special occasions, such as Queen's Day, festivals, and fairs, are also times for eating and drinking well and abundantly.

New Year's

For most of the population New Year's Eve starts with *oliebollen,* doughnut balls that are prepared with and without currants and raisins and eaten fresh, lukewarm, or cold, often sprinkled with powdered sugar. Oliebollen and other fritters such as *appelflappen* (apple fritters), *wafels* (waffles), and pineapple fritters are common and often bought at one of the many temporary stalls that start to appear in cities and towns in autumn. Especially in the provinces the postwar generation remains fixed on a vast number of New Year's dishes and customs. These can vary from eating red cabbage to special stamppot (hotchpotch), herring, and rice pudding, or the paying of New Year's calls to neighbors, friends, and family. Instead of sending each other greeting cards, the Dutch spend the first two weeks of the new year visiting each other and serving oliebollen and (alcoholic) beverages.

New Year's Eve in the Netherlands with champagne and the traditional oliebollen. (iStockPhoto)

Oliebollen (Doughnut Balls)

1 c raisins and/or currants

2 c all-purpose flour

1 tsp salt

1 tbsp dry yeast

2 tbsp sugar

2 c lukewarm buttermilk

5–6 c frying oil, such as canola

Powdered sugar

Soak the raisins and/or currants in hot water.

Combine the flour and salt in a large mixing bowl, and add the yeast and sugar. Make a hole in the center, and slowly pour the buttermilk into it. Use a wooden spoon or electric mixer to stir the ingredients into a smooth batter. Put the raisins and/or currants in a sieve, and then pat them dry. Mix them into the batter.

Cover the bowl with plastic wrap and a kitchen towel, and let the batter rise for about an hour and a half in a warm spot. The batter should double in size.

Heat the oil to 350°F. Stick a soupspoon into the oil for a couple of seconds (this prevents the batter from sticking to the spoon), then fill the spoon with the batter. Carefully dip the batter into the oil. Repeat this process four to five times, and fry the olie-bollen for about 4 to 5 minutes, until golden brown. If necessary, after three minutes, rotate them with a fork. Remove the oliebollen from the oil with a skimmer.

Repeat this step until all of the batter is used.

Put the oliebollen on a plate lined with some paper towels. Serve them hot, sprinkled with powdered sugar.

Carnival

The major rivers, the Lower Rhine, Waal, and Maas, divide the country in two parts, with a largely Calvinist part in the north and primarily Catholic areas in the south, where the beginning of Lent is celebrated with Carnival. Carnival is three days of processions, masquerades, singing, drinking beer, and feasting. At the end of Carnival on Tuesday night, called Vastenavond, pancakes, sausages, and cakes are consumed, as the next day, Ash Wednesday, starts a period of 40 days of fasting, and Vastenavond offers a last chance to eat meat, eggs, and dairy products.

Easter

Easter, the most important religious holiday, is celebrated with eggs and breads. Before Easter, to mark the end of the fast that started on Ash Wednesday, Palm Sunday is commemorated. On Palm Sunday children walk in procession to church carrying sticks that are decorated with sprigs of boxwood, candy, eggs, and a bread rooster on top. *Het Paasontbijt* (Easter breakfast) is the most abundant breakfast and the culinary highlight of the religious calendar year. For Easter, shops, houses, and dinner tables are abundantly decorated with yellow flowers, branches of trees, decorated eggs, chickens, rabbits, and other signs of spring and fertility. In elementary schools and at home, vast quantities of boiled, colored, and chocolate eggs; *paasbroden* (raisin breads); jams; cold cuts; cheeses; and smoked salmon are consumed. Prominent at the Easter breakfast table are round matzo. The Dutch spread the unleavened

Jewish Passover flatbread with butter and sprinkle it with sugar.

Queen's Day

Established in 1885, Queen's Day became a national holiday of unity and togetherness. In honor of the queen, most cities organize children's games, concerts, flea markets, and fireworks. Many times the festivities are organized by the local *Oranje vereniging* (Orange society), a group that supports the Dutch monarchy, which is also known as the House of Orange. Orange became the national color, and for Queen's Day and national sports events, many people nowadays are dressed in orange. Apart from commercial "orange" products, orange candies, cakes, beverages, and snack foods are sold. Best known are the orange tompouce (literally "Tom Thumb," this is pastry filled with custard) of the department store HEMA and *Oranje Bitter* (a liqueur).

Fairs

Once a year most cities and towns have a fair. Fairs are held particularly in summer and during holidays, and they are traditionally organized on market squares, except for in western Friesland, where the fair traditionally is held next to the local bar. At most fairs beer is consumed in vast amounts. Apart from all sorts of attractions, fairgoers eat *kaneelstok* (literally, "cinnamon stick"). These sticks are sold in all kinds of flavors such as cinnamon, licorice, and cherry at stalls that sell candy (*Oud-Hollands snoepgoed*). A regular feature is also the *gebakskraam* (stall that sells baked goods), and many times there are special vendors for cotton candy and popcorn.

Sint Maarten and Sinterklaas

From November until the end of the year, an abundance of *speculaas* (spiced cookies), biscuits, pastry in the shape of letters, chocolate and marzipan figures, *borstplaat* (fondant), and other seasonal specialty sweets, pastry, and confectionery becomes available. On November 11, especially in northwestern parts of the country, on the night of Sint Maarten (Saint Martin) children walk the streets with lanterns they have made. Knocking on doors and singing songs, they are rewarded with all kinds of sweets and candy. Around a week later Sinterklaas (Saint Nicolas) arrives by boat from Spain. "Who behaves sweet gets candy, who behaves bad gets salt" is a line from one of the many songs children sing for Sinterklaas. From his arrival until his departure on December 6, Sinterklaas and his aid, *Zwarte Piet* (Black Pete), hand out lots of specialty sweets and confectionery such as *pepernoten* (spice nuts), *taai taai* (literally, "tough tough"; chewy little cakes), marzipan, confections, chocolate coins, and letters from the alphabet. The highlight of the visit is on December 5, when children receive presents.

Christmas

For the two-day celebration of Christmas, houses are decorated with Christmas trees and lights. On the night of December 24 and on the morning of December 25 many people attend a church service. Baked goods such as *kerststol* (a Christmas loaf with dried fruits and almond paste), *kerstkransjes* (spiced cookies with almonds), or a *kerstkrans* (pastry filled with almond paste) are served. After days of shopping, preparation, and cooking, on the first day of Christmas, most people dine lavishly at home. The 26th, the second Christmas day, is often spent visiting family and friends. In wintertime, if the weather permits, outdoor skating becomes a national sport. On the ice, stalls sell *koek en zopie* (cake and a hot punch that is a mixture of beer and rum), hot chocolate, pea soup, hot smoked sausages, and cakes.

Birthdays

In the past, beschuit (rusk) was considered a rich man's delicacy, but nowadays they are handed out to celebrate a newborn. For the occasion the fragile twice-baked round rusk is spread with butter and sprinkled with pink (for a girl) or blue (for a boy) *muisjes* (literally, "mice," this refers to aniseed sprinkles). One's birthday is celebrated by treating family and friends to cake, drinks, and food, rather than being treated oneself, which is the origin of the expression "Dutch treat." Special breads and cakes in the shape of the biblical figures Abraham or Sarah are presented to people who turn 50. Also typically Dutch is a "do not feel like cooking" party. Nowadays, a pizza or Chinese, Thai, or Surinamese takeout or delivery is ordered, but on days when women do not feel like cooking, they usually prepare pancakes or serve ready-made French fries.

Diet and Health

In the Netherlands, traditionally, nutritional value is considered more important than gastronomic pleasure and the palatability of food. Before and after World War II, many middle-class women were educated in domestic science at schools. Apart from home economics and hygiene, these schools taught and advocated a frugal diet with a high nutritional value. The schools published highly popular cookbooks that greatly influenced domestic cooking and future generations of domestic cooks.

At the same time, so as to prevent chronic diseases, the Dutch government's food policy started strongly focusing on health and food-safety issues. Due to food shortages during World War II and the need to feed the nation, historically the Dutch government and governmental organizations are well enmeshed with the local food industries and factories. Nowadays, a healthy diet is often advocated via media campaigns that promote the consumption of national agricultural produce and industrial products.

During the postwar era, Het Voedingscentrum (the Nutrition Center) became the most important and best-known governmental organization for nutritional information for citizens. Connecting scientific insights with a healthy diet and the daily practice of consumers, in the 1950s it successfully developed a food classification system that informs the general population on how to eat healthy and safely. Nutrition information is provided through *De Schijf van Vijf* (the five disks), via which the so-called whole food assortment is divided. It is comparable to the U.S. Food Pyramid. Depending on the group, the focus is on the amount of dietary fiber, saturated fat, energy, and/or specific micronutrients contained in the food products.

In comparison to other European countries, there are considerable differences in dietary patterns and consumption. Although during the postwar period, the availability of foods and food consumption were subject to drastic changes, the Dutch diet remains relatively high in potatoes but also in animal-derived, processed, sweetened, and refined foods. The consumption of vegetables and fruit is similar to the rest of Europe.

The average Dutch citizen is living a longer and a healthier life than in the past. Like elsewhere in the Western world, consumers are tempted by a huge variety of foods available in a growing number of places and in advertising. Subsequently, the pleasures and palatability of food are becoming more important, but today the risks of chronic diseases such as cancer, diabetes, and obesity, and campaigns that focus on health and food safety, remain dominant issues in the minds of Dutch consumers and food policy makers.

Karin Vaneker

Further Reading

Henne Koene, Ada. *Food Shoppers' Guide to Holland.* 4th ed. Delft, the Netherlands: Eburon, 2003.

Jobse-van Putten, Jozien. *Eenvoudig Maar Voedzaam* [Simple but nourishing]. Nijmegen, the Netherlands: Sun, 1995.

Lans, Jos van der, and Herman Vuijsje. *Lage Landen Hoge Sprongen: Nederland in de Twintigste Eeuw* [Low countries, high leaps: The Netherlands in the twentieth century]. Wormer, The Netherlands: Inmerc, 2003.

"The Netherlands—Agriculture." *Nations Encyclopedia.* http://www.nationsencyclopedia.com/economies/Europe/The-Netherlands-AGRICULTURE.html.

Rose, Peter R. "The Low Countries." *Encyclopedia of Food and Culture,* edited by Solomon H. Katz, 389–96. New York: Charles Scribner's Sons, 2003.

Typical Dutch Recipes. http://tdsrecipes.blogspot.com/.

Norway

Overview

Norway occupies the western part of the Scandinavian Peninsula in the north of Europe. It has a long coast on the Atlantic, high mountains, large forests, rivers and valleys, fjords and glaciers, and only 3 percent arable land. With 4.8 million inhabitants spread out over about 118,000 square miles (305,000 square kilometers), Norway has the lowest population density in Europe after Iceland. Only 2.5 percent of the population is working in agriculture, whereas most of the workforce is in the service sector. The standard of living is very high, and life expectancy is 83 years for women and 78 years for men.

Norway is a monarchy with a democratic constitution and a parliamentary system. Norwegian is a Germanic language in the Indo-European group. Among the aboriginal Saami population, different dialects of a language in the Finno-Ugric group are spoken. Eighty percent of the population belongs to the national Lutheran church, which has dominated in Norway since the 16th century.

🍽 Food Culture Snapshot

Jon and Kari Anderson live in the Oslo region and have two children, Katrine (14) and Fredrik (12). Both parents work outside the home, and they try to concentrate shopping on weekends in one of the big supermarkets. But Kari takes most of the responsibility for both the shopping and the preparation of meals. For weekdays they buy ground meat, sausages, frozen fillets of cod, potatoes and carrots, and bottled sauces. For weekends, pork chops or chicken breasts are popular, particularly in the summer when they are barbecuing in their little garden. Sometimes they buy a pizza to eat with their kids in the evening. They buy mostly coarse-grain brown bread, brown and yellow cheese, salami, and liver paste for breakfast and supper. They also buy apples and bananas and encourage the children to eat more fruit instead of potato chips, pastry, and sweets. To drink they buy milk and coffee, and occasionally beer, and sometimes they go to the state monopoly store and buy a bottle of wine for Saturday night.

Major Foodstuffs

In the area of ingredients available in the Norwegian kitchen, some aspects seem relatively stable, for example, the high consumption of bread, potatoes, milk, and coffee. But a closer look reveals rapidly changing patterns, for example, in the choice of different breads and curdled milk products and in the preparation of potatoes. More important is the increasing variation in fruits, vegetables, and spices. Many ingredients were not on the market only a few decades ago: Some of them were hardly known at all, others were considered exotic foods, consumed only during vacations or on business trips to foreign countries.

Bread is still the fundamental foodstuff: dark bread from rye, as well as white bread and a lot of cookies and biscuits from wheat. One general tendency is to use more whole-grain flour than before. The traditional Norwegian *flatbrød*—unleavened, flat, thin, and crisp breads—and *lefse*—soft, thin breads—are rarely baked at home anymore but are instead produced by small local bakeries. A special small variety of the soft bread is *lompe,* partly used for coffee with a cheese or jam filling but above all known as a wrapping for hot dogs instead of bread.

Fresh meat plays a much more important role than earlier, when preserved products were more common. As a result of growing wealth the consumption of meat has risen since the latter part of the 20th century. There has been a strong increase in pork and chicken consumption, but whole cuts of beef and mutton hold a higher prestige. Reindeer meat from the domestic reindeer flocks owned by Saamis in the northernmost areas is very popular, but the products are rather expensive and not easily available. The total consumption of game per person is of minor importance, but this meat is highly appreciated in the cuisine, above all, red deer, moose, and ptarmigan (similar to partridge). Even if the consumption of preserved meat has dropped, such products are still produced and appreciated, for example, *fenalår,* cured leg of lamb.

Norway has rich fishing grounds with unpolluted water. Of the total ocean fish caught, the most important for human consumption is the Atlantic cod, other codfishes, herring, mackerel, and different flatfish. Sprat (*brisling*) is sold canned in oil under the name of sardines. Of shellfish, prawns or shrimp are very popular, crab and lobster are caught along the coast in summer, and blue mussels and other crustaceans are farmed. Fish farming, which has developed into a big industry since the last part of the 20th

century, has made trout and salmon, exclusive products in the past, available to everybody. The catches of high-quality wild salmon in Norwegian rivers are minimal compared with the farmed salmon.

Fish is sold fresh, frozen, canned, or preserved using old methods. The dried cod from Lofoten (*stokfish*) and the salted and dried cod from the west coast (*klipfish*) are widely exported. A special preservation method is fermentation, which gives the fish a certain soft consistency and a strong aroma. In the valleys of eastern Norway there are lakes and rivers with trout and other fat freshwater fish well suited to such fermentation (*rakefisk*).

Consumption of milk, both fresh and cultured, is very high in Norway, today with emphasis on low-fat products (skim and semiskim). The most common cheeses are the yellowish semihard or hard cheeses of Swiss and Dutch types made from cow milk. The traditional *gammelost* ("old cheese"), produced without the use of rennet, is semihard, with a grainy texture and a brown or dark brown color, often with a pungent flavor reminiscent of ammonia. Another traditional cheese, produced by boiling whey, is the brown cheese (*gjetost*), looking like a small brick. Today, the whey is boiled with cream and milk from cows and goats, so the cheeses are fattier and have a richer, sweet, caramel-like taste.

There has been a sharp rise in vegetable consumption. The rough climate and short seasons made it difficult to grow certain plants in Norway, and the most common were turnips and rutabagas. During the 19th century potatoes conquered the central place in the Norwegian diet, which they still hold.

Partly due to campaigns by the health authorities there has also been a general increase in the consumption of fruits, in particular, fresh fruits. Apples are the most consumed of homegrown fruits. Among the citrus fruits oranges are by far the most important product and are eaten fresh. Oranges are also important in the juice and the marmalade industry. The most appreciated tropical fruit is the banana, with about as large a consumption as apples.

Norway is a coffee-drinking nation; tea plays a very small part in the daily diet. There has been a strong increase in the sales of carbonated soft drinks, but there is also a growing market for uncarbonated

Smoked salmon on bread, a Norwegian delicacy. (Shutterstock)

bottled water, surprisingly enough in an area where water can be drunk from the tap almost everywhere.

Many different beers are produced in Norway, mostly of the pilsner type. There is also a wide selection of beers with a low alcoholic content and in recent years of types with no alcohol at all. This is necessary since driving under the influence of alcohol is severely penalized. Drivers are considered to be under the influence of alcohol if the amount of alcohol in their blood is more than 0.2 per thousand. The characteristic strong alcohol drink is *akevitt,* distilled from potatoes and spiced with caraway seeds.

As producers of beers and spirits, Norwegians have traditionally consumed these drinks to a much higher degree than wine. But in recent years the most characteristic change in alcohol consumption is the increasing part played by imported wines. Norway has a long history of state intervention and control of the importation, production, and distribution of alcoholic beverages. Retail stores selling beverages with high alcoholic contents for off-premises consumption are run by the state monopoly, Vinmonopolet.

Cooking

Most existing cooking methods in Western cuisine are used in Norway: boiling, frying, roasting, baking, grilling, poaching, steaming, sautéing, deep-frying, stir-frying, and so forth. The tendency over the last 150 years has been a decrease in the traditional boiling and an increase in frying and roasting.

Several dishes are still boiled, particularly highly appreciated traditional one-pot dishes. Even if boiling primarily was applied to preserved meat, some fresh meat dishes are also boiled, for example, *fårikål,* a dish with alternating layers of cabbage and chunks of lamb shoulder, sprinkled with peppercorns.

A lot of Norwegian cooking is done with ground meat; in fact, more and more dishes are based on this ingredient. Meatballs are today regarded as a national dish, but ground meat has also met with new types of dishes from abroad, many of them introduced through fast-food culture: taco shells, pitas, pizza crusts, lasagna, and others. These dishes are particularly popular with the younger generation and with children, partly because they represent something new and partly because they may be eaten without the traditional staples and garnishes of potatoes and vegetables, some of them also without a knife and fork.

The cooking of fish differs according to the kind of fish, the size of the fish, the region, the season, and the day of the week. Whole fish, poached or baked, is particularly popular on Sundays. Steaks of cod, halibut, salmon, and many other fish are also poached, as well as baked or steamed. Steaks of halibut, monkfish, and salmon are fried like beefsteaks. In northern Norway "saithe steak" is particularly popular, made from a fillet of saithe that is dredged in flour, fried, and served with browned onion slices, just like the old-fashioned beefsteaks. Fish soups are also widely used; most famous among them is the Bergen recipe:

Palesuppe (Bergen Young Saithe Soup)

Many Bergen citizens will insist that the stock has to be made from the entire fish, not only the trimmings, and that a little veal stock should be added to round out the flavor. Some insist that the vegetables have to be cooked separately, and some that the soup is not complete without small fish balls. There are many ways to make a Bergen fish soup, but one common denominator is the *rømme,* the sour cream.

If saithe is not available, other fishes of the cod family may be used. Instead of or in addition to celeriac, parsnip or leeks may be used.

3 lb young saithe (pollack)

3 pt water

1 tsp salt

2 medium-sized carrots

1 parsley root

1 knob celeriac (celery root)

$1/3$ c flour

$1\frac{1}{3}$ c milk

½ c rømme (sour cream)

Chives

Clean and wash the fish, and remove the gills and the eyes. Cut the head in two, and put it in a pot with the tail. Pour in cold water and salt, and bring to a boil. Cut the rest of the fish in slices an inch thick, add to the pot, and let them simmer for a few minutes, then put them aside. Strain the stock. Cut the vegetables into ½-inch dice, and let them boil 5 minutes in the stock. Whisk flour smooth in cold milk, and beat it into the boiling stock. Let it simmer for 5 minutes. Whisk in the sour cream, and sprinkle finely chopped chives over the soup, if desired. Serve the soup first, then the fish with boiled potatoes.

Ground-up fish is used to make a lot of cakes, balls, and puddings. One-third of all fish dishes served on weekdays are based on ground-up fish. Even if more and more people prefer to buy these products canned or frozen in the supermarkets or fresh at the fishmongers, some enthusiasts continue the old tradition, people along the coast in particular, who do a lot of sport fishing. The fish is ground up in a food processor or in a mortar if a coarser dough is preferred. Codfishes and monkfish make cakes of a light color; saithe, mackerel, and herring make darker and generally coarser cakes.

Since the 1980s there has been an explosion in the sales of barbecues, from the simplest types to big garden installations. Even in a region with such unstable weather conditions, grilling has conquered a unique position in summer cooking. On sunny afternoons and evenings, the aroma of grilled meat (and the stench of fuel) is floating in the air from gardens, terraces, and balconies all over Norway.

In some regions in the north, the Saami population had their own culinary traditions, based on the special conditions of a nomadic life. Today, most Saami people live like other Norwegians, in houses with all possible modern equipment and with access to all sorts of food and cooking methods. Many Saami, however, have continued some of the old culinary traditions, and even outside Saami circles, several of the dishes are popular. The Saami based their food on three products: reindeer meat, reindeer milk, and fish from the rivers and lakes. But they added berries and certain wild plants and thereby got the necessary vitamins. The Saami never roasted their meat. They boiled most of it, often with the offal or other parts of the animal, such as heart, lungs, liver, tongue, udder, marrow, bone, and even blood. Some of the most tender parts were dried or smoked and are considered delicacies today, for example, smoked leg of reindeer. Dried or smoked heart and boiled tongue were cut in fine slices and are still eaten this way, even served in restaurants.

Typical Meals

The Norwegian morning meal is generally based on bread, prepared as a so-called open sandwich, made with butter or margarine and various toppings and spreads. Jams and marmalades are common, cheese is a standard spread, and there are pots with herrings in brine or in different spicy mixtures, or cans of mackerel in tomato sauce and sprat in olive oil. Cod roe and other caviar substitutes are also widely used. Cold cuts of salami and other cured sausages are popular besides boiled or cured ham and liver paste.

An increasing number of people eat packaged cereals with yogurt. Eggs are fairly rare on weekdays, but on Sundays a boiled egg or fried egg with bacon may be served. Fruit is not common except in the form of canned orange juice. Coffee stands out as the number-one morning drink. Coffee is also taken at irregular intervals between meals and snacks during the day. Milk is, according to a survey, the breakfast drink for half of the Norwegian population.

Midmorning or afternoon is the time for a light snack, for example, a sweet pastry. Fruit, ice cream, chocolate, peanuts, or potato chips may also be eaten as a snack. For people constantly on the move, such as taxi drivers, truck drivers, messengers, and couriers, the gas stations offer more and more tempting combinations of coffee with hot or cold snacks.

In Norway most people have a cold lunch, often a lunch pack brought from home or a salad or sandwich bought in a canteen or in a café. Only 6 percent eat two hot meals a day. The hot meals very often consist of only one course: a main component of meat or fish, accompanied by potatoes, vegetables, and a sauce. Ground meat and fish are very popular, fried as cakes or balls. Fish is eaten about one out of four days. Rice and pasta are increasingly substituting for the potatoes. Most vegetables are boiled, and carrots are the most popular for dinner. Many dinners also consist of a one-pot dish or a pizza, combining different animal and vegetable ingredients.

Fårikål (Mutton-in-Cabbage)

2 lb lamb or mutton, preferably from the shoulder or breast

2–3 lb cabbage

2 tbsp whole black peppercorns

2 tsp salt

2 c water

Cut the meat into pieces 2–3 inches square. Rinse the cabbage, and cut into small chunks. Put the fattiest pieces of meat in the bottom of the cooking pot, then cabbage over them, and so on in alternate layers. Sprinkle salt and pepper between the layers. Pour in boiling water. Bring to a boil, and let simmer in 1½–2 hours or until the meat is tender. Serve with boiled potatoes.

Some people keep the peppercorns in a perforated metal container or in a cloth, but much of the charm is in picking the peppercorns out of the cabbage. With the warnings against too much animal fat in mind, one may cut away some of the fattiest parts of the meat.

With hot meals, most people drink water or soft drinks, and to a lesser degree milk and hot beverages. Alcoholic beverages are drunk by only 12 percent of Norwegians on Sundays, 7 percent on weekdays. It seems, however, that this is changing; there is a strong increase in the consumption of wine.

Typical dinners vary according to the occasion and day. Everyday dinner is usually eaten in the kitchen around 5 P.M. from Monday through Thursday. This meal might consist of minced-meat patties, meatballs, meat casserole, or sauce Bolognese, served with boiled potatoes, pasta, or rice. A weekend evening meal might be served in the "cozy corner" of the living room around 8 P.M. on Fridays and Saturdays. Typical dishes are tacos, enchiladas, hamburger, pizza, risotto, lasagna, or something similar. Sunday dinner is served in late afternoon, perhaps in the dining room. Common dishes are homemade meatballs or cabbage rolls with boiled potatoes and boiled root vegetables.

One special form of hot meals eaten at home is the dish delivered to the door or picked up at a take-out outlet. According to a recent Norwegian study, 9 percent of the population eats such hot meals delivered to the door (for example, Chinese, Indian, pizza) at least once a month. A little more, 13 percent, eat food bought at a take-out outlet. But there is a striking contrast between the generations. About three-quarters of the population over 60 years of age never eat this kind of food, compared with 28 percent of the younger group between 16 and 24 years.

The ideal of a family meal is strongly implanted. A family meal is a hot meal eaten in the home in the company of all the other family members. Most Norwegians eat most of their meals in their own home, and approximately half of the population eats all their meals at home. The house is, in other words, the dominant location for Norwegian meals, a different situation from that in the United States, where far less eating takes place in the home.

Eating Out

Eating out does not constitute an important part of Norwegian food consumption or social life. This may partly be explained by historical factors. The country never had the broad restaurant tradition found from the early 19th century on in many European countries with a strong urban culture and a wealthy bourgeoisie. People who had to travel through the country had inns at their disposal along the roads, and, later, hotels grew up in urban centers along the ever-expanding railways. There were also a lot of beer cellars and wine cellars and other watering holes of varying quality and social status, mainly for men, and later also cafés and bars, but most of the important eating was done in the home, as it still is.

However, important changes have taken place in recent years. For most Norwegians, a meal in a fine restaurant is still something special, but more and

A fancy restaurant in Asker, Norway. (Shutterstock)

more are eating out and a greater proportion of the disposable income is spent in cafés and restaurants than ever before. There is a wide choice of alternatives: top gourmet restaurants, cafeterias, hamburger restaurants, and so on. There is, however, a difference in the purpose of eating that also decides the choice of place. In most cases people eat out for practical reasons, out of necessity, because they have to be away from home, not out of a wish to enjoy food.

Most professional people eat their lunch away from home, and they constitute an important segment of the eating-out population. Most people who eat their meals at work or school do so in a cafeteria or, in smaller enterprises, in a room specially designed for lunch and coffee breaks. In a study from 2007, only 4 percent of respondents said they were eating lunch in a café or restaurant once a week or more.

Eating out in the evenings may also be related to work, such as dining with business associates or visitors from abroad, but for most people an evening dinner in a restaurant with family or friends is a treat, often a celebration of an important event. One reason for this is that restaurants are expensive, with a combination of high prices for ingredients, good wages to staff, high taxes, and the service tips included in the total amount on the bill. This is particularly true of the finer and more exclusive restaurants. Young people, couples without children, and single men and women, who eat out often as part of their leisure time and who have been instrumental in prolonging the nightlife by several hours, choose also among the more inexpensive bars and cafés that have grown up in cities and towns in recent years.

The younger generation are among the most frequent visitors to restaurants, when all types of establishments for eating out are considered. A survey found that a very high number of people under 25 years of age eat in pizza restaurants or buy snacks in kiosks, but in the finer restaurants they represent a smaller portion of the customers, whereas people 40 years old and up represent well over the average, and their part is increasing.

Gourmet restaurants and other exclusive restaurants are easy enough to distinguish from the rest, and so are many of the fast-food venues, hamburger restaurants, and pizza restaurants. But between these two groups there are a lot of different concepts, with food of varying quality, and it is difficult to put them into distinct categories. The food they offer at relatively moderate prices is a mixture of traditional home cooking (sausages, meatballs, meat patties, fried battered fish), traditional restaurant dishes (steaks, Wiener schnitzel, cutlets, poached fish), and dishes more recently integrated into Norwegian food culture (pasta, pizza, hamburgers).

A difficulty in classification is that the total restaurant picture is changing, so a typology based on people's perception of different restaurants and the part they play in their lives is more helpful. When people must have something to eat and don't have much time, they frequent fast-food restaurants and kiosks. When it is important to meet and spend time with friends, cafés, pizza restaurants, and ethnic restaurants are chosen. Sometimes Norwegians want something innovative, surprising, or untraditional, for example, organic food, vegetarian dishes, or new and unknown dishes from abroad or from the local area. Finally, for a unique eating venue, when a complete break with everyday life and food is expected, and price is subordinated to the desire for an extraordinary experience, a gourmet restaurant is chosen. Places for drinks, alcoholic or nonalcoholic, hot or cold, are also changing. There are new types of pubs and beer cafés, wine bars, and coffee bars.

In Norway a lot of old seaside hotels, fjord hotels, and mountain hotels have been made into modern establishments with classy restaurants and facilities for conferences and seminars. Many of these restaurants have tried to make their reputation through an excellent cuisine, but they know that quality is not enough; they have to offer something special, a combination of international and local cuisine. In one such hotel in Norway, the cook Arne Brimi in the 1980s developed "nature's cuisine," inspired by French cooking techniques but using Norwegian ingredients, often ignored in classic urban restaurant gastronomy.

The "gourmet" restaurant is an expression from recent decades, when Norwegian cooks have won prizes and awards in Europe, for example, in the competition Bocuse d'Or initiated by French star chef Paul Bocuse. The president of the European Bocuse d'Or, Norwegian chef Eyvind Hellstrøm was the first Scandinavian with two Michelin stars.

Special Occasions

Food has always played a prominent part in the celebrations of rites of passage in the family as well as in the annual festivals based on the secular or the religious calendar. The most important holiday associated with food is Christmastime. Never is so much emphasis put on food and on old habits and customs from the 19th century and earlier.

The weeks immediately before Christmas are filled with baking activity; sweet breads, buns, cakes, and cookies have to be ready when the Christmas bells toll. The small, hard cookies made from an unleavened dough of rye flour, honey, and strong spices (pepper nuts) are popular, as are cookies baked in irons with geometric patterns or fried in liquid fat.

Berlinerkranser (Norwegian Berlin Wreath Cookies)

2 boiled egg yolks (8 minutes)

2 raw egg yolks

½ c sugar

1½ c flour

9 oz butter

Glaze

2 egg whites

Pearl sugar

Crush the boiled egg yolks, mix them with the raw yolks, and blend to a smooth paste. Beat in the sugar. Work in flour and soft butter, but handle the dough carefully. Chill in the refrigerator. Make the dough into rolls about 1/3 inch thick and 5 inches long. Shape them into wreaths. Brush with lightly whipped egg whites and sprinkle with pearl sugar (coarse sugar). Put them on a baking sheet and bake in oven for about 10 minutes (350°F).

Few people eat fish as their main dish on Christmas Eve, but some still eat lutefisk (mainly in the north) or fresh cod (mainly on the south coast). Lutefisk—dried cod softened in a solution of water and lye and then boiled—plays, however, an important part in the pre-Christmas season in the whole country and is served in restaurants and private homes from late October on.

Another traditional dish, porridge, has also changed in form and function throughout history. Since Christmas was a special feast, the grain was supposed to be of better quality than the daily barley or oat flour. Rice was very exclusive but became the rule among the elite in the 18th century, and around 1900 the price of rice was so low that rice porridge became a common festive dish among most people, particularly on Christmas Eve. It used to be strewn with ground cinnamon and sugar, and a lump of butter was put in the middle. A newer dessert variety is served with a red sauce made from berries.

December 24, Christmas Eve, represents the real climax of the season. The social element is still considered as the most important part of the celebration. The extended family gets together, several generations are present, and they distribute Christmas gifts and enjoy the typical Christmas food. The main Christmas meal is served in the late afternoon. Between half and two-thirds of the Norwegians, mainly in the eastern part of the country, eat roast pork rib. The rind is cut up in a pattern of one-inch squares with a sharp knife that cuts through the rind without going into the fat underneath. The goal is to make the rind crackling crisp with a golden color.

In the communities along the western coast of Norway dried and salted (and in some places smoked) rib of lamb is eaten, and in recent decades this Christmas dish has been taken up in other parts of the country, either for Christmas Eve or for one of the other Christmas dinners. The rib is cut into single pieces that must be soaked in water for about 24 hours to soften the meat and drain it of salt. The meat is ready after about two to two and a half hours of steaming, depending on the age of the animal.

New Year's Eve has no set menu. Turkey has become one of the most popular dishes for this evening. Lobster and seafood in general are increasingly popular, as either a starter or a main dish. A special festival cake built as a tower, the *kransekake,* is also often served on this evening.

The old festival drink is beer, well suited to the fatty and salted foods, often followed by a shot or two of akevitt. The temperance movements gained a strong position in the last part of the 19th century, and this led many families to abstain from all alcoholic drinks. Bottled carbonated soft drinks and fruit juices were drunk instead.

For many people most holidays have lost their original connections with the Christian religion. The Shrovetide bun (*fastelavnsbolle*) is the only important culinary remnant of the "Carnival," the last "fat" days before Lent, the fasting period before Easter. The bun is made from sifted wheat flour and filled with whipped cream and raspberry jam. Confectioners' sugar is sprinkled on the top. Some people still bake their own Shrovetide buns, but all bakeries provide them, and consequently they are easy to get.

The most important saint's feast takes place on June 23, celebrating St. John the Baptist. June is a very special month in this region with its long, "blond" nights. In the northernmost areas the midnight sun shines for a shorter or longer time depending on the latitude, but even in the south the night lasts no more than a couple of hours. The feast often includes dancing and, along the coasts, enormous bonfires. In Norway traditional fare at this time is cold cuts of cured meat and *rømmegrøt,* the sour cream porridge

Initiation rituals to important new stages in a person's life are marked with different ceremonies. Except for weddings, most of these celebrations are rather low-key family occasions. Even the funerals, once big events, have been replaced by a simple get-together after the funeral ceremony has taken place.

A wedding may also be a very simple event, a civil ceremony followed by a lunch for the closest friends, the maid of honor, and the best man. But traditional "romantic" weddings on Saturday afternoon are still extremely popular, with brides in white in the church or the city hall, followed by a big banquet in a restaurant or a hotel, or perhaps at home if there is enough room but then with food served by a catering firm.

Diet and Health

Norwegians are increasingly aware of how important a healthy diet is to prevent serious diseases, for instance, cardiovascular diseases and cancer, which account for the majority of deaths for both men and women. Public campaigns encouraging reductions in the intake of fatty foods and recommending a more substantial consumption of vegetables have made some progress. In general, the diet has improved since 1990, but Norwegians still eat too little greens, fish, and whole-grain bread and too much fat and sugar.

Health authorities recognized the basic problems in diet and nutrition early on. They have made efforts to influence food consumption and eating patterns in accordance with the scientifically elaborated norms for a healthy diet. Norway was one of the first in the world to have an official nutrition policy, established in 1975.

Today, the rapid growth in the food-processing industry has led to an increased demand for legal measures to guarantee certain nutritional standards. The technological development within food production has created new processes and made new additives necessary. One consequence is problems with hygiene and the presence of certain toxic bacteria, for instance, salmonella.

Since 1960, health authorities have worked systematically to reduce the intake of fat and, more particularly, to reduce the percentage of fat in the total energy intake. According to the official recommendations a maximum of 30 percent of the total energy intake should come from fat. There has, in fact, been a real reduction in fat intake since the mid-1980s, from about 40 percent down to about 35 percent, or a little less. Since 2000, there seems to have been no further reduction. This means there is still a long way to go before the ideal goal of 30 percent is reached.

The most important sources of fat in the food consumed by Norwegians are milk and milk products, meat and meat products, and various sorts of household fats, margarine in particular. There has been an increase in the consumption of meat over the last decades, but at the same time, there has been a reduction in the consumption of margarine and in the use of lard and tallow in cooking. The fat intake from milk products has been relatively stable. Fats from milk and butter play a far less important part than before, but the consumption of cream and cheese is up.

According to the Nordic Nutrition Recommendations, people should not get more than 10 percent of their total energy from sugar. The actual percentage has decreased in recent years but is still as high as 14 percent, partly a result of an extraordinarily strong increase in the consumption of sweet carbonated drinks, fruit juices, and confections.

There is clear evidence today supporting the hypothesis that consumption of fruits and vegetables

A young girl eats fresh raspberries in Norway. (iStockPhoto)

has a protective effect against diseases such as cancer, coronary heart disease, stroke, and diabetes. Fruits and vegetables have a high content of vitamins, minerals, antioxidants, and dietary fiber. A doubling of the consumption of vegetables is assumed to reduce the risk of cancer and cardiovascular diseases substantially. Increased intake of fruits and vegetables may also have an extra effect in replacing less favorable foods in the dietary pattern.

Between 1999 and 2007 there was an increase in the yearly per-capita consumption of fruits from 152 to 189 pounds (69 to 86 kilograms) and of vegetables from 132 to 141 pounds (60 to 64 kilograms). However, Norwegians still are not eating enough vegetables, particularly as the highest increase was for tomatoes and cucumbers, that is, vegetables with a high water content. Authorities recommend more fiber-rich vegetables and deeper-colored vegetables. The increase in fruit consumption is primarily due to an increase in the intake of fruit juices.

The consumption differs within populations. Women eat more vegetables, fruits, and berries than men. The consumption is higher in the old-age groups than in the young. Men and women with a higher education eat more fruits and vegetables than people with less education. This has to be taken seriously both in the way educational campaigns are run and also politically in price policies. The increase in the price of fruits and vegetables is high enough to discourage certain low-income groups.

The consumption of potatoes has declined during the last decades. But the health authorities are not so much concerned with the total amount of potato consumption as with the way potatoes are consumed. Today, an increasing amount of potatoes are sold as French fries, chips, and other processed potato products. In Norway only half of the potato consumption is of fresh potatoes. The processed products have high amounts of unhealthy saturated fat.

Campaigns for increased consumption of fish have been going on for several decades. There is clear evidence that high consumption of fish has beneficial effects on health. The main reason is the content in fish of omega-3 fatty acids, even if the contents of iodine, selenine, and vitamin D are also considered important. Omega-3 fatty acids from fish reduce the risk of fatal coronary disease (sudden cardiac death).

Fish is the main dish about seven times a month in Norway, but only 21 percent of the population eats fish three times a week. The consumption of fish is lower than that of meat and far below the recommended quantity. The value of the high consumption is also to some extent reduced because fish is often eaten with saturated fats (margarine, butter).

Experts recommend an increase in the intake of carbohydrates, primarily from whole-grain foods. In addition to vitamins and minerals whole-grain cereals provide natural dietary fiber. A high consumption of such cereals seems to have a beneficial role in reducing the risk of coronary heart disease and a protective effect against the development of hypertension and diabetes. Cereals are the most important source for dietary fiber. Even if more than half of the intake of cereals consists of whole-grain products, the intake is below the recommendations from health authorities.

There is a very high awareness in Norway of the importance of adequate intake of vitamins and minerals, and in some foodstuffs vitamins and minerals are added, to make sure the population gets the necessary amount. In general, a varied diet will cover the necessary intake, and the increased consumption of fruits and vegetables has helped in recent years. But the reduced consumption of fish and increased sugar intake work in the opposite direction.

Most Scandinavians eat too much salt, about 10 grams a day. Too much salt increases the blood pressure and may be a contributing factor to heart disease and stroke. Whereas consumption of meat and fat partly is dependent on individual choice, this is not the case with consumption of salt. How much salt is added during cooking or at the table is not so important, when 75 percent of the salt intake comes from industrially produced foods. This means that the higher the consumption of convenience foods, the higher the intake of salt, and to reduce salt involves far more drastic changes in the food habits.

Henry Notaker

Further Reading

Bocuse d'Or Norway. http://www.bocusedornorge. no.

Bugge, Annechen, and Reidar Almås. "Domestic Dinner: Representations and Practices of a Proper Meal among Young Suburban Mothers." *Journal of Consumer Culture* 6, No. 2 (2006): 203–29.

The Culinary Institute of Norway. http://www. gastronomi.no/.

Kjærnes, Unni, ed. *Eating Patterns: A Day in the Lives of Nordic Peoples.* Lysaker, Norway: Lysaker National Institute for Consumer Research, 2001.

Ministry of Agriculture and Food. http://www. regjeringen.no/en/dep/lmd.html?id = 627.

Norwegian Directorate of Health. http://www. shdir.no/.

Notaker, Henry. *Food Culture in Scandinavia.* Westport, CT: Greenwood Press, 2008.

Viestad, Andreas: *Kitchen of Light: New Scandinavian Cooking.* New York: Artisan, 2003.

Poland

Overview

Located in central and eastern Europe, Poland has a unique cultural identity that is due in large part to its turbulent political past. Poland's political borders have shifted, dissolved, and reformed frequently over the last 1,000 years. The story begins in the 9th and 10th centuries, when the group known as the Polians began to dominate the land now known as Poland. In 966 A.D., Mieszko I of the Piast dynasty established a state in the western part of modern Poland at a time when other Slavic groups were beginning to form identifiable states. The next major event in the history of Poland was the royal marriage of a Lithuanian grand duke and a Polish princess. The resulting unified Polish-Lithuanian state would prosper for the next 400 years. Neighboring countries, specifically Austria and Russia, took advantage of decline and internal strife. In 1795, as a result of a series of partitions, the political designation of Poland was dissolved and not fully restored until the end of World War I. World War II saw another division, this time between Nazi Germany and the Soviet Union. After the war, the Polish state was again restored, though as a Soviet vassal. Finally, in 1989, Poland's dependence on the Soviet Union ended, and the country emerged as a completely independent, democratic state with an open, free market economy.

As could be expected, the populace of Europe has changed throughout history, infused with new residents from conquering armies, forced immigrants, and willing relocators from all over the world. Ethnic Poles are the descendants of the founding population, the Slavic group known as the Polians, who adopted Christianity at the same time they established their statehood. In the 13th and 14th centuries, military alliances and battles expanded the boundaries and infused the population with Germanic people. During this time protectionist policies allowed Jews to thrive within Poland's borders. Both of these ethnic groups were mainstays of the population until World War II during the 20th century. Throughout Poland's history, Russians, Lithuanians, Prussians, Ukrainians, and other ethnic groups passed through or settled within Poland's borders. However, shifting borders and political movements of people in Europe, specifically during World War II, have led to a population that today is among the most homogeneous in the world—98 percent are Poles. Similarly, about 95 percent are Roman Catholic. Despite its varied past—or perhaps because of it—Poland today has a distinct and recognizable cultural heritage, including a unique and strong food culture.

🍽 Food Culture Snapshot

Like so much of Polish culture, traditional foodways fit nicely into the lives of modern Poles. Maria and Tomasz Jablonski are office workers in Warsaw, where they live with their four school-age sons. They shop for their food in both traditional open-air markets as well as shiny, new supermarkets. In both kinds of stores, they are able to choose from an abundance of produce, meats, dairy products, and other foodstuffs produced in the fertile lands of Poland and all over the world. The Jablonskis are a young family living in a major urban center, so the food they eat is both traditional and new, Polish and foreign. Polish food culture has always been compatible with new and diverse flavors, ingredients, and dishes.

The family eats their breakfasts of fresh bread with wild berry jam and farmhouse cheeses together each morning at home. Most days they will pack a lunch of smoked meat sandwiches to eat at work or at school. They may, on occasion, dine out for this late-morning meal, similar to lunch in other cultures. The cafés serve cold sandwiches and salads, hot soups, and grain dishes; both typically Polish and ethnically diverse foods are available in restaurants.

Each afternoon, the Jablonskis return home after work, school, and other activities to the biggest meal of their day. Dinner is typically eaten in the late afternoon or early in the evening, much earlier than the third meal of the day in most cultures. This meal, more than any other, is where the diversity of the modern Polish diet is revealed. Traditional meals include hearty soups and stews, meat with vegetables and potatoes, and pierogi. While all of these are enjoyed in traditional Polish preparations, they also can incorporate ingredients and flavors introduced from outside Poland.

Major Foodstuffs

Poland's physical geography is as diverse as the history of its political and social geography. The terrain includes three mountain ranges, four major rivers, a Baltic shoreline with three active ports, many lakes, and plenty of forest; at least half of its land is arable for food production. Interestingly, even while Poland was a Communist state, most of its food was produced on small, private farms. Post-Communist changes in the agriculture of Poland include the consolidation of smaller farms into fewer, larger farms and the modernization of tools and techniques. What has remained the same, though, is the fertile soil, moderate climate, and diverse geography that allow Poland to produce the ingredients of a rich cuisine.

Throughout Poland, there is an abundant variety of foodstuffs that are the foundation of the national cuisine. Wheat and other grains, poppies, mushrooms, root vegetables, fruit, domesticated animals and wild game, dairy, and fish are all part of the agricultural bounty of the temperate climate and fertile soil of Poland.

A wide variety of grains and cereals are available that feature heavily in Polish food culture. Among the cereals grown and used in Poland are rye, buckwheat, barley, oats, lentils, and millet. The grains are used to make breads. Sourdough rye and pumpernickel are especially popular and traditional varieties of bread. Grains are also used in a popular porridge dish called kasha (*kasza*) and as an ingredient in sausage and stuffing.

The cool, temperate climate of Poland is suitable for growing many vegetables, especially cole crops such as kohlrabi, cauliflower, turnips, and cabbage. Other common vegetables grown and enjoyed in Poland are beets, carrots, onions, cucumbers, beans, peas, tomatoes, and potatoes, an ingredient that features in many traditional meals.

Like people in any place that experiences cold winters when plant food is not readily available, Poles have had to learn how to preserve vegetables for the lean times. The favorite method for doing so in Polish food culture is pickling. In fact, the taste for the sour flavor of pickling brine is so great that Poles actually make a pickle soup. Pickled vegetables accompany many dishes in Polish cuisine. Pickled cabbage, or sauerkraut, is the most common, but Poles also enjoy pickled cucumbers, beets, cauliflower, fish, and mushrooms.

In addition to the fertile farmland that Poles use to grow the grains and vegetables that are so important to their cuisine, various geographies throughout the country are suitable for raising a number of different animals including pigs, cattle, sheep, goats, and poultry. Popular preparations for Poland's favorite meat—pork—include breaded cutlets (*kotlet shabowy*) and prune-stuffed roast loin (*shab z sliwkami*). Other roasts of beef, lamb, duck, and goose are also popular. Additionally, regions with heavy forests are populated by game animals that have long been hunted and incorporated into the food culture. Today, game meats like rabbit, pheasant, and boar are more commonly enjoyed in restaurants than prepared at home.

Poles are quite fond of smoked meat in general. In fact, smoke-cured bacon is more common than its salt-cured cousin. Even the meat preparation Poland is known for, kielbasa, is often smoke-cured. *Kielbasa* is actually the generic word for sausage in

Polish, and there are many traditional varieties to be found throughout the country. Sausage is usually eaten cold in Poland, and as pork is the favorite meat in Polish cuisine, most sausage is made entirely or partly of pork. Common varieties include a juniper berry–flavored beef and pork sausage called *mysliwska,* blood sausage with pork and buckwheat called *kiszka,* and a long, thin pork sausage called *kabonosy.* Sausage could be eaten by itself, but it is also a common ingredient in dishes like pierogi, stuffing, and sandwiches.

Domesticated animals in Poland are also raised for their milk. Depending on the region, the milk may come from cattle, sheep, or goats. Poles are fond of the sour flavor of fermented dairy, so sour milk, buttermilk, Polish-style yogurt (kefir), and especially sour cream are quite common in the Polish diet. Sour cream turns up everywhere in Polish cooking. It is used to garnish roast meat, dress salads, thicken soups, bind cakes, flavor kasha, and more. One would be hard-pressed to find a food that a Pole would not enjoy more with at least a dab of sour cream. The varieties of cheeses that are made in Poland vary by region, but one that is common to all Polish cooking is farmer's cheese, or fresh cheese curds made with sour milk. This is the cheese used in cheesecake, cheese fillings, and Polish cheese soup (*polewka z serwatki*).

Foraging, especially in the heavily forested regions of Poland, has always been common. As a result,

A butcher in Poland makes kielbasa by hand. (iStockPhoto)

wild mushrooms and honey are popular ingredients in the cuisine. Mushrooms are used in meat dishes, pierogi, kasha, and sauces. Dried mushrooms are generally available in markets. Popular varieties found in Poland and used in the cuisine are the bolete (*borowik*), morel (*smardz*), milky cap (*rydz*), and golden chanterelle (*kurka*). Wild honey is used to sweeten breads, cakes, and other pastries. It is also fermented into wine (*miod pitny*) and distilled into honey liqueur (*krupnik*).

Poland's many rivers and lakes, as well as its Baltic Sea shoreline, provide an abundance of fish. From the freshwater lakes and rivers, Poles enjoy fish like perch, bream, whitefish, European catfish, salmon, and tench (*lin*), a minnow-like panfish. From the Baltic Sea come flounder, carp, herring, eel, cod, and salmon.

In Polish cooking, a few herbs flavor many of the recipes. Of course, dill, which is used throughout eastern and central Europe, is the most popular herb and is found in just about every Polish kitchen. Many Polish recipes call for parsley. Poles prefer root parsley, which is very versatile because both the leaves and the root of the plant can be used as flavoring. Other common herbs in Polish cuisine include caraway seeds and marjoram, an herb related to oregano though with a subtler and earthier flavor. Juniper berries are utilized in meat sauces and marinades, as they are a great complement to the rich, gamey meats that are still very popular in Poland. Finally, in the grain fields throughout Poland, red poppies are cultivated for their seeds, which are used extensively in Polish cooking, especially in desserts.

Cooking

Cooking in Poland is traditionally done by women. It is through the lineage of mothers teaching daughters and daughters-in-law traditional recipes and foodways that Old Polish cuisine has survived a tumultuous and tenuous history. While the flavors of Polish cuisine are complex, the techniques and ingredients are simple. Time and care are the most essential ingredients in good Polish cooking. Slow-roasting meat and fish, pickling vegetables, souring milk and cream, kneading breads and pastries, and stuffing sausages are all techniques that infuse foods with rich flavors.

Typical Meals

While Poland strongly identifies with the rest of modern Europe and the West, it emerged from Communism with a desire to retain what was uniquely Polish about its culture. As a result, Poland's culture and the lifestyle are a mix of traditional practices and modern conveniences. Life in Poland is not primitive or old-fashioned, but a strong sense of traditions and culture remains.

As was always the case in Poland, most people enjoy four meals a day. As Poland has always been an agrarian economy, mealtimes align with the rhythms of a farm. A typical day begins early with a breakfast, called *sniadanie,* which usually consists of bread with butter and jam, as well as cold meats and cheeses. Most people drink coffee or tea with this meal. This meal is typically eaten at home, before work, just as it would have been eaten in the home before leaving for work in the fields on a farm.

Later in the morning, workers will break for what is generally considered a second breakfast (*drugie sniadanie*). Similar to a lunch in other cultures, this meal consists of a small breakfast that is eaten with coffee, tea, or milk. Unlike a lunch in other countries, the second breakfast is eaten in the late morning and is the smallest of the three meals of the day. It derives from the practice of farmers breaking from their work in midmorning to enjoy a quick snack in the fields.

The third meal is the largest of the day. Dinner (*obiad*) is the meal eaten after work, in the late afternoon. Again, this is slightly different from what is done in the United States and other countries, where dinner is an early evening meal. In Poland, the practice of eating earlier again derives from a farm culture where workers would return from the fields famished and ready to eat as early as 3 P.M. Today, it is usually eaten closer to 5 P.M. A dinner will usually consist of three courses, starting with a hearty soup or stew. Next, diners will enjoy meat and potatoes or pierogi. As is typical in many European cultures, the entrée will be followed by a salad. If dessert is served, it is usually cake with coffee or tea.

In the traditional farm culture of Poland, people likely went to bed with the sun, so even today in smaller villages it is impossible to find food for sale in restaurants after 8 P.M. However, most people will have a fourth meal later in the evening, usually in their homes. This fourth meal, called *kolacja,* is very similar to the early breakfast, with emphasis on cold meat instead of the bread and jam.

Since the fall of Communism, when cultural heritage was suppressed, Poles have taken a renewed interest in their traditional foods. There is a now a whole movement within Polish food culture called old Polish cuisine (*kuchnia staropolska*), emphasizing traditional and sometimes forgotten foodstuffs, recipes, and traditions. Polish food is in many ways typical of all Slavic cuisines, but it is also heavily influenced by other cuisines, particularly Austrian, Hungarian, Russian, Jewish, and German cooking. Poles enjoy little dishes, or appetizers, called *zakaski,* as do Russians. The prevalence of sour cream and dill is also a taste borrowed from Russia. Sausage, potatoes, and sweet and sour flavors found in Polish recipes are familiar to Germans. Paprika is the hallmark of Hungarian cuisine and is also common in Polish recipes. Honey cakes, jellied carp, and other fishes were introduced to Polish cuisine from Jewish culture. And, of course, cakes and pastries come to Poland by way of Austria.

These influences have melded with existing foodways and transformed to create a distinctly recognizable Polish food culture. Among the dishes considered quintessentially Polish are various soups and stews, smoked meats, sausages (kielbasa), pasta

Pierogi, traditional Polish dumplings. (iStockPhoto)

dumplings (pierogi), grain-based dishes (kasza), fish dishes, and pastries. The beverages traditionally enjoyed in Poland include beer and vodka.

Hearty soups play a central role in Polish cooking. Hunter's stew, called *bigos,* is considered by many to be the national dish of Poland. Bigos is traditionally served as an appetizer but may also be eaten as a main course.

Bigos (Hunter's Stew)

Ingredients

½ lb pork shoulder, cubed

½ lb beef chuck (or other stew meat), cubed

½ lb veal, cubed (optional; increase quantity of other meats to ¾ lb if not using veal)

3 medium onions, coarsely chopped

¼ c tomato paste

2 lb Polish sauerkraut

Water

About ½ lb *boczek* (Polish pork belly), chopped (salt pork or bacon may be substituted)

½ lb, or 1 foot of links, kielbasa (Polish-style sausage), chopped

1 c reconstituted dried mushrooms (reserve soaking liquid for stew)

2 stock cubes (not actual stock, as that would be too much liquid)

Peppercorns

1 bay leaf

1 tbsp caraway seeds

10 pitted prunes, chopped

1 c red wine

In a very large pot, brown pork, beef, and veal over high heat, and set aside. Put the onion, tomato paste, and sauerkraut in the pot and just barely cover with water. Bring to a simmer, turn the heat way down, and add all the meats, the boczek, the sausage, the mushrooms and soaking liquid, stock cubes, peppercorns, bay leaf, caraway seeds, and prunes. Simmer on very low heat for 1 to 1½ hours. Stir occasion-

ally. Add red wine, and simmer for another 2 to 3 hours. Turn off the heat, cover, and place in a cool place. The next day, reheat and serve in individual bowls with sour cream.

While Poles enjoy vegetable barley, pea, fermented rye (*zurek*), beer (*zupa piwna*), pickle (*zupa ogorkowa*), and other soups, beet soups are the most popular and common in Polish cooking. Hot beet soup (*barszcz*) was traditionally made with fermented beet juice, but today it is often soured with citrus or vinegar.

Barszcz (Beet Soup)

Ingredients

2–3 lb beets, plus 2 large beets

2 qt warm water

1 slice rye bread

1 clove garlic

1 medium onion, chopped

1 stalk celery, sliced

1 lb butter

1 lb mushrooms

1 tsp salt

1 bunch parsley, chopped

2 tbsp sour cream

To Ferment Beet Juice

Peel and dice beets, setting 2 aside for later. Place in a covered dish with warm water and rye bread. Place in a warm place to ferment for 10 days.

To Make Soup

Sauté garlic, onion, and celery in butter in a medium pot until onions are transparent. Add 2 reserved beets, mushrooms, salt, and parsley to pot, and cover with water. Bring to a boil. Reduce heat to simmer, and cook until beets are soft. Pour contents of the pot through a strainer into another pot. Retrieve beets from the strainer and grate into strained beet stock. Just before serving, add 1 pint fermented beet juice. Serve in individual bowls with 2 tablespoons sour cream.

Another popular beet soup is *botwina,* made with baby beets and their greens. This is usually prepared in early summer when beets are young and small. In summer, Poles eat a cold beet and raw vegetable soup called *chlodnik.* Another iconic Polish dish is stuffed pasta called pierogi. Pierogi are usually half-moon shaped and may be filled with anything including mushrooms, potatoes, onions, sausage, and farmer's cheese. The dish is served with sour cream, sautéed onions, dill, or broth. It can be served as a main dish or a side.

The grains that are abundantly grown in Poland are used in a number of ways that are central to Polish cooking. For example, most meals feature porridge—grain-based dishes called kasha, or kasza. These may be served as a main dish, side dish, or part of a thick, hearty soup. Buckwheat kasha is the most popular variation, but Poles also enjoy dishes of this sort made with barley, lentils, millet, and corn.

Cabbage rolls, called *golabki,* are a signature Polish dish that includes many of the foodstuffs of the cuisine. Cabbage, pork or beef, and barley are the standard ingredients of this dish.

Golabki (Cabbage Rolls)

Ingredients

1 medium onion, minced

2 tbsp butter

1 lb ground beef

1 lb ground pork

2 c barley or rice

2 eggs

1 sprig fresh thyme (or 2 tsp dried thyme)

Salt and pepper to taste

2 c pureed tomatoes

1 c chicken stock

1 head green cabbage, core removed

Sauté the onion in butter until translucent. Remove to a large bowl and cool. Add the ground meats, barley, eggs, thyme, salt, and pepper to the sautéed onions, and mix well.

Mix the tomatoes and stock, and add salt and pepper. Place about ¼ of the sauce in the bottom of a large baking dish.

Remove 10–12 whole leaves from the cabbage, and boil in salted water for about 5 minutes, until just wilted. Remove the leaves to a colander, and rinse them with cold water to stop the cooking process. Press the large vein on the back of each leaf to make it flush with the surface of the leaf. Lay a cabbage leaf out on a work surface, vein side down, and put about ¼ cup of meat mixture in the center of the leaf. Fold the bottom of the leaf up over the filling, fold each side in, and roll the leaf up over the mixture. Be careful not to roll up the cabbage tightly around the mixture as the barley will expand as it cooks.

Place all of the cabbage rolls, seam side down, tightly into the baking dish. Pour remaining sauce over the rolls. Cover and bake for 2 hours. Add stock to the dish as needed to keep it from drying out as the barley will soak up liquid as it cooks. Serve hot with sour cream.

Poland has developed its own repertoire of delicious desserts. The most well-known Polish cake is a bundt cake called *babka.* Another popular dessert is *mazurek,* a flaky crust topped with nuts, jam, or poppy seeds. Glazed doughnuts called *pączki* are filled with rose marmalade or plums and are especially popular during Lent. Polish cheesecake has a unique texture and taste because of the famous farmer's cheese used in its making. Poland has its own spin on cream-filled puff pastry that is popular throughout eastern and central Europe.

Like most of the rest of the world, Poles enjoy coffee and tea; however, in Poland, tea is the more popular of the two. Polish vodka is a traditional beverage that is still enjoyed in Poland today. Beer, especially pilsner style and other lagers, is also brewed and drunk in Poland. A popular beverage that is somewhat unique is fruit stewed in sugar water, called *kompoty.*

Like any cuisine, Poland enjoys regional variations that are the result of history and geography. However, it should be noted that the country is not that large, so the cuisine throughout Poland is similar, with regional specialties. Great Poland is the region in the western part of the country that is the original hub of Poland since its inception in the 10th century. The region is a flat, lowland river basin that is known for its fertile soil and has always been a major agricultural center. Because this region had been consumed and colonized by Prussia, German influence on the food here is especially strong. Some of the regional specialties include soft sausage (*kielbasa tatarowa*) and sweet and sour pork and prune soup (*kwasna*). The southeastern part of the nation, called Little Poland, consists of fertile lowlands, plus highlands, valleys, and the foothills of the Carpathian Mountains. The longtime home of shepherds, dairy—specifically cheese—is an important ingredient of the regional food culture. Two in particular are *oszczypek,* an aged, ewe-milk cheese, and *bryndza,* a soft, salty cheese. Kefir, a milk product similar to yogurt, also features in many of the dishes of the local cuisine. Silesia, or Slask, in the southwestern part of Poland, is the country's largest industrial area. Heavily influenced by Prussian and Austrian inhabitants throughout its history, Silesia is known for German-style dishes like mashed potato dumplings (*kluski slaskie*), sour wheat soup (*zurek stryszewski*), and potato pancakes with goulash (*jadlo drwali*). Silesia is also the major brewing region of Poland. Pomerania lies in northwestern Poland along the Baltic Sea and is heavily influenced by its proximity to the sea. Regional specialties include herring and cream (*kartofle w mundurkach*) and tench (lin). Mazovia and Podlaise lie in the east-central part of Poland. This region has the least arable land in the country, though it is heavily forested and therefore suitable for hunting and foraging. Wild honey, green-capped mushrooms, and wild game are important ingredients in the region's cuisine. Signature dishes include cabbage rolls (golabki), tripe with vegetables and cream sauce (*sastka warsawska*), and potato pancakes with sour cream (*placki ziemniaczane po mazowiecku*). The region is also known for a sweet, wild grass–flavored vodka called *zubrowska.* Masuria and Warmia are located in the northeastern part of Poland on the border with Russia. Like Mazovia, they are heavily

forested. The area contains many lakes, so freshwater fish like perch, salmon, and tench are common ingredients in local recipes. Regional dishes include baked perch and bacon (*okon po mazursku*) and creamed carrots with dill (*marchew po mazursku*).

Eating Out

Today, there are dining-out options for every taste and budget, especially in urban areas of Poland. As Polish food culture has always been about comfort and family, it is typical for diners to choose a seat or table in a restaurant rather than being seated by a host. Similarly, diners tend to take their time eating and drinking in Polish restaurants, so meals can last several hours.

Most Poles eat breakfast at home, so most restaurants, even those that serve breakfast food, don't open until 9 A.M. In addition to formal and more home-style restaurants and cafés offering full menus of traditional and neo-Polonaise cuisine, there are restaurants throughout Poland that serve Italian, French, Asian, and even American-style cuisine.

A unique kind of dining facility in Poland is the *bar mleczny,* or milk bar. Inexpensive food can be found at canteen-style facilities. These are often still state subsidized, so everyone from workers on break to tourists to homeless people can be found eating in milk bars.

Special Occasions

As most of the people living in Poland are Roman Catholic, important celebrations are traditional church holidays. Easter, of course, is the most important feast day, around which Poles have developed a rich food culture. Food has become part of the rite of Easter in Polish culture. The formal food ritual begins the day before Easter, on Holy Saturday, with a ceremony called Swieconka, or the Blessing of the Basket, in which some of the foods that will be served on Easter are brought to the local parish to be consecrated by the priest. The blessed foodstuffs include butter sculpted into a lamb's shape, cross-shaped Easter bread, smoked meats, salt, horseradish, and hard-boiled eggs. The ceremony includes a blessing for cakes and breads, one for meats, and another for eggs. Each item holds a symbolic meaning, the most important of which is the egg, representing the Resurrection. It will be the first thing eaten at the Easter feast. The meal begins with a ceremonial Sharing of the Egg, or Dzielenie Sie Jajkiem. A hard-boiled egg is divided and shared with everyone present, who in turn share well wishes with one another. Most Poles will have fasted for the 40 days of Lent and spent all morning at mass, so the Easter feast that follows is eagerly anticipated. The hungry feasters arrive home from church to a traditional spread that includes all of the items consecrated the day before, as well as many others. To accommodate morning worship, most of the foods at the feast are prepared ahead of time and are served cold. The meal will feature colored eggs, sausages, ham, smoked bacon, yeast cakes, pound cakes, poppy seed cakes, and the butter or sugar lamb. In addition to the cold spread, the feast will feature Polish Easter soup (zurek).

The other important feast day in Polish culture is Christmas. As for most Europeans, the major Christmas celebration occurs on Christmas Eve. On the day before Christmas, Poles will fast until the evening star—the Star of Bethlehem—rises. At this point, a feast called *wigilia* begins. Traditionally, this is a meatless feast and is served in 13 courses representing the 12 apostles and Jesus. Not every family can pull off a 13-course feast, so tradition allows for any odd number of courses. Conversely,

Pickled herring with olives and onion on a festive Christmas table in Poland. (Shutterstock)

the number of guests seated at the meal should be an even number.

Much like the Sharing of the Egg at Easter, the Christmas Eve meal begins with thin wheat wafers called *oplatki* that are distributed to all the diners. Each guest offers a blessing and piece of wafer to the rest of the diners. The foods served at the Christmas Eve meal include pickled creamed herring, smoked salmon, caviar, pickled vegetables and mushrooms, dried fruit compote, clear beet soup (*barszcz z uszkami*), a fish dish, sauerkraut, noodles, and grain-based dishes.

Diet and Health

Traditional Polish food is rich and heavy. Foods are thickened, flavored, and garnished with dairy, especially sour cream. Meats, including fatty sausages, are daily staples of the national diet. And hardly a dinner is served and eaten without potatoes, pierogi, or both. Time was that most people worked hard to produce the food they ate, and they needed the fat, calories, and protein these foods afforded to survive.

However, modern Poles are not unlike people in the rest of the Western world. They no longer toil each day in the fields. Most Poles are now office and factory workers and don't need the high fat and calories of their culture's traditional diet. Also, most Poles are as concerned with fitness as they are with health; they value thin waistlines more than hearty meals. So Poles now eat much less meat than they once did, and their consumption of sour cream and dairy is also down.

Interestingly, though, many elements of traditional Polish cuisine are quite compatible with a modern, healthy diet. For example, in the middle of the last century, the kasha that had long been a staple in Polish diets started to fall out of favor as an old-fashioned, peasant food. Recently, it has experienced a resurgence in popularity due to the increased concern Poles have about dietary fiber and health. Similarly, the traditional cooking oil made with the rapeseed grown on Polish farms is high in the unsaturated fats favored for keeping unhealthy cholesterol levels down. Also, Polish yogurt called kefir has been rediscovered and is gaining popularity among health-conscious Poles.

R. J. Krajewski

Further Reading

Dembinska, Maria. *Food and Drink in Medieval Poland: Discovering the Cuisine of the Past.* Philadelphia: University of Pennsylvania Press, 1999.

Knab, Sophie Hodorowicz. *Polish Customs, Traditions, and Folklore.* New York: Hippocrene Books, 1996.

Lemnes, Maria, and Henryk Vitry. *Old Polish Traditions in the Kitchen and at the Table.* New York: Hippocrene Books, 1996.

Ochorowicz-Monatowa, Marja. *Polish Cookery: Poland's Bestselling Cookbook Adapted for American Kitchens.* New York: Crown, 1968.

Peterson, Joan, and Michael Peterson. *Eat Smart in Poland: How to Decipher the Menu, Know the Market Foods, and Embark on a Tasting Adventure.* Madison, WI: Gingko Press, 2000.

West, Karen. *The Best of Polish Cooking.* New York: Hippocrene Books, 2000.

Portugal

Overview

The Republic of Portugal lies at the southwestern corner of continental Europe and includes the autonomous regions of the Madeira Islands and Azores, which lie hundreds of miles to the west and southwest, respectively. Continental Portugal is bordered on the north and east by Spain, while its 1,114 miles of Atlantic coastline beckon westward and southward. At a latitude of 39°30′N, it enjoys a temperate climate. It is one Europe's smaller countries. Having a total area of 35,503 square miles (92,090 square kilometers), it is slightly smaller than the state of Indiana. It is poorer than most fellow European Union member nations, though its standard of living has risen considerably since the country attained European Union membership in 1986.

Fewer of Portugal's 10.4 million citizens live in urban areas than in other European Union countries: only 63 percent, compared to the European Union average of approximately 77 percent. Many still make a subsistence living from fishing or from small family farms. But industry and technology are growing at a rapid rate, and the Portuguese share a deep pride in their country, its history, and its heroes.

In earliest historic times, Portugal's mainland, which is surrounded on its northern and eastern borders by its larger neighbor Spain and situated at the western edge of the Iberian Peninsula, was settled by various groups. The earliest settlements were established by the Phoenicians in the third century B.C. Later, Romans, Celts, Germanic tribes, Visigoths, and Muslim North Africans also settled in Portugal. Even today, one will encounter a greater number of fair, blond, blue-eyed Portuguese in the northern part of the country than in the southern part, where more have darker skin and hair, though the general population is fairly homogeneous. Immigrants from Portugal's former African colonies and an influx of Brazilians and western and eastern Europeans have added to the mix in recent years. The national language is Portuguese, and although religious freedom is guaranteed by law, most citizens are Roman Catholic.

From the Romans came the roots of Portugal's language, its olive groves, and viticulture. From the Moors came almonds, sugar, art, and architecture. Under the leadership of ambitious royals, Portuguese sailors discovered valuable new sea routes throughout the world and gained riches for their kings and country through the trading of spices, Asian goods, and African slaves. Until the 1400s, Arabs ruled the Indian Ocean trade. It was Portugal's Prince Henry (1394–1460) who envisioned a possible sea route to India and, toward this end, established a naval school at Sagres around 1418. There, sailors were trained in navigation, astronomy, and mapmaking. Swift-sailing Portuguese caravels were dispatched in every direction in a quest for sailing routes to the Spice Islands and the treasures of Africa and the Far East.

Successful explorations by Bartholomeu Dias (ca. 1457–1500), Vasco da Gama (ca. 1469–1524), and Pedro Álvares Cabral (ca. 1460–1520) and subsequent conquests in Africa, India, the Americas, and the Far East brought Portugal fabulous wealth. They also paved the way, navigationally speaking, for Spain's future explorations, led by Christopher Columbus (1451–1506), Vasco Núñez de Balboa (1474–1519), and Ferdinand Magellan (1480–1521). Magellan, a Portuguese sea captain hired by Spain to seek a naval passage around the world, was killed en route, but his goal of global circumnavigation was completed by his crew and proved the theories proposed at Sagres.

These courageous explorers first opened global trading routes toward the exchange of goods and ideas that has continued to the present, as well as an era of Portuguese colonization in Africa, South America, and Asia. But it was Portuguese traders who first introduced many of the New World plants, animals, and African and East Asian herbs and spices that flavor its own cuisine and that of the entire world today. Portuguese traders monopolized the trade in cinnamon, nutmeg and mace, pepper, grains of paradise (a peppery spice from the West Coast of Africa), and other spices.

Under weak leadership over the following centuries, Portugal lost its prominence and wealth. To this day, in Portuguese cabarets and clubs, the *fado,* a national type of ballad, can be heard. It echoes ancient Arabic and North African tones and is at once sadly haunting and melancholic. It has been likened by some to the American blues, in that it reflects the common people's collective sensibility, or *saudade.* The word is difficult to translate but roughly means a melancholic longing for those things that make the soul complete. One place where the Portuguese do find and celebrate fulfillment today is at the table, in the love of family and good food that reflects the country's illustrious past and all the world's flavors.

🍽 Food Culture Snapshot

Eduardo and Vitoria de Oliveira Beirão live in a flat in Oeiras, near the coastal bay formed at the mouth of the Tagus River. Eduardo is a pharmaceutical researcher, and Vitoria works part-time in marketing for a computer firm. They have two school-age boys, aged 7 and 10. They enjoy seaside sports as well as their proximity to Lisbon, which can be reached in less than half an hour by car or public transportation.

Vitoria learned to cook from her mother and grandmother, whom she helped in the kitchen as the eldest daughter with four siblings. She enjoys cooking with the wide variety of fresh produce and seafood available in Oeiras. She most frequently shops at a well-stocked supermarket, where, when Eduardo is traveling on business, she sometimes picks up prepared foods such as mild pepper-roasted chicken for herself and the boys. She also frequents small specialty shops, where she buys salted cod and specialty produce, and a local bakery whose fresh-baked breads and *pastéis de nata* (custard tarts) are family favorites.

On weekends, when Eduardo is home, the family enjoys barbecuing sausages and *sardinhas* (sardines) on their small patio in good weather or goes to a favorite café near the park or beach to meet friends. Holidays as well as some feast days and birthdays are generally spent with Vitoria's family at her parents' home outside Lisbon, when large midday meals are enjoyed. Most of Eduardo's family lives near Porto, Portugal's second-largest city, which is several hours north by car or train, and visits with them are less frequent.

Eduardo eats lunch at his company's cafeteria, as do the boys at their school. Their evening supper, served around 7:30 or 8 P.M., is the main meal at home. It is lighter, without as many courses or as large portions as Vitoria and Eduardo grew up with during their own childhoods, mainly because help is more expensive and not as readily available, food costs are higher, and the family's lifestyle is more active. But Vitoria still enjoys making traditional soups, and she freezes extra portions to keep on hand.

In its 2001 national population census, the average Portuguese family consisted of 2.8 persons, very near the average of 2.4 for all European Union countries. Larger families that include several generations may sometimes live in the same home, however, particularly in rural areas or where unemployment is high.

Women's traditional roles have eased over the past several decades as increasing numbers of them have gained employment and increased economic equality. Still, it is generally the wife and mother's responsibility to see to all things domestic, including all homemaking and childrearing tasks. Although the father remains the traditional head of the family, the family home remains the mother's domain, and food shopping and home cooking are a woman's job. Meal preparation is taken seriously because the Portuguese have a choice of high-quality, fresh ingredients, and they enjoy long meals that feature many simply prepared, delicious traditional dishes.

Major Foodstuffs

Mainland Portugal is divided into three parts: northern, central, and southern Portugal, with district divisions within each of these. The Madeira Islands and Azores are politically autonomous, with their own regional governments. Of Portugal's 35,503 square miles of land, about 30 percent is arable. Current efforts by the government, tourist industry, and private groups aim to identify specific regional specialties in order to enhance marketing and promote gastronomic tourism.

Major food crops include almonds, corn, olives, potatoes, rice, tomatoes, and wheat. Commercial and independent fishing produce a great variety of Atlantic fish and shellfish for Portuguese tables, most notably sardines and tuna. Codfish, long a staple of

Fresh mussels, a traditional Portuguese dish, in Cataplana. (iStockPhoto)

the Portuguese diet, is now imported principally from Norway and Iceland due to threats to the sustainability of the Atlantic's Grand Banks fisheries. Beef, poultry, lamb, and pork are raised in Portugal. Still, given the area and climate, the country's agricultural production lags behind the European Union average, due to the need for increased agricultural education and modernization of farming practices.

Caldo verde, Portugal's closest thing to a national soup, hails from northern Portugal's Minho region. Trout, salmon, and lampreys thrive in the Minho's rivers, and the latter are prepared in a popular regional rice dish, *arroz de lampreia.* Other specialties from the area include *caldeirada de peixe,* a hearty fish soup made with the day's catch of firm white fish; *canja,* a brothy chicken soup with rice, lemon, and mint; *arroz de pato,* a duck and rice dish; and *bacalhau à moda de viana,* one of the country's favorite salt cod offerings, with onions, white wine, and cabbage.

In the Douro and Trás-os-Montes regions, also to the north but below the Minho, one will see miles of vineyards, for the Douro is the home of port and other Portuguese wines. In addition, however, there will be cattle and pig farms in the rugged Trás-os-Montes, and smoked ham and sausages from the region are superb. Specialties from these regions include *cozida à Portuguesa,* a meat, vegetable, and sausage soup that is considered to be another national dish; *tripas à moda do Porto,* tripe with chicken, *chouriço* (a spicy sausage), and beans; *arroz com lebre,* or hare with rice; and *bolo de castanhas,* a chestnut cake.

In the Beiras region of central Portugal there will be egg cakes and pastries, ham, sausages, and the world-famous Serra da Estrela, a raw ewe-milk cheese. Kid or goat may be served roasted, and a sunken but delicious sponge cake, *pao de-ló,* is a frequent dessert.

In the Estremadura, also in central Portugal and with an Atlantic coastline, fish of all kinds will be prepared. *Escabeche,* or marinated and preserved fish such as sardines, mackerel, or tuna, is popular. Shellfish soups and caldeirada de peixe are common fare. The salt cod specialty here is *bacalhau à brás,* a casserole of shredded dried salt cod with French-fried potatoes and scrambled eggs.

The Ribatejo region is a rich agricultural land where melons, tomatoes, rice, olives, olive oil, market garden produce, livestock, figs, and, of course, grapes are grown. Some of the area's specialties include pork sausages and smoked ham, eel, potato cakes, and dumplings made with cornbread.

In the coastal Lisbon region, fishing, rice growing, and salt panning are the primary agricultural endeavors. Pastries here are most tempting, and national favorites that hail from the area are pastéis de nata, or egg-custard tarts.

In southern Portugal, there is the Alentejo district. Olives, olive oil, wheat, wines, oranges, and wild boar come from this area. Specialties include *requeijão,* a breakfast of ricotta cheese and honey cake, sausages, and cheese; chicken empanadas (pies or turnovers); *açorda à Alentejana,* a garlicky bread soup flavored with coriander, olive oil, greens, and eggs; *carne de porco à Alentejana,* another nationally favored dish of pork with clams and coriander that is steam-cooked in a hammered copper *cataplana,* a pan that itself looks like a clamshell.

In the southernmost region of the Algarve, where tourism has taken over and culinary internationalism prevails, fewer and fewer traditional dishes are found. Still, there is excellent seafood to be found, with grilled sardines at their peak, as well as clams, oysters, mussels, squid, and octopus. Arabic-influenced sweetmeats such as *morgados,* made of almonds and figs, can be found in local confectioners' shops.

For home cooking, the Portuguese pantry is well supplied by farmers' markets, specialty shops, and, in larger towns and cities, supermarkets or even hypermarkets. Among the ingredients commonly used are *bacalhau* (salt cod) and a variety of other fish and shellfish; meat and poultry; bread; olives and olive oil; rice and beans; herbs and spices; eggs, butter, and cheese; potatoes, vegetables, and fruits; and condiments.

Salt cod is said to be prepared in 100 ways in Portugal. Other fish and shellfish are extremely popular as well. Sardines, tuna, squid, red mullet, swordfish, sea perch, cuttlefish, eels, octopus, prawns, lobster, and clams can be bought fresh in fish markets. Rabbit, ham, pork sausages (chouriço and *linguiça,* the latter a thinner version of the former), and blood sausage (*morcelas* or *chouriços de sangue*) are cooked in various ways, as are chicken, turkey, and duck.

Bread and potatoes are traditionally served at every meal. Bread is usually a wheat loaf with a chewy crust, though in the Minho, cornbread, *broa,* will be served. Bread is used in soups as well as at the table. Potatoes are kept on hand or grown throughout the year in home gardens or farms. Kale is also a popular home garden crop and is used in the national soup, caldo verde. Rice is kept on hand for use in soups, stews, and desserts. Goat and ewe-milk cheeses are served frequently as appetizers, in sandwiches, or with fruit at the end of a meal.

Among condiments, olive oil is by far the most popular. It is served, usually along with wine or cider vinegar, to flavor soups, fish, and salads. *Piri piri,* a red pepper sauce, is often available for seasoning. Honey is harvested in the Alentejo, and the home cook from that region may often substitute it for sugar in sweet desserts. Herbs and spices most commonly found in Portuguese kitchens include salt and pepper, saffron, cumin, curry powder, paprika, cinnamon, cloves, nutmeg, allspice, rosemary, garlic, coriander, mint, bay leaves, parsley, sage, oregano, and red chili peppers.

The home cook will most often use garlic and onions in her cooking but also prepare pumpkins, squashes, carrots, cauliflower, onions, kale, spinach, green beans, broad beans, turnip greens, and tomatoes for use in a variety of soups or dishes or to accompany meats and fish. With its mild, temperate climate, and the semitropical Madeira Islands and Azores nearby, Portugal produces many fruits for home cooks to purchase in season throughout the year. These include grapes, apricots, peaches, plums, figs, oranges, lemons, strawberries, cherries, pineapple, and bananas. Chestnuts, peanuts, pine nuts, and walnuts are served in dishes and eaten out of hand.

Pastries can be purchased from many bakeries and tea salons; they are often very sweet and egg-filled. Today's home cook will buy them mainly for special occasions. Wine is used in cooking and is commonly served with lunch and dinner. Beer is also a popular beverage. Espresso, coffee, and tea are widely enjoyed throughout the day. Mineral water is also kept on hand for serving with meals.

Cooking

Most kitchens are fairly small and basically equipped, with cookstoves powered by natural gas, propane, or electricity. Decades ago, ovens might not even have been found in the home kitchen; in rural homes a *forno* (wood-burning outdoor oven) was instead located in the yard behind the kitchen. For this reason, many dishes are boiled, fried, stewed, or pan-braised on the cooktop. Today, modern appliances may be found throughout the country. Modern kitchens with the latest amenities may be found in newer construction or in renovated older homes in more affluent areas.

Long cooking methods such as simmering or braising are required for the success of many Portuguese dishes. Many popular dishes that are served daily in most homes are soups and stews that have been allowed to cook slowly so that flavors develop fully. If salt cod is to be used in a dish, and it often is, it must be soaked in water, usually overnight, with the water being changed at least twice to remove the salt before cooking. Meats may be roasted, grilled or stewed, and cooked in soups. Chicken, or *frango,* that is marinated in a piri piri (hot pepper) marinade and then grilled, is a popular dish. Fish are usually grilled, oven-roasted, or panfried and are often cooked in soups as well.

For roasting and simmering, earthenware cooking dishes are used as well as metal pots and pans. A small earthenware spirit-burning grill may be used to cook chouriço or other sausages atop the table. Some mixing bowls and stew pots may also be made of earthenware. The cataplana, a clamshell-like hammered copper-clad pan, is particular to Portugal. It can be likened to a pressure cooker of sorts, as it allows dishes to be slow-steamed to completion. It is most often used in preparing shellfish and rice dishes.

In traditional home cooking, salads are not served as often as cooked vegetables. They are usually simple combinations of lettuce, tomatoes, and sliced onions served with olive oil and wine or cider vinegar. Egg desserts are popular and are often made with a curd made from egg yolks cooked with sugar syrup. *Membrillo,* or quince paste, similar to that in Spain, is made by slowly stewing quinces with sugar, then pouring the mixture onto a plate until it congeals into a solid gel, owing to the fruit's high pectin content.

Dinnerware utensils, especially at fine restaurants but also in some homes, may include fish knives and forks.

Caldo Verde (Kale and Potato Soup)

Serves 12

12 oz chouriço or linguiça sausages

1 large bunch kale

2 tbsp olive oil

1 large onion, chopped

2 cloves garlic, minced

3 large russet potatoes, peeled and diced into large pieces, to yield 3 c

2 large (49-oz) cans chicken broth

½ tsp freshly ground pepper

Score each sausage lengthwise with a sharp paring knife, and peel off and discard its casing. Cut the sausages lengthwise in half, then slice crosswise into ¼-inch-thick slices. (They'll be half-moon shaped.) In an 8-quart soup pot, sauté sausage slices slowly until lightly browned, stirring often. Drain off the fat that renders out, and wipe excess from pan and sausage with paper towels. Remove sausage to a plate.

Strip green leaves from hard stems of kale, and discard stems. Chiffonade leaves (cut into thin strips). This should produce about 2 quarts of shredded greens.

Add oil to pan, and sauté onion until translucent, then add garlic and continue sautéing for another minute or two. Add kale, and stir-fry for a minute or two until the leaves begin to wilt. Add potatoes, chicken broth, sautéed sausage, and pepper. Bring to a boil, then reduce heat and simmer, covered, at least 30 minutes. With back of spoon or potato masher, mash potatoes to thicken soup. Remove lid and continue simmering for about another ½ hour. Season with salt and pepper to taste.

Typical Meals

Pequeno almoço, or breakfast, will be a quick, light meal. For most people, it is just a piece of bread or buttered toast accompanied by coffee with milk. Many people stop at a bakery or café to get a quick cup of coffee and a roll on their way to work. A full breakfast with rolls, cheese, fruit, butter, and preserves, and perhaps dry cakes, will usually be found only in a hotel.

For *almoço,* or lunch, the traditional three-hour break at midday in which a hearty meal can be enjoyed at home or in a restaurant still occurs for some. Today's workers, however, often have less time to take for lunch, but even so, that time is spent eating. Lunch may include soup, meat and sometimes seafood, potatoes or occasionally rice, and a vegetable or small, simple salad. Beverages will be wine and mineral water. At a small workers' restaurant, there will usually be a fixed-price menu of the day in addition to à la carte choices, and tables may be shared by strangers. At home, it is customary for the meal to be served with bread and to end with a simple dessert such as fruit and cheese, followed by coffee.

Jantar, or dinner, will be another hearty meal. It is served late, perhaps not quite as late as in Spanish homes, but from 7:30 or 8 P.M. until perhaps 10 P.M. In many restaurants, however, especially on weekends, dining begins around 10 P.M. Dishes similar to those at lunch will be served, and they will be accompanied by wine. Dessert, if served, may be followed, perhaps, by a glass of port or *aguardiente* (brandy).

Weekend dinners are an important time for family to gather for long meals. Meals take time because the Portuguese not only enjoy their food but also view mealtimes as a social occasion, even with family. Meals are not hurried, and everyone participates in the conversation.

Eating Out

Dining out can mean anything from stopping at a café or teahouse, or even a fast-food restaurant, of which there are an increasing number, especially in the larger towns and cities, to dining at a *típico*

Chicken piri-piri (peri-peri) with french fries, served in a restaurant in Albufeira, Portugal. (iStockPhoto)

(traditional restaurant) or a multistarred restaurant. Only the more expensive restaurants take reservations; for all others, service is on a first-come, first-served basis.

At an *adega,* or wine cellar, there may be a small restaurant where the proprietor's wine will be served with local fare. These may be open only on weekends or seasonally, or for special events. Cafés serve coffee from morning until late at night or into the early morning hours. They may also serve lunch and light snacks. The most common type of coffee ordered throughout the day is *uma bica,* a small espresso. *Casas* or *salons de chá* (teahouses) serve tea, coffee, juices, and soft drinks as well as pastries and snacks. They are popular for morning or late-afternoon breaks. *Pastelarias,* or pastry shops, also sometimes serve similar offerings, but they may have a greater range of pastry choices.

Inexpensive to moderately priced restaurants include *casas de pasto* (diners), *cervejarias* (beer houses), *churrascarias* and grills (barbecue restaurants), *fumeiros* (smokehouse taverns, mainly found in the Alentejo district), and *marisquerias* (seafood restaurants). Full-service restaurants and típicos (regional specialty restaurants) range in price from moderate to expensive.

Special Occasions

Many festival days throughout the year require special foods and/or feasting at community gatherings or with family. On Dia de Ano Novo, or New Year's Day, the family gathers for dinner and shares a *bolo rei,* or king's cake, which has been purchased from a bakery. In this favorite spiced fruit bread, a prize token or fava bean will have been baked. The person who gets the prize supposedly has to provide next year's bolo rei.

Carnival is held on Shrove Tuesday, toward the end of February, or 40 days before Easter. Similar to Rio de Janeiro's Carnival or Mardi Gras in New Orleans, it is celebrated with floats, parades, dancing, and costumes, especially in Lisbon, the Algarve, and Funchal on the island of Madeira. Seafood and cozida á Portuguesa are popular at this celebration. For Páscoa (Easter), the family gathers for favorite traditional dishes. This might include a roast piglet, lamb, or kid, or casseroles and breads with eggs baked into them.

In June, several summer saint's days are celebrated with *festas,* or festivals: São Gonçalo, Santo António, and, finally, São João. The latter two are the larger, more widely celebrated feast days, with roast kid or grilled sardines being special treats.

Natal (Christmas) is the biggest family festival of the year. On Christmas Eve, families gather for a traditional dinner of salt cod, boiled potatoes, bitter greens (kale or turnip greens sprinkled with olive oil and vinegar), and hard-cooked eggs. Seafood such as octopus with rice or fried salt cod fritters may also be served, along with *vinho verde,* the spritzy young wine of the most recent vintage, and special desserts such as *arroz doce* (rice pudding with cinnamon), honey cakes, or doughnut-like fried cakes.

Two-thirds of all weddings take place in a church. They are followed by a festive gathering of family and friends. The dinner to follow will often be a feast, both for the eyes and for the digestion. Although these vary according to means and region, a wedding reception might feature a cocktail hour with wine or *vinho spumante* (sparkling wine) and hearty appetizers, many of which will feature seafoods and shellfish. The wedding party and guests will be seated, and dinner will follow, possibly beginning with soup such as caldo verde, followed by a fish course, then a meat course. A wedding cake will be cut, and other desserts and pastries are served as well. At a celebration following a baptism, vinho spumante, hors d'oeuvres, cakes, and pastries may be served in the family home.

Diet and Health

Although the Portuguese eat a basically Mediterranean-style diet, it tends to be heavy in carbohydrates and sugar. Egg-based desserts are common, and a day's food intake may be more than what is required. The diet is varied, with adequate protein and vitamins from many vegetables and fruits. Although fish is eaten often, many Portuguese may

Sliced traditional Portuguese Christmas cake, called Bolo Rei, made with candied fruits. (iStockPhoto)

Fishing bounty from Portugal's waters. (Corel)

consume excessive amounts of cholesterol from eggs and saturated fats in meats. Portugal's men have a lower rate of death by heart attacks than those in other European Union countries but a considerably higher rate of strokes.

Pamela Elder

Further Reading

Anderson, Jean. *The Food of Portugal.* New York: William Morrow, 1986.

Goldstein, Joyce. *Savoring Spain and Portugal.* San Francisco: Weldon Owen, 2000.

Leite, David. *The New Portuguese Table.* New York: Clarkson Potter, 2009.

Luard, Elisabeth. *The Food of Spain and Portugal.* London: Kyle Cathie, 2005.

Poelzl, Volker. *Culture Shock, A Guide to Customs and Etiquette: Portugal.* Portland, OR: Graphic Arts Center, 2004.

Robertson, Carol. *Portuguese Cooking: The Traditional Cuisine of Portugal.* Berkeley, CA: North Atlantic Books, 2008.

Robertson, Ian. *Portugal: A Traveller's History of Portugal.* London: Cassel, 2002.

Scott-Aitken, Lynelle, and Clara Vitorino. *World Food Portugal.* Footscray, Australia: Lonely Planet, 2002.

Turismo Portugal/Portuguese National Tourist Office. http://www.visitportugal.com/Cultures/en-US/default.html.

Virtual Portugal. http://www.portugalvirtual.pt.

Romania

Overview

Romania is situated in the region of eastern Europe and is considered part of the Balkans. It is bordered by Bulgaria to the south, Serbia to the southwest, Hungary to the west and northwest, Moldova and Ukraine to the north and northeast, and the Black Sea to the east. The total area of Romania is 59 million acres (23.8 million hectares), of which 60 percent is dedicated to agriculture. Romania was formed after the joining of Walachia and Moldavia in 1859. However, it wasn't recognized as a nation-state until 1878 after the Russo-Turkish War, which saw Romania as a Russian ally and resulted in Romania's freedom from the Ottoman Empire. Romania was a Warsaw Pact state under the sway of the Soviet Union until 1989, when Communism was overthrown. The population in 2007 was 21.5 million. The main ethnic minorities are Hungarian, German, Romani (Gypsy), Jewish, and diverse Slavic populations. A large population of Romanians lives outside of Romania, mainly in Serbia, Moldova, Ukraine, the United States, Canada, and Australia. Romanian food culture has been shaped over time by these historical, social, and geographic features.

The most distinctive trait of Romanian food is its diverse origins. Romanian food, on the one hand, is a mix of Balkan, Turkish, Greek, and Eastern influences and, on the other hand, has been influenced by western Europe, namely, French cuisine. It is heavily grounded in peasant cooking and its eastern European location. Many foods and food habits are shared with its neighboring country, Moldova. Variations in regional foods can be detected and are explained by the fact that different ethnic groups throughout history have traversed or occupied the territory of modern-day Romania. For example, in Transylvania, clear Germanic and Hungarian influences can be perceived, and in the north a Russian influence is evident.

A history of occupation as well as times of political instability has played a key role in Romania's food culture. Roman colonists settled in the area in 106 A.D. and left their mark on many facets of Romanian culture, including food. From the 14th century, the Ottoman Empire had a significant impact on Romanian cuisine, and for many years Romania was its main food supplier. The Turkish influences that can be seen today include a fondness for sweet pastries, the practice of eating appetizers (meze), and foods like pilaf, meat patties, stuffed grape leaves, caviar, coffee, and many introduced spices and vegetables, as well as the cooking utensils used to prepare these foods.

The Soviet occupation also played its part in shaping Romanian food culture. This took the form of the restructuring of a largely peasant agrarian society into a centralized economy, characterized by large cooperative farms. Many food customs were undermined in this period, and obtaining basic nutritional requirements became the focus. However, in the face of food crises, Romanians have upheld a strong sense of food traditions that can be seen today. The aftermath of Communism and the opening of Romania to a free market economy have been the most recent influence on Romanian food culture. This influence manifested initially in the struggle to obtain enough food as the restructuring of agriculture and the economy took place and then, in recent years, in the appearance of many Western food trends.

With 86 percent of the population following the Romanian Orthodox Church, religion has significantly shaped Romanian eating habits. Fasting and feasting make up the rhythm of the year and influence choices of what is eaten when. Today, however, like other aspects of Romanian food culture, the practice of traditions, such as fasting, is more common among the rural population than for urban dwellers.

Food Culture Snapshot

Romania has seen an immense shift in shopping and eating habits since the transition from a centralized market economy to a free market economy in 1989. These changes are most evident in the urban setting. International supermarket chains and fast-food establishments have entered Romania. Convenience foods, such as precooked meals, have become more popular among working city residents, replacing home-cooked traditional foods. There is evidence to suggest that Romanian food habits, along with those of other former Communist nations, will move toward a more western European pattern. However, in Romania there exist two different patterns of food shopping and eating, the rural and the urban.

Stefan and Ana Radu live in a middle-class neighborhood in Bucharest. They both work full-time; Stephan is employed by Transelectrica, and Ana works for an information technology company. Once bills have been paid, food purchases account for over half of their income. These days they have a variety of places to buy their food. They split their shopping between supermarkets and more traditional small shops and open-air markets. For fresh fruit and vegetables they go to the open-air market. From supermarkets or sometimes even larger hypermarkets (as they are called in Europe), they purchase coffee, milk, and wine; sometimes precooked meals for dinner; condiments; cornmeal for *mamaliga* (corn porridge/polenta); some canned foods; meat (mainly pork); and sugar. Bread is bought from a bakery to have for breakfast as toast with jam and coffee. Some mornings a pastry and Western-style coffee are purchased on the way to work. A small amount of their food, mainly *tuica*

(plum brandy), some wine, and occasionally meat, comes from relatives who live in the country.

Petar and Elena Ionescu live in the Apuseni Mountains in the region of Transylvania; Petar is 56 years old, and Elena is 54. They live with their son, Emil, and his wife, Daniela. They are both practicing members of the Romanian Orthodox Church and spend more than half of the year fasting. Almost half of their food is either produced by them or exchanged with neighboring farms. Their farm consists of two cows that provide them with milk. The milk is drunk fresh or with coffee, or served cold on mamaliga for breakfast, and it is sometimes used in cooking and is also made into cheese, cottage cheese, or sour cream, which is used frequently in their meals. The Ionescus sell their milk at a local street market and sometimes direct to customers from their farm. They keep chickens that provide them with eggs, which they eat boiled or made into an omelet for breakfast or made into baked mamaliga for lunch or supper. For nonfasting days, their meat comes from the chickens they raise, which may be made into a *ciorba* (sour soup) and served for lunch or supper. They also purchase pig meat from a nearby farm and on special occasions buy a whole suckling pig to roast. As they live in Transylvania, where sheep are herded, they sometimes purchase mutton as well. They grow most of the fruit and vegetables they eat, including apples, plums, potatoes, cabbage, peppers, onions, garlic, tarragon, and dill; the rest is bought from a nearby market. Sugar, cooking oil, coffee, and occasionally soft drinks and beer are bought from a small local shop. Cornmeal is purchased to make into mamaliga, which is eaten frequently at breakfast, lunch, and dinner. Bread is purchased from a bakery or made for special occasions. Much of their day revolves around food procurement and the cooking of food. All meals are made at home and are generally quite time-consuming. Plums from their farm are used to make tuica (plum brandy), and other fruits are made into jams and *dulceata* (sweet preserved fruits). Wine is bought in bulk directly from a local vineyard, and either wine or tuica is served with most meals.

Major Foodstuffs

With more than 60 percent of its land dedicated to agriculture, Romania is fundamentally an agrarian

Farm produce market, Baia Mare, Romania. (Corel)

society. The percentage of people employed by agriculture has decreased since 2000. However, farming is still an important means of existence for many Romanians. Nearly half of the population live rurally, and 79 percent of agricultural land is used by fully or semisubsistent households.

Cereals have always been a major foodstuff for most Romanians. Cereals account for over half of the dietary calories the population consumes, especially in rural areas. Apart from cultural reasons for the high consumption of cereals, the other main motive is economic. Romania is a country in transition from a Communist regime to a free market economy. With this transition has come a removal of food subsidies that has created fluctuating food prices. The result is a decrease in real income for most of the population and an increase in the percentage of income spent on food. On average, spending on food accounts for half of household expenditures. Thus, cereals provide a cheap source of daily calories.

Wheat and maize are the main cereals both produced and consumed in Romania. In households today, cereals are mainly consumed in the form of bread (most commonly made of wheat flour) and mamaliga. Bread is central to Romanian culture and is divided into ritual bread (*colaci*) and regular bread. Maize, in the form of mamaliga or cornbread (*turta de mamaiu*), was for a long time the dietary staple of most Romanians. Today, the consumption of wheat has increased and is more or less balanced with maize consumption. There are some demographic differences in the consumption of wheat

and maize. In the rural population, maize features more heavily than for the urban population, who are generally exposed to more Western foods.

The dairy industry is Romania's largest agricultural activity in terms of both value and quantity. Only a small portion of the milk produced is exported. Consequently, Romanians use a lot of cow milk. According to the Food and Agriculture Organization (FAO) of the United Nations, domestic consumption of whole milk in 2007 was 58 gallons (220 liters) per capita, whereas in the United Kingdom, the population consumed 33 gallons (124 liters) per capita. Milk is used in the form of sour cream, cottage cheese, *telemea* (a traditional Romanian cheese made from either cow, buffalo, or sheep milk). Milk is used in cooking, in coffee, and for breakfast, or it is drunk fresh. Some other milks, such as sheep and buffalo, are used but to a lesser extent. Sheep are raised in the north and west of the Carpathian Mountains. Sheep milk is used to make typical Romanian cheeses, such as *cascaval* (a hard, sharp cheese like Italian *cacciocavallo*) and *brinza* (a younger white cheese).

Fertile soils and a temperate-continental climate allow a wide range of fruit and vegetables to grow. Many fruit and vegetables have been grown in Romania for a long time. The cultivation and consumption of many fruits and vegetables dates as far back as the Roman period. In the past, Romania provided Europe with a significant amount of its food. Today, exports are low compared to other European nations. Vegetables are grown mainly for domestic use and include potatoes, beets, cabbage, eggplant, peppers, onions, and tomatoes, among others. Vegetables are ubiquitous in Romanian cooking, and this is perhaps a legacy of Turkish rule and Balkan influences. It may also be a result of the tradition of fasting in Romania, which prohibits the consumption of meat and meat products on specific days of the year.

Orchards cover much of Romania, especially in the south of the Carpathian Mountains. Plums, cherries, peaches, nectarines, apricots, pears, melons, and apples are grown here. In the 1930s Romania was responsible for a significant export of plums and walnuts. However, today, Romania's exports are very low. Therefore, most fruits are used domestically and are popular in the form of preserves, syrups, and spirits. Plums are used to make tuica (plum brandy) as well as *cozonaci* (sweet bread).

Meat consumption in Romania has fluctuated in relation to social circumstances. It is still fairly low compared to the European average. Pork is the preferred meat for most Romanians. It is used on festive occasions, especially at Christmas, as well as being consumed regularly. Romania produces some of its pig meat; however, it is one of the country's largest food imports. Poultry, mainly chicken, is quite popular, especially among the peasant population, who often rear their own chickens. Beef is consumed to a lesser extent, although there are regional differences. Beef is eaten more frequently in the north of Romania. Other animal products eaten regularly include eggs, a small amount of mutton, and animal fats, which are used for cooking.

The Danube Delta is the second-largest delta in Europe after the Volga. The majority of the delta lies within Romania, with a small part in the Ukraine, and provides a rich source of seafood. Sturgeon, pike, carp, tuna, bream, perch, mackerel, and sterlet are all found here. Herring and mackerel are commonly eaten, often pickled, and there is a long history of eating caviar, which dates back to the Ottoman era.

In Romania wine is often served with meals. Grapes are grown mainly in the eastern part of the country and include common international varieties, such as sauvignon blanc and cabernet sauvignon, as well as indigenous varieties, such as Feteasca Alba, Grasa de Cotnari, and Feteasca Neagra. The Romanian sweet wine, *cotnari,* is compared to some of Europe's finest wines. However, tuica is Romania's national drink and is served for special occasions as well as with daily meals. Much of the tuica drunk is homemade. *Palinca,* a stronger twice-filtered plum brandy, is also commonly drunk. Soft drinks have become a popular beverage since the opening of Romania to the free market economy. Milk is also consumed fresh, especially in rural areas, where people produce much of the milk they use.

Much of Romanian food is characterized by the use of sour ingredients. Sour cream is abundant in Romanian cooking and can be served on top of mamaliga or with crepes, stewed meat, and *bors* (sour beef soup). Sometimes sorrel or sour cabbage is added to food or used as a side dish to give it a sour tang. Spices are also frequently used, especially paprika, although there are regional differences in the strength and frequency of use.

Cooking

As with Romanian food culture in general, cooking was largely shaped by social circumstances and the customs and culture of different peoples. For example, the commonly eaten Romanian grilled meats have their origins in techniques introduced by Gypsies, who were slaves in the kitchens of the nobles up until the 19th century. A French style of cooking is evident and is a result of the culinary exchanges between France and Romania in the 19th century. During this period, many Romanians traveled to France to learn about French cuisine. Bucharest became known as "the little Paris" after French influences swept through the city in the 19th and 20th centuries. Buildings were designed by French architects, and many French restaurants opened their doors. In the 19th century French cooks were brought into many aristocratic kitchens. However, it was the Ottoman Empire that was responsible for introducing many common cooking implements as well as the use of the spices that are prevalent today.

For much of Romania's history there has been a large peasant population. This has influenced styles of cooking and the types of implements used as well as the cultural value of hospitality, which centers around the kitchen. Traditionally, women are the main cooks both in their homes and for occasions involving the community. Today, the kitchens in Romania vary from a very rustic style to standard modern ones. However, they are generally more straightforward and simple compared to the western European standards.

Soups, stews, and mamaliga are made either in a deep pot on the stovetop or in a *caldare* (large pot) on an open fire. Mamaliga is stirred continuously with a wooden spoon or stick called a *facalet* while the cornmeal is added. A typical peasant kitchen traditionally consists of an open fire in the center, over which the mamaliga can be cooked. Mamaliga may be placed onto a wooden board, eaten hot and served directly onto plates, or left to cool and sliced. Mamaliga is also sometimes baked in the oven with cheese. Some dishes, such as pilaf, make use of both the stovetop and the oven. Foods such as *cascaval pane* (breaded cheese) are fried in a pan, although baking and grilling are more common.

In a rural setting, ovens may be wood fired inside or outside the house, or they may be standard electric or gas ovens. The oven is used widely in Romanian cooking for baking *sarmale* (stuffed cabbage leaves), *ardei umpluti* (stuffed peppers), *morun pescaresc* (baked sturgeon), and *budinca* (baked savory or sweet puddings) and for roasting meat. Breads and cakes, both ritual and daily, are baked either in regular ovens or in special wood-fired bread ovens. *Colac* molds or bread tins are used to shape the colaci, the most common ritual bread used for special occasions in Romania. The bride's colaci is ritually prepared by the groom's mother or the bride's mother, or the marriage godmother. It is often knotted or circular (special molds are used), and it is decorated with motifs.

Grilling is a common way to cook meats. The Romanian mixed grill is a popular dish containing the ubiquitous *mititei* (sausage-shaped patties of pork and/or beef) served with grilled pork ribs, pork chops, sausage, and, sometimes, grilled pig kidneys, liver, and brain. As in many other eastern European and Balkan countries, Romanians have a tradition of cooking outdoors. Temporary or permanent structures are made to roast meat, sometimes a whole pig or lamb over a wood fire. The men traditionally do this. Fishermen living near the Danube Delta sometimes cook *uha* (fish soup) over an open fire.

Preserving has its place in Romanian cooking, allowing seasonal produce that is harvested to be eaten throughout the year. Vegetables are often pickled in vinegar and served alongside meats. Fruits are made into syrups, jams, or dulceata. A traditional Romanian kitchen is well stocked with dulceata to serve with coffee in anticipation of the arrival of guests.

Stuffing is a common cooking method in Romania. Vegetables such as peppers, cabbage, mushrooms, and grape leaves are filled with rice, meats, and spices. One of the most common Romanian dishes is sarmale, or stuffed cabbage leaves. This dish is commonly found in other Balkan cuisines but holds a special place in Romanian cooking and is usually accompanied by mamaliga.

Sarmale cu varza (Stuffed Cabbage Leaves)

Ingredients

1 large savoy cabbage

2 tbsp olive oil

2 onions, finely chopped

2 stalks celery, finely chopped

1 tbsp white rice

½ c hot water

1½ lb ground beef, veal, or pork

1 tbsp parsley, finely chopped

Salt

Pepper

½ tbsp paprika

5 fresh tomatoes, coarsely chopped

3 tbsp tomato paste

Juice of half a lemon

2 cloves garlic

Break off the cabbage leaves, and cut out the hard spine of each leaf. In a large pot, bring to a boil enough water to cover the cabbage. Immerse cabbage in salted boiling water. Cover and cook over medium-high heat for 5 to 10 minutes. Gently remove leaves as they become tender. Drain well; let cool and dry.

In a large frying pan over medium heat, add oil, onions, celery, and rice, and sauté until light golden brown; add hot water and cover, allowing the rice to absorb the water. Remove from heat and let cool.

In a bowl, mix together the meat, parsley, salt, pepper, paprika, and the rice mixture. Lay out the cabbage leaves on a wooden board, reserving the small leaves. Place a spoonful of the meat filling in the center of a cabbage leaf. Fold the right-hand side of the leaf over the filling, then roll from the base to the bottom of leaf, then with the index finger gently tuck the left-hand side of the leaf into the cabbage roll to make a nice neat roll. Repeat until all meat is used up.

Chop the small cabbage leaves and any leftovers, and place half in the bottom of a casserole dish along with half the tomatoes. Arrange cabbage rolls tightly on top of the mixture in a casserole dish, seam side down. Then sprinkle the rest of the cabbage and tomatoes on top. Dilute the tomato paste in 4 cups of water, add the lemon juice and garlic, and pour over the rolls. Cover and bake for 1 hour at 325°F. Serve with sour cream and mamaliga.

Typical Meals

Typical meals in Romania need to be divided according to two demographics: urban and rural. There are vast differences between urban and rural meal patterns in terms of what is eaten and the manner in which it is eaten. The rural population is characterized by a more traditional eating pattern. Since 2000, the urban populations have been increasingly exposed to foods typical of the West. Breakfasts in an urban setting are generally light and consist of a coffee, either Western or Turkish style, a pastry or toast, and less frequently a boiled egg or omelet. Yogurt and breakfast cereals have also become more popular recently. In a rural setting, the breakfast is more substantial. A typical rural household may serve hot mamaliga with cold fresh milk, or breakfast could consist of wheat bread, eggs made into an omelet or boiled, vegetables, cold meats, and cheese. Turkish-style coffee is common here.

Romania is still largely a religious nation, with 86 percent of the population identifying themselves as members of the Romanian Orthodox Church. Fasting is a central part of the religion, which has dramatically shaped the culture of Romanian meals. Today, it is not practiced as widely in urban settings. Up to 192 days of the year, meals without meat, dairy, or eggs must be eaten, and fish can be eaten only on some days.

Lunch has traditionally been the most important meal of the day. It is usually eaten in the early afternoon but can vary between 1 and 4 P.M. In its

complete form, lunch will consist of four courses. However, not all Romanians will partake of all four courses daily. Where people live and what their financial situation is will affect what and how much is typically eaten. Today, many people employed in urban centers do not have the time or the financial capacity for such lunches.

Lunch regularly starts with a glass of tuica, which is drunk with snacks called *mezea* (from the Turkish *meze*). The mezea was introduced by the Turks and means a selection of light foods that are accompanied by a beverage. The Romanian mezea often features up to eight items. Most commonly found on the mezea plate is mititei, small sausages or sausage-shaped patties of pork and/or beef that are grilled. Other mezea items include cheese, such as cascaval, telemea, and brinza, which are sometimes cooked or served as fresh slices; *pastrama* (dried cured meats, typically made with beef or mutton); caviar, which is popular; fish served in a variety of ways; ham; preserved vegetables; salads; and fruits. Often the mezea are followed by a soup course. Ciorba is the most common soup in Romania. Ciorba is a sour soup made in a variety of styles with many different ingredients and sometimes topped with sour cream. There is *ciorba de burta* (with tripe), *ciorba de perisoare* (spicy and made with meatballs), *ciorba de legume* (with vegetables), and more. Soup may be followed by mamaliga and sarmale (stuffed cabbage leaves) or a meat or fish dish. Either Turkish or

Decorated Easter eggs in a basket displayed for sale at a Romanian country fair. (iStockPhoto)

Western coffee is served with a dessert. Desserts tend to be sweet pastry, such as baklava or *papanasi* (cheese- or cream-filled pastry), *clatite* (crepes), *cozonac* (sweet bread served at Easter), or *kuros kalacs* (large donuts). Supper or dinner is often lighter than lunch and is eaten around 9 P.M.

Mititei (Grilled Sausage Rolls)

Mititei is one of the most common Romanian foods. They can be served as part of a mezea, in the center of a mixed grill of meats, or as a main dish.

9 oz minced pork

9 oz minced beef

I onion, finely chopped

2 garlic cloves, crushed

½ tsp baking powder

¼ tsp thyme

I tsp paprika

Salt and pepper

I slice white bread, moistened with a little water

I tbsp olive oil, for frying

3 tbsp chicken or vegetable stock

Method
Combine all the ingredients, apart from the olive oil and stock, together in a large mixing bowl. Knead for about 5 minutes. The ingredients must be very well combined. Let the mixture sit for at least I hour. Divide the mixture into small handfuls, and roll into small sausage shapes. Brush with oil, and grill on a barbecue or fry in a pan for 10–15 minutes. Turn them several times during cooking, and baste with a little stock to keep them moist, if you like. Serve with pickled vegetables and salad or as an appetizer.

Typical meals change from region to region, revealing some of Romania's history as well as that of its neighboring countries. In Transylvania there is a distinct cuisine that reflects the history of its inhabitants: Hungarians, German Saxons, and Romanians. Foods are commonly flavored with tarragon, dill, lovage, savory, mustard, and horseradish. A Germanic influence can be seen in dishes like *knodeln* (dumplings), bratwurst (beef or pork sausages), and *auflauf* (baked pudding). In the regions of Maramures and Moldavia in the north and northeast of Romania, a Russian influence is evident in the greater use of beef as in dishes such as bors (beef soup) and *galusti* (Russian *galoushki,* or dumplings). Foods are generally spicier in the Banat region. In the Danube Delta region, meals typically feature a lot of fish.

Mamaliga is still considered the national dish by many Romanians. It is a versatile food, often served on the side of meat or vegetables or topped with cheese and sour cream. It is served either hot or cold and for breakfast, lunch, or dinner. It is made by cooking cornmeal with water (sometimes milk) and salt and is similar to Italian polenta. Mamaliga is commonly known as a peasant food, since during much of the 19th and 20th centuries, peasants, who made up the majority of the population, ate mamaliga on a daily basis.

Eating Out

A culture of eating out was prevalent among travelers and the elite in the 19th and early 20th centuries. Many accounts of foods in Romanian restaurants, inns, hotels, and cafés in the 19th century came from travelers, who noticed the diversity of cultural influences. They also noted sophistication and a cosmopolitan choice in large cities and good simple fare in the country. Throughout history Bucharest was a rich melting pot of cuisines and was the location where restaurants first opened in the first half of the 19th century. Many other food establishments and food merchants proliferated in Bucharest at this time. French, Romanian, and German restaurants were found, alongside Turkish and Greek cafés and street vendors, wine merchants, and bakeries. Even though the Communist regime saw the closing of many restaurants, today Bucharest is a thriving multicultural culinary destination.

For a lot of Romanians today, eating out is a luxury and reserved for special occasions. With many people struggling to provide basic food requirements, there is not much left in the budget for dining out. In many rural settings, in the past and at present, eating out means eating at the house of family or friends, since there is a strong culture of home cooking. However, there is a growing pattern, in large cities, of Romanians working longer hours in order to increase their income. The result is that people have less time to cook at home and may rely on take-out food or sometimes restaurants for dinners. Fast-food outlets are becoming popular, which is demonstrated by the increasing number of McDonald's, Pizza Hut, KFC, and other less-known outlets. The small upper class in Romania has the opportunity to eat out more frequently. Large cities provide many options for eating out in restaurants and cafés. People living in or visiting Bucharest can choose from a range of international cuisines as well as Romanian when they eat out.

Special Occasions

In Romania, food is strongly linked to life transitions and celebrations, especially weddings, births, and deaths, and to religious holidays. In these contexts, food holds significant symbolic meaning for people. The most common foods of traditional ceremonies are colaci (ritual bread), cake, honey, milk, eggs, and wine or tuica. Where religious holidays are concerned, periods of fasting are broken with the preparation and eating of certain meats.

Ritual bread, known as colaci or *colac*, is a fundamental element of all Romanian customary events. The making of the bread as well as the breaking of bread, looking through the central hole in the bread, and the kissing of bread are all significant activities seen in traditional ceremonies. Colaci is usually circular or ring shaped and often adorned with motifs, such as flowers, birds, and the cross, or with fresh basil. In the context of a wedding, colaci, known as bride's colaci, is often pleated, and considerable time goes into its decoration. It is a principal symbol within the wedding feast and sometimes sits in the center of the wedding table. Ritual bread features at significant moments throughout the wedding, which can last up to three days.

Weddings today are varied, from traditional long weddings to more modern, simplified, and shorter occasions. However, key foods are still commonly used. Sarmale (stuffed cabbage) is commonly part of a wedding feast. In traditional settings chicken features in a ceremonial part of the wedding called *horea gainii* (the song of the hen). The cook brings out a roasted chicken that is adorned with greenery and plates of bread, and then a series of songs and theatrical interactions follows. Toasting is also a very important part of the wedding and is usually done with wine or tuica. Sour soup, ciorba, is frequently served on the final day of three-day weddings to revive revelers.

In a funeral setting, colaci with a coin baked into it is sometimes placed in the coffin. In some regions small colaci are given out to the guests. The traditional food at a funeral is *coliva,* which is a cake made specifically for funerals. Coliva is made from boiled wheat, sugar, honey, and pounded nut kernels. Wine or contemporarily tuica is used in funeral settings and is drunk by the mourners as well as offered to the dead. A funeral meal often takes place preceding the funeral.

The traditional Romanian year is characterized by periods of fasting and feasting. In the Communist era many of these patterns were disrupted; however, many traditions relating to food are still practiced, especially in rural settings. At its strictest, fasting can occupy 192 days out of the year. This includes 40 days leading up to Christmas, six weeks leading up to Easter, and Wednesdays and Fridays, along with other religious saint's days. Fasting is less common today, but many of the food traditions associated with the breaking of fasts are still practiced. At Christmastime a whole pig is roasted. In a rural setting the pig may be slaughtered and roasted on an open-fire spit; otherwise, it is cooked in an oven. Cozonac is a ceremonial sweet bread that is eaten at Christmas and Easter. Easter is followed in a traditional Eastern Orthodox manner. The most important food traditions include painting chicken eggs, usually in red; making and eating *pasca,* a traditional Easter cake; eating lamb; and bringing foods to church in baskets to be blessed.

Diet and Health

Many Romanians who lived through the Communist period and its aftermath know too well the close relationship between food and health. In the harshest years of the regime, food shortages were a part of daily life. Under the presidency of Nicolae Ceausescu from 1967 to 1989, money was being spent on the development of grand buildings, and food was being exported to pay off debt, while programs such as the Rational Nourishment Commission were implemented to hide the fact that there was not enough food for the nation. Understandably, today, many Romanians view health and nutrition campaigns with suspicion. The Communist period continued to influence health in Romania even after the expulsion of Ceausescu and the opening of Romania to a free trade economy. From the early 1990s Romania had to completely rebuild systems of health care and food production and distribution. Subsidies that had been in place for many foods were removed. Real incomes were low, and food prices high. In the mid-1990s more than half the population lived below the poverty line, and many households spent as much as 70 percent of their income on food. All of this had a negative impact on the health of much of the Romanian population. Low life expectancies and high levels of diseases related to lifestyle have been reported for much of the period after the collapse of the Communist regime.

The situation today has largely improved. However, the health of Romanians, and people living in many other former Soviet states, is still below the European Union average, based on a number of health indicators. Diet plays an important part in this. Romania has registered a high number of diseases that relate to poverty and inadequate nutrition. Many studies indicate that poor diet and alcohol and tobacco consumption, particularly among men, have contributed to poor health in Romania. The high consumption of fats and oils and calories of low quality from the point of view of nutritional standards is likely to be a contributing factor.

Fruit and vegetable consumption in Romania has fluctuated and at times has been considerably lower than the recommended daily intake. This is partly due to issues of food scarcity and high prices and partly due to the style of the cuisine. While vegetable intake has increased in recent years, the percentage of potatoes that contribute to this has, too. The higher consumption of potatoes and cereals as major caloric items means that intake of many vitamins and minerals is reduced. Low fruit and vegetable intake, according to the World Health Organization, is one of the leading factors in many of the health issues faced by Romania today. However, the produce that is eaten is normally fresh, since much of it is produced locally, and it generally contains low levels of chemicals because of the high costs of herbicides and pesticides.

Kate Johnston

Further Reading

Alexandri, Cecilia, and Cornelia Alboia. "The Romanian Food Consumption Model in the Context of European Union Integration." In *Traditional Food Production and Rural Sustainable Development, A European Challenge,* edited by Theresa de Noronha Vaz, Peter Nijkamp, and Jean-Louis Rastoin, 151–64. Farnham, Surrey, UK: Ashgate, 2009.

Cazacu, Matei. *The Story of Romanian Gastronomy.* Bucharest: Romanian Cultural Foundation, 1999.

Chamberlain, Lesley. *The Food and Cooking of Eastern Europe.* London: Penguin, 1989.

Kavena-Johnson, Maria. *Romania: The Melting Pot, Balkan Food and Cookery.* Totnes, Devon, UK: Prospect Books, 1999.

Petrovici, Dan A., and Christopher Riston. "Food Consumption Patterns in Romania." *British Food Journal* 102 (2000): 290–308.

"Romanian Cuisine." Balkan-Cuisine.com. http://romania.balkan-cuisine.com/.

Sperber, Galia. *The Art of Romanian Cooking.* Gretna, LA: Pelican, 2002.

Russia

Overview

Once considered a gastronomic wasteland, Russia's remarkable and delectable cuisine again is finding its way onto the world stage through commerce, travel, and media coverage. Moscow is becoming a center of culinary innovation in the early 21st century, quickly erasing bitter images of the empty food shelves and state-run restaurants of the Soviet era. Centuries of scarcity, deprivation, and hardship have shaped Slavic culinary aesthetics. Therefore, Russians approach every meal with an unrivaled gusto and sincere appreciation—be it beer and crayfish, or champagne and caviar.

Russia is an inscrutable land on many levels, beginning with the sheer quantity and quality of available foodstuffs. The size of its territory, the variety of its ethnic groups, and its stark history challenge the imagination. The 19th-century Russian Empire included Ukraine, the Baltic nations, the Caucasus, Central Asia, and Siberia. The nation was blessed with an abundance of fish from its waters; fruits and nuts from the southern regions; endless variations of grains and hearty breads; the wild game of the forest; and the rewarding berries and mushrooms of the woods. These ingredients remain in Russia today to form the basis of its extraordinary cuisine.

The Russian Federation is the political remnant of the Russian and Soviet empires. Geographically, the Russian Federation stretches from the Baltic Sea to the Pacific Ocean and spans 11 time zones. Siberia alone makes up 10 percent of the earth's inhabited landmass. Culturally, however, Russia is larger still, extending beyond its imperial boundaries via Russian-language media, established trade patterns,

and the presence of its military on the former borders of the Soviet Union.

The 2002 census counted 160 different nationalities in the country, although Russians comprise almost 80 percent of the 145.2 million total citizens. Kazan Tatars number almost six million citizens, making them the second most numerous nationality. Other ethnic groups in Russia that exceed one million people include Ukrainians, Bashkirs, Chuvash, Chechens, and Armenians. This demographic diversity allows Russians to claim most any dish as their own national foods, such as pilaf, dumplings (*pelmeni*), eggplant "caviar," or Baltic herring. Incomes and lifestyles in Russia are very stratified, especially since the fall of Communism in 1991. Social stratification is the single most important factor in understanding Russian society throughout its history.

🍽 Food Culture Snapshot

Sergei and Katya Aleksandrov are a well-to-do married couple in their late thirties living in a suburb of Moscow with their twins, Sofia and Vassili, who are three years old. Katya works part-time as an accountant, and Sergei sells cars through one of Moscow's larger dealerships. Their combined incomes allow them to employ a full-time nanny to care for the children and help with housekeeping. Their salary also allows them to eat better-quality food and to afford occasional imported European gourmet items, but their core food choices are very mainstream and representative of the larger population. Russians are very particular about their diet and expend much energy in the acquisition

A woman makes pelmeni, a traditional Russian dumpling, by hand. (iStockPhoto)

and preparation of food. Russians, on average, spend more than one-third of their income on food, a much higher amount than in Britain or the United States.

At a minimum, the Russian pantry will always have potatoes, carrots, onions, butter, and sunflower oil. No traditional dish can be prepared without these basic ingredients. Ketchup, mustard, and spicy horseradish are popular as condiments, and mayonnaise is always on hand for use in traditional Russian potato salads. No spices are really necessary save for salt and ground black pepper, although some families, like the Aleksandrovs, like to experiment with Asian ingredients and various spice mixes.

For the parents, breakfast is dominated by bread and dairy, specifically, traditional Russian soft farmer's cheese, *tvorog*, mixed with sour cream and honey. The

children eat freshly prepared hot cereal. Popular varieties of hot cereal include oatmeal, cream of wheat, and porridges made from buckwheat, barley, or millet. Hot sweet black tea is the preferred breakfast drink, although sometimes adults prepare instant coffee. The twins drink whole milk.

During the day, Katya and Sergei eat lunch at work. Most large offices have their own cafeterias with a selection of hot dishes, sandwiches, and salads. The nanny makes a hot lunch for the children, often one of the following dishes: vegetable or chicken noodle soup, meatballs with mashed potatoes, beef stew, or chicken cutlets. All main dishes are accompanied by bread and fresh tomatoes and cucumbers. Lunch concludes with a snack of fresh fruit.

Generally, everyone gathers for the main meal of the day around eight o'clock in the evening. Katya is a good cook with a well-developed repertoire of dishes that are hearty yet quick to prepare. Even with full-time help at home, Katya prefers to do most of the cooking herself. She always prepares cereal in the morning, which can take up to an hour (there is no instant oatmeal), and she makes the majority of family dinners. Sometimes the leftovers are served for lunch the next day.

Almost daily the family purchases bread, both wheat and rye, and fresh vegetables such as cucumbers, tomatoes, and dill fronds, parsley, and green onions. Broccoli and cauliflower have only recently become staples of the Russian diet. Pickled vegetables are enjoyed year-round, and cabbage, carrots, and beets dominate the winter menu. The family consumes fruits regularly until the season changes: strawberries, cherries, raspberries, apricots, and peaches in the summer; apples and melons in the fall; and oranges, apples, grapes, and bananas in winter and spring.

The Aleksandrov household would grind to a halt without sour cream and kefir (fermented milk). The amount of milk and milk products Russians consume is surpassed only by the quantity of bread they eat, whether they are city dwellers or country folk. Where the cow is sacred in India, it is part of the family in Russia. Cattle provide some of the products most dear to Russians—milk, cream, fermented drinks, cheese, butter, yogurt, sour cream, and ice cream. Dairy products are the largest segment of Russian agricultural exports after sunflower oil, namely, condensed milk and cream, yogurt, butter and milk fats, sour milk, cheese, and curds.

The Aleksandrovs' main protein choices are usually beef, pork, lamb, and chicken. The family enjoys smoked fish as an appetizer. Another important kitchen ingredient is ground beef. The Aleksandrovs use it to make meatballs and cutlets, stuffed vegetables, and the gem of Russian cuisine, pelmeni, similar to ravioli or Chinese dumplings. In a pinch, store-bought frozen pelmeni with sour cream make for a modest dinner. The Aleksandrovs, unusual for a Russian family, have recently sworn off any kind of processed meats—sausages, hams, salami, and so on. Sausage is a daily staple of the Russian diet: for breakfast with cheese and bread, as part of a lunch, as a snack, and for appetizers. Initially, the Aleksandrovs were prompted to forgo sausage in response to their son's suspected allergic reactions, but after a while they realized that they did not miss it much and felt better without it. For a typical Russian family, several types of sausage would be among the daily food purchases.

Approximately twice a month, Sergei does bulk shopping in METRO, which is similar to warehouse stores in the United States. He buys grains, dried pasta, tea, coffee, sugar, household supplies, basic toiletries, and some canned goods. Like most Russians, the Aleksandrovs use few canned or prepared foods. They buy all their meats, dairy, fruit, and vegetables fresh on a daily basis. Usually Katya buys whatever is needed for the day on her way home from work. Produce is frequently purchased at roadside stands. Occasionally, the family will make a weekend trip to a large farmers' market for a larger selection of produce, fresh dairy, and meats.

Major Foodstuffs

The foods generally associated with Russia include hearty breads; fresh, smoked, and cured sausages; and winter vegetables such as cabbage, beets, and potatoes. Although the beverage that immediately comes to mind with Russia is vodka, the national drink is actually tea. Russians today without difficulty consider all the following foods to be part of their cuisine: Baltic herring and rye breads, Pacific salmon, Siberian ferns and pine nuts, Asian dumplings, Korean pickled vegetables, Central Asian pilaf, shish kebabs from the Caucasus, Romanian *brynza* (feta cheese), Bulgarian peppers, and eggplant from the Middle East.

Throughout the seasons, the markets present an amazing variety of foodstuffs. Starting with the unprocessed or bulk section, the pantry traditionally contains a selection of grains and flours; pulses and dried beans; vegetable oils sold in reused plastic bottles; walnuts, almonds, and pistachios; macaroni and vermicelli for soups; rice; and dried apricots, raisins, and dates. The vegetables, in order of quantities sold, include potatoes, cabbage, carrots, tomatoes, cucumbers, beets, turnips, and radishes. Besides apples, pears, and berries, most fruits come from the southern regions or are imported. Though rarely perfect in shape, marked with minor external blemishes, and small in size, most of the fruits and vegetables have a vibrant and distinctive taste.

Pickled garlic, peppers, and cucumbers are almost always locally produced and homemade. Most markets have a Korean food section with prepared dishes of spicy pickled vegetables and fish. In the dairy-products section, vendors sell sour cream, fresh cheese (tvorog), aged cheeses, yogurt, and kefir by volume in recycled glass bottles or larger plastic containers.

Grains—specifically, rye, buckwheat, barley, oats, millet, and wheat—are the main staples. Cereals (seeds of cultivated grasses) are of central importance to Russia, so much so that they in many ways define the national cuisine. They form the basis for the delectable breads, filling gruels, savory pies, pancakes (*bliny*), and dumplings.

Bread buttresses the Russian diet, symbolizing sustenance and hospitality. Russians consume an amazing two pounds of bread per person a day. It is the ubiquitous delight of every meal. The very word for hospitality, *khlebosol'stvo,* derives from the roots *khleb* (bread) and *sol'* (salt), which were traditionally presented to guests as a sign of welcome, warmth, and generosity. In almost-endless varieties, most tables are graced with slices of both white wheat bread and dark rye or black bread.

Kasha, or boiled buckwheat groats, is a Russian cultural superfood, and it is difficult to overrate the symbolic importance of a food that has nourished a people for more than 1,000 years. It can be boiled with milk or water, prepared sweet or savory, and served for breakfast or as a side dish. Smaller groats are often used to make a more liquid kasha with only milk. Buckwheat kasha can be prepared with almost anything mixed in—eggs, pork, pork fat, liver, onions, mushrooms, fruits, cheese, and so forth. The first buckwheat varieties originated in parts of Siberia and China. As the largest consumer of buckwheat worldwide, Russia is also the number-one producer of the crop. Today, kasha can refer to almost any porridge made from any groats, such as cream of wheat, rice pudding, hot oatmeal, or less commonly barley or millet porridge.

Pies (*pirogi*) in Russia come in a dizzying array of preparations and presentations. The dough can be leavened or not, salty or sweet. Pies can be round, square, triangular, open, closed, large, small, or fully enclosed like the classic salmon *kulebyaka* (*coulibiac*—a complex pastry with salmon, spinach, and rice), for example.

Bliny, one of the few Russian foods known internationally, are small pancakes a little larger in size than a compact disc (five to six inches in diameter). They are a traditional dish at the spring equinox folk festival, Maslenitsa, perhaps symbolizing the sun with their round shape. The yeast batter is what makes the taste and texture distinctive. Piled high with a pat of butter between the pancake layers, bliny provoke a festive reaction. Though traditionally made with buckwheat flour, wheat-flour bliny are now more common.

Macaroni and vermicelli are made from wheat flour and are commonly added to soups. Buttered macaroni is a common side dish that may be served with any meal. The most famous Slavic pasta dishes are pelmeni and *vareniki*, boiled, filled dumplings. Vareniki are usually larger and often half-moon or triangular shaped, and they come from Ukraine. During the summer, vareniki are filled with cherries, plums, or berries. They can also be made with potatoes, mushrooms, soft cheese, cabbage, and meat. Pelmeni and savory vareniki are generally topped with melted butter or sour cream, but vinegar, mustard, and ketchup are also possible additions.

Russians have a hearty appetite for vegetables, usually served in soups or separately as a pickled dish. Cooked vegetables are also a main component of many salads. Fresh salads are generally made with sliced cucumbers and tomatoes, not leafy greens. Turnips, cabbages, radishes, and cucumbers are considered traditional Russian vegetables. Carrots, onions, and garlic provide the flavors for many savory dishes. One salad that incorporates almost all the customary Russian vegetables is *vinegret* (made from potatoes, pickled cabbage, and beets in oil).

Potatoes, after bread, sustain the population. The most common and preferred method of preparation is peeled boiled potatoes, garnished with butter, dill, and sour cream. Fried potatoes, similar to home fries, are also widespread. They become exceptionally enticing when fried with bacon and mushrooms.

Russia and cabbage are inextricably bound, and rightfully so. No self-respecting Russian can survive long without fermented or sour cabbage (*kvashenaya kapusta*). Cabbage is an extremely versatile vegetable, great in soups, stews, salads, stuffings, and side dishes. The sulfurous scent of cooked cabbage seems to permanently saturate most modern apartment blocks in Russia. Cabbage soup (*shchi*) rates among the most popular national dishes.

Cucumbers, especially the pickled variety, also have a special place in the Russian culinary psyche. Russian pickled cucumbers, like sauerkraut, are pickled in brine and not vinegar. Fresh and pickled cucumbers are added to many hot and cold dishes. It is not uncommon to find salads that contain both pickled and fresh cucumbers.

Whereas potatoes, cabbages, and cucumbers are essential components of the Russian table, mushrooms create magic in the meal. Mushrooms, or *griby*, are neither plants nor animals, but Russians would swear they have a soul. Many civilizations, including the Slavs, have relied on mushrooms for medicinal purposes, and mushroom hunting in Russia remains a national obsession. Considering the expanse of forest and the assortment of mushrooms, many a lazy day can pass in search of the perfect mushroom patch.

The turnip (*repa*), rutabaga (*bryukva*), and red beet (*svyokla*) form the rearguard of traditional Russian vegetables. Turnips, often pureed or cooked together with meat dishes, were the staple crop of northern Russia until well into the 18th century. Beets were better known in the area of Ukraine, although they are now firmly established as part of the Russian culinary repertoire. The most famous dish from beets is borscht, a beef-based soup with beets, cabbage, and bell pepper.

Countless other vegetables are grown on private plots or at the dacha (small vacation house). Tomatoes, squash, zucchini, radishes, bell peppers, peas, green beans, cauliflower, and leafy greens add color and zest to the Russian table. Many vegetables, especially eggplant, are made into spreads or a "caviar," which is a cooked mixture of vegetables with tomatoes, onions, garlic, oil, and vinegar that preserves well.

Fruit production is difficult in northerly climes. Therefore, apples, pears, and forest berries are the most common fruits in Russia. Many other fruits are brought in from the southern regions, particularly peaches, cherries, plums, and melons. Watermelons from Astrakhan on the Volga River delta near the Caspian Sea compete with those from Central Asia and the Caucasus in Russian markets. The best melons, however, are imported from Central Asia, along with grapes, dried apricots, and raisins.

Berries and cherries are the quintessential fruits of Russia. The sour cherry (*vishnya*) and the black cherry (*chereshnya*) are the most common varieties. The bountiful assortment of berries is similar to that of Scandinavia, Canada, and the northern United States. Popular varieties include the raspberry (*malina*); the gooseberry (*kryzhovnik*); the cranberry (*klyukva*); the berry known variously as the lingonberry, bilberry, huckleberry, and whortleberry (*brusnika*); the blueberry (*chernika*); the rowanberry or ashberry (*ryabina*); and currants—red, black, and white (*smorodina*). The delicious strawberry (*klubnika*) and the wild strawberry (*zemlyanika*) are a special treat. The berries can be eaten raw as well as frozen or dried for later use. But more often than not they are made into rich preserves, jams, and jellies used in desserts and to sweeten tea.

Fish is most commonly served as a smoked, cured, or salted appetizer. Salted Baltic herring (*sel'd'* or *selyodka*), by far the most abundant and popular, is found in many cold salads or served plain with oil and onions. A mixed platter of cold smoked fish (*rybnoe assorti*) served as appetizers may include thin slices of eel, mackerel, sturgeon, whitefish, turbot (*paltus*), shad, and salmon.

Other familiar fish are prepared by panfrying, broiling, or baking, such as salmon trout (*forel'*), carp (*sazan*), perch (*sudak* and *okun'*), cod (*navaga* and *nalim*), flounder, northern pike (*shchuka*), and catfish (*som*). Caviar, or fish eggs, is the product most often associated with Russia. The familiar dark or black caviar comes from three particular species of sturgeon: *beluga, osetra,* and *sevruga.* The larger, bright red-orange caviar is roe harvested from the Siberian salmon (*keta*). It is considerably less expensive than black caviar. Recently, trout roe has become a popular addition to the caviar line in Russia.

A family of freshwater fish, abundant in rivers, lakes, canals, and reservoirs, the roach fish (*vobla*) is perhaps the most humble yet emblematic Russian fish. Salted and dried, it is sold in every market. Paired with beer, it is analogous to the American combination of nuts and beer. Nothing promises a

A Russian delicacy, borscht, is a beet root soup served with sour cream. (Shutterstock)

better evening than several whole dried vobla laid out on a newspaper tablecloth.

It is difficult to exaggerate the importance of meat in the Russian diet. Whether meat is served as an entrée or an appetizer, or simply a frankfurter or a sausage, no meal is considered fully satisfying without some form of meat on the plate. Russia is among the world's leading producers, consumers, and importers of meat. Beef, pork, poultry, and mutton—in order of preference and consumption—constitute the primary protein types. Shish kebabs (*shashlyk*) are the ideal method for preparing any meat or poultry in Russia. Marinated meat threaded onto metal skewers is slowly grilled, roasted, and smoked over the gentle heat of charcoal embers.

In addition to shashlyk, beef is generally prepared as fried or baked individual cuts, as part of soups and stews, or as mincemeat for meatballs or various fillings. *Zharkoe* is a stew of roasted meat, potatoes, and vegetables, traditionally baked in small earthenware pots for hours on the Russian hearth. Sautéed ground beef patties, *kotlety,* are perhaps the most common meat dish. Ground beef is mixed with breadcrumbs and diced onions and panfried. *Frikadelki,* from the German *Frikadellen,* are small meatballs simmered in broth. Ground meat mixed with onions also creates the common fillings for *pirozhki* (dumplings), *golubtsy* (cabbage rolls), and *chebureki* (Crimean Tatar fried meat pies).

Internationally, Russia is probably best known for its sausages. Although the brunt of foreign jokes and derision, Russian *kolbasa* can rival the finest Italian salami and German wurst in quality. Sausage is generally made from both pork and beef. Rows of fresh sausages, liverwurst, frankfurters, and links fill store display cases. The most prevalent is the cured sausage—smoked, dried, or both. Ham (*vetchina*) is the most common cured pork product. Among the most flavorful, however, is *buzhenina,* salted and smoked pork loin. The Ukrainian love for pork has made its way into Russia in the form of *salo,* cured pork backfat.

The primary herbs in Russian cuisine are parsley and dill (*pertrushka* and *ukrop*). They are found on almost every table in a variety of guises: as a dish of whole stalks, an ingredient in most salads, an added flavor for soups and stews, and a garnish for these same dishes. Bay leaves and sweet paprika are often added to soups and stews. In making many Central Asian or Caucasian dishes, cilantro (fresh coriander) is essential. Seasonings are minimal; usually only salt and black or red (paprika) pepper are used in cooking and also found in shakers on the dining tables. Anise, allspice, cloves, cinnamon, and nutmeg are sparingly applied to some pastries and baked goods. Sweeteners traditionally include honey, jams, jellies, and dried or preserved fruits. The most common condiments are mayonnaise, sour cream, butter, vinegar, horseradish, mustard, ketchup, and a couple of Georgian spicy sauces. Mayonnaise is found in every sort of Russian salad, sometimes mixed with sour cream. Horseradish (*khren*) is grated and mixed with vinegar and served with meat dishes.

In marketing terms, Russia and vodka are inextricable. In reality, however, tea retains the title of the Russian national drink. Beer is the trendy and affordable beverage of choice of the younger generations, while traditional drinks such as *kvas* (made from fermented rye bread), *kisel'* (made from berries), *sbiten'* (made from honey and spices), and mead (*myod*) still hold an important, if not purely symbolic and nostalgic, place in Russian culinary thought and action. Tea (*chai*) is consumed at breakfast, lunch, and dinner. It is served in the afternoon and as a late-night drink. Russian tea, with lemon and sugar cubes, is served piping hot in porcelain cups with saucers or in glasses with metal holders. It is usually strong and well sweetened with sugar, or perhaps jam and honey. Everyone drinks tea. Even children learn from an early age to enjoy it, no doubt because it is often served with chocolate, candy, wafers, cookies, or other pastries.

Cooking

The kitchen is the principal domestic space for a Russian woman. A great part of her day is spent at the market looking for products, preparing the raw ingredients, cooking, and cleaning. Without the convenience of electric kitchen appliances, Russian women exert tremendous effort in basic kitchen preparation work. Despite the arrival of processed foods and semiprepared dishes in the 1990s, Russians have taken to them with caution. Whether they distrust foreign products or simply prefer to cook from scratch is open to debate, but the fact is that almost all food is still made at home using only fresh ingredients. This is a time-consuming task, one that only increases as the summer draws to an end. In addition to their daily workload of meal preparation, women are also expected to pickle and preserve fresh produce to last throughout the winter months. Fruits and vegetables are purchased at the height of the season to ensure the best price. Some are eaten fresh, but most are dried, pickled, or preserved.

The staples of the Russian pantry include flour, salt, sugar, and tea. Rice, macaroni, and cereal grains are common dry goods, the culinary term for all items that do not require refrigeration. As living space is always a rare commodity and refrigerators are exceedingly small, many apartment dwellers also use their balconies for food storage. With nine months of cool or cold weather a year, the balcony offers an ideal area for keeping overflow items. Freezer space is even smaller, and most families cycle through their fresh food supplies within a week. Russians forgo putting leftovers into Tupperware or other storage containers, instead placing the cookware or serving dish in the refrigerator.

As most people in the former Soviet Union live in apartments, the kitchen occupies a very small space in terms of total square footage. In the early years after the revolution of 1917, large city houses were transformed into communal apartments, where several families would share the residence, including a kitchen and bathroom. By the 1980s, after a tremendous two-decade-long effort to house its citizens, most of the Soviet population lived in single-family apartments. The standard kitchen equipment is a sink, a gas stove, and a small refrigerator. Most of the preparatory work is done on the kitchen table since counter space is limited or nonexistent. Some wealthy families have added dishwashers if space permits, but in general, all dishes are washed by hand.

The brilliance of Russian women lies in their ability to produce delicious and healthful food with crude cookware and shoddy supplies. The most indispensable kitchen tool in the Russian kitchen is the manual meat grinder. It is used to make ground beef and fillings for pies and pastries. The main cookware generally includes a large stockpot for soup, a cast iron skillet for fried foods, a tea kettle, and perhaps a baking dish. Knives, also made of aluminum or soft steel, quickly dull, no doubt because they also function as a hammer and can opener. Spatulas and cooking utensils are either wood or aluminum. Daily dishware is simple, and the fine china is brought out only for special occasions.

Typical Meals

The quintessential Russian lunch or dinner contains bread, soup, and hot tea. Bread is required at every meal and is placed on a plate or in a basket in the middle of the table and covered with a cloth or paper napkin. At the end of the meal, tea is regularly offered in china cups with saucers.

Breakfast can be as modest as bread and tea, or as elaborate as yesterday's dinner leftovers such as salads, pickles, fish, and cold cuts. More often than not, most Russians enjoy a simple open-faced sandwich of cheese, ham, or salami with hot tea and a boiled or fried egg. Coffee, generally instant, is also popular, and serving juice in the morning has been on the rise in recent years. Consumption of fermented dairy drinks such as kefir (fermented milk) and *prostokvasha* (sour milk) generally correlates to the age of the individual. Boiled eggs, omelets, and fried eggs are some of the more familiar offerings. Also exceedingly common, especially for children, is some sort of hot cereal, such as kasha—oatmeal, rice pudding, cream of wheat, and buckwheat. Among the first choices for sweet offerings are tvorog (farmer's cheese) mixed with sour cream and sugar and three types of pancakes—*syrniki* (made with tvorog), bliny (thin), and *olad'i* (thicker). Still, day in and day out, the overwhelming majority of Russians simply have tea and bread for breakfast, perhaps accompanied by cheese or tvorog.

Lunch generally occurs around noon on weekdays and may be served as late as two o'clock on the weekends. Many people eat lunch at work since numerous large companies and institutions have their own cafeterias. In some new, more prosperous offices, lunch is catered. Since women often work outside the home, few men go home for lunch even if they have the opportunity. Lunch usually consists of soup as a first course (*pervoe*); a protein (meat or poultry), a starch (potatoes, rice, pasta), and a salad, sometimes with *kompot* (a dried or fresh fruit infusion) to drink, as the second course (*vtoroe*); and tea and dessert as the common third course (*tret'e*).

Dinner is served around seven in the evening, after people have had time to come home from work. The mother, or a grandmother if she lives with the family, prepares the meal. Generally it follows the same pattern as lunch: soup, a meat dish and a starchy side, finished off with tea and something sweet for dessert. The ubiquitous bread basket adds bulk and calories to the meal. Potatoes—boiled, mashed, fried, or part of a salad—serve the same satisfying function. The usual condiments for pork, beef, or chicken are ketchup, mustard, or horseradish. Hot dogs, without a bun, are a common dish, with green peas, potatoes, macaroni, or rice served on the side.

Common salads include "vinegret" or the Russian salad (*oliv'ye*) of boiled and diced potatoes and carrots, peas, pickles, and chicken, mixed with mayonnaise. Beets in oil with a hint of garlic make a superb salad, side dish, or garnish. The most universal salad, however, is made from freshly shredded cabbage, perhaps with carrots or a touch of onion, dressed with oil or mayonnaise. Fermented cabbage in salt, less stringent than sauerkraut, is made at home and always ready for the table. Cabbage can also be the primary ingredient for filling savory pies (pirogi) or smaller baked pastries (pirozhki). Mushrooms, when in season, are equally adaptable, being served as the main course, used for fillings, or eaten pickled. The most familiar appetizers are dill pickles and lightly brined cucumbers, but any pickled vegetable can stand in. Cheese, sardines, smoked fish, or cold cuts are the standby appetizers (*zakuski*) on a daily basis. The vegetable menu is generally limited to cabbage, cucumbers, tomatoes, beets, cauliflower, squash, and eggplant.

Potato and Mushroom Pirozhki

Pirozhki (sing. *pirozhok*) are the smaller, individual-sized cousins of the larger Russian savory pies, pirogi.

Pirozhki are a baked or fried dough with any number of fillings. They may be served with soup and stews or eaten as a snack or appetizer. Some of the more common contents are meat, mushrooms, buckwheat, potatoes, liver, cheese, eggs, and cabbage.

Filling

6 small potatoes

1 large onion, medium dice

1 lb mushrooms, chopped

6 tbsp butter

3 tbsp tvorog or thick yogurt

3 tbsp dill, chopped

Salt and black pepper to taste

Dough

3 c all-purpose flour

½ tsp baking powder

½ tsp salt

1½ sticks butter

3 egg yolks

½ c sour cream

1 tbsp water

To Make Potato Filling

Peel and cut potatoes evenly into large cubes. Boil in salted water until tender. In a separate pan, sauté onions and mushrooms in 4 tablespoons butter. Combine potatoes with tvorog and mash in 2 tablespoons butter, leaving the potato mixture chunky. Mix with sautéed onions, mushrooms, and dill. Season to taste with salt and pepper.

To Make Dough

Mix flour, baking powder, salt, and butter until the dough is mealy. Whisk 2 egg yolks and the sour cream together. Add the liquid to the flour mixture until it forms a rich dough. Chill the dough for at least one hour.

Preheat oven to 375°F. Flatten a piece of dough to make a 3-inch circle. Put a tablespoon of filling in the center. Press the edges together to seal them, creating a football shape. Place the pirozhok on a buttered cookie sheet, seam side down. Make an egg wash with the remaining egg yolk and water and brush on pirozhki with a pastry brush. Bake in the upper third of the oven for 15–20 minutes or until golden brown. Serve while still warm.

Eating Out

Once stereotyped as the land of shortages and sausage queues, Russia now presents an exceptional opportunity to explore dining out as an intersection of economics and culture, of consumption and national identity. From white-tablecloth restaurants to cafeterias to street food, the culinary influences of Russia, the Caucasus, and Central Asia play off each other to create a dynamic restaurant scene. Eating out in Russia is a major event—fun, fascinating, and full of surprises, mostly pleasing ones.

Big plate with red and black caviar, seafood, and vegetables at a Russian restaurant. (iStockPhoto)

The types of restaurants in Russia can be roughly divided into a few sectors: exclusive restaurants and private clubs, international cuisine, fast-food chains and cafés, restaurant chains, independent midrange restaurants, and, the latest arrivals, coffee shops and beer halls. After European and American businesses' initial entry into the market, Russian companies quickly countered to dominate urban offerings. Prevailing trends include more midrange restaurants for the ever-expanding middle class, while new fast-food outlets are offering more Russian dishes in response to market demand. Restaurants are also an attractive area of investment for successful Russian businessmen seeking to diversify their holdings. International cuisine ranges from typical European fare (Italian and French) to the Asian options of Chinese, Japanese, Thai, and even Tibetan.

Russian restaurant menus follow a typical format: cold appetizers, hot appetizers, a first course (usually soup), a second or main course, garnitures or side dishes, and desserts. An extensive list of alcoholic beverages is common, including vodka, Crimean wine, brandy, and champagne. Whiskey, gin, and beer and wine from abroad are making major inroads into the beverage market. Many menus even contain sections for cigarettes and cigars.

Until recently, menus varied little. The meal begins with zakuski, literally "small bites," which are both hot and cold hors d'oeuvres. The cold appetizers often include sturgeon black caviar and salmon red caviar, pickled and fresh vegetables, a dish of assorted smoked or cured fish, assorted cold cuts, mushrooms, and beef tongue with horseradish.

The first course (pervoe) is invariably a hot soup of borscht, cabbage soup (shchi), or boiled dumplings in broth (pelmeni). Main courses of beef, pork, chicken, lamb, and fish—baked, boiled, braised, or fried—are most common. Desserts in a typical restaurant may include fresh fruit or berries, ice cream, and a pastry or two. Sponge cake and simple chocolate candies are also fairly common. Tea and coffee are served as the final course.

Special Occasions

Ask Russians what their favorite celebrations are, and the answer varies little: New Year's, May Day holidays, and birthdays. For children, the birthday party is the most important festive occasion of the year, rivaled only by New Year's. Even during the Communist reign of the 20th century, religiously devout people in the Soviet Union celebrated their holidays, be it Easter, Ramadan, or Passover. Religious holidays have now rebounded, yet many secular Soviet ones remain deeply embedded, too. The Russian Orthodox Church still retains the older Julian calendar system to mark the main periods of feasting and fasting. Christmas, therefore, is celebrated on January 7; it is second only to Easter in religious significance.

The typical Russian celebratory meal requires much planning and preparation. The region is well acquainted with famine and hardship, and consequently feasts are intensely appreciated. Finding all the necessary ingredients, not to mention budgeting for them, demands great sacrifice and scheduling. The hosts of a family celebration may spend a week or more getting ready for the big day. The hosts intend not only to impress their guests but also to ensure an unforgettable experience. The table, decorated with a white tablecloth, is usually wholly covered with small plates of appetizers (zakuski), salads, cold cuts, pickled vegetables, and bread. Selections of vodka, wine, or champagne are proudly displayed. The finest crystal and china, usually stored in the living-room cabinets, are dusted and shined for maximum pageantry. Once everyone is seated, a glass is raised in honor of the host or honored guest. Diners help themselves to the hors d'oeuvres, and the plates are passed family style. The evening is often a noisy affair as dishes clang, music or television drones in the background, conversation builds, and more toasts are offered and accepted. A main hot course follows the toasts. Hot tea with dessert completes the evening.

Grechnevye Bliny (**Russian Buckwheat Pancakes/Crepes**)

2 c buckwheat flour

4 c milk

1½ packages dry active yeast

2 tbsp sugar

5 eggs, separated

4 tbsp unsalted butter, melted

1 tsp salt

2 c all-purpose flour

Mix buckwheat flour with 1 cup cold milk. Then stir 2 cups of warm milk into the flour mixture. Mix in the yeast and only ½ teaspoon of the sugar. Cover and set aside in a warm place for 30 minutes. Blend the egg yolks with the remaining sugar, melted butter, salt, and all-purpose flour until smooth, and add to the buckwheat mixture. Adjust consistency with remaining milk. Cover and set aside for 45 minutes. Fold whipped egg whites into the batter a little bit at a time. Drop 2–3 tablespoons of batter onto a hot, buttered skillet. Cook for 1½ minutes; flip and cook other side for 30–60 seconds. Serve with the usual garnishes of sour cream, fish, jam, caviar, tvorog, and so forth.

Maslenitsa has become the Russian equivalent of Fat Tuesday or Mardi Gras, the pre-Lenten festival of Shrove Tuesday, arriving in February or March, depending on the Easter date. In general, Maslenitsa is a holiday of gluttony and excess that dates to the pre-Christian era. The pancake (*blin*) represents the sun, and dozens of bliny are consumed throughout the week. Bliny are eaten with liberal amounts of butter, sour cream, caviar, smoked fish, and jams. They are made with buckwheat or wheat flour, or a mixture of both, with yeast or baking soda as the leavening agent. Orthodox Christianity adopted this holiday, and it was given an additional meaning as the last week before Lent.

During the seven decades of the Communist experiment, all holidays celebrated the glory of labor as well as specific professions, special days of Communist history, and memorials to war, particularly World War II. The grandest of contemporary holidays in Russia is New Year's Eve, which has become a combination of the Christmas and the Western New Year's holidays. New Year's is considered a family holiday, and the table features all the favorite and traditional Russian dishes, including a wide array of appetizers, salads, and bread. A standard

Perestroika allowed western companies to venture into Russia. McDonald's was a huge success when it opened in Moscow on January 31, 1990. (Hulton Archive | Getty Images)

menu often includes red and black caviar, *salat oliv'ye, salat vinegret,* trays of assorted smoked fish and cold cuts, and pickled cucumbers and other brined vegetables. By the time the main course arrives, hunger has long since passed. Dessert and tea are obligatory at the end of every festive meal, and New Year's is no exception. The meal usually runs up to and beyond the stroke of midnight. Right before the clock strikes 12 at midnight, a toast with vodka, wine, or brandy is raised to the old year—an appreciative farewell. The first toast of the new year is made with champagne, proclaiming, "With the new year comes new happiness" (*s novym godom, s novym schast'em*).

Diet and Health

In Russia, food is not only treated as a source of nourishment and fuel but also valued for its preventative and curative role. Eating healthfully keeps a body fit and free of disease. Should they fall ill, Russians have numerous cures using a wide range of foods and medicinal herbs. The variety, purity, and freshness of food in Russia unfortunately are not enough to ensure proper health. Despite the conscious and continual efforts of mothers, wives, and grandmothers to feed and care for their families, health has generally deteriorated since 2000. Food, however, is only one part of the equation for good health.

Russians have several health-related problems in common: a short life expectancy, cardiovascular disease, and general nutritional deficiencies, as well as high rates of tobacco and alcohol use. Specific nutritional problems include the lack of affordability of certain healthful and essential food items, the suspect quality of some foodstuffs, and the absence of public awareness of what constitutes a healthful and balanced diet. Much of the overall decline in health, without a doubt, may be attributed to the social and economic disruptions since 1991. The Soviet experiment can be credited with improving the general diet of the lowest economic classes but not until well into the 1960s.

Quantity and freshness have priority over quality and finesse on the Russian table. Although restaurants and cafés are numerous in the big cities, hearty homemade meals are the ideal both in the countryside and in urban areas. A well-balanced meal should have a main course of fish or meat for flair, a starch (potatoes, pasta, or rice) for energy, and vegetables (often in the form of a cooked vegetable salad) for vitamins. Soup and tea are the bookends of a meal. Dessert would make it complete in the minds of most Russians. At least one hot meal a day is crucial to maintaining good digestion and health. Lunch, according to an earlier Russian tradition, was the main meal of the day. A light lunch is usually taken at work. The daily menu of most Russian families includes a meat or sausage dish. Therefore, the typical diet is very high in protein and animal fat, mostly from low-quality processed, smoked, or cured meats. Most people consume dairy products (usually fermented) daily, including cheese, dairy drinks (kefir, prostokvasha, *ryazhenka*), farmer's cheese (tvorog) and, more recently, yogurt. The most common vegetables are potatoes, cabbage, onions, tomatoes, and cucumbers. Vegetables are almost always cooked (and often overcooked), except for tomatoes, cucumbers, and radishes, which are used in fresh salads.

Glenn R. Mack and Asele Surina

Further Reading

Boeckmann, Susie, and Natalie Rebeiz-Nielsen. *Caviar: The Definitive Guide.* New York: John Wiley, 2000.

Glants, Musya, and Joyce Toomre, eds. *Food in Russian History and Culture.* Bloomington: Indiana University Press, 1997.

Goldstein, Darra. *A Taste of Russia: A Cookbook of Russian Hospitality.* Montpelier, VT: Russian Information Services, 1999.

Gronow, Jukka. *Caviar with Champagne: Common Luxury and the Ideals of the Good Life in Stalin's Russia. Leisure, Consumption and Culture.* New York: Berg, 2004.

"International Food Consumpton Patterns." Economic Research Service (ERS) of the U.S. Department of Agriculture. http://www.ers. usda.gov/Data/InternationalFoodDemand/.

Mack, Glenn R., and Asele Surnia. *Food Culture in Russia and Central Asia.* Westport, CT: Greenwood Press, 2005.

"Russian Customs, Holidays, and Traditions." Russian Crafts. http://russian-crafts.com/rus sian-traditions.html.

Russian Foods.com. The Russian Department Store and Gourmet Food Network. http://www. russianfoods.com/.

Smith, R.E.F., and David Christian. *Bread and Salt: A Social and Economic History of Food and Drink in Russia.* Cambridge: Cambridge University Press, 1984.

Toomre, Joyce, trans. and ed. *Classic Russian Cooking: Elena Molokhovets' a Gift to Young Housewives.* Bloomington: Indiana University Press, 1992.

von Bremzen, Anya, and John Welchman. *Please to the Table: The Russian Cookbook.* New York: Workman, 1990.

Williams, Robert. *Russia Imagined: Art, Culture, and National Identity, 1840–1995.* New York: Peter Lang, 1997.

Saami

Overview

The Saami are an indigenous people of northern Scandinavia. The names *Sami, Sàmi, Saame,* and *Lapp* have all been used to describe the Saami, although the last of these is considered derogative. There are nine different recognized Saami languages, which fall into three main groups—eastern Saami, central Saami, and southern Saami—and are all of the Finno-Ugric language family. The Saami call the territory they live in Sapmi; it is sometimes referred to as Lapland or Fennoscandia. It spans four countries (northern Norway, Sweden, Finland, and the Kola Peninsula of Russia) and is part of the Arctic Circle. Sapmi is not officially recognized by the nation-states within which it exists. There are strong indications that the Saami have lived and managed resources in this territory for at least 2,000 years. There are approximately 70,000 Saami: 35,000 in Norway, 17,000 in Sweden (2,000 in Stockholm), 5,000 in Finland, and 2,000 in Russia. There are also Saami living in Canada and the United States. Rights to resources and land continue to shape the food culture of the Saami.

The Saami have developed a cuisine linked strongly to nature. The conditions in which the diet has evolved include a harsh arctic environment, where winters are cold, snow covers the land most of the year, and the sun is absent for two months in the far north. The Saami are commonly known as reindeer herders, and traditionally this along with hunting and fishing has been the primary food activity of the Saami. For centuries the Saami have led a seminomadic lifestyle following reindeer on their seasonal migrations, but today fewer Saami are herding.

In contemporary society many Saami live in modern housing and have access to a variety of foods and cooking methods, and often their eating habits are influenced by the cuisines of the dominant countries as well as the impact of globalization on agriculture and food production. Yet tradition still plays a key role in defining a specifically Saami food culture, and often those who lead a more urban lifestyle still have links to Sapmi and their cultural heritage.

🍽 Food Culture Snapshot

A typical Saami family will differ in what they buy to eat depending on where they live and their occupation. A Saami family living in the urban environment of Stockholm has all the conveniences and variety of foods that large European cities offer. This family would typically shop and eat in a similar way to other non-Saami living in Stockholm. A typical reindeer-herding family, in contrast, has stocks of reindeer meat to eat daily. The meat is obtained from their reindeer and is eaten fresh after slaughter, and the rest is preserved. After the slaughter period, the family relies on stores of frozen and dried or smoked reindeer meat throughout the year. Reindeer herders are generally self-sufficient with supplies of reindeer meat, elk, and fish, but they will buy in other supplies such as potatoes, onions, salt, coffee, sugar, barley, milk, and flour. Reindeer meat can be bought in supermarkets throughout Sapmi and large cities in Norway, Sweden, and Finland; it is usually bought in frozen slices to be made into sautéed reindeer or reindeer stew.

In coastal areas fish are either caught or bought directly from fishermen or frozen from a supermarket. In the past many Saami who fished also farmed, which provided a good supply of vegetables and dairy for their diet. Today, many foods that are available in large international cities in Scandinavia can also be bought in supermarkets in the north, but sometimes prices are high.

Major Foodstuffs

The landscape of Sapmi is environmentally varied, and because it spans four countries, it is also culturally varied. Changes in the dietary staples correspond to the environmental and cultural changes in territory. The Saami diet has traditionally been high in animal protein and fat, and low in carbohydrates. Reindeer-herding Saami still have a diet characterized in this way. Many other Saami have adopted a diet similar to that of the Scandinavian countries they live in. There is a commonly held assumption that reindeer meat forms the basis of protein consumption among the Saami; however, for many, protein is obtained from fish as well, especially for the people living in coastal areas, who get most of their protein from fish. The protein intake of the urban population is more balanced between fish and meat. Inland Saami consume meat, predominantly reindeer, as their main source of protein.

Reindeer meat is a central component of the Saami food culture and is symbolic for the culture as a whole. Even though not all Saami consume it today, reindeer meat is a dietary staple for reindeer herders and many other Saami. Currently only 10 percent of Saami make their living from reindeer herding, yet it is considered an important industry, since reindeer are well suited to the arctic environment and provide the main meat source here. The Saami have undertaken nomadic reindeer herding since the early 1600s; prior to this time, instead of herding, they hunted reindeer. Today, many herders use modern technology such as helicopters and snowmobiles to manage their herds, which has significantly changed the food culture associated with a nomadic life. Reindeer herding is an exclusive Saami right in Sweden and Norway but not in Finland. In Russia, where approximately two and a half million of the world's three million reindeer live, many different indigenous groups undertake reindeer herding. Even though a large population of Saami lives in cities (Stockholm has the greatest concentration, with 2,000 Saami living there), people living in cities often have links to relatives who herd reindeer. In traditional practices the entire reindeer is used: Skins and furs can be used for clothes; the flesh, innards, marrow, blood, bones, milk, and linings for food; and bones for implements.

Many of the coastal waters, in particular, the Atlantic Ocean and Barents Sea, offer a rich source of fish that Saami and non-Saami both eat. Fishing was once a means of subsistence, but today, many Saami who live along the coast are employed outside of the fishing industry. Salmon, trout, char, whitefish, grayling, burbot, pike, and cod are all commonly eaten. Inland, there are many lakes, rivers, and marshes, which also provide a rich source of fish. The Tenojoki and Tornionjoki rivers offer a good source of salmon, a fish commonly found in the Saami cuisine. In traditional practices roe from freshwater fish are dried and then used by soaking them in water when needed. In the past fish offered more than just food for many Saami, who in the Middle Ages often paid their taxes using dried fish.

Due to climatic conditions agriculture is extremely difficult in Sapmi territory. However, attempts have been made by Norway, Sweden, and Finland since the mid-1600s to promote agriculture in the north. At best, the growing season is 110–120 days when the temperature is above 41 degrees Fahrenheit (5 degrees Celsius): Short, warm summers with six weeks of continuous sunshine allow some crops, mainly barley, potatoes, oats, turnips, and fodder, to grow. Any other cereals, such as wheat, must be brought in. Potatoes continue to form a major dietary staple for coastal, inland, and urban Saami. Most Saami who have been farmers in coastal Norway and northern Finland learned quickly to rely on a mixed economy and also undertook hunting, fishing, and berry picking, or today buy foods from supermarkets to supplement their subsistence.

Traditionally, fruit and vegetables have not featured heavily in the meals of the Saami. Potatoes, some root vegetables, sorrel, and angelica have complemented meat and fish. Berries have always offered the Saami a good local source of vitamins and minerals and have been a major element of the diet. Berries such as the cloudberry, lingonberry, bilberry, and crowberry continue to be used and are also a source of income. Berries harvested and consumed include the lingonberry, crowberry, blueberry, bog whortleberry, cloudberry, cranberry, rowanberry, raspberry, juniper berry, wild strawberry, bilberry, and arctic bramble. Today, globalization has led to an increased variety of fruit and vegetables available and consumed throughout Scandinavia.

Milk from reindeer was used traditionally to supplement meat and fish as a protein source. Reindeer milk can be made into cheese and used in cooking, and it can be mixed with cloudberries and frozen to form a type of ice cream that preserves both the cloudberries and the milk. It is a good clotting agent and traditionally is used in a dish called *juobmo* (*juopmu*), which combined sorrel with reindeer milk to form a thick souplike dish. Today, joubmo is sometimes made using cow milk and sweetened with sugar and served as a dessert. Today, the milking of reindeer is not common. The movement toward agriculture in the 1950s resulted in a small economy of cow and goat milk in parts of northern Norway and Finland. The Saami through much of the 20th century used goat and cow milk.

Coffee is a major beverage for most Saami; it is consumed in large quantities and is typically very strong. Reindeer herders survive long hours looking after reindeer by drinking coffee. Coffee was traditionally and sometimes still is served with reindeer cheese instead of milk.

Cooking

Today, most Saami live in modern housing, and cooking is done in modern kitchens. Equipment, cooking methods, and access to foods reflect a Scandinavian lifestyle. Traditional Saami society was based on the *siida* system. The siida consisted of a number of families working together to procure food. The traditional Saami kitchen is part of the *goatte,* a tepee-like construction. The hearth is in the center of the area, and a cauldron is suspended from the roof. The smoking of meat sometimes takes place here. Men and women both undertake cooking activities. Traditionally, women were in charge of baking the bread and the overall preparation of daily household meals, and men were in charge of preserving and boiling meat. Today, men largely do the reindeer herding and husbandry, and women tend to manage activities surrounding the household.

Fire plays an important role in traditional Saami cooking. A stone slab or wooden board is placed by the fire for baking bread or cheese bread and for grilling fish. Thin cheese bread is made with cheese and potato and is eaten either hot with cloudberries or cold with hot coffee.

"Cheese Bread"

Ingredients

2 gal unpasteurized milk

1 tbsp potato flour

1 tbsp salt

1 tbsp liquid rennet

Method

Heat the unpasteurized milk to 100°F. Mix potato flour with a small amount of milk, and add with salt and rennet to the heated milk. Stir for 1–1½ minutes, and leave to curdle for about ½ hour. Make a few slits in the curd with a ladle or long knife and leave for 10 minutes to let the whey rise to the surface. Then break the mixture up into small pieces and let stand to allow the whey to collect on the surface. Skim off the whey.

When the curds have formed a cake of cheese, pour onto a wooden cheese board with holes in it, to allow the whey to drain. Bake the curds at 500°F until the surface turns a speckled brown. Turn the cheese over onto a second cheese board, and bake the other side the same way.

A Saami woman cooking over an open fire in Lapland, Finland. (StockPhotoPro)

Pots and frying pans are useful utensils in Saami cooking because of the large amount of boiling and frying done. Reindeer meat is most commonly boiled or fried. Thin frozen pieces of reindeer meat are often fried in a saucepan with brown sauce. A more traditional method still practiced today is carving thin slices from a frozen shoulder and frying them in a saucepan over a fire or on a stovetop.

Preserving plays a big part in Saami food preparation. Reindeer meat, fish, and sometimes cheese are smoked, salted, dried, or frozen. Historically, preserving has been necessary to provide food supplies throughout the year. Today, many households have freezers where meat can be stored, but in the past the low temperatures and snow provided a natural freezer. Meat is often smoked or dried in small hutlike constructions off the ground and outside the house or on drying racks. Dried reindeer meat is commonly taken to eat while herding reindeer. Dried meat is also boiled with barley to make

a soup. Blood is boiled or made into sausages occasionally. Entrails from reindeer and fish are more commonly boiled than fried.

Spoons used for eating porridge, soup, or milk-based foods are traditionally part of the Saami kitchen. They are made from either silver or antlers, and they are typically shaped with a wide curve and uniquely decorated. Other traditional kitchen utensils include a reindeer-milking bowl; a coffee-carrying bag; a brass coffeepot; and a cauldron or pot.

Typical Meals

Defining a typical Saami meal and eating pattern today is difficult since many Saami live like the rest of the population in Norway, Sweden, Finland, or Russia, and there are also regional and seasonal differences in Saami meals. On the coast, fish is the main component of daily meals and is often accompanied by potatoes. Meat is more widely available today, but traditionally in northern coastal Norway it was reserved for holidays and Sundays. Porridge was a typical meal well into the 20th century, sometimes cooked with berries. In the Kola Peninsula of Russia, for breakfast, some Saami eat salted or smoked fish, or sometimes fish mashed with berries to form a type of porridge. Fish is a major part of a meal in the summer and spring for Saami who herd reindeer. Salmon, arctic char, whitefish, trout, and pike are cooked, poached, or fried for dinner and also smoked or salted. It is common to find coffee brewing on the stove or fire for consumption throughout the day.

Saami who eat reindeer meat as their main protein source often eat it daily. The way it is consumed changes with the seasons. After slaughtering, the meat is eaten fresh, and then it is frozen, dried, or smoked. Reindeer meat is often accompanied by potatoes, berries, or barley and is either sautéed or boiled and made into a soup or gruel. A typical meal, especially for herders, is sautéed reindeer. It is often served with lingonberries or cowberries and mashed potato.

Sautéed Reindeer

Ingredients

Butter or oil for frying

Reindeer, thinly sliced (This is easier when the meat is frozen. Reindeer can be bought in frozen pieces or shaved off a frozen shoulder piece.)

Water or beer

Mashed potatoes

Lingonberry jam (available in Ikea) or crushed cowberries in sugar

Method

Melt butter or oil in a pan. (Reindeer was traditionally sautéed in reindeer fat.) Add the reindeer slices, and stir so that the meat does not stick together. Put the lid on, and simmer until cooked. Add some water or beer to the pan at the end, and let reduce to a sauce. Serve with mashed potatoes and berry jam.

Eating Out

The practice of eating out that is typical throughout much of North America and western Europe today is not part of traditional Saami food culture. Historically, eating out was more likely to involve communal eating as part of the siida system that organized nomadic existence.

Saami living in major cities like Stockholm, Gothenburg, and Helsinki have access to a wide range of dining options from typical Western fast-food venues like McDonald's to the many lunchtime restaurants of Sweden. Similarly, large towns across the northernmost parts of Scandinavia offer a wide range of restaurants serving everything from Nordic fare and pizza to Thai food, a more recent arrival. Traditional Saami foods are also easy to come by in many towns and cities across the northern parts of Norway, Sweden, and Finland. Some restaurants and cafés serve typical national dishes alongside local Saami dishes, with reindeer featuring heavily on the menu. There are also many tourist attractions surrounding Saami food, such as eating traditional meals in a goatte, or reindeer herding, fishing, or hunting; however, there is controversy over the authenticity of some of these attractions and the benefit to Saami people.

Special Occasions

There are many festivals, holidays, and events in modern Saami culture. Saami and non-Saami share some special occasions, like midsummer, Easter, and Christmas. There are other occasions that are particular to the Saami culture, such as the Saami National Day on February 6. Food is a part of celebrating all of these occasions.

Many special occasions celebrated by the Saami relate to the seasons and nature. Easter is especially important since it marks the change in seasons from the harsh winter months. The time of the year when the reindeer are slaughtered also marks a special occasion when fresh meat is eaten. The bone marrow along with the tongue has for a long time been considered a delicacy. After the reindeer are slaughtered fresh meat is boiled with the bones, and the marrow is eaten. The liver is also eaten at this time, along with blood balls, which consist of milk, flour, blood, and salt.

Diet and Health

The Saami belief system is heavily linked to nature and features shamanism and the use of medicinal plants. Today, however, shamanism is not commonly practiced, and most Saami rely on the national health system. The World Health Organization acknowledges that many indigenous populations, including the Saami, often have a higher risk of health problems, and this is partly due to social inequalities. In the case of the Saami, sociopolitical rights are closely linked to territory and resources and thus to food and health. Resources and rights to land have been issues at the heart of reindeer herding, fishing, and hunting for centuries. The outcomes for Saami people today are different in the different countries. Policies relating to the Saami have influenced their diet and well-being through herding and hunting restrictions, land disputes, and cultural oppression.

The Saami traditionally have a diet high in animal protein and fat and low in carbohydrates. Fruit and vegetable intake is low even compared with Swedish and Norwegian populations, who are already known to consume low quantities. This type of diet is contrary to most national dietary recommendations, yet there are reported low levels of coronary heart disease in Saami populations who live off a more traditional diet; it is suggested this could be partly due to a high diet of reindeer meat. Reindeer meat has high levels of α-tocopherol and selenium and has a fatty acid composition likely to aid cardiovascular

protection. Berries have high levels of vitamins and minerals and are important in areas where the sun does not rise for some months of the year.

Environmental pollutants affect the food chain that many Saami rely on. A major health problem occurred in 1986 after the Chernobyl nuclear disaster. Dangerous radioactive substances were scattered across parts of Europe, including Scandinavia. Lichens, which form the basis of the reindeer diet, absorbed high levels of radioactive substances and in return had a major impact on the Saami diet and reindeer consumption. The Arctic Monitoring and Assessment Program has recorded a decline in radioactive substances caused by past nuclear disasters but is concerned about other pollution risks in the arctic food chain.

Kate Johnston

Further Reading

Encyclopaedia of Saami Culture. University of Helsinki, 2003–2004. http://www.helsinki.fi/~sugl_smi/senc/en/index.htm.

Kuoljok, Sunna, and John-Erling Utsi. *The Sami People of the Sun and Wind.* Jokkmokk, Sweden: Ajtte Mountain and Saami Museum, 1993.

Notaker, Henry. *Food Culture in Scandinavia.* Food Culture around the World. Westport, CT: Greenwood Press, 1997.

Paine, Robert. *Herds of the Tundra: A Portrait of Saami Reindeer Pastoralism.* Washington, DC: Smithsonian Institute, 1994.

Reindeer Blog. http://www.reindeerblog.org/category/food-culture/.

Vitebsky, Piers. *The Saami of Lapland.* New York: Thomson Learning, 1994.

Scotland

Overview

Scotland, a part of the United Kingdom, covers 30,414 square miles (78,772 square kilometers) of land and encompasses roughly 6,214 miles (10,000 kilometers) of coastline, 2,423 miles (3,900 kilometers) of which constitute the mainland coast. Geographically, Scotland can be divided into roughly three main regions: the Highlands, the Central Lowlands, and the Southern Lowlands. Scotland also includes upward of 800 islands, with 130 of them inhabited. The Shetland and Orkney Islands to the northeast, and the Inner and Outer Hebrides to the west, include most of the populated islands. Glasgow and Edinburgh are Scotland's largest cities and centers of government and culture. Of its 5,116,900 inhabitants, roughly 1.2 million reside in the Greater Glasgow metropolitan area, and almost 500,000 reside in Edinburgh.

Geography and climate historically have played a significant role in the Scottish diet. Rivers and the coastline supply countless varieties of fish, seafood, and edible seaweeds; the Highlands supply game as well as the barley for hundreds of whiskey distilleries; the southwestern region is known for its dairy farming; and the Lowlands supply much of the nation's soft fruits and vegetables.

🍽 Food Culture Snapshot

Ron, Sarah, and their four-year-old daughter Fiona live in the town of Peebles in the Scottish Borders. Ron is a veterinarian, and his wife, a former schoolteacher, stays at home to care for Fiona. Their diet and eating habits are representative of middle-class, educated Scots.

Ron and Sarah start their day at 7 A.M., with porridge or a bowl of cold cereal, bananas, toast and butter, and hot tea. Their daughter usually prefers a soft-boiled egg, toast "soldiers" (strips of toast) to dip in the yolk, and a mug of warm milk. The family typically eats breakfast together before Ron leaves for his practice around 7:45. At 10 A.M., Ron often takes a short break to enjoy a cup of tea with his assistants before returning to his rounds. Sarah likewise often enjoys a midmorning break, taking her daughter with her to a local coffee shop where she meets with other young mothers and their children. While Sarah drinks a mug of coffee and talks to friends, Fiona has a hot cocoa and biscuit (cookie). Around noon, Ron takes a 45-minute lunch break, often eating a cheese and cucumber, or cheese and cress, sandwich that he brings from home, along with a bag of crisps (potato chips) and an apple. He drinks a half-liter of mineral water with his meal. Sarah eats a similar meal at home with Fiona.

Sarah begins dinner preparation around 4 P.M., often making two meals: one for her daughter and one for her and her husband. Like many families, they refer to their dinner meal as "tea" unless they are having a rare "dinner party" later in the evening for friends. Fiona likes many of the foods her parents have later for their dinner, including mashed potatoes with butter, roast chicken, macaroni and cheese, or pasta with cream sauce and peas, but oftentimes Sarah prepares a simple tea for her daughter of porridge and milk with bananas, or toasted cheese and ham with carrot sticks and applesauce. The family generally avoids sweets, but on special occasions, Sarah might make a pudding (a generic word for a dessert) or buy a pastry from a favorite baker and give her daughter a small serving. Raspberry tart is Fiona's favorite.

Fiona's tea is at 5:30, and while she eats, Sarah prepares the rest of her and Ron's dinner, often cooking the main dish in the oven and keeping it warm until their teatime around 6:30, after Ron has returned home and the two have had a moment to sit down for a glass of wine while talking and watching Fiona play. They eat a green salad almost every night and follow it with a main dish such as pasta and mushrooms, lentil soup, grilled lamb chops with sautéed spinach, or roast chicken with carrots and potatoes. When Ron and Sarah entertain friends for dinner, they start with an aperitif and an appetizer such as pâté and French bread in the living room around 7:00, and then proceed to their formal dining room for a more elaborate meal that will include a soup, a salad, a main dish, and pudding. Sarah's favorite company dish is baked salmon with a teriyaki glaze and rice pilaf, along with fresh-steamed Asian vegetables, particularly snow peas and bok choy. To commemorate his family's Highland heritage, Ron likes to follow such dinners by serving *cranachan,* oftentimes considered Scotland's national dessert: a parfait-like concoction made with a soft cheese called crowdie, sweetened lightly with heather honey, accented with malt whiskey and toasted oatmeal, and folded in with fresh raspberries. Coffee, whiskey, and a cheese selection with oatcakes follow.

For reasons of health and economy, Ron and Sarah limit eating out to three to four times a month, often traveling into Edinburgh to take in the lively restaurant scene. Italian or Indian restaurants are Ron and Sarah's favorite choices. When Ron is particularly late at his practice or Sarah has volunteer work, Ron will sometimes stop at their neighborhood fish-and-chip shop to pick up a fish supper (fish, chips, and peas) for the sake of convenience.

Major Foodstuffs

In spite of its small geographic size, Scotland's numerous microclimates and landscapes result in an extraordinary diversity of raw foodstuffs, many of which are exported throughout the United Kingdom and Europe and also find their way into Scotland's

most famous specialties. Scotland's mild summers allow for optimal production of both barley and oats. Barley has been Scotland's main cereal crop since Neolithic times; the Romans are thought to have introduced oats. Roughly 35 percent of the country's barley is malted for whiskey production, while 55 percent is used for animal feed. In remote areas, including the Highlands and Orkney, some people still use barley flour to make bread, and Orkney is known for its *bere*-meal bannocks, a griddle cake or scone made with a variety of barley known as bere. Oats remain a popular staple throughout Scotland, with many older people eating slow-cooked porridge with milk and a dash of salt for breakfast and oatcakes with cheese for a snack. Younger people often eat instant porridge, made by emptying a serving-size packet of oats into a bowl and heating it in the microwave with water. Oats are used to make drop scones (pancakes), *skirlie* (fried oatmeal and onions), and bannocks and are a key ingredient in several of Scotland's best-known dishes, particularly haggis, a savory blend of sheep's pluck (heart, liver, and/or lungs) and oatmeal boiled in a sheep's stomach or, more likely today, in a synthetic casing. Oatmeal is also an ingredient of black pudding (a sausage of oats, suet, spices, and pork blood) and white, or mealy, pudding (a sausage of oats, suet, spices, and onion). Although wheat production is limited in Scotland because of the climate, many

A cooked haggis with diced turnips and mashed potatoes—the traditional "tatties and neeps" of a Burns supper. (Shutterstock)

Scots prefer breads, cakes, pies, and biscuits made of wheat flour.

Oatmeal Biscuits

1 c unbleached white flour

½ tsp sugar

½ tsp salt

¼ tsp baking powder

1 c old-fashioned rolled oats

5 tbsp vegetable shortening

¼ c heavy cream

Water to mix

Preheat oven to 400°F. Sift the flour, sugar, salt, and baking powder together in a large bowl. Add oats. Add vegetable shortening. Rub the shortening into the flour and oats. Add heavy cream, and stir lightly. Add ice water until dough is pliable but still stiff. Roll out to ⅛ inch thick. Prick dough all over with fork tines. Cut into squares, and place on a greased baking tray. Bake approximately 12 minutes until brown and crisp. Best topped with butter and a dollop of jelly or marmalade or served with Scottish cheeses.

Pairs of golden brown haddock hanging on metal rods over a barrel of burning hardwood and being smoked in the traditional manner of Arbroath smokies. (Thomas Langlands | Dreamstime.com)

Scotland's rivers, lochs (lakes), and coasts provide some of the highest-quality fish and seafood in the world. The nation is best known for its salmon, trout, herring, langoustines, oysters, and mussels. Scotland's Arbroath smokies (smoked haddock) have been awarded Protected Geographical Indication (PGI) status by the European Commission (meaning the name is legally protected) and are highly sought after by locals and food connoisseurs alike. Several varieties of seaweed, including dulse and kelp, are staples in northeastern coastal communities, as well as throughout the Western Isles, Inner and Outer Hebrides, the Northern Isles, Orkney, and Shetland.

Before the Clearances of the mid-1700s, Highland clans survived by eating venison, game birds, wild boar, and dairy products from their domesticated livestock. They supplemented their diet with wild foods such as nettles and brambles (blackberries) and with the kale, onions, and leeks that families planted in their *kailyards* (garden plots). Today, many Scots still eat venison, both wild and farmed, along with hare and rabbit. Butchers also sell pheasant, grouse, and partridge when these birds are in season, for those who can afford it. Hunting and fishing are both popular sports.

Scotland is also renowned for its domesticated meats, with Scotch beef having been awarded PGI status in 2004. Aberdeen Angus, Scotch Shorthorn, Galloway, and Highland cattle are esteemed breeds, and many of Scotland's roasts and rich stews depend on Scotch beef for their depth of flavor. The nation's highest-quality lamb comes from crossbred sheep, with Cheviot one of the most important breeds. The southwest is distinguished for its dairying industry, and the by-products of cheese and butter have been used to feed pigs. The distinctive rolled Ayrshire back bacon is created from Great White premium-grade pigs that are raised in part on these dairy by-products.

Up to World War II, many Scots produced their own butter, milk, and cheese, particularly crowdie, a pot cheese still popular in the Highlands. Today, the bulk of Scotland's dairy farming is situated in Dumfries and Galloway, where pastureland is abundant. Artisanal cheese making has been revived due to the efforts of individuals intent on saving or resurrecting Scotland's culinary traditions. Bonchester and Kelsae cheeses from the Borders; Caboc, a cream cheese from the Highlands; Dunlop from Ayrshire; Dunsyre Blue and Lanark Blue from Lanarkshire; Orkney farmhouse cheeses; and cheddar-style cheeses from the Isles of Mull and Iona are only some representatives of a thriving artisan cheese industry. Ice cream became an established part of Scottish culinary culture in the 19th century when Italian immigrants who settled in Glasgow and Edinburgh sold it first from carts and then from cafés. Scotland continues to be known for high-quality ice cream, and due to the health of their vast dairy herds, ice cream from Orkney, Dumfries, and Galloway is particularly esteemed.

Over half of Scotland's soft fruit comes from Perthshire. Raspberries—considered Scotland's national fruit—as well as strawberries, currants, gooseberries, brambles, and tayberries (a cross between a raspberry and a blackberry) are consumed throughout the United Kingdom. Many Scottish desserts blend soft fruits with cream or crowdie. Much of the country's vegetable production extends south from Lothian, through the Borders and into the southwestern region. The Solway Firth benefits from the Gulf Stream, resulting in milder temperatures. Overall, the Scottish climate lends itself to growing potatoes, onions, leeks, turnips, rutabagas, and cabbages, with these vegetables raised both on industrial and small-farm scales.

Contemporary Scottish cooks showcase the bounty of these native foods while celebrating the Norwegian, English, French, Dutch, and Italian influences that have defined this country's cuisine since the 9th century. The taste for salted, dried fish and mutton, the prevalence of cabbage in many dishes such as *kailkenny* (a savory mashed potato and cabbage dish), and recipes for pickled herring are vestiges of Viking influence, evident in the Northern Highlands, the Hebrides, Orkney, and Shetland. Scottish food also owes much to French influence in both technique and dishes, the result of the Auld Alliance formalized in 1295 when Scotland and France united against English invaders. Hotchpotch (a vegetable soup), for example, is similar in composition and name to the French *hochepot*. Italian restaurants are among the most popular restaurants in Scotland and have been so for many decades running.

Seasonings remain straightforward and simple if one is preparing traditional Scottish specialties. Mace and nutmeg are used in a variety of sweet and savory dishes, from white sauces to puddings. Salt and pepper are the most frequent spices, with garden herbs such as thyme, parsley, sage, rosemary, savory, and chives gracing any number of dishes. Scots also prefer the sharp-sweet taste of native berries, such as rowan, as an accompaniment to game dishes.

Cooking

Up through the mid-18th century, Scots cooked by boiling food in a pot or baking it on a griddle. They preserved food by salting, drying, smoking, or pickling. Many Scottish foods, including *clootie* pudding (a sweet flour-and-suet pudding boiled in a cloth), porridge, haggis, bannocks, *cullen skink* (dried haddock and cream soup), and *tattie scones* (potato pancakes), continue to be prepared according to these ancient methods. In addition to boiling food in a pot or baking it on a griddle, today's cooks also fry, sauté, braise, grill, broil, and bake foods in an oven, on a cooker, or in a microwave.

In addition to an electric or gas cooker, oven, and microwave oven, a typical Scottish kitchen includes a sink, a refrigerator and freezer combination unit, and sometimes an electric dishwasher. People also use a variety of countertop electrical appliances, including toasters, mixers, blenders, drip coffeemakers, teakettles, and food processors. For those with large gardens (yards), an outdoor barbecue grill is also common.

From the 1990s on, the sale of convenience foods has spiked. The British Council notes that frozen meals, take-out meals, and boxed dinners (such as macaroni and cheese) were worth £11 billion in 2001 and estimated to grow by 33 percent throughout the decade. A wealth of shortcut products, such as prewashed lettuces and preshredded cheese, have cut the average time that a person may spend preparing a meal down to around 13 minutes. These trends reflect practices in the entire United Kingdom.

Typical Meals

Traditionally, Scottish women were in charge of shopping for food, cooking it, serving meals, and cleaning up. That strict gender demarcation has waned, and in many homes, men are likely to be involved in some or all of these tasks. Contemporary Scottish families often keep diverse schedules, with teenage children and their parents working various shifts and/or involved in an assortment of daily commitments that make it hard for them to cook and eat all of their meals together. Therefore, it is difficult to describe a typical Scottish meal. But there are some commonalities. Most Scots consume three daily meals: breakfast, lunch, and dinner (which might also be called "tea" or "supper"). They likely take a midmorning and midafternoon break for tea or coffee and a snack. Breakfast can range from a substantial meal to little more than a cereal bar, as can lunch. However, most Scots treat dinner as the day's most important and substantial meal.

Many Scottish families attempt to convene around the table for dinner, where they help themselves to a variety of foods, with meat often the main course and vegetables and a starch such as rice, pasta, or potatoes as sides. Many people end the meal with a sweet as well, perhaps a chocolate, a slice of cake, or a tart. Over the decades, however, as tastes have widely diversified and many Scots have become more health conscious, dinners might no longer feature meat, or meat plays a secondary role. Roughly 5 percent of adults in the United Kingdom identify themselves as vegetarians, with countless more limiting meat in their diets to as little as once or twice a week.

While most people drink hot tea or coffee for breakfast, their lunch and dinner might be accompanied by a wide range of beverages, from water and fruit juices to soft drinks, particularly Irn-Bru, a bright orange soda reputedly flavored with iron. Spirits such as wine and whiskey are more likely to be consumed with dinner than with lunch.

Aside from these general features of Scottish meals, what people eat and when they eat it depends on their tastes, ethnicity (especially recent immigrants), knowledge about nutrition, age, and affluence. Because of upward mobility and the nature of a global economy, people often move throughout the United Kingdom, and increasingly throughout Europe, on the basis of where they work. Fluidity of movement disrupts or challenges regional customs as well as distinctive regional food traditions. Furthermore, irrespective of geographic location, most Scots have access to a staggering variety and quantity of food, much of it name-brand, prepackaged, and sold in nationally recognized supermarket chains. Seventy percent of Scotland's food retailing is done in five of these chains.

The following are examples of typical meals of families living in Scotland's Central Lowlands, a region where the population density is the highest. For those who eat breakfast at home, cold cereal and milk, instant porridge, or toast is common. Orange juice is universally popular at breakfast, as is coffee or tea. Commuters might eat in transit, buying a *buttery* (roll) and cup of coffee or tea, or a breakfast sandwich of fried egg and bacon placed inside a bap (a soft floury roll). On weekends, breakfast might be a more substantial affair, with some enjoying a "fry up," or full Scottish breakfast that includes eggs, bacon, *lorne* sausage (a square sausage slice of minced beef and pork), black pudding, tattie (potato) scones, grilled tomatoes, baked beans, toast, and hot tea or coffee.

Noonday lunch often consists of no more than a sandwich, a Scotch pie (a hot pie of minced beef and gravy), a pizza slice, a salad, a kebab, or a small order of chicken tikka masala (roast chicken curry). Many workers pack a lunch to eat at work, or they order a meal in a work canteen. Others purchase something ready-made from a take-out place or sandwich bar. Occasionally, people make time for a more elaborate restaurant lunch, particularly if the meal involves business. Those remaining at home often pause around noon and eat a sandwich or snack. Primary-school children eat a prepared lunch at their cafeteria, while older children might leave the grounds to find lunch at a take-out shop.

The dinner hour (anywhere from 5 to 7 P.M.) remains an important meal, and families will often attempt to eat together if possible. Typical meals include minced beef simmered in gravy and served with mashed potatoes and peas, poached salmon with rice and a side salad, grilled sausage with fried potatoes and brussels sprouts, pasta with sautéed mushrooms, a cheese omelet with steamed vegetables, or vegetable-lentil soup and whole-grain rolls. Likewise, a variety of ethnic foods are as typical on a Scottish dinner table as would be more traditional fare, perhaps even more so. Scots often cook or bring in ready-made Asian foods such as stir-fried shrimp, beef pad Thai, or lamb curry. Italian food, such as lasagna, minestrone soup, and spaghetti, is also popular.

Eating Out

As Europe's first industrialized nation, the United Kingdom was also the first to see its traditional culinary customs give way to consumption patterns that ultimately defined other western European nations. Thousands of rural people throughout Scotland migrated to large industrial centers to find work in factories and shipyards, and in doing so they gave up the space, time, and effort necessary to raise and cook much of their own food. In the 19th and early 20th centuries, the streets of Scottish towns and cities were thronged with food venders selling an extraordinary variety of cheap, filling food, from eel pies to thick slices of steamed currant-studded pudding. Many 19th-century Italian food venders were so successful selling fish and chips and ice cream that that they could leave their barrows and food stalls to build restaurants, cafés, and ice cream parlors. By the 20th century, Scotland had become a restaurant nation, catering to citizens and visitors alike. Of roughly 3,500 restaurants in Scotland, 330 are Italian. Indian and Chinese immigration to Scotland has also made a strong mark on the country's restaurant scene, with over 400 Indian and 350 Chinese restaurants scattered throughout the country.

Scotland's restaurant history has also been influenced by its ties to France. The art of French pastry and confectionery making, the interest that the French have long given to haute cuisine, and the restaurant culture that has defined Paris since the 1700s

have all directly influenced Scottish gastronomy. In the 1800s, Edinburgh was as renowned for its fine bakeries as were Paris and Vienna. Many of Scotland's finest restaurants today champion the nation's abundance of high-quality fresh ingredients by showcasing them in sophisticated dishes that blend Scottish tastes and French culinary technique.

Edinburgh's oldest and most respected pubs and restaurants were initially coach stops that served meals and offered overnight accommodations to travelers. The Grasmarket District houses some of the capitol city's oldest continuing pubs and restaurants, including the White Hart Inn and the Beehive Inn, both from the early 1500s. Glasgow likewise has a famous and established restaurant history, with some of its oldest dining establishments likewise originally coach inns. Sloan's, in Glasgow's city center, was originally Morrison's Coffee House, dating from 1797, and is reputed to be on the site of the city's oldest eating establishment.

While Indian, Chinese, and Scottish-French fusion food are all popular, Scotland's restaurant culture still centers largely around the fish and chip shops, or "chippies" as they are commonly known. Italian and Jewish immigrants often established themselves in Scotland by mastering the art of frying haddock and cod in batter alongside thick wedges of potatoes. The "fish supper" (fried fish, chips, a side of mushy peas) remains for many Scots the most common and popular fast food, and several chippies have become internationally famous. Chippies also sell black and white puddings, Scotch pies, sausages, and, more recently, deep-fried Mars bars. Also very popular are Chinese and Indian take-out places and kebab stands.

Tourism enhances the Scottish restaurant business. Many hotel restaurants have become chief purchasers of traditional Scottish foods, such as oysters, mussels, and venison, that had in earlier times been produced almost exclusively for export. Creative Scottish chefs champion all manner of Scottish foodstuffs, and their consistent purchase of locally prepared gourmet cheeses, sausages, ice creams, and other specialty items in turn helps a now-thriving culture of farmers' markets and a cottage food industry.

Special Occasions

Scottish holidays and special occasions often involve an abundance of food. Scots' generosity toward their guests hearkens back to the days of clans, when chieftains plied visitors with food, drink, and good will. The most important holiday is Hogmanay, or New Year's Eve. Prior to the street parties leading up to the New Year, many Scots eat a celebratory dinner with friends and family. No one dish stands out as traditional, but the time of year lends itself to hearty dishes such as steak pie or lamb stew. Shortbread, oatcakes, an array of cheeses, smoked salmon, and rich puddings are often also on offer. Wine, whiskey, and ale are popular libations. "First footing" (meaning the first person to step over the threshold) occurs after midnight and lasts into the New Year. Many communities still hold to the tradition of considering it good luck when a dark-haired male is the first through their door, bearing gifts of shortbread and whiskey.

Although Christmas was not traditionally a significant holiday, it is now one of the most popular. Christmas dinner often includes roast turkey, "kilted pigs" (*chipolata* sausages wrapped in bacon), dressing, mashed potatoes and gravy, and a variety of side dishes, perhaps *clapshot* (potatoes and turnips layered or mashed together), as well as buttered kale. Mince pies, fruitcake, gingerbread, and plum pudding are English foods also associated with the Scottish Christmas feast.

Burns Night, on January 25, is another important Scottish holiday. Started in 1801 to commemorate the birthday of Scottish poet Robert Burns, the holiday quickly built momentum and is currently celebrated worldwide by Scots, who pay homage to Scotland and its most famous bard. Upon being seated for supper, someone is selected to read Burns's "Selkirk Grace": "Some hae meat and canna eat, / And some wad eat, that want it, / But we hae meat, and we can eat, / Sae let the Lord be thankit." The first course is a Scottish soup, perhaps cock-a-leekie (chicken, leeks, and prunes) or a Scotch broth of lamb neck meat, barley, dried peas, onions, leeks, and root vegetables. After the soup is cleared and side dishes of *bashed neeps* (mashed turnips) and

champit tatties (creamed potatoes) are placed on the table, it is common for a piper to "pipe in" the haggis with bagpipes. The host then recites Burns's "Address to the Haggis," after which he plunges a knife or dagger into the steaming pudding, cutting the shape of St. Andrew's cross in the top. A celebratory sweet, typically cranachan, ends the supper. Whiskey is the beverage of choice, as guests make toasts and recite favorite poems by Burns. Restaurants, fraternal organizations, and individual families throughout Scotland participate in this event, with butchers taking orders for haggis several weeks in advance of the supper itself.

Cranachan

⅓ c medium oats

1¼ c heavy cream

¼ c heather honey (warmed)

5 tbsp whiskey

6 oz fresh raspberries

Toast oats on a heavy baking tray for roughly 8 minutes at 400°F until lightly toasted. Cool and set aside. Whip cream until soft peaks form. Slowly add honey and whiskey as the cream thickens. Fold in the oatmeal. In four parfait glasses, put a tablespoon of raspberries at the bottom, add the whipped cream mixture, top with some more raspberries, and finish

A Burns Night supper of Cock-a-leekie soup, eel pie, smoked salmon and shortbread cookies. (Paul Cowan | Dreamstime.com)

off with more whipped cream and raspberries. Chill thoroughly.

While Burns Night is celebrated throughout Scotland, Up-Helly-Aa is Shetland's most important holiday, replete with traditional Shetland foods. This midwinter celebration is held in Shetland's capital, Lerwick, but communities throughout Shetland hold their own smaller festivals. Up-Helly-Aa involves burning a life-size wooden replica of a Viking longboat, thus commemorating Shetland's Nordic heritage. The blaze begins roughly at 8 P.M., after 800 or so local men dressed as Vikings proceed through the street carrying the boat to the town center. "Attending the halls" takes place after the burning, when residents and tourists alike go to the many parties for feasting. *Reestit mutton* (a dish of dried, reconstituted mutton), homemade mutton soup, Shetland bannocks, and oatcakes are common fare.

Weddings and birthdays are influenced by English as well as western European traditions and customs. Cake is the most important food for both events, with candles placed on top of a birthday cake to symbolize the celebrant's age. Wedding cakes are often white with white icing, although the bride and groom's personal preferences now take precedence over tradition. Because of earlier United Kingdom laws that stipulated a couple marry before noon, the wedding reception is still often called the wedding breakfast, irrespective of the time of day it occurs. Along with cake and champagne, many couples offer their guests a lavish buffet or a sit-down banquet. The bride and groom might choose to invite their families and friends to partake of the loving cup, or *quaich,* as it is called in Gaelic. Whiskey or wine is poured into the large two-handled bowl or cup (often a family heirloom), and a minister or friend blesses the couple, who drink from the cup first, and then the families and guests, who pass the quaich and take a sip in honor of the couple.

Diet and Health

A strong social welfare system ensures that few in the United Kingdom go to bed hungry; however, a lack of education, cooking skills, and limited access to affordable, healthy food does mean that a significant portion of the population suffers from malnourishment. The government estimates that in 2005, 30 percent of patients admitted to hospitals or nursing homes were clinically malnourished. In Scotland specifically, eating habits are the second major cause of poor health after smoking.

Scotland's early industrialization not only made it more difficult for people to grow, store, and cook their own food but also altered people's understanding of their relationship to the land. The vestiges of that legacy are evident in the Scottish love of takeout, restaurants, and ready-made meals and in their penchant to eat quickly. An alarming number of Scots give set mealtimes or well-balanced meals little, if any, priority. People simply eat when they are hungry; they eat what tastes good, what is cheap, and what is readily available. While 40 percent of

In front: homemade pickled vegetables with carrot, cucumbers, peppers, cauliflower, and horseradish. Behind: red peppers in mustard and chopped roasted red peppers. (Goran Andjelic | Dreamstime.com)

the Scottish population consumes fried food two or more times a week, a mere 10 percent eats whole wheat bread. Soft drink consumption has also gone up for both men and women. Younger Scots might have no more than a quick juice-type drink for breakfast, a package of crisps and a sausage for lunch, and a microwaved Scotch pie with chips for dinner, again with a soft drink or a beer.

An aggressive effort is underway to educate the public about the dangers of malnutrition and the importance of eating vegetables, fruit, lean meat, and whole grains. The 1991 white paper, "Towards a Healthier Scotland," has set a number of goals aimed at stopping Scotland's rapidly increasing obesity and incidence of type 2 diabetes, including doubling its citizens' intake of whole-grain breads, whole-grain breakfast cereals, and consumption of fruits and vegetables.

Andrea Broomfield

Further Reading

Eat Scotland. http://eatscotland.visitscotland.com/.

Geddes, Olive M. *The Laird's Kitchen.* Edinburgh: National Library of Scotland, University of Edinburgh School of Scottish Studies, 1998.

Lawrence, Sue. *Cook's Tour of Scotland: From Barra to Brora in 120 Recipes.* London: Headline Books, 2006.

Maw Broon's Cookbook. New Lanark, Scotland: Waverley Books, 2007.

"Section H4 Diet." In *Scottish Health Statistics 2000.* http://isd.scot.nhs.uk/isd/files/H4_2000.pdf.

Wilson, Carol, and Christopher Trotter. *The Food and Cooking of Scotland.* London: Southwater, 2008.

Serbia

Overview

The landlocked Republic of Serbia is located in central Europe on the Balkan Peninsula, bordered by Hungary to the north, Romania and Bulgaria to the east, the Republic of Macedonia to the south, and Croatia, Bosnia and Herzegovina, and Montenegro to the west. Serbia has had a tumultuous history punctuated by foreign invasions, economic instability, political battles, and disputed land battles between Serbia and other former Yugoslavian states including Kosovo and Montenegro. On June 5, 2006, Serbia claimed independence, and, consequently, the state of Yugoslavia was dissolved.

Serbia has an estimated population of 11 to 12 million people; however, all data dealing with population are subject to considerable error due to the dislocations caused by military action and significant political instability. In mid-2003, Serbia's population was estimated at 10.5 million people, with 50 percent residing in urban areas and 40 percent living within rural areas. Serbia has an ethnic Serb majority with the country's population also including substantial minorities of Hungarians, Roma, Albanians, and Bosniaks. There is also a substantial number of refugees and internally displaced persons, many of them ethnic Serbs from the former war zones of Croatia, Bosnia and Herzegovina, and Kosovo. Belgrade is the capital of Serbia and is the largest city in the country, with an estimated population of 1.5 to 2 million. It takes its name, which translates as "white fortress," from the large stone walls that enclose the old part of the city. It is in the north of the country, on a cliff overlooking the meeting of the Danube and Sava rivers.

Consistency and growth in food production, processing, and distribution and in food-safety control are real challenges in the process of Serbian economic development, with the food industry making up 60–80 percent of primary agricultural production; the favorable natural and climatic conditions represent a solid basis for agricultural development. Climate and geography have a significant influence on Serbian food production. Serbia has a continental climate of cold, dry winters and warm, humid summers with well-distributed rainfall and a long growing season, as well as mountainous terrain. This facilitates extensive cereal production as well as fodder crops to support intensive beef and dairy production. The fertile plains of Vojvodina supply much of the nation's grain and sugar beets, while the hilly central areas of Serbia specialize in dairy, fruit, and livestock. Key foodstuffs include grain, cotton, oilseeds, maize, sugar beets, wheat, potatoes, chicory, grapes, plums, vegetables, tobacco, olives, rice, and fodder. Livestock include sheep, cattle, and goats.

🍽 Food Culture Snapshot

Bojan and his wife, Ljiljana, have been married for 14 years and live in the town of Novi Sad, near the Danube. Bojan works as a policeman, while Ljiljana, like the majority of Serbian women, is responsible for all domestic duties, including cooking.

Breakfast is usually taken early, around 6–7 A.M. Before breakfast Bojan and Ljiljana will almost always have a black coffee called *Turska kafa*. With breakfast they will have either tea, milk, or juice and *rakija* (clear spirits)—both of which are homemade and in which Ljiljana takes great pride. These accompany several pastries or bread served with butter, jam, yogurt, sour cream, and cheese, accompanied by bacon, sausages, salami, scrambled eggs, and *kajmak* (clotted cream).

Ljiljana prepares the family lunch between 10 and 11 A.M. Lunch predominantly consists of three courses—soup, a meat-based dish, and a dessert, which in most cases will be a baked cake or pastry such as baklava. Dinner is eaten between 8 and 10 P.M. and consists of many of the same foods eaten at breakfast, unless, of course, dinner is a celebration, in which case Ljiljana and her husband will prepare a proper meal (similar to that taken at lunch).

Major Foodstuffs

The swift collapse of the Yugoslav federation has been accompanied by bloody ethnic warfare, the destabilization of republic boundaries, and the breakup of important inter-republic trade flows, resulting in serious impingements on the development of a sustainable food industry in Serbia. Consequently, current food production in Serbia is variable, closely following fluctuations in political and economic stability. Largely, Serbian food-production levels meet both direct consumption and demand from the food-processing industry, with sufficient surpluses to allow for exports. However, the low standard of living and purchasing power of the Serbian population prevent significant growth in demand for agricultural products and foodstuffs.

Despite impingements on growth, the agri-industries represent one of the most important economic footholds in Serbia, accounting for approximately 35 percent of the gross domestic product in 2005, with agricultural production at 14.5 percent and the food-processing industry at 20 percent. Crop production dominates the gross agricultural product (58%) with livestock production at 42 percent.

With well-distributed rainfall, Serbia has a long growing season for the production of fruit, grapes, and cereals as well as for livestock and dairy farming. The fertile plains of Vojvodina produce 80 percent of the cereals and most of the cotton, oilseeds, and chicory; Vojvodina also produces fodder crops to support intensive beef and dairy production.

Cooking

Serbian cuisine is largely heterogeneous with heavy Mediterranean (Byzantine/Greek), Oriental (Turkish), and Hungarian influences. The cuisine is varied because of the turbulent historical events influencing the food and people, with each region having its own subtle peculiarities and differences in traditional dishes.

A number of foods, notably pickled fruits and jams, are made at home in Serbia. Accompaniments such as rakija (fruit brandy), *slatko* (fruit or rose petal preserves), jams, jellies, various pickled foods (notably, *kiseli kupus,* or sauerkraut), *ajvar* (eggplant and pepper relish), and even sausages are all homemade.

Different dishes made with beans are popular, as well as peppers and sour cabbage (sauerkraut) leaves stuffed with ground meat, rice, and spices (*sarma*). There are various salads: The most popular, *srpska,* is made of tomatoes, peppers, onions, and dressing; the variation with cheese is called *sopska. Pitas* are made with many fillings, salty or sweet, the most common sort being *gibanica* (pita leaves filled with cheese, cream, and eggs); those filled with paprika, cheese, and sour milk (yogurt) are also a popular cooking choice both at home and in local restaurants. Peppers are a common ingredient in many dishes.

Meat is eaten in all forms (boiled, fried, roasted), in many kinds of dishes. Traditional sausages and meat-based dishes are made of pork, beef, mutton, kid, or chicken, all of which Serbs prefer roasted on a spit. Fish is also popular, and regions along the Danube are famous for their fishermen's pots (*alaska corba*).

The national dish, called *cevapcici,* is a small meat patty, highly spiced and prepared on a grill. Other Serbian specialties include *proja,* a type of cornbread; gibanica, a thin, crispy dough often filled with cheese and eggs; sarma, cabbage leaves filled with meat; and *djuvéc,* a vegetable stew. Pita (a type of strudel) and *palacinke* (crepes) are popular desserts. After a meal, coffee is prepared in the Turkish style, boiled to a thick, potent liquid and served in small cups.

Family meals play an important social role in Serbian culture, with food preparation having a strong part in Serbian family tradition. Families, depending on their economic standing, will pay between 8 and 40 dollars per day on food, and the women are generally responsible for preparing meals. Food preparation often involves daily trips to the markets, with many families visiting markets after 11 A.M. to find cheaper foodstuffs, before the markets close.

Families and friends use the meal as a celebration feast and an opportunity to exchange ideas, celebrate friendships, and often sing traditional Serbian folk songs. Daily meals are often improvised in a simple manner, with lunch (the main meal) consisting of maize bread and cottage cheese, and two or three types of pork sausages with peppers, onions, and boiled eggs. Slatko and sweet bread is also common.

Celebration meals or meals for special occasions tend to be copious and consist of numerous dishes from entrée-style soups in winter to cabbage salads during summer or the sopska salad—a salad of tomatoes, cabbage, and cheese. Main dishes generally consist of grilled meats cooked on wood fires and fish such as carp, perch, and trout from the rivers of Serbia.

Typical Meals

Serbian cuisine is heavily influenced by Greek and Croatian cooking. Despite these strong influences, Serbian food items and dishes have evolved, achieving their own culinary identity. Food preparation is a strong part of the Serbian family tradition. Serbia has its own gastronomic tradition founded in processing of milk into white cheese and kajmak (a kind of cream cheese similar to clotted cream). Other specialties include proja (cornbread), *kacamak* (corn-flour porridge), gibanica (cheese and kajmak pie), *prsuta* (local smoked ham), čvarci (cracklings), and *pihtije* (meat aspic). Staples of the Serbian diet include bread, meat, fruits, vegetables, and dairy products.

The majority of Serbians consume three meals daily, breakfast, lunch, and dinner, with lunch being the largest, following Mediterranean fashion. In rural areas, up to five meals are consumed particularly during the exhausting summer work in the fields. Breakfast generally consists of eggs, meat, and bread, with a dairy spread called kajmak. Lunch is the main meal of the day and usually is eaten at about 3 P.M. in the afternoon. A light supper is eaten at about 8 P.M.

Serbs eat a lot of wheat bread, made with or without yeast. Bread is the basis of all Serbian meals and is part of everyday meals as well as special celebrations and when hosting guests. Although pasta, rice, potatoes, and similar side dishes have entered everyday Serbian cuisine, bread is still served with these meals. Bread is often made in the home or purchased from bakeries and shops; making bread at home using barley, millet, and rye is more common in Serbian rural households. A traditional Serbian welcome is to offer guests bread and salt. Bread also plays an important role in religious rituals. Some people believe that it is sinful to throw away bread regardless of how old it is.

The national food of Serbia is cevapcici. This caseless sausage is made of minced meat, which is grilled and seasoned. Many Serbian dishes comprise various sorts of meat such as lamb, pork, and veal.

Cevapcici (Sausage)

1 lb minced lamb

1 lb minced pork

1 lb minced veal

3 cloves fresh garlic, peeled and finely chopped

1 large onion, peeled and finely chopped

Salt to taste

2 tbsp freshly ground black pepper

3 tbsp hot Hungarian paprika or sweet paprika

1 tsp freshly grated nutmeg

Mix together lamb, pork, veal, garlic, chopped onions, salt and spices until thoroughly combined. Roll meat mixture into a long, ¾-inch cylinder. Cut links at 4-inch intervals. Or you can use a sausage extruder. Place on a plastic wrap–lined plate, cover with more plastic wrap, and refrigerate for 1 hour to firm. Panfry in a large nonstick frying pan for 8 minutes, turning frequently until brown on all sides. Serve with yogurt sauce.

Yogurt Sauce

1 pt plain yogurt

Juice of 1 lemon

½ cucumber, peeled, grated, and drained for 1 hour

2 cloves fresh garlic, peeled and crushed

Salt and white pepper to taste

Combine all yogurt ingredients in a bowl. Serve immediately with cevapcici.

Eating Out

Dining out in Serbia is considered a serious opportunity for social bonding and a feast, with Serbs having a strong passion for eating meat in as many ways as they can think of cooking it. A typical restaurant meal might begin with kajmak—a salty cream cheese spread—on bread. This is followed by smoked meats such as ham and meat preserves such as jellied pork and garlic. For the main course, the most popular dish is meat patties, grilled and served with onion and mixed vegetables. This is usually accompanied by vegetable dishes such as chopped tomatoes with onion and cheese. Fish dishes are rare and are significantly more expensive given that the fish has to be brought in from the coastal regions. Dessert is usually a choice of fresh fruit, sweet pastries, and cakes.

Special Occasions

Food plays a central role in the cultural life of Serbians, particularly during ceremonial occasions such as Christmas, Easter, religious holidays, and weddings. The Christmas feast is an elaborate occasion. On Christmas Eve, people eat Lenten foods (no meat or dairy products) and drink hot toddies (warm brandy with honey). The following day, the meal generally consists of roast pork and a round bread called *cesnica*. On Krsna Slava, a family's patron saint's day, another round bread, called *kolac*, is served, as well as *zito*, a boiled, sweetened wheat dish. For Easter, boiled eggs are a traditional food. The shells are dyed and decorated in elaborate patterns.

"Wedding feast cabbage" is a special dish consisting of large chunks of cabbage mixed with many different kinds of meat and spices, which is boiled for many hours. On feast days or special celebrations an abundance of different dishes are prepared and can include cheese, kajmak, boiled eggs, and ham (smoked or dry), which are all served as starters. These dishes may be followed by soups such as the famous Backa soup, which is made with four kinds of meat. Vegetable dishes made of string beans, potatoes, and cabbage are very popular. Dessert includes a variety of cakes accompanied by *slivovica* (plum brandy), served hot or cold depending on the season; local wines; homemade fruit juices; and coffee.

Diet and Health

Since the early 1990s Serbia has undergone considerable demographic, economic, and nutritional transitions that compromised the population's food supply, especially for low-income socioeconomic groups. Reliable food production, processing, and distribution and food safety are real challenges in the development of the Serbian economy. Consequently, during the last decades many demographic, social, economic, and political changes influenced the food supply as well as dietary patterns in Serbia and resulted in a nutrition transition with an increase in the number of noncommunicable diseases. These have been the leading causes of morbidity, disability, and mortality for decades. The available data clearly indicate that smoking, hypertension, and physical inactivity as well as obesity are responsible for the greatest mortality burden, contributing 5.5 percent of total years of life lost in males and 7 percent in females. Diet represents one of the most relevant lifestyle risk factors contributing to the double burden of diet-related noncommunicable diseases. Overweight and obesity represent important public health challenge in Serbia.

Prevention of nutrition-related disorders is one of the major concerns of the Ministry of Health. There are several health-promotion and prevention programs in which regulation of body weight is an important issue; therefore, prevention of overweight and obesity is included as one of the high-priority objectives. According to the findings of the 2006 Serbian Health Survey, based on the body mass index (BMI), 38.3 percent of adult Serbians had an optimum body weight, while one in two adults in Serbia was overweight or obese (54.5%), with 36.2 percent categorized as pre-obese and 18.3 percent as obese.

In 2005 the Ministry of Health set up an expert task force to develop the "Nutrition Action Plan for the Republic of Serbia." Key objectives of this action plan with respect to diet and health include ensuring a safe, healthy, and sustainable food supply and promoting healthy nutrition for all age groups. The key focus is to stop the increasing tendency toward obesity in children and adolescents, to eliminate micronutrient deficits across the population, and to monitor dietary habits.

The most frequent intestinal infectious diseases in 2006 in Serbia were diarrhea and gastroenteritis (44.55%) followed by bacterial intestinal infections (26.51%), bacterial alimentary intoxications (12.06%), and salmonellosis (9.41%)

Katrina Meynink

Further Reading

Davies, Trish. *Cooking around the World: Romanian, Bulgarian and Balkan.* London: Lorenz Books, 2005.

Hawkesworth, Celia, trans. *Colović.* London: Hurst, 2002.

Hawkesworth, Celia. *Voices in the Shadows: Women and Verbal Art in Serbia and Bosnia.* Belgrade, Serbia: Central European University Press, 2000.

Mitchell, Lawrence. *Bradt Travel Guide to Serbia.* Chalfont St. Peter, UK: Bradt Press, 2007.

Wachtel, Andrew. *Making a Nation, Breaking a Nation: Literature and Cultural Politics in Yugoslavia.* Stanford, CA: Stanford University, 1998.

Slovakia

Overview

The Slovak Republic has the unique distinction of being the geographic center of Europe and one of its youngest countries. Roughly halfway between the North Sea and the Urals, the Mediterranean and the Arctic seas, this country has had many different political borders and has been influenced politically and culturally by both eastern and western Europe.

A tumultuous political existence has strengthened cultural markers in the region. The Slovak nation, whether recognized politically or not, has a strong connection with language, cuisine, and religion. Slovak foodstuffs and cooking are upheld and cherished as an emblem of its people and deeply tied into folk sentiments. As the country is increasingly integrated into the European Union, the foodscape is also rapidly changing. This "meat-and-potatoes" cuisine is being supplemented with imported foods through the marketing and Western supply chains of multinational food retailers.

Slovakia's high mountains extend across its northern border with Poland. The Danube River forms the border with Austria. The Czech Republic borders Slovakia in the northwest, and the Ukraine in the east. The southern low hills and plains that border Hungary offer rich farmland for raising livestock and growing grains as well as for a strong regional viticulture.

The Slovak Republic has been a parliamentary democracy since 1993, when it broke with the Czech Republic following the Velvet Revolution in 1990. Due to conservative leadership following the breakup, Slovakia was slower to warm to relations with western Europe. Not until a pro-Western government was elected in 1998 did Slovakia start to track into becoming a member of the European Union. The country joined the European Union in May 2004; it has been a member of the Schengen area since 2007 and adopted the Euro at the opening of 2009. The opening up of the borders to the West has rapidly changed the foodscape. More Slovaks are commuting across borders, more students are traveling to the West to study, and more foreign workers are moving into the small country. As such, the foodstuffs that are available and being consumed are becoming more similar to those of western Europe.

While the larger cities in western Slovakia are becoming more cosmopolitan, the remote and inaccessible mountain towns remain set in traditional foodways. In central Europe, Slovakia has the most people living in rural areas. Forty-five percent of the people live in towns of 5,000 or less, and 14 percent in villages of 1,000 or less. Many Slovak dishes are tied to folk traditions of the rural regions, which are celebrated with performances of song and dance troupes in traditional dress. Regional dishes are served, such as stuffed cabbage rolls from the east, Hungarian goulash from the south, and schnitzel from the west.

Slovakia is ethnically uniform with 85.5 percent considering themselves Slovak, 9.7 percent Hungarian, 1.7 percent Roma (although some estimates put that number closer to 10%). The country is 69 percent Roman Catholic and 9 percent Protestant. There are 3,000 Jews who still remain in the country, reduced from a population of approximately 120,000 before World War II.

Each cuisine is tied closely to ethnicity. The birth of the Slovak consciousness was tied up in the revolutions in the mid-19th century. Pan-Slavism was a dominant philosophy at the time. Aiming to rebel against the Hungarian political influence, religious leaders, philosophers, and poets helped to codify the Slovak language through literature, song, religion, and other cultural markers. Cuisine is a cultural marker by which Slovaks have also made themselves ethnically distinct.

🍽 Food Culture Snapshot

Katerina and Martin Jurov live in a village of less than 1,000 people in the central southern hills of Slovakia. Martin works as a wine inspector for the government among the local vintners in the wine-growing region. The couple owns a single-family home sitting on approximately one acre of land.

Katerina's food sources come from a combination of products grown at home, grown by her friends and

neighbors, purchased in the small village market, and purchased in a large supermarket about 15 miles away. The Jurovs have a large vegetable and fruit garden as well as a small barn where they raise a few pigs a year. Their sons live in the capital, Bratislava, and in the United States. Katerina spends time in both places and eats a wide range of food from around the world, but she likes traditional Slovak meals, too.

Major Foodstuffs

Slovak cuisine is extremely seasonal and follows the harvest through the winter months with different foodstuffs. Using simple ingredients many hearty dishes are made that are appropriate to the season. For example, in the northern hills people gather mushrooms and dry them to add to soups throughout the year. Beets, peppers, peas, and cucumbers are popular vegetables.

Local fruits, such as apricots, walnuts, cherries, Italian plums, and apples, are abundant in farmers' markets during the harvest. Imported fruits are very popular as many people remember the managed food systems under Communism, which deprived people of tropical fruits throughout the year. Today, these fruits, such as pineapples and mandarin oranges, are cherished and eaten year-round.

Although the number of vegetarians is growing, meat and poultry are still nearly ubiquitous on the dinner plate. Beef, turkey, lamb, and chicken are popular, but pork makes the most regular appearance on the plate. The sausage, *kolabasa,* is used in soups and served with brown bread as pub fare. Roasted pork is served with stewed stone fruits and dumplings, and ham is a common topping on pizza. Bacon is also a common topping for dumplings and *pirogues* (stuffed dough pockets). It is also served in breakfast breads like *pagačik,* which is made from lard and bacon bits.

Staple starches are potatoes, rice, and wheat breads. Potatoes are used in dumplings, soups, and latkes (a fried potato pancake). Rice is not native to the country, but it is very popular. It is served beside roasted meats and usually prepared with Vegeta, a spice mixture made of onion, garlic, parsley, and chicken

A man makes wine using a traditional method in Slovakia. (Shutterstock)

flavoring. Wheat is found in pastas and breads in the region. Brown and rye breads are served with sausages and soups, but a dietary staple is *roshky.* These are small, oblong-shaped buns made from bleached white flour. They are served beside cold meats or are stuffed with hot dogs for snacks.

Fats used in Slovak cooking are mostly canola oil, lard, and butter. While lard was the traditional fat, many health-conscious cooks have turned to olive oil and other healthier fats in their cooking.

Slovakia produces a wide variety of regional cheeses. Cheeses have become an important folk-heritage item for which producers have gained political protection under European Union geographical status. The most popular of these cheeses are *bryndza* and Slovensky Oštiepok, a smoked sheep's cheese. A popular dish is *vyprazene syr,* or fried cheese. This is a small block of hard cheese such as Gouda that is breaded and deep-fried and served with sauce.

Cooking

Home processing is still widely practiced to preserve the flush that a harvest brings. Many city dwellers have weekend cottages with small kitchen gardens, and rural villages are composed of single-family homes with large yards. The produce from these kitchen gardens is seasonally consumed as well as preserved as jams, pickled vegetables, smoked meats, and alcohol. Equipment for preserving and processing foods is kept in these weekend homes.

Slovaks have a few pieces of equipment that are essential to traditional cooking. When the American company Kmart opened in 1993 in downtown Bratislava, the company allocated three yards of space to displaying meat grinders to accommodate Slovak cooks. They also carried special tools to grind poppy seeds and nuts for filling pastries. A special *halušky* strainer to make the small potato/wheat dumplings is also unique to the region.

Vegetables were traditionally processed or pickled for consumption, but with the rise in Western retailing, many vegetables and salads are now served fresh. Most meals in restaurants are served with some shredded cabbage with vinegar, a radish, and some corn.

Slovaks are very careful to not waste food, and processing fruit into alcohol is another means of preserving excess food. Slivovica and *jablakovica,* eaus de vie from plums and apples, are the most commonly made liquors. Despite being illegal, many distilleries exist in private homes. Some towns have set up local distilleries for people to process their own mash. Furthermore, in the western hills, the people make homemade wine, usually in soda bottles, to be consumed at everyday meals. Although home beer brewing is not as common, manufactured Slovak beers are popular at home and in pubs.

In the ethnically Hungarian south, the dishes are spicier, with hot paprika adding heat. Goulashes, pepper salads, and Tokaj wine are common. Although Hungary has the reputation as the major wine producer in the region, the Tokaj wines produced in the Hungarian areas of Slovakia are rivals to those of the southern neighbor. This is a white wine with a distinctly musky sweetness.

The Roma (Gypsy) population has a cuisine that is difficult to describe as the Roma exist in several different economic strata within the Slovak state and have very diverse eating habits. Most Roma live in various states of poverty. Slovakia has had a dubious human rights record in its policies aimed at the Roma populations, and this ethnic group tends to be underrepresented and given little attention in official reports. Some Roma families are fully assimilated to the foodways of modern Slovakia, shopping, eating, and celebrating within the mainline traditions, but some settlements in underdeveloped Roma villages in the east do not have modern kitchens. The cooking is done mostly in a pot over an open fire with cabbage, potatoes, and roasted meats as dietary staples, supplemented by fresh fruits and sweetened tea.

Typical Meals

Breakfast starts early, with hot coffee and tea served with cold cereals, muesli, bread, butter, and ham. Lunch is the largest meal of the day, and it is customary to take this in two courses. Soup is served as a first course followed by a larger plate with a meat, a starch, and maybe a vegetable. It is common

Traditional Slovak food—dumpling (halusky) with sheep cheese (bryndza), bacon, chives, onion, and Zincica. (iStockPhoto)

to sit together as a company or a group to take the meal. Dinner is smaller and consists of only a bowl of soup or a sandwich served around seven or eight in the evening.

Slovaks have an unofficial national dish, *bryndzové halušky,* which is tied into the shepherding traditions of the mountainous north. This dish is composed of dumplings made of potato and wheat flour, topped with lardoons (small strips or cubes of pork) or bacon, onions, and an unpasteurized sheep-milk cheese, bryndza. This cheese won European Union geographical status in 2008 as a regional food of Slovakia.

Bryndzové Halušky (Dumplings)

Serves 4

Ingredients

2 lb russet potatoes

⅓ c milk

2 eggs

1 tsp salt

1 c flour

½ lb bryndza cheese (or feta)

⅓ lb bacon or lardons, cubed

1 tbsp oil

Equipment: Large pot, wooden cutting board or specialized halušky strainer

Boil water in a large pot.

Peel the potatoes, and grate them into a bowl. Mix with milk, eggs, and salt. Add flour in spoonfuls until a stiff dough forms, and knead into a ball.

Method 1: On a wet cutting board spread out dough. With a knife cut off small ½-inch pieces into the boiling water.

Method 2: Push dough through a halušky strainer into boiling water.

Boil for 4–5 minutes, until the dough comes to the surface. Scoop the dumplings out of the water. Fry the bacon until crisp. Caramelize the onion. Top dumplings with bryndza cheese, bacon, and onions.

Eating Out

The restaurant culture died during the 75 years of Communism, but it is growing back at a fast pace. Although Slovakia has a number of pubs and restaurants in many towns, it is uncommon for families to go out to dine together. The family meal is usually eaten at home. People will congregate with friends and coworkers to go to a pub or a restaurant.

Today, the streets of Bratislava are lined with Mexican, Italian, Chinese, and vegetarian choices catering to the many tourists and business travelers to the city. But smaller towns may have only a pub, which will serve a simple meal. All of this is changing with rapid globalization. With the opening of the borders, the migration of its peoples, and integration of Western supermarkets, there will be a lot more change to come into the region in the future. But for now, the foods and foodways of the Slovak republic are tied to the rich traditions of a people attached to their mountainous home.

Special Occasions

Celebrations and banquets in Slovakia are multicourse sit-down dinners. Weddings are large affairs with the celebration lasting all day into the next morning. It is traditional for a family to have a special pig slaughter for the occasion, preparing sausages for the guests.

The Slovak Christmas is similar to that of its northern neighbors in the Czech Republic. A traditional carp meal will start at the Christmas market, where the family will buy a 10–20-pound carp from a pool in the market. The fish is then kept in the bathtub for several days before Christmas Eve, when it is then roasted or fried and served with potatoes and *kapusnica,* a spicy cabbage soup. Dessert is *vianočka,* a braided yeast cake.

Kapusnica

Serves 10

2 tbsp lard

2–3 medium onions, diced

1½ lb fresh pork (a fatty cut), cubed

2 tbsp sweet paprika

1 tsp caraway seeds

1 small ham hock

2 lb sauerkraut

2 8-in. kolabasa (Polish sausage), sliced into small rounds

3–4 garlic cloves, pressed

1 full handful dried mushrooms

10–12 prunes

2 diced apples

2–3 grated potatoes

1. In a large pot heat the lard over medium heat until it melts. Add onions. Cook until translucent.

2. Add fresh pork with paprika and caraway. Cook until the meat is browned. Cover with water, add the ham hock, and simmer for ½ hour.

3. Add sauerkraut and cook another 15 minutes.

4. Add kolabasa, garlic, mushrooms, prunes, and apples, and simmer for 1 hour.

5. Add potatoes, and cook another 15 minutes until soft.

6. Serve this immediately, or let it sit for a day while the flavors fully develop. Serve with warm rye bread.

Many Slovak families in villages or with ties to villages have performed a *zabjiacka.* In this ceremony, a family or community comes together to slaughter a pig. The whole animal is used. The fresh meat and tenderloin will be eaten in the coming days, but smoked sausages made from the pig, as well as the lard, can sustain a family for months. These ceremonies take place during the late fall and winter so the slaughter can be done outside without the need for refrigeration.

Brelyn Johnson

Further Reading

Henderson, Karen. *Slovakia: The Escape from Invisibility.* New York: Routledge, 2002.

Kirschbaum, Stanislav. *A History of Slovakia: The Struggle for Survival.* New York: Palgrave McMillan, 1994.

Lorinc, John, and Sylvia Lorinc. *The Best of Slovak Cooking.* New York: Hippocrene Books, 2000.

Polvany, Marina. *All along the Danube: Recipes from Germany, Austria, Czechoslovakia, Yugoslavia, Hungary, Romania and Bulgaria.* New York: Hippocrene Books, 1994.

Slovak Cooking. http://www.slovakcooking.com.

Slovenia

Overview

A part of central Europe, the Republic of Slovenia is situated at the crossroads of the Alpine, Pannonian, and Mediterranean areas. Prior to its independence in 1991, it had been a part of the state known for decades as Yugoslavia. The current population of Slovenia amounts to 2,053,740 people inhabiting an area of about 7,722 square miles (20,000 square kilometers). With over 90 percent of its population being Slovene, Slovenia is a not a multicultural country. Autochthonous Slovenes also live in the neighboring countries of Italy, Austria, and Hungary; about 500,000 Slovene immigrants live in other parts of the world. Since 57 percent of the population is Catholic, 2.3 percent Serbian Orthodox, and 2.4 percent Muslim, religion does not play a key role in the life of many Slovenes.

In the first half of the 20th century, Slovenia was predominantly agrarian, with most of its population living in the countryside and tilling the land. Larger towns were scarce. Although the gradual industrialization after World War I changed this situation to a certain extent, 66 percent of Slovenes still worked in agriculture in 1921. At present, their number amounts to only around 4 percent.

🍽 Food Culture Snapshot

Marko, Alenka, and Tina Novak are the members of a Slovene family living in Ljubljana, the capital of Slovenia. Marko and Alenka are university graduates, while their 14-year-old daughter Tina is in the ninth grade. At approximately 7 A.M. the family meets for breakfast. The first common meal of the day, breakfast is usually prepared by Alenka. It consists of bread or toast spread with butter and jam, or with honey, and occasionally the bread is eaten with salami and cheese. Tina usually eats muesli, cornflakes, or another cereal with milk or yogurt. While the parents drink coffee with milk, the daughter drinks fruit tea or juice.

Between 10 and 11 A.M., each family member eats a light meal. Marko and Alenka eat at their workplace, and Tina, like all students, eats a school lunch. This meal usually consists of a sandwich or a roll with yogurt, milk, or juice. Sometimes they also eat a piece of fresh fruit such as an apple, a pear, or an orange.

The principal meal in Slovenia is lunch. After returning from work and from school, Marko, Alenka, and Tina have lunch together, which generally takes place around 3:30 or 4 P.M. It is mostly prepared by Alenka, with occasional assistance from Marko and Tina. Lunch is made up of several warm courses. Many times it starts with a vegetable, beef, or chicken soup. The main course usually consists of either pasta with meat or vegetable sauce; potatoes with fried meat or with cutlets and gravy; or risotto with chicken meat or with mushrooms. Consumed simultaneously with the main course, the most common salad is made with lettuce or with radicchio; in the summer, the salad can be made from tomatoes, cucumbers, or green peppers while in winter it is mainly made from sauerkraut or pickled garden beets. Lunch occasionally ends with fruit or with dessert such as ice cream, fruit salad, or pudding topped with whipped cream.

In Slovenia, dinner is a less important meal than lunch. Each member of the family usually eats it separately, mostly around 8 P.M. Dinner customarily does not consist of warm dishes; instead, it is often bread with different spreads or with cheese, ham, or salami, combined with tea, fruit, or yogurt. Alenka occasionally prepares foods from her childhood that are very popular with her family: milk rice or groats; cornmeal with milk or coffee substitutes; pancakes with jam; or *Kaiserschmarrn* (a light, eggy pancake, shredded and served with fruit preserves).

In recent years, the family has tried to eat more wholesome foods. Marko frequently buys foodstuffs, particularly vegetables and fruit, in an open-air market where vendors sell their organically grown food. Family members eat less sugar, especially white sugar, and less animal fats. Dishes are often prepared with olive or rapeseed (canola) oil. They try to include sea fish, for instance, mackerel, cod, or sole, in their weekly menus at least once; the fish are usually fried or grilled. With the exception of bread, fruit, and vegetables, which are bought daily from smaller grocery stores, the family habitually purchases food in large supermarkets once a week. Believing that homegrown food is tastier and of higher quality, Alenka, Marko, and Tina are especially glad to be able to obtain certain vegetables and fruits from their country relatives.

Major Foodstuffs

Until the 1960s, Slovene farmers worked the land for their own household needs, primarily to feed their families and less to market their crops. Until this time food culture in Slovenia was still very much geographically differentiated, and staples were not yet being bought in stores. According to ethnological classification, there were traditionally four major types of food culture in Slovenia. The eastern, Pannonian type was based on crops like wheat and buckwheat. Meals made from wheat and buckwheat flour consisted of different types of pasta, leavened pies (which were often filled with cottage cheese), and breads. Dishes were flavored with sour cream and cottage cheese, red pepper powder, or poppy seeds. Abundant crops of pumpkins, not grown anywhere else in Slovenia, yielded excellent pumpkin oil, which was widely used in cooking.

The northern, or Alpine type, was typical for the hills, mountains, and forest areas of the north. With the exception of corn and buckwheat, its harsh climate does not provide adequate conditions for agriculture but is suitable for animal husbandry and alpine dairy farming. The food culture of this region was thus based mainly on dairy products such as milk, sour milk, curd, and cheese and on corn and buckwheat mush. Venison, which was rarer in other parts of Slovenia, could also be found on the tables of local households. Game meat was also cured and made into sausages and other meat products.

In central Slovenia, farmers planted tuberous vegetables such as potatoes and turnips. Buckwheat and millet porridge, boiled in water or milk, was prepared frequently, as were cabbage and turnips. This was the first Slovene region to include the potato in its daily meals, starting in the 19th century. Prepared in a number of ways, potatoes quickly became very popular.

With its warm Mediterranean climate and karstic soil (limestone with many fissures), western Slovenia's food culture was much like that in neighboring Mediterranean countries. The barren soil, not rich enough to produce cereals, is suitable for raising sheep and for growing olive trees and certain kinds of vegetables and fruits: tomatoes, zucchini, chicory, figs, *kakis* (persimmons), and pomegranates; farmers also grow many different types of grapevines. Among the most frequently consumed foods, usually included in most meals, were polenta, which substitutes for bread; thick vegetable soups called minestrone; vegetable and meat sauces; fish; and the widely used olive oil.

Changes in the traditional food culture were introduced gradually and were connected with the growing mobility of the rural population. More perceptible changes started to take place at the end of the 1950s, and especially in the 1960s, when the rising standard of living in Slovenia resulted in an increase in its population's purchasing power.

During this period people gradually stopped baking their own bread and certain other foods themselves. Instead of making sauerkraut and sour turnips; sour milk, cream, and cottage cheese; meat products (for example, several varieties of sausages made from pigs raised and butchered at home); and beverages such as apple cider, made from home-grown apples, people purchased these foods from stores. Like bread, which was obtained in bakeries and grocery stores, people increasingly bought meat products, for instance, salami, sausages, and cold cuts; dairy foods, such as yogurt, sour cream, and whipping cream; industrially made pasta; rice; pastries and other sweets; and industrially made beverages such as beer, mineral water, and other soft drinks, particularly sodas.

At present, Slovenes' food culture mainly consists of bread and farinaceous products, potatoes, meat and meat products, and dairy products. Vegetables, pulses, and fruit are less important. Slovenia has over 100 varieties of bread, prepared by large as well as family-owned bakeries. Wheat flour is an ingredient of pasta whose many kinds are either handmade or made by machines, for example, certain types of dumplings such as *žlikrofi, krpice,* and *fuži;* and noodles. There are also other popular and widely consumed wheat-based dishes, for instance, *mlinci* (dried pancakes), crepes, the Kaiserschmarrn, different strudels, and the so-called *gibanice,* leavened pies with a variety of fillings. The once widely popular porridge and mush, which in the past represented the basic Slovene dishes and were prepared from buckwheat, millet, and cornmeal, are now seldom consumed.

The potato was first used in the first half of the 19th century as a food for human rather than animal consumption, but it was already widely popular by the end of that century. Slovenes prepare it in a number of ways. It can be cut into pieces and boiled; mashed; roasted; prepared as French fries; or cooked as home fries, namely, boiled, sliced, and then fried with onions, which is by far the most popular potato dish in Slovenia.

Until approximately the 1920s, most Slovene families consumed meat and meat products only on rare occasions, generally on Sundays and holidays. The meat served at those times was inexpensive, for example, the meat of home-raised rabbits and pigs or store-bought beef. Due to their high price, venison, veal, and poultry were far too expensive for most people. Many families reared one or two pigs, which were butchered in wintertime to provide a supply of meat,

meat products, and lard. A variety of sausages—for example, blood sausages, liverwurst, the *pečenice* (sausages that are boiled and then fried), hams, prosciuttos, stuffed stomachs, salamis, and bacon—were also made. Equally important was the preparation of lard, particularly of cracklings and minced lard; as a substitute for meat, these were used in the preparation of all daily meals. Due to a higher standard of living and animal farm factories, which in the 1960s brought meat prices down, meat-consumption patterns changed considerably. Many Slovene families now eat meat several times a day. Eaten frequently, pork and various processed pork products (for example, sausages, spareribs, the shoulder blade, prosciuttos, salamis, and the like) are still very popular. There is also an increasing consumption of poultry, particularly chicken and turkey meat, whereas beef, veal, and venison can be found on Slovene dining tables more rarely.

Fish was less prominent in the diet of Slovenes. Until the 1930s, freshwater fish, for instance, trout, sheatfish, *huchen* (in the salmon family), pike, barbell, and carp, was consumed almost throughout the Slovene territory. Along the Drava and Cerknica Lake, barbell and carp were also dried to be eaten in winter. Inhabitants of the coastal region of Primorska ate mostly sea fish, particularly sardines, European anchovies, mackerel, codfish, and tuna. First preserved in salt, the fish were kept in stone receptacles or dried to be used in winter, when they were prepared in a sauce. After World War II, sea fish became widely popular throughout Slovenia, partly due to a growing interest in, and the promotion of, healthy nutrition.

In the past, milk and dairy products were more important ingredients of meals than they are today. Most milk is now consumed for breakfast and with a light snack before noon. The consumption of yogurt and whipping cream has generally increased. Sour cream and cottage cheese, which are also eaten with bread, are used to prepare many Slovene dishes such as dumplings and strudel. Slovenia also produces butter and a variety of cheeses; two of them, the *mohant* (semisoft, yellowish, and pungent) and the *tolminc* (similar to Swiss cheese), were each given the status of products with the designation of origin.

As in the past, vegetables and fruit play no major role in the food culture of Slovenia. Legumes, particularly broad beans, lentils, kidney beans, chickpeas, and green peas, which were once eaten very frequently, were no longer grown in large quantities after World War II. By far the most frequently consumed legume of today, the kidney bean is one of, or the principal, ingredient of soups, sauces, and salads. Prepared with fat, it is eaten together with sauerkraut and potatoes. Salad is eaten frequently, particularly iceberg-type lettuce, but also spring lettuce, lamb's lettuce, endive, and radicchio. Slovenes often eat kale, sauerkraut, and turnips in wintertime. In the period after World War II, Slovene menus started to include vegetables that had come to Slovenia from other parts of Europe, for example, tomatoes, green peppers, cauliflower, broccoli, eggplant, zucchini, spinach, and *mangelwurzel* (a kind of beet).

Written reports on fruit growing and fruit consumption date from as far back as the 17th century. Mentioned are apples, pears, plums, cherries, sour cherries, peaches, apricots, walnuts, quinces, currants, and gooseberries. Just as important were forest fruits, particularly raspberries, huckleberries, strawberries, and mushrooms. While most of these fruits used to be dried or boiled, they are increasingly eaten fresh. The consumption of other fresh fruits, such as imported oranges, tangerines, clementines, and bananas, is equally on the rise.

Spices were already used when the Slavs settled the territory of present-day Slovenia. In the late Middle Ages, spices used for seasoning were the following: garlic, onions, juniper berries, anise, celery, cumin, capers, mustard, mint, lovage, rue, parsley, bay leaves, and cress. More affluent families were already using expensive imported spices such as cinnamon, pepper, saffron, nutmeg, cloves, and ginger. However, until the middle of the 20th century, Slovene homemakers generally seasoned dishes with domestic herbs, most of which were grown in their own gardens or yards: yarrow, basil, parsley, cumin, marjoram, chives, tarragon, thyme, sorrel, chervil, onion, and garlic.

In the more distant past, Slovenes drank mostly water, sometimes also beer, mead, and cider. It was

A delicious cake with apple, curd, and nuts named Gibanica. (iStockPhoto)

not until modern times that wine and hard liquor became more widely drunk. Richer families also drank coffee, hot chocolate, and tea. Until the middle of the last century, Slovenes ordinarily drank only what they had at home, for example, water, homemade cider, and cheap homemade wine. After that period, the consumption of store-bought beverages, particularly beer, mineral water, sodas, and juices, has been steadily increasing. Since the 1960s, coffee has become widely popular among Slovenes.

Cooking

Before the introduction of kitchen stoves and with the exception of the western part of the Slovene territory, where food was cooked over an open hearth, food was generally cooked in ovens. The clay pots used for this purpose could be placed on a sill in front of, or next to, the stove door and pushed into the stove itself when necessary.

By far the simplest way of preparing food was boiling; it was also the least expensive because it required neither lard nor cooking oil. Needing less attention, the simmering food also enabled the homemaker to do other chores. Since most homemakers also worked in the fields and tended farm animals, the finished dishes could easily be reheated upon their return. In certain areas local homemakers prepared food solely in the morning before leaving for the field or the family vineyard. When family members returned home the food was ready to be reheated and served. Some of the most common dishes, prepared in this manner at least until the middle of the 20th century, were gruel, mush, barley, dumplings, boiled potatoes, cabbage, turnips, soups, and sauces. Farinaceous foods, for instance, *zlivanka* (a type of cottage cheese cake), Kaiserschmarrn, leavened pies, and dumplings, were baked in the *pekva,* a clay baking pan, or in pans. Meat and meat products such as blood sausages, the pečenice, and the *mavžlji,* which were made of chopped pork or intestines and wrapped in pork membrane, were also prepared in the pekva but were consumed on very rare occasions.

Frying was not as popular as boiling and baking. Employing lard, either plain or mixed with minced meat, homemakers generally made roast potatoes, cabbage, cold mush, polenta, and occasionally offal, for example, liver. In a small part of the Slovene territory, food was cooked in kettles, suspended on a chain, over an open hearth; some dishes were baked under a large lid called the *čepnja.* Separate pieces of meat or even whole animals were spitted and roasted; this traditional way of cooking has been preserved up to the present.

First introduced in more affluent Slovene households in the middle of the 19th century, wood- and coal-burning stoves became very popular after World War I. Such modern stoves and greater availability of cooking oil, which made baking and frying cheaper and more accessible to most households, made it possible to more often prepare the dishes that up to the 1960s were made mostly on holidays. Today, the most popular types of kitchen stoves are electric and gas ranges and electric ovens. Electric or gas barbecue grills, pressure cookers, deep-fryers, and electric bread makers are also widely used.

Typical Meals

Due to their great variety it is extremely difficult to describe the daily meals typical for Slovenia in the past and in the present. Meals varied according to regions, the financial and social position of households, and their rural or urban origin. Generally speaking, Slovenes eat three meals a day: breakfast, lunch, and dinner. Students also eat a light meal at school, while some adults consume it during their working hours. The principal meal is a hot lunch, which is the heaviest meal of the day. Dinners are generally more modest.

In the past, farmers' breakfasts usually consisted of mush or polenta with milk or sour milk and ersatz coffee made of barley. Some families also ate boiled potatoes or mush and sauerkraut. This breakfast did not significantly differ from the one eaten by poorer urban dwellers, who had mostly corn mush or bread, and ersatz coffee. White bread was consumed only in wealthier families, who also ate rolls and croissants; butter, jam, and honey; and at times eggs, cold cuts, and cheeses. The usual morning beverages in these families were coffee or cocoa.

In the second half of the 20th century, breakfast started to change significantly. The main ingredients of breakfast have become bread or rolls spread with butter or margarine, jam, or liver or other kinds of pâtés, or topped with salami, sausage, or cheese; eggs are eaten occasionally. Ersatz coffee has been replaced by real coffee or tea. Some people now include in their breakfast various kinds of cereal, yogurt, and fruit. While breakfast used to be eaten very early in the morning, it is now consumed between 6:30 and 7:30 A.M.

In the past, farmers used to eat lunch at noon. It consisted of different kinds of soups and starchy dishes made from potatoes, sour turnips, kidney beans or fava beans, barley, millet, or buckwheat. These might be made into porridge or dumplings, or some other variety of mealy dishes, for example, zlivanka or *kvasenica* (both are a type of cottage cheese cake). In the summertime they ate salad greens. Meat was eaten sparingly. During the period of heavy farming chores, homemakers served smoked pork. In towns, less-well-to-do families ate potato or vegetable soups with Kaiserschmarrn, dumplings, or strudels; sometimes they ate mush or potatoes served with sauerkraut or turnips. In prosperous families, soup was always followed by a main course consisting of meat dishes such as cutlets, boiled beef, or roast meat, served with potatoes or rice, bread dumplings, pasta, or vegetable side dishes such as peas, cauliflower, spinach, or asparagus and salad. These meals always ended with dessert.

In the present, Slovene families have lunch upon returning from work, which is between 3 and 4 P.M. Since lunch is their main meal, all family members try to eat it together, which owing to the many obligations of adults and children alike is becoming increasingly difficult. Lunch is usually made by the mother. It consists of soup made from beef or chicken, potatoes, kidney beans, or kohlrabi. Soup is followed by the main course, which can be stewed meat, goulash, fricassee, cutlets, or ragout made from minced meat, and so on. Meat is served with pasta, potatoes, or rice and with a salad. Once very popular, mush, polenta, and porridge are now very seldom seen on Slovene dining tables. They have been replaced by new dishes and ingredients, particularly those that have been taken over from Italian cuisine and have become very popular: pizza, tortellini, lasagna, and gnocchi, all served with a variety of sauces. Some urban families also like Asian food.

Dinner has always been less important than lunch. Farmers used to eat dinner after they had finished their chores and returned to their house at dusk. Their dinner often consisted of dishes such as corn or buckwheat mush, boiled potatoes served with sauerkraut or turnips, salad, pumpkins prepared with flour and lard, or porridge made from millet boiled in milk. Poorer urban families ate mush with ersatz coffee; kidney bean or potato salad; or grits made with milk. Well-situated urban families ate bread, sausage, eggs, cheese, crepes, omelets, or rice pudding.

Family members now often eat dinner separately. It usually takes place between 7 and 9 P.M., depending on their hunger or when they were able to return home. Their dinner generally consists of bread with a variety of spreads or with salami, cheese, or ham. It can also be yogurt, a salad, or at times also pancakes or milk pudding.

Eating Out

Roadside inns have offered simple dishes and beverages to passing merchants and travelers since ancient times. Sources from the Middle Ages to the 18th century bear witness that the food offered to the guests in inns was bad, tasteless, and quite expensive. More important than the food was the sale of drinks, mostly wine and low-quality beer. At the beginning of the 18th century these two commercial areas were separated. This was due to an increase in road and river traffic, and in trade. The construction of the South Railway from Vienna to Trieste in the period between 1846 and 1857 significantly influenced the development of the catering trade in the Slovene territory.

Dishes that were being offered in Slovene inns before World War II were typical of the so-called Viennese cuisine. Important were novel meat dishes, among which goulash and cutlets, particularly the Wiener schnitzel, were the most popular. Lunch at an inn noted for its "good plain family cooking" consisted of the following dishes. To start there were soups such as beef soup with homemade noodles, pea soup, soup with groats or liver dumplings, or perhaps cauliflower, spinach, or tomato soup. Then there would be meats, such as roast pork, veal, venison, Wiener and Parisian schnitzel, fried or roast chicken, capon, roast turkey, goose, or duck. Side dishes included potatoes, especially fried, mashed in skins, or French fried, which appeared at the beginning of the 20th century; boiled or stewed rice; fried potato rolls or bun dumplings; and salad. Guests could also choose among different puddings, Kaiserschmarrn, crepes with homemade jam, stewed fruit, and so on.

Certain foods were also sold in the street. Street vendors offered rolls with cooked sausages, particularly frankfurters, and rolls with sausages made of horse meat or of grilled meat, for instance the *čevapčici* (meat patties) and the *ranjii* (roasted skewered meat).

Among the most popular restaurants since the mid-1970s are those that serve Italian food, particularly pizza and lasagna. In the last decade and a half, a segment of the Slovene population started to frequent restaurants serving Chinese, Indian, Thai, and Mexican food.

Special Occasions

Until the middle of the 20th century, the food culture of the Slovene population depended on the days of the week. While Slovenes generally observed the fast on Fridays, their Sunday diet was richer than during the week, with the meals usually including food that was pricier and of better quality. The same can be said of festive foods served on holidays; those that celebrated the end of difficult farm chores, for example, harvest and vintage; and those prepared when farmers butchered their pigs in wintertime. In contrast, birthdays and name days ordinarily did not require any special food; the only exceptions were weddings and sometimes baptism feasts.

Families tried to include in their Sunday meals richer meat dishes and farinaceous desserts generally not eaten on weekdays. Although there were people who ate meat, for example, sausages, spareribs, or ham, even for breakfast, meat dishes were generally served only for lunch and dinner. A typical Sunday lunch started with a meat soup, usually a beef broth with homemade noodles or with grits or liver dumplings. The main course could be the beef that had been boiled to make the soup, for instance, or smoked pork with horseradish; prosperous families also ate roasted veal or pork, tenderloin, or fried chicken. The homemakers baked dessert, for example, a bundt cake, an apple or cottage cheese strudel, or a leavened pie with filling. Dinner often consisted of food that had been left over from lunch: leftover pieces of cold roast or chicken, a salad, and dessert. Many Slovene families still eat very similar dishes on Sundays.

Christmas and Easter have always been among the most important Slovene holidays. Christmas preparations started several days ahead of time with the making of Christmas bread, cookies, and the *potica* (nut roll). This was also the time when most Slovene families butchered a pig to have an abundance of fresh meat and sausages for Christmas and New Year's celebrations. The day before Christmas was traditionally a fast day that was devoutly observed. During the day, people ate only legumes, vegetable soups, or mush; some of the more affluent families had fish. On Christmas Eve, meat was allowed once again, particularly after families returned from midnight mass. Traditionally it was either blood sausages or the pečenice, or roasted pork; the urban middle class sometimes ate fish such as boiled trout or fried carp. The festive meal ended with the potica

Potica, or nut roll pound cake, with walnuts. (iStockPhoto)

(a roll filled with nuts, poppy seeds, or a chocolate filling, more rarely with a carob, hazelnut, or coconut filling), homemade festive cookies, and fruit bread. Fasting is generally no longer observed, and new dishes have become a part of Christmas menus: for example, beefsteak tartare; French salad, which is a mixture of diced potatoes, peas, cucumbers, eggs, and mayonnaise; and sponge and layer cakes.

Another important Slovene holiday is Easter. Traditionally, the foods consumed on Easter have not changed for centuries. Families prepare a basketful of Easter food, the so-called *žegen*. The žegen consists of boiled or baked ham, or of the *šoblek* (filled pork stomach) in alpine regions, or prosciutto in Istria; homemade sausages; white bread made with or without milk; horseradish; and the *pirhi* (boiled colored eggs). Traditional Easter pastries are the potica, the *ptički,* and the *menihi* (small pasties made from leavened dough made of fine flour). A typical Easter dish from central Slovenia and Primorsko is the *aleluja*. Made of dried turnip peels, the aleluja evokes the memory of the time of severe famine during the Easter of 1529.

Aleluja

Ingredients

1 lb dried turnip peels

1 c flour (for example, buckwheat)

¾ qt water

4 tbsp lard with bacon cracklings

Salt

Wash turnip peels, and soak them in water for 3 days; the water needs to be changed every day. Boil them, then strain and chop. Add them to salted water or to water in which the Easter ham was boiled. When the water starts boiling, add flour. Make a hole in the middle, and pour in hot lard and cracklings. Serve immediately.

Diet and Health

In the past centuries, the main preoccupation of the Slovene population was to ensure enough food, which, despite the meager means generally available for its purchase or cultivation, had to be prepared in a way that would provide enough energy for the heavy physical work that was required daily. Not much attention was paid to health or special diets. The two general exceptions were childbirth and severe illness. New mothers and the sick were given special food and beverages to restore their health as soon as possible so that they could return to work.

After a woman had given birth, her family had to provide adequate quantities of wine to renew her strength and vigor. The habit of giving wine to new mothers has been documented throughout the Slovene territory. She was also given a loaf of good white bread and a hen for hen soup, which was believed to possess special powers. Another dish recommended for new mothers and for those who were sick was the *tirjet*. It consisted of slices of white bread first dipped in wine and whisked egg and then fried.

Those who had problems with constipation were given pieces of dried pears or prunes soaked in water; equally recommendable were horseradish, which is a strong purgative, and lukewarm whey. Diarrhea was fought with dried huckleberries, dried pears, the *prežganka* (soup made from water and browned flour), and water in which unhusked wheat had been boiled for several hours.

Those who were anemic had to purify their blood with raw meat, particularly horse meat, fresh sauerkraut, and turnip shoots. Certain plants and vegetables, for example, dandelion, watercress, elder shoots, and wormwood buds, were believed to help as well. In case of dropsy, swooning, bronchial disease, nerves, and worms, folk medicine advised substantial quantities of garlic. Onions helped cure pulmonary diseases, colds, and rheumatism.

Today, interest in a healthy diet has increased primarily due to a growing number of articles in the printed and electronic media. According to experts, Slovenes consume too much fat, sugar, pork, and alcohol and too little fruit and vegetables. In view of this, the Ministry of Health has organized different activities and programs to promote the consumption of fruit, vegetables, and unsaturated fats.

Maja Godina-Golija

Further Reading

Bogataj, Janez. "The Festive Table." In *Culinary Cultures of Europe: Identity, Diversity and Dialogue,* edited by Darra Goldstein and Kathrin Merkle, 397–441. Strasbourg, France: Council of Europe Publishing, 2005.

Bogataj, Janez. *Taste Slovenia.* Washington, DC: National Geographic, 2007.

Godina-Golija, Maja. "Food Culture in Slovene Urban Inns and Restaurants between the End of the Nineteenth Century and World War II." In *Eating Out in Europe: Picnics, Gourmet Dining and Snacks since the Late Eighteenth Century,* edited by Peter Scholliers and Marc Jacobs, 125–35. Oxford and New York: Berg, 2003.

Slovenia Info. http://www.slovenia.info/ uzivajmobrezmeja.

Spain

Overview

Spain is a country with a remarkably diverse landscape and climate, from the mountainous snow-capped north to the arid plains of La Mancha to the hot Mediterranean climate of the south, plus the Balearic Islands and Canary Islands. This climate has shaped not only the type of plants and domesticated animals that flourish but also the cooking techniques, mealtimes, and nutritional status of the population.

The culinary culture of Spain is understood through the various peoples who have settled or invaded the Iberian Peninsula through its long history. The original inhabitants may be represented by the surviving Basque culture, whose language and dominant blood type are completely unrelated to those of any other European group, who from prehistoric times utilized the native flora and fauna. Herbs that still grow wild fit the general Mediterranean flavor profile of seasonings and include oregano, thyme, rosemary, and garlic. Spain has also been suggested as a separate independent site of domestication for the fava bean, which is still eaten commonly and featured in stews like the Asturian *fabada*. While wild deer populations have dwindled in the ensuing millennia, wild boar is still highly prized, as are rabbit and hare, not to mention the bounty of shellfish enjoyed along the coasts, which were rigorously exploited by the native inhabitants in prehistoric times.

The first major civilization that settled southern Spain was the Phoenicians, who came originally from what is now Lebanon. After having settled in northern Africa they set up trading posts in Gadir, founded in 1104 B.C. (modern-day Cadiz), and Cartagena, which was named for their African trading hub Carthage. The Phoenicians introduced one of the single most important ingredients in Spanish culture—the olive. Although these probably arrived much earlier, the Phoenicians also brought with them eastern Mediterranean wheat and most likely cattle-rearing techniques, which provided meat from sheep, goats, and cows as well as dairy products. Olives, wheat, and cattle products form the core of Spanish cuisine as they do throughout the Mediterranean.

There were also ancient Greek settlements on the northeastern coast of what is today Catalonia, and evidence suggests that it was the Greeks who introduced the cultivation of grapes and, of course, wine to Spain. Almonds also date to this period as well as cultivated fruits. Celtic groups also settled in Spain in what is today known as Galicia, whose name is cognate with both Gaul (modern-day France) and Wales. Northwestern Spain is thus distantly related also to the Irish and Scots. The tradition of curing hams has often been ascribed to the Gauls, although there is no historical evidence that they were the ones who invented the process.

Thereafter, Spain was conquered by the Romans, who apart from building major metropolitan centers—such as Italica, the remains of which lie outside Seville, replete with amphitheaters, baths, and waterworks—also introduced the large-scale slave-operated plantations known as latifundia. Spain not only supplied much of the empire with food but also was known for certain specialty products such as *garum*—a fermented fish sauce used extensively in Roman cooking. Agricultural authorities such as Columella were Spanish, not to mention writers like Seneca as well as several emperors.

The Romans also encouraged migration to Spain from throughout the empire, and in the case of Jews forced them from their homeland in the province of Judaea after the destruction of the second temple in 70 A.D. For the next millennium and a half Jews would comprise a significant part of the population. They were easily identified by their food practices, in particular, their abstinence from foods considered unclean by kosher dietary laws, namely, pigs, rabbit, and shellfish. There still exist dishes in Spain ultimately descended from Jewish cuisine, particularly stews based on chickpeas, originally called *adafina,* which would have been cooked on Friday night before sundown for consumption the following day on the Sabbath, when fires were not allowed to be lit.

Christianity was another important introduction in late antiquity. Although official dogma and a liturgy had not yet been settled, Christianity introduced a wide variety of fasts and feasts. Eventually these became a set calendar of holy days during which abstinence from meat and meat products was commanded, most importantly during the period of Lent. Asceticism, the conscious denial of bodily pleasures, including food, as an act of penance, became a cultural ideal, though perhaps practiced rigorously only by the holiest of people. The celebration of the Eucharist in the form of bread and wine meant that cultivation of grapes and wheat was required, and it was often monastic communities who carried out these activities in periods of turmoil and social unrest in the wake of the collapse of Roman rule.

With the collapse of the Roman Empire in the fifth century, the Visigoths, a Germanic tribe from central Europe, invaded and set up a kingdom eventually centered in Toledo. Although they never displaced the local inhabitants, they did introduce Germanic taste preferences, such as that for beer, which is very popular in Spain to this day, although one might find that surprising in a Mediterranean culture. A good picture of Visigothic cuisine

can be found in Isidore of Seville's *Etymologies,* a mostly fanciful dictionary of the origins of words that inadvertently reveals many popular ingredients. For example, Isidore believed that the word *malum* (apple) derived from the word *malus,* meaning "evil," in Latin and thus explained the apple as the original fruit of the tree of knowledge in the Garden of Eden.

In 711 the Visigothic Kingdom was conquered by Moors from northern Africa who not only pushed much of the Christian populations far to the north in small, relatively weak kingdoms but also introduced Islam, which has its own variety of fasting (during Ramadan) and dietary laws—abstinence from pork and alcohol. Many Christians and Jews stayed behind and adopted Arabic as their language. For many centuries the three religions coexisted in relative peace in what is known as *convivencia,* exchanging ideas, especially scientific and medical knowledge, as well as recipes. The center of Moorish culture was the flourishing city of Cordoba, not only the largest and most splendid city in Europe at the time, but also a center of learning. The Moors introduced many new foodstuffs, the names of which in modern Spanish are all directly derived from Arabic. Thus, there are artichokes (*alcachofas*), eggplants (*berejenas*) and spinach (*espinacas*), lemon (*limón*), rice (*arroz*), and sugar (*azúcar*). They also used techniques of irrigation and intensive cultivation (especially for fruits), which were well beyond any developed elsewhere in Europe.

Very gradually the small Christian kingdoms in the north, Leon and Castille, Aragon, Navarre, and the County of Catalonia, began to reconquer land from the Moors in a process that took several centuries, the Reconquista. Timed precisely with the Crusades, this was seen not only as a way to gain territory but also as a kind of holy war against the infidel, which especially sought to regain the ancient capital of Toledo. While not complete until the fall of Granada in 1492, the Spanish kingdoms now found themselves ruling over a heterogeneous population of Jews and Muslims as well as culturally Arab Christians called Mozarabs. At times there was peace and continued interchange, at other times forced conversions and persecution. In fact, the Inquisition was founded primarily as an institution to uncover less than thoroughly converted "New Christians," or *conversos,* who might still be lighting candles on the Sabbath or keeping their kosher laws in private. Otherwise, the Middle Ages were a vibrant period in Spanish culinary history, and cookbooks were produced such as the *Libre de Sent Sovi* and eventually another by Rupert of Nola. Medieval Spanish cuisine followed some trends popular throughout Europe, including the heavy use of spices such as pepper, cinnamon, cloves, nutmeg, and ginger imported from Asia; vinegar- and sugar-laden sauces thickened with breadcrumbs; and the use of almond milk and rose water. These were in fact largely inherited from Islamic cuisine, but they would have a permanent impact on Spanish food. Some dishes descend directly from this period, like *escabeche,* fish that is fried, then preserved in vinegar and spices and served cold.

Probably the most important event influencing Spanish cooking, if not the entire world, was the discovery of the Americas by Christopher Columbus in 1492. He was, of course, not trying to discover anything new but sought a west-bound route to Asia across the ocean, which was then thought to be one ocean. This was intended as an easier route than that discovered by the Portuguese, which went around the southern tip of Africa, across the Indian Ocean, and ultimately to the spice islands in what is now Indonesia. Had there been no American continents, Columbus's plan would have made perfect sense—and he knew, as did everyone, that the world is round. It was only the earth's circumference that he miscalculated, and to his dying day Columbus believed his discoveries lay somewhere slightly east of China. Moreover, the long delay of his enterprise was due to the fact that Ferdinand and Isabella were busy conquering Granada and then subsequently expelling the Jews (Sephardim), most of whom went to live under Ottoman rule in Turkey and Greece and through northern Africa.

The introduction of tomatoes, peppers, squash, beans, and, although they took a long time to be adopted, potatoes would transform Spanish cuisine.

From Mexico also came chocolate, which became the preferred drink for the Spanish nobility and thereafter for everyone. Most important, it was sweetened with sugar, grown increasingly in the Caribbean by African slave labor. By the end of the 16th century Spain controlled the first global empire, including most of the Caribbean, Mexico, and Peru as well as the Philippines in Asia and much of Italy as well as the great Portuguese Empire in Africa, India, and Asia after the crowns had been united under a common ruler from 1580–1640.

The 17th century may be considered the golden age of Spanish cuisine. Even though much of the land was depopulated through emigration or natural attrition, the royal court was then the most splendid in Europe and indeed set culinary fashions everywhere. Grand cookbooks by royal chef Francisco Martínez Montiño were published as well as lesser ones like that of Domingo Hernández de Maceras. The quintessential dish of this period is the *olla podrida* (which literally means "rotten pot," or in French *pot pourris*), a wild combination of tongue, lamb, pigeons, sausages, chickpeas, turnips, chestnuts, and other ingredients stewed down into an indistinguishable but utterly delectable stew. Recipes appeared in English, Italian, and French cookbooks as well. This age came to an end only after two civil wars in midcentury and the failure of both the economy and the Hapsburg progeny. A war of succession fought by several European powers ultimately put a French Bourbon on the throne, but it left Spain, ironically, a relatively backward and impoverished nation, as it would remain into the 20th century. The only major cookbook published in this era was by Juan Altamiras, and it was reprinted throughout the 19th century.

The invasion of the French in the 19th century left the country in turmoil and gave its colonies in South America a chance to win independence. Civil war in the early 20th century ensured that Spain would continue to be impoverished. It would not be until the second half of the century that Spain would emerge among the modern industrialized nations of Europe and once again become a world power economically.

🍽 Food Culture Snapshot

Alicia Rios was born in 1943 and grew up in Madrid; although she never suffered from hunger, she was very conscious of the misery and repression around her through the dictatorship of the Franco era. Her father was a geologist from Zaragoza in Aragon who would bring special foods home from his field trips, bought directly from farmers and fishermen. His family would send them cherries and peaches from the mountains in the north, thick red wines from Cariñena and Somontano, and vegetables from the banks of the Ebro. Her mother came from the Costa Blanca, specifically from a village named Benissa near Alicante, where she grew citrus trees, grapes, white and black figs, and melons, as well as tomatoes and eggplants, in a garden near the sea. She also kept chickens and rabbits. Here, there were as many different paellas as there are days of the year, changing from season to season, incorporating whatever mother earth had to offer.

With this love of food Alicia went on to work in vegetarian restaurants and eventually opened her own macrobiotic restaurant, La Biotika, in 1978, followed by Los Siete Jardines in 1982, both in Madrid. She was married in 1970 to a man from Andalusia, from whom she learned a whole new repertoire of traditional bourgeois cooking. He passed away in 1999.

Today, she runs a company of food-performance art (Ali&Cia) that stages edible cityscapes around the world. Participants from neighborhoods throughout the city contribute a building or block made entirely out of foods from their own ethnic traditions, and the events culminate when the whole city is consumed.

She lives by herself in Madrid. Around 9:30 A.M. she eats a breakfast of mostly fresh fruits and porridge with walnuts, a single date, honey, and a dash of extra-virgin olive oil. At 3:30 or 4 P.M. she eats lunch, which starts with raw vegetables, followed by a *potaje,* a kind of solid soup with fresh cod, chickpeas, vegetables, and sometimes lentils or meat. This is accompanied by whole-grain rice, a glass of wine or beer, and some cheese for dessert, after which she takes a brief siesta. She rarely goes out for tapas with friends, as most Spaniards do, but waits for dinner, which may include a vegetable soup, fish, or an omelet with bread, olive oil, and ham, and perhaps some tomato. She also likes intense dark chocolate.

Major Foodstuffs

The staple grain of Spain has always been wheat, despite the cultivation of barley, oats, and other grains throughout history. Wheat is used foremost in bread, which forms the basis of practically every meal in some form, and Spanish cuisine is unthinkable without it. Interestingly, bread is usually served directly on the table rather than by putting it on little plates, nor is it served with butter. In Catalonia it is often toasted and flavored with garlic, salt, a drizzle of olive oil, and tomato, which is cut and rubbed directly onto the bread, which constitutes a kind of signature regional dish called *pa amb tomà-quet.* Wheat also features in rolls (*roscas*), many pastries, fritters, and pies (empanadas). The soft interior crumbs of bread are used for *migas* (fried crumbs) and as a thickener in gazpacho, which is a direct descendant of medieval soups, with the addition of tomato. The Spanish also eat noodles, especially the *fideos* of the east coast, which are thin, short lengths like spaghetti, cooked in a skillet like rice for paella in a dish called *fideuà.*

Rice is another important grain, and the technique for cooking it by frying in oil first and coloring it with saffron as in the classic paella ultimately goes back to medieval Arab cookery and is related to the pilaf and *biryani* introduced from as far away as India. The rice grown here, however, is mostly short-grained; the most revered are called Calasparra and Bomba. Paella recipes vary widely across Spain, though the classic version comes from Valencia. Paella may include shrimp and clams, a spicy sausage called chorizo, beans, and chicken. The classic version should not include fish, though, but rather rabbit and snails. What constitutes a proper paella is a hotly debated topic, and most people would distinguish this kind of mixed paella from a seafood paella. Whatever the ingredients, it must be cooked on a large metal *paellera* pan, preferably outdoors over a fire of vine cuttings. The dish should not be stirred as it cooks, but the rice is left to gradually absorb the liquid, which results in a crispy layer at the bottom of the pan, said to be the best part.

Corn is less important historically and was used mostly for cattle feed, but today Spain is a major producer and importer of corn. Much of this still goes into fodder, corn oil, or other industrial products, but there are some cornbreads, notably in Galicia and Asturias, but most Spaniards seem to dislike corn or consider it a food of poverty or only a porridge for babies (*maizena*). This may be due to the fact that corn that has not been nixtamalized (treated with lime—the mineral calcium hydroxide) does not supply a full range of nutrients, as it would in a Mexican tortilla, and may lead to pellagra if it forms the staple starch.

Potatoes are certainly not as popular as elsewhere in Europe, but they do feature in the classic Spanish tortilla. This word merely means "little tart," and the Mexican corn tortilla simply adopted the Spanish term. In Spain it is basically thinly sliced potatoes and onions fried in olive oil, then drained and mixed with just enough eggs to hold them together. The potato and egg mixture is then returned to the pan, cooked on one side until light brown and then flipped over using a plate and cooked on the other side. It is not really an omelet per se but closer to a frittata, though perhaps the literal translation, "little cake of potatoes," is just as good. It can also be served cold or put on bread for a sandwich.

Spanish chef preparing traditional Spanish seafood paella. (iStockPhoto)

Beans are and always have been central to Spanish cuisine. The first types used were fava beans, black-eyed peas, and other *Vigna* species that are native to Africa. Lentils and chickpeas were introduced from the Middle East, and all other beans that are today classified in the *Phaseolus* genus come from the Americas and include kidney beans, lima beans, black beans, pinto beans, and so on. Spaniards do not generally distinguish these, and many varieties from the Americas are believed to have always been grown in Spain. Beans are featured in soups and stews, often with sausage in many regional classics, or they are served cold marinated in oil as an appetizer.

Spanish cuisine makes great use of vegetables, especially those introduced by the Moors—asparagus and artichokes, spinach, and eggplant in particular. These are usually sautéed or mixed into other dishes, but with the exception of spinach, they can also be grilled and marinated and served cold or battered and fried in fritters. Many vegetables like lettuce, endive, cucumbers, and carrots are served raw in salads. Turnips are often featured in cooked stews like *cocido* or olla podrida, as are mushrooms. To lend flavor, countless Spanish dishes include onions and garlic. Among the New World vegetables the tomato is the most important, but peppers and zucchini are also important, all of which are featured in cooked recipes. Along with these, olives are perhaps the most ubiquitous of Spanish appetizers. Depending on the variety they may be picked just as they begin to turn black, then lightly cracked and soaked in successive changes of water for about a week until the bitterness is gone, then brined with herbs and garlic. But green and completely black olives are also popular, as are capers, the bud of a shrub. Along with olives they are used in cooked dishes as well.

Salmorejo Cordobes (Cold Pureed Salad)

This recipe is a thicker version of the popular gazpacho, often served with ham and bits of hard-boiled egg on top. It can be made in a food processor but is much more fun to make in a big mortar, pounded with a pestle. This should not have any water added and is essentially a cold pureed salad.

Serves 2

4 or 5 perfectly ripe tomatoes

2 slices stale peasant bread with crust removed

I clove garlic

½ c extra-virgin olive oil, preferably Spanish

A dash of vinegar

2 thin slices ibérico or serrano ham

I hard-boiled egg

Start by pounding the tomatoes in your mortar or whizzing them in the food processor. Add the bread, torn into small pieces, and garlic, and continue pounding until you have a smooth consistency. Drizzle in the olive oil; you can add more if you like. Add salt and pepper, and a dash of vinegar to taste. Pour the thick soup into wide bowls, and cover with shreds of ham and thin slices of egg.

The most popular fruits in Spain include apples, grown mostly in the Celtiberian north. Quinces are also popular; they must be cooked, most often in the form of *membrillo,* a solid quince paste that is served with cheese. Citrus fruits like lemons and oranges are grown widely in the south largely due to Arab influence. There are also dates, figs, and pomegranates. The former are also dried, along with peaches and apricots, which are also made into jam. Among nuts, almonds are perhaps the most important, and one typically finds a plate of salted almonds, especially the delicate thin-shelled *marcona,* which have a higher oil content than U.S. almonds, alongside a plate of olives and perhaps some cheese as a favorite snack. But there are also walnuts, hazelnuts, and pistachios as well as pine nuts, which are used often as a garnish with raisins in traditional Arab-influenced dishes. Chestnuts have also been very important historically as a starchy ingredient in stews, and today they are candied.

The most common meats used in Spain are beef, including the meat of bulls that have been killed in bullfights; lamb and mutton; and especially pork. The Spanish have a particular reverence for ham, especially *serrano* and above all else the *jamón ibérico de bellota,* for which the pigs are allowed to eat acorns, which gives their flesh an incomparable nutty flavor. Such hams are always served raw and thinly sliced, much like Italian prosciutto, but quite distinct. Many bars feature a whole ham fixed to a stand from which thin slices are carved to order. Pork is also used to make sausages ranging from spicy chorizo to varieties made from the pig's head or even blood as in the case of *butifarra.* Although familiar cuts of pork provide everyday fare, among the pinnacles of Spanish cuisine is the whole roasted suckling pig, associated mostly with Castile.

Poultry is also popular: chicken, turkey, and smaller game fowl like pigeon and quail. These can be sautéed, stewed, fried, made into broth, or featured in more complex mixed dishes. Rabbit is also very popular and used much like chicken, though its flavor is quite different.

Along with meat, dairy products are important in Spain, above all else cheese. Many types of cheese are eaten frequently, made from either cow, sheep, or goat milk. Manchego made from sheep is the most familiar in this country, but there is also Mahon from Minorca, Zamorano from Castile, Idiazábal from the Basque region, Tetilla from Galicia (in the shape of a woman's breast), and Cabrales, a pungent blue cheese.

Fish is also loved by the Spanish, traditionally eaten fresh along the coasts and rivers and more often cured and transported inland. Dried salted cod is one of the most unique; called *bacalao,* it is actually fished in the North Sea or Newfoundland, or it may be merely dried on the coast of Norway as stockfish. Bacalao provided protein during times of fasting when meat was forbidden, and it is used in many dishes such as *bacalao alla vizcaína* or codfish *pil pil,* which is made with oil, garlic, and chili peppers and served in a little clay dish. Preserved fish are also popular. Anchovies are often marinated in vinegar (*boquerón*) rather than salted and preserved in oil as in Italy. Tuna also is cooked and preserved in oil or dried (*mojana*) and eaten thinly sliced like ham. Fresh fish are also eaten everywhere today, along with squid and octopus, as are shellfish such as shrimp, crabs and langoustines, clams (including the distinctive narrow razor clam) and tiny cockles, sea urchins, conch, oysters and mussels, and

A variety of Spanish cheeses. (Shutterstock)

spice that has gained recent attention abroad is *Pimentón de la Vera,* a smoked paprika that comes in sweet and bitter varieties and lends a beautiful deep flavor and color to cooked dishes.

Wine is central to Spanish culinary culture, ranging from deep ruddy Rioja and Ribera del Duero to light effervescent *cavas*—the Catalonian equivalent of champagne. But wine grapes are grown practically everywhere throughout Spain, from the far western Galician coast to Alicante on the eastern shores of the Mediterranean. There are also a number of specialty wines, the most celebrated of which comes from Xeres and Sanlúcar de Barrameda on the southern tip of Spain, popularly known as sherry. These are made using the *solera* system whereby the barrels are exposed to air and oxidized and constantly refilled as the content evaporates. Then they are fortified with alcohol, making them stronger and more durable than most other wines. They can be either bone dry (fino) with a woody aroma and sometimes even a hint of brinyness to medium amontillado and oloroso and sweet versions known outside Spain as cream sherry.

Spain also produces distilled liquors such as brandy, anise (flavored with the seed of the same name), and absinthe, which is made from the herb *Artemisia absinthum.* Until very recently the active component thujone was believed to be toxic and was outlawed in most of the world, though not in Spain. It is traditionally taken by putting the alcohol into a special glass on top of which sits a perforated spoon and a cube of sugar. Cold water is drizzled on top, which creates a *louche,* or swirling green clouds in the glass.

There are other unique Spanish drinks such as *horchata* made from tiger nuts—actually the tuber called *chufa* (*Cyperus esculentus*). Since the 16th century Spaniards have been avid drinkers of chocolate, made not as it was among the Aztecs with chili peppers and various flowers, but sweetened and flavored with cinnamon. It has been proposed that chocolate was an ideal drink for the Spanish nobility, whose cultural ideals included indolence and the life of leisure, as compared to the northern countries, whose Protestant work ethic led them to drink coffee. In fact, both drinks contain caffeine,

scallops. As the symbol of Saint James (Santiago), the patron saint of Spain, scallop shells were used by pilgrims as a kind of souvenir. Although people along the coast consume shellfish fresh, especially in tapas bars known for their seafood, most Spaniards are also happy to eat these canned and keep a stock in their cupboard.

For flavoring cooks in Spain use a wide array of herbs and spices common throughout the Mediterranean like parsley, thyme, oregano, rosemary, and basil. Fennel seeds and cumin are also used as well as imported spices like cinnamon and cloves. Saffron is the spice most readily associated with Spain, which colors dishes bright yellow. It is the stamen of a crocus flower, meticulously picked by hand, which until recently was the most expensive flavoring in the world until vanilla overtook it. Another

and Spaniards are as avid coffee drinkers as any people in the world. As elsewhere in the world, there is also a great variety of mass-manufactured soft drinks.

Cooking

In Spain, many pots and pans are still made of clay. There are many advantages apart from affordability and beauty. Low-fired earthenware ceramics cook food differently, mostly because the heat is evenly distributed and gently retained rather than directed powerfully from below, creating hot spots that may burn as with modern metal pots. Moreover, food must be cooked gently, so although it takes longer, the flavor is ultimately deeper and richer rather than seared or scorched. Such pans will range from small, flat, shallow pans called *cazuelas* to covered *ollas* for soups or stews to large stewpots called *pucheros*. The cazuela can be placed directly over a gentle fire for cooking with oil or placed in the oven, and it doubles as a serving vessel as well. Other unique vessels include the *porrón,* a glass decanter for wine with a long, straight spout that pours a thin stream of liquid directly into the mouth, and also the bota, a goatskin bag seasoned with pitch on the interior, which is also used to squirt wine into one's mouth.

The mortar and pestle is also an essential Spanish implement and can be made of ceramic, stone, or olive wood. It is used to make cold soups like gazpacho as well as sauces like *allioli,* an emulsified garlic sauce.

A typical way to begin a recipe is with a *sofrito* or *sofregit* in Catalan. It is chopped onions and garlic cooked slowly in olive oil with tomatoes and sometimes other vegetables like red or green peppers. This is then used as a base for soups or stews, or it can be used in fillings for empanadas or even to cook fish like snapper or tuna in a pan.

Stewing is a common and economical technique that takes little more effort than assembling the ingredients and letting them cook slowly together in a pot. The *cocido Madrileño* is a typical example, though unlike most stews, the broth or caldo is served first, sometimes with cooked rice or noodles in it, separate from the vegetables, which are served second, and the meats, served last, arranged on a platter. The typical base is chickpeas along with vegetables like cabbage, carrots, potatoes, and turnips. With these an array of meats are cooked such as pork belly, fresh chorizo sausages, morcilla blood sausages, beef shanks and other soup bones, and a stewing hen.

Sautéing is probably the quickest and easiest cooking method, with ingredients merely placed in a pan with olive oil or rendered lard. Deep-frying is also popular for small fish or vegetables covered in batter and fried. Grilling is used most often for small fish like sardines and sausages as well as vegetables. Roast meat is very highly appreciated, whether small cuts, joints, or whole suckling pigs or lambs; roasting is best done beside an open flame, slowly turning on a spit, but it can also be done in a wood-fired oven. Normally this would be used for baking bread, but traditionally many dishes were simply cooked in an open red earthenware dish, placed directly in the *horno* until crispy and browned.

Before modern canning technologies, food would often be salted and dried for preservation or kept in oil. The former include not only hams and sausages but also dried vegetables like peppers, fish, and legumes; practically anything that could be preserved was, as a means of survival.

Spain is also home to some of the most avant-garde experimental cuisines to be found anywhere, most notably in Ferran Adrià's famed elBulli, often recognized as the best restaurant on earth. Here, one will find scientific instruments used to cook, to deconstruct and reconstruct food into new and exciting forms. Although these techniques have not had a great impact on household cooking, they have become popular in restaurants worldwide and are beginning to be used in homes. The *sous vide* method in which food is gently poached at a low temperature, vacuum sealed in a plastic bag, may soon become familiar.

Typical Meals

Spaniards eat a very small breakfast, or *desayuno,* that usually consists of nothing more than coffee or hot chocolate and maybe a piece of bread or pastry, if anything. It can be eaten at home or quickly at a bar on the way to work. The equivalent of the American breakfast is *almuerzo,* eaten before noon and usually consisting of coffee and a bread roll, but it can be something a little more substantial, and even be accompanied by wine. In the past farmworkers would eat a larger meal in the morning to fortify them for the day of work ahead.

On holidays people may eat a midafternoon snack of tapas, but normally they wait for lunch, or *comida,* eaten around 2 or 3. This is a full meal and can contain several courses and last a few hours. Traditionally people would go home to eat lunch, and they would take a siesta afterward in the hottest part of the day, but increasingly they go out to restaurants and then go back to work. A *merienda,* or snack, may be eaten, mostly by children, late in the afternoon between 5 and 7, mainly because dinner is eaten so late. For the same reason people often go out for tapas (the meal being called *tapeo*) after work, between perhaps 7 and 9. This meal will almost certainly include an aperitif like sherry, wine, or beer, plus several little plates that can include absolutely anything. In Spain the place where tapas are eaten is not a restaurant but more like a bar, and one stands. Commonly the tapas are served with napkins, which are tossed on the floor, and after a crowd passes through the tapas bar, it may look like a disaster hit.

Dinner, which can be as late as 11 P.M., is usually a smaller meal eaten at home with family members,

An assortment of Spanish tapas on a cold buffet. (Shutterstock)

in structure much like lunch. On holidays, however, it can be a much larger meal, eaten out. It will also consist of several courses with soup or salad to start, a meat or fish main course, plus a dessert such as flan or cake but just as often merely a piece of fruit.

Eating Out

Restaurants in Spain range from simple neighborhood joints to Michelin-starred white-tablecloth restaurants. elBulli was rated the best restaurant in the world for several years in succession, and the economic upsurge of Spain has meant that people eat out a lot and demand high-quality food at every type of dining establishment. Spain is currently at the forefront of what is popularly known as molecular gastronomy, cooking using scientific implements, new combinations of unusual ingredients, and plates arranged in novel and surprising ways. Many Spanish chefs dislike this term, though, preferring to call what they do simply *nueva cocina* (new cuisine). Sometimes recipes in such restaurants are variations on traditional dishes, perhaps deconstructed, but just as often they depart completely from traditional Spanish food. Like all food trends there are many imitators whose foams, colloidal suspensions, edible menus, and the like are pale imitations of the real innovators.

Restaurants are open for full meals both late in the afternoon and very late in the evening, and formal multicourse meals are served at both seatings. The Spanish love to eat out and socialize, whether at tapas bars, taverns, *fondas* (a kind of informal restaurant), cafés, or proper restaurants. Quite recently one also finds ethnic restaurants serving Chinese, Indian, Italian, or Turkish food; these may also offer a take-out menu. There are now some fast-food chains and pizzerias, but they are not as successful as elsewhere in Europe, nor can they compete with the local tapas culture.

Tapas bars are a thriving business throughout Spain and can get extremely crowded, with people standing elbow to elbow, packed in like sardines, at the best sites. Spaniards usually visit such bars in the early evening, going in groups, and often hitting several spots in one tapeo. One will find olives and lupins everywhere, as well as pickled vegetables on skewers (*banderillas*), little ceramic dishes of shrimp or fried squid, and slices of toast with tomato, cheese, ham, or blood sausage, but there can also be more substantial dishes that must be eaten with a fork, like cooked seafood, vegetables, or *patatas bravas,* which are fried potatoes served with spicy tomato sauce or garlic mayonnaise. The most renowned tapas bars are found in Andalusia in cities like Seville. The word *tapas* literally means "covers" and may derive from a piece of paper that covered a glass to keep out flies, or hold a little snack. Or it may mean a cover to the stomach when one drinks alcohol. Traditionally one would pay per plate, which were counted by white marks made on the wooden bar. Each plate holds only a few bites, and if one wants a larger portion one orders a *ración.* In the Basque country tapas are called *pintxos* (from the word for toothpicks, used to hold the little mouthfuls together) and nowadays may include wild experimental combinations of exotic ingredients.

Special Occasions

Spain is a largely Catholic country, though increasingly it is becoming secularized. Traditionally this has meant fasting on Fridays, during the entire season of Lent (40 days leading up to Easter, minus Sundays), and, for the especially devout, for the vigils on saint's days, Advent, and several other holy days. To fast in this case meant abstention from meat, cheese and dairy, eggs, and any animal products, like lard for cooking. In much of Spain this was not a terrible hardship as there is abundant oil for cooking, bounteous fish and vegetables, and especially legumes. But it did mean forgoing many favorites like ham and sausages, and in rural and mountainous regions fasting periods could be austere.

The Spanish have also been known for centuries for their parsimonious diet, subsisting on much less food than other Europeans, largely because of the heat. This, at least in the minds of foreigners, was compounded with their intense religiosity, sparing use of alcohol, and preference for many small meals scattered through the day rather than large, hearty, and substantial meals. While there may be some truth to this, the Spanish do have many celebrations. The tradition of Mardi Gras, or Carnival, a huge festival of excess preceding Lent, was abolished in the course of the Catholic Reformation in the 16th and 17th centuries. There have been revivals recently, though, which are essentially street festivals, bereft of their original religious purpose. While these are not as raucous as those of New Orleans or Rio de Janeiro, many Spanish towns manage to throw a big street party.

Street festivals are also popular during the *feria,* or bullfighting season, when stalls line the streets and people cook big pans of paella, grill sausages, and serve various kinds of street food, beer, and wine. There is usually loud music playing and flamenco dancing. The feria was originally solely a religious holiday, though, held during Easter week, or during Advent preceding Christmas. Christmas Day, like elsewhere, is an occasion for a big, formal sit-down meal at home with relatives. Special cookies are made as well as marzipan, nougats (turrón), and crumbly cakes like *mantecados,* which melt in the mouth. Candy and presents arrive on Twelfth Night, or the Feast of the Epiphany, January 5–6, when a king cake (*roscón de reyes*) is served, containing a bean or little ceramic baby. Whoever finds it is crowned king for the day.

Saint's days are also holidays; that commemorating Saint John (San Juan) on June 24 is popular,

A pile of mantecados and polvorones, typical Spanish sweets. (Shutterstock)

as is traditionally Saint James' (Santiago) the next day. As in the rest of the Hispanic world, All Saints' Day is also celebrated, by eating chestnuts, candies in the shape of dead men's bones, puffy *buñuelos* (doughnuts), and other pastries. Likewise rites of passage—baptisms, confirmations, weddings, and funerals—are celebrated with festive foods.

Diet and Health

Much of Spain would until recent decades have been included among those people who ate a so-called Mediterranean diet, consisting of a small amount of animal protein, many fruits and vegetables, healthy oils (predominantly olive), and fish high in omega-3 fatty acids. This was not the case for mountainous parts of Spain and in particular the north, but in general the Spanish diet was parsimonious and healthy, though political turmoil certainly did add its share of poverty and malnutrition. With economic prosperity, Spain can now be said to share with other nations the problems of hypertension, obesity, diabetes, and a diet relatively high in saturated fat, salt, and processed sugar. Cardiovascular disease is on the rise. This is compounded by an increasingly sedentary lifestyle, with people working at desks in an increasingly service economy and fewer people performing manual labor. Even agriculture, which a mere generation ago would have been physically very demanding, has been mechanized on par with industrial-scale farming in the wealthiest of countries. Ironically, the Spanish are also increasingly health conscious, and manufactured foods specifically designed for maintaining an ideal body weight, as well as low-calorie and low-cholesterol foods, are now commonly seen in grocery stores.

Ken Albala

Further Reading

Andres, Jose. *Made in Spain: Spanish Dishes for the American Kitchen.* New York: Clarkson Potter, 2008.

Barrenechea, Teresa. *The Cuisines of Spain.* Berkeley, CA: Ten Speed Press, 2005.

Casas, Penelope. *The Foods and Wines of Spain.* New York: Knopf, 1982.

Castro, Lourdes. *Eat, Drink, Think in Spanish.* Berkeley, CA: Ten Speed Press, 2009.

Medina, F. Xavier. *Food Culture in Spain.* Westport, CT: Greenwood Press, 2005.

Mendel, Janet. *My Kitchen in Spain.* New York: HarperCollins, 2002.

von Bremzen, Anya. *The New Spanish Table.* New York: Workman, 2005.

Sweden

Overview

Located on the peninsula of Scandinavia, the Kingdom of Sweden is one of the largest countries in Europe. Approximately 9.3 million people share a land with many natural resources, forests, mountains, rivers, lakes, and shorelines; Sweden has harsh winters in the north and mild weather in the south. Sweden is one of the least densely populated countries in Europe, and about 80 percent of its inhabitants live in cities, mostly in Stockholm, the capital, on the coast of the Baltic Sea; Malmö, in the southernmost part of the country; and Gothenburg, on the west coast. The climate varies considerably from north to south due to the country's shape, and thus the foodstuffs available to Swedes in different parts of the country also vary greatly. Sweden is divided into three general areas: Götaland in the south, Svealand in the middle, and Norrland in the north, each with its own culinary traditions, strongly influenced by climate, geography, and available foodstuffs. These three areas are in turn politically divided into 21 regions or counties characterized, in part, by their own local gastronomy.

An important aspect of Swedish culture and tradition in general is the Lutheran or Protestant heritage, even though very few Swedes regularly attend church activities. However, the strong Lutheran heritage, more specifically the belief in "not craving more than one needs," has clearly marked Swedish culinary traditions, which may appear simple to foreigners since herbs and spices have been sparingly used. At the same time, there has been a tendency to embrace foreign dishes, which has led to an increase in the variety of herbs and spices on offer, while more traditional Swedish menus are enjoyed during holidays and on special occasions. Since the 1960s, when pizza became a major Swedish dish, Middle Eastern kebabs, Chinese, and more recently Tex-Mex–inspired foods have been incorporated into mainstream Swedish food consumption.

🍴 Food Culture Snapshot

A mainstream family living in downtown Stockholm, the Nyströms consider themselves open to new tastes while maintaining their families' traditions. Sanna and David both work full-time, like most Swedes, and have one 10-year-old daughter, Lisa. Their neighborhood has several supermarkets in which Sanna and David buy most of their food. Several new bakeries sell sourdough bread, which has recently become very trendy; it is expensive by Swedish standards, and the Nyströms seldom buy the bread, but they love the smell that surrounds the bakeries. In the area there are also many coffee shops, all offering take-out *caffe latte* and lunches; however, during weekdays it is almost impossible to get a seat since they serve pasta, pie, and salad lunches that are very popular. Both Sanna and David go out to eat on workdays, even though a few co-workers have lunch boxes with them. The Nyströms spend little time shopping for food and cooking during the week.

Sanna, David, and Lisa usually start their day with a complete breakfast. They are similar to other Swedes who follow the Swedish National Food Administration's food pyramid and nutrition advice. They believe that a good breakfast is important and thus often eat oat porridge with low-fat milk and lingonberry jam, a

359

glass of fruit juice, and coffee or tea. Sometimes they have packaged cereals or toast with boiled eggs. The Nyströms do not worry about lunch since Lisa, like all children in Sweden, is served a free lunch at school. The school lunch menus are varied and include regular Swedish and international dishes, milk, bread, and salad. Since most parents work full-time, children are offered a midafternoon snack in the Child and Youth Center that is located near the school and where Lisa regularly spends her afternoons. Sanna and David arrive home around 6 P.M. and take turns making dinner. They both love food, cookbooks, and watching food programs on the television but lack the time to make elaborate recipes so they settle for ready-made meals or quick and easy dishes such as boiling potatoes and warming frozen fish fingers or Swedish meatballs in the oven.

On Saturdays, the Nyströms visit a nearby farmers' market and purchase different kinds of vegetables. Popular choices are beets, which they boil and eat with melted butter and salt; salad greens, such as spinach; and trendy vegetables, for example, *ramsoms* (a wild relative of chives), which have become very popular. Sanna, David, and Lisa eat lunch at one of the numerous restaurants that serve food from different cultures; a favorite is Lebanese food, but they sometimes purchase take-out sushi. Often, they prepare dinner at home and love to try out new recipes of modern Swedish home cooking, which are quicker to make than more traditional ones.

Major Foodstuffs

Sweden has only 5.93 percent arable land, while the rest of the country is comprised of forests, lakes, mountains, and coastlines. Fish and seafood, especially salmon and shrimp, are inexpensive; wild game is a traditional part of Swedish home cooking; locally grown vegetables are available during the summer months but otherwise are imported, along with fruits and meat.

Sweden's most important grain crops are wheat, rye, barley, and oats. Barley is mostly used for animal feed, but wheat and oats are a part of Swedish daily fare. A very popular breakfast is oatmeal with berry jams and milk, and wheat flour is used in creamy gravies and pastries. Rye is an indispensable ingredient in Swedish *knäckebröd,* or crispbread. Rye and oats also are combined or used as the main ingredient in breakfast porridges. Sugar beets are also cultivated in the southern part of the country. Sweden is practically self-sufficient regarding sugar because of the processing of sugar beets into refined sugar. Swedes consume the most candy and sweets in the world.

Potatoes are a favorite crop in Sweden, even though the yield is not large enough to feed the whole population, and, therefore, a certain percentage is imported. Potatoes are often divided into several categories according to when the potato is harvested and the best use for it. Fresh, early summer potatoes are a must on all Swedish tables during the summer. They are small and their skin is so soft that they do not have to be peeled; just washing the dirt off is usually enough. Starchy potatoes are mostly used in mashes; less starchy, firmer varieties are often boiled or sautéed. These are more frequent during the fall and winter months.

Other root crops frequently used in Swedish cuisine are carrots, rutabagas, and beets. Carrots are often just grated and served as a salad on the side. Rutabaga mash is a traditional Swedish side dish and is sometimes mixed with mashed potatoes. Boiled summer beets are popular with butter and salt, while fall and winter beets are preserved in brine and consumed throughout the year.

All sorts of cabbages are available year-round in Sweden. Spring cabbage, with its tender leaves, is used for making *kåldolmar,* the Swedish interpretation of eastern Mediterranean dolmas. Filled with minced meat and served with creamy gravy, mashed potatoes, and lingonberry jam, this dish is one of the most important in Sweden. Cabbage is also used for making *skånsk kålsoppa,* a winter soup with homemade broth and salted pork. Red cabbage is a delicacy from southern Sweden and is irreplaceable on the Christmas table.

Pork may be the most commonly used meat in Swedish households. Many different varieties of pork sausages are eaten, such as the thick *falukorv* (Falun sausage, similar to bologna), a favorite of children, and the *isterband,* made of pork, rye, and potatoes. Pork steaks appear regularly on Swedish tables, and bacon and salted pork are used to flavor different soups, such as the popular *ärtsoppa* (yellow pea soup), traditionally eaten on Thursdays. Beef is also eaten regularly even though it is more expensive than pork. Swedish *köttbullar,* the traditional meatballs now available throughout the world at IKEA restaurants, are made of one part minced pork and one part minced beef, depending on one's budget and taste. Swedish meatballs must be served with gravy, potatoes, and lingonberry jam.

Wild meats are a staple in the northern parts of Sweden and have seen a comeback in more urban areas. Supermarkets now have different cuts of wild boar, elk, moose, and deer for sale, so Swedes do not have to go hunting to be able to prepare wild game

stews, hamburgers, and steaks. Hunting is a common fall activity, and Swedish homes often have very large industrial freezers in which to preserve the game. Even in urban households, the standard refrigerator does not include a small freezer but is placed beside an independent freezer of the same size.

Several dairy products are part of Swedish daily meals. Milk is a compulsory drink for children and is also used in porridges. Cheese in Sweden is most often made from cow milk and is very popular. Many different varieties, such as *västerbottenost,* a strong aged cheese from northern Sweden, and the mild *hushållsost,* literally "home cheese," are easily available throughout the country. *Messmör* (whey butter), a spread, and *messost* (whey cheese), a cheese, are both made from milk whey, butter, and sugar and are a must on crispbread. Cream with different quantities of fat is used almost every day in Sweden. "Cooking cream" makes gravies creamy, sour cream is used in dips and cold sauces, and whipping cream is irreplaceable in *pannkakstårta,* an easy-to-make birthday pancake cake that originated in Norrbotten (North Bothnia) and is now very popular everywhere in the country.

A young girl eating a delicious winter meal of Swedish meatballs, served with mashed potatoes, gravy, and lingonberry sauce. (iStockPhoto)

Pannkakstårta (Birthday Pancake Cake)

Makes 12–15 medium-sized pancakes

Ingredients

1 c wheat flour

½ tsp salt

2½ c milk

3 medium eggs

3 tbsp butter

In a large bowl, blend the wheat flour and the salt. Add 1¼ cup milk, and beat until the dough is smooth. Add the rest of the milk, and beat again. Add 1 egg at a time, beating well before adding the next. Melt 2 tablespoons butter, and blend it into the batter. Set aside for 30 minutes.

In a large frying pan, melt 1 tablespoon butter on medium heat. Pour approximately ¼ cup batter into the pan, and fry for about 1 minute, then turn over and fry until golden brown. Put aside to cool on a plate.

For the Cake

2 c whipping cream

Sugar to taste

1½ c berry jam or fresh berries of your choice

In a bowl, whip the cream, and add sugar to taste. Place one pancake on a cake plate or other serving dish, spread some berry jam or fresh berries on the pancake, and top with 2 tablespoons whipped cream. Cover with 1 or 2 pancakes and repeat the process until all pancakes have been used. Decorate with whipped cream and fresh berries. Serve cool.

Fish is eaten at least once a week in Sweden, preferably on Tuesdays, and may be prepared in many different manners. Fish casseroles are often served in schools, and fish fingers with mashed potatoes are a children's favorite. Herring, both pickled and fried, has been an important staple in Sweden and is often eaten with potatoes and crispbread. Seafood, mostly shrimp and crayfish, is inexpensive. A delicacy that is available once a year is *surströmming,* fermented herring, served with bread and sometimes potatoes with a glass of milk on the side. Fish roe is also common in Swedish households, mostly in the form of *kaviar,* which, even though the names are similar, does not have anything in common with Russian caviar. Swedish kaviar is a spread eaten on bread with cheese and cucumber slices or on boiled eggs, and it may be used in fish sauces or sour cream seafood dips.

Sweden produces several kinds of alcoholic beverages, of which the most well known is Absolut vodka. Vodka and *akvavit,* the "water of life" made from potatoes, are irreplaceable on holidays. They are served with meals, cold, in small glasses, and are drunk in one shot, followed by a sip of beer. Akvavit is flavored with different kinds of spices, for example, dill, coriander, and caraway seeds; many Swedes make their own spice blends that they add to unflavored akvavit, which is then left to steep for several weeks.

Pickled herring served with tomato, cucumber, and lettuce. (Shutterstock)

Favorite nonalcoholic beverages are *saft,* a berry or fruit concentrate; water flavored with cucumber, lemon, or orange slices; tea; and coffee. Swedes are some of the world's biggest consumers of coffee, and the *fika,* coffee break, is compulsory in most workplaces in the country, where workers take coffee breaks twice a day. There are many varieties of coffee in Sweden: espresso, cappuccino, café au lait, and regular brewed coffee. Coffee shops are found on almost every corner in cities. Coffee and tea are often accompanied by an American-style muffin (called *muffins*), brownies, or more traditional Swedish pastries.

Desserts and sweets, cookies, cakes, and pastries are very popular in Sweden. Many recipes have French origins, though they have been adapted throughout the years. Others are originally foreign, such as Italian *pannacotta* (cooked sweetened cream solidified with gelatin), which is now sold in portion-sized containers in most supermarkets. A favorite in Sweden is *ostkaka,* which is very different from its literal translation of "cheesecake": It is a pudding or curdlike cake of cream, sugar, egg, almond, and bitter almond, served warm with cloudberry jam and sometimes whipped cream.

Cooking

Swedish cuisine has a rural heritage that is simple though time-consuming. Boiling, frying, and baking are the most commonly used techniques, and, in summer, barbecuing meats, vegetables, and fruits has become very popular during the last few years. Most stoves and ovens are electric, though a few households have older gas-fueled stoves, which are becoming quite popular in higher-income households. Microwave ovens are found in almost all Swedish homes and workplaces, where fully furnished kitchens are often available to workers. Preserving food by pickling, drying, and smoking is part of the rural heritage, and the techniques originally became popular in order to store foodstuffs during the harsh winter. Nowadays, foods from all over the world are available in most supermarkets, and preserving food is not necessary. However, the tradition of picking wild berries and mushrooms and preserving them is still very much alive today in Sweden.

Typical Meals

Since Swedes are very health conscious, they believe in starting the day with a good breakfast consisting of at least a couple slices of bread, preferably crispbread, with ham, cheese, and some cucumber slices. Sometimes breakfast consists of boiled eggs or oatmeal porridge with berries or jam and milk. Adults drink tea or coffee, while children often have a cup of hot cocoa.

Lunch is an important meal and is usually eaten around noon. Depending on the day of the week, since Swedes maintain the custom of eating fish on Tuesdays and soup on Thursdays, restaurant lunch menus vary from Thai noodles, sushi, and Swedish meatballs as well as a vegetarian alternative dish to more traditional fish casseroles, yellow pea soup and Swedish pancakes, or light salads or pies. Submarine sandwiches are also popular lunch choices.

Ärtsoppa (Yellow Pea Soup)

Serves 6

Preparation: 2–3 hours

Ingredients

6½ c dried yellow peas

8½–12 c water

1 lb salt pork (or bacon)

2 tsp dried marjoram or thyme

Cull and rinse the yellow peas. Put in a large bowl and cover with water. Leave to soak overnight. Drain the soaking water, and put in a large pot. Cover with 8½ cups cold water, and bring to a boil. Skim. Slice the salt pork or bacon into 1-inch cubes. Add to the soup and cover. Boil on medium heat until the peas feel tender and the soup is creamy, about 2 hours. Skim often and remove any pea shells. Add dried marjoram or thyme, and serve in bowls with some spicy sweet mustard on the side.

Around 2:30 P.M., it is common in Sweden to eat fruit or have a coffee break with something sweet, which may be a couple of cookies or a pastry.

Dinner on weekdays is regularly simple, with many ready-to-heat dishes or take-out foods available. Many Swedes with tight schedules choose to cook during weekends instead. However, some dishes, such as *korv* (sausage) stroganoff with rice and all sorts of meats (beef, pork, chicken) fried with vegetables and often noodles, a Thai- and Chinese-inspired cooking method, are popular weekday meals.

Swedes are very interested in cooking, and weekends are reserved for trying new recipes or creating new menus. Weekends start on Friday evenings, when taco dinners or fajitas are a popular choice. On Saturdays and Sundays, recipes from all around the world are cooked. In urban areas, it is not unusual to make Korean *bibimbap* (rice topped with vegetables and slices of meat) or Peruvian ceviche (raw marinated fish) to share with friends. Traditional Swedish meals are often reserved for holidays.

Eating Out

Swedes often eat out, in particular in cities, where many restaurants serve weekday lunch menus. Also, there are many popular street stands that offer hot dogs, hamburgers, and kebabs that share their customers with McDonald's and Burger King. Most pubs and local bars offer similar menus, of which steak and fries is often the most inexpensive choice, even though they also often serve Swedish home cooking such as *pytt i panna,* a hodgepodge of potatoes and meat leftovers sautéed with onions and served with fried eggs. However, dining out in Sweden is often expensive at regular restaurants, which are often led by well-known chefs, who during the last few years have been inspired by traditional Swedish home cooking to create modern versions of their grandmothers' recipes. Many restaurants specialize in fish and seafood or garlic-based dishes, while others concentrate on serving wild game or vegan food.

As Swedes are very interested in foreign foods, there are many restaurants that have Middle Eastern, Chinese, Korean, Thai, American, Greek, Indian, and Pakistani menus. One of the most popular choices for eating out with friends is restaurants that serve Spanish-inspired tapas.

Special Occasions

Sweden has a Christian heritage, and therefore Swedes celebrate Christmas, Easter, and All Saints' Day. However, Christian celebrations have been influenced by pre-Christian customs and sometimes foreign traditions, which have contributed to create very Swedish holiday festivities.

Christmas is very important in Sweden, even though it is no longer expected for families to celebrate Christmas Eve or share a meal on Christmas Day. Many younger Swedes celebrate with friends or travel abroad during the holidays. Nevertheless, some traditional Christmas customs are irreplaceable for many Swedes. In early December, restaurants begin to serve the traditional *julbord,* Christmas table, which includes many if not all of the compulsory Swedish Christmas dishes. Swedish meatballs, Christmas ham, red cabbage with raisins, several kinds of pickled herring, smoked salmon, sausages, cheese, crispbread, and boiled potatoes are just some examples of the wide variety of dishes on the Christmas table. Almost all employers invite their staff to a Christmas lunch or dinner consisting

of the traditional Christmas table. However, during the last few years new menus have become popular, and it is not unusual to share a Pakistani- or Lebanese-inspired Christmas table. Sweets are also very important during the holidays, and many children bake Swedish *pepparkakor,* gingerbread cookies, at school or at home. These are a must on the festival of Lucia, which celebrates the Italian Saint Lucia as the one who brings the light, on the early morning of December 13.

The Christmas table is a variation of the traditional Swedish smorgasbord that also is a part of the summer festival of *midsommar,* or Feast of St. John, celebrated in late June on Midsummer's Eve. Everywhere in Sweden, people celebrate summer by singing and dancing around a Maypole decorated with flowers and share a meal that consists of a great variety of herring, salmon, and shrimp dishes, the irreplaceable meatballs and boiled spring potatoes, lots of beer and akvavit, and bowls of strawberries and cream for dessert. The festivities begin around noon and stretch well into the night.

Summer is the most important season in Sweden due to the climate, which is cold and very dark through the long winter months. Therefore, starting in early June, fresh produce is a treat, and Swedes look forward to celebrating summer with strawberries and cream cakes, a favorite on summer birthdays; rhubarb pie with vanilla cream; and fresh greens. Summer is also the time for connecting with

Gingerbread cookies, often found in Swedish homes at Christmastime. (Shutterstock)

nature, and it is common to spend as much time as possible outdoors, eating most meals in gardens and on balconies. Swedish forests are rich with many kinds of berries, and families often spend their summer days picking berries and mushrooms. Fishing is also a favorite summer activity, and it is not unusual to see fishermen in downtown Stockholm, which has many good fishing spots.

In August the *kräftskiva,* crayfish party, is celebrated outdoors and in the company of family and friends. The menu is simple: lots of crayfish with dill flowers, crispbread and cheese, and akvavit and beer. The idea is to have a shot of akvavit for each crayfish claw on one's plate and to sing one of the many traditional songs before downing the shot. As the theme is crayfish, the table and its surroundings are decorated with paper tablecloths, napkins, carton plates, bibs, and plastic glasses, all decorated with crayfish and crayfish-related themes, and one or several paper lanterns representing the man-in-the-moon is hung from tree branches.

For Easter, Swedes decorate their homes with twigs and bright-colored feathers, and their children, both boys and girls, dress as *påskkärringar* (Easter witches who according to old Swedish beliefs congregated on the evening before Good Friday) and go out trick-or-treating. The Easter bunny usually makes an appearance on Easter Sunday, and both children and adults receive or trade as presents large cardboard eggs filled with candy and other sweets. Traditionally, Easter is celebrated by eating a variation of the smorgasbord, with cold shrimp, fish, and egg dishes and occasionally a lamb roast. In recent years, other dishes have become popular, and nowadays each family may create their own Easter menu; some may have Tex-Mex food, while others might make Vietnamese spring rolls.

Diet and Health

Swedes are very health conscious; many work out regularly and make mindful choices about the foods they eat. A lot of people are vegetarians or vegan,

and others avoid red meat and pork. Recently, eating foods with a low glycemic index has become very popular, and many restaurants now offer at least one dish with a low glycemic index.

A few years ago, a journalist published a book about additives and preservatives, and Swedes were shocked about the high content of unnatural ingredients in their favorite foods. Therefore, many Swedes now check the ingredients on packaged foods and try to avoid those they do not consider natural. A chain of supermarkets has taken advantage of this trend and is now marking "real food" to make it easier for their customers to find more natural products.

Another important trend is the strong movement toward organic and locally produced foods, which takes up a large part of the media discussions. Many cookbooks that deal with organic, regional, local, and unprocessed foods are published every year in Sweden. Food blogs are also very popular, and there are several that have organic and natural food as their favorite subject.

Sweden has a strong rural tradition, and many Swedes have a passion for nature and everything related to growing and cultivating plants. In many cities people may rent a small patch of land for growing their own food, and it is common for those who do to spend several days at a time in their lots, which most often have a small shed in which to spend the night. Recently, growers have organized small local markets, which have become very popular, in which they sell their surplus. Many who do not have access to arable land grow vegetables and even fruits at home, and it is common to see balconies in Sweden overflowing with cherry tomato plants and different kinds of herbs.

Gabriela Villagran Backman

Further Reading

Förare Winbladh, Lisa. *Safe and Delicious: Good Food the Swedish Way.* Stockholm: Swedish Institute, 2001.

Granqvist, Carl Jan, and Lena Swanberg. *Swedish Culinary Classics: Recipes with History and Originality.* Stockholm: Swedish Institute, 2005.

Henderson, Helene. *The Swedish Table.* Minneapolis: University of Minnesota Press, 2005.

Lundgren Åström, Catarina. *Swedish Homecooking.* Värnamo, Sweden: Arena, 2005.

Mosesson, Anna. *Swedish Food and Cooking: Traditions, Ingredients, Tastes, Techniques, over 60 Classic Recipes.* London: Aquamarine, 2006.

Notaker, Henry. *Food Culture in Scandinavia.* Westport, CT: Greenwood Press, 2008.

Switzerland

Overview

Switzerland is located in central Europe, landlocked between Italy, France, Germany, Austria, and Liechtenstein. The country is divided into three regions—the Alps, the Jura, and the Central Plateau—and 26 cantons. German, French, Italian, and Romansch are the country's four official languages. Its 7.6 million inhabitants are 65 percent Swiss German, 18 percent Swiss French, 10 percent Swiss Italian, 1 percent Romansch, and 6 percent of other origins. Immigrants are numerous in Switzerland, having come most recently from the Balkans. Serbo-Croatian is now the fourth most spoken language in the country, and 4.3 percent of the population is Muslim, compared to about 42 percent Catholic and 35 Percent protestant. The country's quality of living is high, and the average life expectancy is about 80 years.

Much of the country consists of mountains (the Alps cover 65 percent of its surface, with the Jura making up another 12 percent), with its highest peak, the Dufourspitze, towering at 15,203 feet. Many lakes adorn the landscape—the largest are Lake Geneva, Lake Constance, the Lake of Neuchâtel, and Lake Maggiore—which makes for a diet rich in fish specific to each lake and region. About a third of the country's land is farmed.

Switzerland's public transportation is abundant and efficient. The country boasts one of the world's densest rail systems, ranging from intercity express trains that go from Zurich to Geneva, with two stops in between, in about three hours to regional trains that cover medium-size towns, connecting them to larger urban areas. Postal cars serve smaller towns and mountain villages, while boats connect cities around lakes.

What the Swiss cook and eat is still very much influenced by the ingredients found in each region, but immigration, travel, and a large variety of prepared foreign foods available in supermarkets have diversified the Swiss palate. A Chinese hot pot is as likely to be the centerpiece of a dinner among friends as cheese fondue is. Stores close at 6:30 P.M. on weeknights and 4:30 P.M. on Saturdays, and they are closed on Sundays. Convenience stores in major train stations sell a variety of foodstuffs, including fresh fruits and vegetables, allowing commuters to shop on their way home.

Rustic dishes that contain high-calorie foodstuffs, such as potatoes, cheese, pasta, and sausages (sometimes all together), and seasonal vegetables are most typical of Swiss cuisine. These long-standing traditional foods date back to a time when most Swiss worked outside, on farms, in forests, or in the mountains.

🍽 Food Culture Snapshot

Marc and Valérie Münster live in Bern, the Swiss capital, in the top-floor apartment of a three-story house converted into office and residential space near the center of town. Marc is half Swiss German, but they both grew up in the French part of the country and moved to Bern after he finished his master's degree in geology and she her doctoral degree in law. Marc works an hour away, in Bienne (Biel), as a director and area manager for a company that educates corporations and individuals on sustainable development. Valérie works for the government in Bern, as a legal officer,

367

and travels often. They became parents in September 2009 and as a result reduced their work schedules. Marc now stays at home on Wednesdays, while Valérie does so on Tuesdays and Friday afternoons. They are committed to eating local, seasonal foods and buy mostly Swiss-grown products, organic if possible.

Like many Swiss people, their refrigerator is on the small side, so they tend to shop several times a week for quantities of food sufficient for a day or two of meals. They mostly purchase vegetables, cheese products, rice, and pasta, limiting their meat consumption to a couple of times a week. The vegetables they buy are fresh and seasonal rather than frozen, even when shopping at the supermarket, with the exception of dried green beans, a popular Swiss product. They cook dinner every night but sometimes resort to the high-quality prepared foods that are widely available in Swiss supermarkets, such as premade *rösti* (a potato pancake), premade tart dough for savory tarts, pre-cooked vegetables, and jarred sauces.

Like most Swiss urban areas, Bern is still surrounded by agrarian land and farms, even if housing developments are also prevalent in the countryside. Farmers come to the farmers' market that takes place in front of the Federal Palace and in nearby streets every Tuesday and Saturday morning. The Münsters shop there every Saturday morning, unless they are out of town, purchasing vegetables, meat, and cheeses to use during the week, and flowers. They typically buy a variety of sausages (some of which are ground on site at the market by the butcher once they pick their meat) from the region, both fresh and cured. Local cheese-mongers offer both regional specialties, such as Belper Knolle (a spreadable cheese flavored with garlic and pepper), and cheeses that come from other parts of Switzerland.

In addition to cheeses of all sorts, dairy products such as yogurt, milk, and cream figure prominently in the Münsters' refrigerator. They purchase plain or Greek yogurt to mix with cereals and muesli in the morning, and fruit-flavored yogurts to eat at the end of a meal. They rarely purchase or make dessert for weeknight meals, preferring instead to eat a yogurt and a fruit. They also frequently purchase chocolate bars, which they'll eat as an afternoon snack or after dinner.

The Münsters make their own sparkling water with a Soda-Club. They drink it throughout the day and with lunch and dinner. They drink tea and coffee with breakfast and an espresso after a meal. They often have a beer—usually from Appenzell—before or with dinner on weeknights. On weekends or when friends visit, they serve Swiss wines, which they purchase directly from the producers during tastings in Valais.

Major Foodstuffs

Each canton has its own preferred and most well-known foodstuffs, some of which are not available in other regions and might even be the specialty of only one or two producers. Other products that originated in one particular location are available—and loved—in the whole country.

True to the country's image abroad, cheese is a major Swiss foodstuff. Swiss people consume dozens of varieties of cheeses, however, not just Emmental (what is called Swiss cheese in the United States). Gruyère is usually available as salted, semisalted, mild, aged, and from the pastures (made while the cows were pasturing in the mountains in the summer, which makes it distinctly fruity). Sbrinz is another hard cheese that is eaten raw or grated onto dishes that are then cooked. Tilsiter has a softer texture that is closer to that of Emmental. Vacherin Mont d'Or comes from the canton of Vaud, but its distinct round pine box appears in cheese cases everywhere throughout the winter. It is made from lightly cooked milk and has a pale orange rind. It is eaten raw but also baked in its box with garlic and white wine until melted. Tête de Moine, from the Jura, is a round cheese that comes with its own stand and blade that turns around the top of the cheese (the *girolle*) and allows the diner to "shave" it into flower-shaped portions. Tomme Vaudoise is a small, round, soft cheese originally from Vaud that is eaten raw or baked (often breaded in the latter case). Many Swiss eat a piece or two of cheese before or in lieu of dessert on a regular basis. Cheese is also baked, melted, grated, and incorporated into other dishes, allowing for endless variations and preparations.

While cuts of meats such as steaks and roasts are expensive and as such eaten sparingly, sausages feature prominently on the Swiss table. Raw, cured, or smoked sausages, such as the *St. Galler Bratwurst* (a boiled veal sausage that is roasted or grilled), *Landjäger* (a smoked beef and bacon sausage eaten cold), and *longeole genevoise* (a raw pork sausage that includes lard in its composition), are often served alongside röstis or another starchy dish. *Cervelas* is among the country's most beloved foods. This beef-and-pork boiled sausage is a staple of the Swiss barbecue, grilled both in backyards and at campsites. It is also prepared raw in salads, with potatoes, or on its own in the typical *Würstsalat* (sausage salad). A cold-smoked pork and cabbage sausage made in the canton of Vaud is cooked and served with boiled leeks and potatoes, in a typical dish called *papet vaudois*. Sausages of all kinds are as available at local butchers (most towns still have one) as they are in larger supermarkets, which often have a meat counter. Butchers also have stands at farmers' markets.

Bündnerfleisch is one of the most prized Swiss meat products. Legs of beef are cured in salt and spices for several weeks, before being air-dried for 10 to 15 weeks, during which they are also pressed so as to extract moisture. It is traditionally made from cows raised in Switzerland, but cheaper versions, for which the cows are raised abroad, have appeared on the market in recent years.

Thanks to its numerous lakes and rivers, fish figure prominently in the Swiss diet. Perch fillets are one of the characteristic dishes found all around Lake Geneva in the summer. The small fillets are breaded, fried, and served with a squeeze of lemon and French fries. *Ombles-chevaliers,* also from Lake Geneva, are mostly eaten poached with a white wine and cream sauce. Lake and brook trout abound. Blausee Bioforellen, located on the Blausee in the Bernese Alps, are the only organically farmed trout in Switzerland. Its highly acclaimed varieties include rainbow, river, and salmon trout. *Feras* are found in most parts of Switzerland, including the Tessin, where they are sautéed and served with a vegetable marinade, and St. Gallen, where they are served with an onion and tomato sauce.

Grains, such as rice, polenta, oats, wheat, and spelt, are popular both as side dishes and as vegetarian main dishes. Polenta and risotto are traditional to Tessin, the Swiss-Italian canton, but appear on all tables. Most of the oat consumption comes as part of *Birchermüesli,* the traditional Swiss breakfast cereal mix. Potatoes are also used in large quantities, to make dishes such as rösti, potato gratin, and *spätzli* (ragged noodles made from a thick batter).

Bouillon cubes (most likely to be Knorr or Maggi brand) are a staple of the Swiss pantry. While some cooks undoubtedly make their own stocks, many use this shortcut for dishes such as soups, risottos, and stews. Maggi Würze, a sauce similar in color and flavor to soy sauce, is also a frequently used seasoning. A weeknight dish that most children eat consists simply of small macaroni pasta doused in Maggi Würze.

Bakeries and pastry shops abound in Switzerland; no small town is without its fresh bread supply, even if it takes the form of a bread depot where a baker from another town drops off bread for sale (at a convenience store, for example). In larger towns that have several pastry shops, each will often distinguish itself with a specialty. As a result, it is not unusual for customers to frequent several stores depending on what they need. Typical sweets found in the pastry case include *carac* (a ganache tartlet covered in green fondant and adorned with a chocolate pastille more typical of the French part of Switzerland), flaky pastries called mille-feuilles, *baba au rhum* (cylindrical sponge cakes doused in rum), fruit tartlets, and chocolate slices. Most shops also sell petits fours, and the more sophisticated ones add chocolates to their offerings.

Many pastries and cakes retain their origin in their name even though they are available elsewhere. The following are among the most popular ones, available both in mass-produced versions in supermarkets and in independent pastry shops. *Appenzeller Biberli,* a lightly spiced dough shaped as a round or a rectangle and filled with almond paste, is a specialty of Appenzell that makes its way into all treat bags given out for St. Nicholas or Christmas (alongside cookies, chocolates, mandarins, and peanuts in their shells). It is available in supermarkets year-round, but pastry shops often make it just around the holidays and press its top in a special mold that adorns it with a St. Nicholas

A baker is Switzerland makes chocolates by hand. (Shutterstock)

or other seasonal design, for example. Carrot cake (*Rüeblitorte*) is a specialty from Aargau, while Zug is known for its kirsch-flavored cake (*Kirschtorte*). Kirsch is a clear spirit derived from cherries. Walnut tart, from the Grisons (*Engadiner Nüsstorte*), is widely popular around the country. All supermarkets sell mass-produced, snack-size ones, while pastry shops throughout the country make their own version, which consists of *pâte sablée* (a sweet crumbly pastry crust) and a mixture of walnuts and honey. Some versions are open-faced and others completely enclosed in dough. Pear bread (*Birnbrot*) from Glarus has also made its way to the rest of the country; its filling includes pears, kirsch, nuts, and spices, encased in *pâte brisée*. *Basler Leckerli*, originally from Basel, is a hard cookie made from a dough that includes honey, candied citrus peels, and spices.

Fruit syrups, either commercial or artisanal, are popular throughout Switzerland. Elderberry, raspberry, and black currant are among the preferred flavors for these concentrates of fruits and sugar. Because only a small amount of syrup is mixed with water, it is a favored alternative to sodas.

Rivella is among Switzerland's best-known drinks. The soda, whose classic version is Rivella Red, contains milk serum, as well as herb and fruit extracts. Its lighter version, Rivella Blue, was the first low-calorie soda in Europe. Rivella Green (green tea–flavored) and Rivella Yellow (with soy serum rather than milk serum) are more recent and not as widely consumed. Sinalco, a German soda that is the oldest European soft drink, is also a popular beverage, as are Coca-Cola products.

Swiss wines are an important feature of the country's gastronomy. Swiss people drink wine with food rather than on its own. Hot, spiced wine is a staple of street fairs and community events in the winter. The Valais, a canton in southwestern Switzerland, benefits from a warm and dry climate that makes it ideal for wine production (it is also one of the top fruit-producing regions). As such, its wines represent 40 percent of the total Swiss production. Fendant (a white wine made with Chasselas grapes) and Dole (a blend of Pinot Noir and Gamay) are its most well-known wines, but other varietals, such as Sylvaner and Petite Arvine, are gaining in popularity. Chasselas, Pinot Noir, and Gamay are also the varietals most found in Vaud and Geneva, while Merlot is most abundant in Ticino, the other three top wine-producing cantons in Switzerland. Blauburgunder is a reputed Pinot Noir from the Grisons.

Cooking

While their reliance on ready-made products has increased, the Swiss still cook regularly. The Swiss kitchen does not include many appliances and gadgets. A handheld blender, for soups and purees, and a handheld electric whisk are more common than countertop appliances that would perform the same duties. A food processor will typically be the largest appliance in the kitchen, tucked away until needed. Many typical Swiss dishes, as well as weeknight meals, require few special techniques and can be made in one pot. Chopping onions or shallots and garlic might be the most complex task a cook will accomplish while making dinner. Many households will, however, own a fondue *caquelon* and a raclette oven—used for melting cheese, which is scraped onto toast.

Swiss cooking uses the standard techniques of the Western kitchen, including sautéing, boiling, roasting, braising, and grilling. A number of Swiss dishes are stewlike and as such are cooked for a long time on the stovetop. The oven is much used for gratins and baked goods.

Betty Bossi is an essential cooking partner in Swiss kitchens. This fictional woman represents a culinary empire that includes monthly magazines, cookbooks, utensils, and food products. The recipes range from classic Swiss dishes and their modern interpretations to international cuisines and focus on specific dishes, such as cakes. Even if they do not subscribe to the magazine, most Swiss cooks own at least one Betty Bossi cookbook. Many "family" recipes also have their origin with Betty Bossi.

Because eating out is often expensive and apartments are usually of comfortable size, even in cities, Swiss people frequently invite each other over for dinner. A weeknight dinner after work will be simple, such as a *Zürcher Geschnetzeltes* (a veal stew from Zurich), a cheese or onion tart with a salad, or pasta. A weekend meal will include appetizer, or at least hors d'oeuvres to enjoy with a beer or a glass of wine, and dessert, often homemade, but a cake from a nearby pastry shop might also make an appearance.

Zürich Veal Stew

Serves 4

All-purpose flour

⅔ lb veal cutlets, sliced by hand

½ lb veal kidneys, sliced by hand

Salt and freshly ground black pepper

Unsalted butter

4 shallots, finely chopped

⅔ c sliced white mushrooms

1 c dry white wine

1 c heavy cream

Beurre manié (recipe follows)

1. Lightly flour the cutlet and kidney pieces, and season with salt and pepper.

2. Heat butter in a pan over medium-high heat. Add the cutlet pieces, and cook until golden brown, 6 to 8 minutes. Remove to a plate and set aside. Repeat the process with the kidney pieces.

3. Add more butter to the pan, and add the shallots. Cook until translucent, 3 to 4 minutes. Add the mushrooms to the pan, then deglaze with the wine. Return the meats to the pan, then add the cream and stir in the beurre manié until completely incorporated.

4. Season with salt and pepper, and cook until the stew comes together as a creamy mixture. Serve over rösti, spätzli, or rice.

Beurre Manié

½ c flour

½ c butter

Prepare the beurre manié by working the flour into the butter with your hands.

Baking is as essential to the Swiss cook as knowing how to prepare meat and vegetable dishes, particularly during the holidays. The Swiss exchange homemade cookies for St. Nicholas and/or Christmas, so ovens see a flurry of activity in December. Many typical cookies include almond or hazelnut flour, which are available in all supermarkets. During the year, much of the baked goods include fruits and are eaten with coffee or tea in the afternoon and as dessert. Children often assist with the baking process, helping to perpetuate family traditions. Most people buy bread at their local bakeries but still make *Butterzopf* (*tresse*), a bread that looks like and has a texture similar to challah, on weekends.

Gardens are a popular feature of the Swiss landscape. Residents of the country or the suburbs often grow small plots of vegetables and might have a fruit tree (apple, pear, or cherry) in their backyard. Most towns and cities rent plots to apartment dwellers, who garden after work and on weekends. Neighbors often benefit from their generosity in July and August, when even a small plot results in bountiful crops of zucchini, tomatoes, greens, and fruits such as blackberries, currants, and *mirabelles* (a small, yellow plum). Blackberries and wild strawberries grow alongside less trafficked roads and in the mountains, becoming part of the menu

A small garden in a Swiss village and the Matterhorn. (iStockPhoto)

for people out on a stroll. Foraging also applies to mushrooms, which appear in many Swiss dishes, such as meat stews or on their own in a cream sauce and served over bread, for example. Much of these homegrown and foraged vegetables and fruits are cooked right away, but they are also canned (whole or processed into sauces or jams, for example) to be eaten throughout the year. While younger generations do not can as much as their parents and grandparents, food-preservation methods nonetheless are important.

Typical Meals

While not always perfectly so, typical Swiss meals tend to be fairly balanced. A green salad is often served after the main dish, which can be as simple as a vegetable gratin. The Swiss still cook many of their evening meals at home, and as such they like simple, healthful dishes that can feed the whole family with a minimum of fuss.

Coffee, tea, and milk are equally popular for breakfast. Many Swiss households own coffee machines (Nescafé being the most popular brand), which they use in the morning and throughout the day. Nearly all workers take a coffee break at some point in the morning and in the afternoon, often going to a café or cafeteria to sit down with a coffee or espresso. Most major cities now have at least one Starbucks, but coffee on the go is nowhere near as available or popular as it is in the United States. Typical mealtime beverages include still or sparkling water, often mixed with fruit syrups, and wine. Beer is drunk more frequently separate from meals, outside of the home on a weekend afternoon or before dinner when coming back from work. A digestif, most often in the form of a fruit- or herb-based schnapps, such as kirsch, Williamine, or

Appenzeller, often appears at the end of a weekend or special-occasion meal.

Café complet (the French term is used in all languages) is a long-standing staple weekly meal in Switzerland, now often enjoyed on a Sunday night. While its name comes from coffee and that beverage or chicory was likely served, with much milk, in earlier decades, that is no longer always the case. The meal centers on bread and various types of cheeses and spreads, with no cooked items.

When making desserts, fruit- and custard-based preparations prevail among Swiss cooks. *Süssmost-creme* is a classic dessert, originally from Thurgau and mostly found in the German part of the country, that is made with apple juice, eggs (whole or yolks only depending on the versions), cream, and sugar. Crème brûlée and mousses are equally popular at home and in restaurants. Fruit tarts and cakes appear on the Swiss table at least weekly. High-quality prepared doughs are available in the refrigerator (rather than the freezer) cases of supermarkets and can be used immediately, which allows cooks to have dessert ready in minutes once they cut up fruits and spread them over the dough.

Swiss people get up early and often get to work by 8 A.M. Many sit down for a breakfast consisting of bread and jam or cereals, but others will eat a croissant on the go or wait until the morning break to have a yogurt and a fruit. When not working close enough to go home for lunch (the lunch break lasts at least one hour), Swiss workers will eat the prix fixe menu offered by a nearby, inexpensive restaurant or their company's cafeteria. Plenty of shops offer sandwiches, savory tartlets, and hot dishes to go. Because of increased commuting time, many Swiss people don't get home until 6:30 or 7 P.M., but they still take the time to cook. As a result, dinner most often consists of a hot meal, even if it is a simple one that makes use of shortcuts. A weeknight dinner often includes a salad, which is served after the main dish, and fruit for dessert.

Eating Out

Switzerland boasts nearly 19,000 stand-alone restaurants and about 4,200 restaurants located in hotels. Half of all meat products eaten in Switzerland are consumed in restaurants. The high volume of tourists, particularly in larger cities and in mountain towns, is partially responsible for such a large number of eateries. While take-out places and cheaper ethnic eateries (often of the fast-food type) have gained in popularity over the last 20 years, a dinner out is still something that is enjoyed at most once a week, because restaurants tend to be expensive. Many Swiss also work away from home and might eat at their company's cafeteria or in a café at lunchtime. Smaller villages will have at least one tavern, where locals will stop for coffee in the morning and afternoon and beer or wine in the evening—but often after eating at home. Many of the larger taverns, some of which also offer rooms to rent, often have a rustic bar on the first floor and a more formal restaurant upstairs.

It is possible to eat in restaurants that are several hundred years old. The Hotel les Armures in Geneva, whose restaurant offers Swiss specialties, dates back to the 17th century. Landgasthof Löwen, in Heimiswil, is a tavern and inn that dates back to 1340. Their emphasis on typical dishes does not close this type of restaurants to the younger generations, who eat this type of food just as they will sushi and other more contemporary fare in trendier settings.

Pizzerias are extremely popular, thanks to their flavorful yet affordable offerings. Most are still owned by Italian immigrants, who represented the largest immigrant group for more than 100 years, until immigrants from the former Yugoslavia began arriving in larger numbers in the 1990s. Pizzas are available for takeout or delivery in most cities (albeit with limited options), but most people still go out to eat them.

While they do not allow for full meals, pastry shops are an integral part of Swiss eating-out habits. No weekend stroll would be complete without a stop for coffee or tea and a pastry at one of the town's shops.

Special Occasions

The uninitiated might not find special-occasion meals to be much different from regular ones. The ingredients are simple; some more expensive cuts of meats might be used when cooking for a special occasion at home, for example, but seasonal vegetables and a start will accompany it.

Raclette and fondue are not reserved for special occasions, but they are not exactly typical meals that would be consumed weekly either. They are the occasion of a gathering, even if it is a casual one on a Saturday night. Many Swiss households own a raclette oven (an electric contraption that has room for eight small, square, nonstick cheese holders) and an earthenware fondue pot (a caquelon), but people still often enjoy those foods out, at one of the many rustic restaurants and inns that serve them throughout the country. The type of cheese used for raclette bears that name. It is available in supermarkets in vacuumed-sealed packages or freshly sliced from the

local cheesemonger. The type and blend of cheeses used for fondue varies from region to region. A classic combination is the half-and-half (*moitié-moitié*), which features an equal quantity of Vacherin and Gruyère and is typically associated with the canton of Vaud, even if available in other regions.

Cheese Fondue

Serves 4

If you are a real garlic lover, you can also add a clove—thinly sliced or finely minced—to the fondue itself, for a more pronounced taste.

1 clove garlic

¼ tsp cornstarch

⅔ lb Gruyère, cut in small cubes or grated

⅔ lb Vacherin, cut in small pieces (or substitute a soft, ripe cow-milk cheese)

⅓ c dry white wine, preferably Fendant

1 tbsp kirsch or more to taste

Freshly ground white pepper

Plenty of thick-crusted peasant bread, torn or cut in pieces

1. Rub an earthenware fondue pot with the garlic clove.

2. Dissolve the cornstarch in a couple of tablespoons of the wine. Place the Gruyère and Vacherin in the pot, and add the wine, the dissolved cornstarch, and the kirsch.

3. Place the pot on the stovetop over medium-low heat, and stir with a wooden spoon until the cheese melts and everything forms a homogeneous mixture.

4. Light a container of Sterno canned heat or chafing gel, and place in the appropriate receptacle in the fondue burner stand. Place the fondue pot on the stand. Make sure that the cheese doesn't come to a boil. You can control the heat dispersed by turning the cover of the burner to open or close its ventilation holes.

5. Dip the pieces of bread into the fondue by placing them on long-handled forks. Once you finish the

A quaint and cozy scene of bread being dipped into cheese fondue in front of a fire. (Shutterstock)

fondue, be sure to allow the last thin layer of cheese to crust up and form a *religieuse*. You can remove it by poking it with your fork—if you are lucky it will come out in one piece, but otherwise just enjoy the pieces you manage to get.

For special occasions, the Swiss tend to purchase desserts at the local pastry shop rather than make their own. While cakes are not heavily frosted, the ones found in most bakeries for special occasions have buttercream frosting in flavors such as chocolate, coffee, and vanilla. They can also be covered in marzipan. Guests might bring petits fours, to enjoy with coffee and a digestif after the meal.

Several dishes are served for Carnival (usually in February), such as the *Basler Mehlsuppe,* a soup made of roasted flour typical of Basel, and beignets and fried doughs of all kinds. The Bern onion fair features plentiful onion dishes. A chocolate cauldron filled with marzipan vegetables celebrates Geneva's liberation from the Savoyards every December 10, in an occasion called *l'Escalade.*

Diet and Health

Like many European countries, Switzerland has seen its obesity rate rise over the last 20 years. According to the Federal Office of Public Health, 37.3 percent of Swiss adults have a body mass index greater than 25, which makes them overweight. One out of five children is overweight—a number that has quintupled in 20 years. A decline in physical activity, as both work and leisure become more sedentary, and a diet of high-calorie foods rich in fats and sugars are to blame.

Generally, however, the Swiss lifestyle offers a better work-life balance than other Western countries. While freelancing is not very common, employees can often reduce their work schedule once they start having children or to pursue side activities. Having more time at home means that people cook full meals and bake often. Even the larger cities are close to mountains and lakes, so outdoor activities are part of the everyday life of most Swiss citizens, from a simple walk or a multiday hike at high altitude to boating and skiing.

Grains and dairy products appear frequently on Swiss tables, as do vegetables. Because of its cost, meat is typically not consumed daily. Many still take the time to sit down for breakfast, which includes muesli or bread slices with jams rather than sweet pastries. This makes the Swiss diet a generally balanced one.

Anne Engammare McBride

Further Reading

Biner, Béatrice. *Saveurs du Monde: La Suisse.* Aspères, France: Romain Pages Éditions, 2000.

Bossi, Betty. *Cuisine Suisse.* Zurich: Editions Betty Bossi, 2009.

Bossi, Betty. *Spécialités Suisses.* Zurich: Editions Betty Bossi, 1997.

Federal Office of Public Health. http://www.bag.admin.ch.

Haefeli, Alfred, ed. *In Aller Munde: Die 100 beliebtesten Schweizer Lebensmittel.* Lenzburg, Switzerland: Faro, 2009.

Hazelton, Nika Standen. *The Swiss Cookbook.* 1967. New York: Hippocrene Books, 1998.

Nelson, Kay Shaw. *Cuisines of the Alps: Recipes, Drinks, and Lore from France, Switzerland, Liechtenstein, Italy, Germany, Austria, and Slovenia.* New York: Hippocrene Books, 2005.

Patrimoine Suisse. http://www.patrimoinesuisse.ch.

Prade, Georges. *180 recettes de cuisine Suisse de tous les cantons.* Fribourg, Switzerland: Medea Diffusion, 1986.

Style, Sue. *A Taste of Switzerland.* New York: William Morrow, 1992.

Weiss, Martin. *Urchuchi: Schweizer Restaurants mit Geschichten und Gerichten.* Zurich: Rotpunktverlag, 2007–2009.

Ukraine

Overview

Ukraine is a large eastern European country. Its territory covers 233,090 square miles. It is bordered by Russia, Belarus, Poland, Hungary, Slovakia, Romania, and Moldova, as well as the Black Sea and the Sea of Azov. The Dnieper, the Dniester, and the Buh are the three major rivers in Ukraine. Ukraine is a unitary republic divided into 24 provinces (*oblast*s) centered around large cities. Its population of just over 46 million people consists of ethnic Ukrainians (77%), Russians (17.3%), Moldovans, and Romanians (0.8%). There are also significant minorities of Belarusians, Bulgarians, Tartars, Jews, Armenians, and Greeks. This diversity is also reflected in Ukrainian cuisine, its ingredients, and its culinary techniques. Ukraine, throughout its history, has been subject to numerous invasions and domination by foreign powers. These influences also led a diverse and multirooted culinary tradition.

Religion also plays an important role in Ukrainian culinary traditions. Of those Ukrainians who are religious, 76 percent are Ukrainian or Russian Orthodox Christians. Eastern-rite Catholics make up 8 percent of the religious population, while Roman Catholics and Protestants make up 2 percent each. Less than 1 percent of the population is Jewish or Muslim. Under Soviet rule, religion was strongly discouraged, and today over half of Ukrainians claim to be atheist or to belong to no faith. Despite this, religious holidays and holiday dishes remain popular.

Food Culture Snapshot

Oleh and Viktoriya Shevchuk are a young couple living in Kiev, the capital of Ukraine. Oleh owns a small construction company building summer homes outside of Kiev. Viktoriya is an economist working for a private bank. They have no children. Their eating habits have been shaped by both traditional and Soviet foods that their parents served at home, as well as modern influences. Being middle class has allowed the Shevchuks to travel to western Europe and to Mediterranean resorts. They like the gourmet foods they sampled while traveling. Since they both have busy work lives, the Shevchuks also like the new convenience foods that are available in Ukrainian supermarkets.

The Shevchuks live in a typical "bedroom" district of Kiev, on the left shore of the Dnieper River. Like most other people living in the countries of the former Soviet Union, their sources of food are the supermarket, small local shops, and farmers' markets. The Schevchuks shop together at the markets and supermarkets. As they return home after work, they make small, everyday purchases of bread, cookies, and soft drinks at the small local shops. The Shevchuks own a car and once a week drive to the nearest large supermarket, which is a part of the MegaMarket chain. There, they stock up on porridge grains, convenience foods like instant noodles, and cold cuts, milk, and eggs. Since they are young and have had greater exposure to the western European diet, the Shevchuks purchase many items that are not traditionally Ukrainian such as dry breakfast cereal and yogurts. At the Levoberezhny market, which is not far from where they live, the Shevchuks shop for vegetables and fresh meat. Just like their parents, they try to maintain good relationships with specific stall owners, who then supply them with the better and fresher vegetables and cuts of meat.

Major Foodstuffs

Ukraine was traditionally seen as the breadbasket of eastern Europe, and it continued to play this role under Soviet rule. Unlike the relatively cold and poor-soiled terrain of its northern neighbors, Russia and Belarus, Ukraine's land was able to support a wheat-based cuisine. Millet and rice play a popular but secondary role. Rye and oats are much less important as grains in Ukrainian culinary traditions, but sourdough rye breads are also common. Various breads, cakes, and filled and plain dumplings are all usually made of wheat flour, sometimes in combination with milled buckwheat.

Vegetables and legumes are also very important to Ukrainian cookery. Beets are the most iconic and popular of the vegetables used in Ukrainian cooking, providing a key ingredient in its most well-known dish, a rich soup known as *borsch.* Beans and lentils are used in soups but are also mashed and served mixed with fats or in combination with other vegetables. Carrots, tomatoes, pumpkins, potatoes, and corn are also very important in Ukrainian cuisine. In western Ukraine, where the influence of Balkan cuisine is quite strong, corn is a major source of starch in the form of a local version of polenta known as *mamalyga,* which is often eaten with a salty sheep-milk cheese. Potatoes are not as common as is in the cuisine of Russia, or especially Belarus, but they still are very popular and commonly presented as a side dish, often in combination with other vegetables or even fruit. Potatoes are also used to obtain starch for use in jellied desserts. Onions, turnips, and cabbage are also important, with cabbage used either raw, fermented, in soups, or stuffed and stewed. Eggplants were seen as "foreign" in the distant past but have now become quite common in Ukrainian cuisine.

Meat is also a popular ingredient. Pork is the most common meat for Ukrainians. As in other

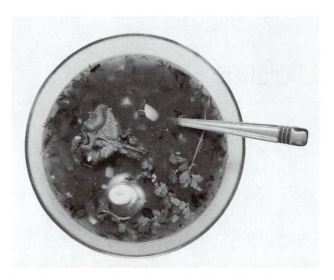

Borsch soup served in a glass dish. (iStockPhoto)

traditional cuisines, every part of the pig is used. Lard, or *salo,* is particularly common in Ukrainian food. It is cooked or preserved, often through salting or smoking. Lard is used as an ingredient or as a fat for frying. Many Ukrainian dishes, including doughnut-like desserts, are fried in rendered lard. Lard is used with other meat ingredients to make them moist. Eating pork became an important source of national and religious identity because, in the early-modern era, Ukrainians constantly fought the Muslim Turks and Tartars. Beef became popular only in the late 19th and 20th centuries, since buffalo (traditional bovines in Ukraine, not to be confused with the American bison) were beasts of burden rather than sources of meat. In the west and the south of Ukraine, lamb is a common source of meat as well. Ukrainians do not eat horse meat, but Ukrainian Tartars still use it as an ingredient in their traditional dishes, usually served only on holidays. Chickens, turkeys, and ducks are also eaten in Ukraine. Fish, especially carp, is a popular ingredient for soups and is also prepared in aspic. Herring, salted or marinated, is a popular appetizer, often associated with Jewish Ukrainian cooking. In the south, on the Black Sea and Sea of Azov coasts, saltwater fish is caught in great variety.

Eggs are also commonly used in the rich dishes of Ukraine. They are either fried plain or prepared as rich, multi-ingredient omelets. Eggs are also an important ingredient in dough for dumplings and holiday breads and pies. Milk is used as a base for soups or a liquid for boiling dumplings. It can be soured and drunk or made into other drinks and cheeses. Cottage cheese, *tvaroh,* is popular throughout the Ukraine, while *bryndzia,* or feta cheese, is popular in the west and in the coastal south of the country.

Fruits such as apples, pears, plums, and cherries are eaten fresh or cooked in drinks and desserts. Berries, such as strawberries, raspberries, blackberries, and currants, are also popular ingredients. Watermelons and an endless variety of other melons are eaten as desserts, preserved, or used in main dishes. Fruit can also be used in savory dishes such as soups and condiments. Sunflower seeds are popular in many dishes but are also eaten roasted as a snack. They are also used as a major source of sunflower oil, which is very common in Ukrainian cooking.

Ukrainian food is not particularly spicy but is quite flavorful. Onions, garlic, dill, caraway seeds, anise, mint, and red and black pepper, as well as bay leaf and cinnamon, are used as common spices and flavoring agents. Vinegar is also a common condiment.

Cooking

Ukrainian dishes tend to be fairly complex, including multiple ingredients that surround, modify, or amplify one central ingredient. This is particularly well illustrated by borsch, the world-renowned soup that became symbolic of Ukrainian food in general. Borsch can contain up to two dozen ingredients in addition to beets, the definitive ingredient of this soup. Borsch is generally based on pork or beef stock, to which other ingredients are added. In some cases, when borsch is prepared in the style of Odessa (a southern port city) or Poltava (a city in central Ukraine), a goose or chicken stock is used. Ukrainian cuisine, unlike Russian food, favors sautéing (*smazhennie*) ingredients before they are introduced into other dishes. Beets are either sautéed or baked before being placed in the stock. Vegetables—carrots, parsnips, tomatoes, and sometimes turnips—are also sautéed and then added to the soup. All ingredients are added in a particular and usually precise order, depending on the recipe. Kievan borsch recipes included beet *kvass* (a fermented malted beverage). Poltava-style borsch is made with goose and wheat-flour dumplings. Chernigov-style borsch features apples, tomatoes, beans, and squash, while Lvov-style borsch, influenced by the cuisine of the Austrian Empire of which it was once a part, has sautéed frankfurter sausage added to it just before serving.

While borsch is perhaps the best-known Ukrainian dish, the cuisine also includes *kulesh,* a somewhat less famous but nonetheless traditional soup. At its most basic, kulesh is a millet, potato, and lard soup-porridge, originally meant to be prepared in the open field. It is very filling and easy to prepare. Since it was developed by the mobile Cossack warriors, kulesh can be prepared from various ingredients on hand. When moving over long distances by water, Cossacks could replace the potatoes and millet with underwater tubers of river plants, and lard could be replaced with almost any other protein.

Kulesh (Millet, Potato, and Lard Soup)

Boil 6 to 8 cups of water with 2 teaspoons of salt. Once the water boils, add half a cup of millet and cook until done. Cube 6 potatoes, add them to the porridge, and cook for an additional half hour. Meanwhile, fry 2 or 3 finely chopped onions in about 5 ounces of *speck* (or other dry-cured smoked ham). Once the potatoes are ready, add the onions, speck, and a tablespoon of chopped parsley to the soup, and cook for an additional 5 minutes before serving.

Ukraine has a great variety of flour-based dishes. Slavic practices, and possibly even some Turkish influences, have mixed to create Ukrainian dumplings: *vareniki,* similar to Polish pierogi. Ukrainians fill vareniki with cherries, sweet or savory cottage cheese, sautéed onions or *shkvarki* (fried poultry or pork skin cracklings), and fat. Almost any filling can be used, including potatoes, liver, cabbage, beans, or sweet fruit and poppy seeds. *Pampushki* are very small buns made of raised yeast dough that can be made from buckwheat or wheat flour and then either boiled or baked. They are often served with butter or oil and garlic-flavored sauce as an accompaniment to borsch. *Halushky* are a typically Ukrainian dish, but similarly named and prepared dishes are known in the rest of eastern Europe. The simplest recipes are boiled squares of dough served with butter, oil, or lard. The dough can also be mixed with cottage cheese, potatoes, and apples.

Halushky (Dumplings)

Make a thick dough from 3 cups flour, 2 eggs, 1/3 cup water, and 1 teaspoon salt. After kneading the dough let it rest for 15 to 20 minutes under a towel, and roll it out to a thickness of a little less than half an inch. Cut into small squares. The cut halushky should rest for another 20 minutes to dry. Then drop into boiling salted water. They should be ready when they float to the surface. They should be eaten hot with butter, fried speck or bacon, or melted lard and cubed ham.

Milk and eggs are important components in Ukrainian cooking. Milk is usually simply drunk or soured into yogurt-like drinks and cottage cheese. A typically Ukrainian milk dish is *ryazhenka*. This is a thick, sour milk that was baked first. This caramelizes the milk sugars, giving ryazhenka a color like café au lait and a lightly sweet-sour flavor. Eggs are traditionally made into *yaishni*, rich omelets with cream or sour cream and flour, with many other ingredients. Hard-boiled eggs can also be baked in sour cream or chopped, mixed with raw eggs, and fried into patties.

Meat in the past had been eaten mostly on holidays, but in the years after World War II it became much more common. Meat, particularly pork, is usually prepared in two stages: first sautéed, then stewed with vegetables and flavorings. Lard may be used as a frying fat. Water, broth, or kvass can be used as a stewing liquid. *Shpundra* is an exemplary dish of this kind: Small cubes of pork are fried in lard and then stewed in kvass with beets. Meat rolls or cabbage rolls stuffed with meat are common preparation techniques as well, producing dishes called *zavivantsy.* German and Polish culinary practices have introduced pattylike dishes of finely chopped ingredients including meat (especially pork) or vegetables, mushrooms, and eggs. Since traditional cuisines call for every part of the animal to be used, Ukrainians prepare *kendiukh,* the stuffed stomach of a pig, filled with spiced and finely chopped head meat. Poultry, whether chickens, ducks, geese, or even turkeys, is commonly made into broths and soups and often stewed with sour cream sauce or together with rice, or halushky. Sausage is a common way to preserve meat. *Kovbasa,* homemade sausage, is made soon after the slaughter of pigs. Cleaned intestines are filled with chopped meat, lard, salt, garlic, and pepper. These sausages are either fried or smoked in ovens. Sausages are preserved by packing them into clay jars and sealing them with lard. *Kyshka,* blood sausage, is also made, as is headcheese (*zeltz*).

The fish served in Ukraine varies by region due to the country's geography. In the north and center of Ukraine, river fish, particularly carp and pike, are popular. In the south, along the Black Sea coast, saltwater fish are more common. Everywhere, salted or marinated herring is popular as an appetizer. Southern Ukrainian cuisine is well known for fresh sea fish that is fried and served very simply with a side of potatoes. Northern and central Ukrainians use a mixture of river fishes to make soups, fried fish, or fish served in aspic.

One of the most popular dishes in Ukrainian cuisine (*salo*), smoked salted pork fat with garlic and bread. (iStockPhoto)

Vegetables are common in the fertile Ukraine. They can be prepared as side dishes with meat or made into soups. Many vegetables are often mashed and dressed with onions, poppy seeds, oil, and vinegar, and served as a main course or an appetizer. Beans, beets, and squash can be prepared as "caviars" of this type. Mashed potatoes mixed with mashed beans and poppy seeds are called *tolchonka*. Vegetables can also be prepared with grains such as wheat berries, millet, or rice to make rich porridges. Finally, vegetables are often preserved in salty or spiced brines. Almost every vegetable can be preserved this way, and Ukrainians are fond of salted tomatoes and cucumbers, and even salted watermelons. Mushrooms are picked in the woods and are dried, pickled, or eaten fresh. Mushrooms are made into soups and can be fried and served with potatoes.

Fruit and berries—apples, plums, strawberries, raspberries, gooseberries, and many others—are often eaten plain. They are added to savory dishes, especially borsch, or served with meats. Fruit and berries are made into the traditional sweet dishes *uzvar,* fruit *kholodets,* and fruit *babki.* Uzvar is made of meticulously cleaned fruit (fresh or dried) and raisins boiled in water and sweetened with sugar or, more traditionally, honey. Spices, such as cinnamon, cloves, and lemon zest, are used to flavor uzvar. The whole mixture is cooked until the fruit is soft and then chilled to thicken the dish. Kholodets is made of fruit, sugar, and spice syrup mixed with pureed fruit and then chilled. Fruit babki are essentially fruit puddings made of mashed fruit mixed with eggs and flour, baked, and eaten while still warm. Fruit is also often made into a jam or *povidlo,* a thick fruit butter most traditionally made out of plums. Sugar is usually added toward the end of cooking the fruit, letting the povidlo remain light-colored.

Ukrainian desserts can also be made out of dough and then either baked or fried and served with a sauce or a topping. Baked pastries are usually made with choux pastry (a light, airy dough made with butter, water, flour, and eggs) rather than yeast-risen dough. These include *bubliki,* small bagels of choux pastry that are baked and topped with powdered sugar. *Puhkeniki* are doughnuts that are either fried and smothered in jam or filled with jam and then fried and topped with powdered sugar. *Shuliki,* simple cookies made of sweet dough with poppy seeds and honey, are broken into pieces and allowed to absorb a sauce of poppy seed, milk, and honey. *Korzhiki* are a slightly thicker version of shuliki, or they can be made with hazelnuts and just served plain. Simple fried cookies, *verguny,* are extremely popular in Ukraine and, like borsch, have many regional variations. They are made of thick, sweet dough made with the addition of rum, brandy, or vodka. The dough is rolled out thinly, cut into small strips, and fried in melted lard. When ready, the cookies are dusted with powdered sugar and can be eaten hot or cold. *Solozheniki* are another common dessert, consisting of light, rich pancakes wrapped around a filling and then baked under a meringue. The pancake dough is runny and made with more milk and eggs than flour, while the fillings tend to be made of one of the traditional Ukrainian ingredients of fruit, fruit jam, or poppy seeds.

Traditional Ukrainian beverages can be divided into alcoholic and nonalcoholic varieties. Vodka, known as *horilka,* has been popular since the 17th century. It is often flavored, most commonly with honey and hot pepper. The Crimean Peninsula is well known for its wines such as the Masandra variety. *Medovukha,* or mead made from fermented honey and water, is an ancient beverage common across Europe and still popular in Ukraine. Beer (*pyvo*) is also very popular among Ukrainians. Nonalcoholic beverages include the traditional fermented kvass, which can be made out of a single or multiple ingredients including bread, beets, and fruit. Yeast is added to the warm mixture, which is then allowed to ferment. Tap water often is seen as unsafe, so most Ukrainians either boil the water they drink or consume the many mineral waters on sale across the country. Tea and coffee are popular beverages, as are more recently introduced sodas, including many of those consumed in western Europe and the United States.

Typical Meals

Breakfast (*snidanok*) in Ukraine traditionally tends to be fairly filling, but this has been changing. Dishes mixing grains and fats are common. These could include buckwheat-flour- and lard-based *lemishky* (a gruel) or buckwheat cooked as porridge with the addition of butter. Farina and oatmeal are also common breakfast porridges. Various egg dishes, whether elaborate yaishni omelets or just eggs boiled or fried sunny-side up, are commonly eaten. French toast is a popular dish, usually served with savory toppings such as meat or cheese, rather than sugar or jam. Meat dishes such as frankfurters or meat patties are often served for breakfast. Sandwiches with sausage, cheese, pâtés, or other toppings are well liked. Ryazhenka and cottage cheese, or cheese fritters, are popular breakfast dishes made with milk. Milk itself, as well as buttermilk, and tea or coffee are commonly served as breakfast beverages. In recent years, yogurts and dry cereals have become more popular, particularly among younger Ukrainians.

Lunch (*obid*), the midday meal, was traditionally the main meal of the day, but with new work schedules this distinction has often been transferred to supper (*vecheria*). The main meals of the day are likely to include a soup, a main dish, and a dessert, and sometimes also an appetizer. As with every meal in Ukraine, bread is an important accompaniment. While vegetables play an important part in Ukrainian cuisine, salads of raw vegetables are less common. They are served as an appetizer, often made of cabbage or tomatoes and cucumbers dressed with salt, pepper, oil, and vinegar. Other appetizers could be salted or marinated fish such as herring or anchovies; marinated mushrooms or vegetables; or rich salads with meat and potatoes dressed with mayonnaise. The appetizer course can be accompanied or even replaced by a shot of vodka (*horilka*). Winter meals usually include a borsch or cabbage soup, such as *kapusniak,* or other soups made with grains or mushrooms. Chicken broth with rice or noodles is also popular, as are soups made with milk and pasta. If in the past a rich soup or stew and bread would be the only food served at an everyday lunch, today there is often a meat-based main dish, served with starch side dishes. Most common today are meat-based stews (especially made with pork) and fried patties (*bitkil*). These are served with a porridge (especially buckwheat), macaroni, or rice. The

stews can also be accompanied by halushky or pampushki. Desserts, depending on the meal, can range from a simple *kompot* (fruit compote), uzvar, or *kissel'* (sweetened juice thickened with starch, with fruit added) to fancier pastries, creams, or cakes. Drinks that are served with dinner could be the traditional kvass, mineral water, or soda, with coffee or tea accompanying dessert. The lighter evening meal is often similar to breakfast. Porridge, eggs, and fritters (meat or vegetable), as well as tea served with cakes, cookies, or preserves, round out the meal.

Modern Ukrainians now have lives scheduled around work patterns similar to those in western Europe or the United States, and their meal patterns have also changed. Many snack foods are now sold, including chips, popcorn, and puffed corn (like corn pops, salty and sweet), as well as the more traditional roasted sunflower or pumpkin seeds. Convenience foods, such as instant soups or noodles, have become the normal midday meal for many students and office workers.

Eating Out

Eating out has increased over the course of the 20th century. Traditionally, Ukraine had some country inns where simple meals were served along with alcohol. In the 19th century, Ukrainian cities acquired more restaurants in the European sense as well as Russian-style *traktiry,* or roadside inns with simple restaurants. In the Soviet era, eating outside the home was encouraged, and communal cafeterias sprang up both in the cities and attached to plants and collective farms. The most recent development has been the appearance of fast-food restaurants such as McDonald's.

The communal canteens and restaurants mixed traditional Ukrainian dishes with those from the rest of the Soviet Union. Ukrainians, when eating out, often expect this mixture of cuisines on the menu, which is likely to include Russian caviar appetizers, grilled meats from the Caucasus, and pilafs from Central Asia. French-influenced dishes such as mushrooms baked in cream sauce (*julliene*) have become iconic for fancy restaurant meals. Even plain canteen-served foods are drawn from many ethnic traditions. An example of an ethnic food served in a canteen would be the Tartar-influenced *azu,* or roasted beef served with a tomato-based sauce and pickles.

Modern Ukraine has fewer Soviet-style canteens and many more cafés serving light foods along with teas and coffees. Fast-food restaurants are very popular. McDonald's and other international chains share space with Ukrainian-owned fast-food establishments that often serve traditional foods such as vareniki (stuffed dumplings) or *bliny* (little pancakes). Simple snack bars selling hot dogs and drinks are often located around major public transportation stops. Beer pubs serving Ukrainian and international beers have become very popular. Kebab stands have become common in large cities, as they are in the rest of Europe.

Special Occasions

Bread, like in other Slavic cultures, is considered sacred and is used to commemorate important life events, with some special breads tied to specific occasions. In the distant past, bread baking was a ritual occasion and seen as a sacred act. Even today, when welcoming guests, Ukrainians serve bread and salt as a sign of hospitality. In addition to special breads, other ritual dishes are made to commemorate many holidays. *Paskha,* the rich Easter bread, is made out of yeast-raised wheat dough, with eggs, milk, and spices, especially ginger and saffron. Western Ukrainians tend to decorate the paskha with dough ornaments such as a cross and keep it low and round, while the Russian-influenced eastern Ukrainians make paskha into a tall but plain glazed bread. This bread is not eaten until it has been blessed in church with other Easter foods during the Easter service. The Easter meal is also the time to serve *babka,* a rich bread made with eggs, raisins, sugar, and spices, which usually includes lemon zest, saffron, and vanilla. Elaborately painted eggs (*pysanki*) are an important part of Ukrainian Easter. Other rich egg and meat dishes are served during Easter, a major ritual feast. Shuliki cookies are the traditional food for church holidays (such as the Feast of Transfiguration) that are celebrated in August.

Traditional decorated Easter basket lined by an embroidered towel, with Easter bread, ham, and eggs. (iStockPhoto)

The Christmas season is a major occasion for ritual foods. On Christmas Eve, meat and milk are not allowed, so the supper that evening is a collection of vegetable and fish-based dishes. Beans or peas are mashed and dressed with onions, garlic, and oil. A meatless borsch flavored with kvass is served, as well as a sauerkraut soup (kapusniak). Porridges, stewed fruit, and dumplings with poppy seeds are also served. The meals on Christmas Day itself are very rich and include roast meats, rich borsch, fried homemade sausages (kovbasa), and *studenets,* meat set in jellied aspic and served cold. Symbolically connecting the meal to the birth of Jesus in a manger, hay is spread under and on the table. As the Christmas season is symbolically connected with the life cycle, certain foods served on Christmas are also served during funerals. Most commonly, these foods include *kalach,* a round, braided bread symbolizing the cyclical nature of life, and *kolyvo* or *kutia,* a dish of boiled grains with poppy seeds and honey. The grains and seeds allude to death, rebirth, and the harvest. Finally, fish dishes, especially carp, are a traditional part of Christmas suppers. As caroling, or *koliaduvannia,* is a common Christmas tradition in Ukraine, the carolers are rewarded with gifts of food: pastries, pancakes (*oladky*), or even whole sausages.

Weddings, with their connections to fertility, are an occasion for special breads and other foods. The *korovai,* primarily a wedding bread, is made of a rich egg dough with sugar and spices for flavoring and color. It is circular in form and has decorations made out of dough on top of it. The bride and groom go around it and are then given pieces of it to eat. In some regions of Ukraine, other traditional breads are used. In the west, *dyven* is a rich bread shaped into a circle or a wheel that is carried by the bride. She looks through it to see a bright future. In other regions, small buns called *shyshky,* or pine cones, are baked, as is *lezhen',* a long bread made with eggs and a coin baked in.

Soviet holidays such as the New Year and Victory Day, celebrating victory during World War II, are important for many Ukrainians. Festive foods introduced during Soviet rule include the *oliv'ie* or *stolichniy* salad, a mixture of potatoes, peas, carrots, and meat dressed with mayonnaise. At family picnics, at summer houses, or on beaches, many Ukrainians like to grill marinated pork or lamb shish kebabs (*shashlyk*).

Anton Masterovoy

Diet and Health

Many younger Ukrainians see the traditional Ukrainian diet of starchy foods along with fatty pork as unhealthy. Today, the population of Ukraine, like that of the rest of Europe, is heavily urbanized. The traditional diet, created to restore the strength of people engaged in heavy farm labor, is no longer relevant to modern work and life. Indeed, in the 20th century, a diet rich in fat and carbohydrates, along with industrial pollution, heavy smoking, and drinking, has contributed to a rise in cardiovascular disease among Ukrainians. Ukrainians also argue that the traditional diet was varied and natural and should be retained instead of consuming industrially processed and imported foods. Pollution from the 1986 nuclear disaster at Chernobyl is also a major concern.

Ukrainians retain many traditional folk remedies for various disorders, as modern medicine is poorly funded and often seen as corrupt. Herbal teas are used to soothe a system out of order. Chamomile tea is used in case of a stomachache. Black tea with honey and lemon is used to soothe sore throats. Alcohol, honey, garlic, and even hot milk are seen as medicinal for many respiratory disorders. Strong-smelling herbs and garlic have been seen as not only medicinal but also useful for scaring away evil spirits. These beliefs have been retained in the Ukrainian countryside and were resurrected after the fall of the Soviet Union.

Further Reading

Farley, Marta Pisetska. *Festive Ukrainian Cooking.* Pittsburgh, PA: University of Pittsburgh Press, 1990.

Ponomarenko, Ninel. *Taste of My Ukrainian Homeland.* Westfield, Tunbridge Wells, UK: Upso, 2004.

Zahny, Bodan. *The Best of Ukrainian Cuisine.* New York: Hippocrene Books, 1998.

About the Editor and Contributors

Ken Albala, Editor, is professor of history at the University of the Pacific in Stockton, California. He also teaches in the gastronomy program at Boston University. Albala is the author of many books, including *Eating Right in the Renaissance* (University of California Press, 2002), *Food in Early Modern Europe* (Greenwood Press, 2003), *Cooking in Europe 1250–1650* (Greenwood Press, 2005), *The Banquet: Dining in the Great Courts of Late Renaissance Europe* (University of Illinois Press, 2007), *Beans: A History* (Berg Publishers, 2007; winner of the 2008 International Association of Culinary Professionals Jane Grigson Award), and *Pancake* (Reaktion Press, 2008). He has co-edited two works, *The Business of Food* and *Human Cuisine.* He is also editor of three food series with 29 volumes in print, including the Food Cultures Around the World series for Greenwood Press. Albala is also co-editor of the journal *Food Culture and Society*. He is currently researching a history of theological controversies surrounding fasting in the Reformation Era and is editing two collected volumes of essays, one on the Renaissance and the other entitled *The Lord's Supper.* He has also coauthored a cookbook for Penguin/Perigee entitled *The Lost Art of Real Cooking,* which was released in July 2010.

Julia Abramson has visited France on a regular basis for more than 25 years to study, research, travel, and eat. She has published essays on aspects of food culture from vegetable carving to gastronomic writing and is the author of the book *Food Culture in France.* Abramson teaches French literature and culture and food studies at the University of Oklahoma, Norman.

M. Shahrim Al-Karim is a senior lecturer of food service and hospitality management at the Universiti Putra Malaysia. His research interests include food and culture, culinary tourism, food habits, and consumer behavior. He received a BS in hotel and restaurant management from New York University; an MBA from Universiti Teknologi MARA, Malaysia; and a PhD in hospitality and tourism from Oklahoma State University, United States.

E. N. Anderson is professor emeritus of the Department of Anthropology, University of California, Riverside.

Laura P. Appell-Warren holds a doctorate in psychological anthropology from Harvard University. Her primary focus of research has been the study of personhood; however, she has also studied the effects of social change on children's play. She has done research among the Bulusu' of East Kalimantan, Indonesia, and among the Rungus Momogon, a Dusunic-speaking peoples, of Sabah, Malyasia. In addition, she has traveled widely throughout Arctic Canada. She is the editor of *The Iban Diaries of Monica Freeman 1949–1951: Including Ethnographic Drawings, Sketches, Paintings, Photographs and Letters* and is author of the forthcoming volume entitled *Personhood: An Examination of the History and Use of an Anthropological Concept*. In addition to her current research on cradleboard use among Native North Americans, she is a teacher of anthropology at St. Mark's School in Southborough, Massachusetts.

Heather Arndt-Anderson is a Portland, Oregon, native who draws culinary inspiration from many world cuisines but prefers cooking from her own backyard. She is a part-time natural resources consultant and a full-time radical homemaker; in her (rare) spare time she writes the food blog *Voodoo & Sauce*.

Michael Ashkenazi is a scholar, writer, and consultant who has been researching and writing about Japanese food since 1990. In addition to books and articles on Japanese society, including its food culture, he has written numerous scholarly and professional articles and papers on various subjects including theoretical and methodological issues in anthropology, organized violence, space exploration, migration, religion and ritual, resettling ex-combatants, and small arms. He has taught at higher-education institutions in Japan, Canada, Israel, and the United Kingdom, directing graduate and undergraduate students. He is currently senior researcher and project leader at the Bonn International Center for Conversion in Germany, with responsibility for the areas of small arms and reintegration of ex-combatants. He has conducted field research in East and Southeast Asia, East and West Africa, the Middle East, and Latin America.

Babette Audant went to Prague after college, where she quickly gave up teaching English in order to cook at a classical French restaurant. After graduating from the Culinary Institute of America, she worked as a chef in New York City for eight years, working at Rainbow Room, Beacon Bar & Grill, and other top-rated restaurants. She is a lecturer at City University of New York Kingsborough's Department of Tourism and Hospitality, and a doctoral candidate in geography at the City University of New York Graduate Center. Her research focuses on public markets and food policy in New York City.

Gabriela Villagran Backman, MA (English and Hispanic literature), was born in Sweden and raised in Mexico and the United States; she currently lives in Stockholm, Sweden. She is an independent researcher, interested in food studies, cultural heritage, writing cookbooks, red wine, and the Internet.

Carolyn Bánfalvi is a writer based in Budapest. She is the author of *Food Wine Budapest* (Little Bookroom) and *The Food and Wine Lover's Guide to Hungary: With Budapest Restaurants and Trips to the Wine Country* (Park Kiado). She contributes to numerous international food and travel publications and leads food and wine tours through Taste Hungary, her culinary tour company.

Peter Barrett is a painter who writes a food blog and is also the Food & Drink writer for *Chronogram Magazine* in New York's Hudson Valley.

Cynthia D. Bertelsen is an independent culinary scholar, nutritionist, freelance food writer, and food columnist. She lived in Haiti for three years and worked on a food-consumption study for a farming-systems project in Jacmel, Haiti. She writes a food history blog, *Gherkins & Tomatoes,* found at http://gherkinstoma toes.com.

Megan K. Blake is a senior lecturer in geography at the University of Sheffield. She has published research that examines the intersections between place and social practices. While her previous work focused on entrepreneurship and innovation, her recent work has examined food practices and family life.

Janet Boileau is a culinary historian who holds a master of arts degree in gastronomy from Le Cordon Bleu Paris and a doctorate in history from the University of Adelaide.

Andrea Broomfield is associate professor of English at Johnson County Community College in Overland Park, Kansas, and author of *Food and Cooking in Victorian England: A History.*

Cynthia Clampitt is a culinary historian, world traveler, and award-winning author. In 2010, she was elected to the Society of Women Geographers.

Neil L. Coletta is assistant director of food, wine, and the arts and lecturer in the MLA in gastronomy program at Boston University. His current research includes food and aesthetics and experimental pedagogy in the field of food studies.

Paul Crask is a travel writer and the author of two travel guides: *Dominica* (2008) and *Grenada, Carriacou and Petite Martinique* (2009).

Christine Crawford-Oppenheimer is the information services librarian and archivist at the Culinary Institute of America. She grew up in Ras Tanura, Saudi Arabia.

Anita Verna Crofts is on the faculty at the University of Washington's Department of Communication, where she serves as an associate director of the master of communication in digital media program. In addition, she holds an appointment at the University of Washington's Department of Global Health, where she collaborates with partner institutions in Sudan, Namibia, and India on trainings that address leadership, management, and policy development, with her contributions targeted at the concept of storytelling as a leadership and evidence tool. Anita is an intrepid chowhound and publishes on gastroethnographic topics related to the intersection of food and identity. She hosts the blog *Sneeze!* at her Web site www.pepperforthebeast.com.

Liza Debevec is a research fellow at the Scientific Research Centre of the Slovene Academy of sciences and arts in Ljubljana, Slovenia. She has a PhD in social anthropology from the University of St. Andrews, United Kingdom. Her research interests are West Africa and Burkina Faso, food studies, Islam, gender, identity, and practice of everyday life.

Jonathan Deutsch is associate professor of culinary arts at Kingsborough Community College, City University of New York, and Public Health, City University of New York Graduate Center. He is the author or editor of five books including, with Sarah Billingsley, *Culinary Improvisation* (Pearson, 2010) and, with Annie Hauck-Lawson, *Gastropolis: Food and New York City* (Columbia University Press, 2009).

Deborah Duchon is a nutritional anthropologist in Atlanta, Georgia.

Nathalie Dupree is the author of 10 cookbooks, many of which are about the American South, for which she has won two James Beard Awards. She has hosted over 300 television shows on the Public Broadcasting Service, The Food Network, and TLC. She lives with her husband, Jack Bass, who has authored 9 books about the American South and helped with her contribution to *Food Cultures of the World.*

Pamela Elder has worked in food public relations and online culinary education and is a freelance writer in the San Francisco Bay area.

Rachel Finn is a freelance writer whose work has appeared in various print and online publications. She is the founder and director of Roots Cuisine, a non-profit organization dedicated to promoting the foodways of the African diaspora around the globe.

Richard Foss has been a food writer and culinary historian since 1986, when he started as a restaurant critic for the *Los Angeles Reader*. His book on the history of rum is slated for publication in 2011, to be followed by a book on the history of beachside dining in Los Angeles. He is also a science fiction and fantasy author, an instructor in culinary history and Elizabethan theater at the University of California, Los Angeles, Extension, and is on the board of the Culinary Historians of Southern California.

Nancy G. Freeman is a food writer and art historian living in Berkeley, California, with a passion for food history. She has written about cuisines ranging from Ethiopia to the Philippines to the American South.

Ramin Ganeshram is a veteran journalist and professional chef trained at the Institute of Culinary Education in New York City, where she has also worked as a recreational chef instructor. Ganeshram also holds a master's degree in journalism from Columbia University. For eight years she worked as a feature writer/ stringer for the *New York Times* regional sections, and she spent another eight years as a food columnist and feature writer for *Newsday*. She is the author of *Sweet Hands: Island Cooking from Trinidad and Tobago* (Hippocrene NY, 2006; 2nd expanded edition, 2010) and *Stir It Up* (Scholastic, 2011). In addition to contributing to a variety of food publications including *Saveur, Gourmet, Bon Appetit,* and epicurious.com, Ganeshram has written articles on food, culture, and travel for *Islands* (as contributing editor), *National Geographic Traveler,*

Forbes Traveler, Forbes Four Seasons, and many others. Currently, Ganeshram teaches food writing for New York University's School of Continuing Professional Studies.

Hanna Garth is a doctoral candidate in the Department of Anthropology at the University of California, Los Angeles. She is currently working on a dissertation on household food practices in Santiago de Cuba. Previously, she has conducted research on food culture, health, and nutrition in Cuba, Chile, and the Philippines.

Mary Gee is a medical sociology doctoral student at the University of California, San Francisco. Her current research interests include herbalism and Asian and Asian American foodways, especially with regards to multigenerational differences. Since 1995, she has actively worked with local and national eating disorders research and policy and advocacy organizations as well as for a program evaluation research consulting firm.

Che Ann Abdul Ghani holds a bachelor's degree in English and a master's degree in linguistics. She has a keen interest in studying language and language use in gastronomy. She is currently attached to the English Department at Universiti Putra Malaysia. Her research interests range from the use of language in context (pragmatics) to language use in multidisciplinary areas, namely, disciplines related to the social sciences. She also carries out work in translation and editing.

Maja Godina-Golija is research adviser at the Institute of Slovenian Ethnology, Scientific Research Centre of Slovenian Academy of Science and Arts, Ljubljana, Slovenia.

Annie Goldberg is a graduate student studying gastronomy at Boston University.

Darra Goldstein is Frances Christopher Oakley Third Century Professor of Russian at Williams College and the founding editor-in-chief of *Gastronomica: The Journal of Food and Culture.*

Keiko Goto, PhD, is associate professor at the Department of Nutrition and Food Sciences, California State University, Chico. Dr. Goto has more than 15 years of work experience in the field of nutrition and has worked as a practitioner and researcher in various developing countries. Dr. Goto's current research areas include food and culture, child and adolescent nutrition, sustainable food systems, and international nutrition.

Carla Guerrón Montero is a cultural and applied anthropologist trained in Latin America and the United States. She is currently associate professor of anthropology in the Department of Anthropology at the University of Delaware. Dr. Guerrón Montero's areas of expertise include gender, ethnicity, and identity; processes of globalization/nationalism, and particularly tourism; and social justice and human rights.

Mary Gunderson calls her practice paleocuisineology, where food and cooking bring cultures alive. Through many media, including the sites HistoryCooks.com and MaryGunderson.com, she writes and speaks about South and North American food history and contemporary creative living and wellness. She wrote and published the award-winning book *The Food Journal of Lewis and Clark: Recipes for an Expedition* (History Cooks, 2003) and has authored six food-history books for kids.

Liora Gvion is a senior lecturer at the Kibbutzim College of Education and also teaches at the Faculty of Agriculture, Food and Environment at the Institute of Biochemistry, Food Science and Nutrition Hebrew University of Jerusalem.

Cherie Y. Hamilton is a cookbook author and specialist on the food cultures and cuisines of the Portuguese-speaking countries in Europe, South America, Africa, and Asia.

Jessica B. Harris teaches English at Queens College/City University of New York and is director of the Institute for the Study of Culinary Cultures at Dillard University.

Melanie Haupt is a doctoral candidate in English at the University of Texas at Austin. Her dissertation, "Starting from Scratch: Reading Women's Cooking Communities," explores women's use of cookbooks and recipes in the formation and reification of real and virtual communities.

Ursula Heinzelmann is an independent scholar and culinary historian, twice awarded the prestigious Sophie Coe Prize. A trained chef, sommelier, and ex-restaurateur, she now works as a freelance wine and food writer and journalist based in Berlin, Germany.

Jennifer Hostetter is an independent food consultant specializing in writing, research, and editing. She has degrees in history and culinary arts and holds a master's degree in food culture and communications from the University of Gastronomic Sciences in Italy. She also served as editorial assistant for this encyclopedia.

Kelila Jaffe is a doctoral candidate in the Food Studies Program at New York University. Originally from Sonoma, California, and the daughter of a professional chef, she has pursued anthropological and archaeological foodways research since her entry into academia. She received a BA with distinction in anthropology from the University of Pennsylvania, before attending the University of Auckland, where she earned an MA with honors in anthropology, concentrating in archaeology. Her research interests include past foodways, domestication, and zooarchaeology, and she has conducted fieldwork in Fiji, New Zealand, and Hawaii.

Zilkia Janer is associate professor of global studies at Hofstra University in New York. She is the author of *Puerto Rican Nation-Building Literature: Impossible Romance* (2005) and *Latino Food Culture* (2008).

Brelyn Johnson is a graduate of the master's program in food studies at New York University.

Kate Johnston is currently based in Italy, where she is an independent cultural food researcher and writer and a daily ethnographer of people's food habits. She has a degree in anthropology from Macquarie University in Sydney, Australia, and a recent master's degree in food culture and communication from the University of Gastronomic Sciences, Italy. She was also editorial assistant for this encyclopedia.

Desiree Koh was born and raised in Singapore. A writer focusing on travel, hospitality, sports, fitness, business, and, of course, food, Koh's explorations across the globe always begin at the market, as she believes that the sight, scent, and savoring of native produce and cuisine are the key to the city's heart. The first and only female in Major League Eating's Asia debut, Koh retired from competition to better focus on each nibble and sip of fine, hopefully slow food.

Bruce Kraig is emeritus professor of history at Roosevelt University in Chicago and adjunct faculty at the Culinary School of Kendall College, Chicago. He has published and edited widely in the field of American and world food history. Kraig is also the founding president of the Culinary Historians of Chicago and the Greater Midwest Foodways Alliance.

R. J. Krajewski is the research services librarian at Simmons College, where among other things he facilitates discovery of food-culture research, especially through the lens of race, class, and gender. His own engagement with food is seasonally and locally rooted, starting in his own small, urban homestead, much like his Polish and German ancestors.

Erin Laverty is a freelance food writer and researcher based in Brooklyn, New York. She holds a master's degree in food studies from New York University.

Robert A. Leonard has a PhD in theoretical linguistics from Columbia. He studies the way people create and communicate meaning, including through food. He was born in Brooklyn and trained as a cook and *panaderia-reposteria* manager in the Caribbean; his doctoral studies led him to eight years of fieldwork in language, culture, and food in Africa and Southeast Asia. In the arts, as an undergraduate he cofounded and led the rock group Sha Na Na and with them opened for their friend Jimi Hendrix at the Woodstock Festival. Leonard is probably one of a very few people who have worked with both the Grateful Dead and the Federal Bureau of Investigation, which in recent years recruited him to teach the emerging science of forensic linguistics at Quantico.

Jane Levi is an independent consultant and writer based in London, England. She is currently working on her PhD at the London Consortium, examining food in utopias, funded by her work on post-trade financial policy in the City of London.

Yrsa Lindqvist is a European ethnologist working as the leading archivist at the Folk Culture Archive in Helsinki. Her research about food and eating habits in the late 1990s, combined with earlier collections at the archive, resulted in 2009 in the publication *Mat, Måltid, Minne. Hundraår av finlandssvensk matkulur.* The book analyzes the changes in housekeeping and attitudes toward food. She has also contributed to other publications focusing on identity questions and has worked as a junior researcher at the Academy of Finland.

William G. Lockwood is professor emeritus of cultural anthropology at the University of Michigan. His central interest is ethnicity and interethnic relations. He has conducted long-term field research in Bosnia-Herzegovina and the Croatian community in Austria and also among Roma and with a variety of ethnic groups in America, including Arabs, Finns, and Bosnians. He has long held a special interest in how food functions in ethnic group maintenance and in reflecting intra- and intergroup relations.

Yvonne R. Lockwood is curator emeritus of folklife at the Michigan State University Museum. Her formal training is in folklore, history, and Slavic languages and literatures. Research in Bosnia, Austria, and the United States, especially the Great Lakes region, has resulted in numerous publications, exhibitions, festival presentations, and workshops focused on her primary interests of foodways and ethnic traditions.

Janet Long-Solís, an anthropologist and archaeologist, is a research associate at the Institute of Historical Research at the National University of Mexico. She has published several books and articles on the chili pepper, the history of Mexican food, and the exchange of food products between Europe and the Americas in the 16th century.

Kristina Lupp has a background in professional cooking and has worked in Toronto and Florence. She is currently pursuing a master of arts in gastronomy at the University of Adelaide.

Máirtín Mac Con Iomaire is a lecturer in culinary arts in the Dublin Institute of Technology. Máirtín is well known as a chef, culinary historian, food writer, broadcaster, and ballad singer. He lives in Dublin with his wife and two daughters. He was the first Irish chef to be awarded a PhD, for his oral history of Dublin restaurants.

Glenn R. Mack is a food historian with extensive culinary training in Uzbekistan, Russia, Italy, and the United States. He cofounded the Culinary Academy of Austin and the Historic Foodways Group of Austin and currently serves as president of Le Cordon Bleu College of Culinary Arts Atlanta.

Andrea MacRae is a lecturer in the Le Cordon Bleu Graduate Program in Gastronomy at the University of Adelaide, Australia.

Giorgos Maltezakis earned his PhD in anthropology with research in cooperation with the Institute Studiorium Humanitatis of the Ljubljana Graduate School of the Humanities. His dissertation was on consumerism, the global market, and food, which was an ethnographic approach to the perception of food in Greece and Slovenia.

Bertie Mandelblatt is assistant professor at the University of Toronto, cross-appointed to the departments of Historical Studies and Geography. Her research concerns the early-modern French Atlantic, with a focus on commodity exchanges at the local and global scales: Her two current projects are the history of food provisioning in the Franco-Caribbean and the transatlantic circulation of French rum and molasses, both in the 17th and 18th centuries.

Marty Martindale is a freelance writer living in Largo, Florida.

Laura Mason is a writer and food historian with a special interest in local, regional, and traditional foods in the United Kingdom and elsewhere. Her career has explored many dimensions of food and food production, including cooking for a living, unraveling the history of sugar confectionery, and trying to work out how many traditional and typically British foods relate to culture and landscape. Her publications include *Taste of Britain* (with Catherine Brown; HarperCollins, 2006), *The Food Culture of Great Britain* (Greenwood, 2004), and *The National Trust Farmhouse Cookbook* (National Trust, 2009).

Anton Masterovoy is a PhD candidate at the Graduate Center, City University of New York. He is working on his dissertation, titled "Eating Soviet: Food and Culture in USSR, 1917–1991."

Anne Engammare McBride, a Swiss native, food writer, and editor, is the director of the Experimental Cuisine Collective and a food studies PhD candidate at New York University. Her most recent book is *Culinary Careers: How to Get Your Dream Job in Food,* coauthored with Rick Smilow.

Michael R. McDonald is associate professor of anthropology at Florida Gulf Coast University. He is the author of *Food Culture in Central America.*

Naomi M. McPherson is associate professor of cultural anthropology and graduate program coordinator at the University of British Columbia, Okanagan Campus. Since 1981, she has accumulated over three years of field research with the Bariai of West New Britain, Papua New Guinea.

Katrina Meynink is an Australia-based freelance food writer and researcher. She has a master's degree in gastronomy through Le Cordon Bleu and the University of Adelaide under a scholarship from the James Beard Foundation. She is currently completing her first cookbook.

Barbara J. Michael is a sociocultural anthropologist whose research focuses on social organization, economics, decision making, and gender. Her geographic focus is on the Middle East and East Africa, where she has done research with the pastoral nomadic Hawazma Baggara and on traditional medicine in Yemen and is working on a video about men's cafes as a social institution. She teaches anthropology at the University of North Carolina Wilmington and has also worked as a consultant for several United Nations agencies.

Diana Mincyte is a fellow at the Rachel Carson Center at the Ludwig Maximilian University-Munich and visiting assistant professor in the Department of Advertising at the University of Illinois, Urbana-Champaign. Mincyte examines topics at the interface of food, the environment, risk society, and global inequalities. Her book investigates raw-milk politics in the European Union to consider the production risk society and its institutions in post-Socialist states.

Rebecca Moore is a doctoral student studying the history of biotechnology at the University of Toronto in Ontario, Canada.

Nawal Nasrallah, a native of Iraq, was a professor of English and comparative literature at the universities of Baghdad and Mosul until 1990. As an independent scholar, she wrote the award-winning *Delights from the Garden of Eden: A Cookbook and a History of the Iraqi Cuisine* and *Annals of the Caliphs' Kitchens* (an English translation of Ibn Sayyar al-Warraq's 10th-century Baghdadi cookbook).

Henry Notaker graduated from the University of Oslo with a degree in literature and worked for many years as a foreign correspondent and host of arts and letters shows on Norwegian national television. He has written several books about food history, and with *Food Culture in Scandinavia* he won the Gourmand World Cookbook Award for best culinary history in 2009. His last book is a bibliography of early-modern culinary literature, *Printed Cookbooks in Europe 1470–1700.* He is a member of the editorial board of the journal *Food and History.*

Kelly O'Leary is a graduate student at Boston University in gastronomy and food studies and executive chef at the Bayridge University Residence and Cultural Center.

Fabio Parasecoli is associate professor and coordinator of food studies at the New School in New York City. He is author of *Food Culture in Italy* (2004) and *Bite Me: Food and Popular Culture* (2008).

Susan Ji-Young Park is the program director and head of curriculum development at École de Cuisine Pasadena (www.ecolecuisine.com); project leader for Green Algeria, a national environmental initiative; and a writer for LAWEEKLY'S Squid Ink. She has written curriculum for cooking classes at Los Angeles Unified School District, Sur La Table, Whole Foods Market, Central Market, and Le Cordon Bleu North America. She and her husband, Chef Farid Zadi, have co-written recipes for *Gourmet Magazine* and the *Los Angeles Times.* The couple are currently writing several cookbooks on North African, French, and Korean cuisines.

Rosemary Parkinson is author of *Culinaria: The Caribbean, Nyam Jamaica,* and *Barbados Bu'n-Bu'n,* and she contributes culinary travel stories to Caribbean magazines.

Charles Perry majored in Middle East languages at Princeton University, the University of California, Berkeley, and the Middle East Centre for Arab Studies, Shimlan, Lebanon. From 1968 to 1976 he was a copy editor and staff writer at *Rolling Stone* magazine in San Francisco, before leaving to work as a freelance writer specializing in food. From 1990 to 2008, he was a staff writer in the food section of the *Los Angeles Times.* He has published widely on the history of Middle Eastern food and was a major contributor to the *Oxford Companion to Food* (1999).

Irina Petrosian is a native of Armenia and a professional journalist who has written for Russian, Armenian, and U.S.-based newspapers. She is the coauthor of

Armenian Food: Fact, Fiction, and Folklore and holds degrees in journalism from Moscow State University and Indiana University.

Suzanne Piscopo is a nutrition, family, and consumer studies lecturer at the University of Malta in Malta. She is mainly involved in the training of home economics and primary-level teachers, as well as in nutrition and consumer-education projects in different settings. Suzanne is a registered public health nutritionist, and her research interests focus on socioecological determinants of food intake, nutrition interventions, and health promotion. She has also written a series of short stories for children about food. Suzanne enjoys teaching and learning about the history and culture of food and is known to creatively experiment with the ingredients at hand when cooking the evening meal together with her husband, Michael.

Theresa Preston-Werner is an advanced graduate student in anthropology at Northwestern University.

Meg Ragland is a culinary history researcher and librarian. She lives in Boston, Massachusetts.

Carol Selva Rajah is an award-winning chef and food writer currently based in Sydney, Australia. She has written 10 cookbooks on Malaysian and Southeast Asian cuisine. Her book *The Food of India* won the gold award for the Best Hardcover Recipe Book at the prestigious Jacob's Creek World Food Media Awards.

Birgit Ricquier is pursuing a PhD in linguistics at the Université Libre de Bruxelles and the Royal Museum for Central Africa, Tervuren, Belgium, with a fellowship from the Fonds de la Recherche Scientifique (FNRS). The topic of her PhD project is "A Comparative Linguistic Approach to the History of Culinary Practice in Bantu-Speaking Africa." She has spent several months in central Africa, including one month in the Democratic Republic of the Congo as a member of the Boyekoli Ebale Congo 2010 Expedition and two months of research focused on food cultures in Congo.

Amy Riolo is an award-winning author, lecturer, cooking instructor, and consultant. She is the author of *Arabian Delights: Recipes and Princely Entertaining Ideas from the Arabian Peninsula, Nile Style: Egyptian Cuisine and Culture,* and *The Mediterranean Diabetes Cookbook.* Amy has lived, worked, and traveled extensively through Egypt and enjoys fusing cuisine, culture, and history into all aspects of her work. Please see www.amyriolo.com, www.baltimoreegypt.org, and diningwithdiplomats.blogspot.com for more information and further reading.

Owen Roberts is a journalist, communications instructor, and director of research communications for the University of Guelph in Guelph, Ontario, Canada. He holds a doctorate of education from Texas Tech University and Texas A&M University.

Fiona Ross is a gastrodetective whose headquarters is the Bodleian Library in Oxford, United Kingdom. She spends her time there investigating the eating foibles of the famous and infamous. Her cookery book *Dining with Destiny* is the result: When you want to know what Lenin lunched on or what JFK ate by the poolside, *Dining with Destiny* has the answer.

Signe Rousseau (née Hansen) is Danish by birth but a long-term resident of southern Africa and is a researcher and part-time lecturer at the University of Cape Town. Following an MA in the Department of English and a PhD (on food media and celebrity chefs) in the Centre for Film and Media Studies, she now teaches critical literacy and professional communication in the School of Management Studies (Faculty of Commerce).

Kathleen Ryan is a consulting scholar in the African Section of the University of Pennsylvania Museum of Archaeology and Anthropology, Philadelphia. She has carried out research in Kenya since 1990, when she began a study of Maasai cattle herders in Kajiado District.

Helen Saberi was Alan Davidson's principal assistant in the completion of the *Oxford Companion to Food*. She is the author of *Noshe Djan: Afghan Food and Cookery;* coauthor of *Trifle* with Alan Davidson; and coauthor of *The Road to Vindaloo* with David Burnett; her latest book is *Tea: A Global History*.

Cari Sánchez holds a master of arts in gastronomy from the University of Adelaide/Le Cordon Bleu in South Australia. Her dissertation explores the global spread of the Argentine *asado*. She currently lives in Jacksonville, Florida, where she writes the food and travel blog *viCARIous* and is the marketing manager for a craft brewery.

Peter Scholliers teaches history at the Vrije Universiteit Brussel and is currently head of the research group "Social and Cultural Food Studies" (FOST). He studies the history of food in Europe in the 19th and 20th centuries. He co-edits the journal *Food and History* and is involved in various ways in the Institut Européen d'Histoire et des Cultures de l'Alimentation (Tours, France). Recently, he published *Food Culture in Belgium* (Greenwood, 2008). More information can be found at http://www.vub.ac.be/FOST/fost_in_english/.

Colleen Taylor Sen is the author of *Food Culture in India; Curry: A Global History; Pakoras, Paneer, Pappadums: A Guide to Indian Restaurant Menus*, and many articles on the food of the Indian Subcontinent. She is a regular participant in the Oxford Food Symposium.

Roger Serunyigo was born and lives in Kampala, Uganda. He graduated from Makerere University with a degree in urban and regional planning, has worked in telecommunications, and is now a professional basketball player for the Uganda National Team. He also coaches a women's basketball team (The Magic Stormers).

Dorette Snover is a chef and author. Influenced by French heritage and the food traditions of the Pennsylvania Dutch country, Chef Snover teaches exploration of the world via a culinary map at her school, C'est si Bon! in Chapel Hill. While the stock simmers, she is writing a novel about a French bread apprentice.

Celia Sorhaindo is a freelance photographer and writer. She was the editor of the 2008 and 2009 *Dominica Food and Drink Guide* magazine and content manager for the Dominica section of the magazine *Caribbean Homes & Lifestyle.*

Lyra Spang is a PhD candidate in the Department of Anthropology and the Food Studies Program at Indiana University. She has written about food, sex, and symbolism; the role of place in defining organic; and the importance of social relationships in small-scale food business in Belize. She grew up on a farm in southern Belize and is a proud promoter of that country's unique and diverse culinary heritage.

Lois Stanford is an agricultural anthropologist in the Department of Anthropology at New Mexico State University. In her research, she has examined the globalization of food systems both in Mexico and in the U.S. Southwest. Her current research focuses on the critical role of food heritage and plant conservation in constructing and maintaining traditional foodways and cultural identity in New Mexico. In collaboration with local food groups, she is currently developing a community food assessment project in the Mesilla Valley in southern New Mexico.

Aliza Stark is a senior faculty member at the Agriculture, Food, and Environment Institute of Biochemistry, Food Science, and Nutrition at the Hebrew University of Jerusalem.

Maria "Ging" Gutierrez Steinberg is a marketing manager for a New York City–based specialty food company and a food writer. She has a master's degree in food studies from New York University and is a graduate of Le Cordon Bleu. Her articles have appeared in various publications in Asia and the United States.

Anita Stewart is a cookbook author and Canadian culinary activist from Elora, Ontario, Canada.

Emily Stone has written about Guatemalan cuisine in the *Radcliffe Culinary Times,* and she is at work on a nonfiction book about chocolate in Central America. She currently teaches journalism and creative writing at Sun Yat-sen University in Guangzhou, China.

Asele Surina is a Russian native and former journalist who now works as a translator and interpreter. Since 1999 she has worked at the Institute of Classical Archaeology at the University of Texas on joint projects with an archaeological museum in Crimea, Ukraine.

Aylin Öney Tan is an architect by training and studied conservation of historic structures in Turkey, Italy, and the United Kingdom. Eventually, her passion for food and travel led her to write on food. Since 2003, she has had a weekly food column in *Cumhuriyet,* a prestigious national daily, and contributes to various food magazines. She was a jury member of the Slow Food Award 2000–2003, with her nominees receiving awards. She contributes to the Terra Madre and Presidia projects as the leader of the Ankara Convivium. She won the Sophie Coe Award on food history in 2008 for her article "Poppy: Potent yet Frail," presented previously at the Oxford Symposium on Food and Cookery where she's become a regular presenter. Currently, she is the curator of the Culinary Culture Section of Princess Islands' City Museum. She is happy to unite her expertise in archaeology and art history from her previous career with her unbounded interest in food culture.

Nicole Tarulevicz teaches at the School of Asian Languages and Studies at the University of Tasmania.

Karen Lau Taylor is a freelance food writer and consultant whose food curriculum vitae includes a master's degree in food studies from New York University, an advanced certificate from the Wine and Spirits Education Trust, and a gig as pastry cook at a five-star hotel after completing L'Academie de Cuisine's pastry arts program. She is working toward a master's degree in public health while she continues to write, teach, test recipes, eat, and drink from her home in Alexandria, Virginia.

Thy Tran is trained as a professional chef. She established Wandering Spoon to provide cooking classes, culinary consultation, and educational programming for culinary academies and nonprofit organizations throughout Northern California. Currently, she is a chef instructor at the International Culinary Schools at the Art Institute of California–San Francisco and Tante Marie's. She is also the founder and director of the Asian Culinary Forum. She co-authored *The Essentials of Asian Cooking, Taste of the World,* and the award-winning guide, *Kitchen Companion.*

Leena Trivedi-Grenier is a Bay-area food writer, cooking teacher, and social media consultant. Her writings have appeared in *The Business of Food: Encyclopedia of the Food and Drink Industry, Culinary Trends* magazine, and the *Cultural Arts Resources for Teachers and Students* newsletter and will be featured in several upcoming titles by Greenwood Press. She also runs a food/travel/gastronomy blog called *Leena Eats This Blog* (www.leenaeats.com).

Karin Vaneker graduated from the AKI Academy of Visual Arts in Enschede, the Netherlands. She later attended Sint-Lukas Hoger Instituut voor Schone Kunsten in Brussels, Belgium. She has written for numerous Dutch newspapers and magazines, specializing in trends and the cultural and other histories of ingredients and cuisines, and has published several books. Furthermore, Vaneker has worked for museums and curated an exhibition about New World taro (L. *Xanthosoma* spp.). At present she is researching its potential in domestic cuisines and gastronomy.

Penny Van Esterik is professor of anthropology at York University, Toronto, where she teaches nutritional anthropology, advocacy anthropology, and feminist theory. She does fieldwork in Southeast Asia and has developed materials on breast-feeding and women's work and infant and young child feeding.

Richard Wilk is professor of anthropology and gender studies at Indiana University, where he directs the Food Studies Program. With a PhD in anthropology from the University of Arizona, he has taught at the University of California,

Berkeley; University of California, Santa Cruz; New Mexico State University; and University College London and has held fellowships at Gothenburg University and the University of London. His publications include more than 125 papers and book chapters, a textbook in economic anthropology, and several edited volumes. His most recent books are *Home Cooking in the Global Village* (Berg Publishers), *Off the Edge: Experiments in Cultural Analysis* (with Orvar Lofgren; Museum Tusculanum Press), *Fast Food/Slow Food* (Altamira Press), and *Time, Consumption, and Everyday Life* (with Elizabeth Shove and Frank Trentmann; Berg Publishers).

Chelsie Yount is a PhD student of anthropology at Northwestern University in Evanston, Illinois. She lived in Senegal in 2005 and again in 2008, when performing ethnographic research for her master's thesis at the École des Hautes Études en Sciences Sociales in Paris, on the topic of Senegalese food and eating habits.

Marcia Zoladz is a cook, food writer, and food-history researcher with her own Web site, Cozinha da Marcia (Marcia's Kitchen; www.cozinhadamarcia.com.br). She is a regular participant and contributor at the Oxford Symposium on Food and History and has published three books in Brazil, Germany, and Holland—*Cozinha Portuguesa* (Portuguese cooking), *Muito Prazer* (Easy recipes), and *Brigadeiros e Bolinhas* (Sweet and savory Brazilian finger foods).

Index

Boldface numbers refer to volume numbers. A key appears on all verso pages.